A First Book of ANSI C

Fourth Edition

Gary J. Bronson
Fairleigh Dickinson University

Andy Hurd
Contributing Editor
Hudson Valley Community College

THOMSON
COURSE TECHNOLOGY™

Australia • Canada • Mexico • Singapore • Spain • United Kingdom • United States

THOMSON
COURSE TECHNOLOGY

A First Book of ANSI C, Fourth Edition
by Gary J. Bronson

Senior Product Manager:
Alyssa Pratt

Development Editor:
Ann Shaffer

Senior Marketing Manager:
Karen Seitz

Production Editor:
GEX Publishing Services

Associate Product Manager:
Jennifer Smith

Editorial Assistant:
Allison Murphy

Cover Design:
Steve Deschene

Compositor:
GEX Publishing Services

Printer:
Webcom Limited

Printed in Canada.

1 2 3 4 5 6 7 8 9 WC 10 09 08 07 06

For more information, contact Thomson Course Technology, 25 Thomson Place, Boston, Massachusetts, 02210.

Or find us on the World Wide Web at: www.course.com

ISBN 1-4188-3556-0

BRIEF TABLE OF CONTENTS

CONTENTS

PREFACE

As with its predecessors, the primary purpose of this edition of *A First Book of ANSI C* is to make C accessible as an applications programming language. The success of past editions, and the many comments I have received from both students and faculty stating that the book really did help them learn and teach C, have been extremely gratifying. Thus, the goal of this fourth edition remains the same as the first three editions: to present all topics clearly, unambiguously, and accessibly to beginning students. This text can be used as an introduction to programming in general, as an introduction to the C language in particular, and as a basis for further study of the C++ language.

This fourth edition includes a number of enhancements, including:

- New case studies illustrating real-world program applications
- A thorough explanation of input data validation techniques
- Expanded exercises that now include both short-answer questions and programming exercises
- A table of Common Compiler Errors (at the end of most chapters), for both Unix- and Windows-based compilers, in addition to the list of Common Programming Errors also provided at the end of most chapters
- Concise introduction to C++ designed to supplement the C++ coverage in Chapters 16 and 17
- Historical Notes relating to computer science topics
- Introductory chapter on Computer Hardware and Software Engineering
- Updates to all programs and descriptions that reflect the latest C99 ANSI standard

To make room for these new features, while keeping the size of the text reasonable, the two advanced chapters on C++ have been made available on the Web at *www.course.com*.

Distinctive Features of This Book

Emphasis: This text presents topics in a manner that helps students in the real-world of programming. I think this emphasis is best described by a reviewer, who wrote. "The depth [of this text] focuses on the kinds of problems that beginning students stumble across. This is in contrast to [many texts] that somehow manage the feat of providing massive volume without including useful hints and short cuts."

Writing Style: I firmly believe that introductory texts do not teach students—professors teach students. An introductory textbook, if it is to be useful, must be the supporting actor to the professor's leading role. Once the professor sets the stage, however, the textbook must encourage the student in mastering the material presented in class. To do this, the text must makes sense to the student. My primary concern, and one of the distinctive features of this book, is that it has been written for the student. As one reviewer said of an earlier edition, "This book addresses the student and not the professional."

Software Engineering: This text introduces students to the fundamentals of software engineering right from the start. In Section 1.3, students learn about algorithms and the various ways that an algorithm can be described.

The emphasis on software engineering continues in Section 1.4, which introduces the Software Development Process, and in all subsequent case studies, which demonstrate practical applications of the Software Development Process.

Introduction to Pointers: One of the unique features of the first edition was the introduction to pointers, in which the `printf()` function was used to initially display the addresses of variables; only then were variables used to actually store these addresses. This approach always seemed a more logical and intuitive method of explaining pointer variables than the indirection description in vogue at the time the first edition was released. Since the first edition, I have been pleased to see that using the `printf()` function to display addresses has become the standard way to introduce pointers. Although this approach, therefore, is no longer a unique feature of my book, I am very proud of its presentation and continue to use it in this new edition.

Program Testing: Every C program in this text has been successfully compiled and run using both Microsoft's Visual C++ .NET and UNIX compilers. All programs have been written following the C99 ANSI standard. Source code files for all program examples used in the text are available online. This permits students to experiment with the programs and more easily modify them as required by a number of end-of-section exercises.

Pedagogical Features

To make C accessible for a first-level course, the text includes the following pedagogical features:

End-of-Section Exercises: Almost every section in the book contains numerous short answer questions, in addition to the programming exercises provided in earlier editions. Additionally, solutions to all short answer questions are provided in Appendix G and the solutions to all programming exercises are available online to instructors.

Pseudocode and Flowchart Description: Pseudocode is stressed throughout the text. Students also learn about flowchart symbols and how to use flowcharts to visually present flow-of-control constructs.

Common Programming and Compiler Errors and Chapter Summary: Each chapter ends with a section on common programming errors. New to this edition is an easy-to-read table of compiler errors and associated error messages generated by both UNIX- and Windows-based compilers. Each chapter also contains a summary of the main topics covered in the chapter.

Programming and Historical Notes: Scattered through the chapters are shaded boxes labeled "Programming Notes" that highlight important concepts, useful technical points, and programming techniques used by professional programmers. Similarly, the "Historical Notes" highlight significant historical events and people related to the history of computer hardware and software development.

Appendices and Solutions: An expanded set of appendices is provided in this fourth edition. These include appendices on operator precedence, ASCII codes, the standard C library, I/O and standard error redirection, floating-point number storage, and creating a personal C library. A final appendix offers solutions to all short answer questions. Solutions for all programming exercises are available at *www.course.com.*

Supplemental Materials The following supplemental materials are available when this book is used in a classroom setting.

Electronic Instructor's Manual. The Instructor's Manual that accompanies this textbook includes:

- Additional instructional material to assist in class preparation, including suggestions for lecture topics
- Solutions to all the end-of-chapter materials, including the Programming Exercises

ExamView®. This textbook is accompanied by ExamView, a powerful testing software package that allows instructors to create and administer printed, computer (LAN-based), and Internet exams. ExamView includes hundreds of questions that correspond to the topics covered in this text, enabling students to generate detailed study guides that include page references for further review. These computer-based and Internet testing components allow students to take exams at their computers, and save the instructor time because each exam is graded automatically.

PowerPoint Presentations. This book comes with Microsoft PowerPoint slides for each chapter. These are included as a teaching aid for classroom presentations, either to make available to students on the network for chapter review, or to be printed for classroom distribution. Instructors can add their own slides for additional topics that they introduce to the class.

Distance Learning. Course Technology is proud to present online courses in WebCT and Blackboard to provide the most complete and dynamic learning experience possible. When you add online content to one of your courses, you're adding a lot: Topic Reviews, Practice Tests, Review Questions, Assignments, PowerPoint presentations, and, most of all, a gateway to the 21st century's most important information resource. For more information on how to bring distance learning to your course, contact your local Course Technology sales representative.

Source Code. The source code for this text is available at *www.course.com* and is also available on the Teaching Tools CD-ROM.

Solution Files. The solution files for all programming exercises are available at *www.course.com*, and are also available on the Teaching Tools CD-ROM.

Acknowledgments This fourth edition is a direct result of the success of the past editions. In this regard, my most heartfelt acknowledgment and appreciation go to the instructors and students who found these editions helpful in their quests to teach and learn C.

Special thanks also to my editor, Alyssa Pratt, at Course Technology. Alyssa's vision, continuous faith, and attention to schedule and detail were instrumental to the successful completion of this edition. Next, Ann Shaffer, the development editor, provided one of the most extensive and professional edits of the original manuscript that I have ever been fortunate to receive.

Additionally, I would like to express my gratitude to the following reviewers:

John Avitabile, The College of Saint Rose
Pamela Carter, University of Colorado at Colorado Springs
Andrew Hurd, Hudson Valley Community College
Thami Rachidi, University of Colorado at Denver
Eric Thompson, University of Colorado at Denver
John H. Town, Blinn College

Each reviewer supplied detailed and constructive reviews of the text. Their suggestions, attention to detail, and comments were extraordinarily helpful to me as the manuscript evolved and matured throughout the editorial process.

Once the review process was completed, the task of turning the final manuscript into a textbook depended on many people other than myself. I especially want to thank Jennifer Roehrig, Production Editor, Serge Palladino, Quality Assurance Tester, Chris Scriver, Quality Assurance Manager, Nicole Ashton, who created the solutions, and once again, Ann Shaffer, the overall coordinator. The dedication of this second team of people was incredible and very important to me. I am very grateful to each of these individuals for the work they did on this text.

Special acknowledgment goes to three of my colleagues who provided material for this text. First, in addition to numerous editing and technical contributions made by Assistant Professor Andrew J. Hurd, of Hudson Valley Community College, I am very grateful for his provision of the compiler errors. I am also extremely grateful to R. Kenneth Walter, now retired from Weber State University, who graciously provided the material used in the Historical Notes. Special thanks must also go to my first mathematics teacher, Marie Scully-Bell, who taught me that any subject, no matter how difficult, can be mastered, both in academics, and in all of life. She is one of those special people that we are blessed to have in our lives. As always, any errors in the text (as in most of my life) rest solely on my shoulders.

I gratefully acknowledge the direct encouragement and support of Fairleigh Dickinson University. This includes the constant encouragement, support, and positive academic climate provided by the campus provost, Dr. Kenneth Greene, and my Chairperson, Dr. Paul Yoon. Without their support, this text could not have been written.

Finally, I deeply appreciate the patience, understanding, and love provided by my friend, wife, and partner, Rochelle.

To: Rochelle, Matthew, Jeremy, David Bronson

Gary Bronson

2006

Photo Credits

Figures 1.1, 1.2, 1.3, 1.7 and 1.8 — Courtesy of IBM Archives
Figure 1.5 — Courtesy of Intel Corporation

Part One

Fundamentals

Chapter 1

Introduction to Computer Programming

1.1 History and Hardware

The process of using a machine to perform computations is almost as old as recorded history. The earliest such tool was the abacus—a device as common in China today as handheld calculators are in the United States. Both of these machines, however, require direct human involvement to be used. To add two numbers with an abacus requires the movement of beads on the device, while adding two numbers with a calculator requires that the operator push both the numbers and the addition operator keys.

The first recorded attempt at creating a programmable computing machine was by Charles Babbage in England in 1822. Ada Byron, daughter of the poet Lord Byron, developed a set of instructions that could, if the machine were ever built, be used to operate the machine. Although this machine, which Babbage called an analytical engine, was not successfully built in his lifetime, the concept of a programmable machine remained. It was partly realized in 1937 at Iowa State University by Dr. John V. Atanasoff and a graduate student named Clifford Berry, using electronic components. (See Figure 1.1.) The machine was known as the ABC, which stood for Atanasoff-Berry Computer, but required a human operator to manipulate external wiring to perform the desired operations. Thus, the goal of internally storing a replaceable set of instructions had still not been achieved.

Figure 1.1 Charles Babbage's analytical engine

The outbreak of World War II led to a more concentrated development of the computer, beginning in late 1939. One of the pioneers of this work was Dr. John W. Mauchly of the Moore School of Engineering at the University of Pennsylvania. Dr. Mauchly, who had visited Dr. Atanasoff and seen his ABC machine, began working with J. Presper Eckert on a computer called ENIAC (Electrical Numerical Integrator and Computer). Funding for this project was provided by the U.S. government. One of the early functions performed by this machine was the calculation of trajectories for ammunition fired from large guns. When completed in 1946, ENIAC contained 18,000 vacuum tubes, weighed approximately 30 tons, and could perform 5,000 additions or 360 multiplications in one second (see Figure 1.2).

Figure 1.2 ENIAC

While work was progressing on ENIAC using vacuum tubes, work on a computer named the Mark I was being done at Harvard University using mechanical relay switches (see Figure 1.3). The Mark I was completed in 1944, but could only perform six multiplications in one second. Both of these machines, however, like the ABC, required external wiring to perform the desired operations.

The final goal of a stored program computer, where instructions as well as data are stored internally within the machine, was achieved at Cambridge University in England on May 6, 1949, with the successful operation of the EDSAC (Electronic Delayed Storage Automatic Computer). In addition to performing calculations, the EDSAC could store both data and the instructions that directed the computer's operation. The EDSAC incorporated a form of memory, whose principles where developed by John Von Neumann, that allowed it to retrieve an instruction and then retrieve the data needed to carry out the instruction. This same design and operating principle is still used by the majority of computers manufactured today. The only features that have significantly changed are the sizes and speeds of the components used to make a computer, and the type of programs that are stored in it. Collectively, the components used to make a computer are referred to as **hardware**, while the programs are known as **software**.

Figure 1.3 Mark I

Computer Hardware

Computers are constructed from physical components referred to as hardware. The purpose of this hardware is to facilitate the storage and processing of data under the direction of a stored program. If computer hardware could store data using the same symbols that humans do, the number 126, for example, would be stored using the symbols 1, 2, and 6. Similarly, the letter that we recognize as "A" would be stored using this same symbol. Unfortunately, a computer's internal components require a different number and letter representation. It is worthwhile to understand why computers cannot use our symbols and then see how numbers are represented within the machine. This will make it easier to understand the actual parts of a computer used to store and process this data.

Bits and Bytes

The smallest and most basic data item in a computer is a bit. Physically, a **bit** is really a switch that can be either open or closed. The convention we will follow is that the open position is represented by 0 and the closed position by 1.[1]

[1]This convention, unfortunately, is rather arbitrary, and you will frequently encounter the reverse correspondence where the open and closed positions are represented as 1 and 0, respectively.

> **Historical Note**
>
> **Binary ABC**
>
> For several years, Dr. Atanasoff agonized over the design of a computing machine to help his Iowa State University graduate students solve complex equations. He considered building a machine based on binary numbers—the most natural system to use with electromechanical equipment that had one of two easily recognizable states, on and off—but feared people would not use a machine that was not based on the familiar and comfortable decimal system.
>
> Finally, on a cold evening at a roadhouse in Illinois in 1937, he determined that it had to be done the simplest and least expensive way, with binary digits (bits). Over the next two years, he and graduate student Clifford Berry built the first electronic digital computer, called the ABC (Atanasoff-Berry Computer). Since that time the vast majority of computers have been binary machines.

A single bit that can represent the values 0 and 1, by itself, has limited usefulness. All computers, therefore, group a set number of bits together both for storage and transmission. The grouping of 8 bits to form a larger unit is an almost universal computer standard and is referred to as a **byte.** A single byte, where each of the 8 bits is either 0 or 1, can represent any one of 256 distinct patterns. These consist of the pattern 00000000 (all eight switches open) to the pattern 11111111 (all eight switches closed) and all possible combinations of 0s and 1s in between. Each of these patterns can be used to represent a letter of the alphabet, other single characters (a dollar sign, comma, etc.), a single digit, or numbers containing more than one digit. The collections of patterns consisting of 0s and 1s used to represent letters, single digits, and other single characters are called **character codes** (one such code, ASCII, is presented in Section 2.1).

Character codes are extremely useful for items such as names and addresses, and any text that must be processed. It almost never is used, however, for arithmetic data. There are two reasons for this. First, converting a decimal number into a character code requires an individual code for each digit. For large numbers, this can waste a computer's memory space. The more basic reason, however, is that the decimal numbering system, which is based on the number 10, is inherently not supported by a computer's internal hardware. Recall that a bit, which is a computer's basic memory component, can take on only one of two possible states, open and closed, which is represented as a 0 and a 1. This would indicate that a numbering system based on these two states makes more sense, and in fact, this is the case. Section 1.8 presents the most commonly used base-two numbering system.

The idea of a computer's internal numbering system differing from our decimal system should not come as a surprise. For example, you are probably already familiar with two other numbering systems, and can easily recognize the following:

- Roman numeral: XIV
- Hash mark system: *### ### ////*

Components

All computers, from large supercomputers costing millions of dollars to smaller desktop personal computers costing hundreds of dollars, must perform a minimum set of tasks and provide the capability to:

1. Accept input, both data and instructions.
2. Display output, both textual and numerical.
3. Store data and instructions.
4. Perform arithmetic and logic operations on either the input or stored data.
5. Monitor, control, and direct the overall operation and sequencing of the system.

Historical Note

The Turing Machine

In the 1930s and 1940s, Alan Mathison Turing (1912–1954) and others developed a theory that described what a computing machine should be able to do. Turing's theoretical machine, known as the Turing Machine, contains the minimum set of operations for solving programming problems. Turing had hoped to prove that all problems could be solved by a set of instructions given to such a hypothetical computer. What he succeeded in proving was that some problems cannot be solved by *any* machine, just as some problems cannot be solved by any person. Turing's work formed the foundation of computer theory before the first electronic computer was built. His contributions to the team that developed the critical code-breaking computers during World War II led directly to the practical implementation of his theories.

Figure 1.4 illustrates the computer components that support these capabilities and collectively form a computer's hardware.

Main Memory Unit This unit stores data and instructions as a sequence of bytes. A program must reside in main memory if it is to operate the computer. Main memories combine 1 or more bytes into a single unit, referred to as a **word**. Although larger word sizes facilitate an increase in overall speed and capacity, this increase is achieved by an increase in the computer's complexity.

Early personal computers (PCs), such as the Apple IIe and Commodore machines, internally stored and transmitted words consisting of single bytes. The first IBM PCs used word sizes consisting of 2 bytes each, while more current Intel-based PCs store and process words consisting of 4 bytes each.

The arrangement of words in a computer's memory can be compared to the arrangement of suites in a large hotel, where each suite is made up of rooms of the same size. Just as each suite has a unique room number that allows patrons to locate and identify it, each word in a computer's memory has a unique numerical address. Like room numbers, word addresses are always positive unsigned whole numbers that are used for location and identification purposes. Also, like hotel rooms with connecting doors that form larger suites, words can be combined to form larger units to accommodate different-sized data types.

As a physical device, main memories are constructed as random access memory, or RAM. This means that every section of memory can be accessed randomly as quickly as any other section. Main memory is also **volatile**; whatever is stored in it is lost when the computer's power is turned off. Your programs and data are always stored in RAM when your program is being executed. The size of the computer's RAM is usually specified in terms of how many bytes of RAM are available to the user. PC memories currently start at 512 million bytes (denoted as megabytes or MB).

A second type of memory is read only memory, or ROM. ROM is nonvolatile; its contents are not lost when the power goes off. As such, ROM always contains fundamental instructions that cannot be lost or changed by the casual computer user. These instructions include those necessary for starting the computer's operation when the power is first turned on, and for holding any other instructions the manufacturer requires to be permanently accessible when the computer is operating.

Central Processing Unit The central processing unit (CPU) consists of two essential subunits, the **control unit** and the **Arithmetic and Logic Unit (ALU)**. The control unit directs and monitors the overall operation of the computer. It keeps track of where in memory the next instruction resides, issues the signals needed to both read data from and write data to other units in the system, and executes all instructions. The ALU performs all of the computations, such as addition, subtraction, comparisons, and so on, that a computer provides.

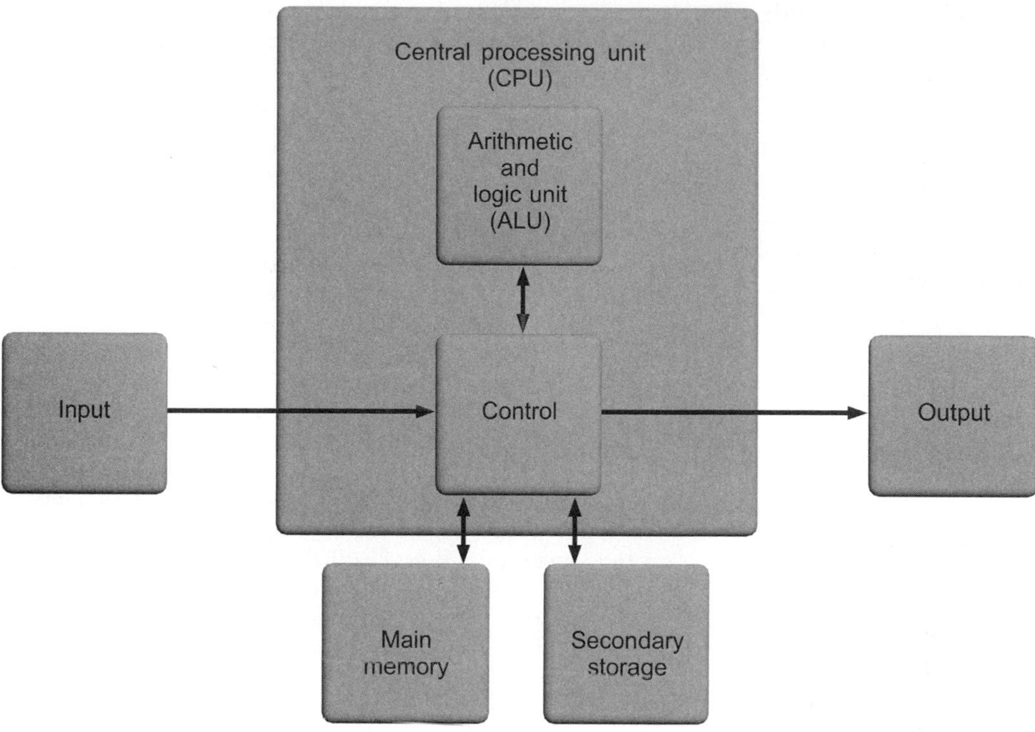

Figure 1.4 Basic hardware units of a computer

The CPU is the central element of a computer and its most expensive part. Currently, CPUs are constructed as a single microchip, which is referred to as a **microprocessor**. Figure 1.5 illustrates the size and internal structure of a state-of-the-art microprocessor chip used in current notebook computers.

Figure 1.5 State-of-the-art Intel microprocessor

Input/Output Unit The input/output (I/O) unit provides access to the computer, allowing it to input and output data. It is the interface to which peripheral devices, such as keyboards, console screens, and printers, are attached.

Secondary Storage Because main RAM memory in large quantities is still relatively expensive and volatile, it is not practical as a permanent storage area for programs and data. Secondary or auxiliary storage devices are used for this purpose. Although data has been stored on punched cards, paper tape, and other media in the past, virtually all secondary storage is now done on magnetic tape, magnetic disks, and CD-ROMs.

The surfaces of magnetic tapes and disks are coated with a material that can be magnetized to store data. Current tapes are capable of storing thousands of characters per inch of tape, and a single tape may store up to hundreds of megabytes. Tapes, by nature, are a sequential storage media, which means that they allow data to be written or read in one sequential stream from beginning to end. Should you want to access a block of data in the middle of the tape, all preceding data on the tape must be scanned to find the block. Because of this, tapes are primarily used for mass backup of historical data.

A more convenient method of rapidly accessing stored data is provided by a **direct access storage device (DASD)**, which allows a computer to read or write any one file or program independent of its position on the storage medium. Until the recent advent of the CD, the most popular DASD was the magnetic disk. A **magnetic hard disk** consists of either a single rigid platter or several platters that spin together on a common spindle. A movable access arm positions the read and write mechanisms over, but not quite touching, the recordable surfaces. Such a configuration is shown in Figure 1.6.

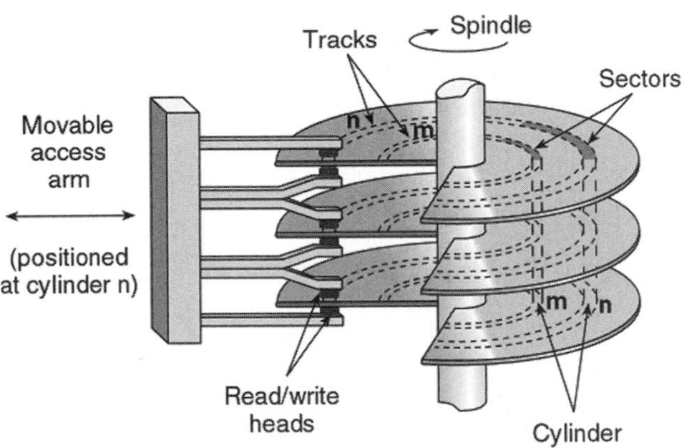

Figure 1.6 Internal structure of a hard disk drive

Initially, the most common magnetic disk storage device was the removable **floppy disk**. The most popular size for these is 3.5 inches in diameter, with a capacity of 1.44 megabytes. More recent removable disks, known as Zip disks, have capacities of 250 megabytes, with 650 to 700 megabyte compact disks (CDs) currently being the auxiliary storage devices of choice. Concurrent with the vast increase in storage capacity has been an equally significant increase in processing speed and a dramatic decrease in computer size and cost. Computer hardware capabilities that cost more than a million dollars in 1950 can now be purchased for less than $500. If the same reductions occurred in the automobile industry, for example, a Rolls-Royce could now be purchased for $10! The processing speeds of current computers have also increased by a factor of thousands over their 1950's predecessors, with the computational speeds of current computers being measured in both millions of instructions per second (MIPS) and billions of instructions per second (BIPS). For comparison, Figure 1.7 shows an early desktop IBM PC of the 1980s, while Figure 1.8 illustrates a current IBM notebook computer.

Figure 1.7 An original (1980s) IBM personal computer

Figure 1.8 A current IBM notebook computer

EXERCISES 1.1

Short Answer Questions

1. Define the term *bit.* What values can a bit assume?
2. Define the term *byte.* How many distinct bit patterns can a byte assume?
3. How is a byte used to represent characters in a computer?
4. Define the term *word.* Give the word sizes for some common computers.
5. What are the two principal parts of the CPU? What is the function of each part?
6. What is the difference between RAM and ROM? What do they have in common?
7. a. What is the input/output unit?
   b. Name three devices that would be connected to the input/output unit.
8. Define the term *secondary storage.* Give three examples of secondary storage.
9. What is the difference between sequential storage and direct access storage? What is the advantage of direct access storage?
10. Define the term *microprocessor.* Name three ways that microprocessors are used in everyday life.

1.2 Programming Languages

A computer, such as the modern notebook shown in Figure 1.8, is a machine made of physical components. Like other machines, such as an airplane, automobile, or lawn mower, a computer must be turned on and then driven, or controlled, to do the task it was meant to do. How this gets done is what distinguishes computers from other types of machinery.

In an automobile, for example, control is provided by the driver, who sits inside of and directs the car. In a computer, the driver is called a **program**. More formally, a **computer program** is a structured combination of data and instructions that is used to operate a computer and produce a specific result. Another term for a program or set of programs is **software**. We will use both terms interchangeably throughout this text.

Programming is the process of writing these instructions in a language that the computer can respond to and that other programmers can understand. The set of instructions that can be used to construct a program is called a **programming language**. Available programming languages come in a variety of forms and types. Each of these different forms and types was designed to make the programming process easier, to capitalize on a special feature of the hardware, or to meet a special requirement of an application. At a fundamental level, however, all programs must ultimately be converted into a machine language program, which is the only type of program that can actually operate a computer.

Historical Note

Ada Augusta Byron, Countess of Lovelace

Ada Byron, daughter of the Romantic poet Lord Byron, was a colleague of Charles Babbage in his attempt throughout the mid-1800s to build an analytical engine. It was Ada's task to develop the algorithms—solutions to problems in the form of step-by-step instructions—that would allow the engine to compute the values of mathematical functions. Babbage's machine was not successfully built in his lifetime, primarily because the technology of the time did not allow mechanical parts to be constructed with necessary tolerances. Nonetheless, Ada is recognized as the first computer programmer. She published a collection of notes that established the basis for computer programming. The modern Ada programming language is named in her honor.

Machine Language

An **executable program** is a program that can operate a computer. Such programs are always written as a sequence of binary numbers, which is a computer's internal language, and are also referred to as **machine language programs**. An example of a simple machine language program containing two instructions is:

```
11000000000000000001000000000010
11110000000000000010000000000011
```

Each sequence of binary numbers that constitutes a machine language instruction consists of, at a minimum, two parts: an instruction part and a data part. The instruction part, which is referred to as the **opcode** (short for operation code), is usually at the beginning of each binary number and tells the computer the operation to be performed, such as add, subtract, multiply, and so on. The remaining part of the number provides information about the data.

Assembly Language

Because each class of computer, such as IBM PCs, Apple Macintoshes, and Hewlett-Packard computers, has its own particular machine language, it is very tedious and time consuming to write machine language programs. One of the first advances in programming was the substitution of word-like symbols, such as ADD, SUB, MUL, for the binary opcodes, and both decimal numbers and labels for memory addresses. For example, in the following set of instructions, word-like symbols are used to add two numbers (referred to as `first` and `second`), multiply the result by a third number known as `factor`, and store the result as `answer`:

```
LOAD first
ADD second
MUL factor
STORE answer
```

Programming languages that use this type of symbolic notation are referred to as **assembly languages**. Because computers can only execute machine language programs, the set of instructions contained within an assembly language program must be translated into a machine language program before it can be executed on a computer (Figure 1.9). Translator programs that translate assembly language programs into machine language programs are known as **assemblers**.

Low- and High-Level Languages

Both machine and assembly languages are classified as **low-level languages**. This is because both of these language types use instructions that are directly tied to one type of computer.[2]

[2]In actuality, the low-level language is defined for the processor around which the computer is constructed.

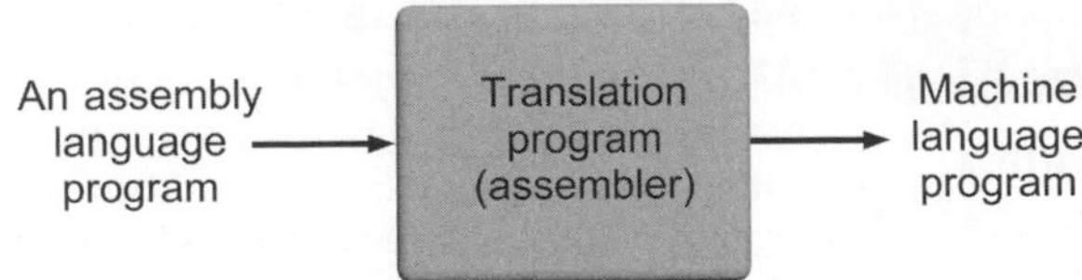

Figure 1.9 Assembly programs must be translated

As such, an assembly language program is limited in that it can only be used with the specific computer type for which the program is written. Such programs do, however, permit using special features of each particular computer type such as an IBM, Apple, or Hewlett-Packard computers, and generally execute at the fastest speed possible.

In contrast to low-level languages, a high-level language uses instructions that resemble human languages, such as English, and can be run on all computers, regardless of manufacturer. C, C++, Visual Basic, and Java are all high-level languages. For example, using C, the assembly language instructions used in the preceding section to add two numbers and multiply by a third number can be written as:

```
answer = (first + second) * factor;
```

Programs written in a computer language (high or low level) are referred to interchangeably as both **source programs** and **source code**. Once a program is written in a high-level language, it must also, like a low-level assembly program, be translated into the machine language of the computer on which it will be run. This translation can be accomplished in two ways.

When each statement in a high-level source program is translated individually and executed immediately upon translation, the programming language is called an **interpreted language**, and the program doing the translation is called an **interpreter**.

When all of the statements in a high-level source program are translated as a complete unit before any individual statement is executed, the programming language is called a **compiled language**. In this case, the program doing the translation is called a **compiler**. Both compiled and interpreted versions of a single language can exist, although typically one predominates. For example, although interpreted versions of C exist, C is predominantly a compiled language.

Figure 1.10 illustrates the process by which a C source program is compiled into a machine language executable program. (This figure does not show the essential steps of planning and analyzing the program design, which should take place before a line of code is typed. You'll learn how to plan a program design in Section 1.4.) As shown, the programmer types the source program using an editor program. This is effectively a word processing program that is part of the development environment supplied by the compiler.

Translation of the C source code into an executable program begins with the compiler. The output produced by the compiler is called an **object program**, which is a machine language version of the source code. Your source code may also make use of additional previously compiled code. This can consist of compiled code provided by another programmer or compiled code provided by a compiler, such as the mathematical code for finding a square root. In such cases this additional machine language code must be combined with the

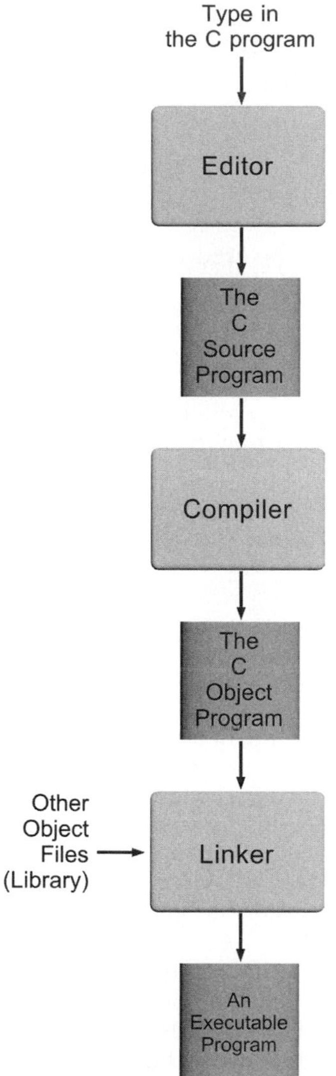

Figure 1.10 Programming steps to create an executable C program

object program to create a final executable program. It is the task of the **linker** to accomplish these steps. The result of the linking process is a completed machine language program, containing all of the code required by your program, ready for execution. It is this final machine language program that is the executable program. The last step in the process is to load this machine language program into the computer's main memory for actual execution.

Procedural and Object-Oriented Languages

High-level languages initially were all procedural languages. In a **procedural language**, the available instructions are used to create self-contained units, referred to as **procedures**. The purpose of a procedure is to accept data as input and transform the data in some manner to produce a specific result as an output. Effectively, each procedure moves the data one step closer to the final desired output along the path shown in Figure 1.11.

The programming process illustrated in Figure 1.11 directly mirrors the input, processing, and output hardware units that are used to construct a computer. This was not accidental, because high-level procedural languages were initially designed to match and directly control corresponding hardware units. Each computer language tends to refer to its procedures by a different name. For example, in C, a procedure is referred to as a **function**; in Java, a procedure is referred to as a **method**; while in C++, the terms **method** and **function** are both used.

A well-written procedure consists of individual instructions that are grouped into specific internal structures according to well-established guidelines. (These guidelines are presented in Section 1.4.) Procedures conforming to these structure guidelines are known as **structured procedures**. High-level procedural languages, such as C, which effectively enforce adherence to these structures, are referred to as **structured languages**. Because of this, we will frequently use the term structured language to denote any high-level procedural languages, such as C, that enforces structured procedures.

Until the early 1990s, all new high-level languages were typically structured languages. More recently, a second approach, known as object orientation, has taken center stage. These languages, which consist of C++, Java, Visual Basic, and C#, are known as **object-oriented languages**.

One of the motivations for object-oriented languages was the development of graphical screens and support for graphical user interfaces (GUIs) capable of displaying multiple windows containing both graphical shapes and text. In such an environment, each window on the screen can be considered an object with associated characteristics, such as color, position, and size. An object-oriented program must first define the objects it will manipulate; this includes describing the general characteristics of the objects and then specifying specific procedures to manipulate them, such as changing size and position and transferring data between objects. Object-oriented languages, however, still retain and incorporate structured features in their procedures. Thus, C++, Java, and C# all used the basic structured procedure types

Figure 1.11 Basic procedural operations

found in C. In fact, C++ was specifically designed as an extension to C that included objects. These extensions are presented in Chapter 15.

C is unique in that it is a structured language that is still used extensively in the arena of these newer languages. In fact, C, in many cases, is preferred by professional programmers, especially when designing programs that handle extensive amounts of data, when dealing with programs that need to be developed quickly or require very targeted results, and for constructing intricate operating system programs. Thus, either as a foundation for learning the newer object-oriented programming languages, or as a programming language that can be used for many applications in its own right, learning C is a valuable addition to a programmer's knowledge base.

Application and System Software

Two logical categories of computer programs are application software and system software. **Application software** consists of programs written to perform particular tasks required by users. Most of the examples in this book would be considered application software.

System software is the collection of programs that must be readily available to any computer system to enable the computer to operate. In the early computer environments of the 1950s and 1960s, a user had to initially load the system software by hand to prepare the computer to do anything. This was done with rows of switches on a front panel. Those initial hand-entered commands were said to boot the computer, a term derived from the expression "pulling oneself up by the bootstraps." Today, the so-called **bootstrap loader** is internally contained in ROM and is a permanent, automatically executed component of the computer's system software.

Collectively, the set of system programs used to operate and control a computer is called the **operating system**. Tasks handled by modern operating systems include memory management; allocation of CPU time; control of input and output units such as the keyboard, screen, and printers; and the management of all secondary storage devices. Many operating systems handle very large programs, as well as multiple users concurrently, by dividing programs into segments, or pages, that are moved between the disk and memory as needed. Such operating systems permit more than one user to run a program on the computer, which gives each user the impression that the computer and peripherals are his or hers alone. This is referred to as a **multiuser system**. Additionally, many operating systems, including most windowed environments, permit each user to run multiple programs. Such operating systems are referred to as both **multiprogrammed** and **multitasking** systems.

The Development of C

The C language was initially developed in the 1970s at AT&T Bell Laboratories by Ken Thompson, Dennis Ritchie, and Brian Kernighan. It has an extensive set of capabilities that permits it to be written as a high-level structured language, while providing abilities to directly access the internal hardware of a computer. Known as the "professional programmer's language," C permits a programmer to "see into" a computer's memory and directly alter data that is stored within his or her own computer's memory. The standard that defines the C language is maintained by the American National Standards Institute (ANSI).

In the 1980s, Bjarne Stroustrup (working at AT&T) developed C++ as an extension to C. This new language contained the extensive set of capabilities provided by C, but was an object-oriented program. This close relationship between C and C++ explains why C++ programs incorporate significant amounts of structured C-type code. Many C programs are now, in fact, written using C++ but are restricted to using only those features that are uniquely defined for the C language.

EXERCISES 1.2

Short Answer Questions

1. Define the following terms:
   a. computer program
   b. programming
   c. programming language
   d. high-level language
   e. low-level language
   f. machine language
   g. assembly language
   h. procedure-oriented language
   i. object-oriented language
   j. source program
   k. compiler
   l. assembler

2. a. Describe the difference between high- and low-level languages.
   b. Describe the difference between procedure and object-oriented languages.

3. Describe the difference between assemblers, interpreters, and compilers.

4. a. Assuming the following operation codes:

   `11000000` means add the 1st operand to the 2nd operand

   `10100000` means subtract the 1st operand from the 2nd operand

   `11110000` means multiply the 2nd operand by the 1st operand

   `11010000` means divide the 2nd operation by the 1st operand

   translate the following instructions into English:

Opcode	**Address of 1st Operand**	**Address of 2nd Operand**
11000000	000000000001	0000000000010
11110000	000000000010	0000000000011
10100000	000000000100	0000000000011
11010000	000000000101	0000000000011

b. Assuming the following locations contain the following data, determine the result produced by the instructions listed in Question 4a.

Address	Initial Value (in Decimal) Stored at this Address
00000000001	5
00000000010	3
00000000011	6
00000000100	14
00000000101	4

5. Rewrite the machine-level instructions listed in Question 4a using assembly language notation. Use the symbolic names ADD, SUB, MUL, and DIV for addition, subtraction, multiplication, and division operations, respectively. In writing the instructions, use decimal values for the addresses.

6. Assuming that A = 10, B = 20, and C = .6, determine the numerical result of the following set of assembly language-type statements. For this exercise, assume that the LOAD instruction is equivalent to entering a value into the display of a calculator, and that ADD means add and MUL means multiply by.

```
LOAD    A
ADD     B
MUL     C
```

1.3 Algorithms

Before a C program is written, the programmer must clearly understand what data is to be used, the desired result, and the steps to be used to produce this result. The steps selected to produce the result is referred to as an algorithm. More precisely, an algorithm is defined as a step-by-step sequence of instructions that describes how the data are to be processed to produce the desired outputs. In essence, an algorithm answers the question: "What method will you use to solve this problem?"

Only after we clearly understand the data that we will be using and select an algorithm (the specific steps required to produce the desired result) can we code the program. Seen in this light, programming is the translation of a selected algorithm into a language that the computer can use. In our case, we will always convert our steps into C language.

To illustrate an algorithm, we will consider a simple problem. Assume that a program must calculate the sum of all whole numbers from 1 through 100. Figure 1.12 illustrates two methods we could use to find the required sum. Each method constitutes an algorithm.

Historical Note

Al-Khwarizmi

About 825 A.D. one of the first great mathematicians, Mohammed Ibn Musa al-Khwarizmi, wrote a treatise called Ilm al-jabr wa'l muqabalah ("The Science of Reduction and Calculation"). The word *algorithm* is derived from al-Khwarismi's name, and our word algebra is derived from the word al-jabr in the title of his work.

Historical Note

The Young Gauss

German mathematical genius Johann Carl Fredrich Gauss (1777–1855) professed that he could "Reckon" before he could talk. When only 2 years old, he discovered an error in his father's business records.

One day in school, young Johann's teacher asked his class to add up the numbers between 1 and 100. To the chagrin of the teacher, who had thought the task would keep the class busy for a while, Gauss almost instantly wrote the number on his slate and exclaimed, "There it is!" He had reasoned that the series of numbers could be written forward and backward and added term-by-term to get 101 50 times. Thus, the sum was 100/2 x 101, and Gauss, at the age of 10 had discovered that 1 + 2 + ... + n = (n / 2)(n+1).

When solving such a problem, most people do not bother to list the possible alternatives in a detailed step-by-step manner (as shown in Figure 1.12) and then select one of the algorithms to solve the problem. That's because most people do not think algorithmically; they think heuristically. For example, if you had to change a flat tire on your car, you would not think of all the steps required—you would simply change the tire or call someone else to do the job. This is an example of heuristic thinking.

Unfortunately, computers do not respond to heuristic commands. A general statement such as "add the numbers from 1 to 100" means nothing to a computer, because the computer can respond only to algorithmic commands written in an acceptable language such as C. To program a computer successfully, you must clearly understand this difference between algorithmic and heuristic commands. A computer is an "algorithm-responding" machine; it is not a "heuristic-responding" machine. You cannot tell a computer to change a tire or to add the numbers from 1 through 100. Instead, you must give the computer a detailed, step-by-step set of instructions that, collectively, forms an algorithm. For example, the set of instructions

Set n equal to 100
Set a equal to 1
Set b equal to 100
Calculate sum = n(a+ b)/2
Display the sum

form a detailed method, or algorithm, for determining the sum of the numbers from 1 through 100. Notice that these instructions are not a computer program. Unlike a program, which must be written in a language the computer can understand, an algorithm can be written or described in various ways.

When English phrases are used to describe the algorithm (the processing steps), as in this example, the description is called **pseudocode**. When mathematical equations are used, the description is called a **formula**. When pictures that employ specifically defined shapes are used, the description is called a **flowchart**. A flowchart provides a pictorial representation of the algorithm using the symbols shown in Figure 1.13. Figure 1.14 illustrates the use of these symbols in depicting an algorithm for determining the average of three numbers.

Because flowcharts are cumbersome to revise, using pseudocode to express an algorithm's logic has gained increased acceptance among programmers. Unlike flowcharts, for which standard symbols are defined, there are no standard rules for constructing pseudocode. Any short English phrase may be used to describe an algorithm using pseudocode. For

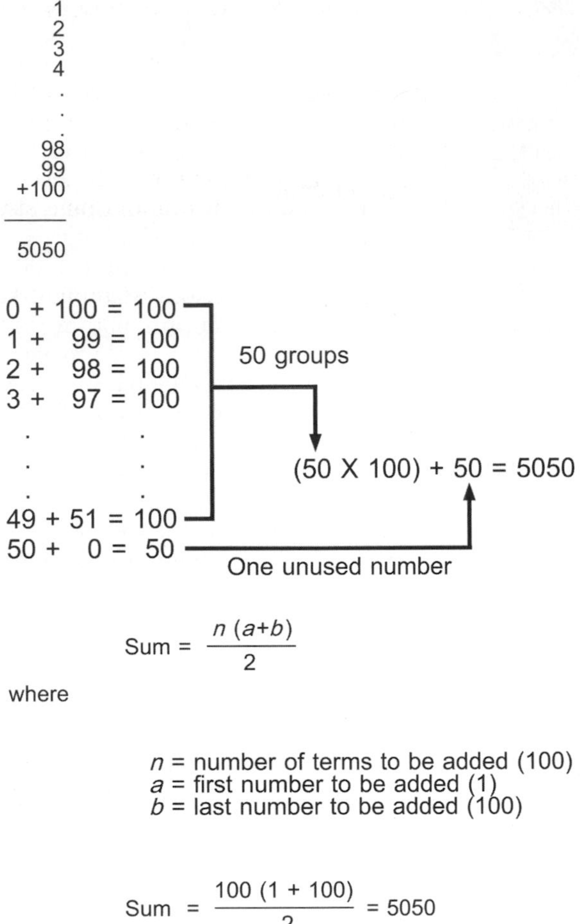

Figure 1.12 Summing the numbers 1 through 100

example, the following is acceptable pseudocode describing the steps needed to compute the average of three numbers:

Input the three numbers into the computer
Calculate the average by adding the numbers and dividing the sum by three
Display the average

Only after the programmer selects an algorithm and understands the required steps can he or she write the algorithm using computer-language statements.

Once selected, an algorithm must be converted into a form that can be used by a computer. Converting an algorithm into a computer program, using a language such as C, is called **coding the algorithm** (see Figure 1.15). The program instructions resulting from this step are referred to as **program code,** or simply **code,** for short. The remainder of this text, starting in the next chapter, is devoted mostly to showing you how to develop algorithms and how to express these algorithms in C.

SYMBOL	NAME	DESCRIPTION
	Terminal	Indicates the beginning or end of an algorithm
	Input/Output	Indicates an input or output operation
	Process	Indicates computation or data manipulation
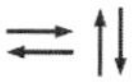 ⇄ ⇅	Flow Lines	Connects the flowchart symbols and indicates the logic flow
	Decision	Indicates a decision point in an algorithm
	Loop	Indicates the initial, final, and increment values of a loop
	Predefined Process	Indicates a predefined process, as in calling a sorting process
	Connector	Indicates an entry to or exit from another part of the flowchart

Figure 1.13 Flowchart symbols

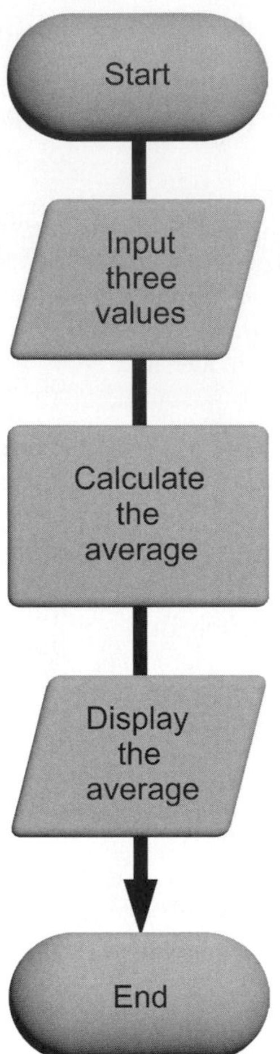

Figure 1.14 Flowchart for calculating the average of three numbers

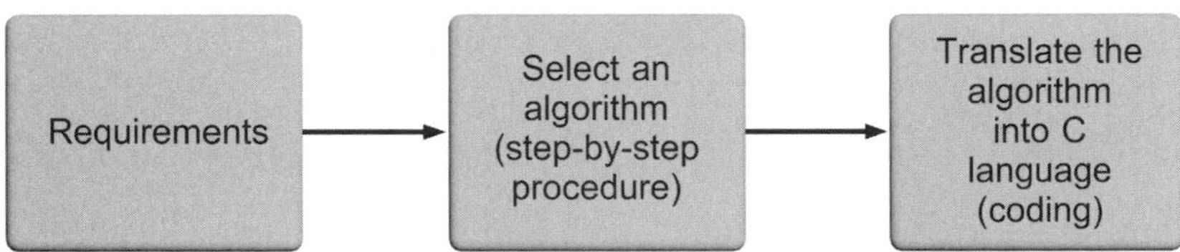

Figure 1.15 Coding an algorithm

EXERCISES 1.3

Short Answer Questions

1. Determine and list a step-by-step procedure to complete the following tasks. (*Note:* There is no single correct answer for each of these tasks. This exercise is designed to give you practice in converting heuristic commands into equivalent algorithms and making the shift between the thought processes involved in the two types of thinking.)
   a. Fix a flat tire
   b. Make a telephone call
   c. Go to the store and purchase a loaf of bread
   d. Roast a turkey

2. Determine and write an algorithm (list the steps) required to interchange the contents of two cups of liquid. Assume that a third cup is available to temporarily hold the contents of either cup. Each cup should be rinsed before any new liquid is poured into it.

3. Write a detailed set of step-by-step instructions, in English, to calculate the dollar amount of money in a piggybank that contains *h* half-dollars, *q* quarters, *n* nickels, *d* dimes, and *p* pennies.

4. Write a detailed set of step-by-step instructions, in English, to find the smallest number in a group of three integer numbers.

5. a. Write a detailed set of step-by-step instructions, in English, to calculate the fewest number of paper bills needed to pay a bill of amount TOTAL. For example, if TOTAL were $97, the bills, in U.S. currency, would consist of one $50 bill, two $20 bills, one $5 bill, and two $1 bills. Assume that only $100, $50, $20, $10, $5, and $1 bills are available if you are using U.S currency; otherwise, use the currency of the country you are living in.
   b. Assume that the bill is to be paid only in $1 bills.

6. a. Write an algorithm to locate the first occurrence of the name "Jones" in a list of names arranged in random order.
   b. Discuss how to improve your algorithm for Question 6a if the list of names was arranged in alphabetical order.

7. Determine and write an algorithm to determine the total occurrences of the letter *e* in any sentence.

8. Determine and write an algorithm to sort three numbers into ascending (from lowest to highest) order.

1.4 The Software Development Process

As modern society becomes more complex, so does its problems. Thus, problem solving has become a way of life. Issues such as solid waste disposal, global warming, international finance, pollution, and nuclear proliferation are relatively new, and solutions to these problems now challenge our best technology and human capabilities.

Most problem solutions require considerable planning and forethought if the solution is to be appropriate and efficient. This is true for most programming problems as well. For example, imagine trying to construct software for a cellular telephone network or creating an inventory management program for a department store by trial-and-error. Such a solution would be expensive at best, disastrous at worst, and practically unrealistic.

Each field of study has its own name for the systematic method used to design solutions to problems. In science this method is referred to as the **scientific method**, while in engineering disciplines the method is referred to as the **systems approach**. The technique used by professional software developers for understanding the problem that is being solved and for creating an effective and appropriate software solution is called the **software development process**. This process consists of the following four phases:

Phase I: Specify the program's requirements

Phase II: Design and development

- **Step 1: Analyze the problem**
- **Step 2: Select an overall solution algorithm**
- **Step 3: Write the program**
- **Step 4: Test and correct the program**

Phase III: Documentation

Phase IV: Maintenance

As shown in Figure 1.16, the first three phases frequently refine and interact with each other until a final design and program have been developed. Also, within the design and development phase itself you may discover that the problem has not been completely specified or analyzed, and further work in an earlier step is required to complete the program. Each of these phases are discussed in the following sections.

Phase I: Specify the Program's Requirements

This phase begins with either a statement of a problem or a specific request for a program, which is referred to as a **program requirement**. Your task is to ensure that the program requirement is clearly stated and that you understand what is to be achieved. For example, suppose you receive a brief e-mail from your supervisor that says: *We need a program to provide information about circles.*

This is not a clearly defined requirement. It does not specify a well-defined problem because it does not tell us exactly what information is required. It would be a major mistake to begin immediately writing a program to solve this poorly formulated problem. To clarify and define the problem statement, your first step would be to contact your supervisor to define exactly what information is to be produced (its outputs) and what data is to be provided (the inputs).

Suppose you do this and learn that what is really desired is a program to calculate and display the circumference of a circle when given the radius. Once you have what you think to be a clear statement of what is required, you may proceed to the next step.

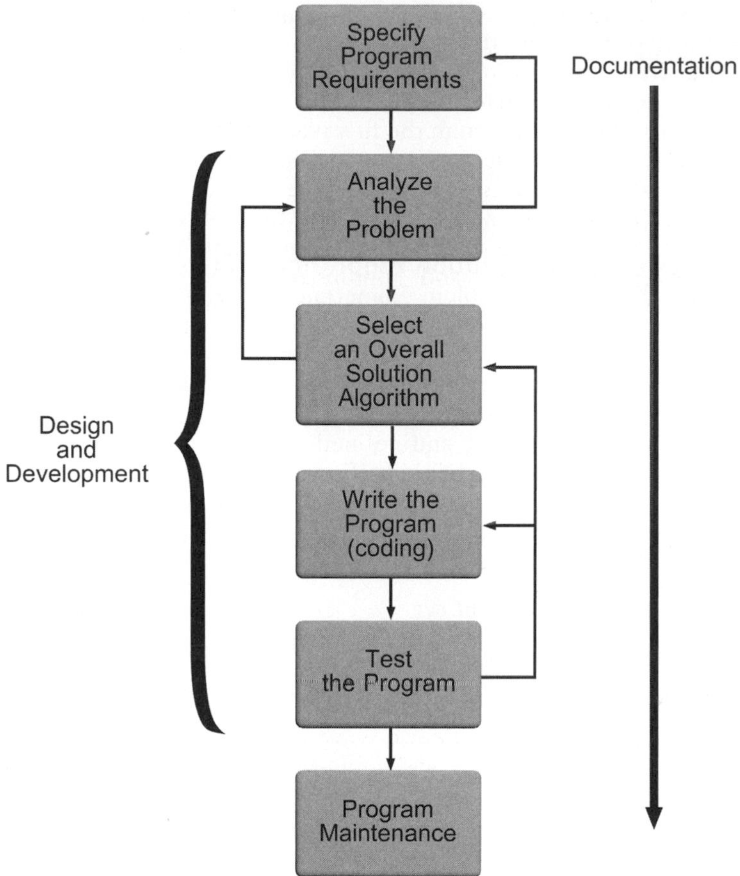

Figure 1.16 The software development process

Phase II: Design and Development

Once a program specification has been completed, the design and development phase, which forms the heart of the programming process, is begun. This phase consists of the following four steps:

Step 1: Analyze the Problem This step is required to ensure that the problem has, in fact, been clearly specified and understood, and to provide the necessary information for selecting an algorithm to solve the problem. The problem is clearly defined only when you understand

- The outputs that must be produced
- The input data that is required to create the desired outputs
- The formulas relating the inputs to the outputs

At the conclusion of the analysis, each of these three items must be clearly defined.

In performing an analysis, many new programmers prefer to determine the input data first, and then determine the desired outputs later, while professional programmers tend to work the other way around. It may seem odd to you to jump ahead to thinking about outputs first, but it is the outputs that the program is supposed to produce; they are the whole purpose of constructing a program in the first place. Knowing this goal and keeping it in mind will keep you focused on what is important in the program. However, if you are more comfortable initially determining the input data, do so.

Step 2: Select an Overall Solution Algorithm In this step, you determine and select an algorithm that will solve the problem. Sometimes determining this overall solution algorithm is quite easy, and sometimes it can be complex. For example, a program for determining the dollar value of the change in one's pocket or determining the area of a rectangle is quite simple. The construction of an inventory tracking and control system for a manufacturing company, however, is more complex. In these more complete cases, the initial solution algorithm is typically improved and refined until it specifies the complete solution in considerable detail. An example of this refinement is provided later in this section.

In its most general form, an overall solution algorithm applicable to most C programs is:

Get the inputs to the problem
Calculate the desired outputs
Report the results of the calculation

These three tasks are the primary responsibility of almost every problem, and we shall refer to this algorithm as the **Problem-Solver Algorithm.** A diagram of this algorithm is shown in Figure 1.17.

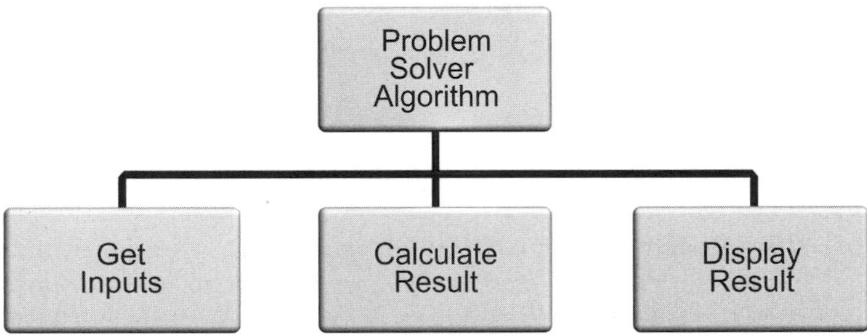

Figure 1.17 The Problem-Solver Algorithm

For example, if you were required to calculate the circumference of a circle with a given radius, the Problem-Solver Algorithm becomes:

Set a radius value, r
Calculate the circumference, C, using the formula C = 2 π r
Display the calculated value for C

For small applications where only one or more calculations must be performed, the Problem-Solver Algorithm by itself is usually sufficient. For larger programs, however, you will have to refine the initial algorithm and organize it into smaller algorithms, with specifications for how these smaller algorithms will interface with each other. This is accomplished by the process of refinement, which is described next.

Refining the Algorithm For larger applications, the initial solution algorithm, which typically starts with the Problem-Solver Algorithm, must be refined and organized into smaller algorithms, with specifications for how the algorithms interface with each other. To achieve this goal, the description of the solution starts from the highest level (topmost) requirement and proceeds downward to the parts that must be constructed to achieve this requirement.

To make this more meaningful, suppose a computer program is required to track the number of parts in inventory. The required output for this program is a description of all parts carried in inventory and the number of units of each item in stock. The inputs are the initial inventory quantity of each part, the number of items sold, the number of items returned, and the number of items purchased.

The program designer could initially organize the overall solution algorithm for this program into the three Problem-Solver Algorithm sections illustrated on the bottom line in Figure 1.18. This is called a **first-level structure diagram** for the algorithm, because it represents the first attempt at an initial, but not yet sufficiently detailed, structure for a solution algorithm.

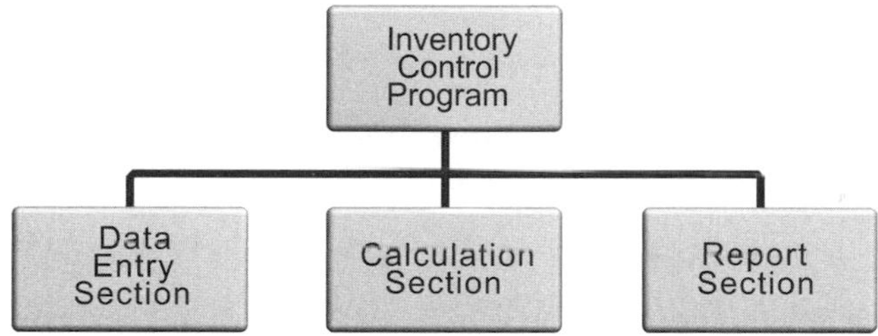

Figure 1.18 First-level structure diagram

Once you have developed an initial algorithm structure, you can then refine it until the tasks indicated in the boxes are completely defined. For example, both the data entry sections in Figure 1.18 would be further refined to specify provisions for entering the data. Because it is the system designer's responsibility to plan for contingencies and human error, provisions must also be made for changing incorrect data after an entry has been made and for deleting a previously entered value altogether. Similar subdivisions for the report section can also be made.

Figure 1.19 illustrates a second-level structure diagram for an inventory tracking system that includes these further refinements.

Notice that the design takes on a treelike structure where the levels branch out as we move from the top of the structure to the bottom. When the design is complete, each task designated in the lower boxes typically represents simple algorithms that are used by algorithms higher up in the structure. This type of algorithm development is referred to as a **top-down algorithm development**; it starts at the topmost level and proceeds to develop more and more detailed algorithms as it proceeds to the final set of algorithms.

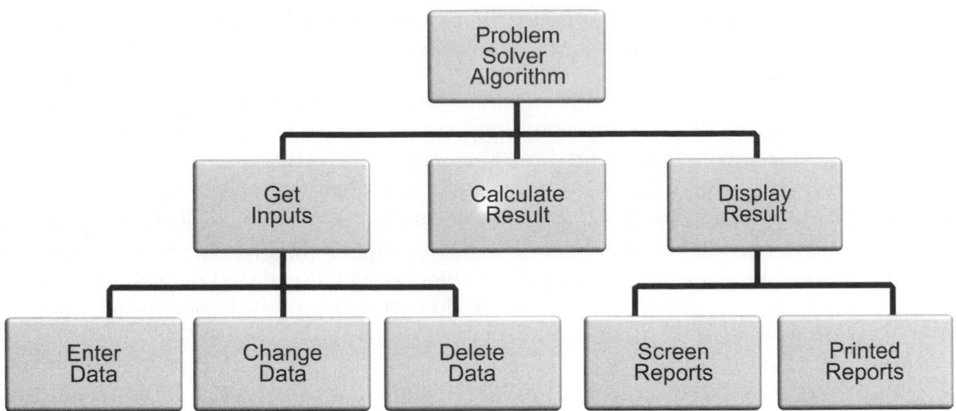

Figure 1.19 Second-level refinement structure diagram

Step 3: Write the Program Writing the program involves translating the chosen solution algorithm into a C language computer program. This step is also referred to as coding the algorithm.

If the analysis and solution steps have been correctly performed, writing the program becomes rather mechanical in nature. In a well-designed program, the statements making up the program will, however, conform to certain well-defined structures that have been defined in the solution step. These structures control how the program executes and consist of the following types:

1. Sequence
2. Selection
3. Iteration
4. Invocation

Sequence defines the order in which instructions are executed by the program. It specifies that instructions will be executed in the order they appear in the code, unless specifically altered by one of the other structures.

Selection provides the capability to make a choice between different instructions, depending on the result of some condition. For example, the value of a number can be checked before a division is performed. If the number is zero, the division will not be performed and a warning message will be issued to the user; otherwise, a division will take place. Selection capabilities and how they are coded in C are presented in Chapter 4.

Repetition, which is also referred to as **looping** and **iteration**, provides the ability for the same operation to be repeated based on the value of a condition. For example, grades might be repeatedly entered and added until a negative grade is entered. In this case the entry of a negative grade is the condition that signifies the end of the repetitive input and addition of grades. At that point a calculation of an average for all the grades entered could be performed. Repetition capabilities and how they are coded in C are presented in Chapter 5.

Invocation involves invoking, or summoning into action, specific sections of code as they are needed. Invocation capabilities and how they are coded in C are presented in Chapters 6 and 7.

Step 4: Test and Correct the Program The purpose of testing is to verify that a program works correctly and actually fulfills its requirements. In theory, testing would reveal all existing program errors (in computer terminology, a program error is called a bug[3]). In practice, this would require checking all possible combinations of statement execution. Because of the time and effort required, this is usually an impossible goal except for extremely simple programs. (We illustrate why this is generally an impossible goal in Section 4.8.)

Exhaustive testing is simply not feasible for most programs. For this reason, different methods of testing have evolved. At its most basic level, testing involves a conscious effort to ensure that a program works correctly and produces meaningful results. You must think carefully about what the test is meant to achieve and the data you will use in the test. If testing reveals an error (bug), you must initiate the process of debugging, which includes locating, correcting, and verifying the correction. It is important to realize that *although testing may reveal the presence of an error, it does not necessarily indicate the absence of one*. Thus, *the fact that a test revealed one bug does not indicate that another one is not lurking somewhere else in the program*.

To catch and correct errors in a program, it is important to develop a set of test data that determines whether the program gives correct answers. In fact, an accepted step in formal software testing is to plan the test procedures and create meaningful test data before writing the code. This helps the programmer be more objective about what the program must do, because it essentially circumvents any subconscious temptation after coding to avoid test data that will cause the program to fail. The tests should examine every possible situation under which a program will be used. This means testing with data within a reasonable range, using data that are at the limits of what is acceptable, and testing with invalid data that the program should detect and report as invalid data. In fact, developing good verifications tests and data for sophisticated problems can be more difficult than writing the program code itself.

Phase III: Documentation

In practice, most programmers forget many of the details of their own programs a few months after they have finished working on them. If they or other programmers must subsequently make modifications to the program, much valuable time can be lost figuring out just how the original program works. Good documentation prevents this from occurring.

So much work becomes useless or lost, and so many tasks must be repeated because of inadequate documentation that it could be argued that documenting your work is the most important step in problem solving. Actually, many of the critical documents are created during the analysis, design, coding, and testing steps. Completing the documentation requires collecting these documents, adding additional material, and presenting it in a form that is most useful to you and your organization.

Although not everybody classifies them in the same way, there are essentially six documents for every problem solution:

1. The requirements statement
2. A description of the algorithms that were coded
3. Comments within the code itself
4. A description of modification and changes made over time

[3]The derivation of this term is rather interesting. When a program stopped running on the MARK I at Harvard University in September 1945, Grace Hopper traced the malfunction to a dead insect that had gotten into the electrical circuits. She recorded the incident in her logbook at 15:45 hours as "Relay #70.... (moth) in relay. First actual case of bug being found."

5. Sample test runs, which include the inputs used for each run and the output obtained from the run
6. A user's manual, which is a detailed explanation of how to use the program

"Putting yourself in the shoes" of a member of a large organization's team that might use your work—anyone from the secretary to the programmer to the user— should help you to make the content and design of the important documentation clear. The documentation phase formally begins in phase I and continues into the maintenance phase.

Phase IV: Maintenance

This phase is concerned with ongoing correction of problems, revisions to meet changing needs, and adding new features. Maintenance is often the major effort, the primary source of revenue, and the longest lasting of the engineering phases. While development may take days or months, maintenance may continue for years or decades. The better the documentation is, the more efficiently this phase can be performed and the happier the customer and user will be.

Figure 1.20 illustrates the relative proportion of time attributable to maintenance as compared to development and design.

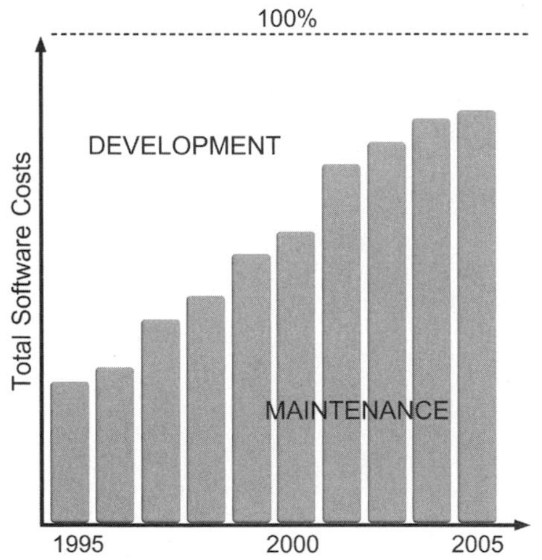

Figure 1.20 Maintenance is the dominant software cost

Figure 1.20 shows that the maintenance of existing programs currently accounts for approximately 70 percent of all programming costs. Students generally find this strange because they are accustomed to solving a problem and moving on to a different one. Commercial and scientific fields, however, do not operate this way. In these fields, one application or idea is typically built on a previous one and may require months or years of work. This is especially true in programming. Once an application is written, which may take weeks or months, maintenance may continue for years as new features are needed. Advances in technology such as communication, networking, fiber optics, and new graphical displays constantly demand updated software products.

How easily a program can be maintained (corrected, modified, or enhanced) is related to the ease with which the program can be read and understood. This, as you have learned, depends on the care with which the program was designed and the availability of high-quality documentation.

Backup

Although not part of the formal software development process, making and keeping backup copies of your work when writing a program is critical. In the course of revising a program, you may easily change the current working version of a program beyond recognition. Backup copies allow you to recover the last stage of work with a minimum of effort. The final working version of a useful program should be backed up at least twice. In this regard, another useful programming proverb is "Backup is unimportant if you don't mind starting all over again." The three fundamental rules of maintaining a program are:

1. *backup!*
2. *Backup!!*
3. *BACKUP!!!*

Many organizations keep at least one backup on site where it can be easily retrieved, and another backup copy either in a fireproof safe or at a remote location.

EXERCISES 1.4

Short Answer Questions

1. List and describe the four principle phases in the software development process.
2. An e-mail note from your department head, Ms. R. Karp, says: "Solve our inventory problems."
   a. What's your first task?
   b. How would you accomplish this task?
3. Suppose you are asked to create a C program that calculates the amount, in dollars, contained in a piggybank. The bank contains half-dollars, quarters, dimes, nickels, and pennies. Do not attempt to code this program. Instead, answer the following questions:
   a. For this programming problem, how many outputs are required?
   b. How many inputs does this problem have?
   c. Determine a formula for converting the input items into output items.
   d. Test the formula written for Question 3c using the following sample data: half dollars = 0, quarters = 17, dimes = 24, nickels = 16, pennies = 12.
4. Suppose you are asked to create a C program that calculates the value of distance, in miles, given the relationship *distance* = *rate* * *elapsed time*. Do not attempt to code this program. Instead, answer the following questions:
   a. For this programming problem, how many outputs are required?
   b. How many inputs does this problem have?
   c. What is the formula for converting the input items into output items?
   d. Test the formula written for Question 4c using the following sample data: rate = 55 miles per hour and elapsed time = 2.5 hours.
   e. How must the formula you determined in Question 4c be modified if the elapsed time is given in minutes instead of hours?
5. Suppose you are asked to create a C program that determines the value of Ergies, given the relationship

   Ergies = Fergies * Lergies

   (*Note:* All terms in this formula are for fictitious items.) Do not attempt to code this program. Instead, answer the following questions:
   a. For this programming problem, how many outputs are required?
   b. How many inputs does this problem have?
   c. What is the formula for converting the input items into output items?
   d. Test the formula written for Question 5c using the following sample data: Fergies = 14.65 and Lergies = 4.

6. Suppose you are asked to create a C program that displays the following name and address:

   Mr. J. Swanson

   63 Seminole Way

   Dumont, NJ 07030

   Do not attempt to code this program. Instead, answer the following questions:
   a. For this programming problem, how many lines of output are required?
   b. How many inputs does this problem have?
   c. Is there a formula for converting the input items into output items? Why or why not?

7. Suppose you are asked to create a C program that determines the distance a car has traveled after 10 seconds assuming the car is initially traveling at 88 feet per second (this equals 60 miles per hour) and the driver applies the brakes to uniformly decelerate at a rate of 12 feet/sec 2. Use the fact that distance = st -(1/2)dt^2, where s is the initial speed of the car, d is the deceleration, and t is the elapsed time. Do not attempt to code this program. Instead, answer the following questions:
   a. For this programming problem, how many outputs are required?
   b. How many inputs does this problem have?
   c. What is the formula for converting the input items into output items?
   d. Test the algorithm written for Question 7c using the data given in the problem.

Many programming problems require both initial negotiations with a client and additional information that the client desires before programming even begins. Questions 8 through 13 are intended to familiarize you with some of the situations you may face, especially if you do any freelance programming.

8. Many people requesting a program or system for the first time consider coding to be the most important aspect of program development. They feel that they know what they need and think that the programmer can begin coding with minimal analysis time. As a programmer, what pitfalls can you envision in working with such people?

9. Many people requesting a program try to contract with programmers for a fixed fee (total amount to be paid is fixed in advance). What is the advantage to the user in having this arrangement? What is the advantage to the programmer in having this arrangement? What are some disadvantages to both user and programmer in this arrangement?

10. Many freelance programmers prefer to work on an hourly rate basis. Why do you think this is so? Under what conditions would it be advantageous for a programmer to give a client a fixed price for the programming effort?

11. People who have experience hiring programmers generally expect a clearly written statement of programming work to be done, including a complete description of what the program will do, delivery dates, payment schedules, and testing requirements. What is the advantage to the user in requiring this? What is the advantage to a programmer in working under this arrangement? What disadvantages does this arrangement pose for both client and programmer?

12. A computer store has asked you to write a sales recording program. The store is open six days a week, each sale requires an average of 100 characters, and, on average, the store makes 15 sales per day. The owner of the store has asked you to determine how many characters must be kept for all sales records for a two-year period. What estimate would you provide to the owner?

13. You are creating a sales recording system for a new client. Each sale input to the system requires that the operator type in a description of the item sold, the name and address of the firm buying the item, the value of the item, and a code for the person making the trade. This information consists of a maximum of 300 characters. The client will have to hire one or more data entry people to convert their existing manual records into computer records. They currently have more than 5,000 sales records, and have asked you how much time it would take to enter these records into your new system. What estimate would you provide? (*Hint:* To solve this problem you must make an assumption about the number of words per minute that an average typist can type and the average number of characters per word.)

1.5 Case Study: Design and Development

In this section we apply the design and development phase (phase II) of the software development process to the following program requirements specification:

> *The circumference, C, of a circle is given by the formula C = 2 π r, where π is the constant 3.1416 (accurate to four decimal places), and r is the radius of the circle. Using this information, write a C program to calculate the circumference of a circle that has a 2-inch radius.*

Step 1: Analyze the Problem

This step verifies that the program specification is complete and that we have a complete understanding of what is required.

a. Determine the Desired Outputs In determining the desired outputs, concentrate on words in the requirements statement such as calculate, print, determine, find, or compare. For our sample program requirement above, the key phrase is "to calculate the circumference of a circle." This identifies an output item (the circumference of a circle). Since there are no other such phrases in the problem, only one output item is required.

b. Determine the Input Items After clearly identifying the desired outputs, you must identify all input items. (If you are more comfortable identifying inputs before outputs, do so.) It is essential, at this stage, to distinguish between input items and input values. An input item is the name of an input quantity, while an input value is a specific number or quantity that can be used as the input item. For example, in our program requirement, the input item is the radius of the circle. Although this input item has a specific numerical value in this problem (the known quantity, which has a value of 2), actual input values are generally not important at this stage.

Input values are not needed at this point because the relationship between inputs and outputs is typically independent of specific input values. The formula depends on knowing the output and input items and whether there are any special constrains. Notice that the relationship between the two, which will be expressed by a formula, is correct regardless of any specific values assigned to the input items (unless there are specific constraints where the formula is valid). Although we cannot produce an actual numerical value for the output item without specific values for the input items, the correct relationship between inputs and outputs is expressed by the formulas relating the two, which are listed next.

c. List the Formulas Relating the Inputs to the Outputs The final step is to determine how to create the output from the inputs. This is answered by knowing the formulas between output and input quantities. In this case the relationship is provided by the single formula $C = 2 \pi r$, where C is the output item and r is the input item. Again, be aware that the formula does not require listing specific input values; it simply identifies the relationship between input and output items.

If you are unsure how to obtain the required outputs from the given inputs, you need a clearer requirements statement. In other words, you need to obtain more information about the problem.

d. Perform a Hand Calculation Having listed the formulas, the next step is to check the formula using specific input values. Performing a manual calculation, either by hand or using a calculator, helps to ensure that you really do understand the problem. An added feature of doing a manual calculation is that the results can be used later to verify program operation in the testing step. Then, when the final program is used with other data, you will have established a degree of confidence that a correct result is being calculated.

It is in this step that we need specific input values that can be assigned to the input items used by the formula to produce the desired output. For this problem one input value is given: a radius of 2 inches. Substituting this value into the formula, we obtain a circumference = 2 (3.1416)(2) = 12.5664 inches for the circle.

Step 2: Select an Overall Solution Algorithm

The general Problem-Solver Algorithm presented in the previous section is:

Get the inputs to the problem
Calculate the desired outputs
Report the results of the calculation

For determining the circumference of a circle, this algorithm becomes:

Set the radius value to 2
Calculate the circumference, C, using the formula $C = 2 \pi r$
Display the calculated value for C

Step 3: Write the Program

Program 1.1 illustrates the code for the algorithm for determining the circumference of a circle having a radius of 2. Because we have not yet introduced the C language, the program will be unfamiliar to you; however, you should be able to understand what the key individual lines are accomplishing. To help you in this, line numbers have been provided. These line numbers are never part of a C program, but will always be inserted for easily identifying individual C statements.

In this case the program follows a sequential order, where each statement is executed in strict sequential order, one after another. To help you understand it, however, comments, which are the text between the `/*` and `*/` symbols, have been included in lines 5, 7, and 8. Although all of the program lines are explained fully in the next chapter, for now, pay attention to these three lines and use the comments to relate these lines to the algorithm selected in the analysis step.

In line 5 the names `radius` and `circumference` are defined for use by the program. The program attaches no significance to these names (the names `r` and `c`, `x` and `y`, or `in` and `out`, for example, could just as well have been defined), but names that are more descriptive and have some meaning to the actual problem should always be chosen. In line 7 a value is assigned to the name `radius`, while in line 8 a value is computed for the item named `circumference`. Finally, in line 9 the value of the circumference is printed.

Program 1.1

```
 1  #include <stdio.h>
 2
 3  int main()
 4  {
 5    float radius, circumference;  /* declare an input and output item */
 6
 7    radius = 2.0;     /* set a value for the radius */
 8    circumference = 2.0 * 3.1416 * radius;  /* calculate the circumference */
 9    printf("The circumference of the circle is %f\n", circumference);
10
11    return 0;
12  }
```

When Program 1.1 is executed, the following output is produced:

```
The circumference of the circle is 12.566400
```

Step 4: Test and Correct the Program

Because only one calculation is performed by the program, testing Program 1.1 really means verifying that the single output is correct. Because the output agrees with our prior hand calculation, we can now use the program to calculate the circumference of circles with different radii and have confidence in the results.

EXERCISES 1.5

Short Answer Questions

1. Assuming a programmer used the names `rad` and `cir` in Program 1.1 instead of the names `radius` and `circumference`, determine the lines that would have to be modified in the program and rewrite these lines to reflect the change in names.

2. Assume that the area of a circle is required in addition to its circumference. What modifications do you think would have to be made to Program 1.1 to accommodate this additional requirement?

3. You have been asked to write a program that converts 86 kilometers to miles, where the formula for converting kilometers to miles is *miles = .625(kilometers)*. Do not attempt to code this program. Instead, answer the following questions:
   a. Write a complete program requirements specification for this problem.
   b. Determine the output required by the program.
   c. Determine how many inputs the program will have.
   d. What is the formula for converting the input items into output items?
   e. Do a hand calculation for the given input value.
   f. Provide a solution algorithm for this problem.

4. In 1627, Manhattan Island was sold to Dutch settlers for approximately $24. Suppose you are asked to create a program that answers this question: If the proceeds of that sale had been deposited in a Dutch bank paying 5 percent interest, compounded annually, what is the principal balance at the end of 2006? The program should display the following output, with an actual value replacing the x's: Balance as of December 31, 2006, is xxxxxx. Do not attempt to code this program. Instead, answer the following questions:
   a. Write a complete program requirements specification for this problem.
   b. Determine the output required by the program.
   c. Determine how many inputs the program will have.
   d. Determine a formula for converting the input items into output items.
   e. Do a hand calculation for the given input value.
   f. Provide a solution algorithm for this problem.

5. Suppose you are asked to create a C program that calculates and displays the weekly gross pay and net pay of two individuals. The first individual is paid an hourly rate of $8.43, and the second individual is paid an hourly rate of $5.67. Both individuals have 20 percent of their gross pay withheld for income tax purposes, and both pay 2 percent of their gross pay, before taxes, for medical benefits. Do not attempt to code this program. Instead, answer the following questions.
   a. For this programming problem, how many outputs are required?
   b. What is the formula for converting the input items into output items?
   c. How many inputs does this problem have?
   d. Test the formula written for Question 5c using the following sample data: The first person works 40 hours during the week and the second person works 35 hours.
   e. Provide a solution algorithm for this problem.

6. The formula for the standard normal deviate, z, used in statistical applications is:

   $z = (X - \mu)/\sigma$

   where µ refers to a mean value and to a standard deviation. Suppose you are asked to write a program that calculates and displays the value of the standard normal deviate where $X = 85.3$, $\mu = 80$, and $\sigma = 4$. Do not attempt to code this program. Instead, answer the following questions:

   a. For this programming problem, how many outputs are required?
   b. How many inputs does this problem have?
   c. What is the formula for converting the input items into output items?
   d. Test the formula written for Question 6c using the data given in the problem.
   e. Provide a solution algorithm for this problem.

7. The equation describing exponential growth is:

   $y = ex$

   Suppose you are asked to create a program that calculates the value of y. Do not attempt to code this program. Instead, answer the following questions:

   a. For this programming problem, how many outputs are required?
   b. How many inputs does this problem have?
   c. What is the formula converting the input items into output items?
   d. Test the formula written for Question 7c assuming $e = 2.718$ and $x = 10$.
   e. Provide a solution algorithm for this problem.

1.6 Common Programming Errors

Part of learning any programming language is making the elementary mistakes that other beginning programmers have made before you. Each language has its own set of common programming errors waiting for the unwary, and these mistakes can be quite frustrating. The most common errors associated with the material presented in this chapter are as follows:

1. Rushing to write and execute a program without spending sufficient time learning about the problem or designing an appropriate algorithm. In this regard, it is worthwhile to remember the programming proverb: "*It is impossible to construct a successful program for a problem that is not fully understood.*" A similar and equally valuable proverb is "*The sooner you start programming an application, the longer it usually takes to debug and complete.*"

2. Forgetting to back up a program. Almost all new programmers make this mistake until they lose a program that has taken considerable time to code.

3. Not understanding that computers respond only to explicitly defined algorithms. Telling a computer to add a group of numbers is quite different than telling a friend to add the numbers. The computer must be given the precise instructions for doing the addition in a programming language.

1.7 Chapter Summary

1. The first attempt at creating a self-operating computational machine was attempted by Charles Babbage in 1822. The concept became a reality with the Atanasoff-Berry Computer built in 1937 at Iowa State University, which was the first computer to use a binary numbering scheme to store and manipulate data.

   The earliest large-scale digital computer was the ENIAC, built in 1946 at the Moore School of Engineering at the University of Pennsylvania. This machine, however, required external wiring to direct its operation.

   The first computer to employ the concept of a stored program was the EDSAC, built at Cambridge University in England. The operating principals used in the design of this machine, developed by the mathematician John Von Neumann, are still used by the majority of computers manufactured today.
2. The physical components used in constructing a computer are called hardware.
3. The programs used to operate a computer are referred to as software.
4. Programming languages come in a variety of forms and types. Machine language programs, also known as executable programs, contain the binary codes that can be executed by a computer. Assembly languages permit the use of symbolic names for mathematical operations and memory addresses. Programs written in assembly languages must be converted to machine language, using translator programs called assemblers, before the programs can be executed. Assembly and machine languages are referred to as low-level languages.
5. Compiler and interpreter languages are referred to as high-level languages. This means that they are written using instructions that resemble a written language, such as English, and can be run on a variety of computer types. Compiler languages require a compiler to translate the program into a machine language form, while interpreter languages require an interpreter to do the translation.
6. An algorithm is a step-by-step sequence of instructions that must terminate and describes how to perform an operation to produce the desired output.
7. The software development procedure consists of the following four phases:
   - Specification of the program's requirements
   - Design and development
   - Documentation
   - Maintenance
8. The design and development phase consists of four well-defined steps:
   - Analyze the problem
   - Select an overall solution algorithm
   - Write the program
   - Test and correct the program

9. Writing (or coding) a program consists of translating the solution algorithm into a computer language such as C.
10. Four fundamental control structures used in writing a program are:
    - Sequence
    - Selection
    - Iteration
    - Invocation
11. Although making copies of a program is not formally a part of the software development process, it is essential that you always keep at least one copy of a program. This copy is referred to as a backup copy, or backup, for short.

1.8 Chapter Appendix: Numerical Storage Codes

The most commonly used code for storing integers within a computer's memory unit is called **two's complement.** This code associates each integer (both positive and negative) with a specific pattern of bits.

A bit pattern, such as 10001011, that is considered to be a numeric value, is referred to as a **binary number.** The easiest way to determine the decimal value of an integer binary number is to first construct a simple device called a **value box.** Figure 1.21 illustrates a value box for a single byte. (For convenience, in the following discussion we will assume words consisting of a single byte, although the procedure also applies to larger-sized words.)

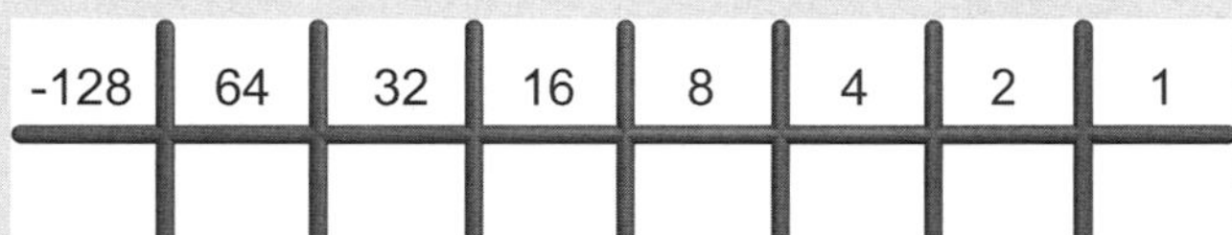

Figure 1.21 An 8-bit value box for two's complement conversion

Mathematically, each value in the box illustrated in Figure 1.21 represents an increasing power of two. Since two's complement numbers must be capable of representing both positive and negative integers, the leftmost position, in addition to having the largest absolute magnitude, also has a negative sign.

Conversion of any binary number, for example 10001101, into its equivalent decimal value simply requires inserting the bit pattern in the value box and adding the only those values that have a 1 under them. Thus, as illustrated in Figure 1.22, the bit pattern 10001101 represents the integer number –115.

Reviewing the value box shows that any binary number with a leading 1 represents a negative number, and any bit pattern with a leading 0 represents a positive number. The value box can also be used in reverse, to convert a base 10 integer number into its equivalent binary bit pattern. Some conversions, in fact, can be made by inspection. For example, the base 10 number –125 is obtained by adding 3 to –128. Thus, the binary representation of –125 is 10000011, which equals –128 + 2 + 1. Similarly, the two's complement representation of the number 40 is 00101000, which is 32 plus 8.

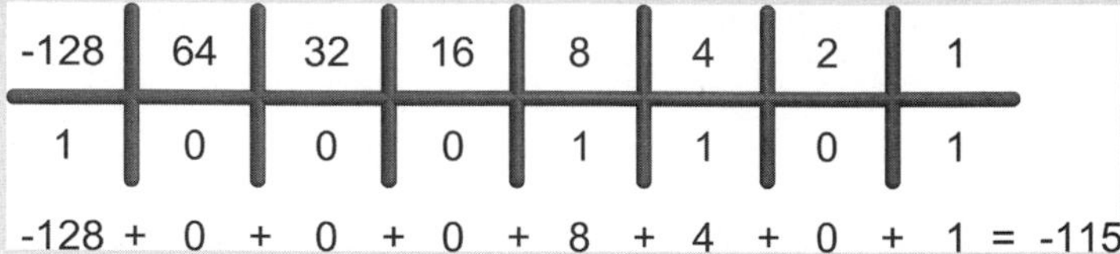

Figure 1.22 Converting 10001101 to a base 10 number

Although the value box conversion method is deceptively simple, the method is directly related to the mathematical basis of two's complement binary numbers. The original name of the two's complement binary code was the **weighted-sign binary code,** which correlates directly to the value box. As the name "weighted sign" implies, each bit position has a weight, or value, of two raised to a power and a sign. The signs of all bits except the leftmost bit are positive and the sign of the leftmost or most significant bit is negative.

Chapter 2

Getting Started in C Programming

A C program is constructed from one or more procedures, which are known as functions. Every program must, however, contain at least one function named `main`. In this chapter we begin our introduction to the fundamentals of C programming by presenting the structure of a `main` function and another function, `printf`, which is used extensively for displaying output on a monitor. Additionally, C's elementary data types, variables, and declarations, which form the basis for almost all computations are presented. The topics in this and the next chapter complete the introduction to basic input, processing, and output statements used in almost all C programs.

2.1 Introduction to C Programming

As noted in Section 1.2, C is a procedural language; this means that the available instructions are used to create self-contained units, which are known as functions in C. The purpose of a function is to accept data as input and transform the data in some manner to produce a specific result.

Figure 2.1 illustrates the construction of a typical C program. Existing functions, which can be created by the programmer or supplied by the C compiler, serve as the basis for new functions, all of which can then be incorporated into a completed source program.

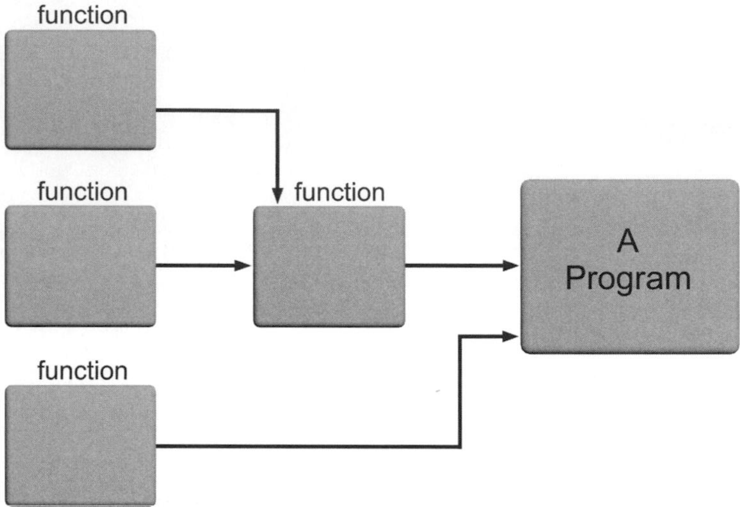

Figure 2.1 C programs are modular

You can think of a function as a small machine that transforms the data it receives into a finished product. Figure 2.2 illustrates a function that accepts two numbers as inputs and multiplies the two numbers to produce one output. As illustrated in Figure 2.2, the interface to the function from the outside consists of the inputs it receives and the outputs it produces. How the inputs are converted to outputs are both encapsulated and hidden within the function. In this regard the function can be thought of as a single unit providing a special-purpose operation.

In fact, C provides a comprehensive set of functions that are collectively stored in a set of files known as the standard library.[1] You'll be able to construct many programs based entirely on the offerings in the standard library, thereby greatly increasing your programming productivity and decreasing programming errors.

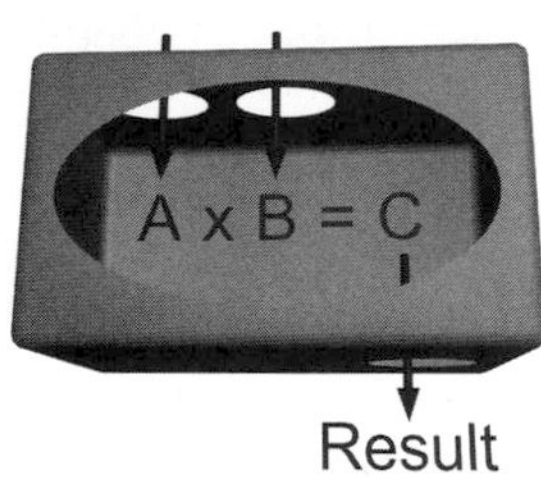

Figure 2.2 A multiplying function

As an example, Program 1.1, which was developed in Section 1.5, is reproduced as Program 2.1. This program computes a value for the circumference of a circle, in line 8, that has a radius of 2, which is set in line 7. The program consists of a single function named `main`, which begins on line 3. Internal to `main`, a second function named `printf` is used in line 9. The `printf` function is provided by C's standard library in a file named `stdio.h` (this is the reason for line 1, which tells the compiler to include this header file when compiling the program). Specifically, `printf` is used to display data on a computer's monitor, and is used in line 9 to display the value of the circumference that was computed in line 8. The line numbers, as was stated in Section 1.5, are not part of a C program and should never

[1] The standard library consists of 15 header files that are described in detail in Appendix C. Each of these header files consists of C source code that you can open and inspect. You can find them on your computer by doing a search for any one of them, such as `stdio.h`.

be entered when writing a program. They have been included simply to help identify individual C statements when these are referenced in the text.

Program 2.1

```
#include <stdio.h>

int main()
{
  float radius, circumference;   /* declare an input and output item */

  radius = 2.0;    /* set a value for the radius */
  circumference = 2.0 * 3.1416 * radius;   /* calculate the circumference */
  printf("The circumference of the circle is %f\n", circumference);

  return 0;
}
```

Program 2.1 consists entirely of words and symbols, such as the pound sign #, angle brackets <> , parentheses, `()`, semicolon, `;`, braces, { and }, the symbols /* and */, as well as = and `*`. The meaning of each of these symbols will be explained in this chapter. The names of functions, as well as all of the words that are permitted in a program, such as `radius` and `circumference` that have special meaning to the compiler are collectively referred to as **identifiers**. It is important in naming functions and data items that you choose identifiers that convey to other programmers some idea about what the function and data item stands for and that conform to C's rules for selecting identifiers. We now see what identifiers are and what these rules are.

Identifiers

Identifiers in C consist of three types: reserved words, standard identifiers, and programmer-created identifiers, each of which has its own special requirements. As these form the basis of all C code, we now consider them individually.

Reserved Words A **reserved word** is a word that is predefined by the programming language for a special purpose and can only be used in a specified manner for its intended purpose.

Attempts to use reserved words for any other purpose will generate an error when the code is compiled. Reserved words are also referred to as **keywords** in C, and we will use these two terms interchangeably.

Table 2.1 presents a complete list of C's keywords. As you progress in your programming studies, you will learn where, why, and how these words are used.

Programming Note

Tokens

In a computer language, a token is the smallest unit of the language that has a unique meaning. Thus, the reserved words, programmer-defined identifiers, and all special mathematical symbols, such as + and -, are considered tokens of the C language.

Table 2.1 Keywords

auto	default	float	register	struct	volatile
break	do	for	return	switch	while
case	double	goto	short	typedef	
char	else	if	signed	union	
const	enum	int	sizeof	unsigned	
continue	extern	long	static	void	

Standard Identifiers **Standard identifiers** are words that are predefined in C. They have a predefined purpose, but a programmer can redefine this purpose. Most of the standard identifiers that you use are the names of functions that are provided in the C standard library. A number of standard identifiers are listed in Table 2.2.

Table 2.2 Sample of C Standard Identifiers

abs	fopen	isalpah	rand	strcpy
argc	free	malloc	rewind	strlen
argv	fseek	memcpy	scanf	tolower
calloc	gets	printf	sin	toupper
fclose	isacii	puts	strcat	ungetc

It is good programming practice to use standard identifiers only for their intended purpose. For example, the standard identifier `rand` is the name of a C function provided in the standard library. This function can be used to create a set of one or more random numbers, which are extremely useful in constructing simulation programs. In certain situations, however, it might be advantageous for a programmer to develop a specialized or more efficient random number generation function and use the name `rand` for this function.

Programmer-created Identifiers A large number of the identifiers used in a C program are selected by the programmer, and are known as **programmer-created identifiers**. These types of identifiers are also referred to as **programmer-created names** and are used for naming data and functions.

Programmer-created names must conform to C's identifier rules (as do reserved words and standard identifiers), which means that they can be any combination of letters, digits, or underscores (_) subject to the following rules:

1. The first character of the identifier must be a letter or underscore (_).
2. Only letters, digits, or underscores may follow the initial character. Blank spaces are not allowed. Additionally, a programmer-created identifier *cannot* be a reserved word (see Table 2.1).

Notice that the names `radius` and `circumference` in Program 2.1, which are programmer-selected, conform to the above rules.

Practically speaking, it's a good idea to limit programmer-selected identifiers to fewer than 14 characters, with 20 characters as an outside maximum. This will help prevent possible typing errors.

It is also helpful to combine words to create an identifier that indicates, at a glance, the purpose of a function or data. In older C programs, programmers typically only used lowercase letters, sometimes with underscores separating individual words in a longer identifier, such as `calculate_payment`. In newer C programs, the underscore is typically not used and the first letter of every word after the first word is capitalized. Examples of valid programmer-created names are:

```
checkItems      displayAMessage       randomNumbers
hoursWorked     tempConversion        multByTwo
```

Examples of invalid C programmer-created names are:

- `4ab7` (begins with a number, which violates Rule 1)
- `e*6` (contains a special character, which violates Rule 2)
- `calculate total` (contains a blank character, which violates Rule 2)
- `while` (this is a reserved word)

You will sometimes encounter identifiers consisting of all uppercase letters. These are usually used to indicate a symbolic constant, a topic covered in Chapter 3.

In addition to conforming to C's identifier rules, a C function name must always be followed by parentheses (the reason for these will be seen shortly). A good function name should convey some idea about how it will be used. Thus, the identifier `degToRadians()` (note that we have included the required parentheses after the identifier, which clearly marks this as a function name) would be a good name for a function that converts degrees to radians. In this case, the name helps identify what the function does. Identifiers such as:

```
easy   duh   justDoIt   mary   bill   theForce
```

provide no indication of their use. They are examples of bad programming and should be avoided. Your identifiers should always be descriptive and indicate their purpose or how they will be used.

Finally, it is important to understand that C is a case-sensitive language. This means that the language distinguishes between uppercase and lowercase letters. Thus, in C, the identifiers TOTAL, total, and TotaL represent three distinct and different identifiers.

The `main()` Function

One of the nice features of C is that we can plan a program by first deciding what functions are needed and how they will be linked. Then we can write each function to perform the task it is required to do.

To provide for the orderly placement and execution of functions and individual statements, each C program must have one and only one function named `main()`. The reserved word main tells the compiler where program execution is to begin. The `main()` function is sometimes referred to as a **driver function**, because it tells the other functions the sequence in which they are to operate (see Figure 2.3).[2]

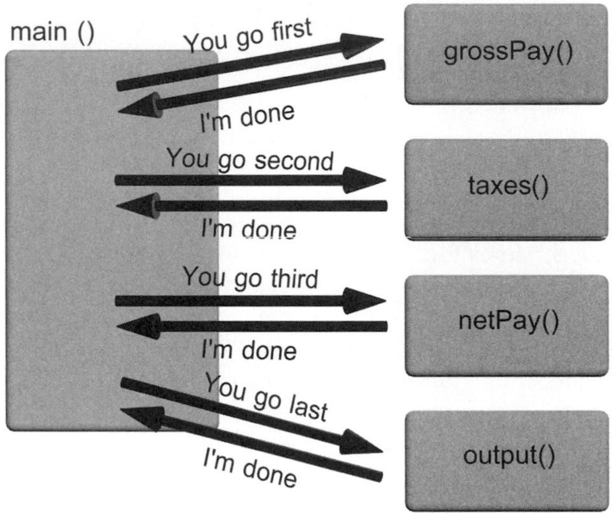

Figure 2.3 The `main()` function controls all other functions

Figure 2.4 illustrates a complete `main()` function that causes each of the functions shown in Figure 2.3 to be executed in the order listed. The first line of the function, in this case `int main()`, is referred to as a function header line. A **function header line**, which is always the first line of a function, contains three pieces of information:

1. What type of data, if any, is returned by the function
2. The name of the function
3. What type of data, if any, is sent into the function

The keyword before the function name defines the type of value the function returns when it has completed operating. When placed before the function's name, the keyword `int` (see Table 2.1) designates that the function returns an integer value. Similarly, empty parentheses following the function name signify that no data will be transmitted into the function when it is run. (Data transmitted into a function at run time are referred to as **arguments of the function**.) The braces, `{` and `}`, enclose the statements that make up the function; as such, they determine the beginning and end of the function. The statements inside the braces

[2] Functions executed from `main()` may, in turn, execute other functions. Each function, however, always returns to the function that initiated its execution. This is true even for `main()`, which returns control to the operating system in effect when `main()` was initiated.

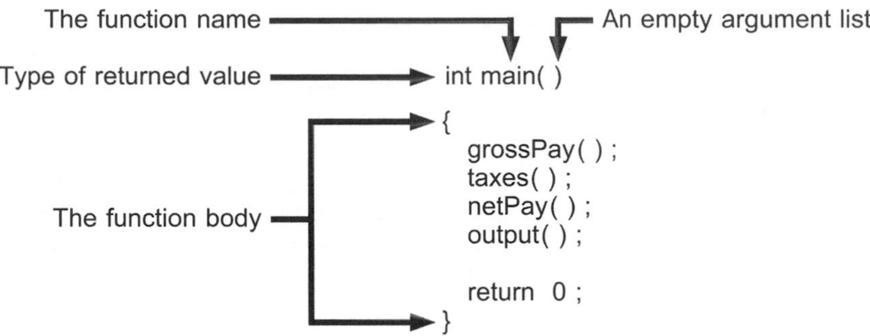

Figure 2.4 A sample `main()` function

determine what the function does. All statements that cause some specific action to be performed by the computer when the function is executed must end with a semicolon (;). Such statements are known as **executable statements**, and will be described in more detail as we progress in our understanding of C.

You will be naming and writing many of your own C functions. In fact, the rest of this book is primarily about how to determine what functions are required, including `main`, how to write the functions, and how to combine them into a working C program. Each program, however, must have a `main()` function. Until we learn how to pass data into a function and return data from a function (the topics of Chapter 6), the header line illustrated in Figure 2.4 will serve us for all the programs we need to write. Using this construction, it is convenient to think of the first two lines

```
int main()
{
```

as designating that "the program begins here," and regard the last two lines

```
  return 0;
}
```

as simply designating the end of the program.

Fortunately, many useful functions have already been written for us and are contained within the standard library. We will now see how to use one of these functions to create a working C program.

The `printf()` Function

One of the most useful functions provided with all C compilers is named `printf()`. This function, as its name suggests, is a print function that formats data and sends it to the standard system display device. For most systems, the display device is the monitor screen. The function prints out whatever data is provided to it by the program. For example, if the message `Hello there world!` is provided to `printf()`, this message is printed (or displayed on your terminal) by the `printf()` function. Inputting data or messages to a function is called **passing data to the function**. The programmer can pass the message `Hello there world!` to the `printf()` function by enclosing the message in double quotes and placing it inside the parentheses in the function's name as follows:

```
printf("Hello there world!");
```

Programming Note

Executable and Nonexecutable Statements

We will be introducing many C statements in this text that can be used to create functions and programs. All statements, however, belong to one or two broad categories: executable statements and nonexecutable statements.

An executable statement causes some specific action to be performed by the computer when the program is executed. For example, a statement that tells the computer to display output or add or subtract a number is an executable statement. Executable statements must always end with a semicolon.

A nonexecutable statement is one that describes some feature of the program or its data, but does not cause the computer to perform any action when a program is executed. An example of a nonexecutable statement is a function header line or a comment. The function header explicitly defines the beginning of a function, but causes no specific action to be taken by the computer when the program is executing. Similarly, a comment is intended for use by anyone reading the program. All comments are ignored by the compiler when it translates source code.

The purpose of the parentheses in all function names is to provide a funnel through which information can be passed to the function (see Figure 2.5). As noted earlier, the items that are passed to the function through the parentheses are referred to as the **function's arguments**.

Now let's put all this together into a working C program that can be run on your computer. Consider Program 2.2. Note that the numbers at the beginning of each line are not part of the program code but are line numbers included to make it easier to refer to individual parts of the program.

Program 2.2

```
/*
File: Pgm2-2.cpp
Description: displays Hello there world!
Programmer: G. Bronson
Date: 6/15/06
*/

#include <stdio.h>
int main()
{
  printf("Hello there world!");

  return 0;
}
```

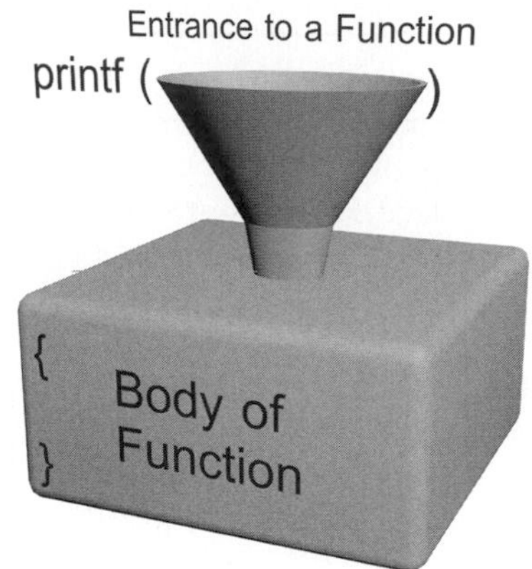

Figure 2.5 Passing a message to `printf()`

The first six lines of program code, starting with the slash and asterisk symbol pair on line one, `/*`, and ending with the matching asterisk slash pair, `*/`, on line six, constitutes a comment block. A **comment** is a note about the code that the programmer includes so that he (or other programmers) can keep track of what the various parts of the program do. Comments are not actual instructions to the computer, but are simply explanations for the programmer. As such, any words within the comment *need not* follow the rules for identifiers.

A comment can consist of one line or multiple lines and consists of all typed characters following the `/*` symbols and ending with the closing `*/` symbol pair. We will have much more to say about comments in the next section, but for now it is important to understand that each source code program should begin with comments similar to those used here. These initial comment lines, at a minimum, should provide the filename under which the source code is saved, a short program description, the name of the programmer, and the date that the program was last modified. For all of the programs contained in this text, the filename refers to the name of the source code file provided with this text.

The seventh line of the program is a blank line, which is inserted to make the program easier for a programmer to read. Blank lines can always be added or eliminated and have no effect on a program's execution.

The eighth line of the program:

```
#include <stdio.h>
```

is a preprocessor command. Preprocessor commands begin with a pound sign, #, and perform some action before the compiler translates the source program into machine code. Specifically, the `#include` preprocessor command causes the contents of the named file, in this case `stdio.h`, to be inserted where the `#include` command appears. The file `stdio.h` is referred to as a **header file** because it is placed at the top, or head, of a C program using the `#include` command. In particular, the `stdio.h` file provides a proper interface to the `printf()` function and should be included in all programs using `printf()`. As indicated in Program 2.2, preprocessor commands do not end with a semicolon.

Following the preprocessor command is the start of the program's `main()` function. The word `main` in a C program tells the computer where the program starts. Because a program can have only one starting point, every C language program must contain one and only one `main()` function. The `main()` function has only two statements. Remember that statements end with a semicolon (`;`). The first statement in `main()` initiates execution of the `printf()`function and passes one argument to it. As described in Section 1.4, this is formally referred to as **invoking** a function, which is also more commonly referred to as **calling the function.** In this particular case, the `printf()` function, which is provided as part of the standard C library, is called and the statements within this function are executed. The argument passed into the function is the message `Hello there world!`. When the `printf()` function displays this message and is finished executing, the computer encounters the `return` statement in line 13. The return statement completes the processing within the `main()` function by returning control to the operating system.

> **Programming Note**
>
> **What Is Syntax?**
>
> A programming language's **syntax** is the set of rules for formulating statements that are "grammatically correct" for the language. A syntactically correct C statement has the proper form specified for the compiler. Thus, the compiler will accept the statement and not generate an error message.
>
> An individual statement or program can be syntactically correct and still be logically incorrect. Such a statement, though correctly structured, would produce an incorrect result. This is similar to an English statement that is grammatically correct but makes no sense. For example, although the sentence "See the tree running" is grammatically correct and contains a noun and verb, it makes no sense.

Because `printf()` is provided as part of the standard C library, we do not have to write it; it is available for use just by calling it correctly. Like all C functions, `printf()` was written to do a specific task, which is to print results. It is versatile and can print results in many different forms. When a message is passed to `printf()`, the function sees to it that the message is correctly printed on your screen.

Messages are known as **strings** in C, because they consist of a string of characters made up of letters, numbers, and special characters. The beginning and end of a string of characters is marked by double quotes. Thus, in line 11 of Program 2.2,

```
11  printf("Hello there world!");
```

the message passed to the function is placed inside the function's parentheses, in double quotes, as shown. The program output (that is, the result displayed on the screen) is

```
Hello there world!
```

Let's take a look at another program to get a sense of `printf()`'s versatility. Read Program 2.3 to determine what it does. To make the program easy to read, we have placed a blank line before the `return` statement, and will continue to do this in all remaining programs.

Program 2.3

```
/*
File: Pgm2-3.cpp
Description: Test program
Programmer: G. Bronson
Date: 6/15/06
*/

```

```
#include <stdio.h>

int main()
{
  printf("Computers, computers everywhere");
  printf("\n as far as I can C");

  return 0;
}
```

When Program 2.3 is run, it produces the following output:

```
Computers, computers everywhere
as far as I can C
```

You might be wondering why the `\n` did not appear in the output. The two characters `\` and `n`, when used together, are called a **newline escape sequence**. They tell `printf()` to start on a new line. In C, the backslash (\) character provides an "escape" from the normal interpretation of the character following it by altering the meaning of the next character. If the backslash was omitted from the second `printf()` call in Program 2.3, the `n` would be printed as the letter `n` and the program would display:

```
Computers, computers everywheren as far as I can C
```

Newline escape sequences can be placed anywhere within the message passed to `printf()`. See if you can determine what the next program prints.

```
#include <stdio.h>
int main()
{
  printf ("Computers everywhere\n as far as\n\nI can see");

  return 0;
}
```

The output for this program is

```
Computers everywhere
as far as

I can see
```

EXERCISES 2.1

Short Answer Questions

1. State whether the following are valid function names. If they are valid, state whether they are descriptive names. A descriptive function name conveys some idea about what the function might do. If they are invalid names, state why.

```
m1234()   invoices()     abcd()     A12345()   1A2345()
power()   salestax()     do()       while()    int()
add5()    newBalance()   newBal()   netPay()   12345()
taxes()   a2b3c4d5()     absVal()   amount()   $taxes()
```

2. Assume that the following functions have been written:

   `input(), salestax(), balance(), calcbill()`

   From the functions' names, what do you think each of these function might do?

3. Select valid identifier names for functions that do the following:
   a. Find the maximum value in a set of numbers.
   b. Find the minimum value in a set of numbers.
   c. Convert a lowercase letter to an uppercase letter.
   d. Convert an uppercase letter to a lowercase letter.
   e. Sort a set of numbers from lowest to highest.
   f. Alphabetize a set of names.

4. In response to a newline escape sequence, `printf()` positions the next displayed character at the beginning of a new line. This positioning of the next character actually represents two distinct operations. What do you think they are?

Programming Exercises

1. a. Use the `printf()` function to write a C program that prints your name on one line, your street address on a second line, and your city, state, and zip code on the third line.
   b. Run the program you have written for Exercise 1a on a computer.

2. a. Write a C program to print the following verse:

```
Computers, computers everywhere
as far as I can see
I really, really like these things,
Oh joy, Oh joy for me!
```

   b. Run the program you have written for Exercise 2a on a computer.

3. a. How many `printf()` statements would you use to print the following:

```
Part No.   Price
T1267      $6.34
T1300      $8.92
T2401      $65.40
T4482      $36.99
```

b. What is the minimum number of `printf()` statements that could be used to print the table in Exercise 3a? Why would you not write a program using the minimum number of `printf()` function calls?
c. Write a complete C program to produce the data shown in Exercise 3a.
d. Run the program you have written for Exercise 3c on a computer.

4. a. Most computer operating systems provide the capability for redirecting the output produced by `printf()` either to a printer or directly to a hard disk file. Read the first part of Appendix D for a description of this redirection capability.
b. If your computer supports output redirection, run the program written for Exercise 4a using this feature. Have your program's display redirected to a file named "poem."
c. If your computer supports output redirection to a printer, run the program written for Exercise 4a using this feature.

2.2 Programming Style

As a programmer, you constantly need to keep in mind the importance of making your programs easy for users to interpret. Long after you've forgotten the details of a particular program, you may be called on to expand or revise it for some other purpose. If you're not available for the job, another programmer, who has never seen your code before, may be called into action. Two important features that make programs easier for programmers to read are indentation consistency and comments.

Indentation

As we have seen, all statements that make up the `main()` function are included within the braces, `{}`, following the function name. Although the `main()` function must be included in every C program, C does not require that the word `main`, the parentheses, `()`, or the braces, `{}`, be placed in any particular form. The form used in the last section

```
int main()
{
  program statements in here;

  return 0;
}
```

was chosen strictly for clarity and ease in reading.[3] For example, the following general form of a `main()` function also works:

```
int main
(
){ first statement;second statement;
third statement;fourth
statement;}
```

Note that more than one statement can be put on a line, or one statement can be written across lines. Except for messages contained within double quotes, function names, and reserved words, C ignores all white space, where **white space** refers to any combination of one or more blank spaces, tabs, or new lines. For example, changing the white space in Program 2.2 while making sure not to split the message `Hello there world!` or the function names `printf` and `main` across two lines, as well as omitting all comments, results in the following valid program:

```
int
main
(
){printf
("Hello there world!"
);return 0;}
```

Although this version of `main()` does work, it is an example of extremely poor programming style. It is difficult to read and understand. For readability, the `main()` function should always be written in standard form as

```
int main()
{
  program statements in here;

  return 0;
}
```

In this standard form, the function name is placed, with the required parentheses, on a line by itself starting at the left-hand corner. The opening brace of the function body follows on the next line and is placed under the first letter of the function name. Similarly, the closing function brace is placed by itself at the start of the last line of the function. This structure serves to highlight the function as a single unit.

Within the function itself, all program statements are indented two spaces. Indentation is another sign of good programming practice, especially if the same indentation is used for similar groups of statements. Review Program 2.3 to see that the same indentation was used for both `printf()` function calls.

As you progress in your understanding and mastery of C, you will develop your own indentation standards. Just keep in mind that the indentation within your programs should be consistent. Your goal should be to create well-designed programs that are easy for you and other programmers to understand.

---

[3] If one of the program statements was a call to `printf()`, the `#include <stdio.h>` preprocessor command would have to be used. If the `main()` function did not return any value before completing, the appropriate first line would be `void main()`.

Comments

As you have learned, comments are explanatory remarks made within a program. When used carefully, comments help clarify what the complete program does, what a specific group of statements is meant to accomplish, or what one line is intended to do.

The symbols /*, with no white space between them, designate the start of a comment, while the symbols */, as a single unit with no intervening white space, designate the end of a comment.[4] For example, all of the following are comment lines:

```
/* this is a comment */
/* this program prints out a message */
/* this program calculates a square root */
```

Comments can be placed anywhere within a program and have no effect on program execution. The computer ignores all comments—they are there strictly for the convenience of anyone reading the program.

A comment can be written either on a line by itself, or on the same line containing a program statement, as

```
printf("Hello there world!");  /*  this is a call to printf() */
```

or it can be continued across two or more lines as illustrated below.

```
/* this comment is used to illustrate a
comment that extends over two lines */
```

Under no circumstances may comments be **nested**—one comment containing another comment. For example, the following will create a compiler error:

```
/* this nested comment is /* always */ invalid */
```

Because C comments can span multiple lines, they are categorized as block comments. Program 2.4 illustrates the use of comments within a program.

Program 2.4

```
/*
File: Pgm2-4.cpp
Description: Test program - this program displays a message
Programmer: G. Bronson
Date: 6/15/06
*/

#include <stdio.h>

int main()
```

[4] Additionally, some compilers permit the start of a comment to be designated by double slashes (//). Such comments extend to the end of the line on which they are written.

```
11  {
12    printf("Hello there world!"); /* a call to  printf() */
13
14    return 0;
15  }
```

The first comment (lines 1 through 6) spans multiple lines at the top of the program. As you saw earlier in this chapter, this is a good place to put a short comment describing the programmer, date of last modification, the file where the source code is stored, and a short description of what the program does. (To save space in this book, because all programs were written by the author, this initial program comment will be used only for short descriptions at the top of a program when they are needed to supplement the accompanying text.) The second comment, at the end of the `printf()` function call, is an example of a comment on the same line as an executable statement.

A program's structure should serve to make the program easy for people to read and understand, making extensive comments unnecessary. The structure itself will be even more self-explanatory if function and variable names, described in Section 2.5, are carefully selected to convey their meaning to anyone reading the program. However, even with careful planning, a program's structure, function names, and variable names still may not provide all the explanation necessary. In that case, you should include comments for additional clarification. Obscure code with no comments is a sure sign of bad programming. Excessive comments are also a sign of bad programming because they imply that insufficient thought was given to choosing descriptive programmer-selected identifiers and to making the code self-explanatory.

EXERCISES 2.2

Short Answer Questions

1. a. Will the following program work?

```
#include <stdio.h>
int main() {printf("Hello there world!"); return 0;}
```

b. Why is the program given in Question 1a not a good program?

2. a. When used in a message, the backslash character alters the meaning of the character immediately following it. If we wanted to print the backslash character, we would have to tell `printf()` to change, or escape from, the way it normally interprets the backslash. What character do you think is used to alter the way a single backslash character is interpreted?

b. Using your answer to Question 2a, write the escape sequence for printing a backslash.

Programming Exercises

1. a. Rewrite the following program to conform to good programming practice.

```
#include <stdio.h>
int main(
){
printf
(
"The time has come"
return 0;
);
```

b. Compile and execute the program you have written for Exercise 1a.

2. a. Rewrite the following program to conform to good programming practice.

```
#include <stdio.h>
int main
(){printf("Newark is a city\n");printf(
"In New Jersey\n"); printf
(It is also a city\n"
); printf(In Delaware\n"
);return 0;}
```

b. Compile and execute the program you have written for Exercise 2a.

3. a. Rewrite the following program to conform to good programming practice.

```
#include <stdio.h>
int main(){printf("Reading a program\n");printf(
"is much easier\n"
);printf("if a standard form for main is used\n")
;printf ("and each statement is written\n");printf(
"on a line by itself\n")
);return 0;}
```

b. Compile and execute the program you have written for Exercise 3a.

4. a. Rewrite the following program to conform to good programming practice.

```
#include <stdio.h>
int main
(){printf("Every C program"
);printf
("\nmust have one and only one"
);
printf("main function"
);
printf(
"\n the escape sequence of characters")
;printf(
```

```
"\nfor a new line can be placed anywhere"
);printf
("\n within the message passed to  printf()"
);return 0;}
```

b. Compile and execute the program you have written for Exercise 4a.

2.3 Data Types

C programs can process different types of data in different ways. For example, calculating the interest on a bank balance requires mathematical operations on numerical data, while alphabetizing a list of names requires comparison operations on character-based data. Additionally, some operations are not applicable to certain types of data. For example, it makes no sense to add names together. Thus, C allows only certain operations to be performed on certain types of data.

The types of data permitted and the appropriate operations defined for each type are referred to as a data type. Formally, a **data type** is defined as a set of values *and* a set of operations that can be applied to these values. For example, the set of all integer (whole) numbers constitutes a set of values. This set of numbers, however, does not constitute a data type until a set of operations is also included. These operations, of course, are the familiar mathematical and comparison operations. The combination of a set of values *plus* operations results in a true data type.

A **built-in data type** is one that is provided as an integral part of the language. Built-in types are also known as **primitive types**. C's built-in data types consist of the two basic numerical types shown in Figure 2.6 and the operations listed in Table 2.3. As seen in Table 2.3, the majority of operations for built-in types use conventional mathematical symbols. The table also lists bit operations, which are discussed in detail in Section 14.2.

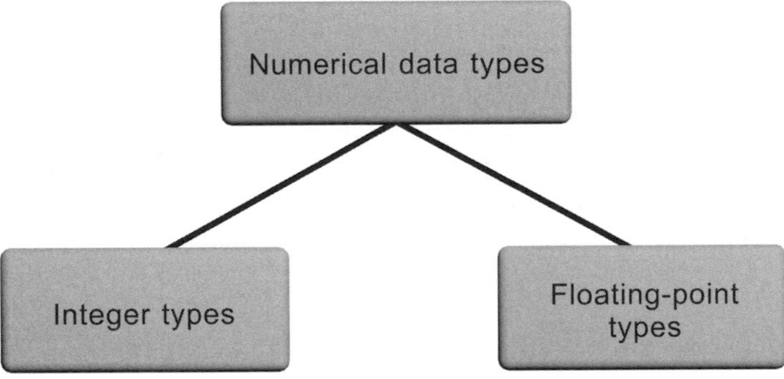

Figure 2.6 Built-in data types

Table 2.3 C's Built-in Data Types

Data Type	Supplied Operations

Integer	`+, -, *, /,`
	`%, =, ==, !=,`
	`<=, >=, sizeof(),`
	`and bit operations`
	`(see Sec. 14.2)`

Floating Point	`+, +, -, *, /,`
	`=, ==, !=,`
	`<=, >=, sizeof()`

In introducing C's built-in data types, we will make use of literals. A **literal** is an acceptable value for a data type. The term "literal" reflects the fact that such a value explicitly identifies itself. (Another name for a literal is a **literal value**, or **constant**.) For example, all numbers, such as 2, 3.6, and –8.2, are referred to as literal values because they literally display their values. Text, such as `"Hello World!"` is also referred to as a literal value because the text itself is displayed. You have been using literal values throughout your life and have commonly referred to them as numbers and words. In Section 2.5 you will see some examples of non-literal values—that is, values that do not display themselves but are stored and accessed using identifiers.

Integer Data Types

C provides seven built-in integer data types, as shown in Figure 2.7. The essential difference among the various integer data types is the amount of storage used for each type, which directly affects the range of values that each type is capable of representing. The two most important integer data types are the `int` and `char` types, which are explained in the following sections. These two integer types are used almost exclusively in the majority of applications.

The reason for the remaining types is essentially historical, as they were originally provided to accommodate special situations (a very small or a very large range of numbers). This permitted a programmer to maximize memory usage by selecting the data type that used the smallest amount of memory consistent with an application's requirements. When computer memories were very small relative to today's computers and extremely expensive, this was a major concern. Although no longer a concern for the vast majority of programs, it still provides a programmer the ability to optimize memory usage when necessary. Typically these situations occur in engineering applications, such as control systems used in home appliances and automobiles.

The `int` Data Type The set of values supported by the `int` data type are whole numbers, which are mathematically known as integers. An integer value consists of digits only and can optionally be preceded by either a plus (+) or minus (–) sign. Thus, an integer value can be the number zero or any positive or negative numerical value without a decimal point. Examples of valid integers are:

0	–10	1000	–26351
5	+25	253	+36

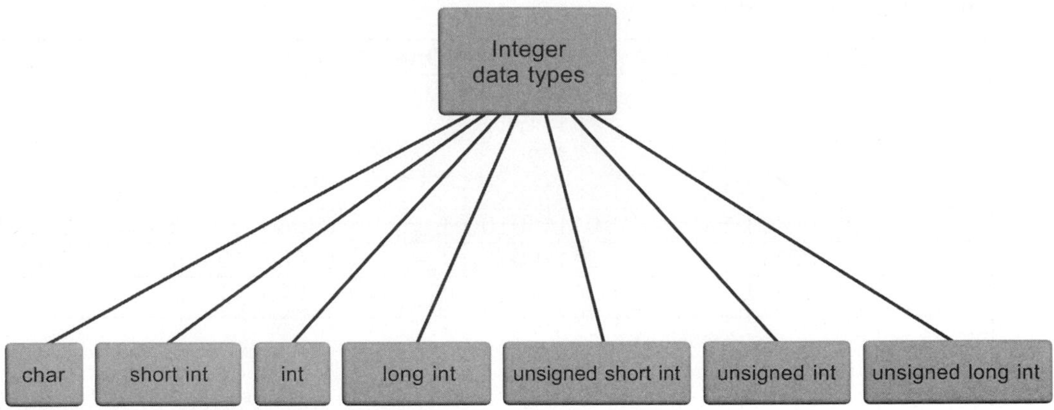

Figure 2.7 C's integer data types

As these examples illustrate, integers may contain an explicit sign. No commas, decimal points, or special symbols, such as the dollar sign, are allowed. Examples of invalid integers are:

$255.62	3.	1,492.89
2,523	6,243,892	+6.0

Different compilers have their own internal limit on the largest (most positive) and smallest (most negative) integer values that can be stored in each data type.[5] The most common current storage allocation for most current C compilers permits integers in the range of

-2,147,483,648 to 2,147,483,647.[6]

The `char` Data Type The `char` data type is used to store individual characters. Characters include the letters of the alphabet (both uppercase and lowercase), the ten digits 0 through 9, and special symbols such as + $. , - !. A single character value is any one letter, digit, or special symbol enclosed by single quotes. Examples of valid character values are:

```
'A'   '$'   'b'   '7'   'y'   '!'   'M'   'q'
```

Character literals are typically stored in a computer using either the ASCII or ANSI codes. ASCII, pronounced ASS-KEE, is an acronym for American Standard Code for Information Interchange. ANSI, pronounced ANN-SEE, is an acronym for American National Standards Institute and is an extended set of 256 codes, the first 128 of which are the same as the ASCII codes. Each of these codes assigns individual characters to a specific pattern of 0s and 1s. Table 2.4 lists the correspondence between bit patterns and the uppercase and lowercase letters of the alphabet used by both the ASCII and ANSI codes.

---

[5] The limits imposed by your compiler can be found in the `limits.h` header file and are defined as `INT_MAX` and `INT_MIN`. They can also be displayed from within a C program (see Program 2.11 in Section 2.9).

[6] Interestingly, in all cases the magnitude of the most negative integer number is always one more than the magnitude of the most positive integer. This is due to the two's complement method of integer storage, which is described in Section 1.8.

Table 2.4 ASCII and ANSI Letter Codes

Letter	Code	Letter	Code	Letter	Code	Letter	Code
a	01100001	n	01101110	A	01000001	N	01001110
b	01100010	o	01101111	B	01000010	O	01001111
c	01100011	p	01110000	C	01000011	P	01010000
d	01100100	q	01110001	D	01000100	Q	01010001
e	01100101	r	01110010	E	01000101	R	01010010
f	01100110	s	01110011	F	01000110	S	01010011
g	01100111	t	01110100	G	01000111	T	01010100
h	01101000	u	01110101	H	01001000	U	01010101
i	01101001	v	01110110	I	01001001	V	01010110
j	01101010	w	01110111	J	01001010	W	01010111
k	01101011	x	01111000	K	01001011	X	01011000
l	01101100	y	01111001	L	01001100	Y	01011001
m	01101101	z	01111010	M	01001101	Z	01011010

Using Table 2.4, we can determine how the characters 'J', 'O', 'N', 'E', and 'S', for example, are stored inside a computer that uses the ASCII character code. This sequence of five characters requires five individual codes of storage (one code for each letter) and would be stored as illustrated in Figure 2.8.

Figure 2.8 The letters JONES stored inside a computer

The Escape Character The backslash character, \, also known as the **escape character**, has a special meaning in C. When the backslash is placed directly in front of a select group of characters, it tells the compiler to escape from the way these characters would normally be interpreted. The combination of a backslash and these specific characters is called an **escape sequence**. We have already encountered an example of this in the newline escape sequence, `\n`, in Section 2.1. Table 2.5 lists C's most common escape sequences. Although each escape sequence listed in Table 2.5 is made up of two distinct characters, the combination of the two characters, with no intervening white space, causes the compiler to create the single code listed in the ASCII Code column of Table 2.5.

Table 2.5 Escape Sequences

Escape Sequence	Character Represented	Meaning	ASCII Code
`\n`	Newline	Move to a new line	00001010
`\t`	Horizontal tab	Move to next horizontal tab setting	00001001
`\v`	Vertical tab	Move to next vertical tab setting	00001011
`\b`	Backspace	Move back one space	00001000
`\r`	Carriage return	Carriage return (moves the cursor to the start of the current line—used for overprinting)	00001101
`\f`	Form feed	Issue a form feed	00001100
`\a`	Alert	Issue an alert (usually a bell sound)	00000111
`\\`	Backslash	Insert a backslash character (places an actual backslash character within a string)	01011100
`\?`	Question mark	Insert a question mark character	00111111
`\'`	Single quotation	Insert a single quote character (places an inner single quote within a set of outer single quotes)	00100111
`\"`	Double quotation mark	Insert a double quote character (places an inner double quote within a set of outer double quotes)	00100010
`\nnn`	Octal number	The number *nnn* (*n* is a digit) is to be considered an octal number	—
`\xhhhh`	Hexadecimal number	The number *hhhh* (*h* is a digit) is to be considered a hexadecimal number	—
`\0`	Null character	Insert the null character, which is defined as having the value 0	00000000

Floating-Point Data Types

A **floating-point value**, which is also called a **real number**, can be the number zero or any positive or negative number that contains a decimal point. Examples of floating-point numbers are:

```
+10.625    5.    -6.2    3251.92    0.0    0.33    -6.67    +2
```

Notice that the numbers 5., 0.0, and +2. are classified as floating-point values, but the same numbers written without a decimal point (5, 0, +2) would be integer values. As with integer values, special symbols such as the dollar sign and the comma are not permitted in real numbers. Examples of invalid real numbers are:

```
5,326.25    24    6,459    $10.29    7.007.645
```

C supports three floating-point data types: float, double, and long double. The difference between these data types is the amount of storage that a compiler uses for each type. Most compilers use twice the amount of storage for doubles than for floats, which allows a double to have approximately twice the precision of a float. For this reason, a float value is sometimes referred to as a **single-precision** number and a double value as a **double-precision** number. The actual storage allocation for each data type, however, depends on the compiler. (Using the sizeof() operator, which is presented in Section 2.9, you can display the amount of storage provided by your compiler for each data type.) The ANSI C standard only requires that a double have at least the same amount of precision as a float and that a long double have at least the same amount of precision as a double. The range of values typically provided by current C compilers is listed in the right-hand column of Table 2.6.[7]

Table 2.6 Floating-point Data Types

Type	Range of Values
float	-1.4012984643e-45 to 3.4028234663e+38
double and long double	-4.9406564584124654e-324 to 1.7976931348623158e+308

A float literal is indicated by appending either an f or F after the number and a long double is created by appending either an l or L to the number. In the absence of these suffixes, a floating-point number defaults to a double.[8] For example:

- 9.234 indicates a double literal.
- 9.234f indicates a float literal.
- 9.234L indicates a long double literal.

The only difference in these numbers is the amount of storage the computer may use to store them. If you require numbers with more than six significant digits to the right of the decimal point, this storage becomes important, and you should use double-precision values. Appendix E describes the binary storage format used for floating-point numbers and its impact on number precision. Because the precision supplied by the float data type is more than adequate for most applications, we will always use this data type for all floating-point numbers in any program that we write that requires a floating-point number.

Exponential Notation

Floating-point numbers can also be written in exponential notation, which is similar to scientific notation and is commonly used to express both very large and very small values in compact form. Table 2.7 illustrates how numbers with decimals can be expressed in exponential notation.

In exponential notation, the letter *e* stands for *exponent*. The number following the *e* represents a power of 10 and indicates the number of places the decimal point should be moved to obtain the standard decimal value. The decimal point is moved to the right if the number after the *e* is positive or moved to the left if the number after the *e* is negative. For

---

[7] The limits imposed by your compiler for maximum floating-point values can be found in the float.h header file and are defined as FLT_MAX, DBL_MAX, and LDBL_MAX. The minimum negative values must be computed using the information provided in Appendix E.

[8] In earlier compilers the default was a float, while appending an L to the number created a double.

Programming Note

What Is Precision?

In numerical theory, the term **precision** typically refers to numerical accuracy. In this context, a statement such as "this computation is accurate, or precise, to the fifth decimal place" is used. This means that the fifth digit after the decimal point has been rounded, and the number is accurate to within ±0.00005.

In computer programming, precision can refer either to the accuracy of a number or the amount of significant digits in the number, where significant digits are defined as the number of clearly correct digits plus 1. For example, if the number 12.6874 has been rounded to the fourth decimal place, it is correct to say that this number is precise (that is, accurate) to the fourth decimal place. In other words, all of the digits in the number are accurate except the fourth decimal digit, which has been rounded. Similarly, it can be said that this same number has a precision of six digits, which means that the first five digits are correct and the sixth digit has been rounded. Another way of saying this is that the number 12.6874 has six significant digits.

The significant digits in a number need not have any relation to the number of displayed digits. For example, if the number 687.45678921 has five significant digits, it is only accurate to the value 687.46, where the last digit is assumed to be rounded. In a similar manner, dollar values in many very large financial applications are frequently rounded to the nearest hundred-thousand dollars. In such applications, a displayed dollar value of $12,400,000, for example, is not accurate to the closest dollar. If this value is specified as having three significant digits, it is only accurate to the hundred-thousands digit.

example, the *e*3 in 1.625*e*3 means move the decimal place three places to the right so that the number becomes 1625. The *e*-3 in 7.31*e*-3 means move the decimal point three places to the left so that 7.31*e*-3 becomes .00731.

Table 2.7 Decimal Numbers Expressed in Exponential Notation

Decimal Notation	Exponential Notation
1625.	1.625e3
63421.	6.3421e4
.00731	7.31e-3
.000625	6.25e-4

EXERCISES 2.3

Short Answer Questions

1. What two sets of components are necessary to define a data type?
2. a. What is a built-in data type?
   b. What two basic built-in data types are provided by C?
3. a. What are the two integer data types that are most used in a C program?
   b. What is the data type most used to represent a number having a decimal point?
4. Determine data types appropriate for the following data:
   a. the average of four grades
   b. the number of days in a month
   c. the length of the Golden Gate Bridge
   d. the numbers in a state lottery
   e. the distance from Brooklyn, N.Y. to Newark, N.J.
   f. the single-character prefix that specifies a component type
5. Convert the following numbers into standard decimal form:

   `6.34e5    1.95162e2    8.395e1    2.95e-3    4.623e-4`
6. Write the following decimal numbers using exponential notation:

   `126.    656.23    3426.95    4893.2    .321    .0123    .006789`
7. Show how the name KINGSLEY would be stored inside a computer that uses ASCII code. That is, draw a figure similar to Figure 2.8 for the name KINGSLEY.
8. Repeat Question 7 using the letters of your own last name.
9. Because compilers assign different amounts of storage for integer, floating-point, double precision, and character values, discuss how a program might alert the compiler to the data types of the various values the program will be using.

2.4 Arithmetic Operations

The previous section presented the types and range of values corresponding to each of C's built-in data types. In this section, the set of arithmetic operations that can be applied to these values is provided.

Integers and real numbers can be added, subtracted, multiplied, and divided. Although it is usually better not to mix integers and real numbers when performing arithmetic operations, predictable results are obtained when using different data types in the same arithmetic expression. Surprisingly, you can also add character data to, or subtract it from, both character and integer data to produce useful results. (For example, 'A' + 1 results in the character 'B'.) This is possible because characters are stored using integer storage codes.

The operators used for arithmetic operations are called **arithmetic operators**, and are as follows:

Operation	Operator
Addition	+
Subtraction	-
Multiplication	*
Division	/
Modulus Division	%

Don't be concerned at this stage if you don't understand the term "modulus division" in the preceding list of operators. You'll learn more about this operator later in this section. All of the operators in this list are referred to as **binary operators**. This term reflects the fact that the operator requires two operands to produce a result. An **operand** can be either a literal value or an identifier that has a value associated with it. A **simple binary arithmetic expression** consists of a binary arithmetic operator connecting two literal values in the form:

`literalValue` *`operator`* `literalValue`

Examples of simple binary arithmetic expressions are:

```
3 + 7
18 - 3
12.62 + 9.8
.08 * 12.2
12.6 / 2.
```

The spaces around the arithmetic operators in these examples are inserted strictly for clarity and can be omitted without affecting the value of the expression. Notice that an expression in C must be entered in a straight-line form. Thus, for example, the C expression equivalent to 12.6 divided by 2 must be entered as 12.6 / 2 and *not* as the algebraic expression

$$\frac{12.6}{2}$$

Displaying Numerical Values

The value of any arithmetic expression can be displayed using the `printf()` function. Doing this requires passing two items to `printf()`: a control string that tells the function where and in what form the result is to be displayed, and the value that is to be displayed. Recall that items passed to a function are always placed within the function name parentheses and are called **arguments**. Arguments must be separated from one another with commas so that the function knows where one argument ends and the next begins. For example, in the statement

```
printf("The total of 6 and 15 is %d", 6 + 15);
```

the first argument is the string `The total of 6 and 15 is %d`, and the second argument is the expression `6 + 15`.

The first argument passed to `printf()` must always be a string. A string that also includes a **conversion control sequence**, such as `%d`, is termed a **control string.**[9] Conversion control sequences have a special meaning to the `printf()` function. They tell the function what type of value is to be displayed and where to display it. Conversion control sequences are also referred to as **conversion specifications** and **format specifiers.**

A conversion control sequence always begins with a `%` symbol and ends with a conversion character (`c, d, f,` etc.). Table 2.8 lists the three conversion control sequences used most frequently for displaying integer and floating-point numerical values, respectively. As we will see in the next chapter, additional conversion characters exist and formatting characters can be placed between the `%` symbol and the conversion character to more precisely determine the placement of values in the output display. It is the percent sign, `%,` in a conversion control sequence that tells `printf()` to print a value at the place in the string where the `%` is located. The letter following the % tells `printf()` the type of value to display. As listed in Table 2.8, a `d`, placed immediately after the `%`, tells `printf()` to display an integer value in decimal format.

Table 2.8 Conversion Control Sequences

Sequence	Meaning
%d	Display an integer as a decimal (base 10) number
%c	Display a character
%f	Display the floating-point number as a decimal number with six digits after the decimal point (pad with zeros, if necessary)

When `printf()` sees a conversion control sequence in its control string, it substitutes the value of the next argument in place of the conversion control sequence. Because this next argument is the expression 6 + 15, which has a value of 21, it is this value that is displayed. Thus, the statement

```
printf("The total of 6 and 15 is %d", 6 + 15);
```

produces the printout

```
The total of 6 and 15 is 21
```

Just as the `%d` conversion control sequence alerts `printf()` that an integer value is to be displayed, the conversion control sequence `%f` (`f` stands for floating point) indicates that a number with a decimal point is to be displayed. For example, the statement

```
printf ("The sum of %f and %f is %f", 12.2, 15.754, 12.2 +
15.754);
```

produces the display

```
The sum of 12.200000 and 15.754000 is 27.954000
```

As this display shows, the `%f` conversion control sequence causes `printf()` to display six digits to the right of the decimal place. If the number does not have six decimal digits, zeros

[9] More formally, a control string is referred to as a **control specifier**. We will use the more descriptive term, control string, to emphasize that a string is being used.

are added to the number to fill the fractional part. If the number has more than six decimal digits, the fractional part is rounded to six decimal digits.

Caution: The `printf()` function does not check the values it is given. If an integer conversion control sequence is used (`%d`, for example) but the value given the function is either a floating-point or double-precision number, the value displayed is compiler dependent. This means that the displayed value depends on your compiler's implementation of `printf()`, although most compilers display a value of 0 regardless of the floating-point value. Similarly, if the floating-point conversion control sequence, %f, is used and the corresponding number is an integer, the value displayed is compiler dependent (most compilers display a value of 0.0, regardless of the integer value).

Program 2.5 illustrates using `printf()` to display the results of an expression within the statements of a complete program.

Program 2.5

```
1  #include <stdio.h>
2  int main()
3  {
4    printf("%f plus %f equals %f\n", 15.0, 2.0, 15.0 + 2.0);
5    printf("%f minus %f equals %f\n", 15.0, 2.0, 15.0 - 2.0);
6    printf("%f times %f equals %f\n", 15.0, 2.0, 15.0 * 2.0);
7    printf("%f divided by %f equals %f\n", 15.0, 2.0, 15.0 / 2.0);
8
9    return 0;
10 }
```

The output of Program 2.5 is

```
15.000000 plus 2.000000 equals 17.000000
15.000000 minus 2.000000 equals 13.000000
15.000000 times 2.000000 equals 30.000000
15.000000 divided by 2.000000 equals 7.500000
```

Each of the four `printf()` statements in Program 2.5 (lines 4 through 7) passes four arguments to the `printf()` function: one control string and three values. Within each control string are three `%f` conversion control sequences (one for each value that is to be displayed). The escape sequence `'\n'` within each `printf()` statement simply causes a new line to be started after each line is displayed.

As listed in Table 2.8, character data is displayed using the `%c` conversion control sequence. For example, the statement

```
printf("The first letter of the alphabet is an %c.", 'a');
```

produces the display

```
The first letter of the alphabet is an a.
```

Because characters are stored as an integer data type, the numerical code used for the character can be displayed using any of the integer conversion sequences listed in Table 2.8. For example, Program 2.6 displays the integer codes used to store the characters `'a'` and `'A'`.

Program 2.6

```
#include <stdio.h>
int main()
{
  printf("\nThe first letter of the alphabet is %c", 'a');
  printf("\nThe decimal code for this letter is %d", 'a');
  printf("\nThe code for an uppercase %c is %d\n", 'A', 'A');

   return 0;
}
```

The output produced by Program 2.6 is

```
The first letter of the alphabet is a
The decimal code for this letter is 97
The code for an uppercase A is 65
```

You can check these values with those listed in Appendix B to see that the displayed decimal values do, in fact, correctly correspond to the ASCII integer code for the designated letters. As shown, using the `%c` conversion sequence causes `printf()` to display the text value of the letter rather than its numerical value.

Expression Types

In its most general form, an **expression** is any combination of operators and operands that can be evaluated to yield a value. An expression that contains only integer values as operands is called an **integer expression**, and the result of the expression is an integer value. Similarly, an expression containing only floating-point values (single and double precision) as operands is called a **floating-point expression** (the term **real expression** is also used), and the result of such an expression is a double-precision value. An expression containing both integer and floating-point values is called a **mixed-mode expression**. Although it is usually better not to mix integer and floating-point values in an arithmetic operation, the data type of each operation is determined by the following rules:

1. If both operands are integers, the result of the operation is an integer.
2. If one operand is a real value, the result of the operation is a double-precision value.

Notice that the result of an arithmetic expression is never a single-precision number. This is because during execution a C program temporarily converts all single-precision numbers to double-precision numbers when an arithmetic expression is being evaluated.

Integer Division

The division of two integer values can produce rather strange results for the unwary. For example, the expression 15/2 yields the integer result 7. Because integers cannot contain a fractional part, a value of 7.5 cannot be obtained. The fractional part obtained when two integers are divided (that is, the remainder) is always dropped (truncated). Thus, the value of 9/4 is 2, and 18/3 is 5.

Often, however, we may need to retain the remainder of an integer division. To do this, C provides an arithmetic operator having the symbol %. This operator, called both the **modulus** and **remainder operator**, captures the remainder when an integer number is divided by an integer (using a noninteger value with the modulus operator results in a compiler error). For example:

- `9 % 4 is 1` (that is, the remainder when 9 is divided by 4 is 1)
- `17 % 3 is 2` (that is, the remainder when 17 is divided by 3 is 2)
- `15 % 4 is 3` (that is, the remainder when 15 is divided by the 4 is 3)
- `14 % 2 is 0` (that is, the remainder when 14 is divided by 2 is 0)

More precisely, the modulus operator first determines the integer number of times that the dividend, which is the number following the % operator, can be divided into the divisor, which is the number before the % operator. It then returns the remainder.

Negation

In addition to the binary arithmetic operators, C also provides unary operators. A **unary operator** is one that operates on a single operand. One of these unary operators uses the same symbol as binary subtraction (–). The minus sign in front of a single numerical value negates (reverses the sign of) the number.

Table 2.9 summarizes the six arithmetic operations we have described so far and lists the data type for the result produced by each operator, based on the data type of the operands involved.

Table 2.9 Summary of Arithmetic Operators

Operation	Operator	Type	Operand	Result
Addition	+	Binary	Both are integers One operand is not an integer	Integer Double-precision
Subtraction	–	Binary	Both are integers One operand is not an integer	Integer Double-precision
Multiplication	*	Binary	Both are integers One operand is not an integer	Integer Double-precision
Division	/	Binary	Both are integers One operand is not an integer	Integer Double-precision
Modulus	%	Binary	Both are integers One operand is not an integer	Integer Double-precision
Negation	B	Unary	Integer or floating point	Same as operand

Operator Precedence and Associativity

In addition to such simple expressions as 5 + 12 and .08 * 26.2, more complex arithmetic expressions can be created. C, like most other programming languages, requires you to follow certain rules when writing expressions containing more than one arithmetic operator. These rules are:

1. Two binary arithmetic operator symbols must never be placed side by side. For example, 5 * % 6 is invalid because the two operators, * and %, are placed next to each other.
2. Parentheses may be used to form groupings, and all expressions enclosed within parentheses are evaluated first. This permits parentheses to alter the evaluation to any desired order. For example, in the expression (6 + 4) / (2 + 3), the 6 + 4 and 2 + 3 are evaluated first to yield 10 / 5. The 10 / 5 is then evaluated to yield 2.
3. Sets of parentheses may also be enclosed by other parentheses. For example, the expression (2 * (3 + 7)) / 5 is valid and evaluates to 4. When parentheses are included within parentheses, the expressions in the innermost parentheses are always evaluated first. The evaluation continues from innermost to outermost parentheses until the expressions in all parentheses have been evaluated. The number of closing parentheses [ )] must always equal the number of opening parentheses [( ] so that there are no unpaired sets.
4. Parentheses cannot be used to indicate multiplication; rather, the multiplication operator, *, must be used. For example, the expression (3 + 4) (5 + 1) is invalid. The correct expression is (3 + 4) * (5 + 1).

Parentheses should specify logical groupings of operands and indicate clearly, to both the compiler and programmers, the intended order of arithmetic operations. Although expressions within parentheses are always evaluated first, expressions containing multiple operators, both within and without parentheses, are evaluated by the priority, or **precedence**, of the operators. There are three levels of precedence:

- P1—All negations are done first.
- P2—Multiplication, division, and modulus operations are computed next. Expressions containing more than one multiplication, division, or modulus operator are evaluated from left to right as each operator is encountered. For example, in the expression 35 / 7 % 3 * 4, the operations are all of the same priority, so the operations will be performed from left to right as each operator is encountered. Thus, the division is done first, yielding the expression 5 % 3 * 4. The modulus operation is performed next, yielding a result of 2. And finally, the value of 2 * 4 is computed to yield 8.
- P3—Addition and subtraction are computed last. Expressions containing more than one addition or subtraction are evaluated from left to right as each operator is encountered.

In addition to precedence, operators have an **associativity**, which is the order in which operators of the same precedence are evaluated, as described in rule P2. For example, does the expression 6.0 * 6 / 4 yield 9.0, which is (6.0 * 6)/4, or 6.0, which is 6.0 * (6/4)? The answer is 9.0, because C's operators use the same associativity as in general mathematics, which evaluates multiplication from left to right, as rule P2 indicates.

Table 2.10 lists both the precedence and associativity of the operators considered in this section. As we have seen, the precedence of an operator establishes its priority relative to all other operators. Operators at the top of Table 2.10 have a higher priority than operators at the bottom of the table. In expressions with multiple operators of different precedence, the operator with the higher precedence is used before an operator with lower precedence. For example, in the expression 6 + 4 / 2 + 3, because the division operator has a higher precedence (P2) than addition, the division is done first, yielding an intermediate result of 6 + 2 + 3. The additions are then performed, left to right, to yield a final result of 11.

Table 2.10 Operator Precedence and Associativity

Operator	Associativity
unary –	Right to left
* / %	Left to right
+ B	Left to right

Finally, let us use Table 2.10 to evaluate an expression containing operators of different precedence, such as 8 + 5 * 7 % 2 * 4. Because the multiplication and modulus operators have a higher precedence than the addition operator, these two operations are evaluated first, using their left-to-right associativity, before the addition is evaluated. Thus, the complete expression is evaluated as:

```
8 + 5 * 7 % 2 * 4 =
   8 + 35 % 2 * 4 =
        8 + 1 * 4 =
            8 + 4 =12
```

EXERCISES 2.4

Short Answer Questions

1. Listed below are correct algebraic expressions and incorrect C expressions corresponding to them. Find the errors and write corrected C expressions.

	Algebra	C Expression
a.	(2)(3) + (4)(5)	(2)(3) + (4)(5)
b.	$\frac{6 + 18}{2}$	6 + 18 / 2
c.	$\frac{4.5}{12.2 - 3.1}$	4.5 / 12.2 - 3.1
d.	4.6(3.0 + 14.9)	4.6(3.0 + 14.9)
e.	(12.1 + 18.9)(15.3 - 3.8)	(12.1 + 18.9)(15.3 - 3.8)

2. Determine the value of the following integer expressions:
   a. 3 + 4 * 6
   b. 3 * 4 / 6 + 6
   c. 2 * 3 / 12 * 8 / 4

d. 10 * (1 + 7 * 3)
e. 20 - 2 / 6 + 3
f. 20 - 2 / (6 + 3)
g. (20 - 2) / 6 + 3
h. (20 - 2) / (6 + 3)
i. 50 % 20
j. (10 + 3) % 4

3. Determine the value of the following floating-point expressions:
   a. 3.0 + 4.0 * 6.0
   b. 3.0 * 4.0 / 6.0 + 6.0
   c. 2.0 * 3.0 / 12.0 * 8.0 / 4.0
   d. 10.0 * (1.0 + 7.0 * 3.0)
   e. 20.0 - 2.0 / 6.0 + 3.0
   f. 20.0 - 2.0 / (6.0 + 3.0)
   g. (20.0 - 2.0) / 6.0 + 3.0
   h. (20.0 - 2.0) / (6.0 + 3.0)

4. Evaluate the following mixed-mode expressions and list the data type of the result. In evaluating the expressions, be aware of the data types of all intermediate calculations.
   a. 10.0 + 15 / 2 + 4.3
   b. 10.0 + 15.0 / 2 + 4.3
   c. 3.0 * 4 / 6 + 6
   d. 3 * 4.0 / 6 + 6
   e. 20.0 - 2 / 6 + 3
   f. 10 + 17 * 3 + 4
   g. 10 + 17 / 3. + 4
   h. 3.0 * 4 % 6 + 6
   i. 10 + 17 % 3 + 4.

5. Assume that `amount` stores the integer value 1, `m` stores the integer value 50, `n` stores the integer value 10, and `p` stores the integer value 5. Evaluate the following expressions:
   a. `n / p + 3`
   b. `m / p + n - 10 * amount`
   c. `m - 3 * n + 4 * amount`
   d. `amount / 5`
   e. `18 / p`
   f. `-p * n`
   g. `-m / 20`
   h. `(m + n) / (p + amount)`
   i. `m + n / p + amount`

6. Repeat Question 5 assuming that `amount` stores the value 1.0, `m` stores the value 50.0, `n` stores the value 10.0, and `p` stores the value 5.0.

7. Determine the errors in each of the following statements:
   a. `printf("%d," 15)`
   b. `printf("%f", 33);`
   c. `printf(526.768, 33, "%f %d");`

8. Determine the output of the following program:

```
#include <stdio.h>
int main() /* a program illustrating integer truncation */
{
  printf("answer1 is the integer %d", 27/5);
  printf("\nanswer2 is the integer $d", 16/6)

  return 0;
}
```

9. Determine the output of the following program:

```
#include <stdio.h>
int main() /* a program illustrating the % operator */
{
  printf("The remainder of 9 divided by 4 is %d", 9 % 4);
  printf("\nThe remainder of 17 divided by 3 is %d", 17 % 3);

  return 0;
}
```

10. Although we have concentrated on operations involving integer and floating-point numbers, C allows characters and integers to be added or subtracted. This can be done because a character is stored using an integer code (it is an integer data type). Thus, characters and integers can be freely mixed in arithmetic expressions. For example, if your computer uses the ASCII code, the expression 'a' + 1 equals 'b', and 'z' - 1 equals 'y'. Similarly, 'A' + 1 is 'B', and 'Z' - 1 is 'Y'. With this as background, determine the character results of the following expressions (assume that all characters are stored using the ASCII code).
    a. 'm' – 5
    b. 'm' + 5
    c. 'G' + 6
    d. 'G' – 6
    e. 'b' – 'a'
    f. 'g' – 'a' + 1
    g. 'G' – 'A' + 1

11. In addition to the `%d` conversion control sequence for displaying integer values, the `%o` sequence forces an integer value to be displayed as an octal (base 8) number and the `%x` sequence forces an integer value to be displayed as a hexadecimal (base 12) number. Using this information and Table 2.11, which lists the correspondence between the decimal numbers 1 through 15 and their octal (base 8) and hexadecimal (base 12) representations, determine the output of the following program.

```
#include <stdio.h>
int main()
{
  printf("The value of the decimal number 9 in octal is %o.\n", 9);
  printf("The value of the decimal number 9 in hexadecimal is %x.\n",9);
  printf("The value of the decimal number 14 in octal is %o.\n",14);
  printf("The value of the decimal number 14 in hexadecimal is %x.\n", 14);

  return 0;
}
```

Table 2.11 Correspondence Between Number Representations

System	Values
Decimal (base 10)	1 2 3 4 5 6 7 8 9 10 11 12 13 14 15
Octal (base 8)	1 2 3 4 5 6 7 10 11 12 13 14 15 16 17
Hexadecimal (base 12)	1 2 3 4 5 6 7 8 9 A B C D E F

Programming Exercises

1. Enter and execute Program 2.5.

2. Enter and execute Program 2.6.

3. Write a C program that displays the results of the expressions 3.0 * 5.0, 7.1 * 8.3 - 2.2, and 3.2 / (6.1 * 5). Calculate the value of these expressions manually to verify that the displayed values are correct.

4. Write a C program that displays the results of the expressions 15 / 4, 15 % 4, and 5 * 3 - (6 * 4). Calculate the value of these expressions manually to verify that the display produced by your program is correct.

5. **a.** Write a C program that uses the `%d` conversion control sequence to display the decimal integer values of the lowercase letters *a*, *m*, and *n*, respectively. Do the displayed values for these letters match the values listed in Appendix B?
   b. Expand the program written for Exercise 16a to display the integer value corresponding to the newline escape sequence `'\n'`.

6. Enter and execute the following program to determine the maximum and minimum integer values that are supported by your compiler.

```
#include <stdio.h>
#include <limits.h>   /* contains the minimum and maximum
                         specifications for an int data type */
int main()
{
  printf("The smallest integer value that can be stored is %d\n", INT_MIN);
  printf("The largest integer value that can be stored is %d\n",  INT_MAX);


  return 0;
}
```

2.5 Variables and Declarations

All data used in a computer program must be stored and retrieved from the computer's memory unit. Each memory location has a unique address, which is analogous to a hotel room number. Consider the memory storage illustrated in Figure 2.9. For purposes of illustration, assume that a set of memory locations, the first of which has the addresses starting with the address 1652, is used to store one integer number and that a second set of memory locations, starting with the address 2548, is used to store a second integer.

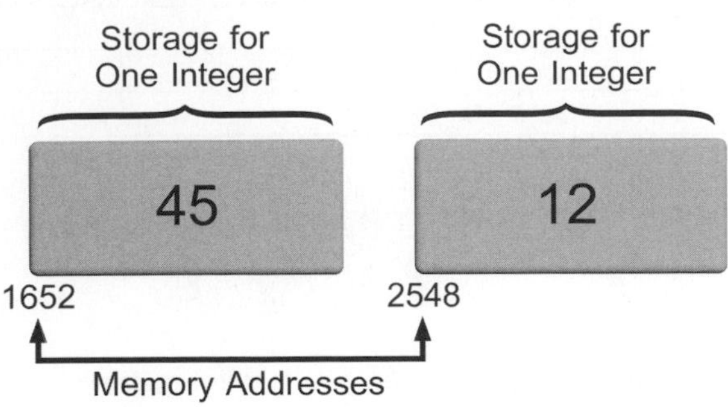

Figure 2.9 Enough storage for two integers

Before high-level languages such as C existed, memory locations were referenced by the address of the first location in the set of locations reserved for each data value. For example, storing the number 45 in the first set of locations illustrated in Figure 2.9 and 12 in the second set required instructions equivalent to

Put a 45 in location 1652
Put a 12 in location 2548

Only the first address in each set of locations is needed because it provides the starting point for storage or retrieval. Once this starting point is known, the correct number of locations reserved for each type of value can then be automatically retrieved.

Adding the two numbers just stored and saving the result in another set of memory locations, for example those starting at location 45, required a statement comparable to

Add the contents of location 1652 to the contents of location 2548
and store the result in location 3000

Clearly, this method of storage and retrieval was cumbersome. In a high-level language such as C, symbolic names are used in place of actual memory addresses. These symbolic names are called variables. **Variables** are simply names given by programmers to computer storage locations. The term "variable" is used because the value stored in the variable can change, or vary. For each name that the programmer uses, the computer keeps track of the memory locations corresponding to that name. Naming a variable is equivalent to putting a name on the door of a hotel room and referring to the room (or suite of rooms) by this name, such as the Blue Room, rather than using the actual room number.

The selection of variable names is left to the programmer, as long as the rules for naming programmer-created identifiers is observed. For convenience, these rules are repeated from Section 2.1:

1. The variable name must begin with a letter or underscore (_) and may contain only letters, underscores, or digits. It cannot contain any blanks, commas, or special symbols, such as ( ) & , $ # . ! \ ? .
2. A variable name cannot be a keyword (see Table 2.1).

Typically there is a limit of 255 characters for a variable's name, but this is compiler dependent. As a practical matter, a variable name should always be descriptive and be limited to approximately no more than 20 characters. (A more comprehensive set of naming rules is provided in this section's Programming Note.) For example, a good name for a variable used to store the total of a group of grades would be `gradesSum` or `gradesTotal`. Variable names that give no indication of the value stored, such as `goForIt`, `linda`, `bill`, and `duh`, should never be selected. As with all identifiers, variable names are case sensitive.

Now assume that the first memory location illustrated in Figure 2.10, which has address 1652, is given the name `num1`. Also assume that memory location 2548 is given the variable name `num2`, and memory location 3000 is given the name `total`, as illustrated in Figure 2.10.

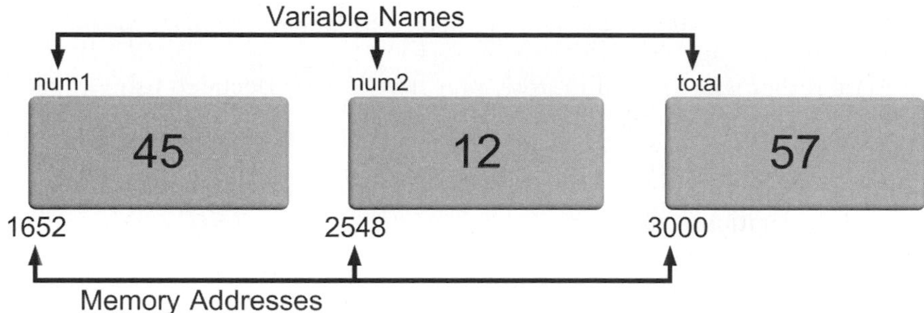

Figure 2.10 Naming storage locations

Using these variable names, the operation of storing 45 in location 1652, storing 12 in location 2548, and adding the contents of these two locations is accomplished by the C statements

```
num1 = 45;
num2 = 12;
total = num1 + num2;
```

Each of these three statements is called an **assignment statement** because it tells the computer to assign a value to (that is, store a value in) a variable. Assignment statements always include an equal sign, =, and one variable name immediately to the left of this sign. The value to the right of the equal sign is determined first, and this value is assigned to the variable to the left of the equal sign. Blank spaces in the assignment statements are included to make the code easier to read, but are not strictly necessary. We will have much more to say about assignment statements in the next chapter, but for now we can use them to store values in variables.

A variable name is useful because it frees the programmer from concern over where data are physically stored inside the computer. We simply use the variable name and let the compiler worry about where in memory the data are actually stored. Before storing a value into a variable, however, C requires that we clearly declare the type of data to be stored in it. We must tell the compiler, in advance, the names of the variables that will be used for characters, the names that will be used for integers, and the names that will be used to store floating-point data.

Declaration Statements

Naming and specifying the data type that can be stored in each variable is accomplished using declaration statements. Declaration statements within a function appear immediately after the opening brace of a function, and like all C statements must end with a semicolon. A C function containing declaration statements has the general form

```
function name()
{
  declaration statements;
  other statements;
}
```

Declaration statements, in their simplest form, provide a data type and variable name, and have the syntax

```
dataType    variableName;
```

where *dataType* designates a valid C data type and *variableName* is a user-selected identifier.

Variables that will be used to store integer values are declared using the keyword `int` to specify the `int` data type and have the form

```
int  variableName;
```

Thus, the declaration statement

```
int sum;
```

declares `sum` as the name of a variable capable of storing an integer value.

Variables that hold single-precision values are declared using the keyword `float`, whereas variables that hold double-precision values are declared using the keyword `double`. For example, the statement

```
float firstNumber;
```

declares `firstNumber` as a variable that will store a single-precision number. Similarly, the statement

```
double secondNumber;
```

declares that the variable `secondNumber` will store a double-precision number.

Declaration statements perform both software and hardware tasks. From a software perspective, declaration statements provide a convenient, up-front list of all variables and their data types. In this software role, variable declarations also eliminate an otherwise common and troublesome error caused by the misspelling of a variable's name within a program, because any misspelled name will be flagged by the compiler as an invalid name.

In addition to their software role, declaration statements can also perform a distinct hardware task. Since each data type has its own storage requirements, the compiler can allocate sufficient storage for a variable only after knowing the variable's data type. Declaration statements used for this hardware purpose are also known as **definition statements**, because they define or tell the compiler how much memory is needed for data storage.

The declarations that we are considering in this section all perform this hardware role; as such, they are also definition statements. In Chapter 7 we will see declaration statements that do not cause any new storage to be allocated and are used simply to declare or alert the program to the data types of previously created and existing variables.

Figure 2.11 illustrates the series of operations set in motion by declaration statements that also perform a definition role. The figure shows that definition statements (or, if you prefer, declaration statements that also cause memory to be allocated) "tag" the first memory location of each set of reserved locations with a name. This name is, of course, the variable's name and is used by the computer to correctly locate the starting byte of each variable's reserved memory area.

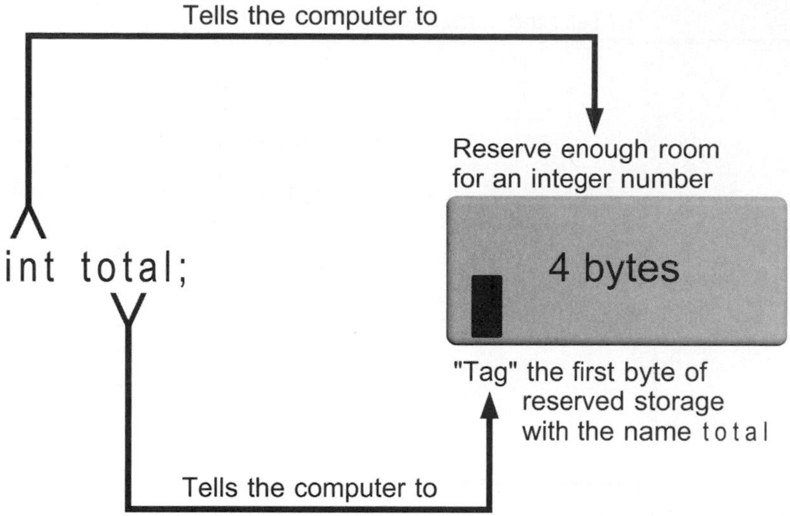

Figure 2.11a Defining the integer variable named `total`

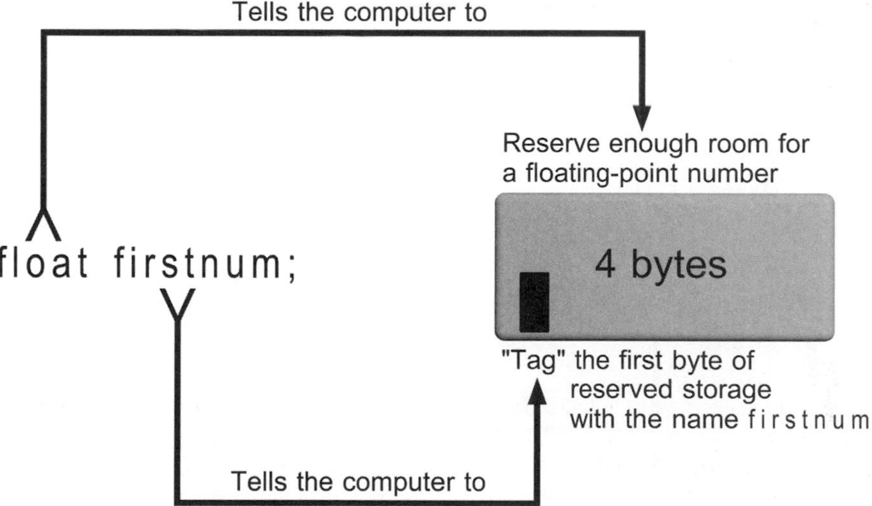

Figure 2.11b Defining the floating-point variable named `firstnum`

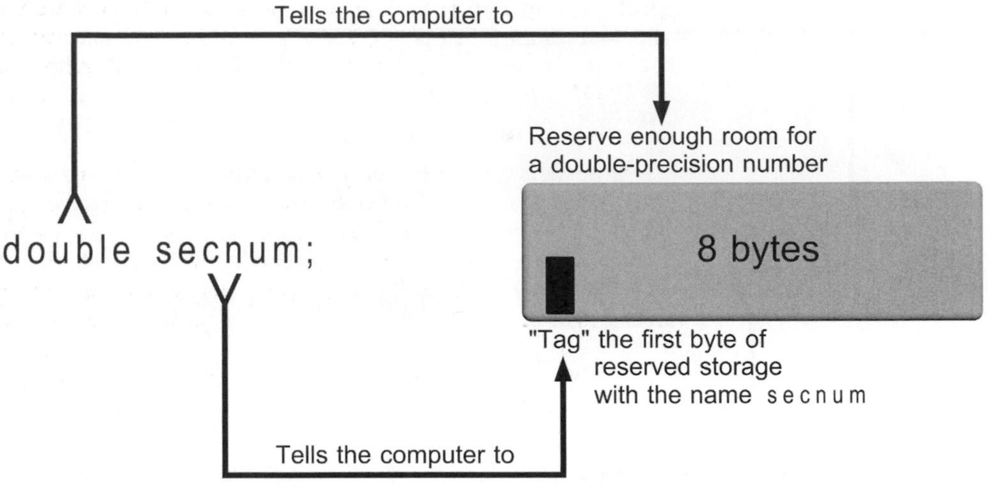

Figure 2.11c Defining the double-precision variable named `secnum`

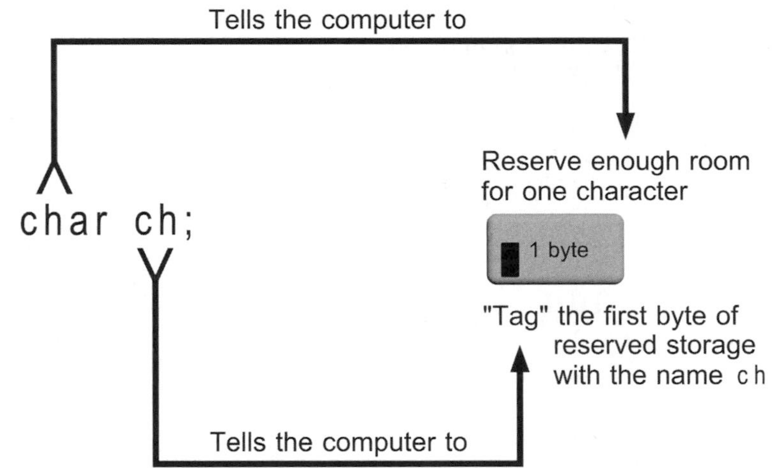

Figure 2.11d Defining the character variable named `ch`

After a variable has been declared within a program, it is typically used by a programmer to refer to the contents of the variable (that is, the variable's value). Where in memory this value is stored is generally of little concern to the programmer.

Program 2.7 illustrates the declaration and use of four floating-point variables. The `printf()` function is then used to display the contents of one of these variables.

Placement of the declaration statements in Program 2.7 is straightforward, although we will shortly see that the four individual declarations can be combined into a single declaration. When Program 2.7 is run, the following output is displayed:

```
The average grade is 91.250000
```

Program 2.7

```
1  #include <stdio.h>
2  int main()
3  {
4    float grade1;   /* declare grade1 as a double variable */
5    float grade2;   /* declare grade2 as a double variable */
6    float total;    /* declare total as a double variable */
7    float average;  /* declare average as a double variable */
8
9    grade1 = 85.5f;
10   grade2 = 97.0f;
11   total = grade1 + grade2;
12   average = total/2.0;
13   printf("The average grade is %f\n",average);
14
15   return 0;
16 }
```

Two comments regarding the `printf()` function call made in Program 2.7 should be mentioned here. First, if a variable name is one of the arguments passed to a function, as it is to `printf()` in Program 2.7, the function receives only a copy of the value stored in the variable. It does not receive the variable's name. When the program sees a variable name in the function parentheses, it first goes to the variable and retrieves the value stored. This value is then passed to the function. Thus, when a variable is included in the `printf()` argument list, `printf()` receives the value stored in the variable and then displays this value. Internally, `printf()` does not know where the value it receives came from or the variable name under which the value was stored.

The second comment concerns the `%f` conversion control sequence in Program 2.7. Although this conversion control sequence works for both single-precision and double-precision numbers, the conversion control sequence `%lf` may also be used for displaying the values of double-precision variables. The letter `l` indicates that the number is a long floating-point number, which is what a double-precision number really is. Omitting the `l` conversion character has no effect on the `printf()` function when double-precision values are displayed. As we shall see, however, it is essential in entering double-precision values when the input function `scanf()` is used. This function is presented in the next chapter.

The final comment concerning Program 2.7 is the assignment of values to the variables `grades1` and `grades2`. Because both of these variables were declared as floats in lines 4 and 5

```
4  float grade1;
5  float grade2;
```

they have been assigned floating-point values in lines 9 and 10

```
9   grade1 = 85.5f;
10  grade2 = 97.0f;
```

Programming Note

Selecting Variable Names

1. Make your variable names descriptive so that you (or other programmers) can immediately understand the purpose of each variable.
2. Limit variable names to approximately 20 characters. This prevents needless typing and minimizes typing errors.
3. Start the variable name with a letter, rather than an underscore (_). Underscores are frequently used as the first letter by compiler-supplied variables so you should ***not*** use underscores as the first character in your variable names. This will prevent any potential name conflicts.
4. In a variable name consisting of several words, capitalize the first letter of each word after the first. Thus, the variable name `gradesSum` is preferable to `gradessum`.
5. Use variable names that indicate ***what*** the variable corresponds to, rather than ***how*** it is computed. Thus, a variable name such as `area` is acceptable, while a variable name such as `computeArea` is not.
6. Add qualifiers, such as `Avg`, `Min`, `Max`, and `Sum` to complete a variable's name where it is appropriate. Thus, a variable name such as `gradesAvg` is preferable to `average`, if the variable is used to store the average of a set of grades.
7. Use single-letter variable names, such as `i`, `j`, and `k`, for loop indexes (as explained in Chapter 5).

These floating-point values are denoted by the `f` following the numbers 85.5 and 97.0, respectively.[10] The reason for this, as explained in Section 2.3, is that if the default for floating-point numbers is a `double`, which is the case for most Windows-based compilers, any number with a decimal point will be considered as a double-precision value.

Generally, however, many C programmers simply omit the `f`, and let the compiler convert the double-precison value into a `float` value when the assignment is made. The only downside to this is that the compiler will issue a warning (not an error) message. Thus, when your receive this message, simply note that it occurred because you are using `floats` where your compiler would default to a `double`, and ignore the warning message[11].

Just as integer, single-precision, and double-precision variables must be declared before they can be used, a variable used to store a character must also be declared. Character variables are declared using the reserved word `char`. For example, the declaration

```
char ch;
```

declares `ch` to be a character variable. Program 2.8 illustrates this declaration and the use of `printf()` to display the value stored in a character variable.

[10] As presented in Section 2.3, compilers that use `floats` rather than doubles as the default floating-point data type, the `f` is not needed, because all numbers with decimal points are assumed to be `floats`.

[11] Another option, to avoid the warning messages entirely, is to use only floating-point variables that have been declared as `doubles`.

Program 2.8

```
#include <stdio.h>
int main()
{
  char ch; /* this declares a character variable */

  ch = 'a'; /* store the letter a into ch */
  printf("\nThe character stored in ch is %c.", ch);
  ch = 'm'; /* now store the letter m into ch */
  printf("\nThe character now stored in ch is %c.", ch);

  return 0;
}
```

When Program 2.8 is run, the following output is produced:

```
The character stored in ch is a.
The character now stored in ch is m.
```

Notice in Program 2.8 that the first letter stored in the variable `ch` is `a` and the second letter stored in `ch` is `m`. Because a variable can store only one value at a time, the assignment of `m` to the variable `ch` automatically causes the `a` to be overwritten.

Variables having the same data type can always be grouped together and declared using a single declaration statement. For example, the four separate declarations used in Program 2.7

```
float grade1;
float grade2;
float total;
float average;
```

can be replaced by the single declaration statement

```
float grade1, grade2, total, average;
```

Declaring multiple variables in a single declaration requires that the data type of the variables be given only once, that all the variables be separated by commas, and that only one semicolon be used to terminate the declaration. The space after each comma is inserted for readability and is not required.

Initialization

Declaration statements can also be used to store an initial value into declared variables. For example, the declaration statement

```
int numOne = 15;
```

both declares the variable `numOne` as an integer variable and provides a value of 15. This value, which is referred to as an **initial value**, will be stored in the variable when the variable is first created. When a declaration statement provides an initial value, the variable is said to be **initialized**. Thus, in this example, it is correct to say that the variable numOne will be initialized to 15 when it is created. Similarly, the declaration statements

```
float grade1 = 87.0f;
float grade2 = 93.5f;
float average;
```

declare three double-precision variables and provide initial values for two of them.

Literals, expressions using only literals such as 87.0 + 12 − 2, and expressions using literals and previously initialized variables can all be used as initializers within a declaration statement.

EXERCISES 2.5

Short Answer Questions

1. State whether the following variable names are valid or invalid. If they are invalid, state the reason.

```
proda    c1234   abcd     c3       12345
newbal   while   $total   new bal  a1b2c3d4
9ab6     sum.of  average  grade1   finGrad
```

2. State whether the following variable names are valid or invalid. If they are invalid, state the reason. Also indicate which of the valid variable names should not be used because they convey no information about the variable.

```
Salestax  a243   r2d2    firstNum  ccA1
Harry     sue    c3p0    average   sum
Maximum   okay   a       awesome   goforit
3sum      for    tot.a1  c$five    netpay
```

3. **a.** Write a declaration statement to declare that the variable count will be used to store an integer.
   b. Write a declaration statement to declare that the variable grade will be used to store a floating-point number.
   c. Write a declaration statement to declare that the variable yield will be used to store a double-precision number.
   d. Write a declaration statement to declare that the variable initial will be used to store a character.

4. Write declaration statements for the following variables:
   a. num1, num2, and num3 used to store integer numbers
   b. grade1, grade2, grade3, and grade4 used to store floating-point numbers
   c. tempa, tempb, and tempc used to store double-precision numbers
   d. ch, let1, let2, let3, and let4 used to store character types

5. Write declaration statements for the following variables:
   a. `firstnum` and `secnum` used to store integers
   b. `price`, `yield`, and `coupon` used to store single-precision numbers
   c. `maturity` used to store a double-precision number

6. Rewrite each of these declaration statements as three individual declarations:
   a. `int month, day = 30, year;`
   b. `double hours, rate, otime = 15.62;`
   c. `float price, amount, taxes;`
   d. `char in_key, ch, choice = 'f';`

7. a. Determine what each statement causes to happen in the following program:

```
#include <stdio.h>
int main()
{
  int num1;
  int num2;
  int total;

  num1 = 25;
  num2 = 30;
  total = num1 + num2;
  printf("The total of %d and %d is %d\n.",num1,num2,total);

  return 0;
}
```

   b. What is the output that will be printed when the program listed in Question 7a is run?

8. Every variable has at least three items associated with it. What are these items?

9. a. A statement used to clarify the relationship between squares and rectangles is "All squares are rectangles but not all rectangles are squares." Write a similar statement that describes the relationship between definition and declaration statements.
   b. Why must definition statements be placed before any other C statements using the defined variable?

Programming Exercises

1. Write and execute a C program that calculates and displays the circumference of a circle that has a radius of 2.57 inches. The relevant formula is *circumference* = *(2* π *) radius*, where π is the value 3.1416. Use the variable names `radius` and `circumference` in your program. (*Hint:* See Program 2.1.)

2. Write and execute a C program that calculates and displays the area of a circle with a radius of 2.57 inches. The relevant formula is *circumference* = π * *radius*^{2}, where π is the value 3.1416. Use the variable names `radius` and `circumference` in your program. (*Hint:* To compute the value of *radius*^{2}, use the expression *radius* * *radius*.)

3. a. Write and execute a C program that calculates and displays the area of a rectangle that has a width of 3.5 inches and a length of 5.48 inches. The relevant formula is *area = length * width*. Use the variable names `length`, `width`, and `area` in your program.
   b. Modify the program written in Exercise 3a to also compute and display the perimeter of the rectangle. The relevant formula is *perimeter = 2(length + width)*.

4. Write and execute a C program that calculates and displays the number of minutes in a year.

5. You purchase a laptop computer for $889. The sales tax rate is 6 percent. Write and execute a C program that calculates and displays the total purchase price.

6. The dollar change remaining after an amount `paid` is used to pay a restaurant bill of amount `check` can be calculated using the following C statements:

```
/* determine the amount of pennies in the change */
change = (paid - check) * 100;
/* determine the number of dollars in the change */
dollars = change / 100;
```

   a. Using the previous statements as a starting point, write a C program that calculates the number of dollar bills, quarters, dimes, nickels, and pennies in the change when $10 is used to pay a bill of $6.07.
   b. Without compiling or executing your program, check the effect, by hand, of each statement in the program and determine what is stored in each variable as each statement is encountered.
   c. When you have verified that your algorithm works correctly, compile and execute your program. Verify that the result produced by your program is correct. After you have verified your program is working correctly, use it to determine the change when a check of $12.36 is paid using a $20 bill.

7. a. Write a C program that stores the integer value 15 in the variable `num1` and the integer value 18 in the variable `num2`. (Make sure to declare these two variables as integers.) Have your program calculate the total of these numbers and their average. The total should be stored in the variable named `total` and the average in the variable named `average`. (Use the statement `average = total/2.0;` to calculate the average.) Use the `printf()` function to display the total and average.
   b. What data type did you have to declare for the average to ensure that the correct answer was calculated and displayed?

2.6 Case Study: Temperature Conversion

This case study applies the software development procedure presented in Section 2.5 in creating a complete C program using double-precision variables.

> *A friend of yours is going to Spain, where temperatures are reported using the Celsius temperature scale. She has asked you to provide her with a list of temperatures in degrees Fahrenheit, and the equivalent temperature in degrees Celsius. The formula relating the two temperatures is Celsius = 5/9(Fahrenheit – 32). Initially, you are to write and test a program that correctly converts the Fahrenheit temperature of 75 degrees into its Celsius equivalent.*

(In the next chapter you will see how to enter temperatures while the program is running, and in Chapter 5 you will see how to create a complete list of equivalent temperatures.)

Step 1: Analyze the Problem

This is a very straightforward problem that has the following components.

a. Required outputs

```
float celsius       /* the Celsius temperature */
```

b. Input data

```
float fahrenheit    /* the Fahrenheit temperature */
```

c. Formulas relating inputs to outputs

```
  Celsius = 5.0/9.0 * (fahrenheit - 32.0)   /* notice we have  used */
/* all floating-point values */
```

The reason we have made all of the quantities floating-point is that the Celsius value corresponding to any integer Fahrenheit temperature can be a noninteger. It also permits us to use noninteger Fahrenheit temperatures should we need to later.

Step 2: Select a Solution Algorithm:

This problem can be solved using the Problem-Solver Algorithm introduced in Section 1.5. As applied to this problem the algorithm becomes:

Set the Fahrenheit temperature to 75
Calculate the equivalent Celsius temperature using formula:
Celsius = 5.0/9.0 * (Fahrenheit - 32.0)
Display the equivalent Celsius temperature

To ensure that we have completely specified the algorithm, we now do a hand calculation. Using the conversion formula with a Fahrenheit value of 75, yields an equivalent Celsius value of 23.89 degrees. The result of this calculation will be used to verify the output of the program, so that once verified, we can confidently use the program to convert other Fahrenheit temperatures.

Step 3: Write the Program

Program 2.9 provides the necessary code.

Program 2.9

```
1  /* convert a Fahrenheit temperature to Celsius */
2
3  #include <stdio.h>
4  int main()
5  {
6    float celsius;
7    float fahrenheit = 75;  /* declaration and initialization */
8
9    celsius = 5.0/9.0 * (fahrenheit - 32.0);
10   printf("The Celsius equivalent of %5.2f degrees Fahrenheit\n",
11                                                       fahrenheit);
12   printf("   is %5.2f degrees\n", celsius);
13
14   return 0;
15 }
```

Lines 1 through 5 in Program 2.9 follow our standard format for the start of a C program. Lines 6 and 7

```
6  float celsius;
7  float fahrenheit = 75;  /* declaration and initialization */
```

provide two declaration statements that declare the variables `celsius` and `fahrenheit` as type `float`, and initializes the value of `fahrenheit` to 75.[12] This is followed by an optional blank line to separate the declaration statements from the rest of the program.

In line 9,

```
9  celsius = 5.0/9.0 * (fahrenheit - 32.0);
```

a value of `celsius` corresponding to the value currently stored in `fahrenheit` (that is, 75) is computed, using the formula listed in our algorithm. This is followed by two output statements to display the value of both the Fahrenheit and equivalent Celsius temperature.

When Program 2.9 is compiled and executed, the following output is produced:

```
The Celsius equivalent of 75.0 degrees Fahrenheit
   is 23.89 degrees
```

Notice that some assumptions as to the format of the output display have been made that were not specified in the requirements specification. This is not uncommon. Frequently the requirements specification will not completely state how the output is supposed to look. When this is the case, as it is here, the programmer is initially free to not only make assumptions about the exact format, but is frequently expected to do so. When you do this, however, you should always show a sample output to the person requesting the program or ask for more guidance in how the output is to be formatted. This provides the person requesting the program either to approve the final output display or to make adjustments to it. Be prepared for this to happen in your programming career, because many users will get upset if they do not have a final say in the output displays.

[12] Note that on compilers that use a default type of double this will generate a compiler warning message that can be ignored (the correct initialization should use a value of 75f). On compilers that use a default type of float, no warning is issued.

Step 4: Test and Debug the Program

The last step in the development procedure is testing the program output. As the displayed value agrees with the previous hand calculation, we have established a degree of confidence in the program. This permits us to use the program for different values of Fahrenheit temperatures. If the parentheses were not correctly placed in the assignment statement that calculated a value for `celsius`, the displayed value would not agree with our previous hand calculation. This would have alerted us to the fact there was an error in the program.

EXERCISES 2.6

Programming Exercises

1. a. Enter and execute Program 2.9.
   b. Modify Program 2.9 to convert 86.5 degrees Fahrenheit into its equivalent Celsius value.

2. In 1955, the Brooklyn Dodgers baseball team won 98 games and lost 55. Using this information, write, compile, and execute a C program that calculates and displays the team's winning percentage for 1955.

3. a. Write, compile, and execute a C program to calculate the dollar amount contained in a piggy bank. The bank currently contains 12 half-dollars, 20 quarters, 32 dimes, 45 nickels, and 27 pennies.
   b. Check the values computed by your program by hand. After you have verified that your program is working correctly, modify it to determine the dollar value of a bank containing no half-dollars, 17 quarters, 19 dimes, 10 nickels, and 42 pennies.

4. The distance that light travels in one year is called a light year. Given that light travels at a speed of 3 * 108 meters in one second, determine the distance of a light year. The relevant formula is *distance = speed * time*. (*Hint:* Make sure that the time corresponds to the number of seconds in one year.)

5. a. Write and execute a C program that calculates and displays the elapsed time it took to make a 150-mile trip. The equation for computing elapsed time is *elapsed time = distance/average speed*. Assume the average speed was 65 miles/hour, and use the variable names `time`, `distance`, and `avgSpeed` in your program.
   b. Check the values computed by your program by hand. After you have verified that your program is working correctly, modify it to determine the elapsed time of a 204-mile trip, where the average speed was 68 miles per hour.

6. a. Write and execute a C program that calculates and displays the sum of the numbers from 1 to 100. The formula for calculating this sum is $sum = (n/2)\ (2*a + (n - 1)d)$, where n = number of terms to be added, a = the first number, and d = the difference between each number.
   b. Check the values computed by your program by hand. After you have verified that your program is working correctly, modify it to determine the sum of the integers from 100 to 1000.

7. a. Write a C program to calculate and display the value of the slope of the line connecting the two points whose coordinates are (3,7) and (8,12). Use the fact that the slope between two points having coordinates (*x*1,*y*1) and (*x*2,*y*2) is *(y2 – y1) / (x2 – x1)*.
   b. How do you know that the result produced by your program is correct?
   c. Once you have verified the output produced by your program, modify it to determine the slope of the line connecting the points (2,10) and (12,6).
   d. What do you think will happen if you use the points (2,3) and (2,4), which results in a division by zero? How do you think this situation can be handled?

8. a. Pendulums used in clocks, such as grandmother and grandfather clocks, keep fairly accurate time for the following reason: When the length of a pendulum is relatively large compared to the maximum arc of its swing, the time to complete one swing is independent of both the pendulum's weight and the maximum displacement of the swing. When this condition is satisfied, the relationship between the time to complete one swing and the length of the pendulum is given by the formula

   $$length = g\ [time/(2\pi)]^2$$

   where π, accurate to four decimal places, is equal to 3.1416 and *g* is the gravitational constant equal to 32.2 ft/sec^2. When the time of a complete swing is given in seconds, the length of the pendulum is in feet. Using the given formula, write a C program to calculate and display the length of a pendulum needed to produce a swing that will be completed in one second. The length should be displayed in inches and should have the following format:

   ```
   The length to complete one swing in one second is: ______
   ```

   where the underlined blank spaces are replaced by the actual value calculated by your program.
   b. Compile and execute the program written for Exercise 8a on a computer. Make sure to do a hand calculation so that you can verify the results produced by your program.

9. a. Modify the program written for Exercise 8 to calculate the length of a pendulum that produces an arc that takes two seconds to complete.
   b. Compile and execute the program written for Exercise 9a on a computer.

10. A directly connected telephone network is one in which all telephones in the network are directly connected and do not require a central switching station to establish calls between two telephones. For example, financial institutions on Wall Street use such a network to maintain direct and continuously open phone lines between firms.

    The number of direct lines needed to maintain a directly connected network for *n* telephones, is given by the formula

    $$lines = n(n-1)/2$$

    For example, directly connecting four telephones requires six individual lines (see Figure 2.12). Adding a fifth telephone to this network would require an additional four lines for a total of 10 lines.

    Using the given formula, write a C program that determines the number of direct lines required for 100 telephones, and the additional lines required if 10 new telephones were added to the network.

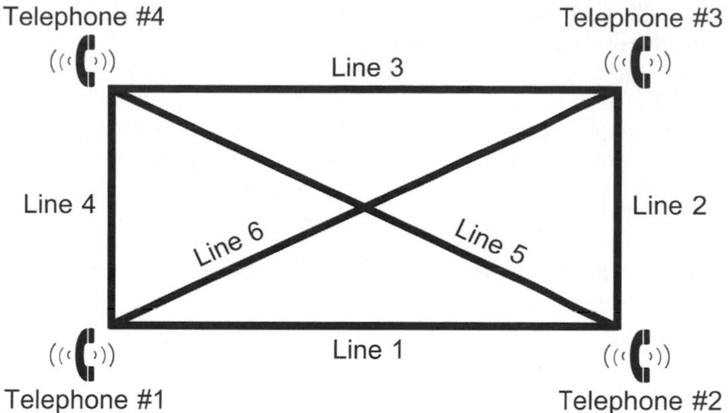

Figure 2.12 Directly connecting four telephones

11. a. Modify the program written for Exercise 10 to calculate and display the total number of lines needed to directly connect 1000 individual phones to each other.
    b. Compile and execute the program written for Exercise 11a on a computer.

2.7 Common Programming and Compiler Errors

In using the material presented in this chapter, be aware of the following programming and compiler errors.

Programming Errors

1. Omitting the parentheses, `()`, after `main` (see the Compiler Errors section).
2. Omitting or incorrectly typing the opening brace, {, that signifies the start of a function body (see the Compiler Errors section).
3. Omitting or incorrectly typing the closing brace } that signifies the end of a function (see the Compiler Errors section).
4. Misspelling the name of a function; for example, typing `print()` instead of `printf-()`(see the Compiler Errors section).
5. Forgetting to close a string passed to `printf()` with a double quote symbol (see the Compiler Errors section).
6. Omitting the semicolon at the end of each executable statement (see the Compiler Errors section).
7. Forgetting to include `\n` to indicate a new line.

8. Forgetting to declare all the variables used in a program. This error is detected by the compiler, and an error message is generated for all undeclared variables (see the Compiler Errors section).

9. Storing an incorrect data type in a declared variable. This error is not detected by the compiler. The assigned value is converted to the data type of the variable to which it is assigned.

10. Using a variable in an expression before a value has been assigned to the variable. Whatever value happens to be in the variable will be used when the expression is evaluated, and the result will be meaningless.

11. Dividing integer values incorrectly. This error is usually disguised within a larger expression and can be very troublesome to detect. For example, the expression

    ```
    3.425 + 2/3 + 7.9
    ```

    yields the same result as the expression

    ```
    3.425 + 7.9
    ```

    because the integer division of 2/3 is 0.

12. Mixing data types in the same expression without clearly understanding the effect produced. Since C allows expressions with "mixed" data types, it is important to be clear about the order of evaluation and the data type of all intermediate calculations. As a general rule it is better never to mix data types in an expression unless a specific effect is desired.

13. Not including the correct conversion control sequence in `printf()` function calls for the data types of the remaining arguments.

14. Not closing the control string in `printf()` with a double quote symbol followed by a comma when additional arguments are passed to `printf()`.

15. Forgetting to separate all arguments passed to `printf()` with commas. In the author's experience, the third, fifth, sixth, and seventh errors in this list are the most common. It's useful to write a simple program and specifically introduce each of these errors, one at a time, to see what error messages are produced by your compiler. Then, when these error messages appear because of inadvertent errors, you will have had experience in understanding the message and correcting the errors.

Compiler Errors

The following table summarizes typical compiler error messages in Unix- and Windows-based compilers.

Error	Typical Unix-based compiler error message	Typical Windows-based compiler error message
Omitting the parentheses,(), in the header line for the `main` function.	`(S) Definition of function main requires parentheses.`	`error:: 'main' : looks like a function definition, but there is no formal parameter list; skipping apparent body`
Omitting the opening `{` in the `main` function body.	`(S) Syntax error: possible missing ';' or ','` `(S) Parameter declaration list is incompatible with declarator for main.`	Note: The error message you will receive depends on the statements in the function. The line numbers for these errors start at the line immediately following the header line. Typical error messages will include: `syntax error : missing ';' before identifier ...` `missing storage-class or type specifiers` `syntax error : 'return'` `syntax error : '}'`
Omitting the `}` at the end of the `main` function.	`(S) Syntax error: possible missing ';' or ','? (S) Unexpected end of file.`	`end of file found before the left brace '{' was matched`
Misspelling `printf`.	`ERROR: Undefined symbol`	`identifier not found, even with argument-dependent lookup`
Omitting either the opening or closing double quotes in the string passed to `printf()`.	`(S) String literal must be ended before the end of line.` `(S) Syntax error: possible missing ')'?`	`newline in constant`
Omitting the `;` at the end of an executable statement.	`(S) Syntax error: possible missing ';' or ','?`	`syntax error : missing ';'`
Forgetting to declare all the variables used in a program.	`(S) Undeclared identifier`	`undeclared identifier`

Error	Typical Unix-based compiler error message	Typical Windows-based compiler error message
Omitting the opening `/*` at the beginning of a comment.	`(S) Definition of function this requires parentheses. (S) Syntax error: possible missing '{'?` Note: The compiler is basically telling you that it cannot recognize any of the lines following the mistake.)	Note: The error message you will receive depends on the statements following the comment. The line numbers for these errors will start at the line missing the `/*`. A warning, similar to the following, will also be issued `warning: '*/' found outside of comment`
Omitting the closing `*/` in a comment.	`(S) Comment that started on line .. must end before the end of file.`	`unexpected end of file found in comment`
Initializing a numeric variable with a comma in the initializer. For example, `int val = 1,234;` will generate an error.	`(S) Syntax error.`	`syntax error : 'constant'`

2.8 Chapter Summary

1. A C program consists of one or more modules called functions. One of these functions must be called `main()`. The `main()` function identifies the starting point of a C program.
2. A function is a C language description of an algorithm.
3. Many functions, like `printf()`, are supplied in a standard library of functions provided with each C compiler.
4. Simple C programs consist of the single function named `main()`.
5. Following the function name, the body of a function has the general form:
```
{
   All program statements in here;
}
```
6. An executable statement causes some specific action to be performed by the computer when the program is executed.
7. All executable C statements must be terminated by a semicolon.
8. The `printf()` function is used to display text or numerical results. The first argument to `printf()` can be text, which is enclosed in double quotes. The text is displayed directly on the screen and may include newline escape sequences for format control.

9. The two basic numerical data types used almost exclusively in current C programs are integers and double-precision numbers. (Older C programs used single-precision numbers rather than double-precision.) Compilers typically assign different amounts of memory to store each of these types of data.

10. An expression is a sequence of one or more operands separated by operators. An operand is a constant, a variable, or another expression. A value is associated with an expression.

11. Expressions are evaluated according to the precedence and associativity of the operators used in the expression.

12. The `printf()` function can be used to display all of C's data types. The conversion control sequence for displaying integer, floating-point (both single-precision and double-precision), and character values are `%d`, `%f`, and `%c`, respectively.

13. Every variable in a C program must be declared as to the type of value it can store, and a variable can only be used after it is declared. Additionally, variables of the same type may be declared using a single declaration statement. Variable declaration statements have the general syntax:
    ```
    dataType variableName(s);
    ```
    Additionally, variables may be initialized when they are declared.

14. A simple C program containing declaration statements has the form:
    ```
    #include <stdio.h>
    int main()
    {
      declaration statements;

      other statements;

      return 0;
    }
    ```

15. Declaration statements always play the software role of informing the compiler of a function's valid variable names. When a variable declaration causes the computer to set aside memory locations for the variable, the declaration statement is also a definition statement. (All the declarations we have encountered so far have also been definition statements.)

2.9 Chapter Supplement: Memory Allocation

A unique feature of C is that it permits you to see where and how values are stored. This allows a programmer to both inspect the computer's internal storage and use C, when necessary, as a low-level language that can directly manipulate a computer's internal hardware.

In this section we introduce these features, so that you can see, when you want or need to, how and where a variable's data is stored during program execution. For many beginning programmers, these features offer useful insight into the inner workings of their programs. For professional programmers, they provide capabilities and programming power not found in most other high-level languages, and are invaluable for advanced programming applications.

Integer Data Types

The range of permitted values typically provided by most current C compilers for the `int` data type was listed in Section 2.3 as -2,147,483,648 to +2,147,483,647. In this section, we provide the ranges for all C's integer data types and show how you can check each one of them for your particular compiler.

Table 2.12 lists the typical range of values for each integer data type in the second column. The standard identifiers provided by each C compiler, listed in the `limits.h` header file, that defines these values are provided in the third column. Finally, the fourth column provides the number of bytes used to store each data type. It is the amount of storage listed in this column that directly determines the range of values listed in the second column.

You can directly check the range of values provided by your compiler for each data type in two ways: (1) locate and then inspect the `limits.h` header file for the identifier names listed in the third column, or (2) use a C program to display the values defined by these identifiers. A program to check the range of values for each data type is presented below. Additionally, the storage size for each data type, listed in the fourth column, can be determined using the `sizeof()`. A program for determining the storage size for each data type is presented in this section.

Table 2.12 Integer Data Type Storage

Name of Data Type	Range of Values	Identifier (in limits.h)	Storage Size (in bytes; see Section 1.8)
`char`	-128 to +127	SCHAR_MIN SCHAR_MAX	1
`short int`	-32,768 to +32,767	SHRT_MIN SHRT_MAX	2
`int`	-2,147,483,648 to +2,147,483,647	INT_MIN INT_MAX	4
`long int`	-2,147,483,648 to +2,147,483,647	LONG_MIN LONG_MAX	4
`unsigned short int`	0 to 65,535	USHRT_MAX	2
`unsigned int`	0 to 4,294,967,295	UINT_MAX	4
`unsigned long int`	0 to 4,294,967,295	ULONG_MAX	4

Before providing a program to check the range of values, two items should be addressed. First, notice in Table 2.12 that a `long` integer provides the same range of values and uses the same amount of storage (4 bytes) as an `int`. The only requirement of the ANSI C standard is that an `int` must provide at least as much storage as a `short int`, and that a `long int` must provide at least as much precision as an `int`. On the first desktop computer systems (1980s), where memory capacity was limited, the allocation for a `short int`, `int`, and `long int` were different, with a `short int` typically using 1 byte of storage, an `int` 2 bytes, and a `long int` 4 bytes.

Second, note the difference between a `short int`, `int` and `long int` and their unsigned equivalents (the last three data types in the table). An **unsigned data type** provides only for nonnegative (that is, zero and positive) values. To distinguish these unsigned data types from their counterparts, the `short int`, `int`, and `long int` data types are formally referred to as **signed data types.**

All of the unsigned integer types in Table 2.12 provide a range of positive values that is, for all practical purposes, double the range provided for their signed counterparts. This extra positive range is made available by using the negative range of its signed counterpart for additional positive numbers.

The keywords `short`, `long`, and `unsigned` are known as **qualifiers**, because they qualify the meaning of the keyword `int`. The meaning of these qualifiers is not altered if the keyword `int` is omitted. Thus, the `short int` data type can also be specified as the `short` data type, the `unsigned short int` data type can be specified as the `unsigned short` data type, and so on for the `long` integer data types. All of these qualified integer types are now rarely used. They were important in early desktop applications that provided a limited range of `int` values from –32,768 to +32,767. With the current range of `int` values in the –2 to +2 billion range, the doubling of positive values using an `unsigned int`, or the doubling of both positive and negative values using a `long` is no longer a consideration.

Program 2.10 uses the standard identifiers listed in Table 2.12 to display the actual range of values provided by the author's compiler for each of C's signed integer data types. Notice that the `limits.h` header file has been included (line 2). The header file is necessary because it contains the standard identifiers being accessed and displayed.

Program 2.10

```
 1  #include <stdio.h>
 2  #include <limits.h> /* contains the minimum and maximum specifications */
 3  int main()
 4  {
 5    printf("The smallest character code that can be stored is %d\n", SCHAR_MIN);
 6    printf("The largest character code that can be stored is %d\n", SCHAR_MAX);
 7    printf("The smallest integer value that can be stored is %d\n", INT_MIN);
 8    printf("The largest integer value that can be stored is %d\n", INT_MAX);
 9    printf("The smallest short integer value that can be stored is %d\n",SHRT_MIN);
10    printf("The largest short integer value that can be stored is %d\n", SHRT_MAX);
11    printf("The smallest long integer value that can be stored is %d\n", LONG_MIN);
12    printf("The largest long integer value that can be stored is %d\n", LONG_MAX);
13
14    return 0;
15  }
```

The output provided by Program 2.10 is

```
The smallest character code that can be stored is -128
The largest character code that can be stored is 127
The smallest integer value that can be stored is -2147483648
The largest integer value that can be stored is 2147483647
The smallest short integer value that can be stored is -32768
The largest short integer value that can be stored is 32767
The smallest long integer value that can be stored is -2147483648
The largest long integer value that can be stored is 2147483647
```

Notice that the displayed values correspond to those listed in Table 2.12.[13]

The `sizeof()` Operator

Using C's `sizeof()` operator, you can directly determine the number of bytes reserved by your compiler for any data type (integer and floating point) or variable. This is accomplished by including the data type or variable's name within the operator's parentheses, and then displaying the returned value. The `sizeof()` operator is a built-in operator that does not use an arithmetic symbol to perform its operation. Program 2.11 uses this operator to determine the amount of storage reserved for the `int`, `char`, `short`, and `long` integer types.

Program 2.11

```
#include <stdio.h>
int main()
{
  printf("Data Type        Bytes\n");
  printf("---------        -----\n");
  printf("char               %d\n", sizeof(char));
  printf("short int          %d\n", sizeof(short));
  printf("int                %d\n", sizeof(int));
  printf("long int           %d\n", sizeof(long));
  printf("float              %d\n", sizeof(float));
  printf("double             %d\n", sizeof(double));
  printf("long double        %d\n", sizeof(long double));

  return 0;
}
```

[13] The standard identifiers for the unsigned integer data types are usually provided as hexadecimal numbers in the `limits.h` header file. As such, their display requires conversion to a decimal (base 10) value to match the values listed in Table 2.12.

The output of Program 2.11 is compiler dependent. That is, each compiler will correctly report the amount of storage that it allocates for the data type under consideration. When run on the author's computer, which uses Microsoft's current Visual C.net compiler, the following output was produced:

```
Data Type        Bytes
---------        -----
char               1
short int          2
int                4
long int           4
float              4
double             8
long double        8
```

The `sizeof()` operator returns the number of bytes relative to a character, where a character is defined as using 1 byte. As almost all compilers currently do use 1 byte per character, the value returned by `sizeof()` is a true byte count.[14]

Addresses[15]

Three major items associated with every variable are its data type, the value stored in it, and where it is stored in memory. The number of memory bytes used by a variable depends on the variable's data type. It is the address of the first memory byte used for storing the variable that is known as the **variable's address**. The relationship between these items is illustrated in Figure 2.13.

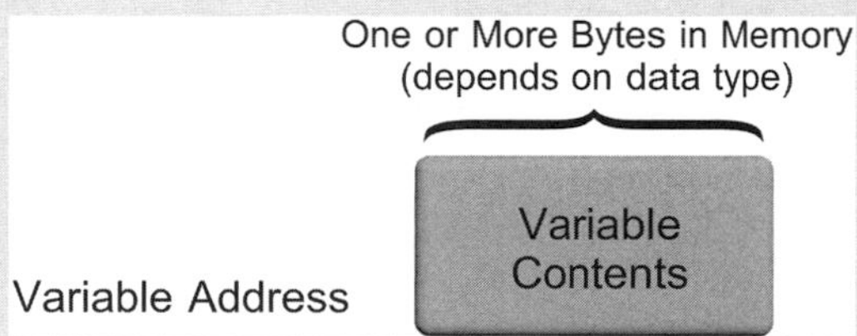

Figure 2.13 A typical variable

Programmers are usually concerned only with a variable's data type and its value, giving little attention to where the value is stored (its address). For example, consider Program 2.12.

[14] The number of bits reserved for a char data type is specified in the `limits.h` file as `CHAR_BIT`.
[15] This section is optional. Understanding it requires an understanding of bytes and words presented in Section 1.8.

Program 2.12

```
#include <stdio.h>
int main()
{
  int num = 22;

  printf("The value stored in num is %d.",num);
  printf("\nThe computer uses %d bytes to store this value", sizeof(int));

  return 0;
}
```

When Program 2.12 is run, the output displayed is

```
The value stored in num is 22.
The computer uses 4 bytes to store this value
```

Program 2.12 displays both the number 22, which is the value stored in the integer variable num (its contents), and the amount of storage used for an integer. The information provided by Program 2.12 is illustrated in Figure 2.14.

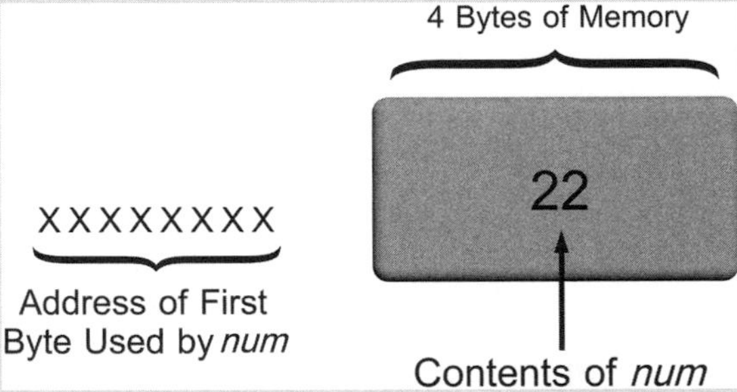

Figure 2.14 Information provided by Program 2.12

We can go further and actually obtain the address corresponding to the variable num. The address that is displayed corresponds to the address of the first byte set aside in the computer's memory for the variable. The ability to display addresses is unique to C (it is really an offshoot of the ability to directly manipulate addresses, using pointers, that is presented in Chapters 11 and 13). Nevertheless, displaying addresses provides a useful tool, in itself, to effectively see into a computer's main memory and gain a clearer perspective of where data is actually stored.

To determine the address of a variable, such as num, we must use C's address operator, &, which means the address of, directly before the variable's name (no space between & and the variable). For example, & means the address of num, &total means the address of total, and &price means the address of price. Program 2.13 uses the address operator to display the address of the variable num.

Program 2.13

```
#include <stdio.h>
int main()
{
  int num = 22;

  printf("num = %d The address of num is %d\n.", num, &num);

  return 0;
}
```

The output produced by Program 2.13 is

```
num = 22 The address of num is 124484.
```

Figure 2.15 illustrates the additional address information provided by the output of Program 2.13.

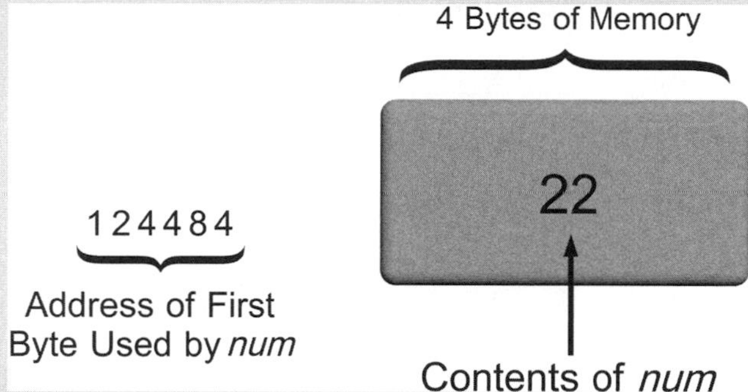

Figure 2.15 A more complete picture of the variable `num`

Clearly, the address output by Program 2.13 depends on the computer used to run the program. Every time Program 2.13 is executed, however, it displays the address of the first byte used to store the variable `num`. Note also that the address is printed using the conversion control sequence `%d`. This conversion control sequence forces the address to be displayed as an integer number, and what is displayed is `printf()`'s representation of the address in a decimal format.[16] The display has no impact on how addresses are used internally to the program and merely provides us with a representation that is helpful in understanding what addresses are.

---

[16] More correctly, the `%p` conversion control sequence should be used, which is the conversion control sequence provided for addresses. The reason for this is that an address is not an integer data type, but a unique data type that may or may not require the same amount of storage as an integer. Because the `%p` control sequence displays the address as a hexadecimal (base 12) number, and it is usually more instructive to see the address as a decimal (base 10) number, we have used a `%d`. In its place, a `%u` conversion control sequence can be used, which forces the address to be treated as an unsigned integer data type.

As we shall see, using addresses as opposed to only displaying them provides the C programmer with an extremely powerful programming tool. Addresses provide the ability to enter directly into the computer's inner workings and access its basic storage structure. This gives the C programmer capabilities and programming power that are not available in most other computer languages.

EXERCISES 2.9

Programming Exercises

1. Enter, compile, and execute Program 2.10 on your computer to determine the range of values provided by your compiler for each of C's signed integer data types.

2. Enter, compile, and execute Program 2.11 on your computer to determine how many bytes of storage your compiler allocates for each of C's data types.

3. Enter, compile, and execute Program 2.13 on your computer to determine where in memory your computer has stored the variable `num`.

4. a. Write a C program that includes the following declaration statements:

```
char key, choice;
int num, count;
long date;
float yield;
double price;
```

   Have the program use the address operator and the `printf()` function to display the addresses corresponding to each variable.

   b. After running the program written for Exercise 4a, draw a diagram of how your computer has set aside storage for the variables in the program. On your diagram, fill in the addresses displayed by the program.

5. Modify the program written in Exercise 4a to display the amount of storage your computer reserves for each data type (use the `sizeof()` operator). With this information and the address information provided in Exercise 4b, determine if your computer set aside storage for the variables in the order they were declared.

Chapter 3

- **3.1** Assignment
- **3.2** Mathematical Library Functions
- **3.3** Interactive Input
- **3.4** Formatted Output
- **3.5** Symbolic Constants
- **3.6** Case Study: Interactive Input
- **3.7** Common Programming and Compiler Errors
- **3.8** Chapter Summary
- **3.9** Chapter Supplement: Introduction to Abstraction

Processing and Interactive Input

In Chapter 2 we explained how data is stored, introduced variables and declaration statements, and described how the `printf()` function is used to display output data. This chapter continues our introduction to C by explaining how data is processed using both assignment statements and mathematical functions and presenting the `scanf()` function that makes it possible for a user to enter data while a program is running. You'll also learn more about the `printf()` function, which permits precise formatting of output data.

3.1 Assignment

As you learned in Chapter 2, assignment statements are used to assign a value to a variable. An assignment statement is also the most basic C statement for performing a computation. The general syntax for an assignment statement is

```
variable = operand;
```

where the equal sign, =, is the assignment operator and the operand to the right of the assignment operator can be a constant, a variable, or an expression. Examples of assignment statements using a constant as an operand are

```
length = 25;
width = 17.5;
```

In each of these assignment statements, the value of the constant to the right of the equal sign is assigned to the variable on the left side of the equal sign. It is extremely important that the equal sign in C does not have the same meaning as an equal sign in algebra. The equal sign in an assignment statement causes the computer to first determine the value of the operand to the right of the equal sign and then to store (or assign) that value in the variable to the left of the equal sign. In this regard, the C statement `length = 25;` is read "length is assigned the value 25." The blank spaces in the assignment statement are inserted for readability only.

Recall from the Section 2.5 that an initial value can be assigned to a variable when it is declared. If an initialization is not done from within a declaration statement, the variable is initialized the first time a value is assigned using an assignment statement. Subsequent assignment statements can, of course, be used to change the value assigned to a variable. For example, assume the following statements are executed one after another and that no value has previously been assigned to `length`:

```
length = 3.7;
length = 6.28;
```

The first assignment statement assigns the value of 3.7 to the variable named `length`. Because this is the first time a value is assigned to this variable it is also correct to say that "length is initialized to 3.7." The next assignment statement causes the computer to assign a value of 6.28 to `length`. The 3.7 that was in `length` is overwritten with the new value of 6.28, because a variable can only store one value at a time. In this regard it is sometimes useful to think of the variable to the left of the equal sign as a temporary parking spot in a huge parking lot. Just as an individual parking spot can only be used by one car at a time, each variable can only store one value at a time. The "parking" of a new value in a variable automatically causes the computer to remove any value previously "parked" there.

In addition to being a constant, the operand to the right of the equal sign in an assignment statement can be a variable or any valid C expression. Thus, the expression in an assignment statement can be used to perform calculations using the arithmetic operators introduced in Section 2.4. Examples of assignment statements using expressions containing these operators are

```
sum = 3 + 7;
diff = 15 - 6;
product = .05 * 14.6;
tally = count + 1;
newTotal = 18.3 + total;
taxes = .06 * amount;
interest = principal * rate;
average = sum /items;
slope = (y2 - y1) / (x2 - x1);
```

As always in an assignment statement, the value of the expression to the right of the equal sign is computed first and then the calculated value is stored in the variable to the left of the equal sign. For example, in the assignment statement `interest = principal * rate;` the expression `principal * rate` is first evaluated to yield a value. This value is then stored in the variable `interest`.

In writing assignment statements, you must be aware of two important considerations. Because the expression to the right of the equal sign is evaluated first, all variables used in the expression must be initialized if the result is to make sense. For example, the assignment statement `interest = principal * rate;` will cause a valid number to be stored in the variable `interest` only if the programmer first takes care to put valid numbers in `principal` and `rate`. Thus, the sequence of statements

```
principal = 1000;
rate = .035;
interest = principle * rate;
```

ensures that we know the values being used to obtain the number that will be stored in the variable to the left of the equal sign.

The second consideration is that because the value of an expression is stored in the variable to the left of the equal sign, one variable must be listed immediately to the left of the equal sign. For example, the expression

```
amount + 1892 = 1000 + 10 * 5
```

is invalid. Here, the expression on the right-hand side of the equal sign evaluates to the integer 1050, which can be stored only in a variable. Because `amount + 1892` is not a valid variable name, the computer does not know where to store the calculated value.

Program 3.1 illustrates the use of assignment statements in calculating the area of a rectangle.

Program 3.1

```
#include <stdio.h>
int main()
{
  float length, width, area;

  length = 27.2;
  width = 13.8;
  area = length * width;
  printf("The length of the rectangle is %f", length);
  printf("\nThe width of the rectangle is %f", width);
  printf("\nThe area of the rectangle is %f", area);

  return 0;
}
```

When Program 3.1 is run, the output obtained is

```
The length of the rectangle is 27.200000
The width of the rectangle is 13.800000
The area of the rectangle is 375.360000
```

Notice the order in which statements are executed in Program 3.1. The program begins with the keyword `main` and continues sequentially, statement by statement, until the closing brace. This is an example of sequential flow of control that is true for all programs. The computer works on one statement at a time, executing that statement with no knowledge of what the next statement will be. This explains why all operands used in an expression must have values assigned to them before the expression is evaluated.

When the computer executes the statement `area = length * width;` in line 8, it uses whatever value is stored in the variables `length` and `width` at the time the assignment is executed. If no values have been specifically assigned to these variables before they are used in the expression `length * width`, the computer uses whatever values happen to occupy these variables when they are referenced.[1] The computer does not "look ahead" to see that you might assign values to these variables later in the program.

In C, the equal sign, =, used in assignment statements is itself an operator, which differs from the way most other high-level languages process this symbol. In C, the = symbol is called the **assignment operator**. As an operator, it has the lowest precedence of all the binary and unary arithmetic operators introduced in Section 2.4, which explains why all of the arithmetic operations in an assignment statement are performed before the assignment is completed.

Because the equal sign is an operator in C, multiple assignments are possible in the same statement. For example, in the statement `a = b = c = 25;` all the assignment operators have the same precedence. Using the operator's right-to-left associativity, the final evaluation proceeds in the sequence

```
c = 25;
b = c;
a = b;
```

This has the effect of assigning the number 25 to each of the variables individually, and can be represented as

```
a = (b = (c = 25));
```

Thus, the single statement `a = b = c = 25;` is equivalent to the three individual statements

```
c = 25;
b = 25;
a = 25;
```

Implicit Type Conversions

Data type conversions take place across assignment operators. This means that the value of the expression on the right side of the equal sign is converted to the data type of the variable to the left of the equal sign. For example, consider the assignment statement `result = 4;`

[1]Most compilers will issue a warning that an uninitialized variable is being used, but the program will compile.

> **Programming Note**
>
> **lvalues and rvalues**
>
> You will encounter the terms **lvalue** and **rvalue** frequently in almost all programming languages that define an assignment using an operator that permits multiple assignments in the same statement. The term lvalue refers to any quantity that is valid on the left side of an assignment operator. An rvalue refers to any quantity that is valid on the right side of an assignment operator.
>
> For example, each variable we have encountered so far can be either an lvalue or rvalue (that is, a variable, by itself, can appear on both sides of an assignment operator). As we will see in Chapter 8, a variable declared for an array cannot be either an lvalue or an rvalue, while individual array variables can be both.
>
> Individual numbers can only be an rvalue and, more generally, any expression that yields a value can be an rvalue.

where `result` has been declared as a double-precision variable. Here, the integer value 4 will be converted to the double-precision value 4.0, and it is this value that gets assigned to `result`. This automatic conversion across an assignment operator is referred to as an **implicit type conversion.** Conversion from an integer to a floating-point data type rarely, if ever, causes a problem. The reverse, however, can cause computational problems. This is because implicit conversion from a floating-point value to an integer results in the loss of the fractional part of the number.

For example, consider the assignment statement `answer = 2.764;` where `answer` has been declared as type `int`. Because the left side of the assignment operator is an integer variable, the double-precision value 2.764 is truncated to the integer value 2 and stored in the variable `answer.` In this case, where the implicit conversion is one from a higher precision to a lower precision data type, the compiler will issue a warning.

Explicit Type Conversions (Casts)

In addition to implicit data type conversions that are automatically made across assignment operators, C also provides for explicit user-specified conversions. The operator used to force the conversion of a value to another type is the **cast** operator. This is a unary operator having the syntax

```
(dataType) expression
```

where *`dataType`* is the desired data type of the expression following the cast. For example, if `sum` is a double-precision variable, the value of the expression `(int) sum` is the integer value determined by truncating `sum`'s fractional part.

Assignment Variations

Although only one variable is allowed immediately to the left of the equal sign in an assignment expression, the variable on the left of the equal sign can also be used on the right of the equal sign. For example, the assignment expression `sum = sum + 10` is valid.

Clearly, in an algebra equation a variable could never be equal to itself plus 10. But in C, the expression `sum = sum + 10` is not an equation—it is an expression that is evaluated in two major steps. The first step is to calculate the value of `sum + 10`. The second step is to store the computed value in sum. See if you can determine the output of Program 3.2.

Program 3.2

```
#include <stdio.h>
int main()
{
  int sum;

  sum = 25;
  printf("\nThe number stored in sum is %d.",sum);
  sum = sum + 10;
  printf("\nThe number now stored in sum is %d.\n",sum);

  return 0;
}
```

The assignment statement `sum = 25;` tells the computer to store the number 25 in sum, as shown in Figure 3.1. The first call to `printf()` in Program 3.2 causes the value stored in sum to be displayed by the message `The number stored in sum is 25.` The second assignment statement, `sum = sum + 10;` causes the computer to retrieve the `25` stored in sum and add `10` to this number, yielding the number `35`. The number `35` is then stored in the variable on the left side of the equal sign, which is the variable sum. The `25` that was in sum is simply erased and replaced with the new value of `35`, as shown in Figure 3.2.

sum

25

Figure 3.1 The integer 25 is stored in sum

Assignment expressions like `sum = sum + 25`, which use the same variable on both sides of the assignment operator, can be written using the following assignment operators:

```
+=     -=     *=     /=     %=
```

For example, the expression `sum = sum + 10` can be written as `sum += 10`. Similarly, the expression `price *= rate` is equivalent to the expression `price = price * rate`.

Figure 3.2 `sum = sum + 10;` causes a new value to be stored in sum

In using these new assignment operators, note that the variable to the left of the assignment operator is applied to the complete expression on the right. For example, the expression `price *= rate + 1` is equivalent to the expression `price = price * (rate + 1)`, not `price = price * rate + 1`.

Accumulating

Assignment expressions like `sum += 10` or its equivalent, `sum = sum + 10`, are common in programming. These expressions are required in accumulating subtotals when data is entered one number at a time. For example, if we want to add the numbers 96, 70, 85, and 60 in calculator fashion, the statements in Table 3.1 could be used.

Table 3.1 Statements and Resulting Value when Adding 96, 70, 85, and 60

Statement	Value in sum
`sum = 0;`	0
`sum = sum + 96;`	96
`sum = sum + 70;`	166
`sum = sum + 85;`	251
`sum = sum + 60;`	311

The first statement initializes `sum` to 0. This removes any previously stored value in `sum` that would invalidate the final total (such a previously stored number, if it has not been initialized to a specific and known value, is frequently referred to as a **garbage value**) . As each number is added, the value stored in `sum` is increased accordingly. After completion of the last statement, `sum` contains the total of all the added numbers.

Program 3.3 illustrates the effect of these statements by displaying `sum`'s contents after each addition is made.

Program 3.3

```
#include <stdio.h>
int main()
{
  int sum;

  sum = 0;
  printf("\nThe value of sum is initially set to %d.", sum);
  sum = sum + 96;
  printf("\n sum is now %d.", sum);
  sum = sum + 70;
  printf("\n sum is now %d.", sum);
  sum = sum + 85;
  printf("\n sum is now %d.", sum);
  sum = sum + 60;
```

```
    printf("\n The final sum is %d.\n", sum);

    return 0;
}
```

The output displayed by Program 3.3 is

```
The value of sum is initially set to 0.
sum is now 96.
sum is now 166.
sum is now 251.
The final sum is 311.
```

Although Program 3.3 is not a practical program (it is easier to add the numbers by hand), it does illustrate the subtotaling effect of repeated use of statements having the form

`variable = variable + newValue;`

We will find many uses for this type of statement when we become more familiar with the repetition statements introduced in Chapter 5.

Counting

A special type of assignment statement that is very similar to the accumulating statement is the **counting statement.** Counting statements have the form

`variable = variable + fixedNumber;`

Examples of counting statements are

```
i = i + 1;
n = n + 1;
count = count + 1;
j = j + 2;
m = m + 2;
kk = kk + 3;
```

In each of these examples, the same variable is used on both sides of the equal sign. After a statement is executed, the value of the respective variable is increased by a fixed amount. In the first three examples the variables `i`, `n`, and `count` have all been increased by 1. In the next two examples, the respective variables have been increased by 2, and in the final example the variable `kk` has been increased by 3.

For the special case in which a variable is either increased or decreased by one, C provides two unary operators. Using the **increment operator**, ++, the expression `variable = variable + 1` can be replaced by the either the expression `variable++` or `++variable`. Examples of the increment operator are shown in Table 3.2.

Table 3.2 Examples of the Increment Operator

Expression	Alternative
`i = i + 1`	`i++ and ++i`
`n = n + 1`	`n++ and ++n`
`count = count + 1`	`count++ and ++count`

Program 3.4 illustrates the use of the increment operator.

Program 3.4

```
#include <stdio.h>
int main()
{
  int count;

  count = 0;
  printf("\nThe initial value of count is %d.", count);
  count++;
  printf("\n count is now %d.", count);
  count++;
  printf("\n count is now %d.", count);
  count++;
  printf("\n count is now %d.", count);
  count++;
  printf("\n count is now %d.\n", count);

  return 0;
}
```

The output displayed by Program 3.4 is

```
The initial value of count is 0.
count is now 1.
count is now 2.
count is now 3.
count is now 4.
```

When the ++ operator appears before a variable, it is called a **prefix increment operator**; when it appears after a variable, it is called **postfix increment operator**. The distinction between a prefix and postfix increment operator is important when the variable being incremented is used in an assignment expression. For example, the expression `k = ++n` does two things in one expression. Initially, the value of n is incremented by 1 and then the new value of n is assigned to the variable k. Thus, the statement k = ++n; is equivalent to the two statements

```
n = n + 1;       // increment n first
k = n;           // assign n's value to k
```

The assignment expression k = n++, which uses a postfix increment operator, reverses this procedure. A postfix increment operates after the assignment is completed. Thus, the statement k = n++; first assigns the current value of n to k and then increments the value of n by 1. This is equivalent to the two statements

```
k = n;          // assign n's value to k
n = n + 1;      // and then increment n
```

In addition to the increment operator, C also provides a decrement operator, --. As you might expect, the expressions variable-- and --variable are both equivalent to the expression variable = variable - 1.

Examples of the decrement operator are shown in Table 3.3.

Table 3.3 Examples of the Decrement Operator

Expression	Alternative
i = i - 1	i-- and --i
n = n - 1	n-- and --n
count = count - 1	count-- and --count

When the -- operator appears before a variable, it is called a **prefix decrement operator**. When the decrement appears after a variable, it is called a **postfix decrement operator**. For example, both of the expressions n-- and --n reduce the value of n by 1. These expressions are equivalent to the longer expression n = n - 1. As with the increment operator, however, the prefix and postfix decrement operators produce different results when used in assignment expressions. For example, the expression k = --n first decrements the value of n by 1 before assigning the value of n to k, while the expression k = n-- first assigns the current value of n to k and then reduces the value of n by 1.

The increment and decrement operators can often be used advantageously to significantly reduce storage requirements and increase execution speed. For example, consider the following three statements:

```
count = count + 1;
count += 1;
count++;
```

All perform the same function; however, when these instructions are compiled for execution, the storage requirements are generally highest for the first statement and lowest for the last statement.

EXERCISES 3.1

Short Answer Questions

1. Determine and correct the errors in the following programs.

a.
```
#include <stdio.h>
int main()
{
  width = 15

  area = length * width;
  printf("The area is %d",area
  return 0;
}
```

b.
```
#include <stdio.h>
int main()
{
  int length, width, area;

  area = length * width;
  length = 20;
  width = 15;
  printf("The area is %d",area);
  return 0;
```

c.
```
#include <stdio.h>
  int main()
  {
    int length = 20; width = 15, area;

    length * width = area;
    printf("The area is %d",area);

    return 0;
  }
```

2. For a = 10.6, b = 13.10, c = -3.42, determine the value of:

a. `(int) a`
b. `(int) b`
c. `(int) c`
d. `(int)(a + b)`
e. `(int) a + b + c`
f. `(int)(a + b) + c`
g. `(int) (a + b + c)`

3. Determine why the expression `a - b = 25` is invalid but the expression `a - (b = 25)` is valid.

Programming Exercises

1. a. Write a C program to calculate and display the average of the numbers 32.6, 55.2, 67.9, and 48.6.
   b. Run the program written for Exercise 1a on a computer.

2. a. Write a C program to calculate the volume of a pool. The equation for determining the volume is *volume = length * width * depth*. Assume that the pool has a length of 25 feet, a width of 10 feet, and a depth of 6 feet.
   b. Run the program written for Exercise 2a on a computer.

3. a. Write a C program to convert temperature in degrees Fahrenheit to degrees Celsius. The equation for this conversion is *Celsius = 5.0/9.0 * (Fahrenheit – 32.0)*. Have your program convert and display the Celsius temperature corresponding to 98.6 degrees Fahrenheit.
   b. Run the program written for Exercise 3a on a computer.

4. a. Write a C program to calculate the distance, in feet, of a trip that is 2.36 miles long. One mile is equal to 5,280 feet.
   b. Run the program written for Exercise 4a on a computer.

5. a. Write a C program to calculate the dollar amount contained in a piggy bank. The bank currently contains 12 half-dollars, 20 quarters, 32 dimes, 45 nickels, and 27 pennies.
   b. Run the program written for Exercise 5a on a computer.

6. a. Write a C program to determine the distance an airplane travels on a runway before takeoff. The equation for determining the distance, *d*, in meters, is $d = \frac{1}{2} a t^2$, where *a* is the acceleration of the airplane in meters per second squared, and *t* is the time, in seconds, that the airplane remains on the runway before lifting off. Use an acceleration of 3.5 meters/sec^2 and a time of 30 seconds.
   b. Run the program written for Exercise 6a on a computer.

7. a. One of the longest suspension bridges in the world is New York City's Verrazano-Narrows Bridge, which links Brooklyn to Staten Island. In building this bridge, which is made of steel, allowance had to be made for the expansion of the steel due to changes in temperature. The change in the length of the bridge, ΔL, in meters, is given by the formula $\Delta L = L * 12*10^{-6} * \Delta T$, where L is the length, in meters, that the bridge must span, $12*10^{-6}$ is the thermal expansion coefficient for steel, and ΔT is the range of temperature, in degrees Celsius, that the bridge will experience. Using this equation, write a C program to determine the expansion that the bridge will undergo if it spans a length of 13,000 meters and can undergo temperature changes of 100 degrees Celsius. (*Note:* The expansion is provided for by expansion joints placed in the surface of the bridge, which automatically expand and contract as the temperature changes.)
   b. Run the program written for Exercise 7a on a computer.

8. a. The work, *W*, in joules, required to stretch a spring a distance, *d*, in meters, is given by the equation, $W = \frac{1}{2}k\, d^2$, where *k* is a spring constant, in newtons per meter, that provides a measure of the spring's stiffness. Using this equation, write a C program to determine the work required in stretching a spring .55 meters, for a spring having a spring constant of 300 newtons per meter.
   b. Run the program written for Exercise 8a on a computer.

3.2 Mathematical Library Functions

Although computations requiring addition, subtraction, multiplication, and division are easily accomplished using C's arithmetic operators within an assignment statement, no such operators exist for raising a number to a power, finding the square root of a number, or determining absolute values. To facilitate such calculations, C provides standard mathematical functions to incorporate into your programs. The most useful of these functions are summarized in Table 3.4 (a more complete set, including trigonometric functions is provided in Section 6.2). All of the functions in this table, except for the last one listed, expect floating-point (single- or double-precision) values to be passed to them and return a single value of type double. Only the last function listed, `abs()`, requires an argument of type `int` and returns a single value of the type `int`.

Table 3.4 Commonly Used Mathematical Functions (all functions require the math.h header file)

Function	Description	Example	Returned Value	Comments
sqrt(x)	Square root of x	sqrt(16.00)	4.000000	an integer value of x results in a compiler error
pow(x,y)	x raised to the y power (x^y)	pow(2, 3) pow(81, .5)	8.000000 9.000000	integer values of x and y are permitted
exp(x)	e raised to the x power (e^x)	exp(-3.2)	0.040762	an integer value of x results in a compiler error
log(x)	Natural log of x (base e)	log(18.697)	2.928363	an integer value of x results in a compiler error
log10(x)	Common log of x (base 10)	log10(18.697)	1.271772	an integer value of x results in a compiler error
fabs(x)	Absolute value of x	fabs(-3.5)	3.5000000	an integer value of x results in a compiler error
abs(x)	Absolute value of x	abs(-2)	2	a floating-point value of x returns a value of 0

Figure 3.3 Passing data to the `sqrt()` function

To illustrate the use of C's mathematical functions, consider the function named `sqrt()`, which calculates the square root of a number. The square root of a number is computed using the expression

```
sqrt(number)
```

where the function's name, in this case `sqrt`, is followed by parentheses containing the number for which the square root is desired. The parentheses following the function name, as we have already seen for the `printf()` function, effectively provide a "funnel" through which data can be passed, and are known as the function's arguments. This concept is illustrated in Figure 3.3 for the `sqrt()` function.

The function itself can be regarded as a "black box," where the arguments constitute the inputs to the box. The output from the box is the square root of the input value; how the function performs its operations to convert the input to the output is effectively hidden within the box.

The argument to the `sqrt` function must be a floating-point value (single- or double-precision); attempting to pass an integer value results in a compiler error. The `sqrt()` function computes the square root of its argument and then returns this value as a double-precision value. For example, Table 3.5 lists the values returned by the `sqrt()` function for a number of argument values.

Table 3.5 Examples Using `sqrt()`

Expression	Returned Value
`sqrt(4.0)`	`2.000000`
`sqrt(17.0)`	`4.123106`
`sqrt(25.0)`	`5.000000`
`sqrt(1043.29)`	`32.300000`
`sqrt(6.4516)`	`2.540000`

To access the mathematical functions listed in Table 3.5, you must include the following preprocessor statement in your program:[2]

```
#include <math.h>
```

Once this header file is included, you can call any of the mathematical functions by specifying the name of the function and, in the parentheses after the function name, place any data you want to pass to it (see Figure 3.4).

functionName (data passed to function)

This identifies the called function — **This passes data to the function**

Figure 3.4 Using and passing data to a function

Because all mathematical functions return a numerical value, they can be used anywhere that an expression is valid. Formally, they can always be used as an rvalue, but never as an lvalue, as these terms are defined in the Section 3.1's Programming Note.) For example, in Program 3.5 the values returned by `sqrt()` and `pow()` are directly displayed in lines 7 and 8, while in line 10 the returned value is assigned to the variable `result`.

[2]Additionally, if you are using a Unix or Linux operating system, you must include the `-lm` option when compiling your program.

Program 3.5

```
#include <stdio.h>
#include <math.h>
int main()
{
  double result;

  printf("The square root of 6.456 is %f\n", sqrt(6.456));
  printf("7.6 raised to the 3rd power is %f\n", pow(7.6, 3));

  result = fabs(-8.24);
  printf("The absolute value of -8.24 is %f\n", result);

  return 0;
}
```

The output produced by Program 3.5 is

```
The square root of 6.456 is 2.540866
7.6 raised to the 3rd power is 438.976000
The absolute value of -8.24 is 8.240000
```

The arguments passed to a mathematical function need not be single constants, as they are in Program 3.5. Instead, the arguments can be an expression, provided that the expression can be computed to yield a value of the required data type. For example, the following list shows functions having valid expressions as arguments:

- `sqrt(4.0 + 5.3 * 4.0)`
- `sqrt(x)`
- `pow(y, z)`
- `fabs(2.3 * alpha)`
- `fabs(theta - phi)`

The expressions in parentheses are first evaluated to yield a specific value. Thus, values would have to be assigned to the variables `x`, `y`, `z`, `alpha`, `theta`, and `phi` before their use in the preceding expressions. After the value of the argument is calculated, it is passed to the function.

Additionally, functions themselves may be included as part of larger expressions. For example, both of the following statements are valid:

```
x = 3.0 * sqrt(5 * 33 - 13.91) / 5;
```

and

```
y = 3.0 * log(30 * .514)/ pow(2.4, 3);
```

The step-by-step evaluation of the expression

```
3.0 * sqrt(5 * 33 - 13.91) / 5
```

is

Step	Result
1. Perform multiplication in argument	`3.0 * sqrt(165 - 13.91) / 5`
2. Complete argument calculation	`3.0 * sqrt(151.090000) / 5`
3. Return a function value	`3.0 * 12.2918672 / 5`
4. Perform the multiplication	`36.8756017 / 5`
5. Perform the division	`7.3751203`

Program 3.6 illustrates the use of the `sqrt()` function to determine the time it takes a ball to hit the ground after it has been dropped from an 800-foot tower. The mathematical formula used to calculate the time, in seconds, that it takes to fall a given distance, in feet, is *time = sqrt(2 * distance/g)*,where *g* is the gravitational constant equal to 32.2 ft/sec^2.

Program 3.6

```
#include <stdio.h>   /* this line may be placed second instead of first */
#include <math.h>    /* this line may be placed first instead of second */
int main()
{
  int height;
  double time;

  height = 800.0;
  time = sqrt(2.0 * height / 32.2);
  printf("It will take %f seconds", time);
  printf(" to fall %d feet.\n", height);

  return 0;
}
```

The output of Programs 3.6 is

```
It will take 7.049074 seconds to fall 800 feet.
```

In Program 3.6, the value returned by the `sqrt()` function is assigned to the variable `time`. In addition to assigning a function's returned value to a variable or using the returned value within a larger expression, the returned value may also be used as an argument to another function. For example, the expression

```
sqrt( pow(fabs(x),y) )
```

is valid. Because parentheses are present, the computation proceeds from the inner to the outer pairs of parentheses. Thus, the absolute value of x is computed first and used as the first argument to the `pow()` function. The value returned by the `pow()` function is then used as an argument to the `sqrt()` function.

EXERCISES 3.2

Short Answer Questions

1. Write C statements to determine:
   a. The square root of 6.37.
   b. The square root of x – y.
   c. The value of 3.62 raised to the 3rd power.
   d. The value of 81 raised to the .24 power.
   e. The absolute value of $a^2 - b^2$.
   f. The value of e raised to the 3rd power.

2. Write C statements for the following:
   a. $c = \sqrt{a^2 + b^2}$
   b. $p = \sqrt{|m - n|}$
   c. $sum = \frac{a(r^n - 1)}{r - 1}$

Programming Exercises

1. a. Write, compile, and execute a C program that calculates and returns the fourth root of the number 81.0, which is 3. (*Hint:* The fourth root of a number can be obtained by raising the number to the ¼, or .25 power).
   b. When you have verified that your program works correctly, use it to determine the fourth root of 1,728.896400.

2. Write, compile, and execute a C program that calculates the distance between two points whose coordinates are (7, 12) and (3, 9). Use the fact that the distance between two points having coordinates (x1, y1) and (x2, y2) is $distance = sqrt([x1 - x2]^2 + [y1 - y2]^2)$.

3. The formula for calculating the area of a triangle with sides *a*, *b*, and *c* can be calculated using Heron's formula: $area = sqrt(s * (s - a) * (s - b) * (s - c))$, where $s = (a + b + c)/2$. Using this formula, write, compile, and execute a C program that calculates and displays the area of a triangle having sides of 3, 4, and 5 inches.

4. A model of world population, in billions of people, after 2000 is given by the equation
   $Population = 6.0e^{.02\ [Year\ -\ 2000]}$

   Using this formula, write, compile, and execute a C program to estimate the world population in the year 2010.

5. The time, *T*, in seconds, that a donut-sized space station must make one rotation in gravity-free space to provide a human with the same gravitational force as that experienced on Earth is given by the equation $T = 2\pi\ sqrt(r/g)$, where *g* is the gravitational force on the Earth's surface, in meters/sec^2 and *r* is the outside radius of the space station, in meters. Using this equation write, compile, and run a C program that calculates and displays the rotation time for a donut-sized space station that has an outer radius of 700 meters and g = 9.81 meters/sec^2.

6. Given an initial deposit of money, denoted as *deposit*, in a bank that pays interest annually, the amount of money, *amount*, at a time *n* years later is given by the formula $amount = deposit * (1 + i)^n$ where *i* is the interest rate as a decimal number (for example, 9.5% is .095). Using this formula, write, compile, and execute a C program that determines the amount of money that will be available in four years if $10,000 is deposited in a bank that pays 10% interest annually.

7. a. Newton's law of cooling states that when an object with an initial temperature, *itemp*, is placed in a surrounding substance of temperature *a*, it will reach a temperature *tfin* in *t* minutes according to the formula $tfin = a + (itemp - a)\ e^{-kt}$. In this formula *k* is a thermal coefficient, which depends on the material being cooled. Using this formula, write, compile, and execute a C program that determines the temperature reached by an object after 20 minutes when it is placed in a glass of water whose temperature is 60 degrees. Assume that the object initially has a temperature of 150 degrees and has a thermal constant of 0.0367.

   b. Modify the program written for Exercise 7a to determine the temperature of the same object, with an initial temperature of 150 degrees, after 10 minutes when it is placed in a glass of water whose temperature is 50 degrees.

8. The number of bacteria, *B*, in a certain culture that is subject to refrigeration can be approximated by the equation $B = 300{,}000\ e^{-.032t}$, where *t* is the time, in hours, that the culture has been refrigerated. Using this equation, write, compile, and execute a single C program that calculates the number of bacteria in the culture after it has been in the refrigerator for 8 hours, and displays the result.

3.3 Interactive Input

Data for programs that are only going to be executed once may be included directly in the program. For example, if we wanted to multiply the numbers 300.0 and .05, we could use Program 3.7.

Program 3.7

```
#include <stdio.h>
int main()
{
  float  num1, num2, product;

  num1 = 300.0;
  num2 = .05;
  product = num1 * num2;
  printf("%f times %f is %f\n", num1, num2, product);

  return 0;
}
```

The output displayed by Program 3.7 is

```
300.000000 times .050000 is 15.000000
```

Program 3.7 can be shortened, as illustrated in Program 3.8. Both programs, however, suffer from the same problem: They must be rewritten to multiply different numbers. Both programs lack the facility for entering different numbers to be operated on.

Program 3.8

```
#include <stdio.h>
int main()
{
  printf("%f times %f is %f\n", 300.0, .05, 300.0*.05);

  return 0;
}
```

Except for the practice provided to the programmer of writing, entering, and running the program, programs that do a calculation only once, on one set of numbers, are clearly not very useful. After all, it is simpler to use a calculator to multiply two numbers than to enter and run either Program 3.7 or 3.8.

This section presents the `scanf()` function, which is used to enter data into a program while it is executing. Just as the `printf()` function displays a copy of the value stored inside a variable, the `scanf()` function allows the user to enter a value at the screen (Figure 3.5). The value is then stored directly in a variable.

Like the `printf()` function, the `scanf()` function requires a control string as the first argument inside the function name parentheses. The control string tells the function the type of data being input and uses the same control sequences as the `printf()` function. Unlike

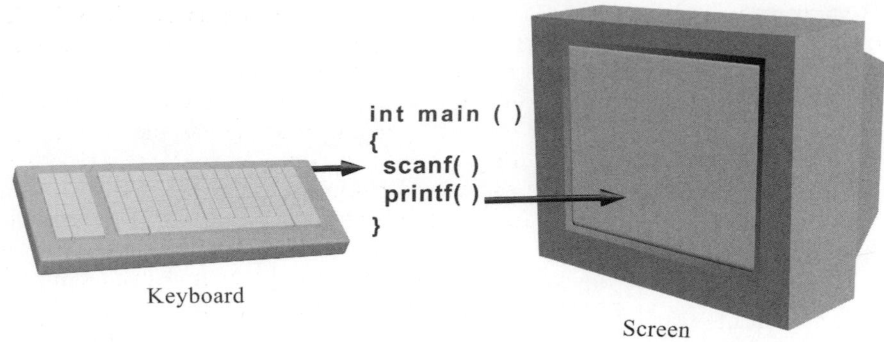

Figure 3.5 `scanf()` used to enter data; `printf()` used to display data

the control string used in a `printf()` function, however, the control string passed to `scanf()` typically consists of conversion control sequences only. Also unlike `printf()`, where a list of variable names can follow the control string, `scanf()` requires that a list of variable addresses follow the control string. For example, the statement `scanf("%d", &num1);` is a call to the `scanf()` function. The conversion control sequence `%d` is identical to the conversion control sequence used in `printf()` in that it tells the `scanf()` function that it will be dealing with an integer number. The address operator `&` in front of the variable `num1` is required for `scanf()`. Recall from Section 2.9 that `&num1` is read *the address of* `num1`.

When a statement such as `scanf("%d",&num1);` is encountered, the computer stops program execution and continuously scans for data entered from the keyboard (`scanf` is short for scan function). When a data item is typed, the `scanf()` function stores the item using the address it was given. The program then continues execution with the next statement after the call to `scanf()`. To see this, consider Program 3.9.

Program 3.9

```
#include <stdio.h>
int main()
{
  float num1, num2, product;

  printf("Please type in a number: ");
  scanf("%f",&num1);
  printf("Please type in another number: ");
  scanf("%f",&num2);
  product = num1 * num2;
  printf("%f times %f is %f\n", num1, num2, product);

  return 0;
}
```

The first call to printf() in Program 3.9 produces a **prompt**, which is a message that tells the person at the screen what should be typed. In this case the user is told to type a number. The computer then executes the next statement, which is a call to scanf().

The scanf() function puts the computer into a temporary pause (or wait) state for as long as it takes the user to type a value. Then the user signals the scanf() function by pressing the Enter key after the value has been typed. The entered value is stored in the variable, num1, whose address was passed to scanf(), and the computer is taken out of its paused state. Program execution then proceeds with the next statement, which in Program 3.9 is another call to printf(). This call causes the next message to be displayed. The second call to scanf() again puts the computer into a temporary wait state while the user types a second value. This second number is stored in the variable num2.

The following sample run was made using Program 3.9:

```
Please type in a number: 300.
Please type in another number: .05
300.000000 times .050000 is 15.000000
```

In Program 3.9, each call to scanf() is used to store one value into a variable. The scanf() function, however, can be used to enter and store as many values as there are conversion control sequences in the control string. For example, the statement

```
scanf("%f %f",&num1,&num2);
```

results in two values being read from the terminal and assigned to the variables num1 and num2. If the data entered at the terminal was

```
0.052 245.79
```

the variables num1 and num2 would contain the values 0.052 and 245.79, respectively. The space in the control string between the two conversion control sequences, "%f %f", is strictly for readability. The control string "%f%f" would work equally well. When actually entering numbers such as 0.052 and 245.79, however, you must leave at least one space between the numbers, regardless of which control string, "%f %f" or "%f%f", is used. The space between the entered numbers clearly indicates where one number ends and the next begins. Inserting more than one space between numbers has no effect on scanf().

The only time that a space can affect the value being entered is when scanf() is expecting a character data type. For example, the statement scanf("%c%c%c",&ch1,&ch2,&ch3); causes scanf() to store the next three characters typed in the variables ch1, ch2, and ch3, respectively. If you type x y z, then x is stored in ch1, a blank is stored in ch2, and y is stored in ch3. If, however, the statement scanf("%c %c %c",&ch1,&ch2,&ch3); was used, scanf() looks for three characters, each character separated by exactly one space.

Any number of scanf() function calls may be made in a program, and any number of values may be input using a single scanf() function. Just be sure that a conversion control sequence is used for each value to be entered and that the address operator is used in front of the variable name where the value is to be stored. The conversion control sequences used in a scanf() control string are the same as those used in printf() calls, with one caution. In printing a double-precision number using printf(), the conversion control sequence for a single-precision variable, %f, can be used. This is not true when using scanf(). If a double-precision number is to be entered, the conversion control sequence %lf must be used.

The scanf() function, like the printf() function, does not test the data type of the values being entered. It is up to the user to ensure that all variables are declared correctly and that any numbers entered are of the correct type. However, scanf() is "clever" enough to make a few data type conversions. For example, if an integer is entered in place of a single-precision or double-precision number, the scanf() function automatically supplies a decimal point at the end of the integer before storing the number. Similarly, if a single-precision or double-precision number is entered when an integer is expected, the scanf() function only uses the integer part of the number. For example, assume the user enters numbers 56, 22.879, and 33.1023 in response to the function call scanf("%f %d %f",&num1,&num2,&num3);.

In this case, the scanf() function converts the 56 to 56.0 and stores this value in the variable num1. The function continues scanning the input, expecting an integer value. As far as scanf() is concerned, the decimal point after the 22 in the number 22.879 indicates the end of an integer and the start of a decimal number. Thus, the number 22 is stored in num2. Continuing to scan the typed input, scanf() takes the .879 as the next double-precision number and stores this value in num3. As far as scanf() is concerned, 33.1023 is extra input and therefore it is ignored until the next scanf(), if any, is encountered. However, if you do not initially type enough data, the scanf() function will continue to make the computer pause until sufficient data has been entered.

Caution: The Phantom Newline Character

Seemingly strange results are sometimes obtained when the scanf() function is used to accept characters. To see how this can occur, consider Program 3.10, which uses scanf() to accept the next character entered at the keyboard, storing it in the variable fkey. This is followed by a second scanf() for a second character.

Program 3.10

```
#include <stdio.h>
int main()
{
  char fkey, skey;

  printf("Type in a character: ");
  scanf("%c", &fkey);
  printf("The keystroke just accepted is %d", fkey);
  printf("\nType in another character: ");
  scanf("%c", &skey);
  printf("The keystroke just accepted is %d\n", skey);

  return 0;
}
```

The following is a sample run for Program 3.10:

```
Type in a character: m
The keystroke just accepted is 109
Type in another character: The keystroke just accepted is 10
```

When Program 3.10 is run, the character entered in response to the prompt `Type in a character:` is stored in the variable `fkey`. At this point the program displays the decimal code for the entered character, which is 109, and everything seems to be working fine. Notice, however, that in response to the first prompt, two keys have been pressed, the `m` key and the Enter key. On most computer systems these two characters are stored in a temporary holding area called a **buffer** immediately after they are pressed, as illustrated in Figure 3.6.

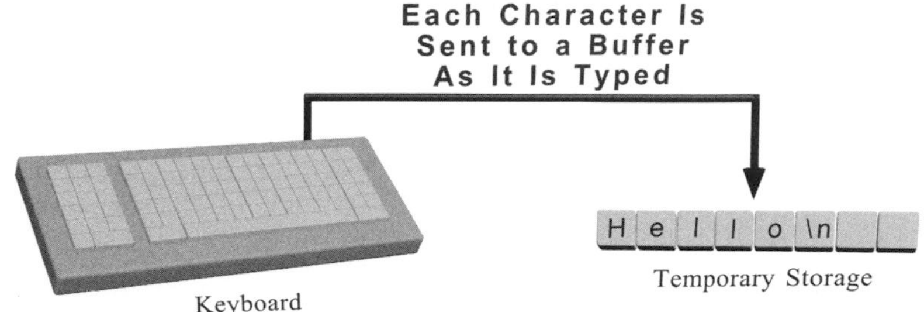

Figure 3.6 Typed keyboard characters are first stored in a buffer

From a character standpoint this represents the entry of two distinct characters. The first character is `m`, which is stored as `109`. The second character also gets stored in the buffer with the numerical code for the Enter key. The second call to `scanf()` picks up this second code, without waiting for any additional key to be pressed. The last call to `printf()` displays the code for this key. The reason for displaying the numerical code rather than the character itself is because the Enter key has no printable character associated with it that can be displayed, but the code stored for it is the newline code, which is 10. Notice that the value 10, the code for the Enter key, will always be displayed, and is not dependent on the `m` being entered first; it is the result of pressing the Enter key after the first letter is pressed.

It is important to remember that every key has a numerical code, including the spacebar, and the Enter, Escape, and Control keys. These keys generally have no effect when entering numbers, because `scanf()` ignores them as leading or trailing white-space input with numerical data. Nor do these keys affect the entry of a single character requested as the first user data to be input. Only when a character is requested after the user has already input some other data, as in Program 3.10, does the usually invisible Enter key become noticeable.

There is a quick solution to the problem of having the Enter key accepted as a legitimate character input. All we have to do is accept the Enter key, store it as a character variable, and then just not use it. Program 3.11 illustrates this technique. The Enter key is accepted along with the first character typed. This clears the computer's buffer and prepares the way for the character input.

In reviewing Program 3.11, observe that the first `scanf()` function call accepts two back-to-back characters. Now when the user types `m` and presses the Enter key, the `m` is assigned to `fkey` and the code for the Enter key is automatically assigned to `skey`. The next call to `scanf()` stores the code for the next key pressed in the variable `skey` also. This automatically erases the code for the Enter key that was previously stored there. From the user's standpoint, the Enter key has no effect except to signal the end of each character input.

Program 3.11

```
#include <stdio.h>
int main()
{
  char fkey, skey;

  printf("Type in a character: ");
  scanf("%c%c", &fkey, &skey); /* the enter code goes to skey */
  printf("The keystroke just accepted is %d", fkey);
  printf("\nType in another character: ");
  scanf("%c", &skey); /* accept another code */
  printf("The keystroke just accepted is %d\n", skey);

  return 0;
}
```

The following is a sample run for Program 3.11:

```
Type in a character: m
The keystroke just accepted is 109
Type in another character: b
The keystroke just accepted is 98
```

The solution to the "phantom" Enter key used in Program 3.11 is not the only solution possible (there is never just one way of doing something in C).[3] All solutions, however, center on the fact that the Enter key is a legitimate character input and must be treated as such when using a buffered system.

A First Look at User-Input Validation

A well-constructed program should validate user input and ensure that a program does not either crash or produce nonsensical output due to unexpected input. The term **validate** means checking that the entered value matches the data type of the variable that the value is assigned to within a `scanf()` function call, and that the value is within an acceptable range of values appropriate to the application. Programs that detect and respond effectively to unexpected user input are formally referred to as **robust programs** and informally as "bullet-proof" programs. One of your jobs as a programmer is to produce such programs.

To understand the importance of validating data that is input by a user, consider Program 3.12, which computes the average of three user-input integer values.

[3]Two other solutions are to replace the last `scanf()` call in Program 3.11 with the statement `scanf("\n%c",&skey);`, or to place the statement `fflush(stdin);` after accepting a one-character input. The `fflush()` function flushes the input buffer of any remaining characters.

Program 3.12

```
#include <stdio.h>
int main()
{
  int num1, num2, num3;
  double average;

  /* get the input data */
  printf("Enter three integer numbers: ");
  scanf("%d %d %d", &num1, &num2, &num3);

  /* calculate the average*/
  average = (num1 + num2 + num3) / 3.0;

  /* display the result */
  printf("\nThe avearge of %d, %d, and %d is %f\n",
                          num1, num2, num3, average);


  return 0;
}
```

As written, Program 3.12 is not a robust program. Let's see why.

The problem with this program becomes evident when a user enters a noninteger value. For example, consider the following sample run using Program 3.12.

```
Enter three integer numbers: 10 20.68 20
The average of 10, 20, and -858993460 is -286331143.333333
```

This output occurs because the conversion of the second input number results in the integer value 20 assigned to `num2` and the value -858993460 assigned to `num3`. This last value corresponds to an invalid character, the decimal point, being assigned to an expected integer value. The average of the numbers 10, 20, and -858993460 is then computed correctly as -286331143.333333. As far as the average user is concerned, this will be reported as a program error. This same problem occurs whenever a noninteger value is entered for either of the first two inputs (it does not occur for any numerical value entered as the third input, because the integer part of the last input is accepted and the remaining input ignored).

You may think that just changing the `int` declaration to `double` will solve the problem. However, if the user enters data such as 12e4, the problem will reappear.

As a programmer your initial response may be, "The program clearly asks the user to enter integer values." This, however, is the response of a very inexperienced programmer. Professional programmers understand that it is their responsibility to ensure that a program anticipates and appropriately handles any and all input that a user can possibly enter. This is accomplished by both thinking about what can go wrong with your own program as you develop it and then having another person or group thoroughly test the program.

The basic approach to handling invalid data input is referred to as **user-input validation**, which means validating the entered data either during or immediately after the data have been entered, and then providing the user with a way of reentering any invalid data. User-input validation is an essential part of any commercially viable program, and if done correctly, it will protect a program from attempting to process data that can cause computational problems. We will see how to provide this type of validation in Sections 5.7 and 9.3 after C's selection, repetition, and string handling capabilities have been presented.

EXERCISES 3.3

Short Answer Questions

1. For each of the following declaration statements, write a `scanf()` function call to correctly accept a user-entered value for the indicated variable.
   a. `int firstnum;`
   b. `double grade;`
   c. `double secnum;`
   d. `char keyval;`
   e. `int month, years;`
      `double average;`
   f. `char ch;`
      `int num1, num2;`
      `double grade1, grade2;`
   g. `double interest, principal, capital;`
      `double price, yield;`
   h. `char ch, letter1, letter2;`
      `int num1, num2, num3;`
   i. `double temp1, temp2, temp3;`
      `double volts1, volts2;`

2. For the following `scanf()` function calls, write appropriate declaration statements.
   a. `scanf("%d",&day);`
   b. `scanf("%c",&firChar);`
   c. `scanf("%f",&grade);`
   d. `scanf("%lf",&price);`
   e. `scanf("%d %d %c",&num1,&num2,&ch1);`
   f. `scanf("%f %f %d",&firstnum,&secnum,&count);`
   g. `scanf("%c %c %d %lf",&ch1,&ch2,&flag,&average);`

3. Given the following declaration statements,

```
int num1, num2;
double firstnum, secnum;
double price, yield;
```

determine and correct the errors in the following `scanf()` function calls.

a. `scanf("%d",num1);`
b. `scanf("%f %f %f",&num1,firstnum,&price);`
c. `scanf("%c %lf %f",&num1,&secnum,&price);`
d. `scanf("%d %d %lf",num1,num2,yield);`
e. `scanf(&num1,&num2);`
f. `scanf(&num1,"%d");`

Programming Exercises

1. a. Write a C program that displays the following prompt:

   `Enter the radius of a circle:`

   After accepting a value for the radius, your program should calculate and display the circumference of the circle.

   (*Hint:* circumference = 2 * 3.1416 * radius.)

   b. Check the value displayed by the program written for Exercise 1a by calculating the result manually. After manually determining that the result produced by your program is correct, use your program to complete the following table:

Radius (inches)	Circumference (inches)
1.0	
1.5	
2.0	
2.5	
3.0	
3.7	

2. a. Write a C program that first displays the following prompt:

   `Enter the temperature in degrees Fahrenheit:`

   Have your program accept a value entered from the keyboard and convert the temperature entered to degrees Celsius, using the equation *Celsius = (5.0 / 9.0) * (Fahrenheit – 32.0)*. Your program should then display the temperature in degrees Celsius, using an appropriate output message.

   b. Compile and execute the program written for Exercise 2a. Verify your program by calculating, by hand, and then using your program, the Fahrenheit equivalent of the following test data:

   Test data set 1: 0 degrees Celsius

   Test data set 2: 50 degrees Celsius

   Test data set 3: 100 degrees Celsius

   When you are sure your program is working correctly, use it to complete the following table:

Celsius	Fahrenheit
45	
50	

Celsius	Fahrenheit
55	
60	
65	
70	

3. a. Write a C program that displays the following prompts:

```
Enter the length of the room:
Enter the width of the room:
```

After each prompt is displayed, your program should use a `scanf()` function call to accept data from the keyboard for the displayed prompt. After the width of the room is entered, your program should calculate and display the area of the room. The area displayed should be included in an appropriate message and calculated using the equation *area = length * width.*

b. Check the area displayed by the program written for Exercise 3a by calculating the result manually.

4. a. Write a C program that displays the following prompts:

```
Enter the miles driven:
Enter the gallons of gas used:
```

After each prompt is displayed, your program should use a `scanf()` function call to accept data from the keyboard for the displayed prompt. After the gallons of gas used has been entered, your program should calculate and display miles per gallon obtained. This value should be included in an appropriate message and calculated using the equation *miles per gallon = miles / gallons used.* Verify your program using the following test data:

Miles	Gas
276	10 gallons
200	15.5 gallons

When you have completed your verification, use your program to complete the following table:

Miles driven	Gallons used	MPG
250	16.00	
275	18.00	
312	19.54	
296	17.39	

b. For the program you wrote for Exercise 4a, determine how many verification runs are required to ensure the program is working correctly and give a reason supporting your answer.

5. a. Write a C program that displays the following prompts:

```
Enter the length of the swimming pool:
Enter the width of the swimming pool:
Enter the average depth of the swimming pool:
```

After each prompt is displayed, your program should use a `scanf()` function call to accept data from the keyboard for the displayed prompt. After the depth of the swimming pool is entered, your program should calculate and display the volume of the pool. The volume should be included in an appropriate message and calculated using the equation *volume = length * width * average depth.*

b. Check the volume displayed by the program written for Exercise 5a by calculating the result manually.

6. a. Write a C program that displays the following prompts:

```
Enter a number:
Enter a second number:
Enter a third number:
Enter a fourth number:
```

After the prompt is displayed, your program should use a `scanf()` function call to accept a number from the keyboard for the displayed prompt. After the fourth number has been entered, your program should calculate and display the average of the numbers. The average should be included in an appropriate message. Check the average displayed by your program using the following test data:

Test data set 1: 100, 100, 100, 100

Test data set 2: 100, 0, 100, 0

Then, use your program to complete the following table:

Numbers	Average
92, 98, 79, 85	
86, 84, 75, 86	
63, 85, 74, 82	

b. Repeat Exercise 6a, making sure that you use the same variable name, `number`, for each number input. Also use the variable `sum` for the sum of the numbers. (*Hint:* To do this, you must use the statement `sum = sum + number;` after each number is accepted. Review the material on accumulating presented in Section 3.1.)

7. Write a C program that prompts the user to type a number. Have your program accept the number as an integer and immediately display the integer using a `printf()` function call. Run your program three times. The first time you run the program, enter a valid integer number; the second time, enter a double-precision number; and the third time, enter a character. Using the output display, see what number your program actually accepted from the data you entered.

8. Repeat Exercise 7 but have your program declare the variable used to store the number as a single-precision variable. Run the program four times. The first time, enter an integer; the second time, enter a decimal number with fewer than six decimal places; the third time, enter a number with more than six decimal places; and the fourth time, enter a character. Using the output display, keep track of what number your program actually accepted from the data you typed in. What happened, if anything, and why?

9. Repeat Exercise 7 but have your program declare the variable used to store the number as a double-precision variable. Run the program four times. The first time, enter an integer; the second time, enter a decimal number with fewer than six decimal places; the third time, enter a number with more than six decimal places; and the fourth time, enter a character. Using the output display, keep track of what number your program actually accepted from the data you typed in. What happened, if anything, and why?

10. a. Why do you think that most successful commercial applications programs contain extensive data input validity checks? (*Hint:* Review Exercises 7, 8, and 9.)
    b. What do you think is the difference between a data type check and a data reasonableness check?
    c. Assume that a program requests that a month, day, and year be entered by the user. What are some checks that could be made on the data entered?

11. Write a C program that uses the declaration statement `double num;`. Then use the function call `scanf("%f",&num);` to input a value into `num`. (Notice that we have used the wrong control sequence for the variable `num`.) Run your program and enter a decimal number. Using a `printf()` function call, have your program display the number stored in `num`. Determine what problem you can run into when an incorrect control sequence is used in `scanf()`.

12. Program 3.9 prompts the user to input two numbers, where the first value entered is stored in `num1` and the second value is stored in `num2`. Using this program as a starting point, write a program that swaps the values stored in the two variables.

3.4 Formatted Output

Most programs are judged by users on the perceived ease of data entry and the style and presentation of their output. Thus, besides displaying correct results, it is important that a program present its results attractively. For example, displaying a monetary result as 1.897 is not in keeping with accepted report conventions. The display should be either $1.90 or $1.89, depending on whether rounding or truncation is used.

The format of numbers displayed by `printf()` can be controlled by **field width specifiers** included as part of each conversion control sequence. For example, the statement

```
printf("The sum of%3d and%4d is%5d.", 6, 15, 21);
```

produces the printout

```
The sum of ∧∧6 and∧∧15 is∧∧∧21.
```

The ∧ symbol is used in this output to indicate blank spaces produced by the field width specifiers 3, 4, and 5 in the control string. The 3 in the first conversion sequence, `%3d`, causes the first number to be printed in a total field width of three spaces, in this case two blank spaces followed by the number 6. The field width specifier for the second conversion control sequence, `%4d`, causes two blank spaces and the number 15 to be printed for a total field width of four spaces. The last field width specifier causes the 21 to be printed in a field of five spaces, which includes three blanks and the number 21. As illustrated, each integer is right-justified within the specified field.

Field width specifiers are useful in printing columns of numbers so that the numbers in each column align correctly. Program 3.13 illustrates how a column of integers would align in the absence of field width specifiers.

Program 3.13

```
#include <stdio.h>
int main()
{
  printf("\n%d", 6);
  printf("\n%d", 18);
  printf("\n%d", 124);
  printf("\n---");
  printf("\n%d\n", 6+18+124);

  return 0;
}
```

The output of Program 3.13 is

```
6
18
124
---
148
```

Because no field widths are given, the `printf()` function allocates enough space for each number as it is received. Forcing the numbers to align on the unit digits requires a field width wide enough for the largest displayed number. For Program 3.13, a width of three suffices. The use of this field width is illustrated in Program 3.14.

Program 3.14

```
#include <stdio.h>
int main()
{
  printf("\n%3d", 6);
```

```
    printf("\n%3d", 18);
    printf("\n%3d", 124);
    printf("\n---");
    printf("\n%3d\n", 6+18+124);

    return 0;
}
```

The output of Program 3.14, where we have used ∧ to denote a blank space, is

```
∧∧6
∧18
124
---
148
```

Formatted floating-point numbers require two field width specifiers. The first specifier determines the total display width, including the decimal point; the second determines how many digits are printed to the right of the decimal point. For example, the statement

```
printf("%10.3f",25.67);
```

produces the printout

```
∧∧∧∧25.670
```

In this display we have once again used the ∧ symbol to mark spaces produced by the conversion control sequence, `%10.3f`. Specifically, the field width specification 10.3 tells `printf()` to display the number in a total field of 10, which includes one decimal point and three digits to the right of the decimal point. Because the number contains only two digits to the right of the decimal point, the decimal part of the number is padded with a trailing zero. To fill out the field, four spaces are displayed at the beginning of the output.

For all numbers (integers, floating point, and double precision), `printf()` ignores the specified field width if the total field width is too small and allocates enough space for the integer part of the number to be printed. The fractional part of both floating-point and double-precision numbers is always displayed with the number of specified digits. If the fractional part contains fewer digits than specified, the number is padded with trailing zeros; if the fractional part contains more digits than called for in the specifier, the number is rounded to the indicated number of decimal places. Table 3.6 illustrates the effect of various field width specifiers.

Table 3.6 Effect of Field Width Specifiers

Specifier	Number	Display	Comments
`%2d`	3	`∧3`	Number fits in field
`%2d`	43	`43`	Number fits in field
`%2d`	143	`143`	Field width ignored
`%2d`	2.3	Compiler dependent	Floating-point number in an integer field
`%5.2f`	2.366	`∧2.37`	Field of 5 with 2 decimal digits

Table 3.6 Effect of Field Width Specifiers (continued)

Specifier	Number	Display	Comments
`%5.2f`	42.3	`42.30`	Number fits in field
`%5.2f`	142.364	`142.36`	Field width ignored but fractional specifier is used
`%5.2f`	142	Compiler dependent	Integer in a floating-point field

Format Modifiers

In addition to the conversion control sequences (`%d`, `%f`, etc.) and the field width specifiers that may be used with them, C also provides a set of format modifiers that provides additional format control, such as left- and right-field justification. Format modifiers, if used, must always be placed immediately after the `%` symbol. The more commonly used format modifiers are discussed here.

Left Justification Numbers displayed using the `printf()` function are normally displayed right-justified with leading spaces inserted to fill the selected field width. To force the output to left-justify the display, a minus sign (–) format modifier can be used. For example, the statement

```
printf("%-10d",59);
```

produces the display

```
59⋏⋏⋏⋏⋏⋏⋏⋏
```

Again, we have used the ⋏ symbol to clearly identify blanks that will be inserted in the display. Notice that the displayed number, 59, is printed at the beginning of the field (left-justification within the field) rather than at the end of the field, as would be obtained in the absence of the format modifier. Also notice that the format modifier within the `printf()` function is placed immediately after the `%` symbol.

Explicit Sign Display Normally, the sign of a number is only displayed for negative numbers. To force both positive and negative signs to be displayed, a plus (+) format modifier must be used. For example, the statement

```
printf("%+10d",59);
```

produces the display

```
⋏⋏⋏⋏⋏⋏⋏+59
```

In the absence of the plus sign immediately after the `%` symbol in the `printf()` function call, the output would not display the sign of the positive number.

Format modifiers may be combined. For example, the conversion control sequence `%-+10d` would cause an integer number to both display its sign and be left-justified in a field width of 10 spaces. Because the order of the format modifiers is not critical, this conversion control sequence could have been written as `%+-10d`.

Other Number Bases [Optional][4]

When outputting integers, several display conversions are possible. As we have seen, the conversion control sequence %d, with or without a field width specifier, causes integers to be displayed in decimal (base 10) form. To have the value of an integer displayed in either a base 8 (octal) or base 16 (hexadecimal) form requires the use of the conversion control sequences %o and %x, respectively. Program 3.15 illustrates each of these conversion control sequences.

Program 3.15

```
#include <stdio.h>
int main() /* a program to illustrate output conversions */
{
  printf("The decimal (base 10) value of 15 is %d.", 15);
  printf("\nThe octal (base 8) value of 15 is %o.", 15);
  printf("\nThe hexadecimal (base 16) value of 15 is %x\n.", 15);

  return 0;
}
```

The output produced by Program 3.15 is

```
The decimal (base 10) value of 15 is 15.
The octal (base 8) value of 15 is 17.
The hexadecimal (base 16) value of 15 is f.
```

The display of integer values in one of the three possible number systems (decimal, octal, and hexadecimal) does not affect how the number is stored inside a computer. All numbers are stored using the computer's internal codes. The conversion control sequences used in `printf()` simply tell the function how to convert the internal code for output display purposes.

Besides displaying integers in octal or hexadecimal form, integer constants can also be written in a program in these forms. To designate an octal integer constant, the number must have a leading zero. The number `023`, for example, is an octal number in C. Hexadecimal numbers are denoted using a leading `0x`. The use of octal and hexadecimal integer constants is illustrated in Program 3.16.

---

[4] This topic may be omitted on a first reading without loss of subject continuity.

Program 3.16

```
#include <stdio.h>
int main()
{
  printf("The decimal value of 025 is %d.\n",025);
  printf("The decimal value of 0x37 is %d.\n",0x37);

  return 0;
}
```

When Program 3.16 is run, the following output is produced:

```
The decimal value of 025 is 21.
The decimal value of 0x37 is 55.
```

The relationship between the input, storage, and display of integers is illustrated in Figure 3.7.

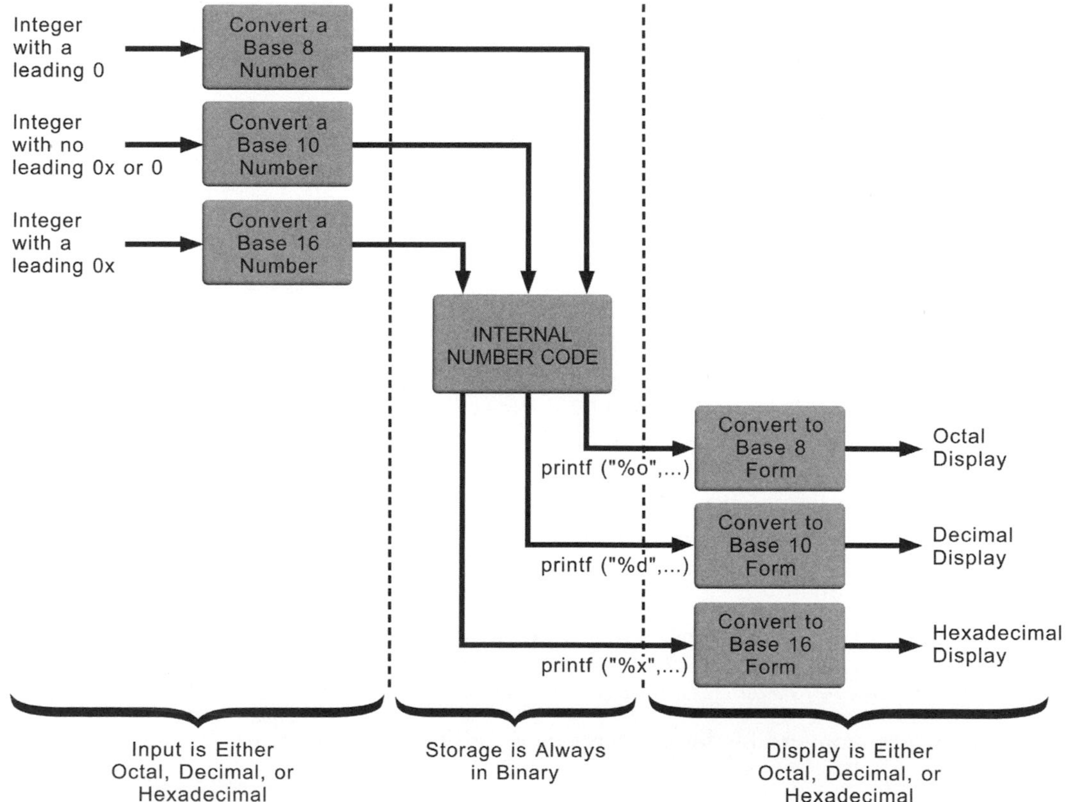

Figure 3.7 Input, storage, and display of integers

To force both octal and hexadecimal numbers to be printed with a leading `0` and `0x`, respectively, the # format modifier must be used. For example, the statement

```
printf("The octal value of decimal 21 is %#o",21);
```

produces the display

```
The octal value of decimal 21 is 025
```

Without the inclusion of the # format modifier within the conversion control sequence `%o`, the displayed octal value would be `25`, with no leading `0`. Similarly, the statement

```
printf("The hexadecimal value of decimal 55 is %#x",55);
```

produces the display

```
The hexadecimal value of decimal 55 is 0x37
```

Without the inclusion of the # format modifier within the conversion control sequence `%x`, the displayed hexadecimal value would be `37`, with no leading `0x`.

The same display conversions available for integers can also be used to display characters. In addition to the `%c` conversion control sequence, the `%d` conversion control sequence displays the value of the internal character code as a decimal number, and the `%o` and `%x` conversion control sequences cause the character code to be displayed in octal and hexadecimal form, respectively. These display conversions are illustrated in Program 3.17.

Program 3.17

```
#include <stdio.h>
int main()
{
  printf("The decimal value of the letter %c is %d.", 'a', 'a');
  printf("\nThe octal value of the letter %c is %o.", 'a', 'a');
  printf("\nThe hex value of the letter %c is %x.\n", 'a', 'a');

  return 0;
}
```

When Program 3.17 is run, the following output is produced:

```
The decimal value of the letter a is 97.
The octal value of the letter a is 141.
The hex value of the letter a is 61.
```

The display conversions for character data are illustrated in Figure 3.8.

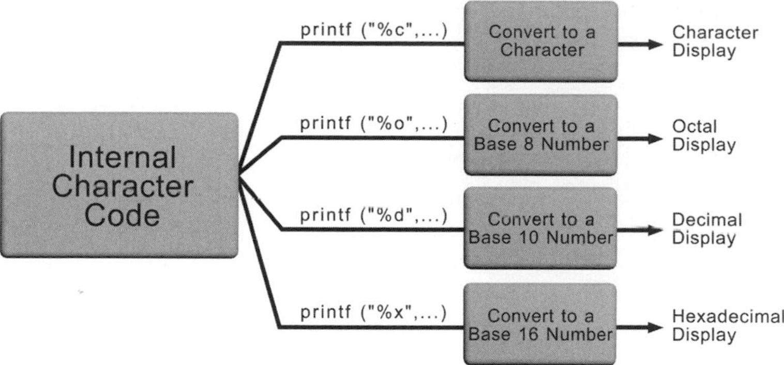

Figure 3.8 Character display options

EXERCISES 3.4

Short-Answer Questions

1. Determine the output of the following program:

```
#include <stdio.h>
int main() /* a program illustrating integer truncation */
{
  printf("answer1 is the integer %d", 27/5);
  printf("\nanswer2 is the integer %d", 16/6);

  return 0;
}
```

2. Determine the output of the following program:

```
#include <stdio.h>
int main() /* a program illustrating the % operator */
{
  printf("The remainder of 9 divided by 4 is %d", 9 % 4);
  printf("\nThe remainder of 17 divided by 3 is %d", 17 % 3);

  return 0;
}
```

3. Determine the errors in each of the following statements:
   a. `printf("%d," 15)`
   b. `printf("%f", 33);`
   c. `printf("%5d", 526.768);`
   d. `printf("a b c", 26, 15, 18);`
   e. `printf("%3.6f", 47);`
   f. `printf("%3.6", 526.768);`
   g. `printf(526.768, 33, "%f %d");`

4. Determine and write out the display produced by the following statements:
   a. `printf("%d",5);`
   b. `printf("%4d",5);`
   c. `printf("%4d",56829);`
   d. `printf("%5.2f",5.26);`
   e. `printf("%5.2f",5.267);`
   f. `printf("%5.2f",53.264);`
   g. `printf("%5.2f",534.264);`
   h. `printf("%5.2f",534.);`

5. Write out the display produced by the following statements:
   a.
   ```
   printf("The number is %6.2f\n",26.27);
   printf("The number is %6.2f\n",682.3);
   printf("The number is %6.2f\n",1.968);
   ```
   b.
   ```
   printf("$%6.2f\n",26.27);
   printf(" %6.2f\n",682.3);
   printf(" %6.2f\n",1.968);
   printf("--------\n");
   printf("$%6.2f\n", 26.27 + 682.3 + 1.968);
   ```
   c.
   ```
   printf("$%5.2f\n",26.27);
   printf(" %5.2f\n",682.3);
   printf(" %5.2f\n",1.968);
   printf("--------\n");
   printf("$%5.2f\n", 26.27 + 682.3 + 1.968);
   ```
   d.
   ```
   printf("%5.2f\n",34.164);
   printf("%5.2f\n",10.003);
   printf("-----\n");
   printf("%5.2f\n", 34.164 + 10.003);
   ```

Programming Exercises

1. Write a C program that displays the results of the expressions 3.0 * 5.0, 7.1 * 8.3 – 2.2, and 3.2 / (6.1 * 5). Calculate the value of these expressions manually to verify that the displayed values are correct.

2. Write a C program that displays the results of the expressions 15 / 4, 15 % 4, and 5 * 3 – (6 * 4). Calculate the value of these expressions manually to verify that the display produced by your program is correct.

3. a. Rewrite the `printf()` function calls in the following program

   ```
   #include <stdio.h>
   int main()
   {
     printf("The sales tax is %f", .05 * 36);
     printf("The total bill is %f", 37.80);

     return 0;
   }
   ```

to produce the display

```
The sales tax is $ 1.80
The total bill is $37.80
```

b. Run the program written for Exercise 3a to verify the output display.

4. a. For display purposes the `%f` conversion control sequence allows the programmer to round all outputs to the desired number of decimal places. This can, however, yield seemingly incorrect results when used in financial program that requires all monetary values be displayed to the nearest penny. For example, the display produced by the statements

```
double a, b;
a = 1.674
b = 1.322
printf("\n%4.2f",a);
printf("\n%4.2f",b);
printf("\n----");
c = a + b;
printf("\n%4.2f\n",c);
```

is

```
1.67
1.32
----
3.00
```

Clearly, the sum of the displayed numbers should be 2.99 and not 3.00. The problem is that although the values in `a` and `b` have been displayed with two decimal digits, they were added within the program as three-digit numbers. The solution is to round the values in `a` and `b` before they are added by the statement `c = a + b;`. Using the `(int)` cast, devise a method to round the values in the variables `a` and `b` to the nearest hundredth (penny value) before they are added.

b. Include the method you have devised for Exercise 4a into a working program that produces the following display:

```
1.67
1.32
----
2.99
```

3.5 Symbolic Constants

As we have seen in Section 2.3, **literal data** refers to any data within a program that explicitly identifies itself. For example, the constants 2 and 3.1416 in the assignment statement

```
circum = 2 * 3.1416 * radius;
```

are also called **literals**. Additional examples of literals are contained in the following C assignment statements. See if you can identify them.

```
perimeter = 2 * length * width;
y = (5 * p) / 7.2;
salestax = 0.05 * purchase;
```

The literals are the numbers `2, 5` and `7.2`, and `0.05` in the first, second, and third statements, respectively.

The same literal often appears many times in one program. For example, in a program used to determine bank interest charges, the interest rate would typically appear repeatedly throughout the program. Similarly, in a program used to calculate taxes, the tax rate might appear in many individual instructions. If either the interest rate or tax rate change, the programmer would have the cumbersome task of changing the literal value everywhere it appears in the program. Multiple changes, however, can lead to errors—if just one rate value is overlooked and not changed, the result obtained when the program is run will be incorrect. Literal values that appear many times in the same program are referred to by programmers as **magic numbers**. By themselves the numbers are quite ordinary, but in the context of a particular application they have a special ("magical") meaning.

To avoid the problem of having a magic number spread throughout a program, C provides the programmer with the capability to define the value once by equating the number to a **symbolic name**. Then, instead of using the number throughout the program, the symbolic name is used instead. If the number ever has to be changed, the change need only be made once at the point where the symbolic name is equated to the actual number value. Equating numbers to symbolic names is accomplished using a `#define` statement. Two such statements are

```
#define SALESTAX 0.05
#define PI 3.1416
```

Note that these two statements do not end in semicolons and do not use an equal sign. Such statements are called either `#define` or **equivalence** statements. The first `#define` statement equates the value `0.05` to the symbolic name `SALESTAX`, while the second `#define` statement equates the number `3.1416` to the symbolic name `PI`. Other terms for symbolic names are **symbolic constants** and **named constants**. We shall use these terms interchangeably.

It is common in C to use all uppercase letters for symbolic constants. Then, whenever a programmer sees all uppercase letters in a program, he or she will know the name is a symbolic constant defined in a `#define` statement, and not a variable name declared in a declaration statement.

The symbolic constants defined above can be used in any C statement in place of the numbers they represent. For example, the assignment statements

```
circum = 2 * PI * radius;
amount = SALESTAX * purchase;
```

are both valid. These statements must, of course, appear after the named constants are defined. Although `#define` statements can be freely intermixed with other statements, they are typically placed immediately before or after all `#include` statements or within a function, such as `main()`, immediately before any variable declaration statements. The `#define` and `#include` statements may be freely intermixed. Thus, in Program 3.18, the `#include` statement could have been placed below the `#define` statement or inside `main()`, above the declaration statement on line 5.

Program 3.18

```
#include <stdio.h>
#define SALESTAX 0.05
int main()
{
  float amount, taxes, total;

  printf("\nEnter the amount purchased: ");
  scanf("%f", &amount);
  taxes = SALESTAX * amount;
  total = amount + taxes;
  printf("The sales tax is $%4.2f",taxes);
  printf("\nThe total bill is $%5.2f\n",total);

  return 0;
}
```

The following sample run was made using Program 3.18:

```
Enter the amount purchased: 36.00
The sales tax is $1.80
The total bill is $37.80
```

Whenever a symbolic constant appears in an instruction, it has the same effect as if the literal value it represents was used. Thus, `SALESTAX` is simply another way of representing the value `0.05`. Since `SALESTAX` and the number `0.05` are equivalent, the value of `SALESTAX` may not subsequently be changed by the program. An instruction such as `SALESTAX = 0.06;` is meaningless, because `SALESTAX` is not a variable, and will result in a compiler error. Since `SALESTAX` is only a stand-in for the value `0.05`, this statement is equivalent to writing the invalid statement `0.05 = 0.06;`.

Notice also that `#define` statements do not end with a semicolon. The reason for this is that `#define` statements are not processed by the regular C compiler used to translate C statements into machine language. The # sign is a signal to a C preprocessor. This preprocessor screens all program statements when a C program is compiled. When the preprocessor encounters a # sign, it recognizes an instruction to itself. The word `define` tells the preprocessor to equate the symbolic constant in the statement with the information or data following it. In the case of a statement like `#define SALESTAX 0.05`, the word `SALESTAX` is equated to the value `0.05`. The preprocessor then replaces each subsequent occurrence of the word `SALESTAX` in the C program with the value `0.05`.

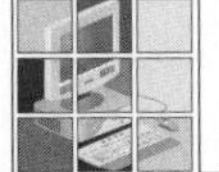

EXERCISES 3.5

Short Answer Questions

1. Write `#define` statements for the following:
   a. The symbolic name `TRUE` is to be equated to the integer value of `1` and the symbolic name `False` is to be equated to the integer value of `2`.
   b. The symbolic name `AM` is to be equated to `0` and the symbolic name `PM` is to be equated to `1`.
   c. The symbolic name `Rate` is to be equated to the value `3.25`.

2. Determine the errors in the following `# define` statements:
   a. `#define YES 1.0;`
   b. `#define 2 NO`
   c. `#define BOOLEAN true`

Programming Exercises

Determine the purpose of the programs given below in Exercises 1 through 3. Then rewrite each program using `#define` statements for appropriate literals.

1.
```
#include <stdio.h>
int main()
{
  float radius, circum;

  printf("\nEnter a radius: ");
  scanf("%f", &radius);
  circum = 2.0 * 3.1416 * radius;
  printf("\nThe circumference of the circle is %f", circum);

  return 0;
}
```

2.
```
#include <stdio.h>
int main()
{
  float prime, amount, interest;

  prime = 0.08; /* prime interest rate */
  printf("\nEnter the amount: ");
  scanf("%f", &amount);
  interest = prime * amount;
  printf("\nThe interest earned is %f dollars", interest);

  return 0;
}
```

3.
```
#include <stdio.h>
int main()
{
  float fahren, celsius;

  printf("\nEnter a temperature in degrees Fahrenheit: ");
  scanf("%f", &fahren);
  celsius = (5.0/9.0) * (fahren - 32.0);
  printf("\nThe equivalent Celsius temperature is %f", celsius);

  return 0;
}
```

3.6 Case Study: Interactive Input

This case study demonstrates creating a complete program that requires interactive input and C's mathematical power function. The program is developed using the software development procedure presented in Section 1.4.

Requirements Specification

Center-Mark Industries is planning an advertising campaign called "Hit The Mark," that includes painting bull's-eye diagrams (see Figure 3.9) on the sides of barns and billboards throughout the Midwest. To mange the cost of the campaign, the company needs to keep track of how much paint is used, an amount that can be calculated based on the size of each sign.

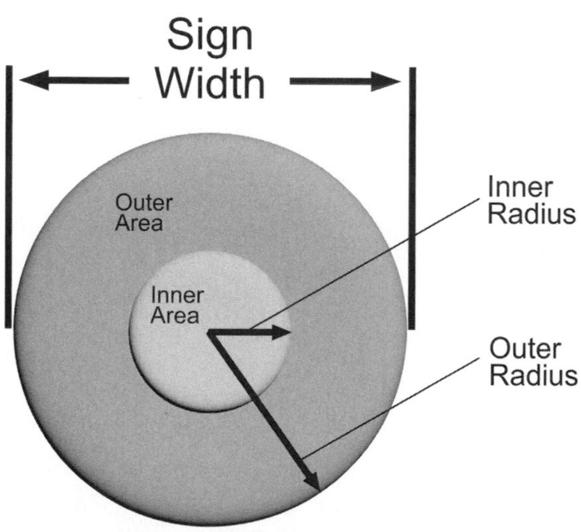

Figure 3.9 The Hit-The-Mark display

To accomplish this, the project director has asked you to prepare a computer program that calculates the area of each circle in the figure and then calculates the amount used of each color of paint. The specifications listed on the paint cans indicate that one quart of paint can cover 400 square feet of sign. Because the company wants each sign covered with two coats of paint, it is assumed that one quart is needed for every 200 square feet.

According to the specification for the bull's-eye design, the inner circle must have a radius that is one quarter of the outer circle's radius. A typical bull's-eye is 8 feet across.

Step 1: Analyze the Problem

Although the inputs and outputs are well defined for this problem, some work is needed to determine the relationship between the two.

a: Determine the Desired Outputs
The following four outputs are required:

1. The area of the inner circle
2. The area of the outer rim
3. The number of quarts of red paint used for the inner circle
4. The number of quarts of blue paint needed for the outer rim

b. Determine the Input Data The only required input value is the width of the display, which corresponds to the diameter of the outside circle.

c. List the Formulas Relating the Inputs to the Outputs

outerRadius = width / 2.0.
*innerRadius = .25 * outerRadius*
totalArea = π **outerRadius*^{2}
innerArea = π * *innerRadius*^{2}
outerRimArea = totalArea - innerArea
redPaint = innerArea / 200;
bluePaint = outerRimArea / 200;

Notice that the computations begin with determining the radius of the outer circle from the input width of the display, proceed to determine three areas, and then calculate the amount of paint needed.

d. Perform a Hand Calculation
Arbitrarily using a sign width of 8 feet, the following results are obtained using the formulas listed in the prior step:

outerRadius = 4
innerRadius = 1
totalArea = 50.26
innerArea = 3.14
outerRimArea = 47.12
redPaint = .016
bluePaint = .236

Step 2: Select an Overall Solution Algorithm

This problem can be solved using the Problem-Solver Algorithm introduced in Section 1.5. As applied to this problem, the algorithm becomes

Input the width of the display
Calculate the inner and outer areas and the paint required using the formulas provided in the analysis stage
Display the inner and outer rim areas and the paint required for each area

Step 3: Write the Program

Program 3.19 provides the necessary code, where the variable names have been selected to reflect their usage.

Program 3.19

```
1  #include <stdio.h>
2  #include <math.h>
3  #define SQFTPERQUART 200.0
4  #define PI 3.1416
5
6  int main()
7  {
8    float width, outerRadius, innerRadius;
9    float totalArea, innerArea, outerRimArea;
10   float blue, red;
11
12   /* get the input data */
13   printf("Enter the width of the display (in feet): ");
14   scanf("%f", &width);
15
16   /* determine the two radii */
17   outerRadius = width/2.0;
18   innerRadius = 0.25 * outerRadius;
19
20   /* determine the two areas */
21   totalArea = PI * pow(outerRadius, 2);
22   innerArea = PI * pow(innerRadius, 2);
23   outerRimArea = totalArea - innerArea;
24
25   /* determine the gallons of paint needed */
26   red =  innerArea / SQFTPERQUART;
27   blue = outerRimArea / SQFTPERQUART;
28
29   /* provide the required outputs */
30   printf("\nThe inner area is %5.2f sq. feet", innerArea);
31   printf("\nThe outer rim area is %5.2f sq feet", outerRimArea);
32   printf("\n\nRed paint required is %6.3f quarts", red);
33   printf("\nBlue paint required is %6.3f quarts\n", blue);
34
35   return 0;
36 }
```

Lines 1 through 7 in Program 3.19 include the two required header files, `stdio.h` and `math.h`. These lines also define two named constants, `PI` and `SQFTPERQUART`, and provide the standard header line we have been using for `main()`. The header line is followed, in line 7, by the opening brace of `main()`'s body.

Within the function's body, lines 8, 9, and 10 declare the variables that are used in the program. Following these declarations, the Problem-Solver Algorithm, as it applies to this application, is coded. Thus, lines 13 and 14 provide a prompt and the code to enter the single input value needed, which is the sign's overall width. This is followed by a computation section, consisting of lines 17 through 27, that code the formulas determined in the analysis step. Finally, lines 30 through 33 provide the required outputs.

Step 4: Test and Debug the Program

The last step in the development procedure is to verify the program's operation. A sample output produced by Program 3.19 is

```
Enter the width of the display (in feet): 8

The inner area is  3.14 sq. feet
The outer rim area is 47.12 sq feet
Red paint required is  0.016 quarts
Blue paint required is  0.236 quarts
```

Because the displayed value agrees with the previous hand calculation, it establishes a degree of confidence in the program and its use in determining the desired outputs for different sized signs.

EXERCISES 3.6

Programming Exercises

1. a. Enter and execute Program 3.19.
   b. Execute Program 3.19 to determine the amount of each color paint needed for an 8-foot display.

2. a. Write a C program to calculate and display the coordinates of the midpoint of the line segment connecting the points (3, 4) and (10, 12). Use the fact that the coordinates of the midpoint between two points having coordinates (x_1,y_1) and (x_2,y_2) are $((x_1+ x_2)/2, (y_1+ y_2)/2)$. Your program should produce the following display:

   ```
   The x midpoint coordinate is __________
   The y midpoint coordinate is __________
   ```

   where the blank spaces are replaced with the values calculated by your program.
   b. How do you know that the midpoint values calculated by your program are correct?
   c. Once you have verified the output produced by your program, modify it to determine the midpoint coordinates of the line connecting the two points (2,10) and (12, 6).

3. Redo Exercise 2a but change the output produced by your program to

   ```
   The x coordinate of the midpoint is xxx.xx
   The y coordinate of the midpoint is xxx.xx
   ```

   where *xxx.xx* denotes that the calculated value should be placed in a field wide enough for three places to the left of the decimal point, and two places to the right of it.

4. Using `scanf()` statements, write, compile, and execute a C program that accepts the x and y coordinates of two points. Have your program determine and display the midpoints of the two points (use the formula given in Exercise 2). Verify your program using the following test data:

   Test data set 1: Point 1 = (0,0) and Point 2 = (16,0)

   Test data set 2: Point 1 = (0,0) and Point 2 = (0,16)

   Test data set 3: Point 1 = (0,0) and Point 2 = (-16,0)

   Test data set 4: Point 1 = (0,0) and Point 2 = (0,-16)

   Test data set 5: Point 1 = (-5,-5) and Point 2 = (5,5)

   When you have completed your verification, use your program to complete the following table:

Point 1	Point 2	Midpoint
(4,6)	(16,18)	
(22,3)	(8,12)	
(-10,8)	(14,4)	
(-12,2)	(14,-31)	
(2,-6)	(20,16)	
(2,-6)	(-16,-18)	

5. Write, compile, and execute a program that calculates and displays the fourth root of a number entered by a user. Recall from elementary algebra that the fourth root of a number can be found by raising the number to the 1/4 power. (*Hint:* Do not use integer division. Can you see why?) Verify your program by calculating the fourth root of the following data: 81, 16, 1, and 0. When you have completed your verification, use your program to determine the fourth root of 42, 121, 256, 587, 1240, and 16256.

6. Write, compile, and execute a C program that calculates and displays the amount of money, A, available in N years when an initial deposit of X dollars is deposited in a bank account paying an annual interest rate of R percent. Use the relationship that $A = X(1.0 + R/100)^N$. The program should prompt the user to enter appropriate values and use `scanf()` statements to accept the data. In constructing your prompts, use strings such as `Enter the amount of the initial deposit.` Verify the operation of your program by calculating, by hand, and using your program, the amount of money available for the following test cases:

   Test data set 1: $1000 invested for 10 years at 0% interest

   Test data set 2: $1000 invested for 10 years at 6% interest

   When you have completed your verification, use your program to determine the amount of money available for the following cases:

   a. $1000 invested for 10 years at 8% interest.
   b. $1000 invested for 10 years at 10% interest.
   c. $1000 invested for 10 years at 12% interest.
   d. $5000 invested for 15 years at 8% interest.
   e. $5000 invested for 15 years at 10% interest.
   f. $5000 invested for 15 years at 12% interest.
   g. $24 invested for 300 years at 4% interest.

7. Write a C program that prompts the user for a cost per item, number of items purchased, and a discount rate. The program should then calculate and print the total cost, discounted total cost, tax due, and amount due. Use the formulas

```
total cost = number of items * cost-per-item
total cost (discounted) = total cost - (discount rate * total cost)
tax due = total cost * TAXRATE
amount due = total cost + tax due
```

For this problem assume that the `TAXRATE` is 6%.

8. The roads of Kansas are laid out in a rectangular grid at exactly 1-mile intervals, as shown in Figure 3.10 . Lonesome farmer Pete drives his 1939 Ford pickup *x* miles east and *y* miles north to get to widow Sally's farm. Both *x* and *y* are integer numbers. Using this information, write, test, and run a C program that prompts the user for the values of *x* and *y* and then uses the formula

```
distance = sqrt(x * x + y * y);
```

to find the shortest driving distance across the fields to Sally's farm. Since Pete does not understand fractions or decimals very well, the answer must be rounded to the nearest integer value before it is displayed.

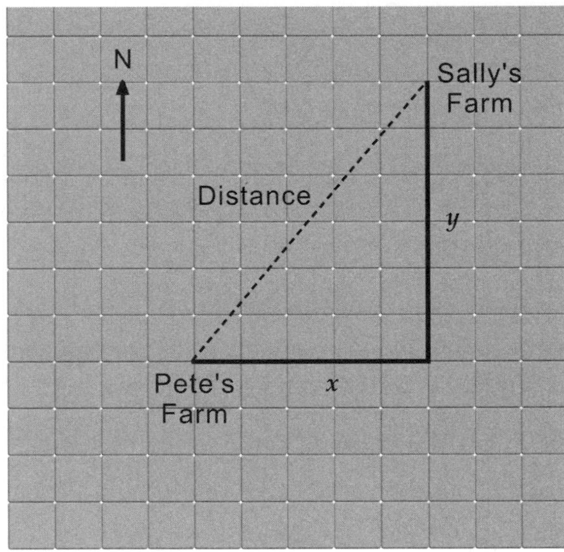

Figure 3.10 Kansas roads

9. When a particular rubber ball is dropped from a given height (in meters), its impact speed (in meters/second) when it hits the ground is given by the formula *speed = sqrt(2 * g * height)*. The ball then rebounds to 2/3 the height from which it last fell. Using this information write, test, and run a C program that calculates and displays the impact speed of the first three bounces and the rebound height of each bounce. Test your program using an initial height of 2.0 meters. Run the program twice and compare the results for dropping the ball on Earth (g = 9.81 meters per sec^2) and on the moon (g = 1.67 meters per sec^2).

3.7 Common Programming and Compiler Errors

In using the material presented in this chapter, be aware of the following possible programming and compiler errors:

Programming Errors

1. Forgetting to assign initial values to all variables before the variables are used in an expression. Initial values can be assigned when the variables are declared, by explicit assignment statements, or by interactively entering values using the `scanf()` function.
2. Calling the `sqrt()` function with an integer argument. This will not cause a compiler error on most Unix-based compilers. On Windows-based compilers, an error message similar to `"ambiguous call to overloaded function"` is generated.
3. Forgetting to use the address operator, `&`, in front of variable names in a `scanf()` function call. Because `scanf()` requires all arguments following the control string to be addresses, it is up to the programmer to ensure that addresses are passed correctly. This programming error will not generate a compiler error but will generate an error when the program is executed. Unix-based systems will display a message similar to `"Memory fault (coredump)"`, while Windows-based systems display a message similar to `"The variable … is being used without being defined."`
4. Not including the correct control sequences in `scanf()` function calls for the data values that must be entered. This typically occurs using a `%f` sequence for a double-precision value rather than the required `%lf`. Although this will not generate a compiler error, it does result in incorrect values being assigned when the statement is executed.
5. Including a message within the control string passed to `scanf()`. Unlike `printf()`, `scanf()`'s control string typically contains only conversion control sequences. Although this does not generate a compiler error, it does result in incorrect values being assigned when the statement is executed.
6. Terminating a `#define` command to the preprocessor with a semicolon. By now you probably end every line in your C programs with a semicolon, almost automatically. But there are cases, such as preprocessor commands, where a semicolon should not end a line.
7. Placing an equal sign in a `#define` command when equating a symbolic constant to a value.

8. Using the increment and decrement operators with variables that appear more than once in the same expression. This more exotic error occurs because C does not specify the order in which operands must be accessed within an expression. This makes the order of operand access compiler dependent, which means the access order depends on how the compiler has been designed to handle the code. For example, the value assigned to `result` by the code

```
i = 5;
result = i  +  i++;
```

can be either 10 or 12 depending on which operand is initially accessed. If your compiler forces initial access to the first operand, this statement is equivalent to

```
result = i + i;    /* calculate result first */
i++;               /* then increment i */
```

However, if your compiler initially forces access to the second operand, the statement is equivalent to

```
i++;               /* increment i first */
result = i + i;    /* then calculate result */
```

As a general rule, you should avoid using either the increment or decrement operators in expressions where the variables they operate on appear more than once in the same expression; rather, separate the expression into two such that the order of expressions clearly designates what you want accomplished.

9. Being unwilling to test a program in depth. After all, since you wrote the program you assume it is correct or you would have changed it before it was compiled. It is extremely difficult to back away and honestly test your own software. As a programmer, you must constantly remind yourself that just because you think your program is correct does not make it so. Finding errors in your own program is a sobering experience, but one that will help you become a master programmer.

Compiler Errors

The following table summarizes common errors that will result in compilation errors and the typical error messages provided by Unix- and Windows-based compiler.

Error	Typical Unix-based compiler error message	Typical Windows-based compiler error message
Attempting to use a mathematical function, such as `pow` without including the `math.h` header file.	`"ERROR: Undefined symbol: .pow` (You can use the `-bloadmap` or `-bnoquiet` options when compiling the program to obtain more information. Additionally, you must use the `-lm` option for correct compilation.)	`"pow identifier not found."`

Error	Typical Unix-based compiler error message	Typical Windows-based compiler error message
Forgetting to close the control string passed to `scanf()` with double quotes.	`"(S) String literal must be ended before the end of line."` `"(S) Syntax error: possible missing ')'?"` (The first error message is attempting to tell you that the string has not been closed using a double quote. The second error message is a result of the string not being terminated, which causes an error on the line following the call to `scanf()`.)	`"newline in constant" "syntax error: missing ')' before identifier…"` (The first error message is attempting to tell you that the string has not been closed using a double quote. The second error message is a result of the string not being terminated, which causes an error on the line following the call to `scanf()`.)
Failing to separate all arguments in `scanf()` with commas as, for example, in the call `scanf("%f%f", &count &n);`	`"(S) Operation between types "unsigned char*" and "float" is not allowed."` (Although very cryptic, this message indicates that the compiler cannot recognize the variable in which the function is trying to store a value.)	`" '&': illegal, left operand has type …"` (Although very cryptic, this message indicates that the compiler cannot recognize the variable in which the function is trying to store a value.)
Placing the parentheses in the wrong location when using the cast operator, as, for example, in the expression `(int count)`	`"(E) Identifier not allowed in cast or sizeof declarations."` `"(S) Syntax error."`	`"syntax error: missing ')' before count" "syntax error:')'"`
Applying the increment or decrement operators to an expression. For example, the expression `(count + n)++`	`"Operand must be a modifiable lvalue."` (This error message is indicates that the expression to the left of the ++ operator can not be modified.)	`"++ needs l-value."` (This error message indicates that the expression to the left of the ++ operator can not be modified.)

3.8 Chapter Summary

1. Arithmetic calculations can be performed using either assignment statements or mathematical functions. They can also be performed using expressions in calculating an argument's value supplied to a function.

2. The assignment symbol, =, is an operator. It has a lower precedence than all mathematical operators (+, -, *, /, %). Because assignment is an operation in C, multiple uses of the assignment operator are possible in the same expression.

3. In addition to the assignment operator, =, C provides the +=, -=, *= and /= assignment operators.

4. The increment operator, ++, adds 1 to a variable, while the decrement operator, --, subtracts 1 from a variable. Both of these operators can be used as prefixes or postfixes. In prefix operation the variable is incremented (or decremented) before its value is used. In postfix operation the variable is incremented (or decremented) after its value is used.

5. C provides library functions for calculating square root, logarithmic, and other mathematical computations. Each program using one of these mathematical functions must either include the statement `#include <math.h>` or have a function declaration for the mathematical function before it is called.

6. Mathematical functions may be included within larger expressions.

7. The `scanf()` function is a standard library function used for data input. The `scanf()` function requires a control string and a list of addresses. The general form of this function call is

   ```
   scanf("control string", &arg1, &arg2, . . . , &argn);
   ```

   The control string typically contains only conversion control sequences, such as `%d`, and must contain the same number of conversion control sequences as the argument addresses.

8. When a `scanf()` function is encountered, the program temporarily suspends further statement execution until sufficient data has been entered for the number of variable addresses contained in the `scanf()` function call.

9. It is good programming practice to display a message, prior to a `scanf()` function call, that alerts the user as to the type and number of data items to be entered. Such a message is called a prompt.

10. Field width specifiers can be included with conversion control sequences to explicitly specify the format of displayed fields. This includes both the total width of the output field and, for floating-point and double-precision numbers, the number of decimal digits to display.

11. Each compiled C program is automatically passed through a preprocessor. Lines beginning with # in the first column are recognized as commands to this preprocessor. Preprocessor commands are not terminated with a semicolon.

12. Expressions can be made equivalent to a single identifier using the preprocessor `#define` command. This command has the form
    `#define identifier expression`

    and allows the identifier to be used instead of the expression anywhere in the program after the command. Generally, a `#define` command is placed at the top of a program or at the beginning of the `main()` function.

3.9 Chapter Supplement: Introduction to Abstraction

A very important programming concept, and one that you will increasingly encounter as you progress in your studies, is the idea of abstraction. This concept is fundamentally applied in two areas: data type abstraction and procedural abstraction—both of which you now have the background to understand. In this section we first introduce the concept of abstraction and then use it to define these two types of abstractions.

In its most general usage, an abstraction is simply an idea or term that identifies general qualities or characteristics of a group of objects, independent of any one specific object in the group. For example, consider the term "car." As a term this is an abstraction: It refers to a group of objects that individually contain the characteristics associated with a car, such as a motor, passenger compartment, wheels, steering capabilities, brakes, etc. A particular instance of a car, such as my car or your car, are not abstractions—they are real objects that are classified as "type car" because they have attributes associated with a car.

Although we use abstract concepts all the time, we tend not to think of them as such. For example, the words "tree," "dog," "cat," "table," and "chair" are all abstractions, just as a car is. Each of these terms refers to a set of qualities that are met by a group of particular things. For each of these abstractions there are many individual trees, dogs, and cats; each instance of which conforms to the general characteristics associated with the abstract term.

In programming, especially in more advanced work, we are much more careful to label appropriate terms as abstractions than we are in everyday life. The first such term that is really an abstraction is a data type. Let us see why this is so.

Just as "my car" is a particular instance or object of the more abstract "type car," a particular integer, say 5 for example, is a specific object or instance of the more abstract "type integer," where an integer is a signed or unsigned number having no decimal point. As such, each data type—integer, character, and double precision—is considered an abstraction that defines a general type of which specific instances can be realized, including operations that can be applied to specific values. Such data types, then, simply identify common qualities of each group and make it reasonable to speak of integer types, character types, and double-precision types.

Although programmers ordinarily assume that mathematical operations such as addition, subtraction, multiplication, and division will be supplied, the designers of C had to consider carefully which operations would be provided as part of each data type. For example, they did not include an exponentiation operator as part of the numerical data types, while this operation was included in Visual Basic's data abstraction for integers (in C, exponentiation is supplied as the mathematical library function `pow()`).

Built-in and Abstract Data Types

Data types provided by the compiler, such as the `int`, `double`, and `char` data types provided in C, are referred to as built-in or primitive data types (the two terms are synonymous). In contrast to built-in types, some programming languages permit programmers to create their own data types; that is, define a type of value with an associated range of values and operations that can be performed on the acceptable values.[5] Such user-defined data types are formally referred to as **abstract data types**. Although C does not provide the capability to create abstract data types, it is provided in C++. In C++ abstract data types are called **classes**, and the ability to create classes is the major enhancement provided to C by C++ (in fact, the original name for C++ was "C with Classes").

Procedural Abstraction

In addition to data abstraction, all programming languages permit assigning a name to a self-contained set of instructions, which in C is known as a function. As a specific example, consider the `printf()` function. This function internally consists of a sequence of instructions that provides for the formatted display of data. This sequence of instructions, however, is invoked as a unit using the single name `printf`.

The assigning of a name to a function or procedure in such a way that the function is invoked by simply using a name with appropriate arguments is formally referred to as **procedural abstraction**.

Procedural abstraction effectively hides the details of how a function performs its task. This hiding of the details is one of the hallmarks and strengths of abstraction in both analyzing a problem and programming a solution algorithm.

On the analysis side, by thinking of tasks as abstract, procedural-level programmers can solve problems at a higher level without immediately being concerned with the nitty-gritty details of the actual solution implementation. For example, a financial application may require the number of days between two dates. Rather than attempting to immediately solve how to compute this day count, it can be designated as a function to be coded later. Doing this permits the designer to concentrate on other aspects of the program and leave the analysis of how to actually calculate the date difference function for later or assign the task to a second person.

On the programming side, procedural abstraction permits a programmer to use an existing function, such as C's mathematical functions, without the need to either know or understand how the functions are internally coded. This saves an enormous amount of coding time by permitting the reuse of preexisting code.

---

[5]The range of allowed values is formally referred to as the data type's domain.

Part Two
Flow of Control

Chapter 4

Selection

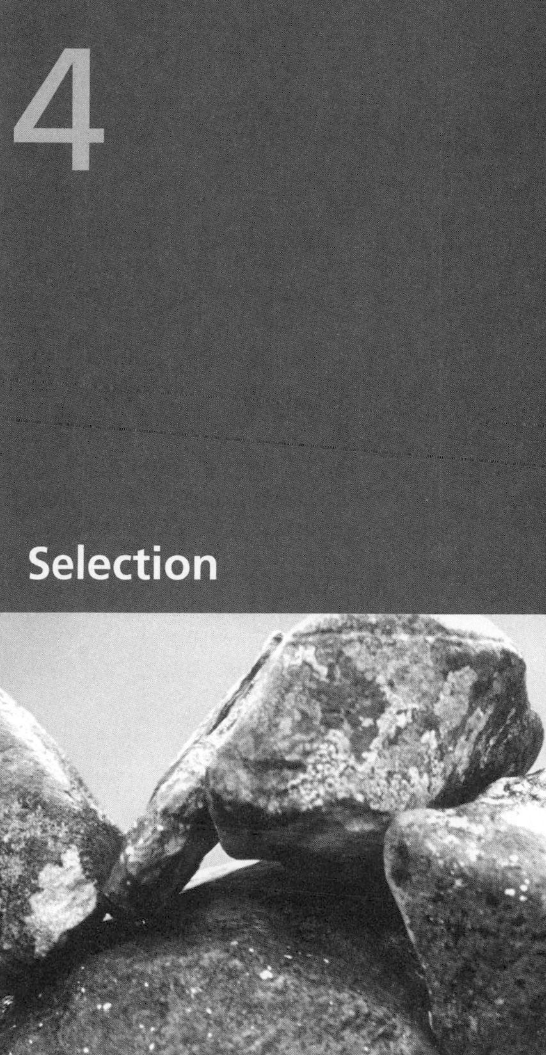

The term **flow of control** refers to the order in which a program's statements are executed. One of the important early advances in programming theory occurred in the late 1960s with the recognition that any algorithm, no matter how complex, could be constructed using combinations of four standardized flow of control structures: sequential, selection, repetition, and invocation.

Unless directed otherwise, the normal flow of control for all programs is *sequential*. This means that statements are executed in sequence, one after another, in the order in which they are placed within the program. Selection, repetition, and invocation statements permit this sequential flow of control to be altered in precisely defined ways.

Selection is used to select which statements are to be performed next based on a condition being true or false, while *repetition* is used to repeat a set of statements. *Invocation*, as we have already seen, means invoking a sequence of instructions using a single statement, as in calling a function. In this chapter we present C's selection statements. Repetition statements are presented in Chapter 5. Finally, in Chapters 6 and 7 we see how to create our own callable functions.

4.1 Relational Expressions

In the solution of many problems, different actions must be taken depending on the value of the data. Examples of simple situations include calculating an area *only if* the measurements are positive, performing a division *only if* the divisor is not 0, printing different messages *depending on* the value of a grade received, and so on.

The `if` statement in C is used to implement such a decision structure in its simplest form—that of selecting a statement to be executed only if a condition is satisfied. The most commonly used syntax of this statement is

if (condition)
statement executed if condition is true

When an executing program encounters the `if` statement, the condition is evaluated to determine its numerical value, which is then interpreted as either true or false. If the condition evaluates to any non-0 value (positive or negative), the condition is considered as a "true" condition and the statement following the `if` is executed; otherwise this statement is not executed.

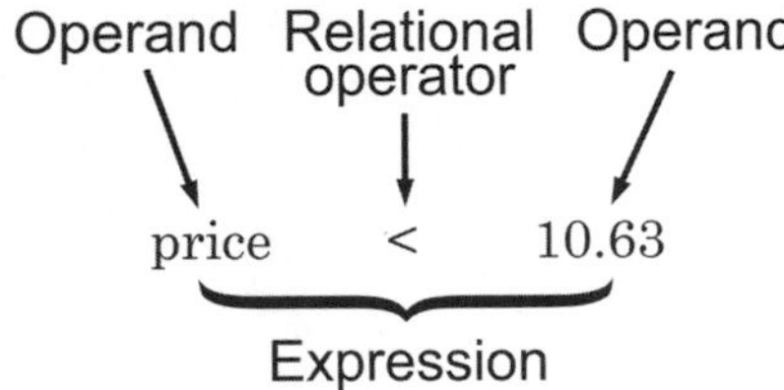

Figure 4.1 Anatomy of a simple relational expression

The condition used in all of C's `if` statements can be any valid C expression (including, as we will see, an assignment expression.) The most commonly used expressions, however, are called relational expressions. A **relational expression** consists of a relational operator that compares two operands as shown in Figure 4.1. Unlike arithmetic expressions that can yield an infinite number of values, a relational expression can yield only one of two values, 0 or 1.

While each operand in a relational expression can be a variable, constant, or any valid C expression, the relational operators must be one of those listed in Table 4.1. These relational operators may be used with each of C's data types, and cover all possible relationships between two operands.

Table 4.1 Relational Operators in C

Relational Operator	Meaning	Example
<	less than	`age < 30`
>	greater than	`height > 6.2`
<=	less than or equal to	`taxable <= 20000`
>=	greater than or equal to	`temp >= 98.6`
==	equal to	`grade == 100`
!=	not equal to	`number != 250`

Historical Note

De Morgan's Laws

Augustus De Morgan was born at Madura, India, in 1806 and died in London in 1871. He became a professor of mathematics in London in 1828 and spent many years performing investigations into a variety of mathematical topics. He was a revered teacher and wrote numerous textbooks containing a wealth of information on mathematics and its history, but his texts generally were very difficult for his students to understand.

De Morgan's contributions to modern computing include two laws by which AND statements can be converted to OR statements and vice versa. They are

1. NOT(A AND B) = (NOT A) OR (NOT B)
2. NOT(A OR B) = (NOT A) AND (NOT B)

Thus, from De Morgan's first law, the statement "Either it is not raining or I am not getting wet" says the same thing as "It is not true that it is raining and I am getting wet." Similarly, from the second law "It is not true that politicians always lie or that teachers always know the facts" becomes "Politicians do not always lie and teachers do not always know the facts."

In computer usage, De Morgan's laws are typically more useful in the following form:

1. A AND B = NOT((NOT A) OR (NOT B))
2. A OR B = NOT((NOT A) AND (NOT B))

The ability to convert from an OR statement to an AND statement and vice versa is extremely useful in many programming situations.

In creating relational expressions, the relational operators must be typed exactly as given in Table 4.1. Thus, although the following relational expressions are all valid:

```
age > 40
length <= 50
temp > 98.6
3 < 4
flag == done
idNum == 682
day != 5
2.0 > 3.3
hours > 40
```

the following are invalid:

```
length =< 50    /* operator out of order */
2.0 >> 3.3      /* invalid operator */
flag = = done   /* spaces are not allowed */
```

Relational expressions are also known as **conditions**, and we will use both terms to refer to these expressions. Like all C expressions, relational expressions are evaluated to yield a numerical result.[1] In the case of relational expressions, as has been noted, the value of the expression always results in only one of two possible values, an integer value of 1 or 0. *A relational expression that we interpret as true evaluates to an integer value of 1, and a false relational expression results in an integer value of 0.* For example, because the relationship 3 < 4 is always true, the expression has a value of 1, and because the relationship 2.0 > 3.3 is always false, the expression has a value of 0. This can be verified using the statements

```
printf("The value of 3 < 4 is %d", 3 < 4);
printf("\nThe value of 2.0 > 3.3 is %d", 2.0 > 3.3);
```

which result in the display

```
The value of 3 < 4 is 1
The value of 2.0 > 3.3 is 0
```

The value of a relational expression such as `hours > 0` depends on the value stored in the variable `hours`.

In addition to numerical operands, character data can also be compared using relational operators. Such comparisons are essential in alphabetizing names or using characters to select a particular choice in decision-making situations.

[1]In this regard C differs from other high-level programming languages that yield a Boolean (true or false) result.

All character sets have either an increasing or decreasing ordering sequence. For example, in ASCII code, letters are coded in increasing order, where the letter "B" is stored using a code having a higher numerical value than the letter "A," the code for a "C" being higher in value than the code for a "B," and so on. For this ordering sequence, the expressions provided in the first column of Table 4.2 have the values listed in the second column. The interpretation of these values as either true or false is provided in the third column.

Table 4.2 Sample Comparisons of ASCII Characters

Expression	Value	Interpretation
'A' > 'C'	0	false
'D' <= 'Z'	1	true
'E' == 'F'	0	false
'g' >= 'm'	0	false
'b' != 'c'	1	true
'a' == 'A'	0	false
'B' < 'a'	1	true
'b' > 'Z'	1	true

Logical Operators

In addition to using relational expressions as conditions, more complex conditions can be created using the logical operations `AND`, `OR`, and `NOT`. These operations are represented by the symbols `&&`, `||`, and `!`, respectively.

When the `AND` operator, `&&`, is used with two expressions, as listed in Table 4.3, the condition is true only if both expressions are true by themselves. Thus, the compound condition

```
(age > 40) && (term < 10)
```

is true (has a value of 1) only if `age` is greater than 40 and `term` is less than 10. Because relational operators have a higher precedence than logical operators, the parentheses in this logical expression could have been omitted.

Table 4.3 The `AND` (`&&`) Operator

If `expressionOne` is:	And `expressionTwo` is:	Then, `expressionOne && expressionTwo` is:
true (that is, non-0)	true (that is, non-0)	true (1)
true (that is, non-0)	false (that is, 0)	false (0)
false (that is, 0)	true (that is, non-0)	false (0)
false (that is, 0)	false (that is, 0)	false (0)

The logical `OR` operator, `||`, is also applied between two expressions. When using the OR operator, as illustrated in Table 4.4, the resulting condition is true if either one or both of the two expressions are true. Thus, the compound condition

```
(age > 40) || (term < 10)
```

is true if either age is greater than 40, term is less than 10, or both conditions are true. Again, the parentheses surrounding the relational expressions are included to make the expression easier to read. Because of the higher precedence of relational operators with respect to logical operators, the same evaluation is made even if the parentheses are omitted.

Table 4.4 The OR (||) Operator

If expressionOne is:	And expressionTwo is:	Then, expressionOne || expressionTwo is:
true (that is, non-0)	true (that is, non-0)	true (1)
true (that is, non-0)	false (that is, 0)	true (1)
false (that is, 0)	true (that is, non-0)	true (1)
false (that is, 0)	false (that is, 0)	false (0)

For the declarations

```
int i, j;
double a, b, complete;
```

the following represent valid conditions:

```
a > b
i == j || a < b || complete
a/b > 5 && i <= 20
```

Before these conditions can be evaluated, the values of a, b, i, j, and complete must be known. Assuming

```
a = 12.0, b = 2.0, i = 15, j = 30, and complete = 0.0
```

the expressions yield the following results:

Expression	Value	Interpretation
a > b	1	true
i == j || a < b || complete	0	false
a/b > 5 && i <= 20	1	true

The && operator has a higher precedence than the || operator, and both operators associate from left to right. Thus, in a logical expression containing && and || operators, the && operators are evaluated first, from left to right, followed by the evaluation of the || operators, again from left to right. Evaluation stops, however, whenever the truth or falsity of an expression containing any of these operators is definitively determined, regardless of how many additional operations may exist. For example, evaluation of the expression age <= 62 && tenure > 10 stops if age is greater than 62, which makes the entire logical expression false no matter what the value of tenure may be. This evaluation feature for the && and || operators is known as **short-circuit evaluation.**

The third logical operator, the NOT operator, is used to change an expression to its opposite state. As listed in Table 4.5, if an expression has any non-0 value (true), !expression produces a 0 value (false). If an expression is false to begin with (has a 0 value), !expression is true and evaluates to 1. For example, assuming the number 26 is stored in the variable age, the expression age > 40 has a value of 0 (it is false), while the expression !(age > 40) has a value of 1. The NOT operator can only be applied to single expressions; as such, it is a unary operator.

Table 4.5 The NOT (!) Operator

If expression is:	Then, !expression is:
true (that is, non-0)	false (0)
false (that is, 0)	true (1)

The relational and logical operators have a hierarchy of execution similar to that of the arithmetic operators. Table 4.6 lists the operators in order of precedence in relation to the other operators we have used. The operator with the highest precedence is at the top of the table, and the operator with the lowest precedence is at the bottom.

Table 4.6 C Operators Listed from Highest Precedence to Lowest Precedence

Operator	Associativity
!, unary -, ++, --	right to left
*, /, %	left to right
+, -	left to right
<, <=, >, >=	left to right
==, !=	left to right
&&	left to right
||	left to right
+=, -=, *=, /=	right to left

The following example illustrates the use of precedence and associativity to evaluate relational expressions, assuming the following declarations:

```
char key = 'm';
int i = 5, j = 7, k = 12;
double x = 22.5;
```

Expression	Equivalent Expression	Value	Interpretation
i + 2 == k - 1	(i + 2) == (k - 1)	0	false
3 * i - j < 22	((3 * i) - j) < 22	1	true
i + 2 * j > k	(i + (2 * j)) > k	1	true
k + 3 <= -j + 3 * i	(k + 3) <= ((-j) + (3*i))	0	false
'a' + 1 == 'b'	('a' + 1) == 'b'	1	true
key - 1 > 'p'	(key - 1) > 'p'	0	false
key + 1 == 'n'	(key + 1) == 'n'	1	true
25 >= x + 4.0	25 >= (x + 4.0)	0	false

As with all expressions, parentheses can be used to alter the assigned operator priority and improve the readability of relational expressions. By evaluating the expressions within parentheses first, the following compound condition is evaluated as:

```
(6 * 3 == 36 / 2) && (13 < 3 * 3 + 4) || !(6 - 2 < 5) =
           (18 == 18) && (13 < 9 + 4) || !(4 < 5) =
                        1 && (13 < 13) || !1 =
                        1 && 0 && 0 =
                        1 && 0 =
                        0
```

EXERCISES 4.1

Short Answer Questions

1. Determine the value of the following expressions. Assume a = 5, b = 2, c = 4, d = 6, and e = 3.
   a. `a > b`
   b. `a != b`
   c. `d % b == c % b`
   d. `a * c != d * b`
   e. `d * b == c * e`
   f. `a * b`
   g. `a % b * c`
   h. `c % b * a`
   i. `b % c * a`

2. Using parentheses, rewrite the following expressions to correctly indicate their order of evaluation. Then evaluate each expression assuming a = 5, b = 2, and c = 4.
   a. `a % b * c && c % b * a`
   b. `a % b * c || c % b * a`
   c. `b % c * a && a % c * b`
   d. `b % c * a || a % c * b`

3. Write relational expressions to express the following conditions (use variable names of your own choosing):
   a. a person's age is equal to 30
   b. a person's temperature is greater than 98.6
   c. a person's height is less than 6 feet
   d. the current month is 12 (December)
   e. the letter input is *m*
   f. a person's age is equal to 30 and the person is taller than 6 feet
   g. the current day is the 15th day of the 1st month
   h. a person is older than 50 or has been employed at the company for at least 5 years
   i. a person's identification number is less than 500 and the person is older than 55
   j. a length is greater than 2 and less than 3 feet

4. Determine the value of the following expressions, assuming a = 5, b = 2, c = 4, and d = 5.
   a. `a == 5`
   b. `b * d == c * c`
   c. `d % b * c > 5 || c % b * d < 7`

4.2 The `if` and `if-else` Statements

The simplest C selection statement is the **one-way `if` statement** having the syntax

```
if (expression)   <———— no semicolon here

  statement;
```

In this construction, the statement following the `if(`*expression*`)` is only executed if the *`expression`* has a non-0 value (a true condition). Examples of this statement are

```
if (age >= 62)
   discount = .20

if (grade > 69)
   ++passTotal;
```

In each of these examples, the statement following the condition contained within the parentheses is only executed if the relational expression is true (that is, evaluates to a numerical value of 1); otherwise, the statement following the condition is not executed at all.

Program 4.1 illustrates a one-way `if` statement within the context of a complete program. This program checks a car's mileage and prints a message if the car has been driven more than 3,000 miles.

Program 4.1

```
#define LIMIT 3000.0
#include <stdio.h>

int main()
{
  int idNum;
  float miles;

  printf("Please type in car number and mileage: ");
  scanf("%d %f", &idNum, &miles);

  if(miles > LIMIT)
    printf(" Car %d is over the limit.\n",idNum);

  printf("End of program output.\n");

  return 0;
}
```

To illustrate the one-way selection criteria in action, Program 4.1 was run twice, each time with different input data.

```
Please type in car number and mileage: 256 3562.8
 Car 256 is over the limit.
End of program output.
```

and

```
Please type in car number and mileage: 23 2562.3
End of program output.
```

Because the data entered for the first run causes the tested expression to be true, the `printf()` function in the line 13

```
printf(" Car %d is over the limit.\n",idNum);
```

is executed and the message `Car 256 is over the limit` is displayed. The data for the second run causes the tested expression to be false; hence, the statement in line 13 is not executed. Notice in both runs that the statement

```
15  printf("End of program output.\n");
```

which immediately follows the `if` statement, is always executed. Thus, the only statement whose execution depends on the value of the condition being tested is the single statement

```
13     printf(" Car %d is over the limit.\n",idNum);
```

The flowchart corresponding to a one-way `if` statement is illustrated in Figure 4.2.

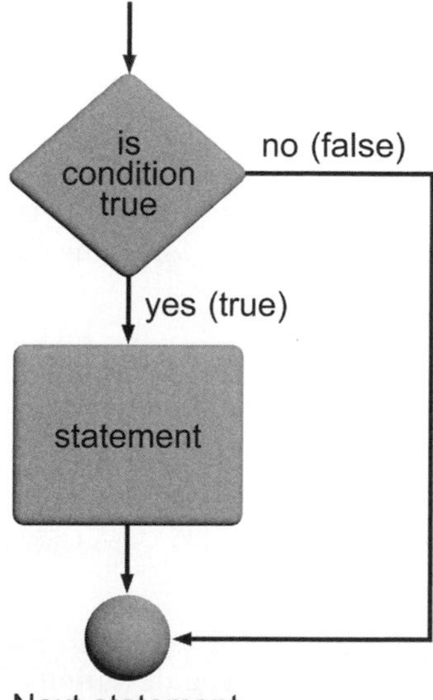

Figure 4.2 One-way `if` statement flowchart

Compound Statements

Although only a single statement is permitted in an `if` statement, this statement can be a single compound statement. A **compound statement** is one or more statements contained between braces as shown in Figure 4.3.

```
{
    statement1;
    statement2;
    statement3;
        .
        .
        .
    last statement;
}
```

Figure 4.3 A compound statement

The use of braces to enclose a set of individual statements creates a single block of statements, which may be used anywhere in a C program in place of a single statement. The general syntax of a compound within a one-way `if` statement is

```
if (expression)
{
  statement1;     /* as many statements as necessary */
  statement2;     /* can be placed within the braces */
      •           /* each statement must end with a ; */
      •
      •
  statementn;
}
```

Some programmers prefer to use this syntax even when only a single statement is required. Doing so permits additional statements to be added later by simply including them within the existing braces. Using this syntax, the following lines in Program 4.1

```
if(miles > LIMIT)
  printf(" Car %d is over the limit.\n",idNum);
```

would be written as

```
if(miles > LIMIT)
{
  printf(" Car %d is over the limit.\n",idNum);
}
```

In general, you should adopt one consistent style in coding `if` statements and adhere to it. Only in one specific instance, however, is a deviation considered acceptable. Because white space is optional in C, you may, for very short statements, code a complete `if` statement placed on a single line, as in the example

```
if (grade > 69) ++passTotal;
```

Programming Note

All Valid Expressions Work

Because of the syntax of C's selection statements, any valid expression will work in an `if` statement and not generate a compiler error. For example, the following `if` statement is syntactically correct:

```
if (age = 40)
  printf("Happy Birthday!");
```

Here the expression `age = 40` is always true (has a non-0 value), because at the completion of the assignment operation the expression itself has a value of 40. Because C considers any non-0 value as true, the call to `printf()` is always made, regardless of the value in `age` before the expression is encountered. Another way of looking at this is to realize that the `if` statement is equivalent to the following two statements:

```
age = 40; /* assign 40 to age */
if (age)  /* test the value of age */
  printf("Happy Birthday!");
```

More generally, all assignment expressions, except those that yield a right-hand side of 0 will be considered as true.

Similarly, code such as `if (tenure + 5)` is also syntactically correct, because the expression `tenure + 5` is valid. Here, the only value of `tenure` that makes the condition false is `-5`. Because a C compiler has no means of knowing that an expression being tested is not the desired one, you must be especially careful in writing conditions that are not only syntactically correct, but also logically correct.

The `if-else` Statement

The `if-else` statement directs the computer to select a sequence of one or more instructions based on the result of a comparison. For example, if a New Jersey resident's income is less than $20,000, the applicable state income tax rate is 2 percent. If the person's income is greater than $20,000, a different rate is applied to the amount over $20,000. The `if-else` statement can be used in this situation to determine the actual tax based on whether the gross income is less than or equal to $20,000. The most commonly used form of the `if-else` statement is

```
if (expression)  <------------  no semicolon here
  statement1;
else  <------------  no semicolon here
  statement2;
```

The *`expression`* is evaluated first. If the value of the *`expression`* is non-0, which corresponds to the expression being true, *`statement1`* is executed. If the value is 0 (which corresponds to the `expression` being false), *`statement2`*, the statement after the reserved word `else`, is executed. Thus, one of the two statements (either *`statement1`* or *statement2*) is always executed depending on the value of the tested expression. Notice that this tested expression must be put in parentheses and that semicolons go only at the end of each statement. The `if-else` statement's flowchart is illustrated in Figure 4.4.

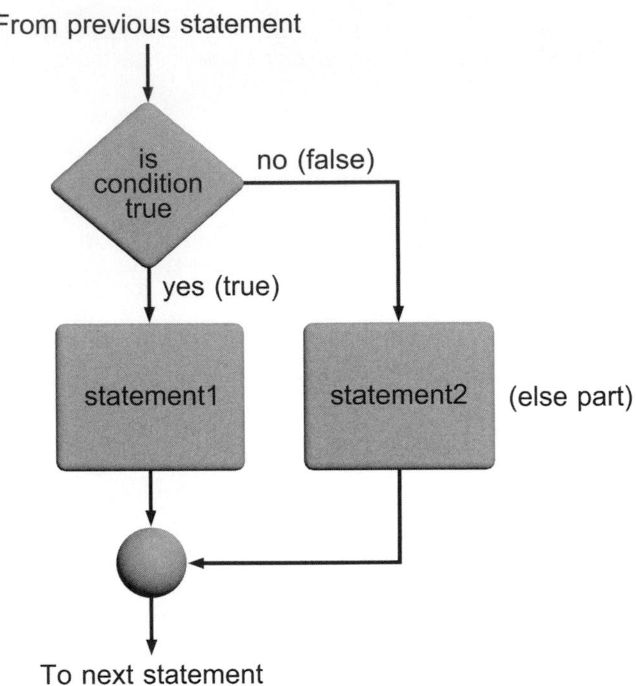

Figure 4.4 The `if-else` flowchart

As an example, let us write an income tax computation program containing an `if-else` statement. As previously described, New Jersey state income tax is assessed at 2 percent of taxable income for incomes less than or equal to $20,000. For taxable income greater than $20,000, state taxes are 2.5 percent of the income that exceeds $20,000 plus a fixed amount of $400 (which is 2 percent of $20,000). The expression to be tested is whether taxable income is less than or equal to $20,000. An appropriate `if-else` statement for this situation is[2]

```
if (taxable <= 20000.0)
  taxes = 0.02 * taxable;
else
  taxes = 0.025 * (taxable - 20000.0) + 400.0;
```

Here we have used the relational operator <= to correctly represent the relation "less than or equal to." If the value of `taxable` is less than or equal to 20,000, the condition is true (has a value of 1) and the statement `taxes = 0.02 * taxable;` is executed. If the condition is not true, the value of the expression is 0, and the statement after the reserved word `else` is executed. Program 4.2 illustrates the use of this statement in a complete program using

[2]In actual practice the numerical values in this statement would be defined as named constants.

named constants for the actual numerical values. A blank line was inserted before and after the `if-else` statement to highlight it in the complete program. We will continue to do this throughout the text to emphasize the statement being presented.

Program 4.2

```
1  #include <stdio.h>
2  #define LOWRATE 0.02    /* lower tax rate */
3  #define HIGHRATE 0.025 /* higher tax rate */
4  #define CUTOFF 20000.0 /* cut off for low rate */
5  #define FIXEDAMT 400    /* fixed dollar amount for higher rate amounts */
6
7  int main()
8  {
9    float taxable, taxes;
10
11   printf("Please type in the taxable income: ");
12   scanf("%f", &taxable);
13
14   if (taxable <= CUTOFF)
15     taxes = LOWRATE * taxable;
16   else
17     taxes = HIGHRATE * (taxable - CUTOFF) + FIXEDAMT;
18
19   printf("Taxes are $%7.2f\n",taxes);
20
21   return 0;
22 }
```

To illustrate this selection in action, Program 4.2 was run twice with different input data. The results are

```
Please type in the taxable income: 10000.
Taxes are $ 200.00
```

and

```
Please type in the taxable income: 30000.
Taxes are $ 650.00
```

Observe that the taxable income input in the first run of the program was less than $20,000, and the tax was correctly calculated in the `if` part of the `if-else` statement

```
15    taxes = LOWRATE * taxable;
```

Programming Note

True and False

Many computer languages provide a logical or Boolean data type that consists of two values only, true and false, for evaluating relational expressions. In these languages relational and logical expressions are restricted to yielding one of these values, and selection statements are restricted to evaluating only relational and logical expressions. This is not the case in C.

In C any expression can be tested within a selection statement, be it a relational, arithmetic, or assignment expression, or even a function call. Within a selection statement, an expression that evaluates to 0 or a function that returns a 0 is considered as false, while any non-0 value (negative or positive) is considered as true. If a relational or logical expression is tested, however, the expression itself will yield only 1 or 0; 1 if the relational or logical expression is true and 0 if it is false.

Sometimes it is convenient to create the following two symbolic constants:

```
#define TRUE 1;
#define FALSE 0;
```

These constants are convenient as values to clearly identify a true or false condition. For example, consider the algorithm

```
if (it is a leap year)
  set yearType to TRUE
else
  set yearType to FALSE
```

A C programmer will automatically understand this to mean "set yearType to 1" and "set yearType to 0," respectively.

as 2 percent of the number entered. In the second run, the taxable income was more than \$20,000, and the `else` part of the `if-else` statement

```
taxes = HIGHRATE * (taxable - CUTOFF) + FIXEDAMT;
```

was used to yield a correct tax computation of

```
taxes = 0.025 * ($30,000. - $20,000.) + $400. = $650.
```

As always in C, a compound statement can be used wherever a single statement is valid. The syntax for an `if-else` statement that uses a compound statement in both of its `if` and `else` parts is

```
if (expression)
{

  statement1;    /* as many statements as necessary */
  statement2;    /* can be placed within each brace pair */
      •
      •
      •
```

```
  statementn;
}
else
{
  statementa;
  statementb;
      •
      •
      •
  statementnn;
}
```

Program 4.3 illustrates using a compound statement within an `if-else` statement.

Program 4.3

```
#include <stdio.h>

int main()
{
  char tempType;
  float temp, fahren, celsius;

  printf("Enter the temperature to be converted: ");
  scanf("%f",&temp);
  printf("Enter an f if the temperature is in Fahrenheit\n");
  printf(" or a c if the temperature is in Celsius: ");
  scanf("\n%c", &tempType);  /* see footnote on page 111 */

  if (tempType == 'f')
  {
    celsius = (5.0 / 9.0) * (temp - 32.0);
    printf("\nThe equivalent Celsius temperature is %6.2f\n", celsius);
  }
  else
  {
    fahren = (9.0 / 5.0) * temp + 32.0;
    printf("\nThe equivalent Fahrenheit temperature is %6.2f\n", fahren);
  }

  return 0;
}
```

Programming Note

Placement of Braces in a Compound Statement

A common practice for some programmers is to place the opening brace of a compound statement on the same line as the `if` and `else` statements. Using this convention, the `if` statement in Program 4.3 would appear as shown below. This placement is a matter of style only—both styles are used and both are correct. However, you should adopt only one of these styles and be consistent in using the same style throughout each of your programs.

```
if (tempType == 'f') {
  celsius = (5.0 / 9.0) * (temp - 32.0);
  printf("\nThe equivalent Celsius temperature is %6.2f", celsius);
}
else {
  fahren = (9.0 / 5.0) * temp + 32.0;
  printf("\nThe equivalent Fahrenheit temperature is %6.2f", fahren);
}
```

Program 4.3 checks whether the value in `tempType` is `f`. If the value is an `f`, the compound statement corresponding to the `if` part of the `if-else` statement, that is, the following lines are executed:

```
{
  celsius = (5.0 / 9.0) * (temp - 32.0);
  printf("\nThe equivalent Celsius temperature is %6.2f\n", celsius);
}
```

Any other letter than an `f` results in the following compound statement, which corresponds to the `else` part of the `if-else` statement, to be executed:

```
{
  fahren = (9.0 / 5.0) * temp + 32.0;
  printf("\nThe equivalent Fahrenheit temperature is %6.2f\n", fahren);
}
```

Following is a sample run of Program 4.3.

```
Enter the temperature to be converted: 212
Enter an f if the temperature is in Fahrenheit
 or a c if the temperature is in Celsius: f
The equivalent Celsius temperature is 100.00
```

Although any expression can be tested by an `if-else` statement, as with the one-way `if` statement, only relational expressions are generally used. However, statements such as

```
if (num)
  printf("Bingo!");
else
  printf("You lose!");
```

are valid. Because `num`, by itself, is a valid expression, the message `Bingo!` is displayed if `num` has any non-0 value and the message `You lose!` is displayed if num has a value of 0.

Programming Note

Avoiding a Common Problem

Almost every professional C programmer, at one time or another, has inadvertently used an assignment symbol, =, in place of the relational symbol, == . Because the resulting expression is valid, the compiler will not flag this with either a warning or error message.

To avoid this error whenever equality to a constant is being tested, you can code the expression with the constant to the left of the relational operator. Thus, instead of coding an expression such as `age == 40`, code the expression as `40 == age`. This simple modification ensures that a compiler error will be generated if the assignment operator, =, is substituted for the relational operator, ==. The error message will be `"the left operand must be an lvalue"` or a similar message informing you that a constant is not valid on the left side of an assignment operator. This error will alert you to your mistake and prevent a syntactically correct, but logically flawed expression from finding its way into your final code.

Many companies that do internal code reviews, in fact, now mandate this coding convention.

EXERCISES 4.2

Short Answer Questions

1. Write appropriate `if` statements for each of the following conditions:
   a. If `angle` is equal to 90 degrees, print the message "The angle is a right angle", else print the message that "The angle is not a right angle".
   b. If the `temperature` is above 100 degrees, display the message "above the boiling point of water", else display the message "below the boiling point of water".
   c. If the number is positive, add the number to `positiveSum`, else add the number to `negativeSum`.
   d. If the slope is less than .5, set the variable `flag` to 0, else set `flag` to 1.
   e. If the difference between `num1` and `num2` is less than .001, set the variable `approx` to `0`, else calculate `approx` as the quantity `(num1 - num2)/2.0`.
   f. If the difference between `temp1` and `temp2` exceeds 2.3 degrees, calculate `error` as `(temp1 - temp2) * factor`.
   g. If `x` is greater than `y` and `z` is less than 20, read in a value for the integer `p`.
   h. If `distance` is greater than 20 and it is less than 35, read in a value for the integer `time`.

2. Write either an `if` or `if-else` statement, as appropriate, for the following flowcharts:

a.

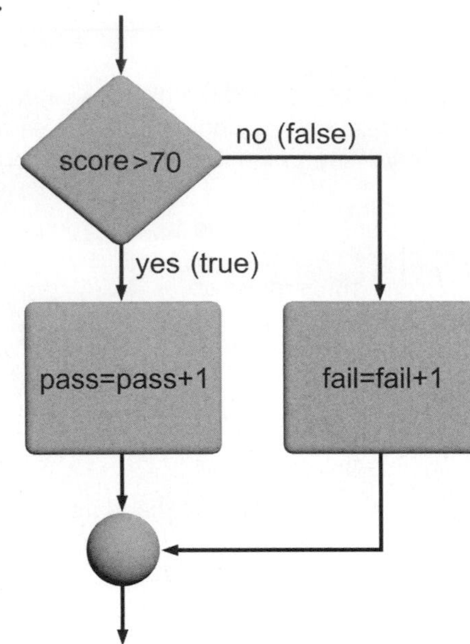

b.

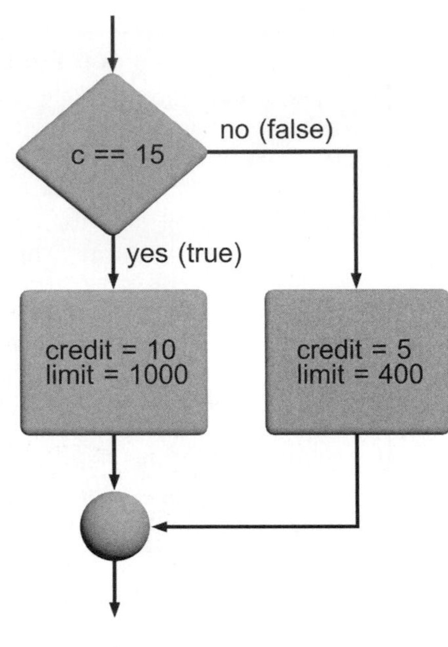

c.

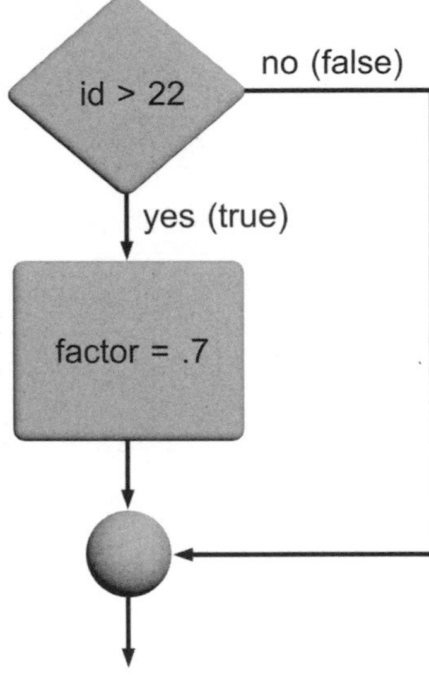

d.

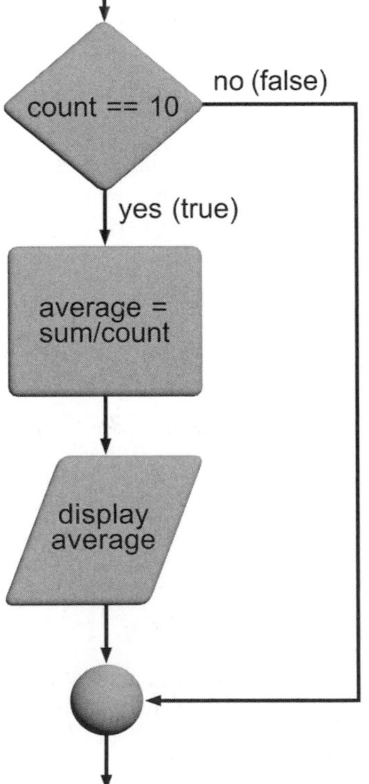

3. The following program displays the message `Hello there!` regardless of the letter input. Determine where the error is and, if possible, why the program always causes the message to be displayed.

```
#include <stdio.h>
int main()
{
  char letter;
  printf("Enter a letter: ");
  scanf("%c",&letter);
  if (letter = 'm') printf("Hello there!");
  return 0;
}
```

Programming Exercises

1. a. If money is left in a particular bank for more than five years, the interest rate given by the bank is 7.5 percent, else the interest rate is 5.4 percent. Write a C program that uses the `scanf()` function to accept the number of years into the variable `numYrs` and display the appropriate interest rate depending on the value input into `numYrs`.
   b. How many runs should you make for the program written in Exercise 1a to verify that it is operating correctly? What data should you input in each of the program runs?

2. a. In a pass/fail course, a student passes if the grade is greater than or equal to 70 and fails if the grade is lower. Write a C program that accepts a grade and prints the message `A passing grade` or `A failing grade`, as appropriate.
   b. How many runs should you make for the program written in Exercise 2a to verify that it is operating correctly? What data should you input in each of the program runs?

3. a. Write a C program to compute and display a person's weekly salary as determined by the following specification:

   If the hours worked are less than or equal to 40, the person receives $8.00 per hour; else the person receives $320.00 plus $12.00 for each hour worked over 40 hours.

   The program should request the hours worked as input and should display the salary as output.
   b. How many runs should you make for the program written in Exercise 3a to verify that it is operating correctly? What data should you input in each of the program runs?

4. a. A senior salesperson is paid $800 a week and a junior salesperson $375 a week. Write a C program that accepts as input a salesperson's status in the character variable `status`. If `status` equals `'s'`, the senior person's salary should be displayed, else the junior person's salary should be output.
   b. How many runs should you make for the program written in Exercise 4a to verify that it is operating correctly? What data should you input in each of the program runs?

5. Write a C program that asks the user to input two numbers. After your program accepts these numbers using one or more `scanf()` function calls, have your program check the numbers. If the first number entered is greater than the second number, print the message `The first number is greater than the second`, else print the message

`The first number is not greater than the second.` Test your program by entering the numbers 5 and 8 and then using the numbers 2 and 11. What will your program display if the two numbers entered are equal?

6. The area of any triangle with sides *a*, *b*, and *c* can be computed using Heron's formula
$area = \sqrt{s(s-a)(s-b)(s-c)}$ where $s = (a + b + c)/2$

Using these formulas, write a C program that accepts values for the sides *a*, *b*, and *c* from the user. Then calculate and display the area for the case where the value of *s(s-a)(s-b)(s-c)* is positive. If the value of this expression is negative, your program should display a message indicating that the three sides entered do not represent the sides of a triangle.

7. **a.** Write a C program that accepts a character using the `scanf()` function and determines if the character is a lowercase letter. A lowercase letter is any character that is greater than or equal to `"a"` and less than or equal to `"z"`. If the entered character is a lowercase letter, display the message `The character just entered is a lowercase letter.` If the entered letter is not lowercase, display the message `The character just entered is not a lowercase letter.`
   b. Modify the program written for Exercise 7a to determine if the character entered is an uppercase letter. An uppercase letter is any character greater than or equal to `"A"` and less than or equal to `"Z"`.

8. **a.** Write a C program that first determines if an entered character is a lowercase letter (see Exercise 7). If the letter is lowercase, determine and print out its position in the alphabet. For example, if the entered letter is `c`, the program should print out `3`, since `c` is the third letter in the alphabet. (*Hint:* If the entered character is lowercase, its position can be determined by subtracting `"a"` from the letter and adding 1.)
   b. Modify the program written for Exercise 8a for uppercase letters. (*Hint:* If the entered character is uppercase, its position can be determined by subtracting `"A"` from the letter and adding 1.)

4.3 The `if-else` Chain

As we have seen, an `if-else` statement can contain any valid single or compound C statements. This means that one or more `if-else` statements can themselves be included within either or both parts of an `if-else` statement. Including one or more `if-else` statements within an `if` or `if-else` statement is referred to as a **nested `if` statement**.

Generally, the most useful nested `if` statement occurs when a second `if-else` statement is placed within the `else` part of an `if-else` statement.

This takes the form

```
if (expression1)
  statement1;
else
  if (expression2)
    statement2;
  else
    statement3;
```

As with all C programs, the white space we have used is not required. In fact, the above construction is so common that it is typically written using the following arrangement:

```
if (expression1)
  statement1;
else if (expression2)
  statement2;
else
  statement3;
```

This construction is called an **`if-else` chain,** and is used extensively in many programming problems. In this construction, each condition is evaluated in order, and if any condition is true, the corresponding statement is executed and all further processing of the chain stops. Thus, the final `else` statement is only executed if none of the previous conditions are satisfied. This serves as a default or catch-all case that is useful for detecting an impossible or error condition. Leaving out this final catch-all can result in some conditions being unhandled; whether this is acceptable or not depends on the application. Figure 4.5 illustrates the flowchart for this `if-else` chain.

The chain can be continued indefinitely by repeatedly making the last statement another `if-else` statement. Thus, the general form of an `if-else` chain is

```
if (expression1)
  statement1;
else if (expression2)
  statement2;
else if (expression3)
  statement3;
  .
  .
  .
else if (expressionn)
  statementn;
else
  lastStatement;
```

As with all C statements, each individual statement can be a compound statement. To illustrate an `if-else` chain, Program 4.4 displays a person's marital status corresponding to a letter input. The following letter codes are used:

Marital Status	Input Code
Married	M
Single	S
Divorced	D
Widowed	W

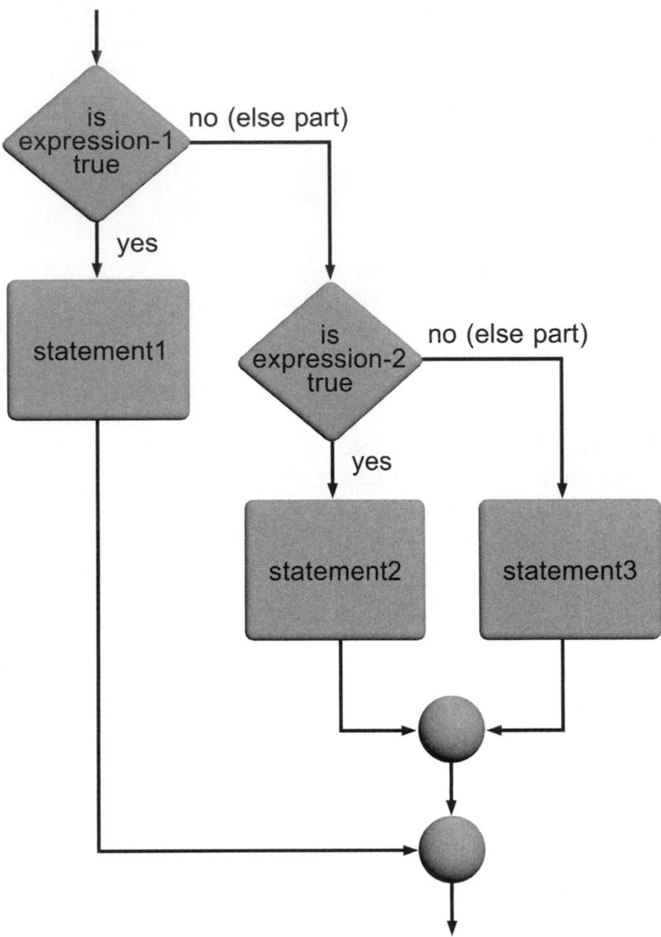

Figure 4.5 The `if-else` chain's flowchart

Program 4.4

```
#include <stdio.h>
int main()
{
  char marcode;

  printf("Enter a marital code: ");
  scanf("%c", &marcode);

  if (marcode == 'M')
    printf("\nIndividual is married.\n");
  else if (marcode == 'S')
```

```
      printf("\nIndividual is single.\n");
    else if (marcode == 'D')
      printf("\nIndividual is divorced.\n");
    else if (marcode == 'W')
      printf("\nIndividual is widowed.\n");
    else
      printf("\nAn invalid code was entered.\n");

    return 0;
}
```

As a final example illustrating an `if-else` chain, let us calculate the monthly income of a salesperson using the following commission schedule:

Monthly Sales	Income
greater than or equal to $50,000	$575 plus 16% of sales
less than $50,000 but greater than or equal to $40,000	$550 plus 14% of sales
less than $40,000 but greater than or equal to $30,000	$525 plus 12% of sales
less than $30,000 but greater than or equal to $20,000	$500 plus 9% of sales
less than $20,000 but greater than or equal to $10,000	$450 plus 5% of sales
less than $10,000	$400 plus 3% of sales

The following `if-else` chain can be used to determine the correct monthly income, where the variable `monthlySales` is used to store the salesperson's current monthly sales:

```
if (monthlySales >= 50000.00)
  income = 575.00 + .16 * monthlySales;
else if (monthlySales >= 40000.00)
  income = 550.00 + .14 * monthlySales;
else if (monthlySales >= 30000.00)
  income = 525.00 + .12 * monthlySales;
else if (monthlySales >= 20000.00)
  income = 500.00 + .09 * monthlySales;
else if (monthlySales >= 10000.00)
  income = 450.00 + .05 * monthlySales;
else
  income =400.000 + .03 * monthlySales;
```

This example makes use of the fact that the chain is stopped once a true condition is found. This is accomplished by checking for the highest monthly sales first. If the salesperson's monthly sales are less than $50,000, the `if-else` chain continues checking for the next highest sales amount until the correct category is obtained.

Program 4.5 uses this `if-else` chain to calculate and display the income corresponding to the value of monthly sales input in the `scanf()` function.

Program 4.5

```
#include <stdio.h>

int main()
{
  float monthlySales, income;

  printf("Enter the value of monthly sales: ");
  scanf("%f", &monthlySales);

  if (monthlySales >= 50000.00)
    income = 575.00 + .16 * monthlySales;
  else if (monthlySales >= 40000.00)
    income = 550.00 + .14 * monthlySales;
  else if (monthlySales >= 30000.00)
    income = 525.00 + .12 * monthlySales;
  else if (monthlySales >= 20000.00)
    income = 500.00 + .09 * monthlySales;
  else if (monthlySales >= 10000.00)
    income = 450.00 + .05 * monthlySales;
  else
    income = 400.00 + .03 * monthlySales;

  printf("The income is $%7.2f\n",income);

  return 0;
}
```

A sample run using Program 4.5 is illustrated below.

```
Enter the value of monthly sales: 36243.89
The income is $4874.27
```

Indentation used within an `if-else` is always irrelevant as far as the compiler is concerned. Whether the indentation exists or not, *the compiler will, by default, associate an* `else` *with the closest previous unpaired* `if`*, unless braces are used to alter this default pairing.* For example, consider the following nested `if` statement code:

```
if (hours < 40)
```

```
  if (hours > 20)
    printf("Snap\n");
else
  printf("Pop\n");
```

Although, the indentation makes it appear that the following is intended:

```
if (hours < 40)
{
  if (hours > 20)
    printf("Snap\n");
}
else
  printf("Pop\n");
```

the code will actually be compiled as

```
if (hours < 40)
{
  if (hours > 20)
    printf("Snap");
  else
    printf("Pop");
}
```

This grouping occurs because the last `else` in the original code is, by default, paired with the closest unpaired `if`, which corresponds to the `if(hours > 20)`. This default pairing can, of course, be altered by explicitly including braces to indicate the desired pairing.

EXERCISES 4.3

Short Answer Questions

1. What output is produced by the following section of code?

```
float x = 22.5f;
float y = 18.2f;
if ( x > y)
  printf(" The if part is true\n");
else
   printf("The else part is true\n");
```

2. Determine the value displayed for `factor` by the following section of code:

```
int a = 2;
int b = 0;
if ( a < b)
   factor = .02;
```

```
else if ( a == b)
  factor = .04;
else if (!a)
  factor = .06;
else if (!b && !a)
  factor = .08;
else if (!b || !a)
  factor = 1.02;
else if(!b)
  factor = 1.04;
else
  factor = 1.06;
printf("factor = %f\n", factor);
```

3. Write C code for the following flowcharts:

a.

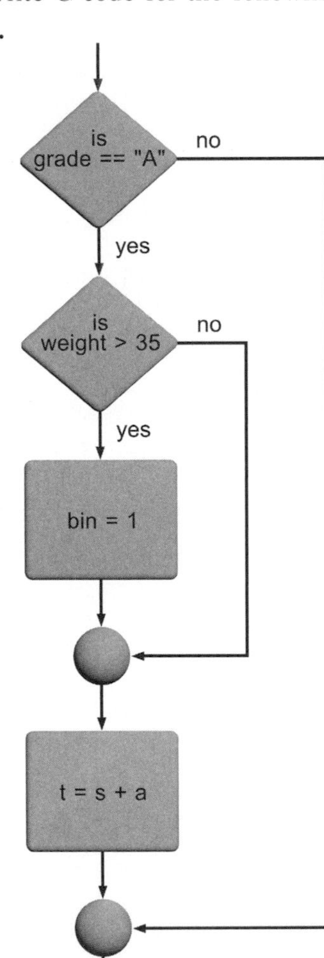

b.

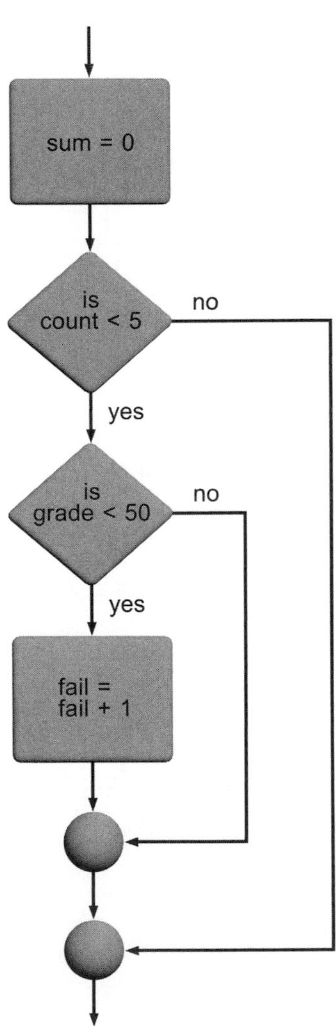

4. Using the commission schedule from Program 4.5, the following program calculates monthly income:

```
#include <stdio.h>
int main()
{
  float monthlySales, income;
  printf("Enter the value of monthly sales: ");
  scanf("%f", &monthlySales);

  if (monthlySales >= 50000.00)
    income = 575.00 + .16 * monthlySales;
  if (monthlySales >= 40000.00 && monthlySales < 50000.00)
    income = 550.00 + .14 * monthlySales;
  if (monthlySales >= 30000.00 && monthlySales < 40000.00)
    income = 525.00 + .12 * monthlySales;
  if (monthlySales >= 20000.00 && monthlySales < 30000.00)
    income = 500.00 + .09 * monthlySales;
  if (monthlySales >= 10000.00 && monthlySales < 20000.00)
    income = 450.00 + .05 * monthlySales;
  if (monthlySales < 10000.00)
    income = 400.00 + .03 * monthlySales;
  printf("The income is $%7.2f\n",income);
  return 0;
}
```

a. Will this program produce the same output as Program 4.5?
b. Which program is better and why?

5. The following program was written to produce the same result as Program 4.5:

```
#include <stdio.h>
int main()
{
  float monthlySales, income;
  printf("Enter the value of monthly sales: ");
  scanf("%f", &monthlySales);
  if (monthlySales < 10000.00)
    income = 400.00 + .03 * monthlySales;
  else if (monthlySales >= 10000.00)
    income = 450.00 + .05 * monthlySales;
  else if (monthlySales >= 20000.00)
    income = 500.00 + .09 * monthlySales;
  else if (monthlySales >= 30000.00)
    income = 525.00 + .12 * monthlySales;
  else if (monthlySales >= 40000.00)
    income = 550.00 + .14 * monthlySales;
  else if (monthlySales >= 50000.00)
    income = 575.00 + .16 * monthlySales;
```

```
    printf("The income is $%7.2f\n",income);
    return 0;
}
```

a. Will this program run?
b. What does this program do?
c. For what values of monthly sales does this program calculate the correct income?

Programming Exercises

1. A student's letter grade is calculated according to the following schedule. Write a C program that accepts a student's numerical grade, converts the numerical grade to an equivalent letter grade, and displays the letter grade.

Numerical Grade	Letter Grade
greater than or equal to 90	A
less than 90 but greater than or equal to 80	B
less than 80 but greater than or equal to 70	C
less than 70 but greater than or equal to 60	D
less than 60	F

2. The interest rate used on funds deposited in a bank is determined by the amount of time the money is left on deposit. For a particular bank, the following schedule is used. Write a C program that accepts the time that funds are left on deposit and displays the interest rate corresponding to the time entered.

Time on Deposit	Interest Rate
greater than or equal to 5 years	.045
less than 5 years but greater than or equal to 4 years	.04
less than 4 years but greater than or equal to 3 years	.035
less than 3 years but greater than or equal to 2 years	.03
less than 2 years but greater than or equal to 1 year	.025
less than 1 year	.02

3. Write a C program that accepts a number followed by one space and then a letter. If the letter following the number is `f`, the program is to treat the number entered as a temperature in degrees Fahrenheit, convert the number to the equivalent degrees Celsius, and print a suitable display message. If the letter following the number is `c`, the program is to treat the number entered as a temperature in Celsius, convert the number to the equivalent degrees Fahrenheit, and print a suitable display message. If the letter is neither `f` nor `c`, the program should print a message indicating that the data entered is incorrect and terminate. Use an `if-else` chain in your program and make use of the conversion formulas

   *Celsius = (5.0 / 9.0) * (Fahrenheit — 32.0)*
   *Fahrenheit = (9.0 / 5.0) * Celsius + 32.0*

4.4 The switch Statement

A switch statement is a specialized selection statement that can be used in place of an if-else chain where exact equality to one or more integer constants is required. Such cases occur with some regularity in real-world applications. An example of such an if-else chain is

```
if (material == 1)
{
  factor = 1.5;
  density = 2.76;
}
else if (material == 3)
{
  factor = 2.5;
  density = 2.85;
}
else if (material == 7)
  factor = 3.5;
  density = 3.14;
{
else
{
  factor = 1.0;
  density = 1.25;
}
```

As was noted in the last Programming Note in Section 4.2, using the == operator can lead to a common programming error when it is inadvertently typed as the assignment operator, =. The main advantages of using a switch statement are that it avoids using the equality operator, ==, avoids the braces needed for compound statements internal to an if-else chain, and frequently results in simpler code.

The general form of a switch statement is

```
switch (integer-expression)
{ /* start of compound statement */
  case value1 :  <----------  terminated with a colon
    statement1;
    statement2;
        .
        .
    break;
  case value2:  <----------  terminated with a colon

    statementm;
    statementn;
        .
        .
    break;
        .
        .
```

```
        .
  case valuen:  <------------  terminated with a colon
    statementw;
    statementx;
        .
        .
    break;
  default:  <------------  terminated with a colon
    statementaa;
    statementbb;
        .
        .
} /* end of switch and compound statement */
```

As seen in this syntax, the `switch` statement uses four new keywords: `switch`, `case`, `default`, and `break`. Let's see what each of these words does.

The keyword `switch` identifies the start of the `switch` statement. The *`integer-expression`* in parentheses following this word is evaluated first. If the expression results in a noninteger value, a compiler error occurs. The integer value of the expression is then compared to each of the values listed after the keyword `case` contained within the compound statement. Again, a compilation error occurs if any of these values are not integer constants or variables.

Thus, internal to the `switch` statement, the keyword `case` identifies the values that will be compared to the value of the `switch` expression. This expression's value is compared to each of these `case` values in the order that these values are listed until a match is found. When a match occurs, execution begins with the statement immediately following the match. Thus, as illustrated in Figure 4.6, the value of the expression determines where in the `switch` statement execution actually begins.

The flowchart corresponding to a `switch` statement is illustrated in Figure 4.7.

Any number of `case` labels may be contained within a `switch` statement, in any order. If the value of the expression does not match any of the `case` values, however, no statement is executed unless the keyword `default` is encountered. The word `default` is optional and operates the same as the last `else` in an `if-else` chain. If the value of the expression does not match any of the `case` values, program execution begins with the statement following the word `default`.

Once an entry point has been located by the `switch` statement, no further `case` evaluations are done; this means that unless a `break` statement is encountered, all statements that follow, until the closing brace of the `switch` statement, will be executed. This is the reason for the `break` statement, which identifies the end of a particular `case` and causes an immediate exit from the `switch` statement. Thus, just as the word `case` identifies possible starting points in the compound statement, the `break` statement determines termination points. If the `break` statements are omitted, all `case`s following the matching `case` value, including the `default` `case`, are executed.

Program 4.6 uses a `switch` statement to select the arithmetic operation (addition, multiplication, or division) to be performed on two numbers depending on the value of the variable `opselect`.

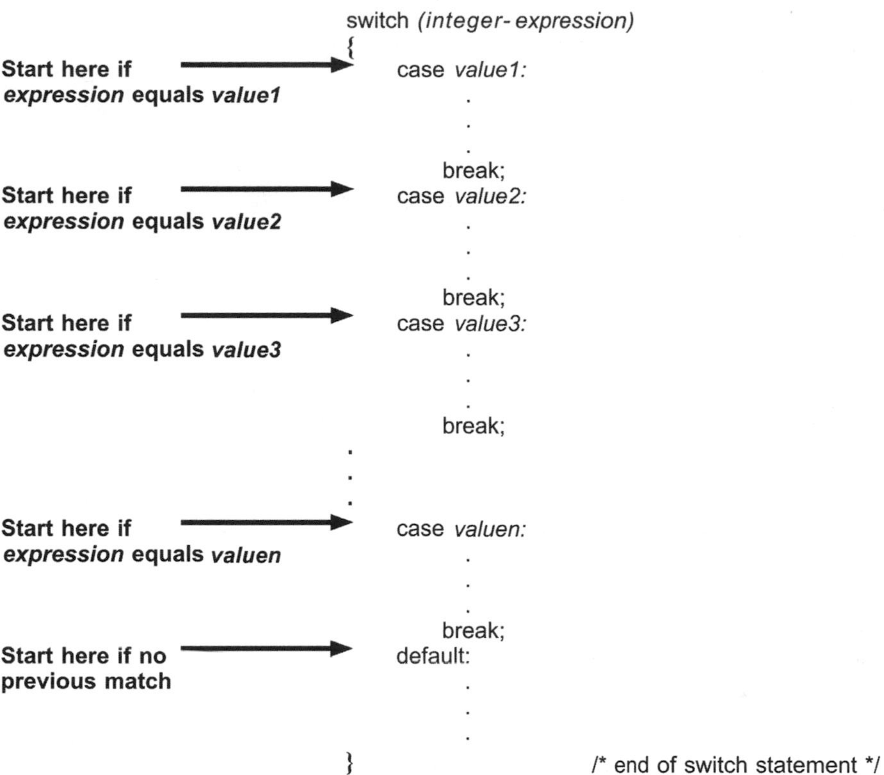

Figure 4.6 The `expression` determines the entry point

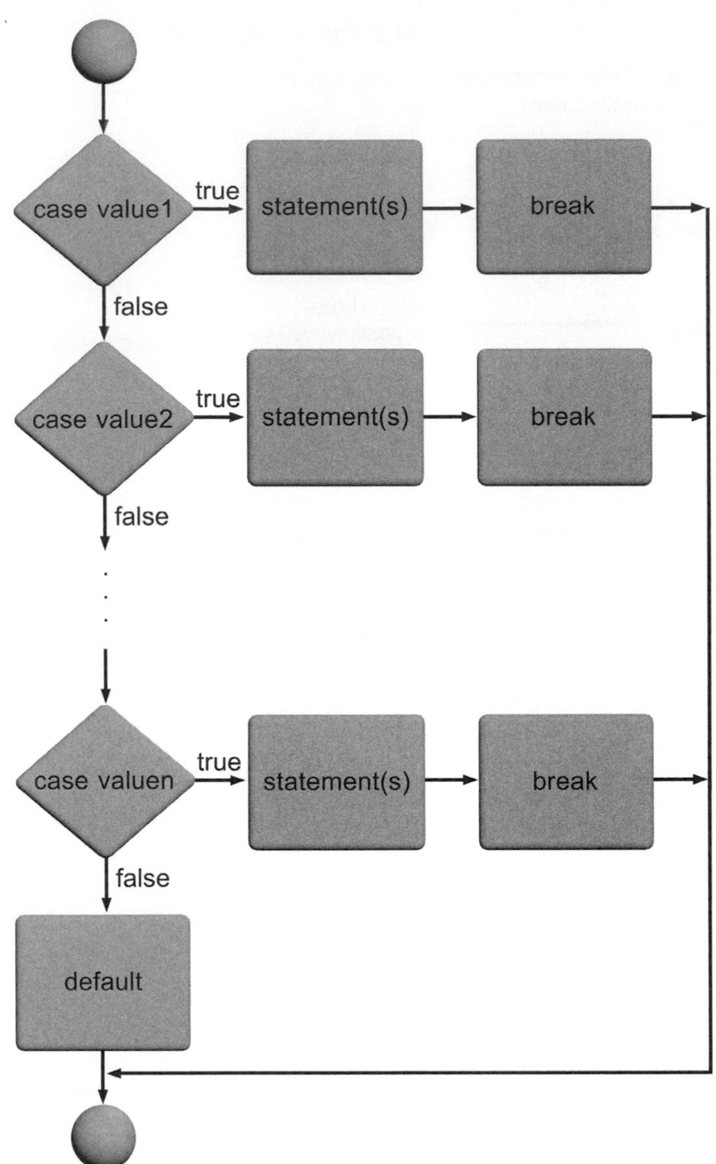

Figure 4.7 The `switch` flowchart

Program 4.6

```
#include <stdio.h>

int main()
{
  int opselect;
  float fnum, snum;

  printf("Please type in two numbers: ");
  scanf("%f %f", &fnum, &snum);
  printf("Enter a select code:");
  printf("\n 1 for addition");
  printf("\n 2 for multiplication");
  printf("\n 3 for division : ");
  scanf("%d", &opselect);

  switch (opselect)
  {
    case 1:
      printf("The sum of the numbers entered is %6.3f\n", fnum+snum);
      break;
    case 2:
      printf("The product of the numbers entered is %6.3f\n", fnum*snum);
      break;
    case 3:
      if (snum != 0.0)
        printf("The first number divided by the second is %6.3f\n",fnum/snum);
      else
       printf("Division by zero is not allowed\n");
      break; /* this break is optional */
  } /* end of switch statement */

  return 0;
} /* end of main() */
```

Program 4.6 was run twice. The resulting displays clearly identify the case selected. The results are

```
Please type in two numbers: 12 3
Enter a select code:
1 for addition
2 for multiplication
3 for division : 2
The product of the numbers entered is 36.000
```

and

```
Please type in two numbers: 12 3
Enter a select code:
1 for addition
2 for multiplication
3 for division : 3
The first number divided by the second is 4.000
```

In reviewing Program 4.6, notice the `break` statement in the last `case` (line 29). Although this `break` is not necessary, it is a good practice to terminate the last `case` in a `switch` statement with a `break`. This prevents a possible program error later if an additional case is subsequently added to the `switch` statement. With the addition of a new `case`, the `break` between `cases` becomes necessary; having the `break` in place ensures you will not forget to include it at the time of the modification.

When constructing a `switch` statement, multiple `case` values can be stacked together, and the `default` label is always optional. For example, consider the following, which stacks together `case 3`, `case 4` and `case 5`, and additionally, does not include a `default` case.

```
switch (number)
{
  case 1:
    printf("Have a Good Morning\n");
    break;
  case 2:
    printf("Have a Happy Day\n");
    break;
  case 3: case 4: case 5:
    printf("Have a Nice Evening\n");
}
```

If the value stored in the variable `number` is `1`, the message `Have a Good Morning` is displayed. Similarly, if the value of `number` is `2`, the second message is displayed. Finally, by stacking the last three `cases` together, the last message is displayed if the value of `number` is `3` or `4` or `5`. Also, because there is no `default`, no message is printed if the value of `number` is not one of the listed `case` values. Although it is good programming practice to list `case` values in increasing order, this is not required by the `switch` statement. A `switch` statement can have any number of `case` values, in any order. Thus, values do not have to be consecutive and only values that need to be tested need to be listed.

Because character data are always converted to their integer values in an expression, a `switch` statement can also be used to "switch" based on the value of a character expression.

For example, assuming that choice is a character variable, the following switch statement is valid:

```
switch(choice)
{
  case 'a': case 'e': case 'i': case 'o': case 'u':
    printf("\nThe character in choice is a vowel");
    break;
  default:
    printf("\nThe character in choice is not a vowel");
} /* end of switch statement */
```

This section of code will correctly identify the character in the variable choice as either a vowel or not.

EXERCISES 4.4

Short Answer Questions

1. Rewrite the following if-else chain (this is the same code listed at the beginning of this section) using a switch statement:

```
if (material == 1)
{
  factor = 1.5;
  density = 2.76;
}
else if (material == 3)
{
  factor = 2.5;
  density = 2.85;
}
else if (material == 7)
  factor = 3.5;
  density = 3.14;
{
else
{
  factor = 1.0;
  density = 1.25;
}
```

2. Rewrite the following `if-else` chain using a `switch` statement:

```
if (letterGrade == 'A')
  printf("The numerical grade is between 90 and 100");
else if (letterGrade == 'B')
  printf("The numerical grade is between 80 and 89.9");
else if (letterGrade == 'C')
  printf("The numerical grade is between 70 and 79.9");
else if (letterGrade == 'D');
  printf("How are you going to explain this one");
else
{
  printf("Of course I had nothing to do with my grade.");
  printf("\nThe professor was really off the wall.");
}
```

3. Rewrite the following `if-else` chain using a `switch` statement:

```
if (bondType == 1)
{
  inData();
  check();
}
else if (bondType == 2)
{
  dates();
  leapYr();
}
else if (bondType == 3)
{
  yield();
  maturity();
}
else if (bondType == 4)
{
  price();
  roi();
}
else if (bondType == 5)
{
  files();
  save();
}
else if (bondType == 6)
{
  retrieve();
  screen();
}
```

Programming Exercises

1. Each disk drive in a shipment of devices is stamped with a code from 1 through 4, which indicates a drive manufacturer as follows:

Code	Disk Drive Manufacturer
1	3M Corporation
2	Maxell Corporation
3	Sony Corporation
4	Verbatim Corporation

Write a C program that accepts the code number as an input and, based on the value entered, displays the correct disk drive manufacturer.

2. Rewrite Program 4.4 in Section 4.3 using a `switch` statement.
3. Determine why the `if-else` chain in Program 4.5 cannot be replaced with a `switch` statement.
4. Repeat Programming Exercise 3 in Section 4.3 using a `switch` statement instead of an `if-else` chain.
5. Rewrite Program 4.6 using a character variable for the select code. (*Hint:* Review data entry of characters in Section 3.3 if your program does not operate as you think it should.)

4.5 Case Study: Data Validation

An important use of C's `if` statements is to validate data by checking for clearly invalid cases. For example, a date such as 5/33/09 contains an obviously invalid day. Similarly, the division of any number by 0 within a program, such as 14/0, should not be allowed. Both of these examples illustrate the need for a technique called **defensive programming**, where the program includes code to check for improper data before an attempt is made to process it further. The defensive programming technique of checking user input data for erroneous or unreasonable data is referred to as **input data validation**. We will show you how to check data, as it is being entered by a user, in Chapter 6. In this case study, we will see how defensive programming is used to check data before using it in a computation.

Requirements Specification

In this case study, you are asked to write a C program to calculate the square root and the reciprocal of a user-entered number. Before calculating these values, you are also required to validate that the number is not negative before attempting to take its square root, and that the number is not 0 before calculating the number's reciprocal value.

Analyze the Problem

The requirements for this problem specify that the program is to accept a single number as an input, validate the entered number, and based on the validation produce two possible outputs: if the number is nonnegative, we are to determine its square root and if the input number is not 0, we are to determine its reciprocal value.

Select an Algorithm

Because the square root of a negative number does not exist as a real number and the reciprocal of 0 cannot be taken, our program will contain input data validation statements that screen the user input data and avoid these two cases. The pseudocode that can be used to achieve this is

```
Display a program purpose message
Display a prompt requesting a user-input number
Accept a user-input number
if the number is negative
    Print a message that the square root cannot be taken
else
   Calculate and display the square root
endif
if the number is zero then
   print a message that the reciprocal cannot be taken
else
   calculate and display the reciprocal
endif
```

Write the Program

The C code corresponding to our pseudocode solution is found in Program 4.7.

Program 4.7

```
#include <stdio.h>
#include <math.h>
int main()
{
  float usenum;

  printf("This program calculates the square root and\n");
  printf("reciprocal (1/number) of a number\n");
  printf("\nPlease enter a number: ");
  scanf("%f", &usenum);

  if (usenum < 0.0)
```

```
    printf("The square root of a negative number does not exist.\n");
  else
    printf("The square root of %f is %f\n", usenum, sqrt(usenum));

  if (usenum == 0.0)
    printf("The reciprocal of zero does not exist.\n");
  else
    printf("The reciprocal of %f is %f\n", usenum, 1/usenum);

  return 0;
}
```

Program 4.7 is a rather straightforward program containing two separate `if` statements. The first `if` statement

```
if (usenum < 0.0)
  printf("The square root of a negative number does not exist.\n");
else
  printf("The square root of %f is %f\n", usenum, sqrt(usenum));
```

checks for a negative input number; if the number is negative, a message indicating that the square root of a negative number cannot be taken is displayed, else the square root is taken.

The second `if` statement

```
if (usenum == 0.0)
  printf("The reciprocal of zero does not exist.\n");
else
  printf("The reciprocal of %f is %f\n", usenum, 1/usenum);
```

determines whether the entered number is 0; if it is a message indicating that the reciprocal of 0 cannot be taken is displayed, else the reciprocal is taken.

Test and Debug the Program

Test values should include an appropriate value for the input, such as 5, and values for the limiting cases, such as a negative and 0 input value. Following are test runs for each of these cases:

```
This program calculates the square root and
reciprocal (1/number) of a number

Please enter a number: 5

The square root of 5.000000 is 2.236068
The reciprocal of 5.000000 is 0.200000
```

and

```
This program calculates the square root and
reciprocal (1/number) of a number

Please enter a number: -6

The square root of a negative number does not exist
The reciprocal of -6.000000 is -0.166667
```

and

```
This program calculates the square root and
reciprocal (1/number) of a number

Please enter a number: 0

The square root of 0.000000 is 0.000000
The reciprocal of zero does not exist.
```

As indicated by these test runs, the program correctly identifies negative and 0 input values.

EXERCISES 4.5

Programming Exercises

1. **a.** Write a program that displays the following two prompts:

   ```
   Enter a month (use a 1 for Jan, etc.):
   Enter a day of the month:
   ```

   Your program should accept and store a number in a variable named `month` in response to the first prompt, and accept and store a number in a variable named `day` in response to the second prompt. If the month entered is not between 1 and 12 inclusive, the program should print a message informing the user that an invalid month has been entered. If the day entered is not between 1 and 31 inclusive, the program should print a message informing the user that an invalid day has been entered.

   b. What will your program do if the user types a number with a decimal point for the month? How can you ensure that your `if` statements check for an integer number?

   c. In a non-leap year, February has 28 days; the months January, March, May, July, August, October, and December have 31 days; and all other months have 30 days. Using this information, modify the program written in Exercise 1a to display a message when an invalid day is entered for a user-entered month. For this program ignore leap years.

2. a. The quadrant in which a line drawn from the origin resides is determined by the angle that the line makes with the positive X axis as follows:

Angle from the Positive X	Quadrant
Between 0 and 90 degrees	I
Between 90 and 180 degrees	II
Between 180 and 270 degrees	III
Between 270 and 360 degrees	IV

Using this information, write a C program that accepts the angle of the line as user input and determines and displays the quadrant appropriate to the input data. (*Note:* If the angle is exactly 0, 90, 180, or 270 degrees, the corresponding line does not reside in any quadrant but lies on an axis.)

b. Modify the program written for Exercise 2a so that a message is displayed that identifies an angle of 0 degrees as the positive X-axis, an angle of 90 degrees as the positive Y-axis, an angle of 180 degrees as the negative X-axis, and an angle of 270 degrees as the negative Y-axis.

3. a. All years that are evenly divisible by 400 or are evenly divisible by 4 and not evenly divisible by 100 are leap years. For example, since 1600 is evenly divisible by 400, the year 1600 was a leap year. Similarly, since 1988 is evenly divisible by 4 but not by 100, the year 1988 was also a leap year. Using this information, write a C program that accepts the year as a user input, determines if the year is a leap year, and displays an appropriate message that tells the user if the entered year is or is not a leap year.

b. Using the code written in Exercise 3a, redo Exercise 1c such that leap years are taken into account.

4. Based on an automobile's model year and weight, the state of New Jersey determines the car's weight class and registration fee using the following schedule:

Model Year Registration	Weight	Weight Class	Fee
1970 or earlier	less than 2,700 lbs	1	$16.50
	2,700 to 3,800 lbs	2	25.50
	more than 3,800 lbs	3	46.50
1971 to 1979	less than 2,700 lbs	4	27.00
	2,700 to 3,800 lbs	5	30.50
	more than 3,800 lbs	6	52.50
1980 or later	less than 3,500 lbs	7	35.50
	3,500 or more lbs	8	65.50

Using this information, write a C program that accepts the year and weight of an automobile and determines and displays the weight class and registration fee for the car.

5. A quadratic equation is an equation that either has the form $ax^2 + bx + c = 0$ or an equation that can be algebraically manipulated into this form. In this equation, x is the unknown variable, and a, b, and c are known constants. Although the constants b and c can be any numbers, including 0, the value of the constant a cannot be 0 (if a is 0, the equation would become a *linear equation* in x). Examples of quadratic equations are

   $5x^2 + 6x + 2 = 0$

   $x^2 - 7x + 20 = 0$

   $34x^2 + 16 = 0$

   In the first equation $a = 5$, $b = 6$, and $c = 2$; in the second equation $a = 1$, $b = -7$, and $c = 20$; and in the third equation $a = 34$, $b = 0$, and $c = 16$.

   The real roots of a quadratic equation can be calculated using the quadratic formula as follows:

   $$rootOne = \frac{-b + \sqrt{b^2 - 4ac}}{2a}$$

   and:

   $$rootTwo = \frac{-b - \sqrt{b^2 - 4ac}}{2a}$$

   Using these equations, write a C program to solve for the roots of a quadratic equation.

6. In the game of blackjack, the cards 2 through 10 are counted at their face values, regardless of suit, all face cards (jack, queen, and king) are counted as 10, and an ace is counted as either a 1 or an 11, depending on the total count of all the cards in a player's hand. The ace is counted as 11 only if the resulting total value of all cards in a player's hand does not exceed 21, else it is counted as a 1. Using this information, write a C program that accepts three card values as inputs (a 1 corresponding to an ace, a 2 corresponding to a two, and so on), calculates the total value of the hand appropriately, and displays the value of the three cards with a printed message.

4.6 Common Programming and Compiler Errors

In using the material presented in this chapter, be aware of the following possible programming and compiler errors:

Programming Errors

1. Using the assignment operator, =, in place of the relational operator, ==. This error can cause an enormous amount of frustration because any expression can be tested by an `if-else` statement. For example, the statement

```
if (opselect = 2)
  printf("Happy Birthday");
else
  printf("Good Day");
```

always results in the message Happy Birthday being printed, regardless of the initial value in the variable opselect. The reason for this is that the assignment expression opselect = 2 has a value of 2, which is considered a true value in C. The correct expression to determine the value in opselect is opselect == 2.

2. Letting the if-else statement appear to select an incorrect choice. Typically when debugging a program, the programmer mistakenly concentrates on the tested condition as the source of the problem. For example, assume that the following if-else statement is part of your program:

```
if (key == 'f')
{
  contemp = (5.0/9.0) * (intemp - 32.0);
  printf("Conversion to Celsius was done");
}
else
{
  contemp = (9.0/5.0) * intemp + 32.0;
  printf("Conversion to Fahrenheit was done");
}
```

   This statement will always display Conversion to Celsius was done when the variable key contains an f. Therefore, if this message is displayed when you believe key does not contain an f, you need to investigate key's value. As a general rule, whenever a selection statement does not act as you think it should, make sure to test your assumptions about the values assigned to the tested variables by displaying the values. If an unanticipated value is displayed, you have at least isolated the source of the problem to the variables themselves, rather than the structure of the if-else statement. From there, you need to determine where and how the incorrect value was obtained.

3. Nesting if statements without including braces to clearly indicate the desired structure. Without braces the compiler defaults to pairing elses with the closest previously unpaired ifs, which can destroy the original intent of the selection statement. To avoid this problem and to create code that is readily adaptable to change, it is useful to write all if-else statements as compound statements in the form

```
if (expression)
{
  one or more statements in here
}
else
{
  one or more statements in here
}
```

   This form ensures that, no matter how many statements are added later, the integrity and intent of the original if statement is maintained.

4. Using a single & or | in place of the logical && and logical || operators, respectively. Although this does not cause a syntax error (because the symbols & and | are themselves valid operators—see Section 14.2), these single symbol operators have significantly different meanings to the compiler than && and ||.

Compiler Errors

The following table summarizes common errors that will result in compilation errors and the typical error messages provided by Unix- and Windows-based compilers.

Error	Typical Unix-based Compiler Error Message	Typical Windows-based Compiler Error Message
Forgetting to surround a tested expression in parenthesis	`(S) Syntax error: possible missing '('?`	`syntax error: identifier ....`
Mistyping relational operators. For example using `=>` instead of `>=`	`(S) Unexpected text '>' encountered.`	`syntax error : 'operator'`

Using a construction such as
`if (expression)`
`  statement1;`
`  statement2;`
`else`
`    statement3`
	`(S) Unexpected text 'else' encountered.`
	(This error message occurs because the `else` keyword does not have a matching `if`. Because of `statement2` the `if` becomes a one-way `if` statement.)
		`illegal else without matching if`
		(This error message occurs because the `else` keyword does not have a matching `if`. Because of `statement2` the `if` becomes a one-way `if` statement.)

Forgetting to use quotes around single characters used in a relational expression	`(S) Undeclared identifier ...`	`'char': undeclared identifier`
Testing a floating-point expression in a `switch` statement	`(S) Expression must be an integral type.`	`switch expression of type '...' is illegal`
Forgetting the braces in a `switch` statement	`(S) Case label cannot be placed outside a switch statement. (S) Break statement cannot be placed outside a while, do, for, or switch statement.`	`illegal break illegal default`

4.7 Chapter Summary

1. Relational expressions, which are also called simple conditions, are used to compare operands. If a relational expression is true, the value of the expression is the integer 1. If the relational expression is false, it has an integer value of 0. Relational expressions are created using the following relational operators:

Relational Operator	Meaning	Example
<	less than	`age < 30`
>	greater than	`height > 6.2`
<=	less than or equal to	`taxable <= 20000`
>=	greater than or equal to	`temp >= 98.6`
==	equal to	`grade == 100`
!=	not equal to	`number != 250`

2. More complex conditions can be constructed from relational expressions using C's logical operators, `&&` (AND), `||` (OR), and `!` (NOT).

3. A one-way `if` statement has the general form

```
if (expression)
  statement;
```

4. A compound statement consists of any number of individual statements enclosed within the brace pair { and }. Compound statements are treated as a single unit and can be used anywhere a single statement is called for.

5. An `if-else` statement is used to select between two alternative statements based on the value of an expression. Although relational expressions are usually used for the tested expression, any valid expression can be used. All of C's selection statements interpret a non-0 value as true and a 0 value as false.

   The general form of an `if-else` statement is

```
if (expression)
  statement1;
else
  statement2;
```

   If the expression has a non-0 value, it is considered as true and `statement1` is executed; otherwise `statement2` is executed.

6. An `if-else` statement can contain other `if-else` statements. In the absence of braces, each `else` is associated with the closest unpaired `if`.

7. The `if-else` chain is a multiway selection statement having the general form

```
if (expression1)
  statement1;
else if (expression2)
  statement2;
else if (expression3)
  statement3;
       .
       .
       .
else if (expressionm)
  statementm;
else
  statementn;
```

Each expression is evaluated in the order it appears in the chain. Once an expression is true (has a non-0 value), the statement between that expression and the next `else if` or `else` is executed, and no further expressions are tested. The final `else` is optional, and the statement corresponding to the final `else` is only executed if none of the previous expressions are true.

8. The `switch` statement is a multiway selection statement. The general form of a `switch` statement is

```
switch (integer-expression)
{ /* start of compound statement */
  case value1:  <-------------- terminated with a colon
     statement1;
     statement2;
         .
    break;
  case value2:  <-------------- terminated with a colon
     statementm;
     statementn;
         .
    break;
         .
  case valuen:  <-------------- terminated with a colon
     statementw;
     statementx;
         .
    break;
  default:  <-------------- terminated with a colon
     statementaa;
     statementbb;
         .
} /* end of switch and compound statement */
```

For this statement the value of an integer expression is compared to a number of integer or character constants or constant expressions. Program execution is transferred to the first matching `case` and continues through the end of the `switch` statement unless an optional `break` statement is encountered. The `case`s in a `switch` statement can appear in any order, and an optional `default` case can be included. The `default` case is executed if none of the other cases is matched.

4.8 Chapter Supplement: Errors, Testing, and Debugging

The ideal in programming is to produce readable, error-free programs that work correctly and can be modified or changed with a minimum of testing. You can work toward this ideal by keeping in mind the different types of errors that can occur, when they are typically detected, and how to correct them.

An error can be detected:

1. Before a program is compiled
2. While the program is being compiled
3. While the program is being run
4. After the program has been executed and the output is being examined

In some cases, an error may not be detected at all. Errors detected by the compiler are referred to as **compile-time errors**, and errors that occur while the program is running are referred to as **run-time errors**. Other names for compile-time errors are **syntax errors** and **parse errors**, terms that emphasize the type of error being detected by the compiler.

By now, you have probably encountered numerous compile-time errors. Although beginning programmers tend to be frustrated by them, experienced programmers understand that the compiler is doing a lot of valuable checking, and that it is usually quite easy to correct any errors the compiler does detect. In addition, because these errors occur while the program is being developed, and not while a user is attempting to perform an important task, no one but the programmer ever knows they occurred; you fix them and they go away.

Run-time errors are much more troubling because they occur while a user is executing the program, and in most commercial systems the user is not the programmer. Although there are a number of error types that can cause a run-time error, such as a failure in the hardware, from a programming standpoint the majority of run-time errors are referred to as logic errors; that is faulty logic, which encompasses not fully thinking out what the program should do or not anticipating how a user can make the program fail, is at fault. For example, if a user inadvertently enters 12e4 in response to a request for an integer value and the program does not include any input-validation code, a run-time error occurs. As a programmer, the only way to protect against run-time errors is to sufficiently anticipate everything a person might do to cause errors, provide input-validation code, and submit your program to rigorous testing. Although beginning programmers tend to blame a user for an error caused by entering obviously incorrect data, professionals do not. They understand that a run-time error is a flaw in the final product that can cause damage to the reputation of both the program and programmer.

There are ways to detect errors both before a program is compiled and after it has been executed. The method for detecting errors before a program is compiled is called **desk checking**. Desk checking, which typically is performed while sitting at a desk with the code in front of you, refers to the process of checking the actual program code for syntax and logic errors. The method for detecting errors either while a program is executing or after it has executed is called **program testing**.

The terms **compile time** and **run time** distinguish between errors based on when the error is detected. In terms of preventing these errors, it is more fruitful to distinguish between them based on what causes them. As we have seen, compile errors are also named **syntax errors**, which refer to errors in either the structure or spelling of a statement. For example the statement

```
1 if ( a lt b
2 {
3   pintf("There are five syntax errors here\n")
4   printf(" Can you find tem);
5 }
```

contains five syntax errors. These errors are

1. The relational operator in line 1 is incorrect; it should be the symbol <.
2. The closing parenthesis is missing in line 1.
3. The function name `printf` is misspelled in line 3.
4. The statement in line 3 is not terminated with a semicolon, ;.
5. The string in line 4 is not terminated with double quotes.

All of these errors will be detected by the compiler when the program is compiled. This is true of all syntax errors because they violate the basic rules of C; if they are not discovered by desk checking, the compiler detects them and displays an error message.[3] In some cases, the error message is clear and the error is obvious; in other cases, it takes a little detective work to understand the error message displayed by the compiler. A very useful aid is that the line number of the statement that triggered the error is also provided. Because syntax errors are the only type of error that can be detected at compile time, the terms *compile-time errors* and *syntax errors* are used interchangeably. Strictly speaking, however, compile-time refers to when the error was detected and syntax refers to the type of error detected.

Note that the misspelling of the word `them` in the `printf()` function call in line 4 is not a syntax error. Although this spelling error will result in an undesirable output line being displayed, it is not a violation of C's syntactical rules. It is a simple case of a **typographical error**, commonly referred to as a "typo."

A **logic error**, unlike a syntax error, can either cause a run-time error or produce incorrect results. Such errors are characterized by erroneous, unexpected, or unintentional output that is a direct result of some flaw in the program's logic. These errors, which are never caught by the compiler, may be detected by desk checking, by program testing, by accident when

[3]They may not, however, all be detected at the same time. Frequently, one syntax error masks another error, and the second error is only detected after the first error is corrected.

a user obtains an obviously erroneous output from the program, or not at all. If the error is detected while the program is executing, a run-time error can occur that results in an error message being generated or premature program termination (or both).

The most serious logic error is caused by an incorrect understanding of the full requirements that the program is expected to fulfill. This is true because the logic contained within a program is always a reflection of the logic on which it is coded. For example, if the purpose of a program is to calculate a mortgage payment on a house or the load-bearing strength of a steel beam, and the programmer does not fully understand how the calculation is to be made, what inputs are needed to perform the calculation, or what special conditions exist (such as what happens when someone makes an extra payment on a mortgage or how temperature affects the beam), a logic error will occur. Because such errors are not detected by the compiler and frequently even may go undetected at run time, they are always more difficult to detect than syntax errors. If they are detected, a logic error typically reveals itself in one of two predominant ways. In one instance, the program executes to completion but produces obviously incorrect results. Generally, logic errors of this type are revealed by

- **No output**—This is caused either by an omission of an output statement or a sequence of statements that inadvertently bypasses an output statement.
- **Unappealing or misaligned output**—This is caused by an error in an output statement.
- **Incorrect numerical results**—This is caused by incorrect values assigned to the variables used in an expression, the use of an incorrect arithmetic expression, an omission of a statement, a round-off error, or the use of an improper sequence of statements.

A second way that logic errors reveal themselves is by causing a run-time error. Examples of this type of logic error are attempts to divide by 0 or to take the square root of a negative number. See if you can detect the logic error in Program 4.8.

Program 4.8

```
#include <stdio.h>
#include <math.h>

int main() /* a compound interest program */
{
  int nyears;
  float capital, amount, rate;

  printf("This program calculates the amount of money\n");
  printf("in a bank account for an initial deposit\n");
  printf("invested for n years at an interest rate r.\n\n");
  printf("Enter the initial amount in the account: ");
  scanf("%f", &amount);
  printf("Enter the interest rate (ex. 5 for 5%): ");
  scanf("%f", &rate);
```

```
   capital = amount * pow( (1 + rate/100.), nyears);
   printf("\nThe final amount of money is $%8.2f\n", capital);

   return 0;
}
```

The problem with Program 4.8 is that the program does not initialize the variable `nyears`. As a result, on Unix-based systems whatever value happens to occupy the storage locations corresponding to the variable `nyears` will be used (a vast majority of the time the allocated storage will contain a 0, but not always). Windows-based systems generally produce a run-time error when the assignment statement that calculates `capital` is executed and the program detects that `nyears` was declared but not initialized.

Testing and Debugging

In theory, a comprehensive set of test runs will reveal all logic errors and ensure that a program will work correctly for any and all combinations of input and computed data. In practice, this requires checking all possible combinations of statement execution. Due to the time and effort required, this is impossible, except for extremely simple programs. Let us see why this is so. Consider Program 4.9.

Program 4.9

```
#include <stdio.h>
int main()
{
  int num;

  printf("Enter a number: ");
  scanf("%d", &num);
  if (num == 5)
    printf("Bingo!\n");
  else
    printf("Bongo!\n");

  return 0;
}
```

Program 4.9 has two paths that can be traversed from when the program is run. The first path, which is executed when the input number is 5, includes the sequence of instructions

```
printf("Enter a number: ");
scanf("%d", &num);
  printf("Bingo!");
```

The second path, which is executed whenever any number except 5 is input, includes the sequence of instructions

```
printf("Enter a number: ");
scanf("%d", &num);
  printf("Bongo!");
```

To test each possible path through Program 4.9 requires two runs of the program, with a judicious selection of test input data to ensure that both paths of the `if` statement are exercised. Adding one more `if` statement in the program increases the number of possible execution paths by a factor of 2 and requires four (2^2) runs of the program for complete testing. Similarly, two additional `if` statements increase the number of paths by a factor of 4, requiring eight (2^3) runs for complete testing, and three additional `if` statements would produce a program requiring 16 (2^4) test runs.

Consider an application program consisting of 10 modules, each containing five `if` statements. Assuming the modules are always called in the same sequence, there are 32 (2 raised to the fifth power) possible paths through each module and more than 1,000,000,000,000,000 (2 raised to the 15th power) possible paths through the complete program (all modules executed in sequence). The time needed to create individual test data to exercise each path and the actual computer run time required to check each path make the complete testing of such a program impossible.

The impossibility of fully testing all combinations of statement execution sequences is summed up in the programming proverb "There is no error-free program." Nevertheless, you can carefully plan your testing to maximize the possibility of locating errors. As you devise your testing strategy, an important corollary to keep in mind is that *although a single test can reveal the presence of an error, it does not verify the absence of one.* The fact that one error is revealed by testing does not indicate that another error is not lurking somewhere else in the program; *the fact that one test reveals no errors does not indicate that there are no errors.*

Once you discover an error, you must determine where the error occurs and then fix it. In computer jargon, a program error is referred to as a **bug,** and the process of isolating, correcting, and verifying the correction is called **debugging.**[4]

Although there are no hard-and-fast rules for isolating the cause of an error, some useful techniques can be applied. The first is a preventive technique. Frequently, many errors are introduced by the programmer in the rush to code and run a program before fully understanding what is required and how the result is to be achieved. A symptom of this haste to get a program entered into the computer is the lack of a clearly defined solution algorithm, using either pseudocode, flowcharts, or formulas. Many errors can also be eliminated simply by desk checking a copy of the program before it is compiled.

---

[4]The derivation of this term is rather interesting. When a program stopped running on the MARK I computer at Harvard University in September 1945, the malfunction was traced to a dead insect that had gotten into the electrical circuits. The programmer, Grace Hopper, recorded the incident in her logbook as, "First actual case of bug being found."

A second useful technique is to imitate the computer and execute each statement by hand, as the computer would. This means writing down each variable as it is encountered in the program and listing the value that should be stored in the variable as each input and assignment statement is encountered. Doing this also sharpens your programming skills because it requires that you fully understand what each statement in your program causes to happen. Such a check is called **program tracing**.

A third and very powerful debugging technique is to include `printf()` function calls in your program that display the values of selected variables. When used in this manner, the function calls are referred to as **diagnostic `printf()` statements** and can be a considerable help in debugging. If the displayed values are incorrect, you can then determine what part of your program generated them, and make the necessary corrections.

In the same manner, you could add temporary code that displays the values of all input data. This technique is referred to as **echo printing**, and it is useful in establishing that the program is correctly receiving and interpreting the input data.

The most powerful of all debugging and tracing techniques is to use a special program called a **debugger**. A debugger program controls the execution of a C program, can interrupt the C program at any point in its execution, and can display the values of all variables at the point of interruption.

Finally, no discussion of debugging is complete without mentioning the primary ingredient needed for successful isolation and correction of errors. This is the attitude and spirit you bring to the task. After you write a program, it is natural to assume it is correct. It is extremely difficult to back away and honestly test and find errors in your own software. As a programmer, you must constantly remind yourself that just because you think your program is correct does not make it so. Finding errors in your own programs is a sobering experience, but one that will help you to become a master programmer. It can also be exciting and fun if approached as a detection problem with you as the master detective.

Chapter 5

Repetition

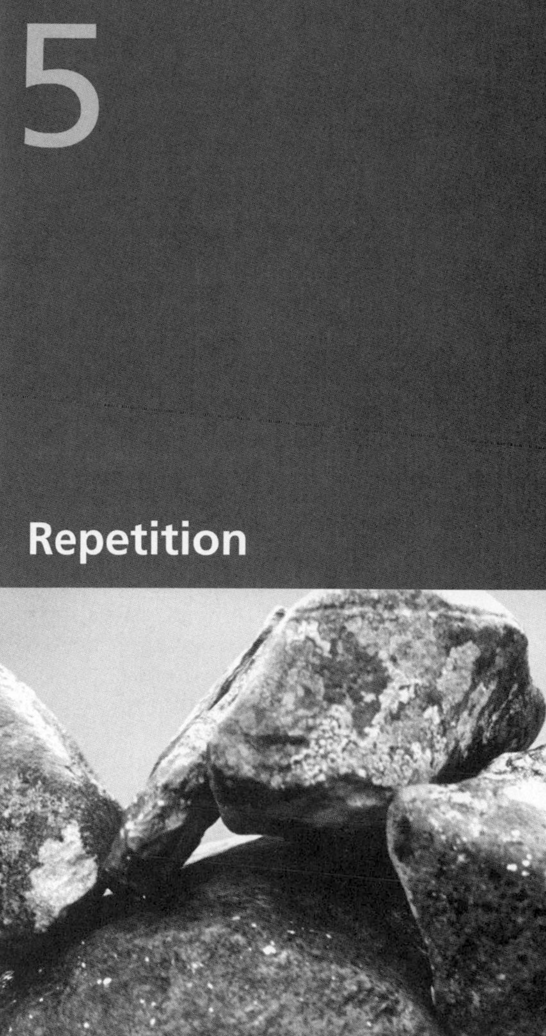

The programs examined so far have illustrated concepts involved in input, output, assignment, and selection capabilities. By this time, you should have gained enough experience to be comfortable with these concepts and the mechanics of implementing them using C. Many problems, however, require a repetition capability, in which the same calculation or sequence of instructions is repeated over and over, using different sets of data. Examples of such repetition include continual checking of user data entries until an acceptable entry, such as a valid password, is entered, counting and accumulating running totals, and constant acceptance of input data and recalculation of output values that only stop on entry of a sentinel value.

This chapter explores the different methods programmers use to construct repeating sections of code and how that code can be implemented in C. More commonly, a section of code that is repeated is referred to as a **loop**, because after the last statement in the code is executed, the program branches, or loops, back to the first statement and starts another repetition through the code. Each repetition is also referred to as an **iteration** or **pass through the loop**.

5.1 Basic Loop Structures

Constructing a repeating section of code requires that four elements be present. The first necessary element is a repetition statement. This repetition statement defines the boundaries containing the repeating section of code and also controls whether the code is executed or not. C provides the following three types of repetition statements:

`while` statement
`for` statement
`do-while` statement

Each of these statements requires a condition that must be evaluated, which is the second element needed for constructing repeating sections of code. Valid conditions are identical to those used in selection statements. If the condition is true, the code contained within the repetition statement is executed; otherwise, it is not.

The third required element is a statement that initially sets the condition being tested. This statement must always be placed before the condition is first evaluated to ensure correct loop execution the first time the condition is evaluated.

Finally, there must be a statement within the repeating section of code that alters the condition so that it eventually becomes false. This is necessary to ensure that, at some point, the repetitions stop.

Once a repetition statement is chosen, the last three elements—condition, initialization, and alteration—are generally controlled by a single loop-control variable, which will be explained shortly. Loop structures can be categorized based on the type of condition being tested and on where the condition is tested within the overall structure. These distinctions are covered next.

Pretest and Posttest Loops

The condition being tested can be evaluated at either the beginning or the end of the repeating section of code. Figure 5.1 illustrates the case where the test occurs at the beginning of the loop. This type of loop is referred to as a **pretest loop** because the condition is tested before any statements within the loop are executed. If the condition is true, the executable statements within the loop are executed. If the initial value of the condition is false, the executable statements within the loop are never executed at all and control transfers to the first statement after the loop. To avoid infinite repetitions, the condition must be updated within the loop. Pretest loops are also referred to as **entrance-controlled loops**.

A loop that evaluates a condition at the end of the repeating section of code, as illustrated in Figure 5.2, is referred to as a **posttest loop** or **exit-controlled loop**. Such loops always execute the loop statements at least once before the condition is tested.

Counter-Controlled and Condition-Controlled Loops

In addition to where the condition is tested (pretest or posttest), repeating sections of code are also classified as to the type of condition being tested. In a **counter-controlled loop**, which is also known as a **fixed-count loop**, the condition is used to keep track of the number of repetitions that have occurred.

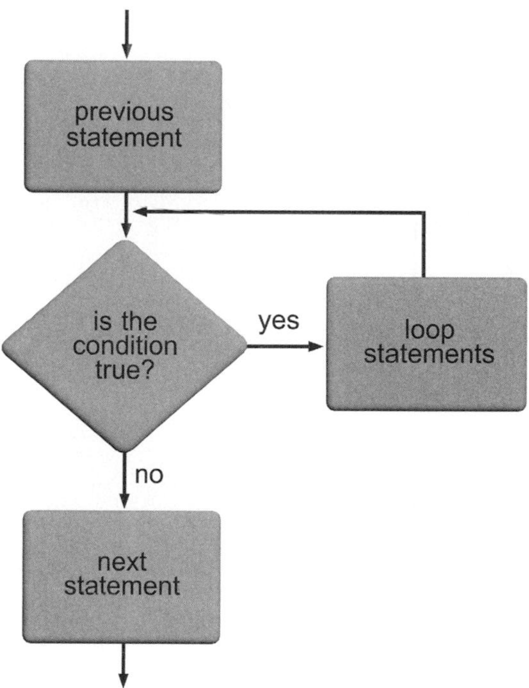

Figure 5.1 A pretest (entrance-controlled) loop

For example, we might want to produce a table of 10 numbers, including their squares and cubes, or a fixed design such as

```
*************************
*************************
*************************
*************************
```

In each of these examples, a fixed number of calculations are performed or a fixed number of lines are printed, at which point the repeating section of code is exited. All of C's repetition statements can be used to produce counter-controlled loops.

In many situations, the exact number of repetitions is not known in advance or the items are too numerous to count beforehand. For example, when entering a large amount of market research data, we might not want to take the time to count the number of actual data items to be entered. In such cases, a condition-controlled loop is used. In a **condition-controlled loop**, the tested condition does not depend on a count being achieved, but rather on a specific value being encountered. When this specified value is met, regardless of how many iterations have occurred, repetitions stop.

In this chapter, we will encounter examples of both counter- and condition-controlled loops and describe the C repetition statements that are typically used to create each loop type. Table 5.1 summarizes the different types of loops that you will commonly encounter in your programming career. The last two loop types are special applications of a condition-controlled loop that are so common that they have their own names.

Table 5.1 Comparison of loop types

Type of Loop	Description
Counter-controlled (Fixed-count)	The number of repetitions is known before the loop executes.
Condition-controlled	The number of repetitions is not known before the loop executes. The loop is terminated when one or more specific values are encountered.
Sentinel-controlled	This is a condition-controlled loop where one specific value is required to terminate the loop.
Input-validation	This is a condition-controlled loop that terminates when a value within a valid range is entered.

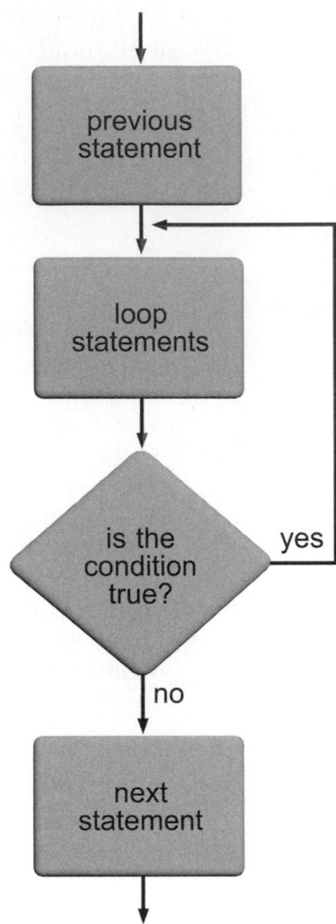

Figure 5.2 A posttest (exit-controlled) loop

EXERCISES 5.1

Short Answer Questions

1. List the three repetition statements that are provided in C.
2. List the four elements that must be present to create repeating sections of code.
3. **a.** What is an entrance-controlled loop?
   b. Which of C's repetition statements produce entrance-controlled loops?
4. **a.** What is an exit-controlled loop?
   b. Which of C's repetition statements produce exit-controlled loops?

5. a. What is the difference between a pretest and posttest loop?
   b. If the condition being tested in a pretest loop is false to begin with, how many times will statements internal to the loop be executed?
   c. If the condition being tested in a posttest loop is false to begin with, how many times will statements internal to the loop be executed?

6. What is the difference between a counter-controlled and a condition-controlled loop?

5.2 The `while` Statement

The `while` statement is a general repetition statement that can be used in a variety of programming situations. The general form of the `while` statement is

```
while (expression)
   statement;
```

The expression contained within the parentheses is evaluated in exactly the same manner as an expression contained in an `if-else` statement; the difference is in how the expression is used. As we have seen, when the expression is true (has a non-0 value) in an `if-else` statement, the statement following the expression is executed once. In a `while` statement, the statement following the expression is executed repeatedly as long as the expression evaluates to a non-0 value. This naturally means that somewhere in the `while` statement there must be a statement that alters the value of the tested expression. As we will see, this is indeed the case. For now, however, considering just the expression and the statement following the parentheses, the process used by the computer in evaluating a `while` statement is

1. test the expression
2. `if` the expression has a non-0 (true) value
a. execute the statement following the parentheses
b. go back to step 1
`else`
exit the `while` statement

Notice that Step 2b forces program control to be transferred back to Step 1. The transfer of control back to the start of a `while` statement to reevaluate the expression is known as a **program loop**. The `while` statement literally loops back on itself to recheck the expression until it evaluates to 0 (becomes false).

The looping process produced by a `while` statement is illustrated in Figure 5.3. A diamond shape is used to show the entry and exit points required in the decision part of the `while` statement.

To make this a little more tangible, consider the relational expression `count <= 10` and the statement `printf("%d ",count);`. Using these, we can write the following valid `while` statement:

```
while (count <= 10)
  printf("%d ",count);
```

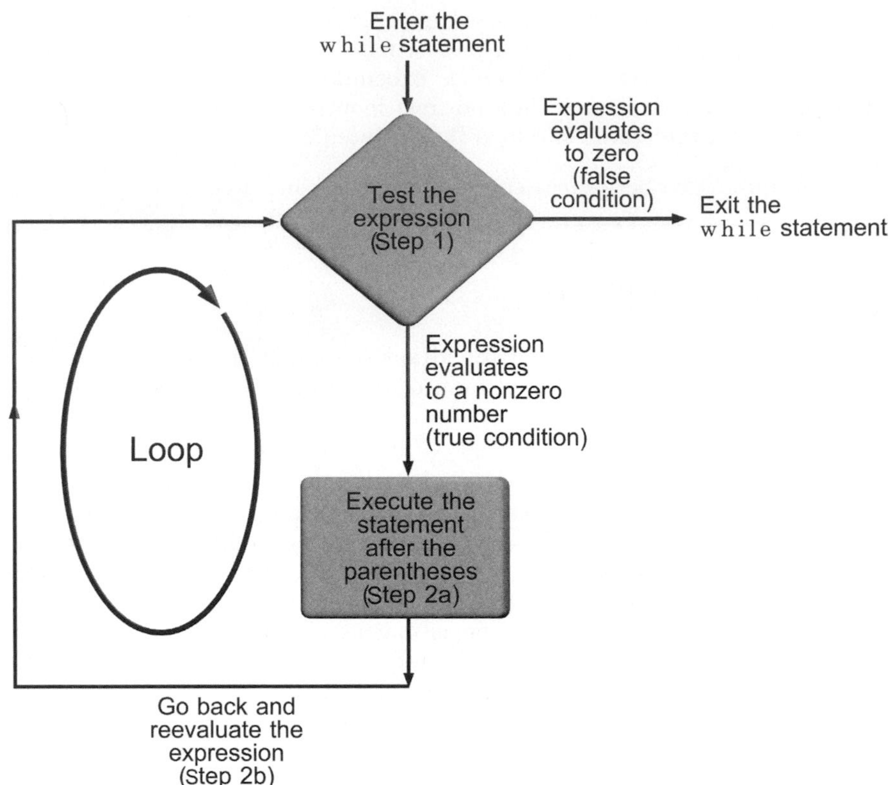

Figure 5.3 Anatomy of a `while` loop

Although the previous statement is valid, the alert reader will realize that we have created a situation in which the `printf()` function is either called forever (or until we stop the program) or is not called at all. Let us see why this happens.

If `count` has a value less than or equal to 10 when the expression is first evaluated, a call to `printf()` is made. The `while` statement then automatically loops back on itself and retests the expression. Since we have not changed the value stored in `count`, the expression is still true and another call to `printf()` is made. This process continues forever, or until the program containing this statement is prematurely stopped by the user. However, if `count` starts with a value greater than 10, the expression is false to begin with and the `printf()` function call is never made.

How do we set an initial value in count to control what the `while` statement does the first time the expression is evaluated? The answer, of course, is to assign values to each variable in the tested expression before the `while` statement is encountered. For example, the following sequence of instructions is valid:

```
count = 1;
while (count <= 10)
  printf("%d ",count);
```

Using this sequence of instructions, we have ensured that count starts with a value of 1. We could assign any value to count in the assignment statement—the important factor is to assign some value. In practice, the assigned value depends on the application.

We must still change the value of count so that we can finally exit the while statement. To do this requires an expression such as count++ to increment the value of count each time the while statement is executed. The fact that a while statement provides for the repetition of a single statement does not prevent us from including an additional statement to change the value of count. All we have to do is replace the single statement with a compound statement. For example

```
1  count = 1; /* initialize count */
2  while (count <= 10)
3  {
4    printf("%d ",count);
5    count++; /* increment count */
6  }
```

For clarity, we have placed each statement in the compound statement on a different line. This is consistent with the convention adopted for compound statements in the last chapter. Let us now analyze the above sequence of instructions.

The first assignment statement, in line 1, sets count equal to 1. The while statement is then entered, and the expression is evaluated for the first time. Becasue the value of count is less than or equal to 10, the expression is true and the compound statement is executed. The first statement in the compound statement, in line 4, is a call to the printf() function to display the value of count. The next statement, in line 5, adds 1 to the value currently stored in count, making this value equal to 2. The while statement now loops back to retest the expression. Because count is still less than or equal to 10, the compound statement is again executed. This process continues until the value of count reaches 11. Program 5.1 illustrates these statements in an actual program.

Program 5.1

```
#include <stdio.h>
int main()
{
  int count;

  count = 1; /* initialize count */
  while (count <= 10)
  {
    printf("%d ",count);
    count++; /* add 1 to count */
  }

  printf("\n");  /* print a blank line */

```

```
    return 0;
}
```

The output for Program 5.1 is

```
1 2 3 4 5 6 7 8 9 10
```

There is nothing special about the name `count` used in Program 5.1. Any valid integer variable could have been used.

Before we consider other examples of the `while` statement, two comments concerning Program 5.1 are in order. First, the statement `count++` can be replaced with any statement that changes the value of `count`. A statement such as `count + = 2` (or, if you prefer, `count = count + 2`), for example, would cause every second integer to be displayed. Second, it is the programmer's responsibility to ensure that `count` is changed in a way that ultimately leads to a normal exit from the `while` loop. For example, if we replace the expression `count++` with the expression `count--`, the value of `count` will never reach 11 and an infinite loop will be created. An infinite loop is a loop that never ends. The computer will not reach out, touch you, and say, "Excuse me, you have created an infinite loop." It just keeps displaying numbers until you realize that the program is not working as you expected.

Now that you have some familiarity with the `while` statement, see if you can read and determine the output of Program 5.2.

Program 5.2

```
#include <stdio.h>
int main()
{
  int i;

  i = 10;
  while (i >= 1)
  {
    printf("%d ",i);
    i--; /* subtract 1 from i */
  }

  printf("\n");   /* print a blank line */

  return 0;
}
```

The assignment statement in Program 5.2 initially sets the `int` variable `i` to 10. The `while` statement then checks to see if the value of `i` is greater than or equal to 1. While the expression is true, the value of `i` is displayed by the call to `printf()` and the value of `i` is decremented by 1. When i finally reaches 0, the expression is false and the program exits the while statement. Thus, the following display is obtained when Program 5.2 is run:

```
10 9 8 7 6 5 4 3 2 1
```

To illustrate the power of the while statement, consider the task of printing a table of numbers from 1 to 10 with their squares and cubes. This can be done with a simple while statement, as illustrated by Program 5.3.

Program 5.3

```
#include <stdio.h>
int main ()
{
  #define TABLESIZE 10
  int num;

  printf("NUMBER SQUARE CUBE\n");
  printf("------ ------ ----\n");
  num = 1;
  while (num <= TABLESIZE)
  {
    printf("%3d %7d %6d\n", num, num*num, num*num*num);

    num++; /* add 1 to num */
  }

  return 0;
}
```

Program 5.3 produces the following display:

```
NUMBER     SQUARE  CUBE
------     ------  ----
   1          1       1
   2          4       8
   3          9      27
   4         16      64
   5         25     125
   6         36     216
   7         49     343
   8         64     512
   9         81     729
  10        100    1000
```

Programming Note

Controlling a Loop with a Symbolic Constant

Symbolic constants can be extremely useful in constructing loops because they indicate what the number in the tested condition represents. For example, if a table of 10 data rows is going to be created, a symbolic constant defined as

```
#define TABLESIZE 10
```

is appropriate. Similarly, if a program is required to test the days in a year, an appropriate symbolic constant definition would be

```
#define DAYSINYEAR 365
```

This symbolic constant clearly identifies what the number 365 is being used to represent. Thus, any programmer examining a loop that uses this constant in its tested expression will understand the relevance of the symbolic constant.

Note that the tested expression in line 10

```
while (num <= TABLESIZE)
```

could have been replaced by either of the expressions `num <= 10` or `num < 11`. Good programming practice, however, dictates both using a symbolic constant and selecting its name to relate to the application. Once this is done, the appropriate relational operator can then be selected for use with the symbolic constant. In this case, as a table of 10 numbers is being prepared, a symbolic constant named `TABLESIZE` is appropriate and the correct choice for this constant is the value 10. This value then leads to the use of the <= relational operator.

If you now wanted to use Program 5.3 to produce a table of 1000 numbers, the only revision that is needed is to change the number 10 to 1000 in line 4, as follows:

```
4  #define TABLESIZE 1000
```

This simple change produces a table of 1000 lines—not bad for a simple five-line `while` statement.

Programs 5.1 through Program 5.3 have all created counter-controlled loops that check for a fixed-count condition. Because any valid expression can be evaluated by a `while` statement, we are not restricted to constructing such loops. In fact, `while` loops are particularly useful in constructing condition-controlled loops. As an example of this type of loop, consider the task of producing a Celsius-to-Fahrenheit temperature conversion table. Assume that Fahrenheit temperatures corresponding to Celsius temperatures ranging from 5 to 50 degrees are to be displayed in increments of 5 degrees. The desired display can be obtained with the series of statements

```
#define ENDVALUE 50

celsius = 5; /* starting Celsius value */
while (celsius <= ENDVALUE)
{
  fahren = (9.0/5.0) * celsius + 32.0;
```

```
  printf("%5d%11.2f",celsius, fahren);
  celsius = celsius + 5;
}
```

In this loop, the expression in the while statement

```
while (celsius <= ENDVALUE)
```

is not being tested for a fixed number of iterations. It is this usage of the tested expression that makes this a condition-controlled loop. As always, however, the while statement consists of everything from the keyword while through the closing brace of the compound statement. Prior to entering the while loop, we have made sure to assign a value to celsius, and there is a statement to alter the value of celsius to ensure an exit from the while loop. Program 5.4 illustrates the use of this code in a complete program.

Program 5.4

```
#include <stdio.h>
 #define ENDVALUE 50
int main() /* program to convert Celsius to Fahrenheit */
{
  int celsius;
  float fahren;

  /* display the heading lines */
  printf("DEGREES DEGREES\n");
  printf("CELSIUS FAHRENHEIT\n");
  printf("------- ----------\n");

  // now fill in the table using a while loop
  celsius = 5; /* starting Celsius value */

  while (celsius <= ENDVALUE)
  {
    fahren = (9.0/5.0) * celsius + 32.0;
    printf("%5d%11.2f\n",celsius, fahren);
    celsius = celsius + 5;
  }

  return 0;
}
```

The display obtained when Program 5.4 is executed is

```
DEGREES DEGREES
CELSIUS FAHRENHEIT
------- ----------
    5       41.00
   10       50.00
   15       59.00
   20       68.00
   25       77.00
   30       86.00
   35       95.00
   40      104.00
   45      113.00
   50      122.00
```

EXERCISES 5.2

Short Answer Questions

1. Do `while` statements produce entrance- or exit-controlled loops? Why or why not?
2. Write a `while` loop that displays the numbers from 10 to 20 on a single line.
3. Write a `while` loop that displays only the even numbers from 10 to 20 on a single line.
4. Write a `while` loop that displays the numbers from 20 to 10 on a single line.
5. Write a `while` loop that displays only the even numbers from 20 to 10 on a single line.
6. For the following program, determine the total number of items displayed. Also determine the first and last numbers printed.

```
#include <stdio.h>
int main()
{
  int num = 0;
  while (num <= 20)
  {
    num++;
    printf("%d ",num);
  }
  return 0;
}
```

Programming Exercises

1. Rewrite Program 5.1 to print the numbers 2 to 10 in increments of two. The output of your program should be

```
2 4 6 8 10
```

2. a. Rewrite Program 5.4 to produce a table that starts at a Celsius value of –10 and ends with a Celsius value of 60, in increments of 10 degrees.
   b. Enter and run the program from Exercise 2a on a computer to verify your answers..

3. Write a C program that converts gallons to liters. The program should display gallons from 10 to 20 in 1-gallon increments and the corresponding liter equivalents. Use the relationship that 1 gallon contains 3.785 liters.

4. Write a C program that converts feet to meters. The program should display feet from 3 to 30 in 3-foot increments and the corresponding meter equivalents. Use the relationship that 1 meter is equivalent to 3.28 feet.

5. A machine purchased for $28,000 is depreciated at a rate of $4,000 a year for seven years. Write and run a C program that computes and displays a depreciation table for seven years. The table should have the form

```
                         END-OF-YEAR  ACCUMULATED
YEAR  DEPRECIATION          VALUE      DEPRECIATION
----  ------------   -----------  ------------
1         4000           24000         4000
2         4000           20000         8000
3         4000           16000        12000
4         4000           12000        16000
5         4000            8000        20000
6         4000            4000        24000
7         4000               0        28000
```

6. An automobile travels at an average speed of 55 miles per hour for four hours. Write a C program that displays the distance driven, in miles, by the car every half-hour until the end of the trip.

5.3 Computing Sums and Averages Using a `while` Loop

One of the major uses of loops is the computation of sums and averages of lists of numeric data. The data is typically either stored in a data file (the topic of Chapter 10) or entered interactively using the `scanf()` function.

To understand the basic concept involved, consider Program 5.5, where a `while` statement is used to accept and then display four user-entered numbers, one at a time. Although it uses a very simple idea, the program highlights the flow-of-control concepts needed to produce programs for calculating sums and averages.

Program 5.5

```c
#include <stdio.h>
#define MAXCOUNT 4
int main()
{
  int count;
  float num;

  printf("\nThis program will ask you to enter %d numbers.\n\n", MAXCOUNT);

  count = 1;
  while (count <= MAXCOUNT)
  {
    printf("Enter a number: ");
    scanf("%f", &num);
    printf("The number entered is %f\n", num);
    count++;
  }

  return 0;
}
```

Following is a sample run of Program 5.5. The italicized numbers were input in response to the appropriate prompts.

```
This program will ask you to enter four numbers.

Enter a number: 26.2
The number entered is 26.200000
Enter a number: 5
The number entered is 5.000000
Enter a number: 103.456
The number entered is 103.456000
Enter a number: 1267.89
The number entered is 1267.890000
```

Let us review the program to clearly understand how the output was produced. The first message displayed is caused by execution of the first `printf()` function call on line 8.

```
8   printf("\nThis program will ask you to enter %d numbers.\n\n", MAXCOUNT);
```

This call is outside and before the `while` statement, so it is executed once before any statement in the `while` loop.

Once the `while` loop is entered, the statements within the compound statement

```
12  {
13    printf("\nEnter a number: ");
14    scanf("%f", &num);
15    printf("The number entered is %f\n", num);
16    count++;
17  }
```

are executed while the tested condition is true.

The first time through the compound statement, the message `Enter a number:` is displayed by the `printf()` function call in line 13. The program then calls `scanf()` in line 14, which forces the computer to wait for a number to be entered at the keyboard. Once a number is typed and the Enter key is pressed, the call to `printf()` in line 15 displays the number just entered. The variable `count` is then incremented by 1 in line 16. This process continues until four passes through the loop have been made and the value of count is 5. Each pass causes the message `Enter a number:` to be displayed, causes one call to `scanf()` to be made, and causes the message `The number entered is` to be displayed. Figure 5.4 illustrates this flow of control.

Rather than simply displaying the entered numbers, Program 5.5 can be modified to process the entered data. For example, we can add the numbers entered and display the total. To do this, we must be very careful in how we add the numbers, since the same variable, `num`, is used for each number entered. Because of this the entry of a new number in Program 5.5 automatically causes the previous number stored in `num` to be lost. Thus, each number entered must be added to the total before another number is entered. The required sequence is

Enter a number
Add the number to the total

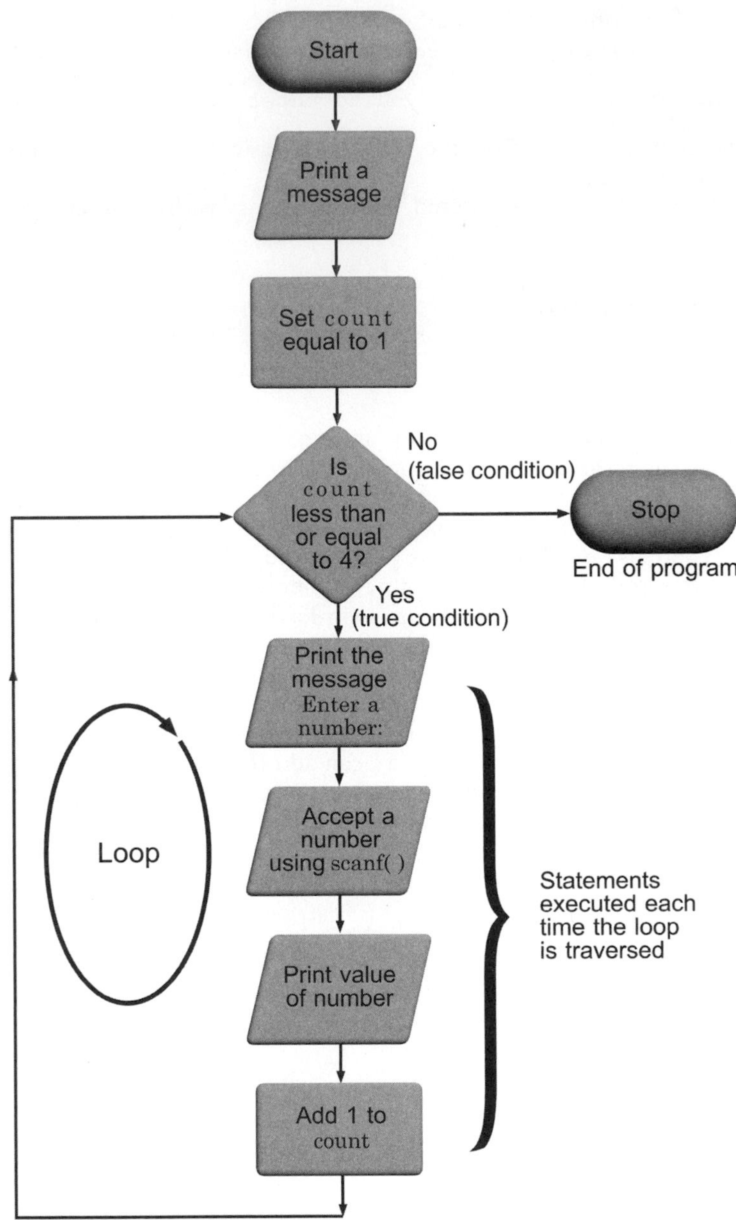

Figure 5.4 Flow-of-control diagram for Program 5.5

How do we add a single number to a total? A statement such as `total = total + num;` does the job perfectly, or its shorter version `total += num;`. These are the accumulating statements introduced in Section 3.1. After each number is entered, the accumulating statement adds the number into the total, as illustrated in Figure 5.5. The complete flow of control required for adding the numbers is illustrated in Figure 5.6.

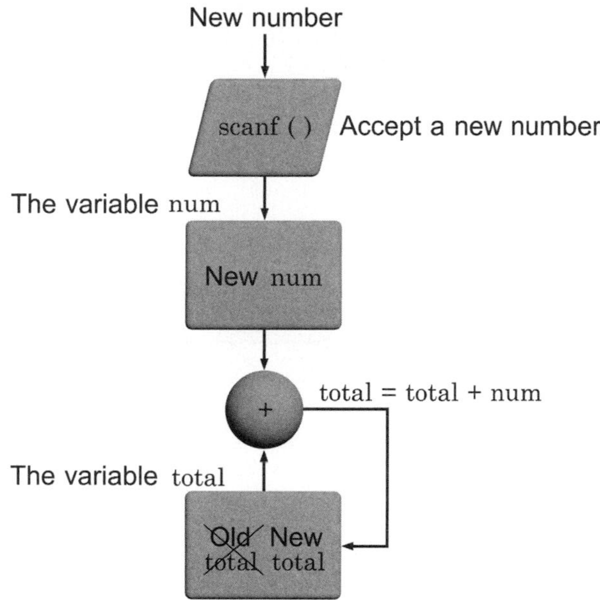

Figure 5.5 Accepting and adding a number to a total

In reviewing Figure 5.6, observe that we have made a provision for initially setting the total to 0 before the `while` loop is entered. If we were to clear the `total` inside the `while` loop, it would be set to 0 each time the loop was executed and any value previously stored would be erased.

Program 5.6 incorporates the necessary modifications to Program 5.5 to total the numbers entered. As indicated in the flow diagram shown in Figure 5.6, the statement `total += num;` is placed immediately after the `scanf()` function call. Putting the accumulating statement at this point in the program ensures that the entered number is immediately "captured" into the total.

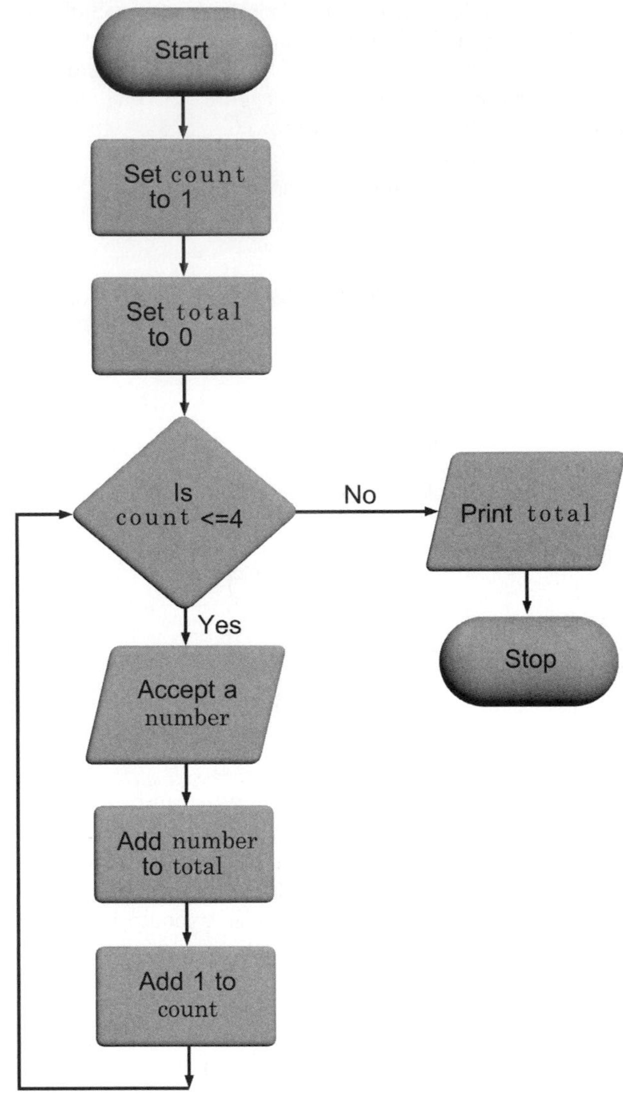

Figure 5.6 Accumulation flow of control

Program 5.6

```
1  #include <stdio.h>
2   #define MAXCOUNT 4
3  int main()
4  {
5    int count;
6    float num, total;
7
8    printf("\nThis program will ask you to enter %d numbers.\n\n", MAXCOUNT);
9
10   count = 1;
11   total = 0.0;
12
13   while (count <= MAXCOUNT)
14   {
15     printf("Enter a number: ");
16     scanf("%f", &num);
17     total += num;
18     printf("The total is now %f\n", total);
19     count++;
20   }
21
22   printf("\n\nThe final total of the %d numbers is %f\n", MAXCOUNT, total);
23
24   return 0;
25 }
```

Let us review Program 5.6. The variable `total` was created to store the total of the numbers entered. Prior to entering the `while` statement, the value of `total` is set to 0 in line 11, as follows

```
11  total = 0.0;
```

This assignment ensures that any previous value present in the storage locations assigned to the variable `total` is overwritten and the total starts at a correct value. When the `while` loop is entered, the statement in line 17:

```
17  total += num;
```

is used to add the value of the entered number into `total`. As each value is entered, it is added into the existing `total` to create a new total. (If you prefer to use the longer statement `total = total + num;`, do so.) Thus, `total` becomes a running subtotal of all the values entered. Only when all numbers are entered does `total` contain the final sum of all the numbers. After the `while` loop is finished, the `printf()` function call in line 22 is used to display the sum.

```
22  printf("\n\nThe final total of the %d numbers is %f\n", MAXCOUNT, total);
```

Using the same data that was entered in the sample run for Program 5.5, the following sample run of Program 5.6 was made:

```
This program will ask you to enter 4 numbers.

Enter a number: 26.2
The total is now 26.200000
Enter a number: 5
The total is now 31.200000
Enter a number: 103.456
The total is now 134.656000
Enter a number: 1267.89
The total is now 1402.546000

The final total of the 4 numbers is 1402.546000
```

Having used an accumulating assignment statement to add the numbers entered, we can now go further and calculate the average of the numbers. Where do we calculate the average—within the `while` loop or outside it?

In the case at hand, calculating an average requires that both a final total and the number of items in that total be available. The average is then computed by dividing the final total by the number of items. At this point, we must ask, "At what point in the program is the correct total available, and at what point is the number of items available?" In reviewing Program 5.6, we see that the correct total needed for calculating the average is available after the `while` loop is finished. In fact, the whole purpose of the `while` loop is to ensure that the numbers are entered and added correctly to produce a correct total. We also have a count of the number of items used in the total that has been defined as the symbolic constant MAXCOUNT. With this as background, see if you can read and understand Program 5.7.

Program 5.7

```
#include <stdio.h>
 #define MAXCOUNT 4
int main()
{
  int count;
  float num, total, average;

  printf("\nThis program will ask you to enter %d numbers.\n\n", MAXCOUNT);

  count = 1;
```

```
    total = 0.0;

    while (count <= MAXCOUNT)
    {
      printf("Enter a number: ");
      scanf("%f", &num);
      total += num;
      count++;
    }

    average = total / MAXCOUNT;
    printf("\nThe average of the %d numbers is %8.4f\n", MAXCOUNT, average);

    return 0;
  }
```

Program 5.7 is almost identical to Program 5.6, except for the calculation of the average. We have also removed the constant display of the total within and after the `while` loop. The loop in Program 5.7 is used to enter and add four numbers. Immediately after the loop is exited, the average is computed and displayed. Following is a sample run using Program 5.7:

```
This program will ask you to enter 4 numbers.

Enter a number: 26.2
Enter a number: 5
Enter a number: 103.456
Enter a number: 1267.89

The average of the 4 numbers is 350.6365
```

Sentinels

A program, such as Program 5.7, can be made much more general by removing the restriction that exactly four numbers are to be entered. This can be done in one of two ways. One method is to have the user enter a value for how many numbers will be averaged. In many situations, however, when the program is being used for many sets of data, it is extremely annoying to stop and determine the exact number of items to be entered for each run. Additionally, the number of items may be too numerous to count beforehand. For example, when entering a large amount of market research data, the exact number of actual data items to be entered may be extremely large. For cases like this, a second approach is used.

In this second approach, the data is continuously entered until, at the end, the user types in a special data value to signal the end of data input. In computer programming, data values used to signal either the start or end of a data series are called **sentinels**. The sentinel values must, of course, be selected so as not to conflict with legitimate data values. For example, if we were constructing a program that accepts student grades, a good sentinel value would be 0.

Once any value less than 0 is entered, the program would stop accepting any further grades. Program 5.8 illustrates this concept. In this program grades are continuously requested and accepted until a negative grade value is entered. Entry of a negative grade alerts the program to exit the `while` loop and display the total of the grades entered.

Program 5.8

```
#include <stdio.h>
int main()
{
  #define CUTOFF -1
  float grade = 0.01;
  float total = 0.01;

  printf("\nTo stop entering grades, type in any negative number.\n\n");

  while (grade > CUTOFF)
  {
    printf("Enter a grade: ");
    scanf("%f", &grade);
    total = total + grade;
  }

  printf("\nThe total of the grades is %f\n", total-grade);

  return 0;
}
```

Following is a sample run using Program 5.8. As long as positive grades are entered, the program continues to request and accept additional data. When a grade less than 0 is entered, the program adds this final number to the total and then exits the `while` loop. Outside of the loop and within the `printf()` function call, this last grade is subtracted so that only the sum of the legitimate grades that were entered is displayed.

```
To stop entering grades, type in any negative number.

Enter a grade: 95
Enter a grade: 100
Enter a grade: 82
Enter a grade: -1

The total of the grades is 277.000000
```

One useful sentinel provided in C is the named constant `EOF`, which stands for End Of File. The actual value of `EOF` is compiler-dependent, but it is always assigned a code that is not used by any other character.

Each computer operating system has its own code for an End Of File mark. In Unix operating systems, this mark is generated whenever the Ctrl and D keys are pressed simultaneously, while in IBM-compatible computers, the mark is generated whenever the Ctrl and Z keys are pressed simultaneously. When a C program detects this combination of keys as an input value, it converts the input value into its own `EOF` code, as illustrated in Figure 5.7.

Figure 5.7 Generation of the `EOF` constant by the `scanf()` function

The actual definition of the `EOF` constant, using the `#define` statement described in Section 3.5, is available in the compiler source file `stdio.h`. Thus, the named `EOF` constant can be used in all programs that have included `stdio.h`. For example, consider Program 5.9.

Notice that the first line in Program 5.9 is the `#include <stdio.h>` statement. Since the `stdio.h` file contains the definition of `EOF`, this constant may now be referenced in the program.

Program 5.9

```
#include <stdio.h>
int main()
{
  float  grade;
  float total = 0.01; /* note the initialization here */

  printf("\nTo stop entering grades, press either the F6 key");
  printf("\n or the ctrl and Z keys simultaneously on PCs");
  printf("IBM compatible computers");
  printf("\n or the ctrl and D keys for UNIX operating systems.\n\n");
  printf("Enter a grade: ");
  while (scanf("%f", &grade) != EOF)
  {
    total += grade;
    printf("Enter a grade: ");
  }

```

```
18    printf("\nThe total of the grades is %f\n",total);
19    return 0;
20  }
```

The EOF symbolic constant is used in Program 5.9 to control the while loop. The expression in parentheses in line 12

```
12  while(scanf("%f", &grades) != EOF)
```

makes use of the fact that the scanf() function returns an EOF value if an attempt is made to read an End Of File mark. From a user's viewpoint, assuming an IBM computer is being used, pressing both the Ctrl and Z keys simultaneously generates an End Of File mark, which is converted to the EOF constant by scanf(). Following is a sample run using Program 5.9.

```
To stop entering grades, press either the F6 key
or the ctrl and Z keys simultaneously on IBM compatible computers
or the ctrl and D keys for UNIX operating systems.

Enter a grade: 100
Enter a grade: 200
Enter a grade: 300
Enter a grade: ^Z

The total of the grades is 600.000000
```

One distinct advantage of Program 5.9 over Program 5.8 is that the sentinel value is never added into the total, so it does not have to be subtracted later.[1] One disadvantage of Program 5.9, however, is that it requires the user to type in an unfamiliar combination of keys to terminate data input.

The break and continue Statements

Two useful statements in connection with repetition statements are the break and continue statements. We have previously encountered the break statement in relation to the switch statement. The general form of this statement is

```
break;
```

A break statement, as its name implies, forces an immediate break, or exit, from switch, while, for, and do-while statements only.

For example, execution of the following while loop is immediately terminated if a number greater than 76 is entered:

```
while(count <= 10)
{
  printf("Enter a number: ");
  scanf("%f", &num);
```

[1] This method of input will be very useful when reading data from files rather than the keyboard. (File input is presented in Chapter 10.)

```
  if (num > 76)
  {
    printf("You lose!");
    break; /* break out of the loop */
    }
  else
    printf("Keep on truckin!");
}
/* break jumps to here */
```

The break statement violates pure structured programming principles because it provides a second, nonstandard exit from a loop. Nevertheless, the break statement is extremely useful for breaking out of loops when an unusual condition is detected. The break statement is also used to exit from a switch statement, but this is because the desired case has been detected and processed.

The continue statement is similar to the break statement but applies only to loops created with while, do-while, and for statements. The general format of a continue statement is

```
continue;
```

When a continue statement is encountered in a loop, the next iteration of the loop begins immediately. For while loops this means that execution is automatically transferred to the top of the loop and reevaluation of the tested expression is initiated. Although the continue statement has no direct effect on a switch statement, it can be included within a switch statement that itself is contained in a loop. Here the effect of continue is the same: the next loop iteration begins.

As a general rule, the continue statement is used less than the break statement, but it is convenient for skipping over data that should not be processed while remaining in a loop. For example, invalid grades are simply ignored in the following section of code, and only valid grades are added into the total[2]:

```
while (count < 30)
{
  printf("Enter a grade: ");
  scanf("%f", &grade);
  if(grade < 0 || grade > 100)
    continue;
  total = total + grade;
  count = count + 1;
}
```

[2]The continue statement is not essential, however, and the selection can be written as:

```
if (grade >= 0 && grade <= 100)
{
  total = total + grade
  count = count + 1
}
```

The Null Statement

Statements are always terminated by a semicolon. A semicolon with nothing preceding it is also a valid statement, called the null statement. Thus, the statement

```
;
```

is a **null statement**. This is a do-nothing statement that is used where a statement is syntactically required, but no action is called for. Null statements typically are used either with `while` or `for` statements. An example of a `for` statement using a null statement is found in Program 5.10c.

EXERCISES 5.3

Short Answer Questions

1. What is the type of assignment statement that is used within a `while` loop for creating a total?
2. What is a sentinel?
3. Describe the differences between a `break` and `continue` statement.
4. By mistake, a programmer put the statement `average = total / count;` within the `while` loop immediately after the statement `total = total + num;` in Program 5.7. Thus, the `while` loop becomes

```
while (count <= MAXCOUNT)
{
  printf("\nEnter a number: ");
  scanf("%f", &num);
  total += total;
  average = total / count;
  count++;
}
```

   Will the program yield the correct result with this `while` loop? From a programming perspective, which `while` loop is better to use, and why?

Programming Exercises

1. Rewrite Program 5.6 to compute the total of eight numbers.
2. Rewrite Program 5.6 to display the prompt

```
Please type in the total number of data values to be added:
```

   In response to this prompt, the program should accept a user-entered number and then use this number to control the number of times the `while` loop is executed. Thus, if the user enters `5` in response to the prompt, the program should request the input of five numbers and display the total after five numbers have been entered.

3. a. Write a C program to convert Celsius degrees to Fahrenheit. The program should request the starting Celsius value, the number of conversions to be made, and the increment between Celsius values. The display should have appropriate headings and list the Celsius value and the corresponding Fahrenheit value. Use the relationship *Fahrenheit = (9.0 / 5.0) * Celsius + 32.0.*
   b. Run the program written in Exercise 3a on a computer. Verify that your program begins at the correct starting Celsius value and contains the exact number of conversions specified in your input data.

4. a. Modify the program written in Exercise 3a to request the starting Celsius value, the ending Celsius value, and the increment. Thus, instead of the condition checking for a fixed count, the condition checks for the ending Celsius value.
   b. Run the program written in Exercise 4a on a computer. Verify that your output starts at the correct beginning value and ends at the correct ending value.

5. Rewrite Program 5.7 to compute the average of 10 numbers.

6. Rewrite Program 5.7 to display the prompt

```
Please type in the total number of data values to be averaged:
```

   In response to this prompt, the program should accept a user-entered number and then use this number to control the number of times the `while` loop is executed. Thus, if the user enters 6 in response to the prompt, the program should request the input of six numbers and display the average of the next six numbers entered.

7. a. Modify Program 5.8 to compute the average of the grades entered.
   b. Run the program written in Exercise 7a on a computer and verify the results.

8. a. A bookstore summarizes its monthly transactions by keeping the following information for each book in stock:
   - Book identification number
   - Inventory balance at the beginning of the month
   - Number of copies received during the month
   - Number of copies sold during the month

   Write a C program that accepts this data for each book and then displays the book identification number and an updated book inventory balance using the relationship:

   New Balance = Inventory balance at the beginning of the month
   + Number of copies received during the month
   – Number of copies sold during the month

   Your program should use a `while` statement with a fixed-count condition so that information on only three books is requested.
   a. Run the program written in Exercise 8a on a computer. Review the display produced by your program and verify that the output produced is correct.

9. Modify the program you wrote for Exercise 8 to keep requesting and displaying results until a sentinel identification value of 999 is entered. Run the program on a computer.

10. a. The following data were collected on a recent automobile trip:

Mileage	Gallons
22495, at start of trip	Full tank
22841	12.2
23185	11.3
23400	10.5
23772	11.0
24055	12.2
24434	14.7
24804	14.3
25276	15.2

Write a C program that accepts a mileage and gallons value and calculates the miles-per-gallon (mpg) achieved for that segment of the trip. The mpg is obtained as the difference in mileage between fill-ups divided by the number of gallons of gasoline received in the fill-up.

b. Modify the program written for Exercise 10a to additionally compute and display the cumulative mpg achieved after each fill-up. The cumulative mpg is calculated as the difference between each fill-up mileage and the mileage at the start of the trip divided by the sum of the gallons used to that point in the trip.

5.4 The `for` Statement

The `for` statement performs the same functions as the `while` statement, but uses a different form. In many situations, especially those that use a counter-controlled loop, the `for` statement format is easier to use than its `while` equivalent. This is because the `for` statement combines all four elements required to easily produce this loop type on the same line. Recall that these elements are

- A repetition statement
- Initialization of variables used in the tested expression
- The expression that will be tested
- Alteration of variable values in the tested expression

All of these elements are contained within the following general syntax of the `for` statement:

```
for (initializing list; tested expression; altering list)
statement;
```

Although this syntax may look a little complicated, it is really quite simple if we consider each of its parts separately.

Within the parentheses of the `for` statement are three items, separated by semicolons. Each of these items is optional and can be described individually, but the semicolons must be present. As we shall see, the items in parentheses correspond to the initialization, tested expression, and altering of expression values that we have already used with the `while` statement.

The middle item in the parentheses, the tested expression, is any valid C expression, and there is no difference in the way for and while statements use this expression. In both statements, as long as the expression has a non-0 (true) value, the statement following the parentheses is executed. This means that prior to the first check of the expression, initial values for the tested expression's variables must be assigned. It also means that before the expression is reevaluated, there must be one or more statements that alter these values. Recall that the general placement of these statements using a while statement follows the pattern:

```
initializing statements;
while (expression)
{
  loop statements;
           .
           .
           .
  expression-altering statements;
}
```

The need to initialize variables or make some other evaluations prior to entering a repetition loop is so common that the for statement allows all the initializing statements to be grouped together as the first set of items within the for statement's parentheses. The items in this initializing list are executed only once, before the expression is evaluated for the first time.

The for statement also provides a single place for all expression-altering statements. These items can be placed in the altering list, which is the last list contained within the for statement's parentheses. All items in the altering list are executed by the for statement at the end of the loop, just before the expression is reevaluated. Figure 5.8 illustrates the for statement's flow-of-control diagram.

The following code comparison illustrates the correspondence between the for and while statements and the relative placement of the four elements that are required to construct a loop. For example, the while loop

```
count = 1;      /* initialization */
while (count <= 10)    /* repetition statement and tested
expression */
{
  printf("%d", count);
  count++:      /* altering statement */
}
```

can be replaced by the following for statement:

```
for (count = 1; count <= 10; count++)
  printf("%d", count);
```

As this example shows, the only difference between the for statement and the while statement is the placement of equivalent expressions. The grouping together of the initialization, expression test, and altering list in the for statement is very convenient when creating counter-controlled loops. This is because the altering expression in such loops is typically a simple increment of the counter, as in this example. As another example, consider the following for statement:

```
for (count = 2; count <= 20; count += 2)
  printf("%d ",count);
```

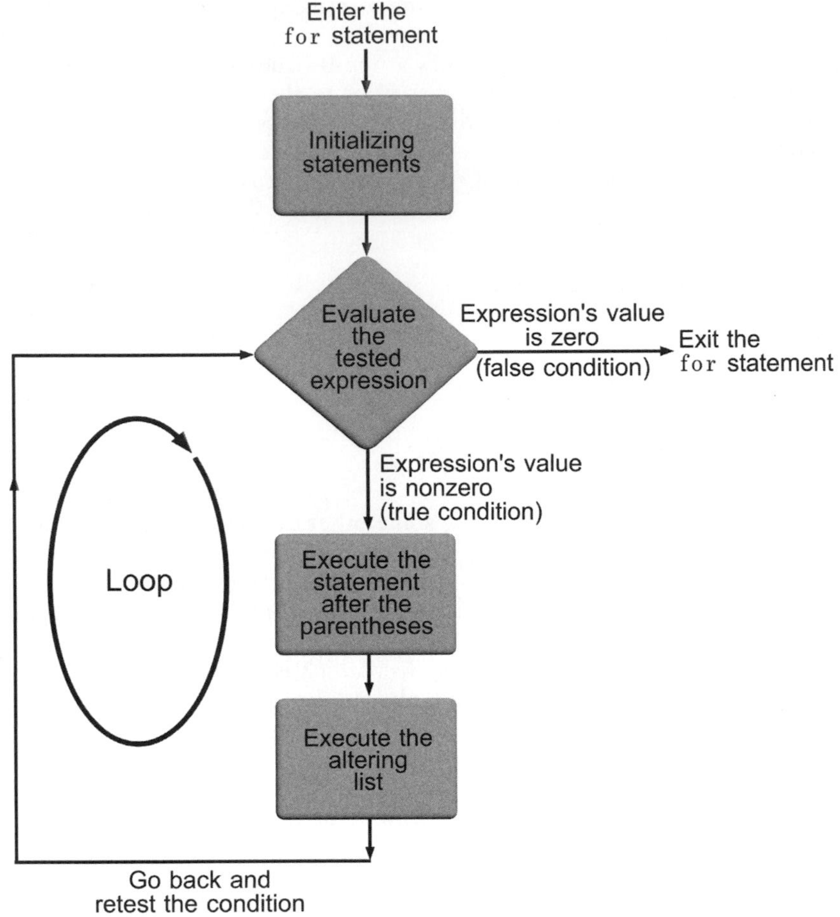

Figure 5.8 `for` statement flow of control

All of the loop control information, which consists of initialization, condition test, and altering statement, is contained within the parentheses. The loop starts with a count of 2, stops when the count exceeds 20, and increments the loop counter in steps of 2. Program 5.10 illustrates this `for` statement in an actual program, where the tested expression makes use of a symbolic constant in place of the literal value 20.

Program 5.10

```
#include <stdio.h>
int main()
{
  #define MAXCOUNT 20
```

```
  int count;

  for (count = 2; count <= MAXCOUNT; count += 2)
    printf("%d ",count);

  return 0;
}
```

The output of Program 5.10 is

```
2 4 6 8 10 12 14 16 18 20
```

The `for` statement does not require that any of the items in parentheses be present or that they actually be used for initializing or altering the values in the expression statements. However, the two semicolons must be present within the `for` statement's parentheses. For example, the construction `for ( ; count <= 20;)` is valid.

If the initializing list is missing, the initialization step is omitted when the `for` statement is executed. This, of course, means that the programmer must provide the required initializations before the `for` statement is encountered. Similarly, if the altering list is missing, any expressions needed to alter the evaluation of the tested expression must be included directly within the statement part of the loop. The `for` statement only ensures that all expressions in the initializing list are executed once, before evaluation of the tested expression, and that all expressions in the altering list are executed at the end of the loop before the tested expression is rechecked. Thus, Program 5.10 can be rewritten in any of the three ways shown in Programs 5.10a, 5.10b, and 5.10c.

Program 5.10a

```
#include <stdio.h>
int main()
{
  int count;

  count = 2; /* initializer outside for statement */
  for ( ; count <= 20; count += 2)
    printf("%d ",count);

  return 0;
}
```

Programming Note

Should I Use a `for` Loop or `while` Loop?

A question issue for beginning programmers is which loop structure to use—a `for` or `while` loop? This is a good question because each of these loop structures in C can be used to construct both fixed-count and variable-condition loops. In almost all other computer languages, the answer is relatively straightforward, because the `for` statement can be used only to construct counter-controlled loops. Thus, in most other languages, `for` statements are used to construct such loops, and `while` statements are generally used only when constructing condition-controlled loops.

In C, this easy distinction does not hold, because each statement can be used to create each type of loop. The answer in C, then, is really a matter of style. Because `for` and `while` loops are interchangeable in C, either loop is appropriate. Some professional programmers always use a `for` statement for every loop they create and almost never use a `while` statement. Others always use a `while` statement and rarely use a `for` statement. Still a third group tends to retain the convention used in other languages—a `for` loop is generally used to create counter-controlled loops and a `while` loop is used to create condition-controlled loops. This is the convention we will adhere to in this text. However, in C it is all a matter of style, and you will encounter all three styles in your programming career.

Program 5.10b

```
#include <stdio.h>
int main()
{
  int count;

  count = 2; /* initializer outside for statement */
  for( ; count <= 20; )
  {
    printf("%d ",count);
    count += 2; /* alteration statement */
  }

  return 0;
}
```

Program 5.10c

```
#include <stdio.h>
int main() /* all expressions within the for's parentheses */
{
  int count;

  for (count = 2; count <= 20; printf("%d ",count), count += 2);

  return 0;
}
```

In Program 5.10a count is initialized outside the for statement and the first list inside the parentheses is left blank. In Program 5.10b both the initializing list and the altering list are removed from within the parentheses. Program 5.10b also uses a compound statement within the for loop, with the expression-altering statement included in the compound statement. Program 5.10c includes all items within the parentheses, so there is no need for any useful statement following the parentheses. Here the Null statement satisfies the syntactical requirement that one statement follow the for's parentheses. Observe also in Program 5.10c that the altering list (the last set of items in parentheses) consists of two items and that a comma separates these items. The use of commas to separate items in both the initializing and altering lists is required if either of these two lists contains more than one item. Such lists in C, where commas are required to separate individual expressions in the list, are referred to as **comma-separated** lists. Finally, note that Programs 5.10a, 5.10b, and 5.10c are all inferior to Program 5.10. The for statement in Program 5.10 is much clearer because all the expressions pertaining to the tested expression are grouped together within the parentheses.

Although the initializing and altering lists can be omitted from a for statement, omitting the tested expression results in an infinite loop. For example, such a loop is created by the statement

```
for (count = 2; ; count++)
  printf("%d",count);
```

As with the while statement, both break and continue statements can be used within a for loop. The break forces an immediate exit from the for loop, as it does in the while loop. The continue, however, forces control to be passed to the altering list in a for statement, after which the tested expression is reevaluated. This differs from the action of a continue in a while statement, where control is passed directly to the reevaluation of the tested expression.

To understand the enormous power of the for statement, consider the task of printing a table of numbers from 1 to 10, including their squares and cubes, using this statement. Such a table was previously produced using a while statement in Program 5.3. You may wish to review Program 5.3 and compare it to Program 5.11 to get a further sense of the equivalence between the for and while statements.

Programming Note

Where Do the Opening Braces Go?

There are two styles of writing `for` loops that are used by professional C programmers. These styles come into play only when the `for` loop contains a compound statement. The style illustrated and used in the text takes the form

```
for (expression)
{
  compound statement
}
```

An equally acceptable style that is used by many programmers places the initial brace of the compound statement on the first line. Using this style a `for` loop appears as

```
for (expression) {
  compound statement
}
```

The advantage of the first style is that the braces line up under one another, making it easier to locate brace pairs. The advantage of the second style is that it makes the code more compact and saves a display line, permitting more code to be viewed in the same display area. Both styles are used, but are almost never intermixed. Select whichever style appeals to you or is specified by your professor or place of work, and be consistent in its use. As always, the indentation you use within the compound statement (two or four spaces, or a tab) should also be consistent throughout all of your programs. The combination of styles that you select becomes a "signature" for your programming work.

Program 5.11

```
#include <stdio.h>
int main()
{
  #define TABLESIZE 10
  int num;

  printf("NUMBER SQUARE CUBE\n");
  printf("------ ------ ----\n");

  for (num = 1; num <= TABLESIZE; num++)
    printf("%3d %7d %6d\n", num, num*num, num*num*num);

  return 0;
}
```

Program 5.11 produces the following display:

```
NUMBER    SQUARE    CUBE
------    ------    ----
  1          1        1
  2          4        8
  3          9       27
  4         16       64
  5         25      125
  6         36      216
  7         49      343
  8         64      512
  9         81      729
 10        100     1000
```

Simply changing 10 in the `#define` statement of Program 5.11 to 1000 creates a loop that is executed 1000 times and produces a table of numbers from 1 to 1000. As with the `while` statement, this small change produces an immense increase in the processing and output provided by the program.

Computing Sums and Averages Using a for Loop

Sums and averages are computed using a `for` loop in the exact same manner as these values are computed using a `while` loop (see Section 5.3). For example, in Program 5.12 a `scanf()` function call is used to input a set of numbers. As each number is input, it is added to a total. When the `for` loop is exited, the average is calculated and displayed.

Program 5.12

```
#include <stdio.h>
#define MAXCOUNT 5
int main()
/* This program calculates the average */
/* of five user-entered numbers.       */
{
  int count;
  float num, total, average;

  total = 0.0;

  for (count = 0; count < MAXCOUNT; count++)
  {
    printf("\nEnter a number: ");
    scanf("%f", &num);
    total += num;
  }
```

☞

```
    average = total / MAXCOUNT;
    printf("\n\nThe average of the %d numbers entered is %f\n",
                                             MAXCOUNT, average);

    return 0;
}
```

The for statement in Program 5.12 creates a loop that is executed five times. The user is prompted to enter a number each time through the loop. After each number is entered, it is immediately added to the total. Although, for clarity, `total` was initialized to 0 before the `for` statement, this initialization could have been included with the initialization of `count`, as follows:

```
for (total = 0.0, count = 0; count < MAXCOUNT; count++)
```

EXERCISES 5.4

Short Answer Questions

1. Write individual `for` statements for the following cases:
   a. Use a counter named `i` that has an initial value of 1, a final value of 20, and an increment of 1.
   b. Use a counter named `icount` that has an initial value of 1, a final value of 21, and an increment of 2.
   c. Use a counter named j that has an initial value of 1, a final value of 100, and an increment of 5.
   d. Use a counter named `icount` that has an initial value of 20, a final value of 1, and a decrement of –1.
   e. Use a counter named `icount` that has an initial value of 21, a final value of 1, and a decrement of –2.
   f. Use a counter named `count` that has an initial value of 1.0, a final value of 16.2, and an increment of 0.2.
   g. Use a counter named `xcnt` that has an initial value of 20.0, a final value of 10.0, and a decrement of –0.5.

2. Determine the number of times that each `for` loop is executed for the `for` statements written for Question 1.

3. Determine the value in total after each of the following loops is executed:
   a.
```
total = 0;
for (i = 1; i <= 10; i += 1)
  total += 1;
```
   b.
```
total = 1;
for (count = 1; count <= 10; count += 1)
  total = total * 2;
```

c.
```
total = 0;
for ( i = 10; i <= 15; i += 1)
  total += i;
```

d.
```
total = 50;
for (i = 1; i <=10; i += 1)
  total -= i;
```

e.
```
total = 1;
for (icnt = 1; icnt <= 8; icnt++)
  total = total * icnt;
```

f.
```
total = 1.0;
for (j = 1; j <= 5; j++)
  total = total / 2.0;
```

4. Determine the output of the following program:

```
#include <stdio.h>
int main()
{
  int i;
  for (i = 20; i >= 0; i = i - 4)
     printf("%d ",i);
}
```

Programming Exercises

1. Modify Program 5.11 to produce a table of the numbers 0 through 20 in increments of 2, with their squares and cubes.

2. Modify Program 5.11 to produce a table of numbers from 10 to 1, instead of 1 to 10, as it currently does.

3. Write and run a C program that displays a table of 20 temperature conversions from Fahrenheit to Celsius. The table should start with a Fahrenheit value of 20 degrees and be incremented in values of 4 degrees. Recall that *Celsius = (5.0/9.0) * (Fahrenheit – 32.0).*

4. Write and run a C program that accepts six Fahrenheit temperatures, one at a time, and converts each value entered to its Celsius equivalent before the next value is requested. Use a `for` loop in your program. The conversion required is *Celsius = (5.0/9.0) * (Fahrenheit – 32.0).*

5. Write and run a C program that accepts 10 individual values of gallons, one at a time, and converts each value entered to its liter equivalent before the next value is requested. Use a `for` loop in your program. There are 3.785 liters in 1 gallon.

6. Write and run a C program that calculates and displays the amount of money available in a bank account that initially has $1000 deposited in it and earns 8 percent interest a year. Your program should display the amount available at the end of each year for a period of 10 years. Use the relationship that the money available at the end of each year equals the amount of money in the account at the start of the year plus .08 times the amount available at the start of the year.

7. A machine purchased for $28,000 is depreciated at a rate of $4,000 a year for seven years. Write and run a program that computes and displays a depreciation table for seven years. The table should have the form

```
                  DEPRECIATION SCHEDULE
                  ---------------------

                         END-OF-YEAR ACCUMULATED
YEAR DEPRECIATION           VALUE     DEPRECIATION
---- ------------ ----------- ------------
1        4000          24000        4000
2        4000          20000        8000
3        4000          16000       12000
4        4000          12000       16000
5        4000           8000       20000
6        4000           4000       24000
7        4000              0       28000
```

8. A well-regarded manufacturer of widgets has been losing 4 percent of its sales each year. The annual profit for the firm is 10 percent of sales. This year the firm has had $10 million in sales and a profit of $1 million. Determine the expected sales and profit for the next 10 years. Your program should complete and produce a display as follows:

```
            SALES AND PROFIT PROJECTION
            ---------------------------

YEAR    EXPECTED SALES      PROJECTED PROFIT
----    --------------      ----------------
  1     $10000000.00          $1000000.00
  2     $ 9600000.00          $ 960000.00
  3           .                    .
  .           .                    .
  .           .                    .
  .           .                    .
 10           .                    .
        -------------       ----------------
Totals: $                   $
```

5.5 Case Studies: Loop Programming Techniques

In addition to the applications that have already been described, this section presents four additional programming techniques associated with pretest (`for` and `while`) loops. Each of these techniques is common knowledge to experienced programmers.

Technique 1: Selection within a Loop

One common programming technique is to use either a `for` or `while` loop to cycle through a set of numbers and select those numbers that meet one or more criteria. For example, assume that we want to find both the positive and negative sums of a set of numbers. The criteria here is whether the number is positive or negative, and the logic for implementing this program is given by the pseudocode

While the loop condition is true
  Enter a number
  If the number is greater than 0
    add the number to the positive sum
  else
    add the number to the negative sum
  EndIf
EndWhile

Program 5.13 describes this algorithm in C for a counter-controlled loop where five numbers are to be entered.

Program 5.13

```
#include <stdio.h>
#define MAXNUMS 5
int main()
/* this program computes the positive and negative sums of a set */
/* of MAXNUMS user entered numbers                                */
{
  int i;
  float number;
  float postotal = 0.0f;
  float negtotal = 0.0f;

  for (i = 1; i <= MAXNUMS; i++)
  {
    printf("Enter a number (positive or negative) : ");
    scanf("%f", &number);
    if (number > 0)
      postotal += number;
    else
      negtotal += number;
  }

  printf("\nThe positive total is %f", postotal);
  printf("\nThe negative total is %f\n", negtotal);

  return 0;
}
```

Following is a sample run using Program 5.13:

```
Enter a number (positive or negative) : 10
Enter a number (positive or negative) : -10
Enter a number (positive or negative) : 5
Enter a number (positive or negative) : -7
Enter a number (positive or negative) : 11

The positive total is 26.000000
The negative total is -17.000000
```

Technique 2: Input Data Validation

A `while` loop is frequently used for input validation purposes, where a user is requested to enter a value within a specified range. For example, the input of a date would require that all month values reside between 1 and 12, while day values reside between 1 and 31.

Such cases are easily handled with a `while` loop, which checks for an invalid value. For example, Program 5.14 repeatedly requests a month value until a valid month is entered.

Program 5.14

```
 1  #include <stdio.h>
 2  int main()
 3  {
 4    int month;
 5
 6    printf("\nEnter a month between 1 and 12: ");
 7    scanf("%d", &month);
 8
 9    while (month < 1 || month > 12)
10    {
11      printf("Error - the month you entered is not valid.\n");
12      printf("\nEnter a month between 1 and 12: ");
13      scanf("%d", &month);
14    }
15
16    printf("The month accepted is %d\n", month);
17
18    return 0;
19  }
```

The `while` statement in line 9

```
9  while (month < 1 || month > 12)
```

checks for an invalid month. Thus, any month value less than 1 or greater than 12 will make the tested expression true, and keeps the `while` loop going. The loop only stops when a valid month is detected.

Following is a sample run using Program 5.14. As indicated, the loop keeps requesting a month value until a valid month is entered.

```
Enter a month between 1 and 12: 14
Error - the month you entered is not valid.

Enter a month between 1 and 12: 0
Error - the month you entered is not valid.

Enter a month between 1 and 12: 7
The month accepted is 7
```

From a programmer's perspective, one annoyance with Program 5.14 is that it repeats the `printf()` and `scanf()` function calls both before and within the `while` loop. That is, lines

```
6   printf("\nEnter a month between 1 and 12: ");
7   scanf("%d", &month);
```

are the same as lines

```
12  printf("\nEnter a month between 1 and 12: ");
13  scanf("%d", &month);
```

This repetition of code is always found in data validation `while` loops that require initialization before the first evaluation of the tested expression. Before the loop is even entered, there must be a prompt and input statement to obtain the first value to be tested.

Professional programmers have two ways around this. One method is to use a `do-while` statement, which is introduced in the next section. More commonly, however, a C programmer will code a `while` loop that is always true, use an `if` statement within the loop to test for a valid data value after a number has been entered, and then use a `break` statement if a valid value has been entered. Program 5.15 uses this technique for detecting a valid month value.

Program 5.15

```
#include <stdio.h>
int main()
{
  #define TRUE 1
  int month;

  while (TRUE)  /* this is always true */
  {
    printf("\nEnter a month between 1 and 12: ");
    scanf("%d", &month);
```

```
11
12        if (month > 1 && month < 12)   /* the test is made here */
13          break;
14
15        printf("Error - the month you entered is not valid.\n");
16      }
17
18      printf("The month accepted is %d\n", month);
19
20      return 0;
21    }
```

Program 5.15 produces the same output as Program 5.14, while avoiding the need to recode the `printf()` and `scanf()` calls in lines 9 and 10 and place them before the `while` statement. Both programs assume, however, that an integer value will be entered. In Chapter 9, we will see how to modify this input data validation to ensure that an integer value is, in fact, entered before attempting to verify a correct value.

Technique 3: Interactive Loop Control

Values used to control a loop may be set using variables rather than constant values. For example, the four statements

```
i = 5;
j = 15;
k = 2;
for (count = i; count <= j; count += k)
```

produce the same effect as the single statement

```
for (count = 5; count <= 15; count += 2)
```

Similarly, the statements

```
i = 5;
j = 15;
k = 2;
count = i;
while (count <= j)
  count = count + k;
```

produce the same effect as the following `while` loop:

```
count = 5;
while (count <= 15)
count += 2;
```

The advantage of using variables in the initialization, condition, and altering expressions is that it allows us to assign values for these expressions external to both the `for` and `while` statements. This is especially useful when a `scanf()` function call is used to set the actual values. To make this a little more tangible, consider Program 5.16.

Program 5.16

```
#include <stdio.h>
int main()
/* this program displays a table of numbers, their squares and cubes */
/* starting from the number 1. The final number in the table is */
/* input by the user */
{
  int num, final;

  printf("Enter the final number for the table: ");
  scanf("%d", &final);

  printf("Number Square Cube\n");
  printf("------ ------ ----\n");

  for (num = 1; num <= final; num++)
    printf("%3d %7d %6d\n", num, num*num, num*num*num);

  return 0;
}
```

In Program 5.16, we have used a variable name within the condition (middle) expression only. Here a `scanf()` statement has been placed before the loop to allow the user to decide what the final value should be. This arrangement permits the user to set the size of the table at run time, rather than having the programmer set the table size at compile time. This also makes the program more general, since it now can be used to create a variety of tables without the need for reprogramming and recompiling.

Technique 4: Evaluating Equations

Loops can be conveniently constructed to determine and display the values of mathematical equations for a set of values over any specified interval. For example, assume that we want to know the values of the equation

$$y = 10x^2 + 3x - 2$$

for x between 2 and 6. Assuming that x has been declared as an integer variable, the following `for` loop can be used to calculate the required values.

```
for (x = 2; x <= 6; x++)
{
  y = 10 * pow(x,2) + 3 * x - 2;
  printf(" %3d        %3d\n", x, y);
}
```

For this loop we have used the variable x as both the counter variable and the independent variable in the equation. For each value of x from 2 to 6 a new value of y is calculated and displayed. This `for` loop is contained within Program 5.17, which also displays appropriate headings for the values printed.

Program 5.17

```
#include <stdio.h>
#include <math.h>
int main()
{
  int x, y;

  printf("x value    y value\n");
  printf("-------    --------\n");

  for (x = 2; x <= 6; x++)
  {
    y = 10 * pow(x,2) + 3 * x - 2;
    printf("%4d %10d\n", x, y);
  }

  return 0;
}
```

The following is displayed when Program 5.17 is executed:

```
x value    y value
-------    --------
   2          44
   3          97
   4         170
   5         263
   6         376
```

Two items are of importance here. First, any equation with one independent variable can be evaluated using a single `for` or an equivalent `while` loop. The method requires substituting the desired equation into the loop in place of the equation used in Program 5.17, and adjusting the counter values to match the desired solution range.

Second, we are not constrained to using integer values for the counter variable. For example, by specifying a noninteger increment, solutions for fractional values can be obtained. This is shown in Program 5.18, where the equation $y = 10x^2 + 3x - 2$ is evaluated in the range $x = 2$ to $x = 6$ in increments of 0.5.

Program 5.18

```
#include <stdio.h>
#include <math.h>
int main()
{
  float x, y;

  printf("x value     y value\n");
  printf("--------   ----------\n");

  for (x = 2.0; x <= 6.0; x += 0.5)
  {
    y = 10.0 * pow(x,2) + 3.0 * x - 2.0;
    printf("%8.6f %13.6f\n", x, y);
  }

  return 0;
}
```

Notice that *x* and *y* have been declared as floating-point variables in Program 5.18, to allow these variables to take on fractional values. The following is the output produced by this program:

```
x value     y value
--------   ----------
2.000000    44.000000
2.500000    68.000000
3.000000    97.000000
3.500000   131.000000
4.000000   170.000000
4.500000   214.000000
5.000000   263.000000
5.500000   317.000000
6.000000   376.000000
```

EXERCISES 5.5

Programming Exercises

1. Modify Program 5.13 so that the number of entries to be input is specified by the user when the program is executed.

2. Modify Program 5.13 so that it displays the average of the positive and negative numbers. (*Hint:* Be careful not to count the number 0 as a negative number.) Test your program by entering the numbers 17, –10, 20, 0, and –4. The positive average displayed by your program should be 18.5 and the negative average, –7.

3. **a.** Enter and run either Program 5.14 or 5.15.
   b. Determine what happens when you enter a floating-point number instead of an integer number when executing either Program 5.14 or 5.15.
   c. Determine what happens when you enter a letter instead of an integer number when executing either Program 5.14 or 5.15.

4. Write and run a C program that requests a day value. Have your program accept only day values between 1 and 31.

5. Write and run a C program that requests both a month and day value. Only month values between 1 and 12 should be accepted. Further, day values between 1 and 28 should only be accepted for month 2 (February); day values between 1 and 30 should only be accepted for months 4, 6, 9, and 11 (April, June, September, and November); and only day values between 1 and 31 should be accepted for all remaining months. (*Hint:* Use a `switch` statement.)

6. **a.** Write a C program that selects and displays the maximum value of five numbers that are to be entered when the program is executed. (*Hint:* Use a `for` loop with both a `scanf()` and `if` statement internal to the loop.)
   b. Modify the program written for Exercise 6a so that it displays both the maximum value and the position in the input set of numbers where the maximum occurs.

7. Write a C program that selects and displays the first 20 integer numbers that are evenly divisible by 3.

8. A child's parents promised to give the child $10 on her 12th birthday and double the gift on every subsequent birthday until the gift exceeded $1000. Write a C program to determine how old the girl will be when the last amount is given, and the total amount she received including the last gift.

9. Modify Program 5.18 to produce a table of y values for the following equations:
   a. $y = 3x^5 - 2x^3 + x$ for x between 5 and 10 in increments of .2
   b. $y = 1 + x + \frac{x^2}{2} + \frac{x^3}{6} + \frac{x^4}{24}$ for x between 1 and 3 in increments of .1
   c. $y = 2e^{.8t}$ for t between 4 and 10 in increments of .2

10. A model of worldwide population, in billions of people, is given by the equation
$Population = 6.0(e^{02*t})$
where t is the time in years ($t = 0$ represents January 2000 and $t = 1$ represents January 2001). Using this formula, write a C program that displays a monthly population table for the months January 2007 though December 2008.

11. The x and y coordinates, as an equation of time, t, of a projectile fired with an initial velocity v at an angle of *theta* with respect to the ground is given by
$x = v\ t\ cos\ \theta$
$y = v\ t\ sin\ \theta$
Using these formulas, write a C program that displays a table of x and y values for a projectile fired with an initial velocity of 500 ft/sec at an angle of 22.8 degrees. (*Hint:* Remember to convert to radian measure.) The table should contain values corresponding to the time interval 0 to 10 seconds in increments of one-half seconds.

12. Modify Program 5.16 to accept the starting and increment values of the table produced by the program.

13. Write a C program that converts Fahrenheit to Celsius temperature in increments of 5 degrees. The initial value of the Fahrenheit temperature and the total conversions to be made are to be requested as user input during program execution. Recall that *Celsius = (5.0/9.0) * (Fahrenheit – 32.0).*

14. **a.** Modify the program written for Programming Exercise 6 of the previous section (Section 5.4) to initially prompt the user for the amount of money originally deposited in the account.
b. Modify the program written for Programming Exercise 6 of the previous section (Section 5.4) to initially prompt the user for both the amount of money originally deposited and the number of years that should be displayed.
c. Modify the program written for Programming Exercise 6 of the previous section (Section 5.4) to initially prompt for the amount of money originally deposited, the interest rate to be used, and the number of years to be displayed.

5.6 Nested Loops

There are many situations in which it is very convenient to have a loop contained within another loop. Such loops are called **nested loops.** A simple example of a nested loop is

```
for(i = 1; i <= 5; i++)          /* start of outer loop <---+ */
{                                /*                         | */
  printf("\ni is now %d\n",i)   /*                         | */
  for(j = 1; j <= 4; j++)        /* start of inner loop     | */
    printf(" j = %d", j);        /* end of inner loop       | */
}                                /* end of outer loop   <---+ */
```

The first loop, controlled by the value of `i`, is called the **outer loop**. The second loop, controlled by the value of `j`, is called the **inner loop**. Notice that all statements in the inner loop are contained within the boundaries of the outer loop and that we have used a different variable to control each loop. For each single trip through the outer loop, the inner loop runs through its entire sequence. Thus, each time the `i` counter increases by 1, the inner `for` loop executes completely. This situation is illustrated in Figure 5.9.

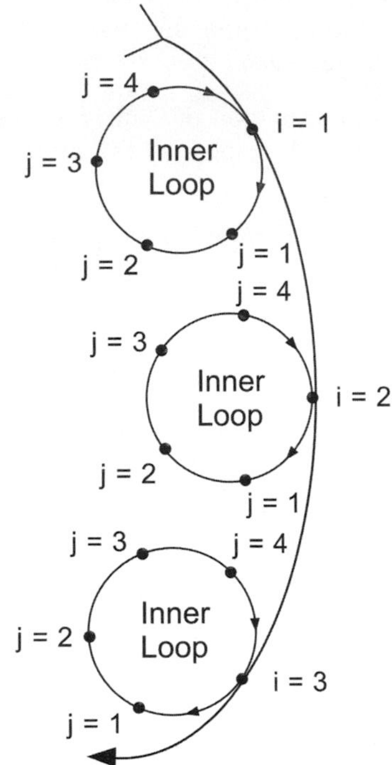

Figure 5.9 `j` loops once for each `i`

Program 5.19 includes the above code in a working program. Following is the output of a sample run of Program 5.19:

```
i is now 1
j = 1 j = 2 j = 3 j = 4
i is now 2
j = 1 j = 2 j = 3 j = 4
i is now 3
j = 1 j = 2 j = 3 j = 4
i is now 4
j = 1 j = 2 j = 3 j = 4
i is now 5
j = 1 j = 2 j = 3 j = 4
```

Program 5.19

```
#include <stdio.h>
int main()
{
  int i,j;

  for(i = 1; i <= 5; i++)          /* start of outer loop <---+ */
  {                                /*                         | */
    printf("\ni is now %d\n",i);  /*                         | */
    for(j = 1; j <=4; j++)         /* start of inner loop     | */
      printf(" j = %d", j);        /* end of inner loop       | */
  }                                /* end of outer loop   <---+ */

  return 0;
}
```

Let us use a nested loop to compute the average grade for each student in a class of 20. Each student has taken four exams during the course of the semester. The final grade is calculated as the average of these examination grades.

The outer loop in our program will consist of 20 passes. Each pass through the outer loop is used to compute the average for one student. The inner loop will consist of 4 passes. One examination grade is entered in each inner loop pass. As each grade is entered, it is added to the total for the student, and at the end of the loop the average is calculated and displayed. Program 5.20 uses a nested loop to make the required calculations.

Program 5.20

```
#include <stdio.h>
  #define NUMSTUDENTS 20
  #define NUMGRADES 4
int main()
{
  int i,j;
  float grade, total, average;

  for (i = 1; i <= NUMSTUDENTS; i++) /* start of outer loop */
  {
    total = 0; /* clear the total for this student */

    for (j = 1; j <= NUMGRADES; j++) /* start of inner loop */
    {
      printf("Enter an examination grade for this student: ");
```

```
16        scanf("%f", &grade);
17        total = total + grade; /* add the grade into the total */
18      } /* end of the inner for loop */
19
20      average = total / NUMGRADES; /* calculate the average */
21      printf("\nThe average for student %d is %f\n\n",i,average);
22    } /* end of the outer for loop */
23
24    return 0;
25  }
```

In reviewing Program 5.20, pay particular attention to the initialization of `total` in line 11

```
11  total = 0; /* clear the total for this student */
```

Because this statement is within the outer loop but before the inner loop is entered, the variable `total` is initialized 20 times, once for each student. Also notice that the average is calculated and displayed in lines 20 and 21 immediately after the inner loop is finished.

```
20  average = total / NUMGRADES; /* calculate the average */
21  printf("\nThe average for student %d is %f\n\n",i,average);
```

Because these two statements are also contained within the outer loop, 20 averages are calculated and displayed. The entry and addition of each grade within the inner loop use techniques we have seen before, so they should now be familiar to you.

EXERCISES 5.6

Programming Exercises

1. Four experiments are performed, each consisting of six test results. The results for each experiment are given below. Write a C program using a nested loop to compute and display the average of the test results for each experiment.

```
1st experiment results: 23.2   31.5   16.9   27.5   25.4   28.6
2nd experiment results: 34.8   45.2   27.9   36.8   33.4   39.4
3rd experiment results: 19.4   16.8   10.2   20.8   18.9   13.4
4th experiment results: 36.9   39.5   49.2   45.1   42.7   50.6
```

2. Modify the program written for Exercise 1 so that the number of test results for each experiment is entered by the user. Write your program so that a different number of test results can be entered for each experiment.

3. a. A bowling team consists of five players. Each player bowls three games. Write a C program that uses a nested loop to enter each player's individual scores and then computes and displays the average score for each bowler. Assume that each bowler has the following scores:

```
1st bowler: 286   252   265
2nd bowler: 212   186   215
3rd bowler: 252   232   216
4th bowler: 192   201   235
5th bowler: 186   236   272
```

   b. Modify the program written for Exercise 3a to calculate and display the average team score. (*Hint:* Use a second variable to store the total of all the players' scores.)

4. Rewrite the program written for Exercise 3a to eliminate the inner loop. To do this, you have to input three scores for each bowler rather than one at a time. Each score must be stored in its own variable name before the average is calculated.

5. Write a C program that calculates and displays the yearly amount available if $1000 is invested in a bank account for 10 years. Your program should display the amounts available for interest rates from 6 percent to 12 percent inclusively, at 1 percent increments. Use a nested loop, with the outer loop having a fixed count of 7 and the inner loop a fixed count of 10. The first iteration of the outer loop should use an interest rate of 6 percent and display the amount of money available at the end of the first 10 years. In each subsequent pass through the outer loop, the interest rate should be increased by 1 percent. Use the relationship that the money available at the end of each year equals the amount of money in the account at the start of the year plus the interest rate times the amount available at the start of the year.

5.7 The `do-while` Statement

Both the `while` and `for` statements evaluate an expression at the start of the repetition loop. There are cases, however, where it is more convenient to test the expression at the end of the loop. For example, suppose we have constructed the following `while` loop to calculate sales taxes:

```
1  #define SENTINEL 0.0
2  #define RATE .06
3  printf("Enter a price:");
4  scanf("%f", &price);
5  while (price != SENTINEL)
6  {
7    salestax = RATE * price;
8    printf("The sales tax is $%5.2f",salestax);
9    printf("\nEnter a price: ");
10   scanf("%f", &price);
11 }
```

Using this `while` statement requires either duplicating the prompt and `scanf()` function calls before the loop (lines 3 and 4) and then within the loop (lines 9 and 10), as we have done, or resorting to some other artifice to force initial execution of the statements within the `while` loop.

The do-while statement, as its name implies, allows us to do some statements before an expression is evaluated. In many situations this can be used to eliminate the duplication illustrated in the previous example. The general form of the do statement is

```
do
  statement;
while (expression);
```

Note that final semicolon after the expression; take care not to omit it. As with all C programs, the single statement in the do may be replaced with a compound statement. A flow-control diagram illustrating the operation of the do-while statement is shown in Figure 5.10.

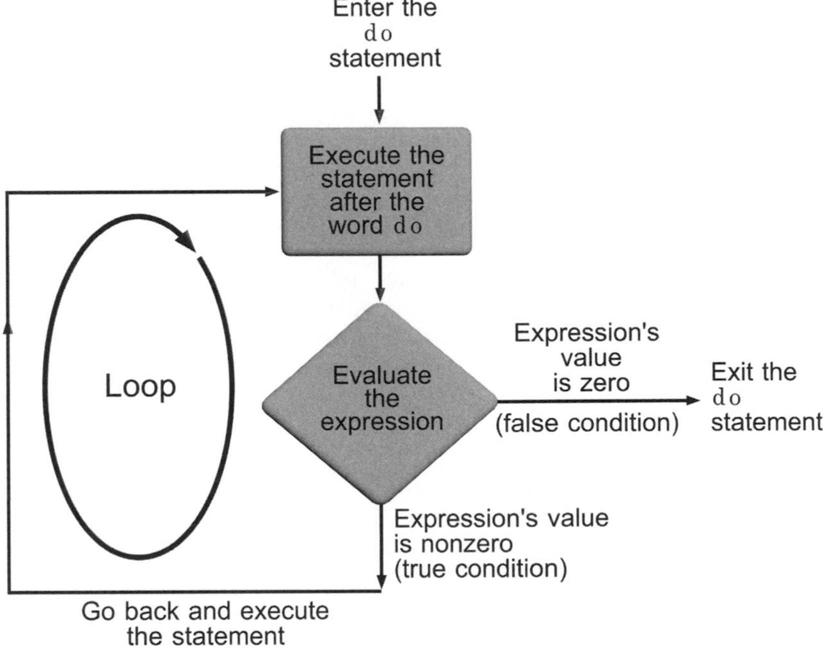

Figure 5.10 do-while statement flow of control

As illustrated in Figure 5.10, all statements within the do-while statement are executed at least once before the expression is evaluated. Then, if the expression has a non-0 value, the statements are executed again. This process continues until the expression evaluates to 0. For example, for the symbolic constant defined as

```
#define SENTINEL 0.0
#define RATE .06
```

consider the do-while statement in the following code segment:

```
do
{
  printf("\nEnter a price or -1 to terminate: ");
```

```
  scanf("%f", &price);

  if (price < SENTINEL)
    break;

  salestax = RATE * price;
  printf("The sales tax is $%5.2f", salestax);
} while (price > SENTINEL);
```

Here the compound statement within the loop will always be executed at least once, regardless of the value of the tested condition. Statements within the compound statement will then be repeatedly executed as long as the tested condition remains true. Calculation of the sales tax and the loop itself is only stopped when any negative value is encountered.

As with all repetition statements, the `do-while` statement can always replace or be replaced by an equivalent `while` or `for` statement. The choice of which statement to use depends on the application and the style preferred by the programmer. In general, the `while` and `for` statements are preferred because they clearly let anyone reading the program know what is being tested "right up front" at the top of the program loop.

Because the `while` and `for` statements evaluate an expression at the start of the repetition loop, they always produce pretest loops. In contrast, a `do-while` statement always creates a posttest loop, in which the condition being tested is always evaluated at the end of the loop, as illustrated in Figure 5.11. This ensures that at least one iteration of statements is completed before the condition is evaluated and the loop is exited when the condition becomes false.

There is one type of application that is ideally suited for a posttest loop, which is the **input data validation application** that was previously listed in Table 5.1 and illustrated using a `while` loop in technique 2 of Section 5.5. For example, assume that an operator is required to enter a valid customer identification number between the numbers 1000 and 1999. A number outside this range is to be rejected and a new request for a valid number made. The following section of code provides the necessary data filter to verify the entry of a valid identification number:

```
do
{
  printf("\nEnter an identification number: ");
  scanf("%f", &idNum);
} while (idNum < 1000 || idNum > 1999);
```

Here, a request for an identification number is repeated until a valid number is entered. This section of code is "bare bones" in that it neither alerts the operator to the cause of the new request for data nor allows premature exit from the loop if a valid identification number cannot be found. As such, it is a trap, where a user cannot exit it until a correct value is entered. An alternative that removes both drawbacks is

```
do
{
  printf("\nEnter an identification number between 1000 and 1999");
  printf("\n  or any negative number to exit the program: ");
  scanf("%d", &idNum);

```

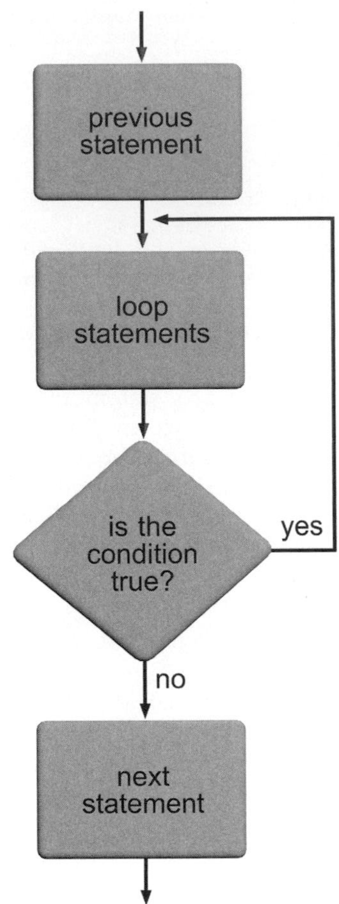

Figure 5.11 A posttest loop structure

```
    if (idNum < 0)
      break;

    if (idNum >= 1000 && idNum <= 1999)
      break;  /* break if a valid id num was entered */
    else
    {
      printf("\n An invalid number was just entered");
      printf("\nPlease check the ID number and re-enter");
      printf("\nA valid ID number is between 1000 and 1999\n");
    }
  } while(1); /* this expression is always true */
```

Because the expression being evaluated by the do-while statement is always 1 (true), an infinite loop has been created that can be exited by a break statement. In this particular code, we have used two `break` statements that exit the loop if the user enters either a negative number or a valid ID. In the first `if` statement in lines 7 and 8

```
7   if (idNum < 0)
8     break;
```

any negative input value causes the loop to stop. This provides a way for the user to get out of the loop whenever a valid ID number is not known. It is the second `if` statement in lines 10 through 17

```
10  if (idNum >= 1000 && idNum <= 1999)
11    break;   /* break if a valid id num was entered */
12  else
13  {
14    printf("\n An invalid number was just entered");
15    printf("\nPlease check the ID number and re-enter");
16    printf("\nA valid ID number is between 1000 and 1999\n");
17  }
```

that causes a break from the loop whenever a valid ID is entered. Clearly, an `if-else` statement would then be required after the `do-while` statement to determine which `break` caused the loop to terminate.[3]

EXERCISES 5.7

Programming Exercises

1. a. Using a `do-while` statement, write a C program to accept a grade. The program should request a grade continuously as long as an invalid grade is entered. An invalid grade is any grade less than 0 or greater than 100. After a valid grade has been entered, your program should display its value.
   b. Modify the program written for Exercise 1a so that the user is alerted when an invalid grade has been entered.
   c. Modify the program written for Exercise 1a so that it allows the user to exit the program by entering the number 999.
   d. Modify the program written for Exercise 1b so that it automatically terminates after five invalid grades are entered.

2. a. Write a C program that continuously requests a grade to be entered. If the grade is less than 0 or greater than 100, your program should print an appropriate message informing the user that an invalid grade has been entered, else the grade should be added to a total. When a grade of 999 is entered, the program should exit the repetition loop and compute and display the average of the valid grades entered.
   b. Run the program written in Exercise 2a on a computer, and verify the program using appropriate test data.

[3]An alternative is to use an `exit()` function call in place of the break in line 8. This will cause termination of the program containing the do statement.

3. a. Write a C program to reverse the digits of a positive integer number. For example, if the number 8735 is entered, the number displayed should be 5378. (*Hint:* Use a `do` statement and continuously strip off and display the units digit of the number. If the variable `num` initially contains the number entered, the units digit is obtained as `(num % 10)`. After a units digit is displayed, dividing the number by 10 sets up the number for the next iteration. Thus, `(8735 % 10)` is 5 and `(8735 / 10)` is 873. The `do` statement should continue as long as the remaining number is not 0.
   b. Run the program written in Exercise 3a on a computer, and verify the program using appropriate text data.

4. Print the decimal, octal, and hexadecimal values of all characters between the start and stop characters entered by a user. For example, if the user enters an `a` and `z`, the program should print all the characters between `a` and `z` and their respective numerical values. Make sure that the second character entered by the user occurs later in the alphabet than the first character. If it does not, write a loop that repeatedly asks the user for a valid second character until one is entered.

5. Repeat any of the exercises in Section 5.4 using a `do-while` statement rather than a `for` statement.

5.8 Common Programming and Compiler Errors

In using the material presented in this chapter, be aware of the following possible programming and compiler errors.

Programming Errors

Six errors are commonly made by beginning C programmers when using repetition statements. The second and third of these errors pertain to the tested expression and you have already encountered them with the `if` and `switch` statements.

1. The most troublesome programming error for new programmers is the "off by one" error, where the loop executes either one too many or one too few times than was intended. For example, the loop created by the statement `for(i = 1; i < 11; i++)` executes 10 times, not 11, even though the number 11 is used in the statement. Thus, an equivalent loop can be constructed using the statement `for(i = 1; i <= 10; i++)`. However, if the loop is started with an initial value of `i = 0`, using the statement `for(i = 0; i < 11; i++)`, the loop will be traversed 11 times, as will a loop constructed with the statement `for(i = 0; i <= 10; i++)`. In constructing loops, you must pay particular attention to both initial and final conditions used to control the loop to ensure that number of loop traversals is not off by one too many or one too few executions.

2. Inadvertently using the assignment operator, `=`, instead of the equality operator, `==`, in the tested expression. An example of this error is typing the assignment expression `a = 5` instead of the desired relational expression `a == 5`. Because the tested expression can be any valid C expression, including arithmetic and assignment expressions, this error is not detected by the compiler.

3. As with the `if` statement, repetition statements should not use the equality operator, ==, when testing single-precision or double-precision operands. For example, the expression `fnum == .01` should be replaced by an equivalent test requiring that the absolute value of `fnum - .01` be less than an acceptable amount. The reason is that all numbers are stored in binary form. Using a finite number of bits, decimal numbers such as .01 have no exact binary equivalent, so that tests requiring equality with such numbers can fail.

4. Placing a semicolon at the end of the `for`'s parentheses if it produces a do-nothing loop. For example, consider the statements

```
for(count = 1; count <= 10; count++);
  total = total + num;
```

Here, the semicolon at the end of the first line of code is a `Null` statement. This has the effect of creating a loop that is traversed 10 times with nothing done except the incrementing and testing of `count`. This error tends to occur because C programmers are used to ending most lines with a semicolon.

It is not always an error to terminate a `for` statement with a semicolon. For example, the following code produces a list of numbers from 1 to 10:

```
for(count = 1; count <= 10; printf("%d  ", count++);
```

5. Using commas to separate the items in a `for` statement instead of the required semicolons. An example of this is the statement

```
for (count = 1, count <= 10, count++)
```

Commas must be used to separate items within the initializing and altering lists, and semicolons must be used to separate these lists from the tested expression.

6. Omitting the final semicolon from the `do` statement. This error is usually made by programmers who have learned to omit the semicolon after the parentheses of a `while` statement and continue this habit when the reserved word `while` is encountered at the end of a `do` statement.

Compiler Errors

The following table summarizes common errors that will result in compilation errors and the typical error messages provided by Unix- and Windows-based compilers.

Error	Typical Unix-based Compiler Error Message	Typical Windows-based Compiler Error Message
Separating the statements in a `for` loop with commas rather than semicolons. For example, `for(init,cond,alt)`	(S) Syntax error: possible missing ';' or ','?	error: syntax error : missing ';' before ')'

Error	Typical Unix-based Compiler Error Message	Typical Windows-based Compiler Error Message

Omitting the parenthesis in a `while` statement. For example,
`while condition`
`{`
`   statement;`
`}`
	(S) Syntax error: possible missing '('?	error: syntax error : missing ';' before '{'

Omitting the `;` at the end of the `do-while` statement. For example,
`do`
`{`
`  statement;`
`}while(condition)`
	(S) Syntax error.
	(This error tends to lead programmers astray. You would expect to get the error generated by a missing semicolon or comma, but instead you get a syntax error.)
		error: syntax error : missing ';'

Omitting the second + or – in a post increment or decrement statement. For example, `val+;` or `val-;`	(S) Syntax error. (Note that `+val;` and `-val;` do not generates a compiler error because these are valid expressions)	error: syntax error : ';'

5.9 Chapter Summary

1. A section of repeating code is referred to as a loop. The loop is controlled by a repetition statement that tests a condition to determine whether the code within the loop will be executed. Each pass through a loop is referred to as a repetition or iteration. The tested condition must always be explicitly set prior to its first evaluation by the repetition statement. Within the loop there must always be a statement that permits altering of the condition so that the loop, once entered, can be exited.

2. The three C repetition statements, which are used to construct their corresponding loop types, are

   a. `while`

   b. `for`

   c. `do-while`

   The `while` and `for` statements are used to create `while` and `for` loops, respectively. Both of these loop types are pretest or entrance-controlled loops. In this type of loop, the tested condition is evaluated at the beginning of the loop, which requires that the tested condition be explicitly set prior to loop entry. If the condition is true, loop repetitions begin; otherwise the loop is not entered. Iterations continue as long as the condition remains true.

The do-while statement is used to create a do-while loop, which is a posttest or exit-controlled loop that tests its condition at the end of the loop. This type of loop is always executed at least once and, as long as the tested condition remains true, do-while loops continue to execute.

3. Loops are also classified as to the type of tested condition. In a counter-controlled loop, the condition is used to keep track of how many repetitions have occurred. In a condition-controlled loop, the tested condition is based on encountering one or more specific values.

4. The most commonly used syntax for a while loop is

```
while (expression)
{
  statements;
}
```

The expression contained within parentheses is the condition tested to determine if the statement following the parentheses, which is generally a compound statement, is executed. The expression is evaluated in exactly the same manner as that contained in an if-else statement; the difference is how the expression is used. In a while statement, the statement following the expression is executed repeatedly as long as the expression retains a non-0 value, rather than just once, as in an if-else statement. An example of a while loop is

```
count = 1;
while (count <= 10)
{
  printf("%d  ", count);
  count++;
}
```

5. A for statement performs the same functions as the while statement, but uses a different form. In many situations, especially those that use a fixed-count condition, the for statement format is easier to use than its while statement equivalent. The most commonly used form of the for statement is

```
for(initializing list; expression; altering list)
{
  statements;
}
```

Within the parentheses of the for statement are three items, separated by semicolons. Each of these items is optional but the semicolons must be present.

The initializing list is used to set any initial values before the loop is entered; generally it is used to initialize a counter. Statements within the initializing list are only executed once. The expression in the for statement is the condition that is tested at the start of the loop and prior to each iteration. The altering list contains loop statements that are not contained within the compound statement: generally it is used to increment or decrement a counter each time the loop is executed. Multiple statements within a list are separated by commas. An example of a `for` loop is

```
for ( total = 0, count = 1; count < 10; count++)
{
  printf("Enter a grade: ");
  scant("%f", &grade);
  total += grade:
}
```

6. The `for` statement is extremely useful in creating counter-controlled loops. This is because the initializing statements, the tested expression, and statements affecting the tested expression can all be included in parentheses at the top of a `for` loop for easy inspection and modification.

7. The `do-while` statement is used to create posttest loops because it checks its expression at the end of the loop. This ensures that the body of a `do` loop is executed at least once. Within a `do` loop, there must be at least one statement that alters the tested expression's value or is a `break` statement.

Chapter 

6.1 Function and Parameter Declarations

6.2 Returning a Value

6.3 Case Study: Calculating Age Norms

6.4 Standard Library Functions

6.5 Common Programming and Compiler Errors

6.6 Chapter Summary

Modularity Using Functions: Part I

Professional programs are designed, coded, and tested very much like hardware, as a set of modules that are integrated to perform as single whole. A good analogy of this is an automobile, where one major module is the engine, another is the transmission, a third the braking system, a fourth the body, and so on. Each of these modules are linked together and ultimately are placed under the control of the driver. (Conceptually, the driver is similar to a supervisor or `main()` program module.) The whole now operates as a complete unit, able to do useful work, such as driving to the store. During the assembly process, each module is individually constructed, tested, and found to be free of defects (bugs) before it is installed in the final product.

Now think what you might do if you wanted to improve your car's performance. You might alter the existing engine or remove it altogether and bolt in a new engine. Similarly, you might change the transmission or tires or shock absorbers, making each individual modification as your time and budget allowed. In each case the majority of the other modules can stay the same, but the car now operates differently.

In this analogy each of the major components of a car can be compared to a function. For example, the driver calls on the engine when the gas pedal is pressed. The engine accepts inputs of fuel, air, and electricity to turn the driver's request into a useful product—power—

and then sends this output to the transmission for further processing. The transmission receives the output of the engine and converts it to a form that can be used by the drive axle. An additional input to the transmission is the driver's selection of gears (drive, reverse, neutral, etc.).

In each case the engine, transmission, and other modules only "know" the universe bounded by their inputs and outputs. The driver need know nothing of the internal operation of the engine, transmission, drive axle, and other modules that are being controlled. The driver simply "calls" on a module, such as the engine, brakes, air conditioning, and steering when that module's output is required. Communication between modules is restricted to passing needed inputs to each module as it is called on to perform its task, and each module operates internally in a relatively independent manner. This same modular approach is used by programmers to create and maintain reliable C programs using functions.

As we have seen, each C program must contain a `main()` function. In addition to this required function, C programs may also contain any number of additional functions, such as `printf()`, `scanf()`, and the mathematical functions introduced in Section 3.2. In this chapter we learn how to write our own functions, which includes passing data to them, processing the passed data, and returning a result.

6.1 Function and Parameter Declarations

In creating a C function, we must be concerned with both the function itself and how it interfaces with other functions, such as `main()`. This includes correctly passing data into a function when it is called and correctly returning a value back from a function. In this section we describe the first part of the interface, passing data to a function and having the function correctly receive, store, and process the transmitted data.

As we have already seen with the `printf()`, `scanf()`, and mathematical functions, a function is called (that is, invoked) by giving the function's name and passing any data to it in the parentheses following the function's name (see Figure 6.1). The called function must be able to accept the data passed to it by the function doing the calling. Only after the called function successfully receives the data can the data be manipulated to produce a useful result.

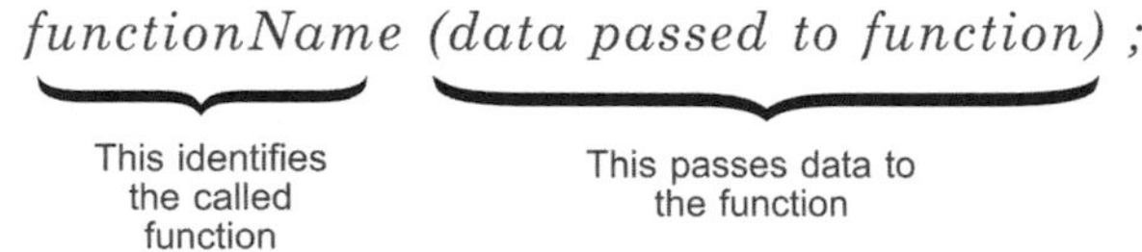

Figure 6.1 Calling and passing data to a function

To clarify the process of sending and receiving data, consider Program 6.1, which consists of two functions, `main()` and `findmax()`.

Program 6.1

```
1  #include <stdio.h>
2  int main()
3  {
4    void findMax(float , float ); /* the function prototype */
5    float firstnum, secnum;
6
7    printf("Enter a number: ");
8    scanf("%f", &firstnum);
9    printf("Great! Please enter a second number: ");
10   scanf("%f", &secnum);
11
12   findMax(firstnum, secnum);     /* the function is called here */
13
14   return 0;
15 }
16
17 /* the following is the function findMax */
18 void findMax(float x, float y) /* this is the function's header line */
19 {
20   float maxnum;
21
22   if (x >= y) /* find the maximum number */
23     maxnum = x;
24   else
25     maxnum = y;
26
27   printf("\nThe maximum of the two numbers entered is %f\n", maxnum);
28 }
```

First, we will examine the code required to declare and call the `findMax()` function from the main() function. We will then examine the `findMax()` function itself to understand how it is coded.

The function `findMax()` is referred to as the **called function**, because it is called or summoned into action by its reference in the `main()` function. The function that does the calling, in this case `main()`, is referred to as the **calling function**. The terms "called" and "calling" come from standard telephone usage, where one party calls the other on the telephone. The party initiating the call is referred to as the calling party, and the party receiving the call is referred to as the called party. The same terms describe function calls.

Now, focus on the three lines of code that have been highlighted in Program 6.1. These include lines 4, 12, and 18, repeated in the following for convenience.

```
4   void findMax(float, float );    /* the function prototype */
12  findMax(firstnum, secnum);      /* the function is called here */
18  void findMax(float x, float y)  /* this is the function's header line */
```

Notice that each of these three lines includes the name of the called function. For each function that you write, you will always code lines similar to these three. Each of these lines performs a specific and distinct task. Line 4 is known as a function prototype. A **function prototype** declares the function to the compiler—it tells the compiler the name of the function, the data type of the value that the function will return (the keyword void indicates that the function will not be returning any value), and the data types of each argument that the function expects to receive when it is called. In the prototype provided in line 4, the function is declared as being named findMax(); it expects to receive two float values and returns no value.

Line 12 is where the function is called. This line should look familiar to you because it is similar to code you have been using to call the printf(), scanf(), and mathematical functions.

Finally, line 18 is the header line for the findMax() function. Each of these statement lines—function prototype, calling statement, and function header—are now described in detail.

Function Prototypes

Before a function can be called, it must be declared, both to the compiler and to the function that will do the calling. The declaration statement for a function is referred to as a **function prototype**. The function prototype declares the data type of the value that will be directly returned by the function, if any, and the data type of the values that need to be transmitted to the called function, if any, when it is invoked. For example, the function prototype in line 4 of Program 6.1

```
4  void findMax(float, float);
```

declares that the function findMax() expects two floating-point values to be sent to it whenever it is called, and that this particular function directly returns no value (void). Function prototypes may be placed with the variable declaration statements of the calling function, as in Program 6.1, or above the calling function name. Thus, the function prototype for findMax() could have been placed either before or after the statement #include <stdio.h> prior to main(), or within main()itself, as in Program 6.1. Placing the prototype before main() makes the declaration available to *all* functions in the file, thus permitting all functions to call findMax(). Placing the prototype within main() makes the declaration available only to main(), which only gives main() the right to call it. Similarly, any other function that needs to use findMax() would then have to include the prototype within itself. The general syntax for a function prototype statement is

returnDataType functionName(list of argument data types);

The *returnDataType* refers to the data type of the value that will be directly returned by the function. The *list of argument data types* defines the number, order, and data types of the data that must be supplied when the function is called. Examples of function prototypes are

```
int fmax(int, int);
```

```
float roi(int, char, char, float);
void display(float, float);
```

In the first example, the function prototype for `fmax()` declares that this function expects to receive two integer arguments and will directly return an integer value. The function prototype for `roi()` declares that this function requires four arguments consisting of an integer, two characters, and a single-precision argument, in this order, and will directly return a floating-point number. Finally, the function prototype for `display()` declares that this function requires two single-precision arguments and does not return any value. Such a function might be used to display the results of a computation directly, without returning any value to the called function.

The use of function prototypes allows the compiler to check for data type errors. If the function prototype does not agree with data types specified when the function is written, an error message (typically `TYPE MISMATCH`) will occur. The prototype also serves another task; it ensures conversion of all arguments passed to the function, when it is called, to their declared argument data types in the prototype.

Historical Note

User-Written Procedures

A function is considered as a user-defined program unit. In more general computer programming terminology, such units are referred to as procedures.

All programming languages provide the ability to create procedures, but they go by different names in different programming languages. In C, as we have seen, procedures are known as functions. In Pascal they were called both procedures and functions. In Modula-2 they were called procedures. In COBOL they were called paragraphs, while in FORTRAN they were referred to as both subroutines and functions.

In more modern languages, this multiple naming convention has continued. Thus, in C++, procedures that are included within a class are referred to as methods, while a procedure that is not part of a class is referred to as a function. In VISUAL BASIC, procedures are referred to as both subroutines and functions, while in Java they are referred to as methods.

Calling a Function

Calling a function is a rather easy operation. The only requirements are that the name of the function be used and that any data passed to the function be enclosed within the parentheses following the function name using the same order, number, and data types as specified in the function prototype. The items enclosed within the parentheses in the call statement, as we have seen, are called **arguments** of the function (see Figure 6.2). Other terms used as synonyms for arguments are **actual arguments** and **actual parameters**. All of these terms refer to the data values supplied to a function within the calling statement when the call is made. It is important to understand that the arguments passed to a C function do not have to be numbers. At their most fundamental level, arguments are expressions that are evaluated when the function is called. Thus, any expression can be used as an argument, provided that the expression can be evaluated to yield an argument of the required data type.

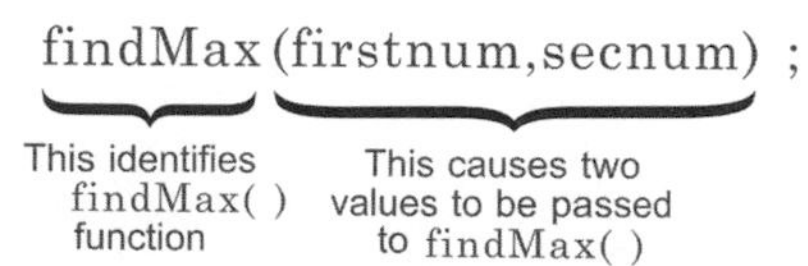

Figure 6.2 Calling and passing two values to `findMax()`

If the expression used as an argument consists of a single variable, the called function receives a copy of the value stored in the variable. Similarly, if one of the arguments consists of a more complicated expression, the expression is evaluated and the value calculated for the expression is passed into the called function. For example, the statement in line 12 of Program 6.1

```
12   findMax(firstnum,secnum);     /* the function is called here */
```

calls the function `findMax()`and causes the values currently residing in the variables `firstnum` and `secnum` to be passed to `findMax()`. The variable names in parentheses are actual arguments that provide values to the called function. After the values are passed, control is transferred to the called function.

As illustrated in Figure 6.3, the function `findMax()` does not receive the variables named `firstnum` and `secnum` and has no knowledge of these variable names.[1] The function simply receives copies of the values in these variables and must determine where to store these values before it does anything else. This is known as a **pass by value** (or a **call by value**). That is, a value is passed into the called function for each argument. Although this procedure for passing data to a function may seem surprising, it is really a safety procedure for ensuring that a called function does not inadvertently change data stored in a variable that is declared in the calling function. The function gets a copy of a value to use. It may change its copy and, of course, change any variables declared within itself. However, unless specific steps are taken to do so, as described in Section 7.3, a function cannot change the contents of variables declared in any other function.

Function Header Line

Each function that you write must begin with a function header line. When a function is written, it is said to be defined. Each function is defined once (that is, written once) and can then be used by any other function in the program for which it is suitably declared.

Like the `main()` function, every C function consists of two parts, a function header and a function body, as illustrated in Figure 6.4. The purpose of the **function header** is to identify the data type of the value returned by the function, if any, provide the function with a name, and specify the number, order, and type of values expected by the function. The purpose of the **function body** is to operate on the passed data and return, at most, one value directly back to the calling function. (We will see in Section 7.3 how a function can be made to indirectly return multiple values.)

The function header line for `findMax()` in line 18 of Program 6.1, which is

```
18  void findMax(float x, float y) /* this is the function's header line */
```

specifies that the function will not directly return any value and is to receive two floating-point values whenever it is called.

---

[1]This is significantly different from other computer languages where functions and subroutines receive access to the variable and can pass data back through them. In Section 7.3 we will see how, using pointer variables, C also permits direct access to the calling function's variables.

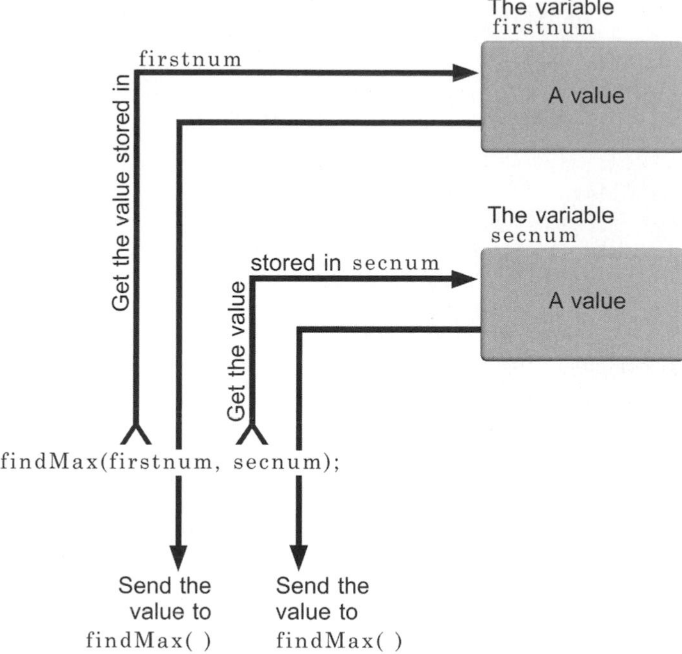

Figure 6.3 `findMax()` receives values

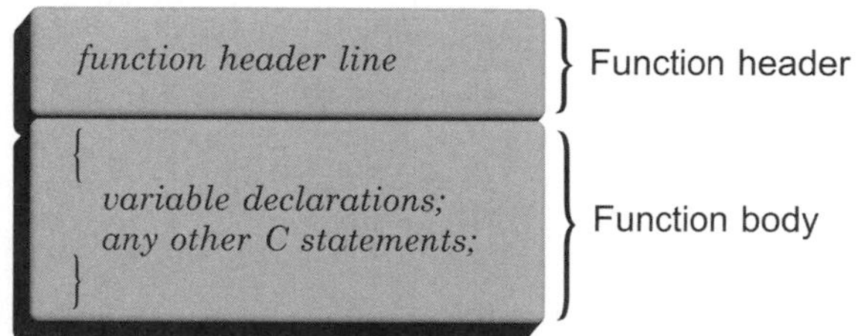

Figure 6.4 General format of a function

The argument names in the header line are known as **parameters** or **formal parameters** and **formal arguments**, and we shall use these terms interchangeably.[2] Thus, the argument `x` will be used to store the first value passed to `findMax()` and the argument `y` will be used to store the second value passed at the time of the function call. The function does not know where the values come from when it is called. The first part of the call procedure executed by the computer involves going to the variables `firstnum` and `secnum` and retrieving the stored values. These values are then passed to `findMax()` and ultimately stored in the parameters named `x` and `y` (see Figure 6.5).

[2]The portion of the function header that contains the function name and parameters is known as a **function declarator**, which should not be confused with a function declaration (prototype).

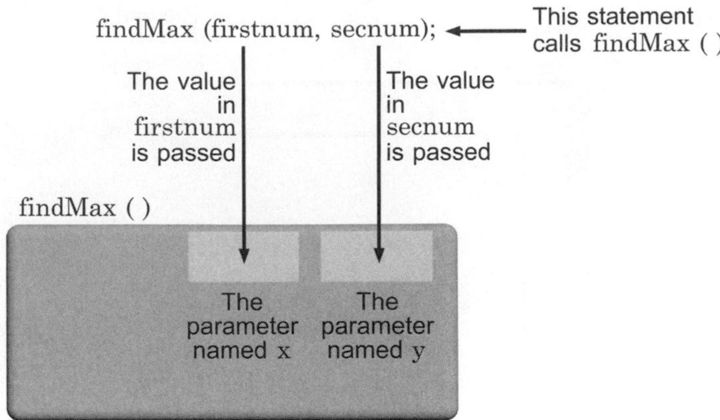

Figure 6.5 Storing values into parameters

The function name and all parameter names in the header line, in this case `findMax`, `x`, and `y`, are chosen by the programmer. Any names selected according to the rules used to choose variable names can be used. All parameters listed in the function header line must be separated by commas and must have their individual data types declared separately.

Having specified the function header for the `findMax()` function, we now examine the body of this function. As illustrated in Figure 6.6, a function body begins with an opening brace, {, contains any necessary variable declarations and other C statements, and ends with a closing brace, }. This should be familiar to you because it is the same structure used in all the `main()` functions we have written. This should not be a surprise, because `main()` is itself a function that must adhere to the rules required for constructing all C functions.

```
{
  variable declarations (if any)
  other C statements
}
```

Figure 6.6 Structure of a function body

Now consider the `findMax()` function previously defined in Program 6.1, which is renumbered and reproduced below for convenience.

```
/* the following is the function findMax */
void findMax(float x, float y) /* this is the function's header line */
{
  float maxnum;

  if (x >= y) /* find the maximum number */
    maxnum = x;
  else
    maxnum = y;

  printf("\nThe maximum of the two numbers entered is %f\n", maxnum);
}
```

Programming Note

Detecting the Difference

A function name is used in three distinct lines of code: within a function prototype, a calling statement, and a function header line. Each use of the function name in these lines of code is distinct and serves a unique purpose.

Initially, you may be confused as to how to recognize each of these three statement types. The key to distinguishing between usages is to notice the difference between argument lists as follows:

Usage	Argument List	Example
Function Prototype	A list of data types only (if any variable names are included, they will be ignored by the compiler). The function prototype is always terminated with a semicolon.	`float roi(int, double);`
Calling Statement	A list of zero or more values. These can be constants, variables, or any valid C expression. It is the value of the constant, variable, or expression that is passed to the called function.	`printf("%f", roi(3, amt));`
Function Header Line	A list of data types and parameter names. The header line is never terminated with a semicolon.	`float roi( int yrs, double rate);`

Within the body of `findMax()`, the variable named `maxnum` is declared as a single-precision number in line 4

```
4   float maxnum;
```

Programming Note

Recognizing Earlier Versions of C Code

In earlier versions of C, function prototypes were not required. Additionally, if a function header line omitted a return data type, the return value was, by default, implicitly declared as being of type `int` (how a function returns a value is presented in the next section). For example, in these earlier versions the header line

```
maxIt(float x, float y)
```

was equivalent to the more complete header line

```
int maxIt(float x, float y)
```

Similarly, omitting a parameter's data type, by default, defined the parameter to be of type `int`. Thus, the function header line

```
float findMax(float x, y)
```

does not declare both of the parameters, `x` and `y`, to be of type `float` ; rather, it declares `x` to be of type `float` and `y` to be of type `int`.

You may encounter this earlier code and your compiler, for compatibility, may still accept it.

This variable will subsequently be used to store the maximum of the two numbers passed to it. Notice that a function's variable declarations are made within the function's body, conventionally placed immediately after the function body's opening brace, while its parameters are declared within the function's header line. This is in keeping with the concept that variables are declared and assigned values from within a function while parameter values are passed to a function from the outside.

The `if-else` statement in lines 6 though 9

```
6  if (x >= y) /* find the maximum number */
7    maxnum = x;
8  else
9    maxnum = y;
```

is then used to find the maximum of the two values passed into `findMax()` when it is called. Finally, the `printf()` function call in line 11 is used to display the maximum value.

Program 6.1 is reproduced below for convenience, in its entirety, as Program 6.2.

Program 6.2 can be used to select and print the maximum of any two floating-point numbers entered by the user. Following is a sample run using Program 6.2:

```
Enter a number: 25.4
Great! Please enter a second number: 5.2

The maximum of the two numbers entered is 25.40000
```

Program 6.2

```
#include <stdio.h>
int main()
{
  void findMax(float, float); /* the function prototype */
  float firstnum, secnum;

  printf("Enter a number: ");
  scanf("%f", &firstnum);
  printf("Great! Please enter a second number: ");
  scanf("%f", &secnum);

  findMax(firstnum, secnum);    /* the function is called here */

  return 0;
}

/* the following is the function findMax */
void findMax(float x, float y) /* this is the function's header line */
{
  float maxnum;

  if (x >= y) /* find the maximum number */
    maxnum = x;
  else
    maxnum = y;

  printf("\nThe maximum of the two numbers entered is %f\n", maxnum);
}
```

The placement of the `findMax()` function after the `main()` function in Program 6.2 is a matter of choice. Some programmers prefer to put all called functions at the top of a program and make `main()` the last function listed. Generally, however, the majority of programmers prefer to list `main()` first because it is the driver function that gives anyone reading the program an idea of what the complete program is about before encountering the details of each function. Either placement approach is acceptable and you will encounter both styles in your programming work. In no case, however, can `findMax()` be placed inside `main()`. This is true for all C functions, which must be defined by themselves outside any other function. Each C function is a separate and independent entity with its own parameters and variables. *It is never permitted to nest one function inside another.*

Programming Note

Function Definitions and Functions Prototypes

When you write a function, you are formally creating a function definition. A function definition begins with a header line that includes a formal parameter list, if any, enclosed in parentheses and ends with the closing brace that terminates the function's body. The parentheses are required whether or not the function uses any parameters. The syntax for a function definition is

```
returnDataType functionName(parameter list)
{
  variable declarations;

  other C statements;

  return value;
}
```

A **function prototype** declares a function. The syntax for a function prototype, which provides the return data type of the function, the function's name, and a list of argument data types, is

```
returnDataType functionName(list of argument data types)
```

The function's prototype, along with pre- and postcondition comments (see next Programming Note) should provide a programmer with all the information necessary to call the function successfully.

In reviewing Program 6.2, it is important for you to again understand the three uses of the function name `findMax()`. The first use is in the function prototype (declaration) for `findMax()` in line 4. This statement, which ends with a semicolon as all statements do, alerts `main()` to the data type that `findMax()` will be returning and the number and type of arguments that must be supplied to `findMax()`. The second use of the function name is found in the call to `findMax()` in line 12, which passes two values into the function. Finally, the third use of the function name is found in the header line for `findMax()` in line 18. This line matches the function's prototype as far as the data types of the return value (none) and declaration of the order and data types of the arguments required by the function is concerned. Additionally, the header line provides parameter names for each of the data types listed in parentheses.

As another example, see if you can identify similar uses of a function name in Program 6.3.

In reviewing Program 6.3, let us start with the definition of the function `tempConvert()`. The complete definition of the function begins with the function's header in line 21:

```
21  void tempConvert(float inTemp) /* function header */
```

Program 6.3

```
1  #include <stdio.h>
2  int main()
3  {
4    #define MAXCOUNT 4
5
6    void tempConvert(float ); /* function prototype */
7
8    int count;              /* start of variable declarations */
9    float fahren;
10
11   for(count = 1; count <= MAXCOUNT; count++)
12   {
13     printf("Enter a Fahrenheit temperature: ");
14     scanf("%f", &fahren);
15     tempConvert(fahren);
16   }
17
18   return 0;
19 }
20
21 void tempConvert(float inTemp) /* function header */
22 {
23   printf("The Celsius equivalent is %6.2f\n", (5.0/9.0) * (inTemp - 32.0) );
24 }
```

This header line specifies that the function will return no value (void) and expects to receive a single floating-point value when it is called. The value will be stored in a parameter named `inTemp`. Because a function header line is not a statement but the start of the code defining the function, the header line does not end with a semicolon. The function's body consists of lines 22 through 24:

```
22 {
23   printf("The Celsius equivalent is %6.2f\n", (5.0/9.0) * (inTemp - 32.0) );
24 }
```

The function prototype for `tempConvert()` in line 6

```
6  void tempConvert(float ); /* function prototype */
```

correctly declares that the function returns no value and expects a single floating-point argument. Finally, the function call in line 15

```
15  tempConvert(fahren);
```

Programming Note

Preconditions and Postconditions

Preconditions are any set of conditions required by a function to be true if it is to operate correctly. For example, if a function uses the named constant MAXCHARS, which must have a positive value, a precondition is that MAXCHARS be declared with a positive value before the function is called.

Similarly, a postcondition is a condition that is true after the function is executed, assuming that the preconditions are met. Pre- and postconditions are typically documented as user comments. For example, consider the following function header line and comments:

```
int leapyr(int year)
/* Precondition: the parameter year must be a year as a four-digit
                 integer, such as 2001
   Postcondition: a 1 is returned if the year is a leap year; otherwise
                  a 0 will be returned
*/
```

Pre- and postcondition comments should be included with both function prototypes and function definitions whenever clarification is needed.

correctly calls the function by passing the value of the floating-point variable fahren into the function at the time of the call. In writing your own functions, you must always keep these three distinct usages of a function's name in mind.

Placement of Statements

C does not impose a rigid statement-ordering structure on the programmer. The general rule for placing statements in a program is simply that all preprocessor directives, variables, named constants, and functions, except main(), must be either declared or defined *before* they can be used. As we have noted previously, although this rule permits both preprocessor directives and declaration statements to be placed throughout a program, doing so results in a very poor program structure.

As a matter of good programming form, the following statement ordering should form the basic structure around which all of your C programs are constructed:

```
preprocessor directives
symbolic constants
function prototypes can be placed here
int main()
{
  function prototypes can be placed here
  variable declarations;

  other executable statements;

  return value;
}
```

As previously mentioned, functions that have their prototypes placed above the `main()` function can be called within any function in the source code file, while functions whose prototypes are placed within the `main()` function can only be called from within `main()`. As always, comment statements can be freely intermixed anywhere within this basic structure.

EXERCISES 6.1

Short Answer Questions

1. For the following function headers, determine the number, type, and order (sequence) of values that should be passed to the function when it is called:
   a. `void factorial(int n)`
   b. `void price(int type, float yield, float maturity)`
   c. `void yield(int type, double price, double maturity)`
   d. `void interest(char flag, float price, float time)`
   e. `void total(float amount, float rate)`
   f. `void roi(int a, int b, char c, char d, float e, float f)`
   g. `void getVal(int item, int iter, char decflag)`
2. Write function headers for the following:
   a. A function named `check()` that has three parameters. The first parameter should accept an integer number, and the second and third parameters should accept single-precision numbers. The function returns no value.
   b. A function named `findAbs()` that accepts a single-precision number passed to it and displays its absolute value.
   c. A function named `mult()` that accepts two single-precision numbers as parameters, multiplies these two numbers, and displays the result.
   d. A function named `sqrIt()` that computes and displays the square of the integer value passed to it.
   e. A function named `powFun()` that raises an integer number passed to it to a positive integer power (also passed as an argument) and displays the result.
   f. A function that produces a table of the numbers from 1 to 10, their squares, and their cubes. No arguments are to be passed to the function, and the function returns no value.
3. Write C function prototypes corresponding to each of the function header lines given in Question 2.

Programming Exercises

1. a. Write a function named `check()` that has three arguments. The first argument should accept an integer number, the second argument a floating-point number, and the third argument a double-precision number. The body of the function should just display the values of the data passed to the function when it is called. (When tracing errors in functions, it is very helpful to have the function display the values that have been passed into it. Quite frequently, the error is not in what the body of the function does with the data, but in the data received and stored.)

b. Include the function written in Exercise 1a in a working program. Make sure your function is called from `main()`. Test the function by passing various data to it.

2. a. Write a function named `findAbs()` that accepts a double-precision number passed to it, computes its absolute value, and displays the absolute value. The absolute value of a number is the number itself if the number is positive, and the negative of the number if the number is negative.
   b. Include the function written in Exercise 2a in a working program. Make sure your function is called from `main()`. Test the function by passing various data to it.

3. a. Write a function called `mult()` that accepts two floating-point numbers as arguments, multiplies these two numbers, and displays the result.
   b. Include the function written in Exercise 3a in a working program. Make sure your function is called from `main()`. Test the function by passing various data to it.

4. a. Write a function named `squareIt()` that computes the square of the value passed to it and displays the result. The function should be capable of squaring numbers with decimal points.
   b. Include the function written in Exercise 4a in a working program. Make sure your function is called from `main()`. Test the function by passing various data to it.

5. a. Write a function named `powfun()` that raises an integer number passed to it to a positive integer power and displays the result. The positive integer should be the second value passed to the function.
   b. Include the function written in Exercise 5a in a working program. Make sure your function is called from `main()`. Test the function by passing various data to it.

6. a. Write a function that produces a table of the numbers from 1 to 10, their squares, and cubes. The function should produce the same display as that produced by Program 5.11.
   b. Include the function written in Exercise 6a in a working program. Make sure your function is called from `main()`. Test the function by passing various data to it.

7. a. Modify the function written for Exercise 6a to accept the starting value of the table, the number of values to be displayed, and the increment between values. Name your function `selecTable()`. A call to `selectTable(6, 5, 2);` should produce a table of five lines, the first line starting with the number 6 and each succeeding number increasing by 2.
   b. Include the function written in Exercise 7a in a working program. Make sure your function is called from `main()`. Test the function by passing various data to it.

8. a. Write a C function that accepts an integer argument, determines whether the passed integer is even or odd, and displays an appropriate message indicating the result of its determination. (*Hint:* Use the `%` operator.)
   b. Include the function written for Exercise 8a in a working C program. Make sure your function is called from `main()` and test the function by passing various data to it and verifying the displayed message.

9. a. Write a function named `hypotenuse()` that accepts the lengths of two sides of a right triangle as the parameters *a*, and *b*, respectively. The function should determine and display the hypotenuse, *c*, of the triangle. (*Hint:* Use Pythagoras' theorem that $c^2 = a^2 + b^2$.)
   b. Include the function written for Exercise 9a in a working C program. Make sure your function is called from `main()` and test the function by passing various data to it and verifying the displayed hypotenuse.

6.2 Returning a Value

Using the method of passing data into a function presented in the previous section, a called function receives only copies of the values contained in the arguments at the time of the call. (Review Figure 6.3 if this is unclear to you.) As stated in Section 6.1, this method of calling a function and passing values to it is referred to as both a **pass by value** and a **call by value** (the terms are used synonymously), and is a distinct advantage of C. Passing only values ensures that a called function has no access to any of the calling function's variables, and so cannot inadvertently change the value of a variable declared outside of itself in the calling function.

When a function is called by value, it may process the data sent to it in any fashion desired and directly return at most one, and only one "legitimate" value to the calling function (see Figure 6.7). In this section we see how such a value is returned to the calling function. (As you might expect, given C's flexibility, it is possible to return more than a single value. You'll learn about this topic in Section 7.3.)

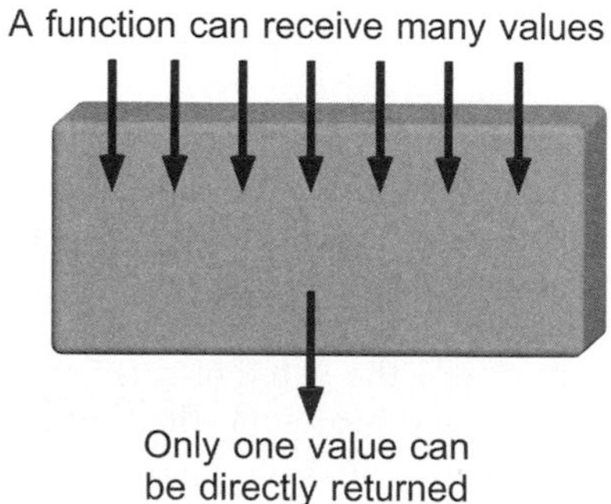
A function can receive many values
Only one value can
be directly returned

Figure 6.7 A function directly returns at most one value when it is called by value

As with the calling of a function, directly returning a value requires that the interface between the called and calling functions be handled correctly. From its side of the return transaction, the called function must provide the following items:

- Data type of the returned value, which is specified in the function's header line
- Actual value being returned, which is specified by a return statement

A function returning a value must specify, in its header line, the data type of the value that will be returned. Recall that the function header line is the first line of the function, which includes both the function's name and a list of argument names. As an example, consider the `findMax()` function written in the last section, which determined the maximum value of two numbers passed to the function. For convenience, the code for this function is listed below.

```
/* the following is the function findMax */
void findMax(float x, float y) /* this is the function's header line */
{
 float maxnum;

  if (x >= y) /* find the maximum number */
    maxnum = x;
  else
    maxnum = y;

  printf("\nThe maximum of the two numbers entered is %f\n", maxnum);
}  /* end of function body and end of function */
```

As written, the function's header line is `void findMax(int x, int y)`, where `x` and `y` are the names chosen for the function's parameters.

If `findMax()` is now to return a value, the function's header line must be amended to include the data type of the value being returned. For example, if an integer value is to be returned, the proper function header line is

```
int findMax(float x, float y)
```

Similarly, if the function is to return a floating-point value the correct function header line is

```
float findMax(float x, float y)
```

and if the function is to return a double-precision value, the header line would be

```
double findMax(float x, float y)
```

Let us now modify `findMax()` to return the maximum value of the two numbers passed to it. To do this, we must first determine the data type of the value that is to be returned and include this data type in the function's header line.

Because the maximum value determined by `findMax()` is stored in the single-precision floating-point variable `maxnum`, it is the value of this variable that the function should return. Explicitly specifying that a single-precision floating-point value will be returned from `findMax()` requires the following function declaration:

```
float findMax(float x, float y)
```

Observe that this is the same as the original function header line for `findMax()` with the substitution of the keyword `float` for the keyword `void`.

Having declared the data type that `findMax()` is to return, all that remains is to include a statement within the function to cause the return of the correct value. To return a value, a function must use a `return` statement, which has the form

```
return (expression);
```

The parentheses in a `return` statement are optional. Thus, the statement `return expression;` and `return (expression);` can be used interchangeably.

When a `return` statement is encountered, the *`expression`* is evaluated first. The value of the expression is then automatically converted to the return value's data type as specified in the function's header line before being sent back to the calling function. After the value is returned, program control reverts to the calling function.

Thus, to return the value stored in `maxnum`, all we need to do is add the statement `return (maxnum);` before the closing brace of the `findMax()` function. The complete function code is

```
        --->float findMax(float x, float y)   /* function
             header line */
These  |    {
should |      float maxnum;
be     |
the    |       if (x >= y)
same   |         maxnum = x;
data   |       else
type   |         maxnum = y;
       |
       |       return (maxnum);   /* return statement */
       |    }          ^
       |               |
        --------------
```

In this new code for `findMax()`, note that the data type of the expression contained within the `return` statement correctly matches the data type specified for the returned value in the function's header line. It is up to the programmer to ensure that this is so for every function returning a value. Failure to exactly match the return value with the function's declared data type can lead to undesired results because the return value is always converted to the data type declared in the function's header line. Usually this is a problem only when the fractional part of a returned floating-point number is truncated because the function was declared to return an integer value.

Having taken care of the sending side of the return transaction, we must now prepare the calling function to receive the value sent by the called function. On the calling (receiving) side, the calling function must

- Be alerted to the type of value to expect
- Properly use the returned value

Alerting the calling function as to the type of return value to expect is properly taken care of by the function prototype. For example, including the function prototype

```
float findMax(float, float);
```

with `main()`'s variable declarations is sufficient to alert `main()` that `findMax()` will return a floating-point value.

To actually use a returned value, we must either provide a variable to store the value or use the value directly in an expression. Storing the returned value in a variable is accomplished using a standard assignment statement. For example, the assignment statement

```
max = findMax(firstnum, secnum);
```

can be used to store the value returned by `findMax()` in the variable named `max`. This assignment statement does two things: (1) the right-hand side of the assignment statement calls `findMax()`, and (2) the result returned by the function is stored in the variable `max`. Because the value returned by `findMax()` is a `float`, the variable `max` should also be declared as a `float` within the calling function's variable declarations.

Alternatively, the value returned by a function need not be stored directly in a variable, but can be used wherever an expression is valid. For example, the expression `2 * findMax(firstnum,secnum)` multiplies the value returned by `findMax()` by 2, and the statement `printf("The maximum value is %f", findMax(firstnum, secnum));` displays the returned value.

Program 6.4 illustrates the inclusion of both prototype and assignment statements for `main()` to correctly declare, call, and store a returned value from `findMax()`. As before, and in keeping with our convention of placing the `main()` function first, we have placed the `findMax()` function after `main()`.

Program 6.4

```
#include <stdio.h>
int main()
{

  float findMax(float, float);  /* the function prototype */
  float firstnum, secnum, max;

  printf("\nEnter a number: ");
  scanf("%f", &firstnum);
  printf("Great! Please enter a second number: ");
  scanf("%f", &secnum);

  max = findMax(firstnum, secnum); /* the function is called here */

  printf("\nThe maximum of the two numbers is %f\n", max);

  return 0;
}

/* following is the function findMax() */
```

```
21
22  float findMax(float x, float y) /* this is the function's header line */
23  {
24    float maxnum;
25
26    if (x >= y)        /* find the maximum number */
27      maxnum = x;
28    else
29      maxnum = y;
30
31    return (maxnum);
32  }
```

In reviewing Program 6.4, it is important to note the four items needed to correctly declare, call, define a header line, and return a value from a called function. The first item is the prototype for `findMax()` within `main()` in line 5

```
5 float findMax(float, float);  /* the function prototype */
```

This statement alerts `main()` to the data type that `findMax()` will be returning. The second item to notice in `main()` is the call to `findMax()` in line 13, which passes the correct number and types of values into the function

```
13  max = findMax(firstnum, secnum); /* the function is called here */
```

We have also made sure to correctly declare `max` as a floating-point variable within `main()`'s variable declarations so that it matches the data type of the returned value.

The last two items of note concern the coding of the `findMax()` function. The header line for `findMax()`, in line 22

```
22  float findMax(float x, float y) /
* this is the function's header line */
```

specifies that the function will return a single-precision floating-point value and expects to receive two single-precision arguments when it is called. Finally, because `maxnum` has been declared as a `float` within the function, the expression in the return statement, in line 31, evaluates to a `float` value

```
31 return (maxnum);
```

Thus, `findMax()` is internally consistent in returning a floating-point value to `main()`, and `main()` has been correctly alerted to receive this value.

In writing your own functions, you must always keep these four items in mind. For another example, see if you can identify these four items in Program 6.5.

Program 6.5

```
1  #include <stdio.h>
2  int main()
3  {
4    #define MAXCOUNT 4
5    float tempConvert(float);  /* function prototype */
6
7    int count;                 /* start of variable declarations */
8    float celsius, fahren;
9
10   for(count = 1; count <= MAXCOUNT; count++)
11   {
12     printf("\nEnter a Fahrenheit temperature: ");
13     scanf("%f", &fahren);
14     celsius = tempConvert(fahren);
15     printf("The Celsius equivalent is %5.2f\n",celsius);
16   }
17
18   return 0;
19 }
20
21 /* convert fahrenheit to celsius */
22 float tempConvert(float inTemp)
23 {
24   return ( (5.0/9.0) * (inTemp - 32.0) );
25 }
```

In Program 6.5 let us first analyze the `tempConvert()` function. The complete definition of the function begins with the function's header line and ends with the closing brace after the `return` statement

```
21  /* convert fahrenheit to celsius */
22  float tempConvert(float inTemp)
23  {
24    return ( (5.0/9.0) * (inTemp - 32.0) );
25  }
```

The function's header line specifies that the function will return a `float`. This means the expression in the function's `return` statement should evaluate to this data type. Because all C compilers perform floating-point evaluations of expressions in double-precision format, the value computed in parentheses in line 24 will be a double-precision number. This will be converted automatically to a `float` to match the return type specified in the function's header line (it may also generate a compiler warning message).[3]

[3]The value of the expression can be explicitly converted into a `float` using the `cast` operator described in Section 3.1. However, in practice you will generally see an implicit conversion as in this `return` statement.

On the receiving side, `main()` has a prototype for the `tempConvert()` function that agrees with the function's header line. As with all declaration statements, multiple declarations of the same type may be made within the same statement. Thus, we could have used the same declaration statement to declare both the variables `celsius` and `fahren`, as well as the function `tempConvert()`, as single-precision data types. If we had done so, the single declaration statement

```
float tempConvert(float), celsius, fahren;
```

could have been used to replace the two individual declarations for `tempConvert()`, `celsius`, and `fahren`. For clarity, however, we will always keep function prototype statements apart from variable declaration statements.

Two further points need to be mentioned here. The first is the call of `tempConvert()` and the display of the returned value in lines 14 and 15

```
14  celsius = tempConvert(fahren);
15  printf("The Celsius equivalent is %5.2f\n",celsius);
```

A professional programmer would combine these two lines into the single statement

```
printf("The Celsius equivalent is %5.2f\n", tempConvert(fahren));
```

This single statement version makes sense when you realize that the only use of each returned value is for display. Thus, it makes little sense to first declare the variable named `celsius`, code a separate assignment statement to store the returned value from the called function into this variable, and then only use the variable once for display. However, if the returned value were to be used a second time, it would make sense to assign it to a variable, because it would save making an additional call to `tempConvert()` to recompute the same value.

The second point is that the purpose of declarations, as we learned in Chapter 2, is to alert the compiler to the amount of internal storage reserved for the data. The prototype within `main()` for `tempConvert()` performs this task and tells the compiler how much storage area must be accessed by `main()` when the returned value is retrieved. Had we placed the `tempConvert()` function before `main()`, however, the function's header line would suffice to alert the compiler to the type of storage needed for the returned value. In this case, the function prototype for `tempConvert()`, could be eliminated. Because we have chosen always to list `main()` as the first function in a file, we must include function prototypes for all functions called by it. This style also serves to document what functions will be accessed by `main()`.

Function Stubs

An alternative to completing each function required in a program is to write the `main()` function first, and add the functions later, as they are developed. The problem that arises with this approach, however, is that the complete program cannot be run until all of the functions are included. For example, reconsider Program 6.4, without the inclusion of the `findMax()` function. (Assume it has not yet been written.)

```
#include <stdio.h>
int main()
{
  float firstnum, secnum, max;
```

```

    printf("Enter a number: ");
    scanf("%f", &firstnum);
    printf("\nGreat! Please enter a second number: ");
    scanf("%f", &secnum);

    max = findMax(firstnum,secnum); /* the function is called here */

    printf("\nThe maximum of the two numbers entered is %f", maxnum);

    return 0;
  }
```

This program would be complete if there were a function definition for `findMax()`. But we really don't need a *correct* `findMax()` function to test and run what has been written; we just need a function that *acts* like it is correct. Thus, a "fake" `findMax()` that accepts the proper number and types of parameters and returns a value of the proper type for the function call is all we need for initial testing. This fake function is known as a stub. A **stub** is the beginning of a final function that is used as a placeholder for the final function until the function is completed. A suitable stub for `findMax()` is

```
float findMax(float x, float y)
{
  printf("In findMax()\n");
  printf("The value of x is %f\n", x);
  printf("The value of x is %f\n ", y);
  return 1.0;
}
```

This stub function can now be compiled and linked with the previously completed code to obtain an executable program. The code for the function can then be further developed, and when it is completed, it replaces this stub function.

The minimum requirement of a stub function is that it compile and link with its calling module. In practice it is a good idea to have a stub display both a message that it has been entered successfully and the value(s) of its received arguments, as in the stub for `findMax()`.

As the function is refined, you let it do more and more, perhaps allowing it to return intermediate or incomplete results. This incremental, or stepwise, refinement is an important concept in efficient program development that provides you with the means to run a program that does not yet meet all of its final requirements.

Functions with Empty Parameter Lists

Although useful functions having an empty parameter list are extremely limited (one such function is provided in Programming Exercise 8), they can occur. The prototype for such a function requires either writing the keyword `void` or nothing at all between the parentheses following the function's name. For example, both prototypes

```
int display(void);
```

Programming Note

Isolation Testing

One of the most successful software testing methods known is always to embed the code being tested within an environment of working code. For example, assume you have two untested functions that are called in the order shown below, and the result returned by the second function is incorrect.

`Function 1` — calls → `Function 2` — `returns` → `An incorrect value`

One or possibly both of these functions could be operating incorrectly. The first order of business is to isolate the problem to a specific function.

One of the most powerful methods of performing this code isolation is to decouple the functions. This is done either by testing each function individually or by testing one function first and, only when you know it is operating correctly, reconnecting it to the second function. Then, if an error occurs, you have isolated the error to either the transfer of data between functions or the internal operation of the second function.

This specific procedure is an example of the basic rule of testing, which states that *each function should only be tested in a program in which all other functions are known to be correct.* This means that one function must first be tested by itself, using stubs if necessary for any called functions, then a second tested function should be tested either by itself or with a previously tested function, and so on. This ensures that each new function is isolated within a test bed of correct functions, with the final program effectively built up of tested function code.

and

```
int display();
```

indicate that the `display()` function takes no arguments and returns an integer. A function with an empty parameter list is called by its name with nothing written within the required parentheses following the function's name. For example, the statement `display();` correctly calls the `display()` function whose prototype is given above.

EXERCISES 6.2

Short Answer Questions

1. For the following function headers, determine the number, type, and order (sequence) of values that should be passed to the function when it is called and the data type of the value returned by the function:
   a. `int factorial(int n)`
   b. `double price(int type, double yield, double maturity)`

c. `double yield(int type, double price, maturity)`
d. `char interest(char flag, float price, float time)`
e. `int total(float amount, float rate)`
f. `float roi(int a, int b, char c, char d, float e, float f)`
g. `void getVal(int item, int iter, char decflag)`

2. Write function headers for the following:
   a. A function named `check()`, which has three arguments. The first argument should accept an integer number, the second argument a single-precision number, and the third argument a double-precision number. The function returns no value.
   b. A function named `findAbs()` that accepts a single-precision number passed to it and returns its absolute value.
   c. A function named `mult()` that accepts two single-precision numbers as arguments, multiplies these two numbers, and returns the result.
   d. A function named `sqrIt()` that computes and returns the square of the integer value passed to it. Use a function prototype and a single-line header for the function's definition.
   e. A function that produces a table of the numbers from 1 to 10, their squares, and cubes. No arguments are to be passed to the function and the function returns no value.

Programming Exercises

1. a. Write a function named `totamt()` that accepts four integer arguments named `quarters`, `dimes`, `nickels`, and `pennies`, which represent the number of quarters, dimes, nickels, and pennies in a piggybank. The function should determine and return the dollar value of the number of quarters, dimes, nickels, and pennies passed to it.
   b. Include the function written for Exercise 1a in a working program. The `main()` function should correctly call and pass the values of 26 quarters, 80 dimes, 100 nickels, and 216 pennies to `totamt`. Do a hand calculation to verify the result displayed by your program.

2. a. Write a function named `distance()` that accepts the rectangular coordinates of two points x_1, y_1 and x_2, y_2 and calculates and returns the distance between the two points. The distance, *d*, between two points is given by the formula

$$d = \sqrt{(x_2 - x_1)^2 + (y_2 - y_1)^2}$$

   b. Include the function written for Exercise 2a in a working C program. Make sure your function is called from `main()` and correctly returns a value to `main()`. Have `main()` display the value returned and test the function by passing various data to it and verifying the returned value. In particular make sure your function returns a value of 0 when both points are the same; for example, $(x_1, y_1) = (5,2)$ and $(x_2, y_2) = (5,2)$.

3. a. Rewrite the function `tempConvert()` in Program 6.5 to accept a temperature and a character as arguments. If the character passed to the function is the letter *f*, the function should convert the passed temperature from Fahrenheit to Celsius, else the function should convert the passed temperature from Celsius to Fahrenheit.
   b. Modify the `main()` function in Program 6.5 to call the function written for Exercise 3a. Your `main()` function should ask the user for a temperature value and the type of temperature being entered (*f* or *c*).

4. a. Write a function named `gallonsToLiters()` that converts gallons of liquid to liters using the relationship that there are 3.7854 liters to the gallon.
   b. Include the function written for Exercise 4a in a working C program. Make sure your function is called from `main()` and correctly returns a value to `main()`. Have `main()` display the value returned and test the function by passing various data to it and verifying the returned value.

5. a. Write a function named `conversions()` that displays a table of miles converted to kilometers. The function should accept the initial mile value to be converted, the number of conversions to be made, and the increment between each mile value. For each conversion the function should call a function named `milesToKm()` that accepts a mile value and returns its equivalent kilometer value. In computing the conversion, use the relationship that there are 1.6093 kilometers per mile.
   b. Include the functions written for Exercise 5a in a working C program. Make sure that `conversions()` is called from `main()` and that it correctly calls `milesToKm()` as needed.

6. a. A common statistical problem is to determine how many ways n objects can be selected from a group of m objects. The number of such possibilities is given by the formula

$$\frac{m!}{n!(m-n)!}$$

For example, using this formula we can determine that the number of committees of three people (n = 3) that can be created from a pool of 8 people (m = 8) is

$$\frac{8.7.6.5.4.3.2.1}{(3.2.1)(5.4.3.2.1)} = 56$$

Using this formula, write a function that accepts values for n and m and returns the number of possibilities.
   b. Include the function written in Exercise 6a in a working program. Make sure your function is called from `main()` and correctly returns a value to `main()`. Have `main()` display the value returned. Test the function by passing various data to it. Then use your program to determine the number of ways 5 people can be selected from a group of 10 people.

7. a. A second-degree polynomial in x is given by the expression $ax^2 + bx + c$, where a, b, and c are known numbers and a is not equal to 0. Write a C function named `polyTwo(a,b,c,x)` that computes and returns the value of a second-degree polynomial for any passed values of a, b, c, and x.
   b. Include the function written in Exercise 7a in a working program. Make sure your function is called from `main()` and correctly returns a value to `main()`. Have `main()` display the value returned. Test the function by passing various data to it.

8. a. A useful function with an empty parameter list can be constructed to return a value for π that is accurate to the maximum number of decimal places allowed by your computer. This value is obtained by taking the arcsine of 1.0, which is π/2, and multiplying the result by 2. In C the required expression is *2.0 * asin(1.0)*, where the

asin() function is provided in the standard C mathematics library (make sure to include the math.h header file). Using this expression, write a C function named Pi() that calculates and displays the value of π.

b. Include the function written for Exercise 8a in a working C program. Make sure your function is called from main() and correctly returns a value to main(). Have main() display the value returned and test the function by passing various data to it and verifying the returned value.

6.3 Case Study: Calculating Age Norms

A well-designed computer program starts like a well-designed term paper, with an outline. Just as a term paper begins with an initial outline that lists the paper's main() topics, a computer program's initial outline provides a listing of the primary tasks that the program must accomplish. This is especially important when using functions, because each task required by the program is typically assigned to a function when it is coded.

As we have already seen, a computer program's initial outline is usually either a pseudocode description or a first-level structure diagram. This initial outline begins the process of defining a more complicated problem into a set of smaller, more manageable tasks. If it is required, each of these tasks can be further subdivided, or refined, into even smaller tasks. Once the tasks are well defined, the actual work of coding can begin, starting with any task, in any order. If there are more tasks than can be handled by one programmer, they can be distributed among as many programmers as required. This is equivalent to having many people work on a large research project, with each person responsible for an individual topic.

In its most general form, a typical outline applicable to most simple programs is the Problem-Solver Algorithm introduced in Section 1.5. Figure 6.8 shows a first-level structure diagram for this algorithm.

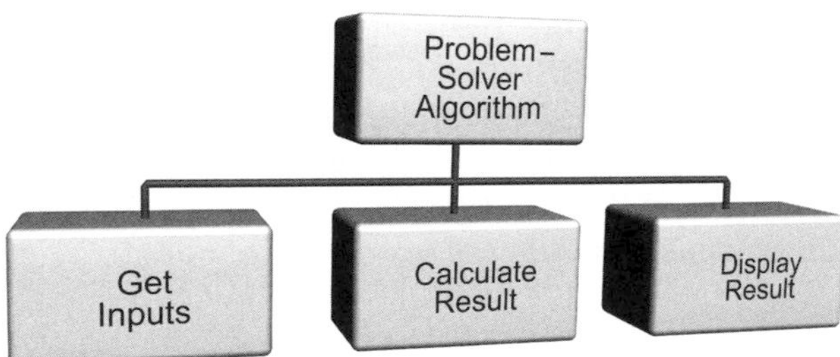

Figure 6.8 First-level structure diagram of the Problem-Solver Algorithm

Each task in the Problem-Solver Algorithm can be worked on independently and can, in turn, be refined and coded in any desired order, although completing the input section first usually makes testing and development easier. We now apply this refinement process to an actual programming problem. A new and very important aspect of this refinement will be the use of stubs (see previous section) as "placeholder" functions. The stubs permit the construction of a working program while also providing for testing the transfer of data between functions. Once the overall program is constructed and running, each function is individually completed, integrated into the program in place of its stub, and tested. We show how this is accomplished with the following case study.

Requirements Specification

A fairly common procedure in child development is to establish normal ranges for height and weight as they relate to a child's age. These normal ranges are frequently referred to as **age norms**. In this case study, we are to develop a program for calculating both the expected height of a child between the ages of 6 and 11 and the deviation of this height norm to an actual child's height.

For this application assume that the group requesting the program has gathered various statistics on a group of normally maturing children between the ages of 6 and 11 and developed the following formula to predict the normal height, in inches, of a child in this age group:

$$Normal\ Height = -\ 0.25\ (Age - 6)^2 + 3.5\ (Age - 6) + 45$$

Using this formula we have been requested to develop a program to calculate and display the normal height for a child between 6 and 11 years old, and the percent difference from a child's actual height. The percent difference is given by the formula

$$PercentDifference = \frac{100\left(ActualHeight - NormalHeight\right)}{NormalHeight}$$

Step 1: Analyze the Problem

a. Determine the Desired Outputs

Two outputs are required: the "normal" height for a child of this age, and the percent difference between the child's actual height and their normal height.

b. Determine the Input Items

At first glance it appears that this problem requires two inputs, the age and height of a child. There is one complication, however, because age is typically given in years and months, while the formula for the normal height requires an age in years. Now we might be tempted to ask the user to enter an age, such as 10 years 6 months, as the number 10.5, but ultimately this will only cause resentment by the user. The correct approach is to permit the user to enter an age in years and months and have the computer convert the data entry into years. Thus, three input items are required

- Age at last birthday (in years)
- Age in months since last birthday
- Height (in inches)

c. List the Formulas Relating the Inputs to the Outputs

The conversion from an age in months and years to an age in years is easily accomplished using the formula

$$Age = years + months/12.0$$

The remaining two formulas given in the problem specification can then be used to calculate a percent difference.

$$Normal\ Height = -\ 0.25\ (Age - 6)^2 + 3.5\ (Age - 6) + 45$$

$$PercentDifference = \frac{100\left(ActualHeight - NormalHeight\right)}{NormalHeight}$$

d. Perform a Hand Calculation

To ensure that we understand how the inputs will be converted into the required outputs, we now do a hand calculation.

Assuming a child is 10 years and 6 months old, which converts to a yearly age of 10.5 years, the equation for calculating a normal height yields $-0.25 * (10.5 - 6)^2 + 3.5(10.5 - 6) + 45 = 55.6875$ inches. Now assuming the child is actually 50 inches in height, the formula for percent difference yields (100) (50 – 55.6875) / 55.6875 = –10.21%. We will use these values as checks against those obtained when we have completed and executed the completed program.

Step 2: Select an Overall Solution Algorithm

This problem is a classic application of the Problem-Solver Algorithm. For this particular application, the problem solution takes the form

Get the child's age and height as inputs
Calculate a normal height and percent difference
Display the calculated values

The top-level structure diagram corresponding to this algorithm is shown in Figure 6.9. Using a modular design approach, each of the tasks specified in the structure can either be directly coded as a function or further developed and refined until all tasks are accounted for.

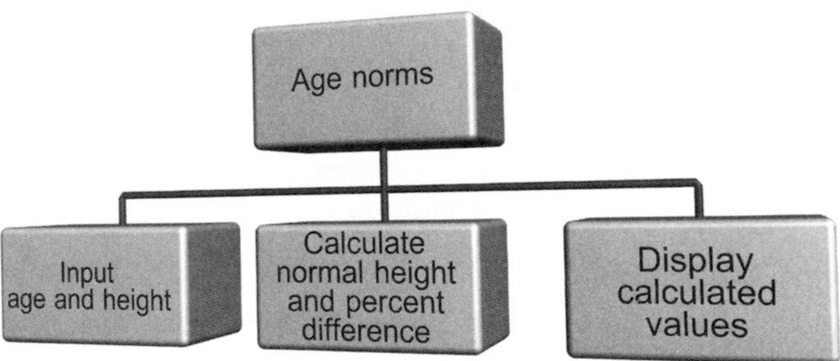

Figure 6.9 Top-level structure diagram for age-norms program

Although our modular development approach permits us to develop functions in any order, the input section is typically constructed first to ensure that we understand the data that we will be working with. At this stage it is convenient to accept these multiple inputs directly into the `main()` function. Thus the requirements for the `main()` function is that it first obtain the child's age and height. It must then convert the age value correctly and pass the child's age and height, as inputs, to a calculation module that must return a normal height and the percent difference between the calculated normal height and actual height.

Because a function can only return one direct value, we must make a choice as to how we will implement the calculation module shown in Figure 6.9. For this application we will construct the calculation module using two functions: one function to calculate and return the normal height, and the second function to calculate and return the percentage difference. (In Section 7.3 we will see how a function can be made to return multiple values). Finally, the `main()` function must pass the two calculated values to a display function. Figure 6.10 shows the refined, final structure diagram for this problem.

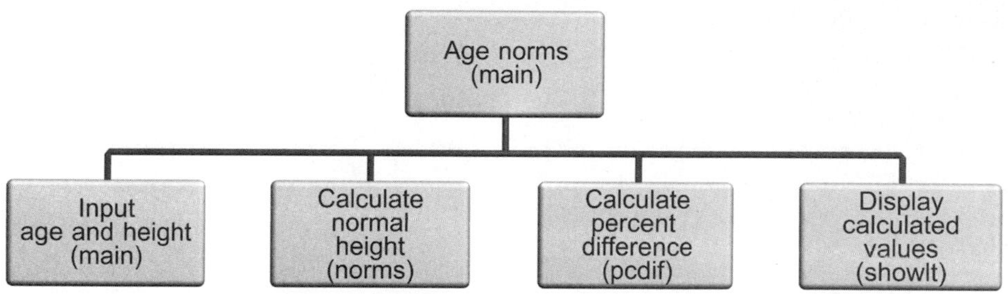

Figure 6.10 Refined structure diagram

Step 3: Write the Program

Arbitrarily naming the calculation and display functions `norms()`, `pcdif()`, and `showit()`, respectively, and using stubs for these functions permits us to write a "skeleton" program, first, before completing the final program defined by Figure 6.10. This is a common practice when a program requires many functions, because it allows us to rapidly construct a program, while leaving the details of completing each function independently until later. As an example, consider Program 6.6.

Program 6.6

```
#include <stdio.h>
#include <math.h>
int main()
{
  float norms(float);        /* here are the function prototypes */
  float pcdif(float, float);
  void showit(float, float);

  int years, months;
  float height, normht;
  float age, perdif;

    /* this is the input section */
  printf("\nHow old (in years) is this child? ");
  scanf("%d", &years);
  printf("How many months since the child's birthday? ");
```

```
  scanf("%d", &months);
  age = years + months/12.0;   /* convert to total years */
  printf("Enter the child's height (in inches): ");
  scanf("%f", &height);

  /* this is the calculations section */
  normht = norms(age);
  perdif = pcdif(height, normht);

  /* this is the display section */
  showit(normht, perdif);

  return 0;
}

/* the following is a stub for norms() */
float norms(float age)
{
  printf("\nInto norms()\n");
  printf("   age = %f\n", age);
  return(52.5);
}

/* the following is a stub for pcdif() */
float pcdif(float actual, float normal)
{
  printf("\nInto pcdif()\n");
  printf("   actual = %f    normal = %f\n", actual, normal);
  return(2.5);
}

/* the following is a stub for showit() */
void showit(float normht, float perdif)
{
  printf("\nInto showit()\n");
  printf("   normht = %f      perdif = %f\n", normht, perdif);
}
```

Notice that the input data required for the problem, year age, month age, and the child's height are obtained from within `main()`. The `main()` function then calls `norms()` with the single age argument that this function will need to calculate a "normal" height for this age. The `pcdif()` function is then called with the two arguments it requires to calculate a percent difference. Finally, it calls `showit()` to display the values calculated in `norms()` and `pcdif()`. The program is then completed by the three stub functions, one for `norms()`, one for `pcdif()`, and one for `showit()`.

Each stub function is constructed to individually display both a message indicating that the function has been called and the values of any passed arguments. Additionally, the stub for `norms()` sets an arbitrary return value, as does the stub for `pcdif()`. When these functions are fully developed, the values will be replaced by correctly calculated ones. For now, however, the values can be passed on to `showit()` to verify correct argument transmission and receipt of all arguments.

Step 4: Test and Correct the Program

Before proceeding with the development of each individual function, we can test the program that we have. If the program works correctly, we can move on to develop each function independently and test and debug it until we are satisfied that what we have is working properly. Then we can move on to the next function.

The following is the output from a sample run of Program 6.6.

```
How old (in years) is this child? 10
How many months since the child's birthday? 6
Enter the child's height (in inches): 50

Into norms()
   age = 10.500000

Into pcdif()
   actual = 50.000000    normal = 52.500000

Into showit()
   normht = 52.500000    perdif = 2.500000
```

This output verifies that the `main()` function is working properly in obtaining an age and height, and converting an age of 10 years and 6 months to an equivalent decimal value of 10.5. Similarly, `norms()` correctly receives the transmitted age and returns a value. The output also verifies that `pcdif()` correctly receives the child's height and the "normal" height returned by `norms()`. These values, in turn, are successfully passed to `showit()` for display.

Having verified that the calling sequence of each function is correct, and that each function correctly receives its argument values, we can now develop them more completely to calculate their return values correctly. Because `showit()` is the simpler of the three required functions, we will develop it first. This "out of order" development is not unusual; in fact, it is the same technique used by motion picture producers to complete a movie. Here we take advantage of the fact that displaying the results is rather trivial if someone else did the actual calculations. Besides, completing the output section gives us the means to verify the calculation section when it is completed. Following is the `showit()` function:

```
void showit(float normht, float perdif)
{
  printf("\nThe average height in inches is: %5.2f\n", normht);
  printf("The actual height deviates from the norm by: %6.2f%c\n", perdif, '%');
}
```

The showit() function can either be placed in its own file and compiled separately, or placed directly into Program 6.6 as a replacement for the showit() stub. In either case, the stub for showit() is removed and the program rerun to test the completed showit() individually. This stub replacement procedure is a major testing technique used by all professional programmers. The procedure permits one to isolate and individually test each function as it is completed. Then, if the program does not act as we expect, we not only have a prior version to fall back on but also have isolated the error to one particular function. This allows us to either continue working on the function or replace it with its stub and use the program as a test bed for one of the other functions. Assuming that our test of showit() verifies its operation, we move on to completing the norms() and pcdif() functions.

We want norms() to calculate and return the normal height given the child's age. Following is a competed norms() function using the formula previously given for calculating a "normal" height:

```
float norm(float age)
{
  #define MINAGE 6.0
  float agedif, avght;

  agedif = age - MINAGE;
  avght = -0.25*pow(agedif,2) + 3.5*agedif + 45.0;
  return (avght);
}
```

This function illustrates a typical calculation function. Also notice that norms() uses a named constant, MINAGE, that defines the "base" age as 6 years old. Once again, having completed this function, we would use it in place of its stub.

The last function, pcdif(), is used to calculate the percent difference of the child's actual height from normal. Notice that the calculation of a percent difference is a general computation that can be used in other applications, so this is a useful function to have programmed because it can be used in other programs where a percentage is required. Here is the completed function

```
float pcdif()(float actual, float base)
{
  return ( (actual - base)) / base * 100.0 );
}
```

Internally, the pcdif() function uses no variables and performs its calculation within its return statement. Again, having completed this function it should be used to replace its stub version and tested.

Program 6.7 illustrates the final evolvement of Program 6.6 with all of the stubs replaced by their final versions.

Program 6.7

```
#include <stdio.h>
#include <math.h>

main()
{
  float norm(float);        /* here are the function prototypes */
  float pcdif(float, float);
  void showit(float, float );

  int years, months;
  float height, normht;
  float age, perdif;

  /* this is the input section */
  printf("\nHow old (in years) is this child? ");
  scanf("%d", &years);
  printf("How many months since the child's birthday? ");
  scanf("%d", &months);
  age = years + months/12.0;  /* convert to total years */
  printf("Enter the child's height (in inches): ");
  scanf("%f", &height);

  normht = norm(age);

  perdif  = pcdif(height, normht);

  showit(normht, perdif);

  return 0;
}

float norm(float age)
{
  #define MINAGE 6.0
  float agedif, avght;

  agedif = age - MINAGE;
  avght = -0.25*pow(agedif,2) + 3.5*agedif + 45.0;
  return (avght);
}

float pcdif(float actual, float base)
{
```

```
  return (actual - base)/base * 100.0;
}

void showit(float normht, float perdif)
{
  printf("\nThe average height in inches is: %5.2f\n", normht);
  printf("The actual height deviates from the norm by: %6.2f%c\n", perdif, '%');
}
```

Following is a sample run using Program 6.7:

```
How old (in years) is this child? 10
How many months since the child's birthday? 6
Enter the child's height (in inches): 50

The average height in inches is: 55.69
The actual height deviates from the norm by: -10.21%
```

As this result agrees with our previous hand calculation, and each function was individually tested for correct input in Program 6.6 and for correct output as the final version replaced the stub version, we have some degree of confidence that our program is correct.

EXERCISES 6.3

Programming Exercises

1. Modify Program 6.7 to calculate a child's normal weight and a percent weight difference, in addition to the calculated height values. Assume the formula for predicting normal weight, in pounds, is given by the formula

   $Normal\ Weight = 0.5\ (Age - 6) + 5.0\ (Age - 6) + 48$

2. Write a function that calculates the area a, of a circle when its circumference, c, is given. This function should call a second function which returns the radius, r, of the circle, given c. The relevant formulas are: $r = c/2\pi$ and $a = \pi R^2$.

3. a. The volume of a right circular cylinder is given by its radius squared times its height times π. Write a function that accepts two single-precision arguments corresponding to the cylinder's radius and height, respectively, and returns the cylinder's volume.
   b. Include the function written for Exercise 3a in a working C program. Make sure your function is called from `main()` and correctly returns a value to `main()`. Have `main()` display the value returned and test the function by passing various data to it and verifying the returned value.

4. **a.** Write a function named `winPercent()` that accepts the number of wins and losses that a team achieves and returns its winning percentage. Use the formula that *winning percentage = 100 * wins / (wins + losses)*
   b. Include the function written in Exercise 4a in a working program. Make sure your function is called from `main()` and correctly returns a value to `main()`. Have `main()` display the value returned. Use your program to determine the winning percentage of the 1927 New York Yankees, who won 110 games and lost 44 games that season, and the 1955 Brooklyn Dodgers, who won 98 games and lost 55 games that season.

5. Write the function named `payment()` that has three parameters named `principal`, which is the amount financed; `intRate`, which is the monthly interest rate; and `months`, which is the number of months the loan is for. The function should return the monthly payment according to the following formula:

$$Payment = \frac{Principal}{\dfrac{1}{\text{int}\,Rate} - \dfrac{1}{\text{int}\,Rate * (1 + \text{int}\,Rate)^{months}}}$$

Note that the interest value used in this formula is a monthly rate, as a decimal. Thus, if the yearly rate were 10 percent, the monthly rate is (0.10/12). Test your function. What argument values cause it to malfunction (and should not be input)?

6. **a.** An extremely useful programming algorithm for rounding a real number to *n* decimal places is

   Step 1: Multiply the number by 10^n
   Step 2: Add 0.5
   Step 3: Delete the fractional part of the result
   Step 4: Divide by 10^n

   For example, using this algorithm to round the number 78.374625 to three decimal places yields

   Step 1: $78.374625 * 10^3 = 78374.625$
   Step 2: $78374.625 + .5 = 78375.125$
   Step 3: retaining the integer part = 78375
   Step 4: 78375 divided by 10^3 = 78.375

   Use this information to write a C function named `round()` that rounds the value of its first parameter to the number of decimal places specified by its second parameter.
   b. Incorporate the `round()` function written for Exercise 6a into a program that accepts a user-entered amount of money, multiplies the entered amount by an 8.675 percent interest rate, and displays the result rounded to two decimal places. Enter, compile, and execute this program, and verify the result for the following test amounts: $1000, $100, $10, and $0.

7. **a.** Write a C function named `whole()` that returns the integer part of any number passed to the function. (*Hint:* Assign the passed argument to an integer variable.)
   b. Include the function written in Exercise 7a in a working program. Make sure your function is called from `main()` and correctly returns a value to `main()`. Have `main()` use `printf()` to display the value returned. Test the function by passing various data to it.

8. a. Write a C function named `fracpart()` that returns the fractional part of any number passed to the function. For example, if the number 256.879 is passed to `fracpart()`, the number .879 should be returned. Have the function `fracpart()` call the function `whole()` that you wrote in Exercise 7. The number returned can then be determined as the number passed to `fracpart()` less the returned value when the same argument is passed to `whole()`. The completed program should consist of `main()` followed by `fracpart()` followed by `whole()`.
   b. Include the function written in Exercise 8a in a working program. Make sure your function is called from `main()` and correctly returns a value to `main()`. Have `main()` use `printf()` to display the value returned. Test the function by passing various data to it.

9. A recipe for making enough acorn squash for four people requires the following ingredients:
   - 2 acorn squashes
   - 2 teaspoons of lemon juice
   - 1/4 cup of raisins
   - 1 1/2 cups of applesauce
   - 1/4 cup of brown sugar
   - 3 tablespoons of chopped walnuts

   Using this information, write and test six functions that each accept the number of people that must be served and return the amount of each ingredient, respectively, that is required.

10. The owner of a strawberry farm has made the following arrangement with a group of students: They may pick all the strawberries they want. When they are through picking, the strawberries will be weighed. The farm will retain 50 percent of the strawberries and the students will divide the remainder evenly among them. Using this information, write and test a C function named `straw()` that accepts the number of students and the total pounds picked as input arguments, and returns the approximate number of strawberries each receives. Assume that a strawberry weighs approximately 1 ounce. There are 16 ounces to a pound. Include the `straw()` function in a working C program.

11. The determinant of the 2-by-2 matrix

$$\begin{vmatrix} a_{11} & a_{12} \\ a_{21} & a_{22} \end{vmatrix}$$

is

$a_{11}a_{22} - a_{21}a_{12}$

Similarly, the determinant of a 3-by-3 matrix

$$\begin{vmatrix} a_{11} & a_{12} & a_{13} \\ a_{21} & a_{22} & a_{23} \\ a_{31} & a_{32} & a_{33} \end{vmatrix}$$

is

$$a_{11}\begin{vmatrix} a_{22} & a_{23} \\ a_{32} & a_{33} \end{vmatrix} - a_{21}\begin{vmatrix} a_{12} & a_{13} \\ a_{32} & a_{33} \end{vmatrix} + a_{31}\begin{vmatrix} a_{12} & a_{13} \\ a_{22} & a_{23} \end{vmatrix}$$

Using this information write and test two functions, named `det2()` and `det3()`. The `det2()` function should accept the four coefficients of a 2-by-2 matrix and return its determinant. The `det3()` function should accept the nine coefficients of a 3-by-3 matrix and return its determinant by calling `det2()` to calculate the required 2-by-2 determinants.

6.4 Standard Library Functions

All C programs have access to a standard, preprogrammed set of functions for handling data input and output, computing mathematical quantities, and manipulating strings of characters. A few of these, the commonly used mathematical functions, have already been introduced in Section 3.2. In this section we present additional mathematical functions,[4] two new input and output functions: character-manipulation functions and conversion routines.

All of the functions presented in this section are part of the standard library provided with each C compiler. The standard library consists of 15 header files that are described in detail in Appendix C. Each of these header files consists of C source code that you can open and inspect. You can find them on your computer by doing a search for any one of them, such as `stdio.h`.

Before using the functions available in the system library, you must know

- The name of each available function
- The arguments required by each function
- The data type of the result (if any) returned by each function
- A description of what each function does
- How to include the library containing the desired function

The first three items are provided by both the function's prototype and its header line. For example, consider the function named `sqrt()`, which was introduced in Section 3.2 and calculates the square root of its argument. The prototype for this function is

```
double sqrt(double)
```

This prototype lists all the information required to call the `sqrt()` function and tells us that the function expects a double-precision argument and returns a double-precision value.

The prototypes for all library functions are contained in at least one of the standard header files that form the standard C library. To include these prototypes into your program, first locate the correct header file for the library functions that you want to use (Appendix C provides a list of these functions) and then include the following statement in your program, where *header-file-name* is replaced by name of the header file you require:

```
#include <header-file-name>        ←——— no semicolon
```

[4]Some of the routines described in this section are actually coded as macros, a topic covered in Section 14.3.

Placing the appropriate `#include` statement at the top of the program ensures proper access to the library functions whose prototypes are contained in the header file.

Mathematical Library Functions

A commonly used set of mathematical functions was presented in Section 3.2. Table 6.1 presents a more complete set of these functions. To access any of the listed functions requires including the `math.h` header file.[5]

As with all C functions, the arguments passed to a mathematical library function do not have to be numbers. Any expression, including another function call, can be an argument provided that the expression can be evaluated to yield an argument of the required data type.

Table 6.1 Mathematical Library Functions (require the `math.h` header file)

Prototype	Description
`double fabs(double)`	Returns the absolute value of its double-precision argument. (Note, the function `int abs(int)` is defined in the `stdlib.h` header file.)
`double ceil(double)`	Returns a floating-point value that is the smallest integer that is greater than or equal to its argument value.
`double floor(double)`	Returns a floating-point value that is the largest integer that is less than or equal to its argument value.
`double fmod(double, double)`	Returns the remainder of its first argument divided by its second argument.
`double exp(double)`	Returns e raised to its double-precision argument.
`double log(double)`	Returns the natural logarithm (base e) of its argument.
`double log10(double)`	Returns the common logarithm (base 10) of its argument.
`double sqrt(double)`	Returns the square root of its argument.
`double pow(double, double)`	Returns its first argument raised to the power of its second argument.
`double sin(double)`	Returns the sine of its argument. The argument must be in radians.
`double cos(double)`	Returns the cosine of its argument. The argument must be in radians.
`double tan(double)`	Returns the tangent of its argument. The argument must be in radians.
`double asin(double)`	Returns the angle (in radians) whose sine is the argument.

[5] Additionally, if you are using a Unix operating system, you must include the `-lm` option when compiling your program.

Table 6.1 Mathematical Library Functions (require the `math.h` header file) (continued)

Prototype	Description
`double acos(double)`	Returns the angle (in radians) whose cosine is the argument.
`double atan(double)`	Returns the angle (in radians) whose tangent is the argument.
`double atan2(double, double)`	Returns the angle (in radians) whose tangent is the first argument divided by the second argument.
`double sinh(double)`	Returns the hyperbolic sine of its argument.
`double cosh(double)`	Returns the hyperbolic cosine of its argument.
`double tanh(double)`	Returns the hyperbolic tangent of its argument.

The `rand()` and `srand()` Functions

In solving many commercial and scientific problems, both probability and statistical sampling techniques are required. For example, in simulating automobile traffic flow or telephone usage patterns, statistical models are required. In addition, applications such as simple computer games and more involved gaming scenarios can only be described statistically. All of these statistical models require the generation of **random numbers**—that is, a series of numbers whose order cannot be predicted.

In practice, it is hard to find truly random numbers. Dice are never perfect, cards are never shuffled completely randomly, and digital computers can handle numbers only within a finite range and with limited precision. The best one can do in most cases is generate **pseudorandom numbers**, which are sufficiently random for the task at hand. All C compilers provide two functions for creating random numbers: `rand()` and `srand()`, which are defined in the `stdlib.h` header file. The `rand()` function produces a series of random numbers in the range 0 < `rand()` < RAND_MAX, where the constant RAND_MAX is a compiler-dependent symbolic constant that is defined in the `stdlib.h` header file. The `srand()` function provides a starting "seed" value for `rand()`. If `srand()` or some other equivalent "seeding" technique is not used, `rand()` will always produce the same series of random numbers.

The general procedure for creating a series of N random numbers using these two functions is illustrated in Program 6.8, which produces a series of 10 such numbers.

Program 6.8

```
#include <stdio.h>
#include <stdlib.h>
#include <time.h>
  #define TOTALNUMBERS 10

int main()
{
```

```
 8      float randValue;
 9      int i;
10
11      srand(time(NULL));   /* this generates the first "seed" value */
12
13      for (i = 1; i <= TOTALNUMBERS; i++)
14      {
15        randValue = rand();
16        printf("%6.0f\n", randValue);
17      }
18
19      return 0;
20    }
```

Notice that in line 11

```
11  srand(time(NULL));   /* this generates the first "seed"
value */
```

`srand()`'s argument function is a call to the `time()` function with a `NULL` argument. The `NULL` argument causes `time()` to read the computer's internal clock time, in seconds. The `srand()` function then uses this time to initialize the `rand()` random-number generator function.[6]

Once `rand()` has been initialized, the `for` loop in lines 13 through 17, repeated below, calls this function 10 times, with each call producing a new random number:

```
13  for (int i = 1; i <= N; i++) /* this generates N random numbers */
14  {
15    randvalue = rand();
16    printf("%f\n", randvalue);
17  }
```

The following is the output produced by one run of Program 6.8:

```
16579
14775
18082
32697
 8029
24680
31569
 5795
11768
25546
```

Each time Program 6.8 is executed, it will create a different series of 10 random numbers.

[6]Alternatively, many C compilers have a `randomize()` routine that is defined using the `srand()` function. If this routine is available, the call `randomize()` can be used in place of the call `srand(time(NULL))`. In either case, the initializing "seed" routine is only called once, after which the `rand()` function is used to generate a series of numbers.

Scaling

In practice you'll typically need to make one modification to the random numbers produced by the `rand()` function. In many applications the random numbers must be integers within a specified range, such as 1 to 100. The method for adjusting the random numbers produced by a random-number generator to reside within a specified range is called **scaling**.

Scaling a random number as an integer value between 1 and `N` is accomplished using the expression `1 + (int)rand() % N`. For example, the expression `1 + (int)rand() % 100` produces a random integer between 1 and 100. Similarly, the expression `1 + (int) rand() % 6` produces a random integer between 1 and 6. Random numbers within this range could be used in a program that simulates the roll of a die. In general, to produce a random integer between the numbers `a` and `b`, you can use the expression

```
a + (int)(rand() % (b - a + 1)).
```

Coin Toss Simulation

A common use of random numbers is to simulate events, rather than going through the time and expense of constructing a real-life experiment. We will illustrate the general concepts and techniques frequently encountered in constructing a simulation by looking at a program that has been designed to simulate the tossing of a coin 1000 times.

From probability theory we know that the probability of having a single tossed coin turn up heads is 50 percent. Similarly, there is a 50 percent probability of having a single tossed coin turn up tails. Using these probabilities, we would expect a single coin that is tossed 1000 times to turn up heads 500 times and tails 500 times. In practice, however, this is never exactly realized for a single experiment consisting of 1000 tosses.

Rather than attempting to toss a coin 1000 times, we will use a program to simulate these tosses. To do this we will generate 1000 random numbers and then devise a means of deciding which random numbers correspond to a head and which a tail. Program 6.9 performs the required simulation, using the two highlighted functions that are called from `main()`.

Program 6.9

```
#include <stdio.h>
#include <stdlib.h>
#include <time.h>

int flip(int);   /* prototype for flip function */
void percentages(int, int) ;   /* prototype for percentage function */

int main()
{
  int numTosses = 1000;
  int heads;

  heads = flip(numTosses);
  percentages(numTosses, heads);
```

```

  return 0;
}

// this method tosses the coin numTimes
// and returns the number of heads
int flip(int numTimes)
{
  int randValue;
  int heads = 0;
  int i;

  srand(time(NULL));

  for (i = 1; i <= numTimes; i++)
  {
    randValue = 1 + (int)rand() % 100;
   if (randValue > 50)
      heads++;
  }

  return (heads);
}

// this method calculates and displays
// the percentages of heads and tails
void percentages(int numTosses, int heads)
{
  int tails;
  float perheads, pertails;

  if (numTosses == 0)
  printf("There were no tosses, so no percentages can be calculated.\n");
  else
  {
    tails = numTosses - heads;
    printf("Number of coin tosses: %d\n", numTosses);
    printf("   Heads: %d   Tails: %d\n", heads, tails);
    perheads = (float)heads/numTosses * 100.0;
    pertails = (float)(numTosses - heads)/numTosses * 100.0;
    printf("Heads came up %6.2f percent of the time.\n", perheads);
    printf("Tails came up %6.2f percent of the time.\n", pertails);
  }
}
```

The lighter highlighted code in Program 6.9 contains the `flip()` function, which is coded according to the following algorithm:

Coin Toss Algorithm :
For numTimes times
Generate a random number between 1 and 100
If the random number is greater than 50,
increment the heads count
End For
Return the heads count

As coded, the `flip()` function accepts the required number of tosses as an argument and returns the number of heads realized when the tosses are made. As indicated in lines 29 through 34, repeated below for convenience,

```
29  for (i = 1; i <= numTimes; i++)
30  {
31    randValue = 1 + (int)rand() % 100;
32   if (randValue > 50)
33      heads++;
34  }
```

the `flip()` function generates the required number of tosses using a `for` loop. Within this loop, line 31

```
31  randValue = 1 + (int)rand() % 100;
```

scales the random number returned by `rand()` to be an integer from 1 to 100. It then uses an `if` statement in lines 32 and 33

```
32  if (randValue > 50)
33     heads++;
```

to increment the heads count whenever an integer above 50 was detected. The condition being tested forces the integers from 51 to 100 to represent a toss as a head, and thus, the integers from 0 to 50 represent a toss as a tail. This split preserves the probability that a single toss has a 50-50 chance of being either a head or tail. Other determinations could certainly have been used, as long as they maintain this single-toss probability.

The `percentages()` function calculates the percentages of heads and tails using the algorithm

Percentage Algorithm:
If the number of tosses equals 0
Display a message indicating that no tosses were made
Else
Calculate the number of tails as the number of tosses minus the number of heads
Display the number of tosses, number of heads, and number of tails
Calculate the percentage of heads as the number of heads divided by the number of tosses x 100%
Calculate the percentage of tails as the number of tails divided by the number of tosses x 100%
Print the percentage of heads and tails
EndIf

Notice in lines 53 and 54 the use of the cast (float)

```
53  perheads = (float)heads/numTosses * 100.0;
54  pertails = (float)(numTosses - heads)/numTosses * 100.0;
```

Without casting at least one of the values in each expression to a floating-point value, the result of each calculation would always be 0. This is because all of the variables in the expression are integer variables, with the numerator always being smaller than the denominator. Making one of the values in the calculation a floating-point value creates a floating-point expression. As described in Section 2.4, this forces the evaluation to yield a double-precision value, which retains the fractional part of the division.

Following are two sample runs using Program 6.9

```
Number of coin tosses: 1000
   Heads: 497   Tails: 503
Heads came up 49.7 percent of the time.
Tails came up 50.3 percent of the time.
```

and

```
Number of coin tosses: 1000
  Heads: 504    Tails: 496
Heads came up 50.4 percent of the time.
Tails came up 49.6 percent of the time.
```

Input/Output Library Functions

We have already made extensive use of two input/output (I/O) library functions, `printf()` and `scanf()`. We now present two additional I/O library routines that are specifically used with character data. These two routines are written and contained within the `stdio.h` header file.[7] The first of these routines is getchar(), which can be used for single character input. The prototype for `getchar()` is

```
int getchar()
```

As indicated by this prototype, `getchar()` expects no arguments to be passed to it and returns an integer data type. The reason for returning characters in integer format is to allow the End-Of-File (EOF) sentinel, previously described in Section 5.3, to be returned. The EOF sentinel has an integer code, and if this sentinel is to be correctly recognized when input, `getchar()` must return integer values.

The `getchar()` routine is used to return the next single character entered at the terminal. For example, a statement such as

```
inChar = getchar();
```

causes the next character entered at the terminal to be stored in the variable `inChar`. This is equivalent to the longer statement `scanf("%c",&inChar);`. The `getchar()` routine is extremely useful when continuously inputting strings of characters from data files, which is the topic of Chapter 10.

---

[7]Formally, these two routines are created as macros within the `stdio.h` header file. The writing of macros is presented in Section 14.3.

The output library routine corresponding to `getchar()` is the `putchar()` routine. This routine expects a single character argument and displays the character passed to it on the terminal. For example, the statement `putchar('a')` causes the letter a to be displayed on the standard output device—it is equivalent to the longer statement `printf("%c",'a')`.

Character Processing Functions

Table 6.2 lists the complete set of the character processing functions whose prototypes are provided in the ctype.h header file.

Table 6.2 Character Functions (require the header file `ctype.h`)

Prototype	Description	Example
`int isalnum(int)`	Returns a non-0 number if the argument is a letter or a digit; otherwise it returns a 0.	`isalnum('9');`
`int isalpha(int)`	Returns a non-0 number if the argument is a letter; otherwise, it returns 0.	`isalpha('a')`
`int iscntrl(int)`	Returns a non-0 number if the argument is a control argument; otherwise, it returns 0.	`iscntrl('a')`
`int isdigit(int)`	Returns a non-0 number if the argument is a digit (0–9); otherwise, it returns 0.	`isdigit('a')`
`int isgraph(int)`	Returns a non-0 value if the argument is a printable character other than a space; otherwise it returns a 0.	`isgraph('@')`
`int islower(int)`	Returns a non-0 number if the argument is lowercase; otherwise, it returns 0.	`islower('a')`
`int isprint(int)`	Returns a non-0 number if the argument is a printable argument; otherwise, it returns 0.	`isprint('a')`
`int ispunct(int)`	Returns a non-0 number if the argument is a punctuation argument; otherwise, it returns 0.	`ispunct('!')`
`int isspace(int)`	Returns a non-0 number if the argument is a space; otherwise, it returns 0.	`isspace(' ')`
`int isupper(int)`	Returns a non-0 number if the argument is uppercase; otherwise, it returns 0.	`isupper('a')`
`int isxdigit(int)`	Returns a non-0 value if the argument is a hexadecimal digit (A–F, a–f, or 0–9).	`isxdigit('b')`

Table 6.2 Character Functions (require the header file `ctype.h`) (continued)

Prototype	Description	Example
`int tolower(int)`	Returns the lowercase equivalent if the argument is uppercase; otherwise, it returns the argument unchanged.	`tolower('A')`
`int toupper(int)`	Returns the uppercase equivalent if the argument is lowercase; otherwise, it returns the argument unchanged.	`toupper('a')`

The functions listed in Table 6.2 are particularly useful in checking individual characters as they are input by a user. For example, Program 6.10 continuously requests that a user enter a character and determines if the character is a letter or a digit. The program exits the `while` loop when either an upper- or lowercase x is entered.

Program 6.10

```
 1  #include <stdio.h>
 2  #include <ctype.h>
 3  int main()
 4  {
 5    char inChar;
 6
 7    do
 8    {
 9      printf("\nPush any key (type an x to stop) ");
10      inChar = getchar(); /* get the next character typed */
11      inChar = tolower(inChar); /* convert to lowercase */
12      getchar(); /* get and ignore the ENTER key */
13
14      if ( isalpha(inChar) ) /* a nonzero value is true in C */
15        printf("\nThe character entered is a letter.\n");
16      else if ( isdigit(inChar) )
17        printf("\nThe character entered is a digit.\n");
18
19    } while (inChar != 'x');
20
21  }
```

A few remarks are in order in reviewing Program 6.10. First, the conditions being tested in the if-else statement in lines 14 through 17

```
14  if ( isalpha(inChar) ) /* a nonzero value is true in C */
15    printf("\nThe character entered is a letter.\n");
```

```
16  else if ( isdigit(inChar) )
17    printf("\nThe character entered is a digit.\n");
```

make use of the fact that a condition is considered true if it evaluates to a non-0 value. Thus, the condition `( isalpha(inChar)` in line 14 is equivalent to the longer expression `(isalpha(inChar) != 0)`, and the condition `( isdigit(inChar) )` in line 16 is equivalent to the longer expression `(isdigit(inChar) != 0)`. The call to `getchar()` in line 12 is used to remove the Enter key.

Because functions return values, a function may itself be an argument to a function (including itself). For example, the two statements in lines 10 and 11 in Program 6.10

```
10  inChar = getchar(); /* get the next character typed */
11  inChar = tolower(inChar); /* convert to lowercase */
```

may be combined into the single statement

```
inChar = tolower(getchar());
```

Conversion Functions

The library functions listed in Table 6.3 are used to convert strings to and from integer and floating-point data types. The prototypes for each of these routines are contained in the `stdlib.h` header file, which should be included in any program that uses these routines.

Table 6.3 String Conversion Functions (require the header file `stdlib.h`)

Prototype[8]	Description	Example
`int atoi(string)`	Converts an ASCII string to an integer. Conversion stops at the first noninteger character.	`atoi("1234")`
`double atof(string)`	Converts an ASCII string to a double-precision number. Conversion stops at the first character that cannot be interpreted as a double.	`atof("12.34")`
`string itoa(int)`	Converts an integer to an ASCII string. The space allocated for the returned string must be large enough for the converted value.	`itoa(1234)`

Program 6.11 illustrates the use of the `atoi()` and `atof()` functions. These functions are illustrated further in Section 9.4, where they are used to ensure that user-entered data is of the correct numerical data type.

[8] There is no C string data type. Formally, a string is an array of characters, which is described in detail in Chapter 9.

Program 6.11

```
#include <stdio.h>
#include <stdlib.h> /* required for string conversion functions */
int main()
{
  int num;
  double dnum;

  num = atoi("1234");   /* convert a string to an integer */

  printf("The string \"1234\" as an integer number is: %d \n", num);
  printf("This number divided by 3 is: %d \n\n", num / 3);

  dnum = atof("1234.96"); /* convert a string to a double */

  printf("The string \"1234.96\" as a double is: %f \n", dnum);
  printf("This number divided by 3 is: %f \n", dnum / 3);

  return 0;
}
```

The output produced by Program 6.11 is

```
The string "1234" as an integer number is: 1234
This number divided by 3 is: 411

The string "1234.96" as a double number is: 1234.960000
This number divided by 3 is: 411.653333
```

As this output illustrates, once a string has been converted to either an integer or floating-point value, mathematical operations on the numerical value are valid.

EXERCISES 6.4

Programming Exercises

1. Write a C function named `root4()` that returns the fourth root of the argument passed to it.

2. Write two C functions, named `dist()` and `angle()`, respectively, to be used in converting the rectangular (x,y) coordinates of a point into polar form. That is, given an `x` and `y` position on a Cartesian coordinate system, as illustrated in Figure 6.11, the `dist()` function must

calculate and return the distance from the origin, r, and the `angle()` function must calculate and return the angle from the x-axis, θ, specified by the point. The values of r and θ are referred to as the point's polar coordinates. Use the relationships that

$$r = \sqrt{x^2 + y^2}$$
$$\theta = tan^{-1}\ (y / x),\ x \neq 0$$

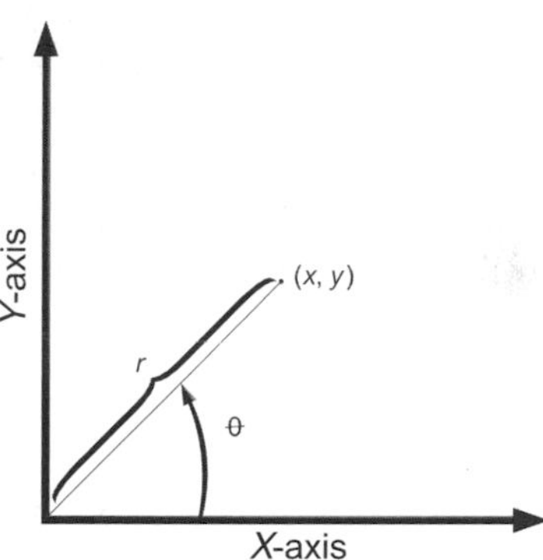

Figure 6.11 Correspondence between polar (distance, *r* and angle, θ) and Cartesian (*x*, *y*) coordinates

3. Enter and execute Program 6.9 on your computer.

4. a. Modify Program 6.9 so that it requests the number of tosses from the user. (*Hint:* Make sure to have the program correctly determine the percentages of heads and tails obtained.)
   b. Execute the modified program written for Exercise 4a five times, each time using 10 tosses per run and notice if the percentages reported by the program differ significantly from the results displayed in the text when 1000 tosses were used.

5. (Central Limit Theorem Simulation) Modify Program 6.9 so that it automatically generates 20 simulations, with each simulation having 1000 tosses. Print out the percentage for each run and the percentages for the 20 runs combined. Determine if the averages for the 20 runs combined are closer to the 50 percent heads and tails than the majority of the individual simulation results.

6. a. Write a C program to create a HI-LO game. In this game the computer produces a random integer between 1 and 100 and provides the user with seven tries to guess the generated number. If the user guesses the correct number, the message, `"Hooray, you have won!"` should be displayed. After each incorrect guess, the computer should display the message, `"Wrong Number, Try Again"` and indicate whether the guess was too high or too low and display the number of guesses left. After seven incorrect guesses, the computer should display the message, `"Sorry, you lose"` and the correct number.
   b. Modify the program written for Exercise 6a to allow the user to run the game again after a game has been completed. The program should display the message `"Would you like to play again (y/n)?"` and restart if the user enters either a Y or y.

7. Write a program that tests the effectiveness of the `rand()` function provided by your compiler. Start by initializing 10 counters, such as `onescount`, `twoscount` to `tenscount`, all to 0. Then generate a large number of random integers between 1 and 10. Each time a 1 occurs, increment `onescount`; when a 2 occurs, increment `twoscount`; etc. Finally, print out the number of 1s, 2s, etc. that occurred and the percentage of the time each number occurred.

8. Write a program to simulate the roll of two dice. If the total of the two dice is 7 or 11 you win; otherwise, you lose. Embellish this program as much as you like, with betting, different odds, different combinations for win or lose, stopping play when you have no money left or reach the house limit, displaying the dice, etc.

9. A value that is sometimes useful is the greatest common divisor (GCD) of two integers n1 and n2, which is the largest integer that can be evenly divided into the two integers. A famous mathematician, Euclid, discovered an efficient method to find the GCD of two integers more than 2000 years ago. Right now, however, we'll settle for a stub. Write the integer function `stubgcd(n1,n2)`. Simply have it return a value that suggests it received its parameters correctly. (*Hint:* n1 + n2 is a good choice of return values. Why isn't n1/n2 a good choice?).

10. Euclid's method for finding the GCD of two positive integers consists of the following steps:
    a. Divide the larger number by the smaller and retain the remainder.
    b. Divide the smaller number by the remainder, again retaining the remainder.
    c. Continue dividing the prior remainder by the current remainder until the remainder is 0, at which point the last non-0 remainder is the GCD.

    For example, assume the two positive integers are 84 and 49, we have:

    Step a: 84/49 yields a remainder of 35

    Step b: 49/35 yields a remainder of 14

    Step c: 35/14 yields a remainder of 7

    Step d: 14/7 yields a remainder of 0

    Thus, the last non-0 remainder, which is 7, is the GCD of 84 and 49.

    Using Euclid's algorithm, replace the stub function written for Exercise 9 with an actual function that determines and returns the GCD of its two integer parameters.

11. In the game of blackjack, the cards 2 through 10 are counted at their face values, regardless of suit, all picture cards (jack, queen, and king) are counted as 10, and an ace is counted as either a 1 or an 11, depending on the total count of all the cards in a player's hand. The ace is counted as 11 only if the total value of all cards in a player's hand does not exceed 21, else it is counted as a 1. Using this information write a C program that uses a random number generator to select three cards (a 1 initially corresponding to an ace, a 2 corresponding to a face card of two, and so on), calculate the total value of the hand appropriately, and display the value of the three cards with a printed message.

12. It has been said that a monkey pushing keys at random on a keyboard, could produce the works of Shakespeare, given sufficient time. Simulate this by having a program select and display letters at random. Count the number of letters typed until the program produces

one of the two-letter words, *at*, *is*, *he*, *we*, *up*, or *on*. When one of these words is produced, stop the program and display the total number of letters typed. (*Hint:* Choose a letter by selecting a random integer number between 1 and 26.)

13. Here is a version of a problem called "the random walk." It can be extended to two or three dimensions and used to simulate molecular motion, to determine the effectiveness of reactor shielding, or to calculate a variety of other probabilities.

    Assume that your very tired and sleepy pet dog leaves his favorite lamppost on warm summer evenings and staggers randomly either two steps in the direction toward home or one step in the opposite direction. After taking these steps, the dog again staggers randomly two steps toward home or one step backward, and does this again, and again. If the pet reaches a total distance of 10 steps from the lamppost in the direction toward home, you find him and take him home. If the dog arrives back at the lamppost before reaching 10 steps in the direction toward home, he lies down and spend the night at the foot of the lamppost.

    Write a C program that simulates 500 summer evenings, and calculate and print the percentage of the time your pet sleeps at home for these evenings. (*Hint:* In a loop determine forward or backward based on the value of a random number.) Accumulate the distance the dog has reached toward your home. If the distance reaches 10, stop the loop and increment the home count. If the distance reaches 0 before it reaches 10, stop the loop but do not increment the home count. Repeat this loop 500 times and find the ratio of (home count)/500.0.

14. Write a C program using the `getchar()`, `toupper()`, and `putchar()` functions that echo back all letters entered in their uppercase form. The program should terminate when either an x or X is entered. (*Hint:* Convert all letters to uppercase and test only for an X.)

15. Rewrite Program 6.10 using a `while` statement in place of the `do-while` statement used in the program.

16. Write a C program that uses the `getchar()` function to input a character from the terminal into the variable `inChar`. Include the function call within a `do-while` loop that continues to prompt the user for an additional character until the + key is pressed. After each character is entered, print the decimal value used to store the character using the function call `printf("%d",inChar);`.

6.5 Common Programming and Compiler Errors

In using the material presented in this chapter, be aware of the following possible programming and compiler errors:

Programming Errors

1. Passing incorrect data types. The values passed to a function when it is called must correspond to the parameters declared for the function. The simplest way to verify that correct values have been received is to display all passed values within a function's body before any calculations are made. Once this verification has taken place, the display can be removed.

2. Omitting a called function's prototype. The called function must be alerted to the data types of the return value and any parameters; this information is provided by the function prototype. This declaration can only be omitted if the called function is physically placed in a program before its calling function or the called function returns an integer or void data type. The actual value returned by a function can be verified by displaying it both before and after it is returned.
3. Terminating a function's header line with a semicolon.
4. Forgetting to include a data type for each parameter listed in a function's header line.
5. Returning a different data type from a function than the data type specified in the function's header line.

Compiler Errors

The following table summarizes common errors that will result in compilation errors and the typical error messages provided by Unix- and Windows-based compilers.

Error	Typical Unix-based Compiler Error Message	Typical Windows-based Compiler Error Message
Terminating a function's header line with a semicolon.	`(S) Syntax error`	`error: missing function header (old-style formal list?)`
Passing the incorrect number of parameters into a function.	`(E) Missing argument(s)`	`error C2660: function does not take … arguments`

Not having a function prototype.	`(S) Syntax error: possible missing ';' or ','`
	Note that each parameter of the function will generate the following error:
	`(S) Undeclared identifier`
		`error: identifier not found, even with argument-dependent lookup`
		`error C2365: redefinition; previous definition was a 'formerly unknown identifier'`

Changing the data types of the parameters between the prototype and the function header.	`(S) Redeclaration of … differs from previous declaration` `(I) The data type of parameter differs from the previous type`	`error: unresolved external symbol referenced in function` `fatal error: unresolved externals`

Error	Typical Unix-based Compiler Error Message	Typical Windows-based Compiler Error Message
Forgetting to separate the parameters in the function header with a comma.	`(S) Syntax error: possible missing ')' or ','? Redeclaration of doit differs from previous declaration on line 3 of "Filename.c" (I) Redeclaration of doit has a different number of fixed parameters than the previous declaration (S) Undeclared identifier b`	`error: syntax error : argument should be preceded by ','`
Using a function name that is a reserved syntax word.	`(S) Redeclaration of function differs from previous declaration`	`error: identifier not found, even with argument-dependent lookup`

6.6 Chapter Summary

1. A function is called by giving its name and passing any data to it in the parentheses following the name. If a variable or expression is one of the arguments in a function call, the called function receives a copy of the variable's or expression's value, respectively.

2. The commonly used form of a user-written function is

   ```
   returnType functionName(parameter list)
   {
   declarations;
   statements;
   return (expression);
   }
   ```

   The first line of the function is called the function header. The opening and closing braces of the function and all statements in between these braces constitute the function's body. The parameter list must include the names of all parameters and their data types.

3. A function's return type is the data type of the value returned by the function. If no type is explicitly declared, the function is assumed to return an integer value. If the function does not return any value, it should be declared as a `void` type.

4. Functions can directly return at most a single value to their calling functions. This value is the value of the expression in the return statement.

5. Functions can be declared to all calling functions by means of a function prototype. The prototype provides a declaration for a function that specifies the data type returned by the function, its name, and the data types of the parameters expected by the function. As with all declarations, a function prototype is terminated with a semicolon and may be

specified as a global declaration or included within a function's local variable declarations. The most common form of a function prototype is

returnDataType functionName(parameter data types);

If the called function is placed physically above the calling function, no further declaration is required because the function's definition serves as a global declaration to all following functions.

6. Arguments passed to a function provide a means of evaluating any valid C expression. It is the expression's value that is then passed to the called function.

7. A set of preprogrammed functions for mathematical calculations, character input and output, character processing, and numerical conversions are included in the standard library provided with each C compiler. To use one of these functions, you must know the name of the function, the arguments expected by the function, the data type of the returned value (if any), and a description of what the function does. You must also include the specific header file containing the function's prototypes and definition.

Chapter 7

Modularity Using Functions: Part II

Any project that requires a computer incurs both hardware and software costs. The costs associated with the hardware consist of all costs relating to the physical components used in the system. These components include the computer itself, peripherals, and any other items such as cabling and associated equipment required by the project. The software costs include all costs associated with initial program development and subsequent program maintenance. As illustrated in Figure 7.1, the major cost of most computer-based projects, be they research, development, or final application, has become the software costs.

Software costs contribute so heavily to *total* project costs because software costs are closely related to human productivity (in other words, they are labor intensive), while hardware costs are more directly related to manufacturing technologies. For example, microchips that cost more than $500 per chip 10 years ago can now be purchased for less than $1 per chip.

It is far easier, however, to significantly increase manufacturing productivity, with the consequent decrease in hardware costs, than it is for people to either double the quantity or quality of their output. So as hardware costs have plummeted, software productivity and their associated costs have remained rather constant. Thus, the percentage of software costs to total system costs (hardware plus software) has increased dramatically.

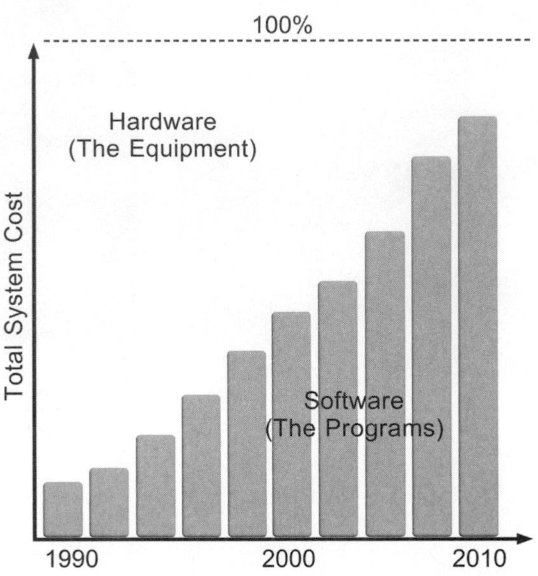

Figure 7.1 Software is the major cost of most computer projects

Looking at just software costs (see Figure 7.2), we find that the maintenance of existing programs accounts for approximately 75 percent of total software costs. Maintenance includes the correction of newly found errors and the addition of new features and modifications to existing programs.

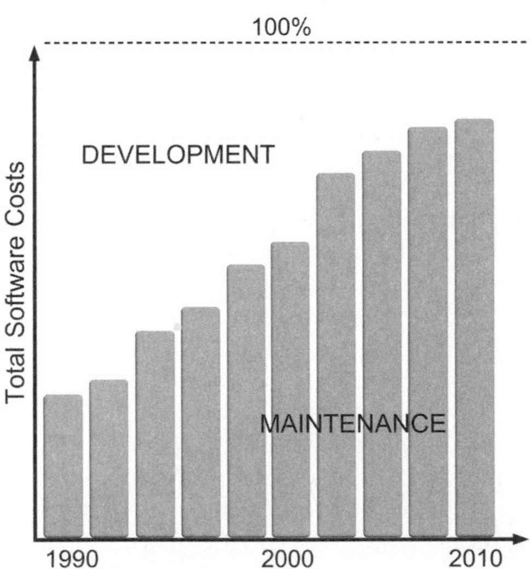

Figure 7.2 Maintenance is the dominant software cost

Students generally find it strange that maintenance is the main software cost because they are accustomed to solving a problem and moving on to a different one. Commercial and engineering fields do not operate this way. In these fields, one application or idea is typically built on a previous one, and may require months or years of work. This is especially true in programming. Once a program is written, new features become evident. Advances in technology such as networking, fiber optics, genetic engineering, and graphical displays also open up new software possibilities.

How easily a program can be maintained (debugged, modified, or changed) is related to the ease with which the program can be read and understood. This, in turn, is directly related to the modularity with which the program was constructed. Modular programs, as we have seen, are constructed using one or more functions, each of which performs a clearly defined and specific task. If each function is clearly structured internally and the relationship between functions clearly specified, each function can be tested and modified with a minimum of disturbance or undesirable interaction with the other functions in the program.

If a bug has been isolated, or if a new feature needs to be added, the required changes can be confined to appropriate functions without radically affecting other functions. Only if the affected function requires different input data or produces different outputs are its surrounding functions affected. Even in this case the changes to the surrounding functions are clear; they must either be modified to output the data needed by the changed function or changed to accept the new output data. Functions help the programmer determine where the changes must be made, while the internal structure of the function determines how easy it will be to make the change.

In this chapter we continue our presentation of functions, providing additional information on specific features that are required for a full understanding of their capabilities.

7.1 Variable Scope

Now that we have begun to write programs containing more than one function, we can look more closely at the variables declared within each function and their relationship to variables in other functions.

By their very nature, C functions are constructed to be independent modules. As we have seen, values are passed to a function using the function's argument list and a value is returned from a function using a `return` statement. Seen in this light, a function can be thought of as a closed box, with slots at the top to receive values and a single slot at the bottom to return a value (see Figure 7.3).

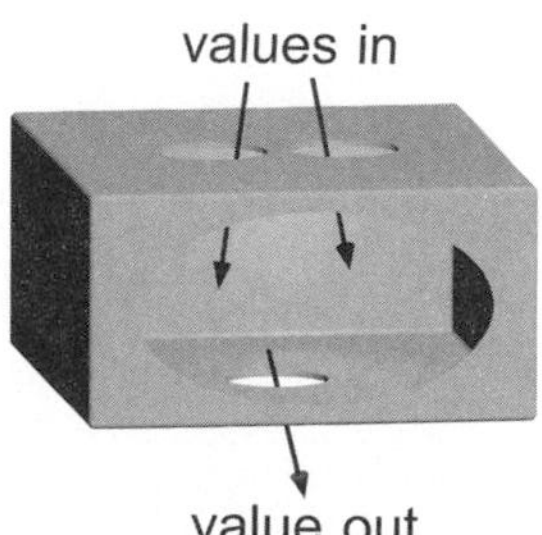

Figure 7.3 A function can be considered a closed box

The metaphor of a closed box is useful because it emphasizes the fact that what goes on inside the function, including all variable declarations within the function's body, is hidden from the view of all other functions. Since the variables created inside a function are available only to the function itself, they are said to be local to the function, or **local variables**. This term refers to the **scope** of a variable, where scope is defined as the section of the program where the variable is valid or "known." A variable can have either a local scope or a global scope. A variable with a **local scope** is simply one that has had storage locations set aside for it by a declaration statement made within a function body. Local variables are only meaningful when used in expressions or statements inside the function that declares them. This means that the same variable name can be declared and used in more than one function. For each function that declares the variable, a distinct variable is created.

All the variables we have used until now have been local variables. This is a direct result of placing our declaration statements inside functions and using them as definition statements that cause the compiler to reserve storage for the declared variable. As we shall see, declaration statements can be placed outside functions and need not act as definitions that cause new storage areas to be reserved for the declared variable.

A variable with **global scope**, more commonly termed a **global variable**, is one whose storage has been created for it by a declaration statement located outside any function. These variables can be used by all functions in a program that are physically placed after the global variable declaration. This is shown in Program 7.1 where we have purposely used the same variable name inside both functions contained in the program.

The variable `firstnum` in Program 7.1 is a global variable because its storage is created by a declaration statement located outside a function. Because both functions `main()` and `valfun()` follow the declaration of `firstnum`, both of these functions can use this global variable with no further declaration needed.

Program 7.1 also contains two separate local variables, both named `secnum`. Storage for the `secnum` variable named in `main()` is created by the declaration statement located in `main()`. A different storage area for the `secnum` variable in `valfun()` is created by the declaration statement located in the `valfun()` function. Figure 7.4 illustrates the three distinct storage areas reserved by the three declaration statements found in Program 7.1.

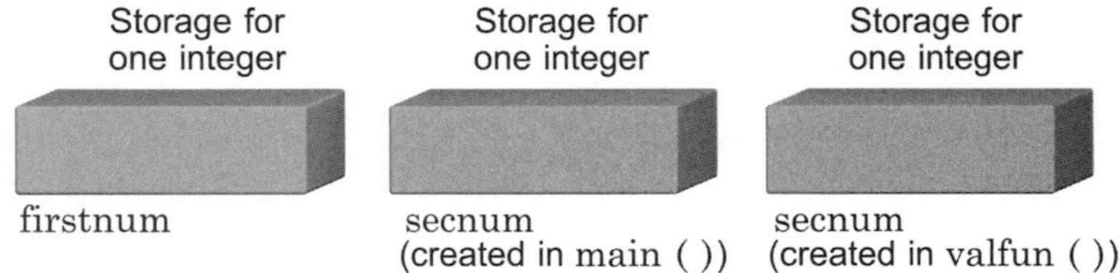

Figure 7.4 The three storage areas created by Program 7.1

Program 7.1

```
#include <stdio.h>
int firstnum; /* create a global variable named firstnum */
void valfun(); /* function prototype */

int main()
{
  int secnum; /* create a local variable named secnum */
  firstnum = 10; /* store a value into the global variable */
  secnum = 20; /* store a value into the local variable */

  printf("\nFrom main(): firstnum = %d",firstnum);
  printf("\nFrom main(): secnum = %d\n",secnum);

  valfun(); /* call the function valfun */

```

```
16    printf("\nFrom main() again: firstnum = %d",firstnum);
17    printf("\nFrom main() again: secnum = %d\n",secnum);
18
19    return 0;
20  }
21
22  void valfun() /* no values are passed to this function */
23  {
24    int secnum; /* create a second local variable named secnum */
25    secnum = 30; /* this only affects this local variable's value */
26
27    printf("\nFrom valfun(): firstnum = %d",firstnum);
28    printf("\nFrom valfun(): secnum = %d\n",secnum);
29    firstnum = 40; /* this changes firstnum for both functions */
30  }
```

Each of the variables named secnum is local to the function in which its storage is created, and each of these variables can only be used from within the appropriate function. Thus, when secnum is used in line 9 in main(), the storage area reserved by main() for its secnum variable is accessed, and when secnum is used in line 25 in valfun(), the storage area reserved by valfun() for its secnum variable is accessed. Program 7.1 produces the following output.

```
From main(): firstnum = 10
From main(): secnum = 20

From valfun(): firstnum = 10
From valfun(): secnum = 30

From main() again: firstnum = 40
From main() again: secnum = 20
```

Let us analyze the output produced by Program 7.1. Because firstnum is a global variable in line 2

```
2 int firstnum; /* create a global variable named firstnum */
```

both the main() and valfun() functions can use and change its value. Initially, both functions print the value 10 that main() stored in firstnum. Before returning, valfun() changes the value of firstnum to 40 in line 29, which is the value displayed when the variable firstnum is next displayed from within main().

Because each function only "knows" its own local variables, main() can only send the value of its secnum to the printf() function, and valfun() can only send the value of its secnum to the printf() function. Thus, whenever secnum is displayed from main(), the value 20 is output, and whenever secnum is displayed from valfun(), the value 30 is output.

C does not confuse the two secnum variables because only one function can execute at a given moment. While a function is executing, only the storage area for the variables and parameters created by this function are automatically accessed. If a variable that is not local to the function is used by the function, the program searches the global storage areas for the correct name.

The scope of a variable in no way influences or restricts the data type of the variable. Just as a local variable can be a character, integer, float, double, or any of the other data types (long/short) we have introduced, so can global variables be of these data types, as illustrated in Figure 7.5. The scope of a variable is determined solely by the placement of the declaration statement that reserves storage for it, while the data type of the variable is determined by using the appropriate keyword (`char`, `int`, `float`, `double`, etc.) before the variable's name in a declaration statement.

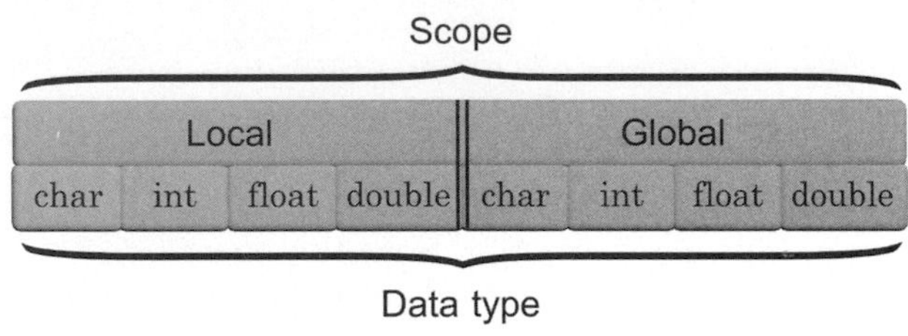

Figure 7.5 Relating the scope and type of a variable

When to Use Global Declarations

The scoping rules for symbolic constants and function prototypes are the same as those for variables. In terms of global declarations, it is precisely for these two items that such a designation makes sense and is used. For example, when a symbolic constant has a general meaning that is applicable throughout an application, it makes good programming sense to declare it globally at the top of a source code file. As such, it can be used in all functions without the need to repeat its declaration within each function. Equally important, such a declaration is very unlikely to cause any unwarranted side effects because, as a constant, it cannot subsequently or inadvertently be altered by any function using it. For example, coding the following declaration as a global

```
#define PI 3.1416
```

makes sense, as the value of `PI` is universally applicable wherever it is used.

Similarly, coding a function prototype as a global makes sense when the function is used by a number of other functions in a source code file. Doing so avoids repeating the prototype within each of the functions that will call it.

Misuse of Global Variables

One caution should be mentioned here. Except for symbolic constants and function prototypes, global variables should almost never be used. This is because global variables allow the programmer to "jump around" the normal safeguards provided by functions. Rather than passing variables to a function, it is possible to make all variables global. *Do not do this.* By making a variable global, you instantly destroy the safeguards C provides to make functions independent and insulated from each other, including the necessity of carefully designating the type of parameters needed by a function, the variables used in the function, and the value returned.

Using global variables can be especially disastrous in larger programs that have many user-created functions. Imagine the horror of trying to track down an error in a large program using global variables. Because a global variable can be accessed and changed by any function following the global declaration, it is a time-consuming and frustrating task to locate the origin of an erroneous value. In general, using global variables except in very restricted and well-defined situations is a sign of extremely bad programming.

EXERCISES 7.1

Short Answer Questions

1. a. For the following section of code, determine the data type and scope of all declared variables. To do this use a separate sheet of paper, and create a three-column table with the headings: Variable name, Data type, and Scope. A sample table, with the information on the first variable filled in for you, follows:

Variable name	Data type	Scope
`price`	Integer	global to `main()`, `roi()`, and `step()`

```
int price;
long int years;
float yield;


int main()
{
  int bondtype;
  float interest, coupon
      .
      .
  return 0;
}

float roi(int mat1, int mat2)
{
  int count;
  float effectiveInt;
      .
      .
  return(effectiveInt);
}

int step(float first, float last)
{
  int numofyrs;
  float fracpart;
      .
      .
  return(10*numofyrs);
}
```

b. Draw boxes around the appropriate section of the above code to enclose the scope of each variable.

c. Determine the data type of the parameters for the functions `roi()` and `step()` and the data type of the value returned by these functions.

2. a. For the following section of code, determine the data type and scope of all declared variables. To do this use a separate sheet of paper, and create a three-column table with the headings: Variable name, Data type, and Scope. A sample table, with the information on the first variable filled in for you, follows:

Variable name	Data type	Scope
key	character	global to main(), func1(), and func2()

```
char key;
long int number;
int main()
{
  int a,b,c;
  float x,y;
     .
     .
  return 0;
}

float secnum;

int func1(int num1, int num2)
{
  int o,p;
  float q;
     .
     .
  return(p);
}

float func2(float first, float last)
{
  int a,b,c,o,p;
  float r;
  float s,t,x;
     .
     .
  return(s*t);
}
```

b. Draw a box around the appropriate section of the above code to enclose the scope of the variables `key`, `secnum`, `y`, and `r`.

c. Determine the data type of the parameters for the functions `func1()` and `func2()` and the data type of the value returned by these functions.

3. Besides speaking about the scope of a variable, we can also apply the term to the parameters declared in a function header. What do you think is the scope of all function parameters?

4. Determine the values displayed by each call to `printf()` in the following program:

```
int firstnum = 10; /* declare and initialize a global variable */
#include <stdio.h>

int main()
{
  int firstnum = 20; /* declare and initialize a local variable */
  void display(); /* function prototype (declaration) */

  printf("\nThe value of firstnum is %d",firstnum);
  display();

  return 0;
}

void display()
{
  printf("\nThe value of firstnum is now %d",firstnum);
}
```

7.2 Variable Storage Class

The scope of a variable defines the location within a program where that variable can be used. Given a program, you could take a pencil and draw a box around the section of the program where each variable is valid. The space inside the box represents the scope of a variable. From this viewpoint, the scope of a variable can be thought of as the space within the program where the variable is valid.

In addition to the space dimension represented by its scope, variables also have a time dimension. The time dimension refers to the length of time that storage locations are reserved for a variable. This time dimension is known as the variable's "lifetime." For example, all variable storage locations are released back to the operating system when a program is finished running. However, while a program is still executing, interim variable storage areas are also reserved and subsequently released back to the operating system. Where and how long a variable's storage locations are kept before they are released can be determined by the **storage class** of the variable.

The four available storage classes are called `auto`, `static`, `extern`, and `register`. If one of these class names is used, it must be placed before the variable's data type in a declaration statement. Examples of declaration statements that include a storage class designation are

```
auto int num; /* auto storage class and int data type */
static int miles; /* static storage class and int data type */
extern int price; /* extern storage class and int data type */
register int dist; /* register storage class and int data type */
auto float coupon; /* auto storage class and float data type */
static float yrs; /* static storage class and float data type */
extern float yld; /* extern storage class and float data type */
auto char inKey; /* auto storage class and char data type */
```

To understand what the storage class of a variable means, we will first consider local variables (those variables created inside a function) and then global variables (those variables created outside a function).

Local Variable Storage Classes

Local variables can only be members of the `auto`, `static`, or `register` storage classes. If no class description is included in the declaration statement, the variable is automatically assigned to the `auto` class. Thus, `auto` is the default class used by C. All the local variables we have used, because the storage class designation was omitted, have been `auto` variables.

The term `auto` is short for **automatic**. Storage for automatic local variables is automatically reserved (that is, created) each time a function declaring automatic variables is called. As long as the function has not returned control to its calling function, all automatic variables local to the function are "alive"; that is, storage for the variables is available. When the function returns control to its calling function, its local automatic variables "die"; that is, the storage of the variables is released back to the operating system. This process repeats itself each time a function is called. For example, consider Program 7.2, where the function `testauto()` is called three times from `main()`.

Program 7.2

```
#include <stdio.h>
void testauto(); /* function prototype */
int main()
{
  int count; /* create the auto variable count */
  for(count = 1; count <= 3; count++)
  testauto();

  return 0;
}

void testauto()
{
  int num = 0; /* create the auto variable num */
               /* and initialize to zero */

  printf("The value of the automatic variable num is %d\n", num);
  num++;
}
```

Program 7.2 produces the following:

```
The value of the automatic variable num is 0
The value of the automatic variable num is 0
The value of the automatic variable num is 0
```

Each time `testauto()` is called, the automatic variable `num` is created and initialized to 0. When the function returns control to `main()`, the variable `num` is destroyed along with any value stored in `num`. Thus, the effect of incrementing `num` in `testauto()`, before the function's return statement, is lost when control is returned to `main()`.

For the majority of applications, the use of automatic variables works just fine. There are cases, however, where we want a function to remember values between function calls. This is the purpose of the `static` storage class. A local variable that is declared as `static` causes the program to keep the variable and its latest value even when the function that declared it is through executing. Examples of static variable declarations are

```
static int rate;
static float taxes;
static float amount;
static char inKey;
static long years;
```

A local static variable is not created and destroyed each time the function declaring the static variable is called. Once created, local static variables remain in existence for the life of the program. This means that the last value stored in the variable when the function is finished executing is available to the function the next time it is called. Within a function such variables are typically used as counters that keep track of an event occurring in the function. For example, a counter might keep track of the number of times that a function has been called to perform a specific task. By using a static counter variable, there is no need to return the counter value and repass it into the function for each function call.

Because local static variables retain their values, they are not initialized within a declaration statement in the same way as automatic variables. To see why, consider the automatic declaration `int num = 0;` in line 14 of Program 7.2. This statement causes the automatic variable `num` to be created and set to 0 each time the declaration is encountered. This is called a **run-time initialization** because initialization occurs each time the declaration statement is encountered. This type of initialization is disastrous for a static variable because resetting the variable's value to 0 each time the function is called destroys the very value we are trying to save.

The initialization of static variables (both local and global) is done only once, when the program is first compiled. At compilation time, the variable is created and any initialization value is placed in it.[1] Thereafter, the value in the variable is kept without further initialization each time the function is called. To see how this works, consider Program 7.3.

Program 7.3

```
#include <stdio.h>
void teststat(); /* function prototype */

int main()
{
  int count; /* count is a local auto variable */
```

[1]Some compilers initialize local static variables the first time the definition statement is executed rather than when the program is compiled.

```
  for(count = 1; count <= 3; count++)
    teststat();

  return 0;
}

void teststat()
{
  static int num = 0; /* num is a local static variable */

  printf("The value of the static variable num is now %d\n", num);
  num++;
}
```

The output produced by Program 7.3 is

```
The value of the static variable num is now 0
The value of the static variable num is now 1
The value of the static variable num is now 2
```

As illustrated by the output of Program 7.3, the static variable num is set to 0 only once. The function teststat() then increments this variable just before returning control to main(). The value that num has when leaving the function teststat() is retained and displayed when the function is next called.

Unlike automatic variables that can be initialized by either constants or expressions using both constants and previously initialized variables, static variables can only be initialized using constants or constant expressions, such as 3.2 + 8.0. Also unlike automatic variables, all static variables are set to 0 when no explicit initialization is given. Thus, the specific initialization of num to 0 in Program 7.3 is not required.

The remaining storage class available to local variables, the register class, is not used as extensively as either the auto or static variable classes. Examples of register variable declarations are

```
register int time;
register float diffren;
register float coupon;
```

Register variables have the same time duration as automatic variables; that is, a local register variable is created when the function declaring it is entered and is destroyed when the function completes execution. The only difference between register and automatic variables is where the storage for the variable is located.

Storage for all variables (local and global), except register variables, is reserved in the computer's memory area. Most computers have a few additional high-speed storage areas located directly in the computer's processing unit that can also be used for variable storage. These special high-speed storage areas are called **registers**. Because registers are physically located in the computer's processing unit, they can be accessed faster than the normal memory storage areas located in the computer's memory unit. Computer instructions that access registers typically require less space than instructions that access memory locations because there are fewer registers that can be accessed than there are memory locations. In general, only special purpose programs that directly interact with a computer's operation, such as an operating system, will use register variables. Application programs rarely, if ever, should use register variables.

Variables declared with the `register` storage class are automatically switched to the `auto` storage class if the compiler does not support register variables or if the declared register variables exceed the computer's register capacity.

The only restriction in using the register storage class is that the address of a register variable, using the address operator &, cannot be taken. This is easily understood when you realize that registers do not have standard memory addresses.

Global Variable Storage Classes

Global variables are, by definition, created by declaration statements external to a function. By their nature, these externally defined variables do not come and go with the calling of any function. Once an external (global) variable is created, it exists until the program in which it is declared is finished executing. Thus, global variables cannot be declared as members of either the `auto` or `register` storage classes, which are created and destroyed as the program is executing. Global variables may, however, be declared as members of the `static` or `extern` storage class (but not both). Examples of declaration statements including these two class descriptions are

```
extern int sum;
extern float price;
static float yield;
```

The global `static` and `extern` classes affect both the scope and time duration of these variables. As with static local variables, all static global variables are initialized to 0 at compile time if no explicit initialization is present.

The purpose of the `extern` storage class is to extend the scope of a global variable declared in one source code file into another source code file. To understand this, we must first note that all of the programs we have written so far have always been contained together in one file. Thus, when you saved or retrieved programs, you needed only to give the computer a single name for your program. This is not required by C.

Larger programs typically consist of many functions that are stored in multiple files. An example of this is shown in Figure 7.6, where the three functions—`main()`, `func1()`, and `func2()`—are stored in one file and the two functions—`func3()` and `func4()`—are stored in a second file.

For the files illustrated in Figure 7.6, the global variables `price`, `yield`, and `coupon` declared in `file1` can only be used by the functions `main()`, `func1()`, and `func2()` in this file. The single global variable, `interest`, declared in `file2` can only be used by the functions `func3()` and `func4()` in `file2`.

Although the variable `price` has been created in `file1`, we may want to use it in `file2`. The `extern` class provides the means of doing this. For example, placing the declaration statement `extern int price;` at the top of `file2`, as shown in Figure 7.7, extends the scope of the variable `price` into `file2` so that it may be used by both `func3()` and `func4()`.

Similarly, placing the statement `extern float yield;` in `func4()` extends the scope of this global variable, created in `file1`, into `func4()`. The scope of the global variable interest, created in `file2`, is extended into `func1()` and `func2()` by the declaration

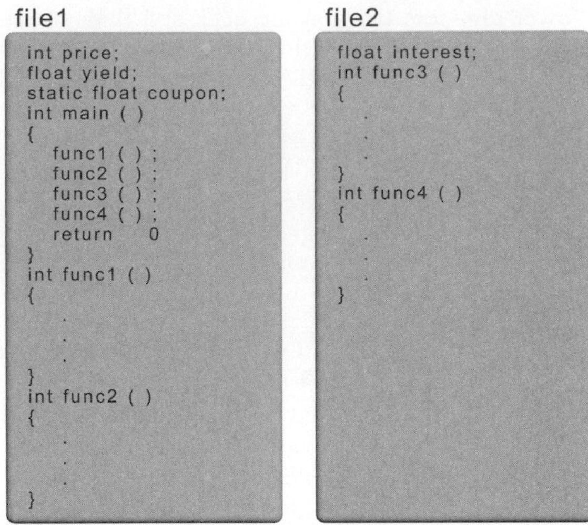

Figure 7.6 A program may extend beyond one file

file1

```
int price;
float yield;
static float coupon;
int main ( )
{
   func1 ( ) ;
   func2 ( ) ;
   func3 ( ) ;
   func4 ( ) ;
}
extern float interest;
int func1 ( )
{
   .
   .
   .
}
int func2 ( )
{
   .
   .
   .
}
```

file2

```
float interest;
extern int price;
int func3 ( )
{
   .
   .
   .
}
int func4 ( )
{
   extern float yield;
   .
   .
   .
}
```

Figure 7.7 Extending the scope of a global variable

statement `extern float interest;` placed before `func1()`. Notice `interest` is not available to `main()`.

A declaration statement that specifically contains the word `extern` is different from every other declaration statement in that it does not cause the creation of a new variable by reserving new storage for the variable. An `extern` declaration statement simply informs the compiler that the variable already exists and can now be used. The actual storage for the variable must be created somewhere else in the program using one, and only one, global declaration statement in which the word `extern` has not been used. Initialization of the global variable can, of course, be made with the original declaration of the global variable. Initialization within an extern declaration statement is not allowed and causes a compilation error.

Programming Note

Storage Classes Rules

1. Variables of the type `auto` and `register` are always local variables.
2. Only nonstatic global variables may be declared as `extern`. Doing so either extends the variable's scope:
   - into another file, which makes the variable global in the new file; or
   - into a function within another file, which makes the variable local to the function.
3. Because global `static` variables cannot be declared as `extern`, these variables are private to the file in which they are declared.
4. Except for `static` variables (global and local), all variables are initialized each time they come into scope.

The existence of the `extern` storage class is the reason we have been so careful to distinguish between the creation and declaration of a variable. Declaration statements containing the word `extern` do not create new storage areas; they only extend the scope of existing global variables.

The last global class, `static`, is used to prevent the extension of a global variable into a second file. Global static variables are declared in the same way as local static variables, except that the declaration statement is placed outside any function.

The scope of a global static variable cannot be extended beyond the file in which it is declared. This provides a degree of privacy for static global variables. Since they are only "known" and can only be used in the file in which they are declared, other files cannot access or change their values. Static global variables cannot be subsequently extended to a second file using an `extern` declaration statement. Trying to do so results in a compilation error.

EXERCISES 7.2

Short Answer Questions

1. a. List the storage classes available to local variables.
   b. List the storage classes available to global variables.

2. Describe the difference between a local automatic variable and a local static variable.

3. What is the difference between the following functions?

```
int init1()
{
  static int yrs = 1;

  printf("\nThe value of yrs is %d", yrs);
  yrs = yrs + 2;

  return 0;
```

```
}

void init2()
{
  static int yrs;

  yrs = 1;
  printf("\nThe value of yrs is %d", yrs);
  yrs = yrs + 2;
  return;
}
```

4. a. Describe the difference between a static global variable and an external global variable.
   b. If a variable is declared with an `extern` storage class, what other declaration statement must be present somewhere in the program?

5. The declaration statement `static float years;` can be used to `create` either a local or global static variable. What determines the scope of the variable `years`?

6. For the function and variable declarations illustrated in Figure 7.8, insert an `extern` declaration statement that that does the following:
   a. Extends the scope of the global variable choice into all of file2.
   b. Extends the scope of the global variable flag into function `pduction()` only.
   c. Extends the scope of the global variable date into `pduction()` and `bid()`.
   d. Extends the scope of the global variable date into `roi()` only.
   e. Extends the scope of the global variable coupon into `roi()` only.
   f. Extends the scope of the global variable `bondType` into all of file1.
   g. Extends the scope of the global variable maturity into both `price()` and `yield()`.

file1

```
char choice;
int flag;
long date, time;
int main ( )
{
    .
    .
    .
}
double coupon;
void price ( )
{
    .
    .
    .
}
void yield ( )
{
    .
    .
    .
}
```

file2

```
char bondType;
double maturity;
void roi ( )
{
    .
    .
    .
}
void pduction ( )
{
    .
    .
    .
}
void bid ( )
{
    .
    .
    .
}
```

Figure 7.8 Files for Exercise 7.6

7.3 Pass by Reference

In the normal course of operation, a called function receives values from its calling function, stores the passed values in its own local parameters, manipulates these parameters appropriately, and directly returns, at most, a single value. As we have seen, this method of calling a function and passing values to it is referred to as a function **pass by value**.

This pass by value procedure is a distinct advantage of C. It allows functions to be written as independent entities that can use any variable and parameter names without concern that other functions may also be using the same names. It also alleviates any concern that altering a parameter or variable in one function may inadvertently alter the value of a variable in another function. In writing a function, parameters can conveniently be thought of as either initialized variables or variables that are assigned values from the outside when the function is called. At no time, however, does the called function have access to any variable contained in the calling function.

There are times, however, when it is convenient to give a function access to the variables of its calling function. Although such cases are the exception, they do occur and sometimes are even necessary (see, for example, the case study in the next section). Providing a called function access to one or more variables of a calling function permits the called function to both use and change the values in these variables without the knowledge of the calling function. This effectively permits a function to return multiple values to any function that calls it.

Providing such access requires that the address of a variable be passed to the called function. Once the called function has the variable's address, it "knows where the variable lives," so to speak, and can access the variable using its address.

Passing an address is referred to as a function **pass by reference**,[2] because the called function can reference, or access, the variable using the passed address. In this section we describe the techniques required to pass one or more addresses to a function and have the function accept and use these addresses.

Passing Addresses to a Function

Passing addresses to a function should be familiar to you because addresses have been used in this manner each time you called the `scanf()` function. As indicated by `scanf()` function calls, passing the address of a variable to the function requires placing the address operator, `&`, in front of the variable's name. Recall that the address operator followed immediately by a variable name means "the address of" the variable. Examples of this are

`&num` *means "the address of* `num`*"*
`&testvals` *means "the address of* `testvals`*"*

Program 7.4 illustrates using the address operator to display the address of the variable named `num`.

[2]It can also be referred to as a *call by reference* when it is clearly understood that the term applies only to those parameters whose addresses have been passed.

Program 7.4

```
#include <stdio.h>
int main()
{
  int num;

  num = 22;
  printf("num = %d\n", num);
  printf("The address of num is %u\n", &num);

  return 0;
}
```

The output of Program 7.4 is

```
num = 22
The address of num is 124484
```

The address indicates where the computer has stored the variable num when the program has been executed. As we will now see, actually using addresses as opposed to only displaying them provides the C programmer with an extremely powerful programming tool. As a starter, addresses provide a means of returning multiple values from a function, when this capability is required. Writing a function to accept, store, and use a passed address, however, requires two new elements—pointers and the indirection operator.

Storing Addresses

Besides displaying the address of a variable, as was done in Program 7.4, we can also store addresses in suitably declared variables. The reason for this is that addresses themselves are values with their own data type; as such, the values can be stored in a variable that has been correctly declared to accept this data type. For example, the statement

```
numAddr = &num;
```

stores the address corresponding to the variable num in the variable numAddr, as illustrated in Figure 7.9. Similarly, the statements

```
messAddr = &message;
tabPoint = &list;
chrPoint = &ch;
```

store the addresses of the variables message, list, and ch in the variables messAddr, tabPoint, and chrPoint, respectively, as illustrated in Figure 7.10.

A variable that can store an address is known as a **pointer variable**. Thus, the variables numAddr, messAddr, tabPoint, and chrPoint are all pointer variables, or **pointers**, for short. Pointers are simply variables that are used to store the addresses of other variables. As we will see, the passing of an address to a function that subsequently stores this address in a pointer is what constitutes a pass by reference.

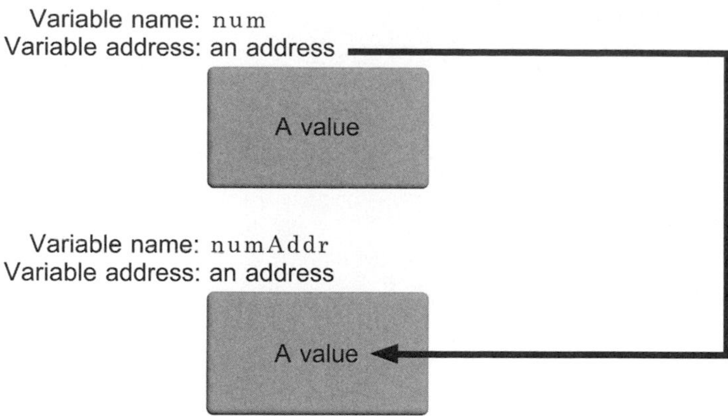

Figure 7.9 Storing num's address in numAddr

Using Addresses

To use a stored address, C provides us with an **indirection operator**, `*`. The `*` symbol, when followed immediately by a pointer (no space allowed between the `*` and the pointer), means *the variable whose address is stored in*. Thus, if `numAddr` is a pointer (remember that a pointer is a variable that contains an address), `*numAddr` means *the variable whose address is stored in* `numAddr`. Similarly, `*tabPoint` means *the variable whose address is stored in* `tabPoint`, and `*chrPoint` means *the variable whose address is stored in* `chrPoint`. In effect, a pointer variable points to a location in memory where the desired variable is located. Figure 7.11 shows the relationship between the address contained in a pointer variable and the variable ultimately addressed.

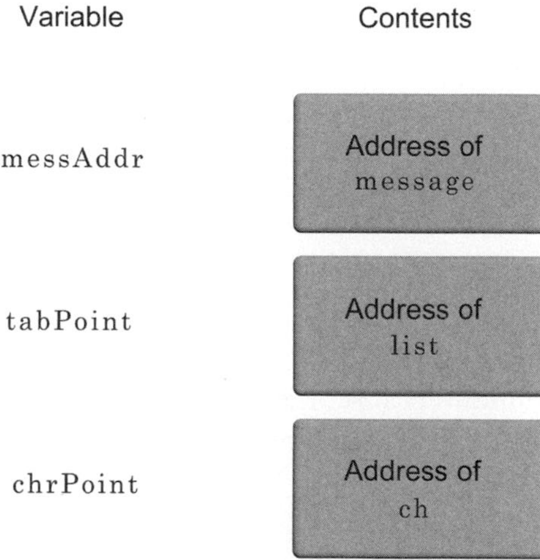

Figure 7.10 Storing more addresses

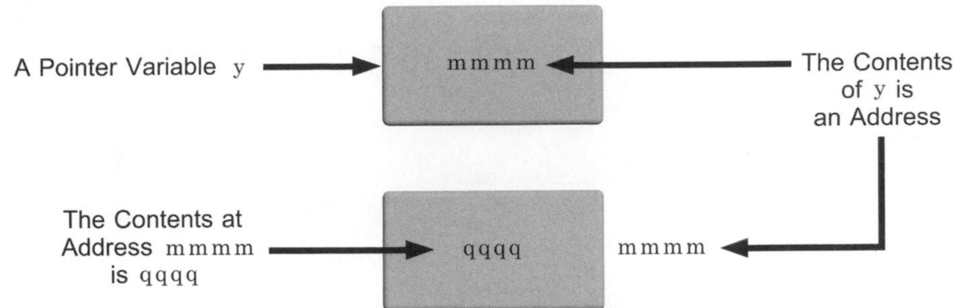

Figure 7.11 Using a pointer variable

Although `*d` literally means *the variable whose address is stored in* `d`, this is commonly shortened to *the variable pointed to by* `d`. Similarly, referring to Figure 7.11, `*y` can be read as *the variable pointed to by* `y`. The value ultimately obtained, as shown in Figure 7.11, is `qqqq`.

When using a pointer variable, the value that is obtained is always found by first going to the pointer for an address. The address contained in the pointer is then used to locate the desired contents. Certainly, this is a rather indirect way of getting to the final value, and not unexpectedly, the term **indirect addressing** is used to describe this procedure.

Declaring and Using Pointers

Like all variables, pointers must be declared before they can be used. In declaring a pointer variable, C requires that we also specify the type of variable that is pointed to. For example, if the address in the pointer `numAddr` is the address of an integer, the correct declaration for the pointer is

```
int *numAddr;
```

This declaration can be read in a number of ways. First, it can be read as *the variable pointed to by* `numAddr` (from the `*numAddr` in the declaration) *is an integer.* This is frequently shortened to the simpler statement that `numAddr` *points to an integer.* In reality it means that `numAddr` can be used to store the address of memory locations that contain an integer. As all of these descriptions of this declaration statement are correct, select and use whichever description makes a pointer declaration meaningful to you. In each interpretation, however, notice that the description effectively is read in reverse starting from the expression `*numAddr` and ending with "*an integer.*"

Also notice that the declaration `int *numAddr;` specifies two things: first, that `numAddr` must be a pointer (because it is used with the indirection operator `*`); and second, that the variable pointed to is an integer. Similarly, if the pointer `ratePoint` points to (contains the address of) a double-precision number and `chrPoint` points to a character variable, the required declarations are

```
double *ratePoint;   /* ratePoint points to a double */
char *chrPoint;      /* chrPoint points to a character */
```

These two declarations can be read as the variable pointed to by `ratePoint` is a double-precision value and the variable pointed to by `chrPoint` is a character.

Now consider Program 7.5, where a pointer is used to change the value in the "pointed to" location.

Program 7.5

```
1  #include <stdio.h>
2  int main()
3  {
4    int *milesAddr; /* declare a pointer to an int */
5    int miles;      /* declare an integer variable */
6
7    miles = 22; /* store the number 22 into miles */
8
9    milesAddr = &miles; /* store the 'address of miles' in milesAddr */
10   printf("The address stored in milesAddr is %u\n",milesAddr);
11   printf("The value pointed to by milesAddr is %d\n\n", *milesAddr);
12
13   *milesAddr = 158; /* set the value pointed to by milesAddr to 158 */
14   printf("The value in miles is now %d\n", miles);
15
16   return 0;
17 }
```

The output of Program 7.5 is

```
The address stored in milesAddr is 1244872
The value pointed to by milesAddr is 22

The value in miles is now 158
```

The only value of Program 7.5 is in helping us understand "what gets stored where." Let's review the program to see how the output was produced.

The declaration statement int *milesAddr; in line 4

```
4  int *milesAddr;
```

declares milesAddr to be a pointer variable that can store the address of (that is, will point to) an integer variable. The selection of the variable's name is arbitrary, and any valid identifier could have been chosen instead.

The statement in line 9

```
9  milesAddr = &miles; /* store the 'address of miles' in milesAddr */
```

stores the address of the variable miles into the pointer milesAddr. This address is displayed in the next line.

```
10  printf("The address stored in milesAddr is %u\n", milesAddr);
```

Because milesAddr is a variable, the value in this variable, which happens to be an address, can be displayed in the same manner as any other variable's value.[3] It is the next statement in Program 7.5 that begins to reveal the usefulness of pointers.

```
11  printf("The value pointed to by milesAddr is %d\n\n", *milesAddr);
```

Here, the indirection operator is used in the expression *milesAddr to retrieve and print out the *value pointed to by* milesAddr. This, of course, is the value stored in the variable miles. At this point you may be asking yourself, why go through all this trouble to display the value in miles, and not just use the variable name miles directly. The answer is that it illustrates that there is another way to access a variable's value without using the variable's name; rather, we can use the variable's address. This feature becomes essential in giving a called function access to a variable in another function because the called function will not know the variable's name, but will know its address. The use of this feature is illustrated in lines 13 and 14.

```
13  *milesAddr = 158; /* set the value pointed to by milesAddr to 158 */
14  printf("The value in miles is now %d\n", miles);
```

In line 13 the value in miles is changed to the number 158 by using its address. That the change in mile's value has been accomplished is verified by displaying its value in line 14. Thus, not only have we displayed the value in miles using its address, we have also altered its value via this address.

It certainly would have been much simpler if the pointer used in Program 7.5 could have been declared as pointer ratePoint;. Such a declaration, however, conveys no information about the storage used by the variable whose address is stored in ratePoint. This information is essential when the pointer is used with the indirection operator, as it is in the expression *milesAddr in both lines 11 and 13. For example, because the address of an integer is stored in milesAddr, 4 bytes of storage are typically retrieved when the address is used. If milesAddr was a pointer to a character, then when the address were used only 1 byte of storage would be retrieved. Similarly, a pointer to a double-precision value would require the retrieval of 8 bytes of storage. The declaration of a pointer must, therefore, include the type of variable being pointed to, which is illustrated in Figure 7.12.

Passing Addresses to a Function

We can now put all of this together to pass an address to a function that will correctly receive and then use the passed address. The function, which we will name newval(), will first be developed as a stub, whose initial task is to verify correct receipt of the passed address. Once this verification is made, we will complete coding the function to use the address. Consider Program 7.6.

---

[3]Although we have used the %u conversion sequence to display this value as an unsigned integer, this is for convenience only in reading the address as a decimal number. Addresses have their own data type that more correctly are displayed in hexadecimal notation using the %p conversion sequence.

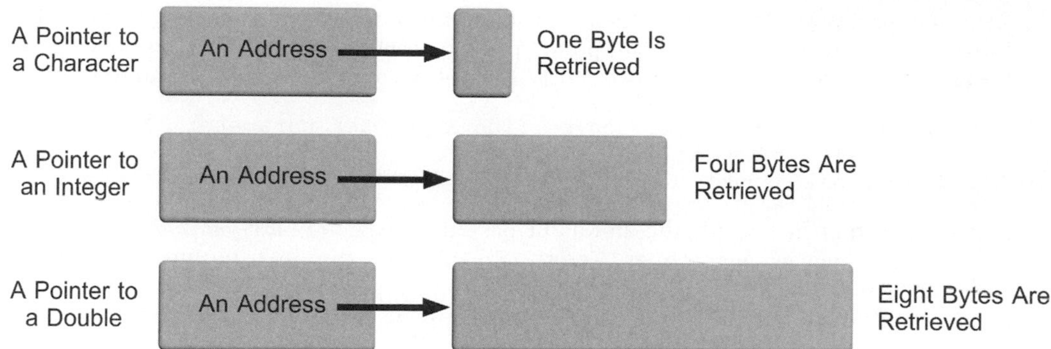

Figure 7.12 Addressing different data types using pointers

Program 7.6

```
#include <stdio.h>
int main()
{
  void newval(float *);  /* prototype with a pointer parameter */
  float testval;

  printf("\nEnter a number: ");
  scanf("%f", &testval);

  printf("The address that will be passed is %u\n\n", &testval);

  newval(&testval);   /* call the function */

  return 0;
}

void newval(float *xnum)   /* function header using a pointer parameter */
{
  printf ("The address received is %u\n", xnum);
  printf("The value pointed to by xnum is: %5.2f \n", *xnum );
}
```

First, observe in Program 7.6 that, as with all function calls, the called function is listed at least three times; once in a function prototype, once each time it is called, and once in its own header line. These three lines, 4, 12, and 17 are highlighted in Program 7.6 and repeated below.

```
 4  void newval(float *);  /* prototype with a pointer parameter */
12  newval(&testval);     /* call the function */
17  void newval(float *xnum)    /* function header using a pointer parameter */
```

Now notice that in line 12, the argument passed to `newval()` is *the address of the variable* `testval`, which is denoted as `&testval`. One of the first requirements in writing `newval()` is to declare a parameter that can store this passed address. Because only pointers can be used to store addresses, this parameter must be a pointer. The parameter declaration `float *xnum` used in `newval()`'s header line (line 17)

```
17  void newval(float *xnum)    /* function header using a pointer parameter */
```

can be used because it declares the parameter named `xnum` to be a pointer to a `float` in the same manner as a variable would be declared as a pointer. Because the address of a `float` variable, in this case `testval`, is being passed, this is a correct pointer type. The choice of the parameter name, `xnum` is, as with all parameter names, up to the programmer. Figure 7.13 illustrates how the passed address will be stored in `xnum` at the time of the call. Because an address is passed, which can be used to reference (that is, access) a variable, it constitutes a pass by reference.

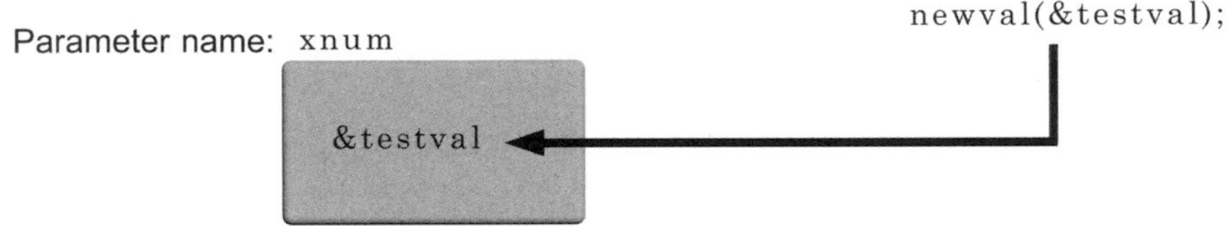

Figure 7.13 Passing and storing passed addresses

Finally, the function prototype for `newval()` in line 4 matches the header line for the function; it declares that the function will not directly return a value and expects one pointer argument (that is, one address), which points to (is the address of) a single-precision variable.

Within `newval()` the call to `printf()` in line 19 displays the address that was received, while the call to `printf()` in line 20 displays the value of the variable that is pointed to.

```
19  printf ("The address received is %u\n", xnum);
20  printf("The value pointed to by xnum is: %5.2f \n" , *xnum );
```

The display produced by line 19 is sufficient to verify correct receipt of the passed address if this address matches that displayed by `main()` in line 10 before the call to `newval()`.

```
10 printf("The address that will be passed is %u\n\n", &testval);
```

That this is indeed the case, is shown by the following sample run of Program 7.6:

```
Enter a number: 24.6
The address that will be passed is 124484

The address received is 124484
The value pointed to by xnum is: 24.60
```

The last line displayed by the program shows that the pointer can be used to correctly locate `testval`'s value from within `newval()` using the indirection operator. The `newval()` function has no knowledge of the variable named `testval`, but it does have the address of `testval` stored in `xnum`. The expression `*xnum` used in line 20 means "the variable whose address is in `xnum`." This is of course the variable `testval`.

Having verified that `newval()` can access `main()`'s local variable `testval`, we can now expand `newval()` to alter this variables' values. This is done in Program 7.7.

Program 7.7

```
#include <stdio.h>
int main()
{
void newval(float *);  /* prototype with a pointer parameter */
float testval;

printf("\nEnter a number: ");
scanf("%f", &testval);

printf("\nFrom main(): The value in testval is: %5.2f \n",
                                              testval);
newval(&testval);   /* call the function */

printf("\nFrom main(): The value in testval has been changed to: %5.2f \n",
                                                 testval);


  return 0;
}

void newval(float *xnum)
{
  printf("\nFrom newval(): The value pointed to by xnum is: %5.2f \n", *xnum);

  *xnum = *xnum + 20.2;
}
```

In calling the `newval()` function within Program 7.7, it is again important to understand the significance of passing the address of `testval` to `newval()`— it gives `newval()` the capability of directly accessing and altering the value stored in the variable `testval`. This is done within the function by the statement

```
*xnum = *xnum + 20.2;
```

This statement can be read as "add 20.2 to the value of the variable pointed to by xnum." The memory locations that are accessed in `newval()` in this statement, using the memory addresses stored in the pointer xnum, are the same ones that are referenced in `main()` using the name `testval`. The following sample run was obtained using Program 7.7:

```
Enter a number: 24.6

From main(): The value in testval is: 24.60

From newval(): The value pointed to by xnum is: 24.60

From main(): The value in testval has been changed to: 44.80
```

As is seen by this output, the value initially stored in `main()`'s variable `testval` has been successfully altered from within `newval()`.

The mechanism used in `newval()` for altering the variables of its calling function provides the basis for returning multiple values from any function. For example, assume that a function is required to accept three values, compute these values' sum and product, and return these computed results to the calling routine. Naming the function `calc()` and providing five parameters (three for the input data and two pointers for the returned values), the following function can be used:

```
void calc(float  num1, float num2, float num3, float *sumaddr, float *prodaddr)
{
  *sumaddr = num1 + num2 + num3;
  *prodaddr = num1 * num2 * num3;
 }
```

This function has five parameters, named num1, num2, num3, `sumaddr`, and `prodaddr`, of which only the last two are declared as pointers. Within the function `calc()` the last two parameters, `sumaddr` and `prodaddr`, are used to directly access and change the values in two of the calling function's variables. Specifically, "the variable pointed to by `sumaddr`" is calculated as the sum of the first three parameters and the variable pointed to by `prodaddr` is computed as the product of the parameters num1, num2, and num3. Program 7.8 includes this function in a complete program.

Within `main()`, the `calc()`function is called in line 10 using the five arguments— `firstnum`, `secnum`, `thirdnum`, the address of `sum`, and the address of `product`.

```
10 calc(firstnum, secnum, thirdnum, &sum,  &prodaddr); /* function call */
```

Program 7.8

```
#include <stdio.h>
int main()
{
  void calc(float, float, float, float *, float *);  /* prototype */
  float firstnum, secnum, thirdnum, sum, product;

  printf("Enter three numbers: ");
  scanf("%f %f %f", &firstnum, &secnum, &thirdnum);

  calc(firstnum, secnum, thirdnum, &sum,  &product); /* function call */

  printf("\nThe sum of the entered numbers is: %6.2f" , sum );
  printf("\nThe product of the entered numbers is: %6.2f\n" , product);

  return 0;
}

void calc(float num1, float num2, float num3, float *sumaddr, float *prodaddr)
{
  *sumaddr = num1 + num2 + num3;
  *prodaddr = num1 * num2 * num3;
}
```

As required, these arguments agree in number and data type with the parameters declared in both `calc()`'s prototype and header line. Of the five arguments passed, only `firstnum`, `secnum`, and `thirdnum` have been assigned values when the call to `calc()` is made. The remaining two variables, whose addresses are passed, were not initialized and will be provided by values calculated within `calc()`. Depending on the compiler used in compiling the program, these arguments will initially contain either 0s or "garbage" values.

Once `calc()` is called, it uses its first three parameters to calculate values for the variables pointed to by `sumaddr` and `prodaddr`, and then returns control to `main()`. Because of the order of its actual calling arguments, `main()` knows the values calculated by `calc()` as `sum` and `product`, which are then displayed. Following is a sample run using Program 7.8:

```
Enter three numbers: 2.5 6.0 10.0

The sum of the entered numbers is:  18.50
The product of the entered numbers is: 150.00
```

Notice that the net effect of `calc()` is that it has returned two values back to `main()`, both of which are passed through the parameter list. The default in C is to make calls by value rather than calls by reference, precisely to limit a called function's ability to alter variables in the calling function. Thus, the standard call by value procedure should be adhered to whenever possible, which means that address arguments should only be used in very restricted situations that actually require multiple return values. The `calc()` function, included in Program 7.8, while useful for illustrative purposes, would more properly be written as two separate functions, each returning a single value.

There are cases, however, where it is absolutely necessary for a function to return multiple values. One of these cases is illustrated in the next section, where a function is required to exchange the values of two variables. Such a function is essential when sorting a list of numbers or names into either ascending (increasing) or descending (decreasing) order.

EXERCISES 7.3

Short Answer Questions

1. If `average` is a variable, what does `&average` mean?
2. For the variables and addresses illustrated in the figure below, determine `&temp`, `&dist`, `&date`, and `&miles`.

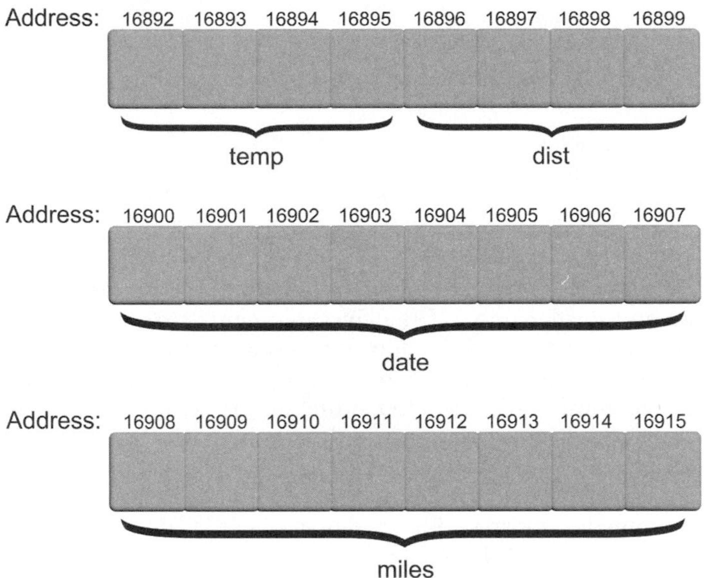

Memory bytes for Exercise 2

3. If a variable is declared as a pointer, what must be stored in the pointer?
4. Write declarations for the following:
   a. A parameter named `amount` that will be a pointer to a single-precision value.
   b. A parameter named `price` that will be a pointer to a double-precision number.
   c. A parameter named `minutes` that will be a pointer to an integer number.
   d. A parameter named `key` that will be a pointer to a character.
   e. A parameter named `yield` that will be used to store the address of an integer variable.

f. A parameter named `coupon` that will be used to store the address of a single-precision variable.
g. A parameter named `rate` that will be used to store the address of a double-precision variable.
h. A parameter named `securityType` that will be used to store the address of a character.
i. A parameter named `datePt` that points to an integer.
j. A parameter named `yldAddr` that points to a double-precision variable.
k. A parameter named `amtPpt` that points to a single-precision variable.
l. A parameter named `ptrchr` that points to a character.

5. Which of the following are declarations for pointers:
   a. `long a;`
   b. `char b;`
   c. `char *c;`
   d. `int x;`
   e. `int *p;`
   f. `double w;`
   g. `float *k;`
   h. `float l;`
   i. `double *z;`

6. Suppose a program function contains the declarations

```
char m1, m2;
float m3, m4;
int m5;
```

and that this function calls the `whatNow()` function. Also, assume the `whatNow()` function makes changes to the variables `m1`, `m2`, `m3`, `m4`, and `m5`. Assume we want these changes available to the calling function.. What should the call to `whatNow()` look like?
   a. Assuming that `whatNow()` directly returns no value, but can directly alter the variables `m1`, `m2`, `m3`, `m4`, and `m5`, what is a correct function header (select parameter names of your own choosing)?
   b. What is the correct function prototype for `whatNow()`?

Programming Exercises

1. a. Write a program that includes the following declaration statements. Have the program use the address operator and the `printf()` function to display the addresses corresponding to each variable.

```
char key, choice;
int num, count;
long date;
float yield;
double price;
```

b. After running the program written for Exercise 1a, draw a diagram of how your computer has set aside storage for the variables in the program. On your diagram, fill in the addresses displayed by the program.

c. Modify the program written in Exercise 1a to display the amount of storage your computer reserves for each data type (use the `sizeof` operator). With this information and the address information provided in Exercise 1b, determine if your computer set aside storage for the variables in the order they were declared.

2. Write a C function named `change()` that accepts a single-precision number and the addresses of the integer variables named `quarters`, `dimes`, `nickels`, and `pennies`. The function should determine the number of quarters, dimes, nickels, and pennies in the number passed to it and write these values directly into the respective variables declared in its calling function.

3. a. Write a function named `secs()` that accepts the time in hours, minutes, and seconds; and determines the `total` number of seconds in the passed data. Write this function so that the `total` number of seconds is returned by the function as an integer number.

   b. Repeat Exercise 3a but also pass the address of the variable `totSec` to the function `secs()`. Using this passed address, have `secs()` directly alter the value of `totSec`.

4. Write a C function named `time()` that accepts an integer number of seconds and the addresses of three variables named `hours`, `min`, and `sec`. The function is to convert the passed number of seconds into an equivalent number of hours, minutes, and seconds and directly alter the value of the respective variables using their passed addresses.

5. Replace the `calc()` function used in Program 7.8 with two functions named `computeSum()` and `computeProduct()`. The `computeSum()` function should calculate and directly return the sum of three values passed to it, while the `computeProduct()` function should calculate and directly return the product of three values passed to it.

6. a. Write a function named `date()` that accepts an integer of the form `yyyymmdd`, such as 20070412; determines the corresponding month, day, and year; and returns these three values to the calling function. For example, if date is called using the statement

```
date(20120411, &month, &day, &year)
```

   the number 4 should be returned in month, the number 11 in day, and the number 2012 in year.

   b. Include the `date()` subroutine written for Exercise 6a in a working program. The `main()` function should correctly call date and display the three values returned by the function.

7. Rewrite Program 6.6 in Section 6.3 so that lines 14 through 20 are replaced by a function named `getData()`. This function should request a child's age, in years and months, as integer values, and the child's height, as a floating-point value. It should return both the child's age in years and the child's height as floating-point values through its parameter list.

7.4 Case Study: Swapping Values

A common programming requirement is the sorting of both numeric values and text, such as names, in either ascending (increasing) or descending (decreasing) order. This is typically accomplished by comparing two values and then switching values if they are not in the correct order.

Requirements Specification

Write a C function that exchanges the values in two single-precision variables of its called function. Thus, if the function has access to two variables of its calling function, the called function should switch the values in these variables.

Analyze the Problem

Because the values of two variables are affected, the function cannot be written as a call by value function that returns only a single value. The desired exchange of values can only be obtained by giving the function direct access to the two variables whose values have to be switched. This is accomplished using pointers.

a. Determine the Input Items Because we are developing a function, the input items will become the function's arguments. In this case the required inputs to the function are two addresses, which are the addresses of the two variables whose values are to be exchanged. Passing addresses will permit the called function to directly access and change the values in the variables whose addresses have been passed.

Thus, one of the first requirements in writing the function, which we will name `swap()`, is to declare two pointer parameters that can store addresses. The following declarations can be used:

```
float *num1Addr; /* num1Addr points to a single-precision variable*/
float *num2Addr; /* num2Addr points to a single-precision variable*/
```

The choice of the parameter names `num1Addr` and `num2Addr` is, as with all parameter names, up to the programmer.

b. Determine the Desired Outputs In this case there is no single value that must be directly returned. Rather, the function must change the values in the calling function using passed addresses.

c. List the Formulas Relating the Inputs to the Outputs The interchange of values stored in two variables is accomplished using the following three-step interchange algorithm:

1. Store the first variable's value in a temporary location (Figure 7.14a).
2. Store the second variable's value in the first variable (Figure 7.14b).
3. Store the temporary value in the second variable (Figure 7.14c).

The reason for Step 1, which uses the temporary variable to hold the first variable's value, is immediately obvious once you consider what happens if this variable were not used. For example, if the value of the second variable were initially moved into the first variable (Step 2) before temporarily saving the first value (Step 1), the first value would be lost.

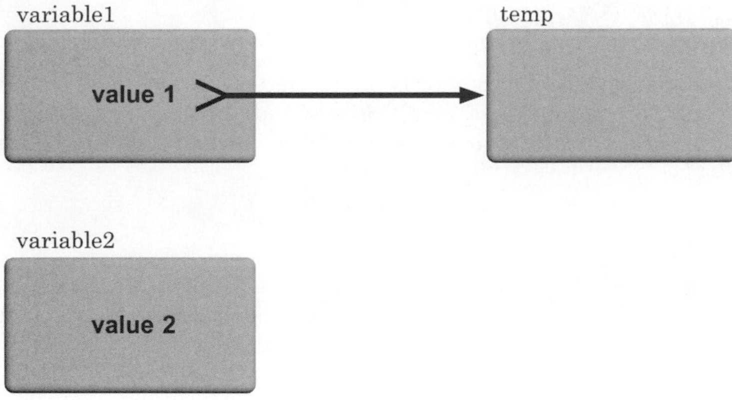

Figure 7.14a Save the first value

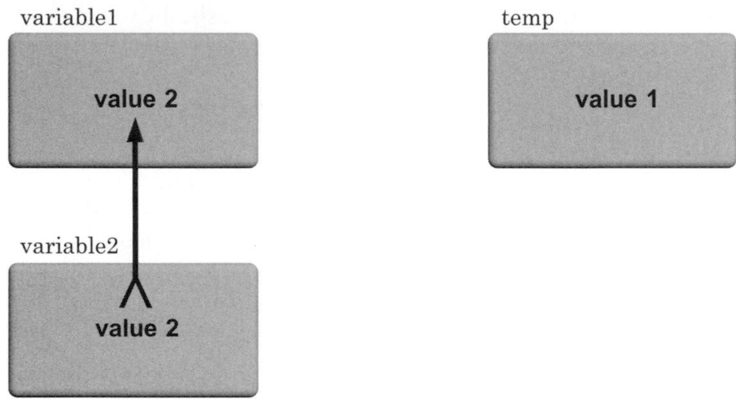

Figure 7.14b Replace the first value with the second value

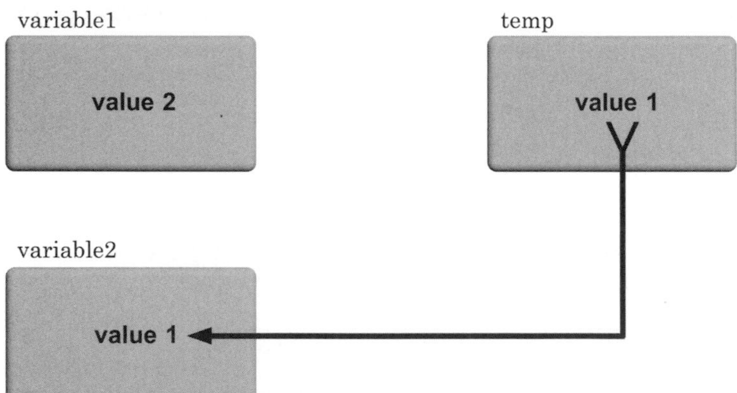

Figure 7.14c Change the second value

Code the Function

We will write the function in two steps. In the first step, we will create a stub function to ensure that the addresses of two variables are correctly passed and received. The function will then be completed to exchange the referenced values.

Using the same technique for passing two addresses into a function that was employed in Programs 7.8, a suitable header for our swapping function, which we have named `swap()` is

```
swap(float *num1Addr, float *num2Addr) /* function header */
```

Using this header, we can now check that the values accessed using the addresses in `num1Addr` and `num2Addr` are correct. This is done in Program 7.9, which contains a stub version for `swap()`.

Program 7.9

```
1   #include <stdio.h>
2   void swap(float *, float *); /* function prototype */
3
4   int main()
5   {
6     float firstnum = 20.0, secnum = 5.0;
7
8     swap(&firstnum, &secnum);
9
10    return 0;
11  }
12
13  void swap(float *num1Addr, float *num2Addr)
14  {
15    printf("The number pointed to by num1Addr is %5.2f\n", *num1Addr);
16    printf("The number pointed to by num2Addr is %5.2f\n", *num2Addr);
17  }
```

The display produced by Program 7.9 is

```
The number pointed to by num1Addr is 20.00
The number pointed to by num2Addr is  5.00
```

In reviewing Program 7.9, note two items. First, the header line

```
13 void swap(float *numAddr1, float *numAddr2)
```

declares that `swap()` returns no value directly and that its parameters, `numAddr1` and `numAddr2`, are each pointers that "point to" single-precision values. As such, when the function is called, it will require that two addresses be passed, and that each address is the address of a single-precision value. Second, within `swap()`, the indirection operator is used, in both lines 15 and 16, to access the values stored in `firstnum` and `secnum`, respectively. The `swap()` function itself has no knowledge of these variable names, but it does have the address of `firstnum` stored in `num1Addr` and the address of `secnum` stored in `num2Addr`. The expression `*num1Addr` used in line 15 as the last argument within the `printf()` call means "the variable whose address is in `num1Addr`." This is of course the variable `firstnum`.

```
15 printf("The number pointed to by num1Addr is %5.2f\n", *num1Addr);
```

Similarly, the last argument to `printf()` in line 16

```
16 printf("The number pointed to by num2Addr is %5.2f\n", *num2Addr);
```

obtains the value stored in `secnum` as "the variable whose address is in `num2Addr`." Thus, in both lines 15 and 16, we have successfully used pointers to allow `swap()` to access variables in `main()`.

Having verified that `swap()` can access `main()`'s local variables `firstnum` and `secnum`, we can now expand `swap()` to exchange the values in the variables whose addresses were passed to `swap()`.

Using the pointers `num1Addr` and `num2Addr`, the swapping algorithm takes the form

1. Store the value held by the variable pointed to by `num1Addr` in a temporary location. The statement `temp = *num1Addr;` does this (see Figure 7.15a).
2. Store the value held by the variable whose address is in `num2Addr` in the variable whose address is in `num1Addr`. The statement `*num1Addr = *num2Addr;` does this (see Figure 7.15b).
3. Store the value in the temporary location in the variable whose address is in `num2Addr`. The statement `*num2Addr = temp;` does this (see Figure 7.15c).

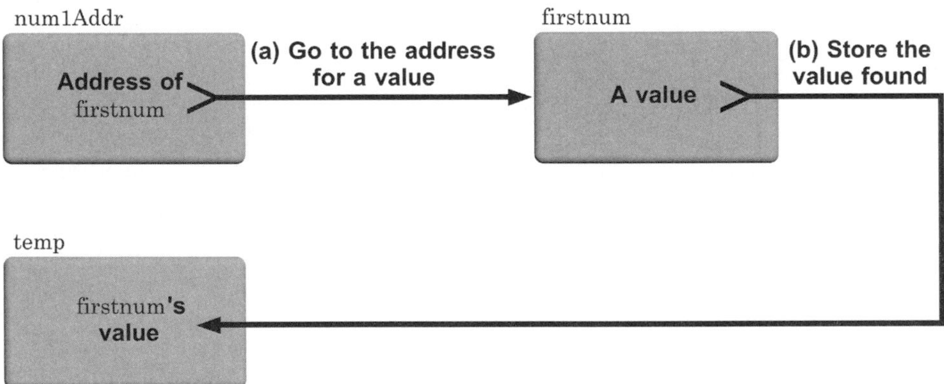

Figure 7.15a Indirectly storing `firstnum`'s value

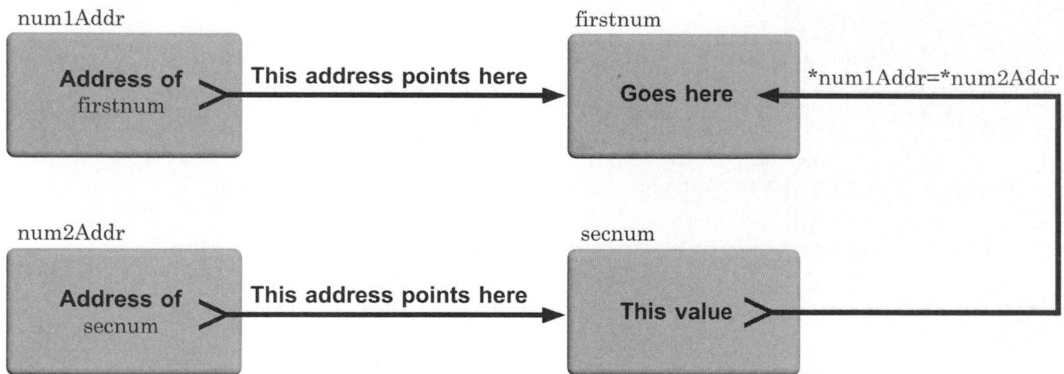

Figure 7.15b Indirectly changing `firstnum`'s value

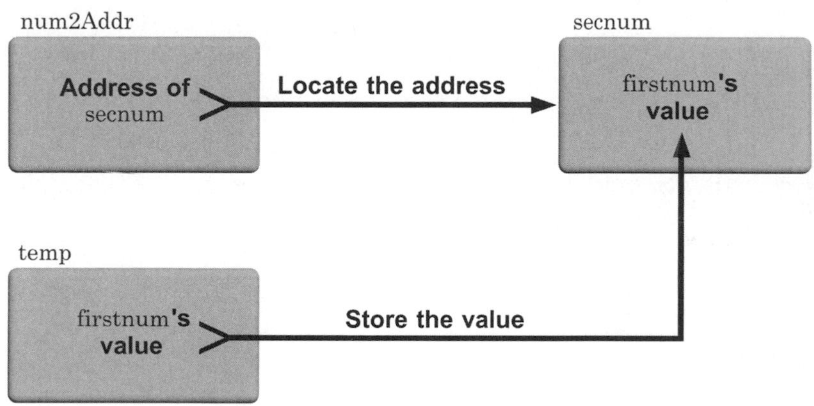

Figure 7.15c Indirectly changing `secnum`'s value

Program 7.10 contains the final form of `swap()`, written according to this algorithm.

Program 7.10

```
#include <stdio.h>

void swap(float *, float *); /* function prototype */

int main()
{
  float firstnum, secnum;

  printf("Enter two numbers: ");
  scanf("%f %f", &firstnum, &secnum);
```

☞

```

  printf("\nBefore the call to swap():\n");
  printf("  The value in firstnum is %5.2f\n", firstnum);
  printf("  The value in secnum is %5.2f\n", secnum);

  swap(&firstnum, &secnum); /* call swap() */

  printf("\nAfter the call to swap():\n");
  printf("  The value in firstnum is %5.2f\n", firstnum);
  printf("  The value in secnum is %5.2f\n", secnum);

  return 0;
}

void swap(float *num1Addr, float *num2Addr)
{
  float temp;

  temp = *num1Addr; /* save firstnum's value */
  *num1Addr = *num2Addr; /* move secnum's value into firstnum */
  *num2Addr = temp; /* change secnum's value */
}
```

Test and Debug the Program

We have already begun the testing of swap() with the stub function written for Program 7.9. The following sample run was obtained using Program 7.10, which completes the verification:

```
Enter two numbers: 20.5 6.25

Before the call to swap():
  The value in firstnum is 20.50
  The value in secnum is  6.25

After the call to swap():
  The value in firstnum is  6.25
  The value in secnum is 20.50
```

As illustrated in this output, the values stored in main()'s variables have been modified from within swap(), which was made possible by the use of pointers. If a call by value had been used instead, the exchange within swap() would only effect swap()'s parameters and would accomplish nothing with respect to main()'s variables. Thus, a function such as swap() can only be written using pointers that provide access to main()'s variables.

In using pointer parameters, one caution needs to be mentioned. Pointers *cannot* be used to change constants. For example, calling swap() with the address of two constants, such as in the call swap(&20.5, &6.5), causes a compiler error. This error also occurs if the address of a symbolic constant is used.

Finally, notice that the header line for the function, as well as the call itself, provides a clear indication that addresses are being passed. Once you see that addresses are being passed, it is a clear indication that the indirection operator, *, will be needed to access the values.

EXERCISES 7.4

Short Answer Questions

1. The addresses of three integer variables are to be used as arguments in a call to a function named `time()`. Write a suitable function header for time, assuming that time accepts these variables as the pointer arguments `sec`, `min`, and `hours`, and returns no value to its calling function.

2. The following program uses the same variable names in both the calling and called functions. Determine if this causes any problem for the computer. What problems might this code pose to a programmer? Also determine the type of data stored in each variable.

```
#include <stdio.h>
void time(int *, int *);
int main()
{
  int min, hour;

  printf("Enter two numbers :");
  scanf("%d %d", &min, &hour);
  time(&min,&hour);

  return 0;
}
void time(int *min, int *hour)
{
  int sec;

  sec = ( (*hour) *60 + *min ) * 60;
  printf("The total number of seconds is %d", sec);

  return;
}
```

3. Assume that the following declaration has been made:

```
int *pt1, *pt2;
```

Since the asterisk, *, is used for both multiplication and indirection, how is the expression

```
* pt1 * * pt2
```

evaluated by the computer? Why does the computer evaluate the expression in the order you have indicated? Rewrite this expression to make its meaning clearer to anyone reading it.

Programming Exercises

1. Enter and execute Program 7.10.
2. Write a C function named `liquid()` that is to accept an integer number and the addresses of the variables `gallons`, `quarts`, `pints`, and `cups`. The passed integer represents the `total` number of cups, and the function is to determine the number of gallons, quarts, pints, and cups in the passed value. Using the passed addresses, the function should directly alter the respective variables in the calling function. Use the relationships of 2 cups to a pint, 4 cups to a quart, and 16 cups to a gallon.
3. Rewrite the `findMax()` function in Program 6.2 so that the variable `max` is declared in `main()` and the maximum value of the two passed numbers is written directly to `max`. (*Hint:* The address of `max` will also have to be passed to `findMax()`.)
4. Modify Program 7.10 to accept a character parameter named `sortOrder`. If `sortOrder` is an `a`, `swap()` should exchange values only if the first value is larger than the second value; that is, the function should return the values in ascending order (smallest number first, largest number second). For any other value, the function should return the values in descending order (largest number first, smallest number second).
5. Write a C function named `yrCalc()` that accepts a longer integer representing the `total` number of days from the date 1/1/1900 and the addresses of the variables `year`, `month`, and `day`. The function is to calculate the current year, month, and day for the given number of days and write these values directly in the respective variables using the passed addresses. For this problem assume that each year has 365 days and each month has 30 days.

7.5 Recursion[4]

Because C allocates new memory locations for arguments and local variables each time a function is called, it is possible for a function to call itself. Functions that do so are referred to as **self-referential** or **recursive** functions. When a function invokes itself, the process is called **direct recursion**. Similarly, a function can invoke a second function, which in turn invokes the first function. This type of recursion is referred to as **indirect** or **mutual recursion**.

In 1936, Alan Turing showed that, although not every possible problem can be solved by computer, those problems that have recursive solutions also have computer solutions, at least in theory.

Mathematical Recursion

The recursive concept is that the solution to a problem can be stated in terms of "simple" versions of itself. Some problems can be solved using an algebraic formula that shows

[4]This topic may be omitted on first reading with no loss of subject continuity.

recursion explicitly. For example, consider finding the factorial of a number n, denoted as n!, where n is a positive integer. This is defined as

```
0! = 1
1! = 1 * 1 = 1 * 0!
2! = 2 * 1 = 2 * 1!
3! = 3 * 2 * 1 = 3 * 2!
4! = 4 * 3 * 2 * 1 = 4 * 3!
```

and so on.

The definition for n! can be summarized by the following statements:

```
0! = 1
n! = n * (n-1)!    for n >= 1
```

This definition illustrates the general considerations that must be specified in constructing a recursive algorithm. These are

1. What is the first case or cases?
2. How is the *n*th case related to the *(n–1)* case?

Although the definition seems to define a factorial in terms of a factorial, the definition is valid, because it can always be computed. For example, using the definition, 3! is first computed as

```
3! = 3 * 2!
```

The value of 2! is determined from the definition as

```
2! = 2 * 1!
```

Substituting this expression for 2! in the determination of 3! yields

```
3! = 3 * 2 * 1!
```

Finally, substituting the expression 1*0! for 1! yields

```
3! = 3 * 2*1*0!
```

0! is not defined in terms of the recursive formula, but is simply defined as being equal to 1. Substituting this value into the expression for 3! gives us

```
3! = 3 * 2 * 1  * 1 = 6
```

To see how a recursive function is defined in C, we construct the function factorial(). In pseudocode, the processing required of this function is

If n = 0
factorial = 1
Else
factorial = n * factorial(n - 1)

Notice that this algorithm is simply a restatement of the recursive definition previously given. In C, this can be written as

```
int factorial(int n)
{
  if (n == 0)
    return (1);
  else
    return (n * factorial(n-1));
}
```

Program 7.11 illustrates this code in a complete program.

Program 7.11

```
#include <stdio.h>
int main()
{
  int n, result;
  int factorial(int);   /* function prototype */

  printf("\Enter a number: ");
  scanf("%d", &n);
  result = factorial(n);
  printf("\nThe factorial of %d is %d\n", n, result);

  return 0;
}

int factorial(int n)
{
  if (n == 0)
    return (1);
  else
    return (n * factorial(n-1));
}
```

Following is a sample run of Program 7.11:

```
Enter a number: 3

The factorial of 3 is 6
```

How the Computation Is Performed The sample run of Program 7.11 invoked `factorial()` from `main()` with a value of 3 using the call

```
result = factorial(n);
```

Let's see how the computer actually performs the computation. The mechanism that makes it possible for a C function to call itself is that C allocates new memory locations for all function arguments and local variables as each function is called. This allocation is made dynamically, as a program is executed, in a memory area referred to as the **stack**.

A memory stack is simply an area of memory used for rapidly storing and retrieving data. It is conceptually similar to a stack of trays in a cafeteria, where the last tray placed on top of the stack is the first tray removed. This last-in first-out mechanism provides the means for storing information in order of occurrence. Each function call simply reserves memory locations on the stack for its arguments, its local variables, a return value, and the address where execution is to resume in the calling program when the function has completed execution. Thus, when the function call `factorial(n)` is made, the stack initially is used to store the address of the instruction being executed (`result = factorial(n);`), a space for the value to be returned by the function, and the argument value for `n`, which is 3. At this stage the stack can be envisioned as shown in Figure 7.16. From a program execution standpoint, the function that made the call to `factorial()`, in this case `main()`, is suspended and the compiled code for the `factorial()` function starts executing.

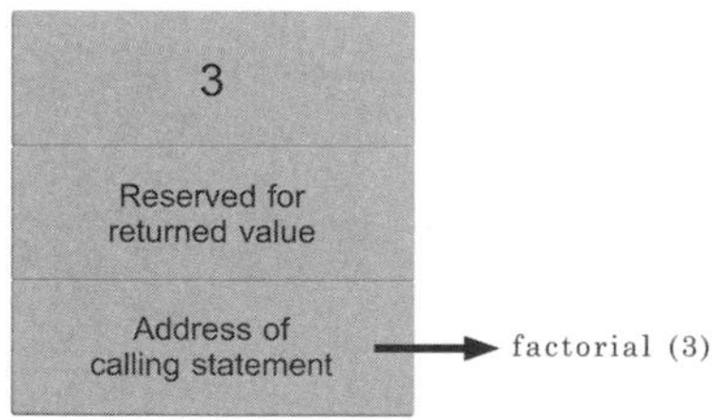

Figure 7.16 The stack for the first call to `factorial()`

Within the `factorial()` function itself, another function call is made. That this call is to `factorial()` is irrelevant as far as C is concerned. The call simply is another request for stack space. In this case the stack stores the address of the instruction being executed in `factorial()`, a space for the value to be returned by the function, and the number 2. The stack can now be envisioned as shown in Figure 7.17. At this point a second version of the compiled code for `factorial()` begins execution, while the first version is temporarily suspended.

Once again, the currently executing code, which is the second invocation of `factorial()`, makes a function call. That this call is to itself is again irrelevant in C. The call is once again handled in the same manner as any function call and begins with allocation of the stack's memory space. Here the stack stores the address of the instruction being executed in the calling function, which happens to be `factorial()`, a space for the value to be returned by the function, and the number 1. The stack can now be envisioned as shown in Figure 7.18. At this point this third called version of the compiled code for `factorial()` begins execution, while the second called version is temporarily suspended.

This third version of `factorial()` makes the fourth and final call to `factorial()`. This last call continues in the same fashion, except, rather than resulting in another call, it results in a returned value of `1` being placed on the stack. This completes the set of recursive calls and permits the suspended calling functions to resume execution and be completed in reverse order. The value of `1` is used by the third invocation of `factorial()` to complete its operation and place a return value of `1` on the stack. This value is then used by the second invocation of `factorial()` to place a return value of 2 on the stack. Finally, this value is then used by the first invocation of `factorial()`to complete its operation and place a return value of 6 on the stack, with execution now returning to `main()`. The original calling statement within `main()` stores the return value of its invocation of `factorial()` into the variable `result`.

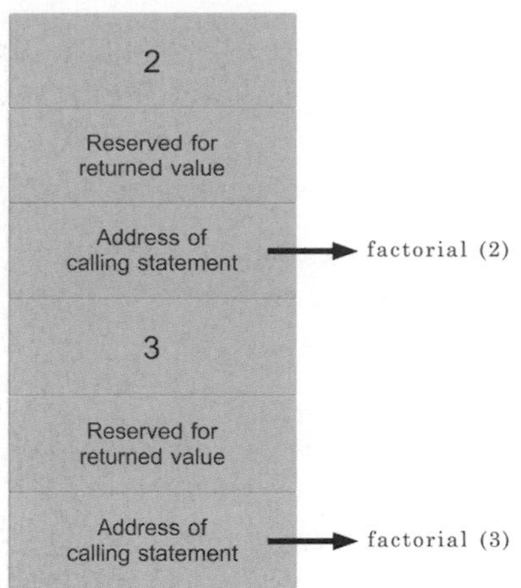

Figure 7.17 The stack for the second call to `factorial()`

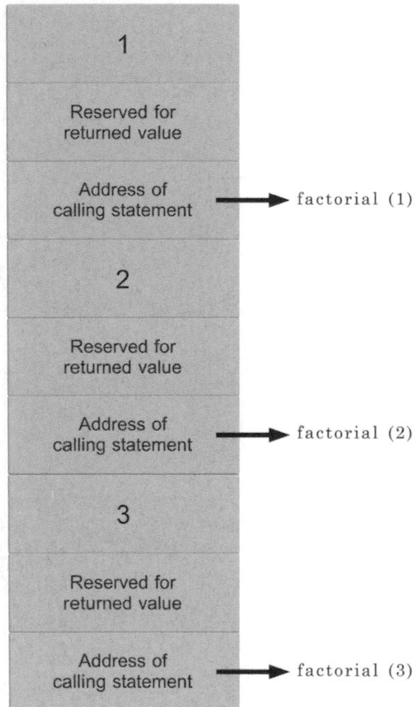

Figure 7.18 The stack for the third call to `factorial()`

Recursion versus Iteration

The recursive method can be applied to any problem in which the solution is represented in terms of solutions to simpler versions of the same problem.

The most difficult tasks in implementing recursion are deciding how to create the process and visualizing what happens at each successive invocation.

Any recursive function can always be written in a nonrecursive manner using an iterative solution. For example, the `factorial()` function can be written using an iteration algorithm as

```
int factorial(int n)
{
  int fact;

  for(fact = 1; n > 0; n--)
    fact = fact * n;
  return (fact);
}
```

Because recursion is usually a difficult concept for beginning programmers, under what conditions would you use it in preference to a repetitive solution? The answer is rather simple.

If a problem solution can be expressed iteratively or recursively with equal ease, the iterative solution is preferable because it executes faster (there are no additional function calls, which consumes processing time) and uses less memory (the stack is not used for the multiple function calls needed in recursion). There are times, however, when recursive solutions are preferable. This typically occurs in more advanced applications where recursion is the only practical means of implementing a solution, because obtaining the same result using repetition would require extremely complicated coding. An example of this is the Quicksort sorting algorithm presented in Section 8.8.

EXERCISES 7.5

Programming Exercises

1. a. The Fibonacci sequence is 0, 1, 1, 2, 3, 5, 8, 13... where the first two terms are 0 and 1, and each term thereafter is defined recursively as the sum of the two preceding terms; that is

```
Fib(n)= n    for n < 2
Fib(n) = Fib(n-1) + Fib(n-2) for n >= 2
```

   Write a recursive function that returns the *n*th number in a Fibonacci sequence when *n* is passed to the function as an argument. For example, when $n = 8$, the function returns the 8th number in the sequence, which is 13.

   b. Write a function that uses repetition to calculate the *n*th term of a Fibonacci sequence.

2. a. The sum of a series of consecutive numbers from 1 to *n* can be defined recursively as

```
sum(1) = 1;
sum(n) = n + sum(n - 1)
```

   Write a recursive C function that accepts *n* as an argument and calculates the sum of the numbers from 1 to *n*.

   b. Test the function written in Exercise 2a with a program that requests the value of *n* from the user and then calculates and displays the sum of the numbers from 1 to *n*.

3. a. Write a function that recursively determines the value of the *n*th term of an arithmetic sequence defined by the terms

```
a, a+d, a+2d, a+3d, ..... a+(n-1)d
```

   The argument to the function should be the first term, *a*, the common difference, *d*, and the value of *n*.

   b. Modify the function written for Exercise 3a so that the sum of the first *n* terms of the sequence is returned. (This is a more general form of Exercise 2.)

4. a. Write a function that recursively determines the value of the *n*th term of a geometric sequence defined by the terms

   $a, ar, ar^2, ar^3, \ldots\ldots ar^{n-1}$

   The argument to the function should be the first term, *a*, the common ratio, *r*, and the value of *n*.

   b. Modify the function written for Exercise 4a so that the sum of the first *n* terms of the sequence is returned.

5. a. The value of x^n can be defined recursively as

```
x^0 = 1
x^n = x * x^(n-1)
```

   Write a recursive function that returns the computes and returns the value of x^n.

   b. Rewrite the function written for Exercise 5a so that it uses a repetitive algorithm for calculating the value of x^n.

6. The following algorithm, discovered by Euclid, provides a simple means of determining the greatest common divisor (GCD) of two positive integers *a* and *b* (the GCD is the largest number that divides evenly into both numbers with no remainders):
   a. Divide the larger number by the smaller and retain the remainder.
   b. Divide the smaller number by the remainder, again retaining the remainder.
   c. Continue dividing the prior remainder by the current remainder until the remainder is 0, at which point the last non-0 remainder is the GCD.

   Write a recursive function named `gcd()` that implements this algorithm.

7. a. A numeric palindrome is a number that is the same when read either forward or backward. For example, the number 4321234 is a numeric palindrome. Use this information to create a recursive function named `numpal()` that accepts an integer number as a parameter and returns a 1 if the parameter is a numeric palindrome and a 0 if it is not.

   b. Test the function written in Exercise 7a with a program that requests five user-input integers, one at a time. After each integer is entered, the program should display a message indicating that the number is or is not a numeric palindrome.

7.6 Common Programming and Compiler Errors

In using the material presented in this chapter, be aware of the following possible programming and compiler errors:

Programming Errors

1. Using the same name for a local variable that has been used for a global variable. Within the function declaring it, the use of the local variable name affects only the local variable's contents. Thus, the value of the global variable can never be altered by the function, unless the scope resolution operator, `::`, is used.

2. Becoming confused about whether a parameter (or variable) *contains* an address or *is an* address. Pointer parameters (as well as pointer variables) contain addresses. Some of the confusion surrounding pointers, used either as parameters or variables is caused by the cavalier use of the word *pointer*. For example, the phrase "a function requires a pointer argument" is more clearly understood when it is realized that the phrase really means "a function requires an address as an argument." Similarly, the phrase "a function returns a pointer" really means "a function returns an address." Addresses can only be stored in pointers. If you are ever in doubt as to what is really contained in a parameter or a variable, or how it should be treated, use the `printf()` function to display its contents. Seeing what is displayed frequently helps sort out what is really in the parameter or

variable. Alternatively, use the indirection operator with the parameter or variable. If the parameter or variable is a valid pointer, the "thing being pointed to" will be displayed; if not, the compiler will issue an error message telling you that the parameter is not a pointer.

3. Declaring a pointer as a function parameter and then forgetting to place the address operator, &, before the argument passed to the function when it is called.

4. Forgetting to specify the initial case when a recursive function is defined.

Compiler Errors

The following table summarizes common errors that will result in compilation errors and the typical error messages provided by Unix- and Windows-based compilers.

Error	Typical Unix-based Compiler Error Message	Typical Windows-based Compiler Error Message
Attempting to take the address of a constant	`(W) Operation between types "int" and "const int*" is not allowed.`	`error: & on constant`
Applying the indirection operator to a nonpointer variable	`(S) Operand of indirection operator must be a pointer expression.`	`error: illegal indirection`
Not passing an address in a call to a function whose parameter is declared as a pointer	`(W) Function argument assignment between types "type*" and "type" is not allowed.`	`error: function cannot convert parameter from dataType to dataType*`
Assigning a value, rather than an address to a pointer	`(W) Operation between types "type*" and "type" is not allowed.`	`error: cannot convert parameter from dataType to dataType*`

7.7 Chapter Summary

1. Every variable used in a program has *scope*, which determines where in the program the variable can be used. The scope of a variable is either local or global and is determined by where the variable's definition statement is placed. A local variable is defined within a function and can only be used within its defining function or block. A global variable is defined outside a function and can be used in any function following the variable's definition. All nonstatic global variables are initialized to 0 and can be shared between files using the keyword `extern`.

2. Every variable has a class. The class of a variable determines how long the value in the variable will be retained. Automatic (`auto`) variables are local variables that exist only while their defining function is executing. `register` variables are similar to automatic variables but are stored in a computer's internal registers rather than in memory. Variables

that are `static` can be either global or local and retain their values for the duration of a program's execution. `static` variables are also set to 0 or blanks when they are defined if they are not explicitly initialized by the user.

3. Every variable has a data type, a value, and an address. In C the address of a variable can be obtained by using the address operator, `&`.
4. A pointer is a variable or parameter that is used to store the address of another variable. Pointers, like all C variables and parameters, must be declared. The indirection operator, *, is used to both declare a pointer and to access the variable whose address is stored in a pointer. For example, the statement `int *datePtr` declares that the identifier named `datePtr` is a pointer to an integer value. This is commonly read as "*datePtr points to an int.*"
5. If a parameter or variable is a pointer, then the indirection operator, `*`, must be used to access the variable whose address is stored in the pointer. For example, if `datePtr` has been declared as a pointer, then the value pointed to by this pointer is accessed by the expression `*datePtr.` This can be read as "*the thing (actually the value) pointed to by* `datePtr`."
6. The address of a variable can be passed to a function. The parameter receiving this address must be declared as a pointer. Passing an address is referred to as a pass by reference.
7. When a called function receives an address, it has the capability of directly accessing the respective calling function's variable. Using passed addresses permits a called function to effectively return multiple values.
8. A recursive solution is one in which the solution can be expressed in terms of a "simpler" version of itself. A recursive algorithm must always specify
   - The first case or cases
   - How the *n*th case is related to the *(n–1)* case
9. If a problem solution can be expressed repetitively or recursively with equal ease, the repetitive solution is preferable because it executes faster and uses less memory. In many advanced applications, recursion is simpler to visualize and the only practical means of implementing a solution.

Part Three

Completing the Basics

Chapter 8

Arrays

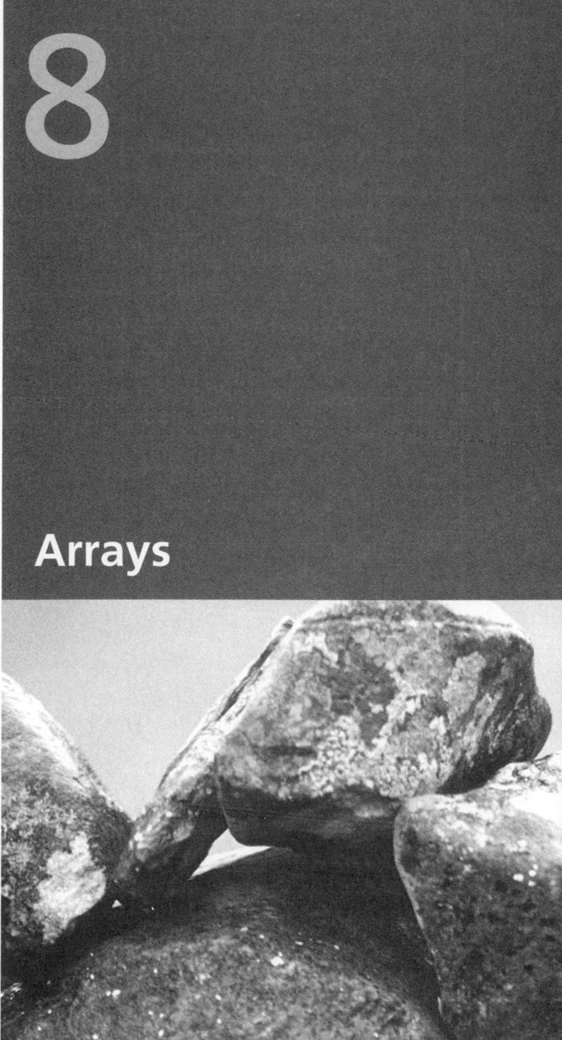

The variables used so far have all had a common characteristic: Each variable can only be used to store a single value at a time. For example, although the variables `inKey`, `counter`, and `price` declared in the statements

```
char inKey;
int counter;
double price;
```

are of different data types, each variable can only store one value of the declared data type. These types of variables are called atomic variables. An **atomic variable**, which is also referred to as a **scalar variable**, is a variable whose value cannot be further subdivided or separated into a built-in data type.

Another method of storing and retrieving data is to use a data structure. A **data structure**, which is also known as an **aggregate data type**, is a data type with two main characteristics. First, its values can be decomposed into individual data elements, each of which is either atomic or another data structure. Secondly, it provides an access scheme for locating individual data elements within the data structure.

Grades	Codes	Prices
98	x	10.96
87	a	6.43
92	m	2.58
79	n	.86
85		12.27
		6.39

Figure 8.1 Three lists of items

One of the simplest data structures, called an **array**, is used to store and process a set of values, all of the same data type, that forms a logical group. For example, Figure 8.1 illustrates three such groups of items. The first group is a list of five integer grades, the second group is a list of four character codes, and the last group is a list of six double-precision prices. Each of these groups can be created as an array.

An array that consists of individual items of the same data type is called a one-dimensional array. In this chapter we describe how one-dimensional arrays are declared, initialized, stored inside a computer, and used. We will explore the use of one-dimensional arrays with example programs and present the procedures for declaring and using multidimensional arrays.

8.1 One-Dimensional Arrays

Grades
98
87
92
79
85

Figure 8.2 A list of grades

A **one-dimensional array**, which is also known as both a **single-dimensional array** and a **single-subscript array**, is a list of values of the same data type that is stored using a single group name.[1] In C, as in other computer languages, the group name is referred to as the array name. For example, consider the list of grades illustrated in Figure 8.2. All the grades in the list are integer numbers and must be declared as such. However, the individual items in the list do not have to be declared separately. The items in the list can be declared as a single unit and stored under a common variable name, which is the array name. For convenience, we will choose `grades` as the name for the list shown in Figure 8.2.

To declare that `grades` is to be used to store five individual integer values requires the declaration statement `int grades[5];`. Notice that this declaration statement gives the data type of the items in the array, the array (or list) name, and the number of items in the array. A common—and good—programming practice is to define the number of array items as a symbolic constant before declaring the array. Using this convention, the previous declaration would be written using two statements, such as

```
#define NUMELS 5 /* this creates the symbolic constant */
int grades[NUMELS]; /* this is the actual array declaration */
```

Here, the symbolic constant name, `NUMELS`, can be replaced with any valid identifier of your choice. Further examples of array declarations are

```
#define NUMCODES 4
char code[NUMCODES]; /* an array of four character codes */

#define NUMELS 6
double prices[NUMELS]; /* an array of six double precision prices */

#define SIZE 100
int amount[100]; /* an array of 100 integer amounts */
```

---

[1]Note that lists can be implemented in a variety of ways. An array is simply one implementation of a list in which all the list elements are of the same type and each element is stored consecutively in a set of contiguous memory locations.

Programming Note

Starting with an Index of 0

In C, the starting index value for all arrays is always 0. This starting index value is fixed by the compiler and cannot be altered. Although other high-level languages, such as Visual Basic, allow the programmer to change this starting value (even permitting negative values), C does not. In C, the first array element is always 0, and negative index values are not permitted.

Although it may seem unusual to force the first element of an array to have an index of 0, doing so actually increases the speed of accessing individual elements. The reason for this is that a starting index value of 0 permits the compiler to directly equate all subsequent index values, without further computation, to an internal offset that is used by the compiler in accessing individual elements.

In these declaration statements, each array is allocated sufficient memory to hold the number of data items given in the declaration statement. Thus, the array named `code` has storage reserved for four characters, the array named `prices` has storage reserverd for six double-precision numbers and the array named `amount` has storage reserved for 100 integers. The named constants, `NUMCODES`, `NUMELS`, and `SIZE` are programmer-selected names.

Figure 8.3 illustrates the storage reserved for the `code` and `grades` arrays. Each item in an array is called an **element** or **component** of the array. The individual elements stored in the arrays illustrated in Figure 8.3 are stored sequentially, with the first array element stored in the first reserved location, the second element stored in the second reserved location, and so on until the last element is stored in the last reserved location. This contiguous storage allocation for the list is a key feature of arrays because it provides a simple mechanism for easily locating any single element in the list.

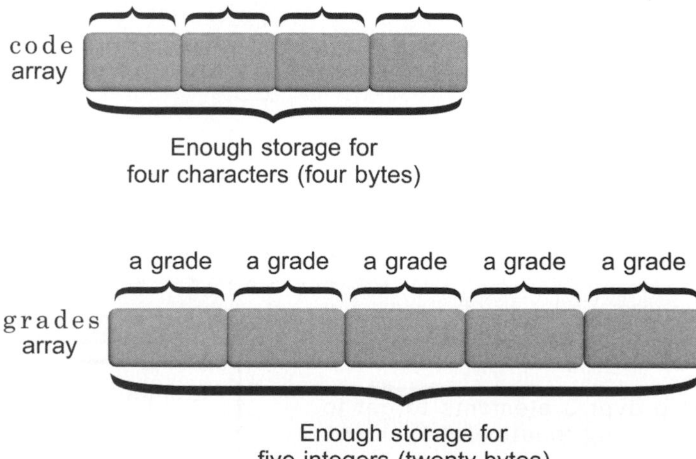

Figure 8.3 The `code` and `grades` arrays in memory

Because elements in the array are stored sequentially, any individual element can be accessed by giving the name of the array and the element's position. This position is called the element's **index** or **subscript** value. (The terms are synonymous.) For a single-dimensional array, the first element has an index of 0, the second element has an index of 1, and so on. In C, the array name and index of the desired element are combined by listing the index in braces after the array name. For example, given the prior declaration for `grades`,

```
grades[0] refers to the first grade stored in the grades array
grades[1] refers to the second grade stored in the grades array
grades[2] refers to the third grade stored in the grades array
grades[3] refers to the fourth grade stored in the grades array
grades[4] refers to the fifth grade stored in the grades array
```

Figure 8.4 illustrates the grades array in memory with the correct designation for each array element. Each individual element is referred to as an **indexed variable** or a **subscripted variable** because both a variable name and an index or subscript value must be used to reference the element. Remember, the index or subscript value gives the *position* of the element in the array.

The subscripted variable `grades[0]` is read both as "grades sub zero" and "grades zero." This is a shortened way of saying "the grades array subscripted by zero." Similarly, `grades[1]` is read as either "grades sub one" or "grades one," `grades[2]` as either "grades sub two" or "grades two," and so on.

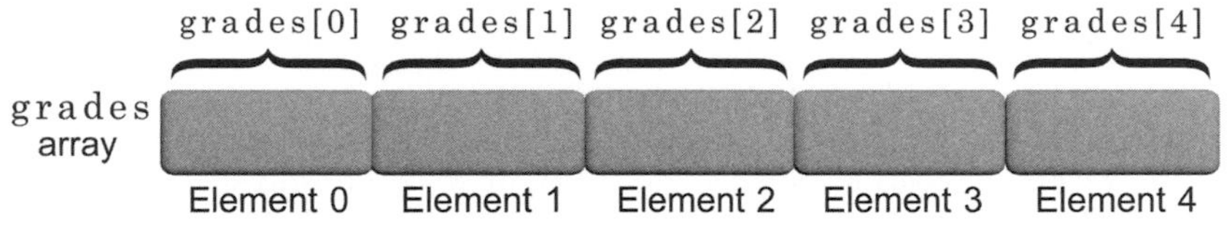

Figure 8.4 Identifying individual array elements

Although it may seem unusual to have the compiler assign the first element in an array with an index of 0, doing so increases the computer's speed of accessing array elements. Internally, unseen by the programmer, the computer uses the index as an offset from the array's starting position. As illustrated in Figure 8.5, the index tells the computer how many elements to skip over, starting from the beginning of the array, to get to the desired element.

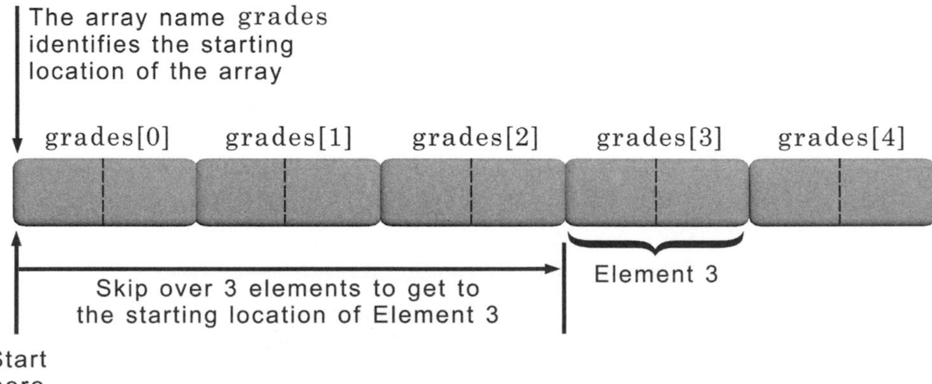

Figure 8.5 Accessing element 3

Programming Note

Structured Data Types

Atomic data types, such as integers and floating-point built-in types, cannot be decomposed into simpler types. In contrast, structured types *can* be decomposed into simpler types that are related within a defined structure. (Other terms used for a structured type is an aggregate or data structure.) Because a structured type consists of one or more simpler types, operations must be available for retrieving and updating the individual types that make up a data structure.

Single-dimensional arrays are examples of a structured type. In a single-dimensional array, such as an array of integers, the array is composed of individual integer values, where the values are related by their position in the array. For arrays, index values provide the means of accessing and modifying individual values.

Subscripted variables can be used anywhere that scalar variables are valid. Examples using the elements of the `grades` array are

```
grades[0] = 98;
grades[1] = grades[0] - 11;
grades[2] = 2 * (grades[0] - 6);
grades[3] = 79;
grades[4] = (grades[2] + grades[3] - 3)/2;
total = grades[0] + grades[1] + grades[2] + grades[3] + grades[4];
```

The subscript contained within square brackets need not be an integer. Any expression that evaluates an integer may be used as a subscript.[2] For example, assuming that `i` and `j` are integer variables, the following subscripted variables are valid:

```
grades[i]
grades[2*i]
grades[j-i]
```

One extremely important advantage of using integer expressions as subscripts is that they allow you to sequence easily through an array, element by element, with a `for` loop. This makes statements such as

```
total = grades[1] + grades[2] + grades[3] + grades[4] + grades[5];
```

unnecessary. The subscript value in each of the subscripted variables in this statement can be replaced by the counter in a `for` loop to access each element in the array sequentially. For example, the code

```
#define NUMELS 5

total = 0; /* initialize total to zero */
for (i = 0; i < NUMELS; i++)
  total = total + grades[i]; /* add in a grade */
```

[2]Some compilers permit double-precision variables as subscripts; in these cases the double-precision value is truncated to an integer value.

sequentially retrieves each array element and adds the element to the total. Here the variable i is used both as the counter in the for loop and as a subscript. As i increases by 1 each time through the for loop, the next element in the array is referenced. The procedure for adding the array elements within the for loop is the same procedure we have used many times before.

The advantage of using a for loop to sequence through an array becomes apparent when you work with larger arrays. For example, if the grades array contains 100 values rather than just 5, simply changing the number 5 to 100 in the #define statement is sufficient to sequence through the 100 grades and add each grade to the total. This single change automatically alters both the array's size and the for loop used to process each array element.

As another example of using a for loop to sequence through an array, assume that we want to locate the maximum value in an array of 1000 elements named price. The procedure we will use to locate the maximum value is to assume initially that the first element in the array is the largest number. Then, as we sequence through the array, the maximum value is compared to each element. When an element with a higher value is located, that element becomes the new maximum.

```
#define NUMELS 1000

maximum = price[0]; /* set the maximum to element zero */
for(i = 1; i < NUMELS; i++) /* cycle through the rest of the array */
  if (price[i] > maximum) /* compare each element to the maximum */
    maximum = price[i]; /* capture the new high value */
```

In this code the for statement consists of one if statement. The search for a new maximum value starts with element 1 of the array and continues through the last element. Each element is compared to the current maximum, and when a higher value is encountered, it becomes the new maximum.

Input and Output of Array Values

Individual array elements can be assigned values using individual assignment statements or, interactively, using the scanf() function. Examples of individual data entry statements are

```
price[5] = 10.69;
scanf("%d %lf", &grades[0], &price[2]);
scanf("%c", &code[0]);
scanf("%d %d %d", &grades[0], &grades[1], &grades[2]);
```

In the first statement, the value 10.69 is assigned to the variable named price[5]. The second statement causes two values to be read and stored in the variables grades[0] and price[2]. The third statement causes a single character to be read and stored in the variable named code[0]. Finally, the last statement causes three values to be read and stored in the variables grades[0], grades[1], and grades[2], respectively.

Historical Note

Handling Lists with LISP

Methods of handling lists have been especially important in the development of computer science and applications. In fact, in 1958, John McCarthy developed a language at the Massachusetts Institute of Technology specifically for manipulating lists. This language was named **LISP**, the acronym for **List Processing**. It has proved valuable for handling problems based on mathematical logic and is used extensively in artificial intelligence and pattern recognition projects.

One simple language related to LISP is named **Logo**, and has been made particularly user friendly. It incorporates a technique called "turtle graphics," by which a pointer is moved around the screen to plot geometric figures. Logo has been used widely to teach programming fundamentals to children.

Alternatively, a `for` statement can be used to cycle through the array for interactive data input. For example, the code

```
#define NUMELS 5

for(i = 0; i < NUMELS; i++)
{
  printf("Enter a grade: ");
  scanf("%d", &grades[i]);
}
```

prompts the user for five grades. The first grade entered is stored in `grades[0]`, the second in `grades[1]`, and so on until all five grades are entered.

One caution should be mentioned about storing data in an array. C does not check the value of the index being used (called a **bounds check)**. If an array has been declared as consisting of 10 elements, for example, and you use an index of 12, which is outside the bounds of the array, C will not notify you of the error when the program is compiled. The program will attempt to access element 12 by skipping over the appropriate number of bytes from the start of the array. Usually this results in a program crash—but not always. If the accessed locations contain a data value, the program will attempt to use this value. This can lead to more errors, which are particularly troublesome to locate, especially if the value has been changed and the variable legitimately assigned to the storage location is used at a different point in the program.

During output, individual array elements can be displayed using the `printf()` function or complete sections of the array can be displayed by including a `printf()` function call within a `for` loop. Examples of this are

```
printf("%lf," price[6]);
```

and

```
printf("The value of element %d is %d", i, grades[i]);
```

and

```
#define NUMELS 20
for(n = 5; n < NUMELS; n++)
     printf("%d %lf", n, price[n]);
```

The first call to `printf()` displays the value of the double-precision subscripted variable `price[6]`. The second call to `printf()` displays the value of `i` and the value of `grades[i]` . Before this statement can be executed, `i` needs to have an assigned value. Finally, the last example includes `printf()` within a `for` loop. Both the value of the index and the value of the elements from 5 to 20 are displayed.

Program 8.1 illustrates these input and output techniques using an array named `grades` that is defined to store five integer numbers. Included in the program are two `for` loops. The first `for` loop is used to cycle through each array element and allows the user to input individual array values. After five values have been entered, the second `for` loop is used to display the stored values.

Program 8.1

```
#include <stdio.h>
int main()
{
  #define MAXGRADES 5
  int grades[MAXGRADES];
  int i;

  /* input the grades */
  for (i = 0; i < MAXGRADES; i++)
  {
    printf("Enter a grade: ");
    scanf("%d", &grades[i]);
  }

  /* display the grades */
  for (i = 0; i < MAXGRADES; i++)
    printf("grades %d is %d\n", i, grades[i]);

  return 0;
}
```

Following is a sample run using Program 8.1:

```
Enter a grade: 85
Enter a grade: 90
Enter a grade: 78
Enter a grade: 75
Enter a grade: 92
grades 0 is 85
grades 1 is 90
grades 2 is 78
grades 3 is 75
grades 4 is 92
```

In reviewing the output produced by Program 8.1, pay particular attention to the difference between the displayed index value and the numerical value stored in the corresponding array element. The index value refers to the location of the element in the array, whereas the subscripted variable refers to the value stored in the designated location.

In addition to simply displaying the values stored in each array element, the elements can also be processed by appropriately referencing the desired element. For example, in Program 8.2, each element's value is accumulated in a total, which is displayed upon completion of the individual display of each array element.

Program 8.2

```
#include <stdio.h>
int main()
{
  #define MAXGRADES 5
  int grades[MAXGRADES];
  int i, total = 0;

  /* input the grades */
  for (i = 0; i < MAXGRADES; i++)    {
    printf("Enter a grade: ");
    scanf("%d", &grades[i]);
  }

  /* display and total the grades */
  printf("\nThe total of the grades ");
  for (i = 0; i < MAXGRADES; i++)
  {
    printf("%d ", grades[i]);
      total += grades[i];
  }

  printf("is %d\n", total);  /* display the total */

  return 0;
}
```

Following is a sample run using Program 8.2:

```
Enter a grade: 85
Enter a grade: 90
Enter a grade: 78
Enter a grade: 75
Enter a grade: 92
The total of the grades 85 90 78 75 92 is 420
```

Notice that in Program 8.2, unlike Program 8.1, only the numerical value stored in each array element is displayed and not their subscript values. Although the second `for` loop was used to accumulate the total of each element, the accumulation could also have been accomplished in the first loop by placing the statement `total += grades[i];` after the `scanf()` call used to enter a value. Also notice that the `printf()` call used to display the total is made outside of the second `for` loop. This ensures that the total is displayed only once, after all values have been added to the total. If this `printf()` call is placed inside the `for` loop, five totals are displayed, with only the last displayed total containing the sum of all of the array values.

EXERCISES 8.1

Short Answer Questions

1. Write array declarations for the following:
   a. A list of 60 double-precision interest rates
   b. A list of 30 double-precision temperatures
   c. A list of 25 characters, each representing a code
   d. A list of 100 integer years
   e. A list of 26 double-precision coupon rates
   f. A list of 1000 double-precision distances
   g. A list of 20 integer code numbers

2. Write appropriate notation for the first, third, and seventh elements of the following arrays:
   a. `int grade[20];`
   b. `double grade[10];`
   c. `double amps[16];`
   d. `double dist[15];`
   e. `double velocity[25];`
   f. `double time[100];`

3. a. Write individual `scanf()` function calls that can be used to enter values into the first, third, and seventh elements of each of the arrays declared in Questions 2a through 2f.
   b. Write a `for` loop that can be used to enter values for the complete array declared in Exercise 2a.

4. a. Write individual `printf()` function calls that can be used to print the values from the first, third, and seventh elements of each of the arrays declared in Questions 2a through 2f.
   b. Write a `for` loop that can be used to display values for the complete array declared in Question 2a.

5. List the elements that will be displayed by the following sections of code:
   a.
   ```
   for (m = 1; m <= 5; m++)
   printf("%d ",a[m]);
   ```
   b.
   ```
   for (k = 1; k <= 5; k = k + 2)
   printf("%d ",a[k]);
   ```
   c.
   ```
   for (j = 3; j <= 10; j++)
   printf("%f ",b[j]);
   ```

d.
```
for (k = 3; k <= 12; k = k + 3)
printf("%f ",b[k]);
```
e.
```
for (i = 2; i < 11; i = i + 2)
printf("%lf ",c[i]);
```

Programming Exercises

1. a. Write a C program to input the following values into an array named `prices`: 10.95, 16.32, 12.15, 8.22, 15.98, 26.22, 13.54, 6.45, 18.59. After the data is entered, your program should output the values.
   b. Repeat Exercise 1a, but after the data is entered, have your program display them in the following form:

```
10.95 16.32 12.15
8.22 15.98 26.22
13.54 6.45 18.59
```

2. a. Write a C program to input 15 integer numbers into an array named `temp`. As each number is input, add the number into the total. After all numbers are input, display the numbers and their average.
   b. Repeat Exercise 2a, but locate the maximum number in the array (do not add the numbers) as the values are being input. (*Hint:* Set the maximum equal to 0 before the `for` loop used to input the numbers.)
   c. Repeat Exercise 2b, keeping track of both the maximum element in the array and the index number for the maximum. After displaying the numbers, your program should print the two messages:

```
The maximum value is: ____
This is element number ____ in the list of numbers
```

   Have your program display the correct values in place of the underlines in the messages.
   d. Repeat Exercise 2c, but have your program locate the minimum value of the data entered.

3. a. Write a C program to input the following integer numbers into an array named `grades`: 89, 95, 72, 83, 99, 54, 86, 75, 92, 73, 79, 75, 82, 73. As each number is input, add the numbers to the total. After all numbers are input and the total is obtained, calculate the average of the numbers and use the average to determine the deviation of each value from the average. Store each deviation in an array named `deviation`. Each deviation is obtained as the element value less the average of all the data. Have your program display each deviation alongside its corresponding element from the `grades` array.
   b. Calculate the variance of the data used in Exercise 3a. The variance is obtained by squaring each individual deviation and dividing the sum of the squared deviations by the number of deviations.

4. Write a C program that declares three one-dimensional arrays named `price`, `quantity`, and `amount`. Each array should be capable of holding 10 elements. Using a `for` loop, input values for the `price` and `quantity` arrays. The entries in the `amount` array should be the product of the corresponding values in the `price` and `quantity` arrays (thus, `amount[i] = quantity[i] * price[i];`). After all of the data has been entered, display the following output:

```
Quantity Price Amount
-------- ----- ------
```

   Under each column heading display the appropriate value.

5. a. Write a program that inputs 10 double-precision numbers into an array named `raw`. After 10 user-input numbers are entered into the array, your program should cycle through `raw` 10 times. During each pass through the array, your program should select the lowest value in `raw` and place the selected value in the next available slot in an array named `sorted`. Thus, when your program is complete, the sorted array should contain the numbers in `raw` in sorted order from lowest to highest. (*Hint:* Make sure to reset the lowest value selected during each pass to a very high number so that it is not selected again. You will need a second `for` loop within the first `for` loop to locate the minimum value for each pass.)
   b. The method used in Exercise 5a to sort the values in the array is very inefficient. Can you determine why? What might be a better method of sorting the numbers in an array?

8.2 Array Initialization

Arrays, like scalar variables, can be declared either within or outside a function. Arrays declared within a function have local arrays, and arrays declared outside a function have global scope. For example, consider the following section of code, which provides the most commonly used array declarations:

```
1  #define SIZE1 20
2  #define SIZE2 25
3  #define SIZE3 15
4
5  int gallons[SIZE1];          /* a global array */
6  static int dist[SIZE2];    /* a static global array */
7
8  int main()
9  {
10   int miles[SIZE3];                /* an auto local array */
11   static int course[SIZE3];     /* a static local array */
12        .
13        .
14   return 0;
15 }
```

As indicated in the code, the `gallons` and `dist` arrays declared in lines 5 and 6 are globally declared arrays, while the `miles` array declared in line 10 is an automatic local array, and the `course` array declared in line 11 is a `static` local array. As with scalar variables, all global arrays, `static` or not, and local `static` arrays are created once, at compilation time, and retain their values until the program declaring them finishes executing. All auto arrays, which can only have a local scope, are created and destroyed each time the function they are local to is called and completes its execution.

The individual elements of all global and static arrays (local or global) are, by default, set to 0 at compilation time. The values within auto local arrays are undefined. This means that, from a programming viewpoint, you must assume that the values in such arrays are effectively "garbage values" and you must explicitly initialize them yourself.

All array elements, no matter whether their scope is local or global, or their storage-class is static or auto, can be explicitly initialized within their declaration statements in the same manner as for scalar variables, except that the initializing elements must be included in braces and can only consist of constants or expressions using only constants. Examples of such initializations are[3]

```
#define NUMGRADES 5
int grades[NUMGRADES] = {98, 87, 92, 79, 85};
```

and

```
#define NUMCODES 6
char codes[NUMCODES] = {'s', 'a', 'm', 'p', 'l', e'};
```

and

```
#define SIZE 7
double width[SIZE] = {10.96, 6.43, 2.58, .86, 5.89, 7.56, 8.22};
```

Initializers are applied in the order in which they are written, with the first value used to initialize element 0, the second value used to initialize element 1, and so on, until all values have been used. Thus, in the declaration

```
int grades[NUMGRADES] = {98, 87, 92, 79, 85};
```

grades[0] is initialized to 98, grades[1] is initialized to 87, grades[2] is initialized to 92, grades[3] is initialized to 79, and grades[4] is initialized to 85.

Because white space is ignored in C, initializations may be continued across multiple lines. For example, the declaration

```
#define NUMGALS 20
int gallons[NUMGALS] = {19, 16, 14, 19, 20, 18, /* initializing values */
                         12, 10, 22, 15, 18, 17, /* may extend across */
                         16, 14, 23, 19, 15, 18, /* multiple lines */
                         21, 5 };
```

uses four lines to initialize all of the array elements.

If the number of initializers is less than the declared number of elements listed in square brackets, the initializers are applied starting with array element 0. Thus, in the declaration

```
#define ARRAYSIZE 7
double length[ARRAYSIZE] = {8.8, 6.4, 4.9, 11.2};
```

only length[0], length[1], length[2], and length[3] are initialized with the listed values. The other array elements will be initialized to 0, except for local auto arrays.

[3]In older versions of C (non-ANSI), only global (static or nonstatic) and local static arrays could be initialized within their declarations statements. Local automatic arrays could not be initialized within their declaration statements.

Unfortunately, there is no method to either indicate repetition of an initialization value or initialize later array elements without first specifying values for earlier elements.

If no specific initializers are given in the declaration statement, all global and static numerical array elements, as has been previously stated, are set to 0. For example, the declaration

```
#define SIZE 100
int distance[SIZE];
```

sets all elements of the `distance` array equal to 0 at compilation time.

A unique feature of initializers is that the size of an array may be omitted when initializing values are included in the declaration statement. For example, the declaration

```
int gallons[] = {16, 12, 10, 14, 11};
```

reserves enough storage room for five elements. Similarly, the following two declarations are equivalent:

```
#define NUMCODES 6
char codes[NUMCODES] = {'s', 'a', 'm', 'p', 'l', 'e'};
```

and

```
char codes[] = {'s', 'a', 'm', 'p', 'l', 'e'};
```

Both of these declarations set aside six character locations for an array named `codes`. An interesting and useful simplification can also be used when initializing character arrays. For example, the declaration

```
char codes[] = "sample"; /* no braces or commas */
```

uses the string "`sample`" to initialize the `codes` array. Recall that a string is any sequence of characters enclosed in double quotes. This last declaration creates an array named `codes` with seven elements and fills the array with the seven characters illustrated in Figure 8.6. The first six characters, as expected, consist of the letters `s`, `a`, `m`, `p`, `l`, and `e`. The last character, which is the escape sequence `\0`, is called the **NULL** character. The **NULL** character is automatically appended to all strings by the C compiler. This character has an internal storage code that is numerically equal to 0 (the storage code of the 0 character has a numerical value of 48, so the two cannot be confused by the computer) and is used as a marker, or sentinel, to mark the end of a string. As we shall see in the next chapter, this marker is invaluable when manipulating strings of characters.

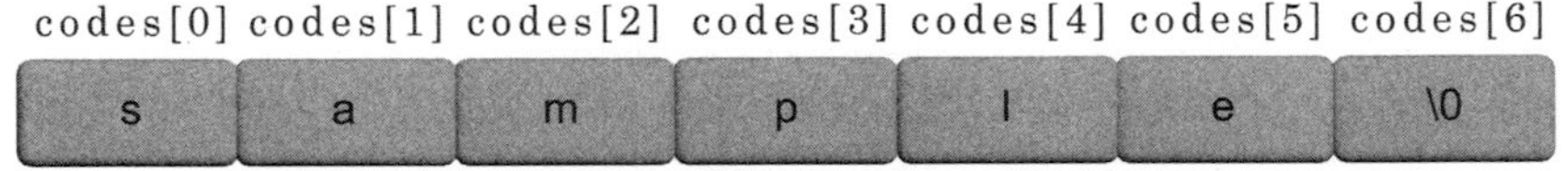

Figure 8.6 A string is terminated with a special sentinel

Once values have been assigned to array elements, either through initialization within the declaration statement or by using interactive input, the array elements can be processed as described in the previous section. For example, Program 8.3 illustrates the initialization of array elements within the declaration of the array and then uses a `for` loop to locate the maximum value stored in the array.

Program 8.3

```
#include <stdio.h>
int main()
{
  #define MAXELS 5
  int nums[MAXELS] = {2, 18, 1, 27, 16};
  int i, max;

  max = nums[0];

  for (i = 1; i < MAXELS; i++)
     if (max < nums[i])
       max = nums[i];

  printf("The maximum value is %d\n", max);

  return 0;
}
```

The output produced by Program 8.3 is

```
The maximum value is 27
```

EXERCISES 8.2

Short Answer Questions

1. Write array declarations, including initializers, for the following:
   a. A list of 10 integer grades: 89, 75, 82, 93, 78, 95, 81, 88, 77, 82
   b. A list of five double-precision amounts: 10.62, 13.98, 18.45, 12.68, 14.76
   c. A list of 100 double-precision interest rates; the first six rates are 6.29, 6.95, 8.25, 8.35, 8.40, 8.42
   d. A list of 64 double-precision temperatures; the first 10 temperatures are 78.2, 69.6, 68.5, 83.9, 55.4, 68.0, 49.8, 58.3, 62.5, 71.6
   e. A list of 15 character codes; the first seven codes are f, j, m, q, t, w, z
2. The string of characters "`Good Morning`" is to be stored in a character array named `goodString`. Write the declaration for this array in three different ways.

Programming Exercises

1. a. Write declaration statements to store the string of characters "Input the Following Data" in a character array named messag1, the string "---------------" in the array named messag2, the string "Enter the Date:" in the array named messag3, and the string "Enter the Account Number:" in the array named messag4.

   b. Include the array declarations written in Exercise 1a in a program that uses the printf() function to display the messages. For example, the statement printf("%s",messag1); causes the string stored in the messag1 array to be displayed. Your program will require four such statements to display the four individual messages. Using the printf() function with the %s control sequence to display a string requires that the end-of-string marker \0 is present in the character array used to store the string.

2. a. Write a declaration to store the string "This is a test" into an array named strtest. Include the declaration in a program to display the message using the following loop:

   ```
   for (i = 0; i <= 14; i++)
     printf("%c", strtest[i]);
   ```

   b. Modify the for statement in Exercise 4a to display only the array characters t, e, s, and t.

   c. Include the array declaration written in Exercise 2a in a program that uses the printf() function to display characters in the array. For example, the statement printf("%s",strtest); will cause the string stored in the strtest array to be displayed. Using this statement requires that the last character in the array be the end-of-string marker \0.

   d. Repeat Exercise 2a using a while loop. (*Hint:* Stop the loop when the \0 escape sequence is detected. The expression while (strtest[i] != '\0') can be used.)

3. a. Write a declaration to store the following values in an array named prices: 16.24, 18.98, 23.75, 16.29, 19.54, 14.22, 11.13, 15.39. Include the declaration in a program that displays the values in the array.

   b. Repeat Exercise 3a, but make the array a global array.

4. Write a C program that uses a declaration statement to store the following numbers in an array named rates: 18.24, 25.63, 5.94, 33.92, 3.71, 32.84, 35.93, 18.24, 6.92. Your program should then locate and display both the maximum and minimum values in the array.

5. Write a C program that stores the following prices in a global array: 9.92, 6.32, 12.63, 5.95, 10.29. Your program should also create two automatic arrays named units and amounts, each capable of storing five double-precision numbers. Using a for loop and a scanf() function call, have your program accept five user-input numbers into the units array when the program is run. Your program should store the product of the corresponding values in the prices and units arrays in the amounts array (for example, amounts[1] = prices[1] * units[1]) and display the following output (fill in the table appropriately):

```
Price    Units    Amount
-----    -----    ------
9.92       .        .
6.32       .        .
12.63      .        .
5.95       .        .
10.29      .        .
                  ------
Total:              .
```

8.3 Arrays as Function Arguments

Individual array elements are passed to a function by simply including them as subscripted variables in the function call argument list. For example, the function call

```
findMin(grades[2], grades[6]);
```

passes the values of the elements `grades[2]` and `grades[6]` to the function `findMin()`.

Passing a complete array to a function is in many respects an easier operation than passing individual elements. The called function receives access to the actual array, rather than a copy of the values in the array. For example, if `grades` is an array, the function call `findMax(grades);` makes the complete `grades` array available to the `findMax()` function. This is different from passing a single variable to a function.

Recall that when a single scalar argument is passed to a function, the called function receives only a *copy* of the passed value, which is stored in one of the function's value parameters. If arrays were passed in this manner, a copy of the complete array would have to be created. For large arrays, making duplicate copies of the array for each function call would waste computer storage, consume execution time, and frustrate the effort to return multiple element changes made by the called program. To avoid these problems, the called function is given direct access to the original array. Thus, any changes made by the called function are made directly to the array itself. For the following specific examples of function calls, assume that the arrays `nums`, `keys`, `units`, and `prices` are declared as:

```
int nums[5]; /* an array of five integers */
char keys[256]; /* an array of 256 characters */
double units[500], prices[500]; /* two arrays of 500 doubles */
```

For these arrays, the following function calls can be made:

```
findMax(nums);
findCh(keys);
calcTot(units, prices);
```

In each case, the called function receives direct access to the named array. On the receiving side, the called function must be alerted that an array is being made available. For example, suitable function headers for the previous functions are

```
int findMax(int vals[5])
char findCh(chr inKeys[256])
void calcTot(double arr1[500], double arr2[500])
```

In each of these function declarations, the names in the parameter list are chosen by the programmer and are local to the function. However, the internal local names used by the functions still refer to the original array created outside the function. This is made clear in Program 8.4.

Program 8.4

```
#include <stdio.h>
#define MAXELS 5

void findMax(int [MAXELS]); /* function prototype */

int main()
{
  int nums[MAXELS] = {2, 18, 1, 27, 16};

  findMax(nums);

  return 0;
}

void findMax(int vals[MAXELS]) /* find the maximum value */
{
  int i, max = vals[0];

  for (i = 1; i < MAXELS; i++)
    if (max < vals[i])
      max = vals[i];

  printf("The maximum value is %d\n", max);
}
```

Notice that the function prototype for `findMax()` declares that `findMax()` returns no value. Only one array is created in Program 8.4. In `main()`, this array is known as `nums`, and in `findMax()`, the array is known as `vals`. As illustrated in Figure 8.7, both names refer to the same array. Thus, in Figure 8.7, `vals[3]` is the same element as `nums[3]`.

The argument and parameter declarations in the `findMax()` prototype and the function header line, respectively, in Program 8.4 actually contain extra information that is not required by the function. All that `findMax()` must know is that the parameter `vals` refers to an array of integers. Because the array has been created in `main()` and no additional storage space is needed in `findMax()`, the declaration for `vals` can omit the size of the array. Thus, an alternative function header is

```
void findMax(int vals[])
```

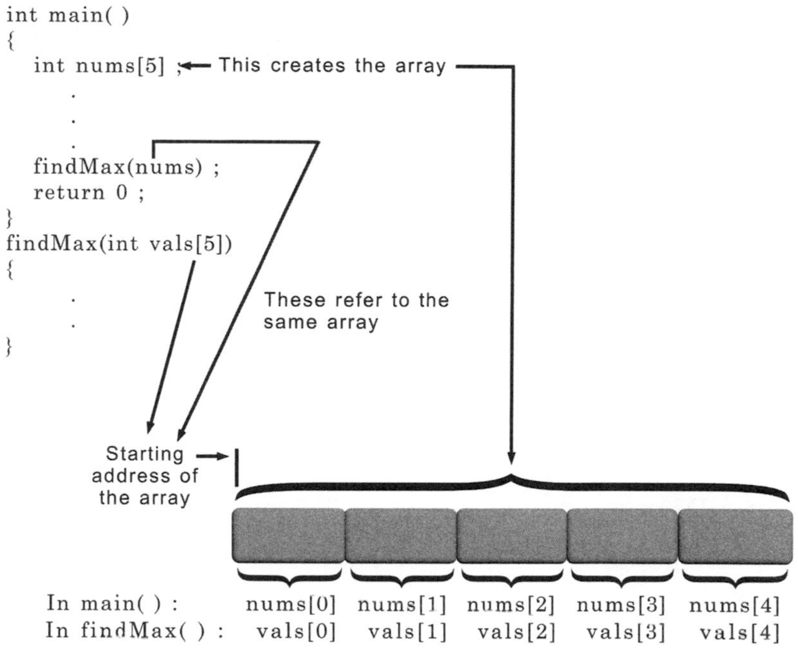

Figure 8.7 Only one array is created

This form of the function header makes more sense when you realize that only one item is actually passed to `findMax()` when the function is called, which is the starting address of the `nums` array, as illustrated in Figure 8.8.

Because only one item is passed to `findMax`, the number of elements in the array need not be included in the declaration for `vals`.[4] In fact, it is generally advisable to omit the size of the array in the function header line. For example, consider the more general form of `findMax()`, which can be used to find the maximum value of an integer array of arbitrary size.

```
int findMax(int vals[], int numels) /* find the maximum value */
{
  int i, max = vals[0];

  for (i = 1; i < numels; i++)
    if (max < vals[i])
      max = vals[i];

  return(max);
}
```

[4]An important consequence of this is that `findMax()` has direct access to the passed array. This means that any change to an element of the `vals` array actually is a change to the `nums` array. This is significantly different from the situation with scalar variables, where the called function does not receive direct access to the passed variable.

This more general form of `findMax()` declares that the function returns an integer value. The function expects the starting address of an integer array and the number of elements in the array as arguments. Then, using the number of elements as the boundary for its search, the function's `for` loop causes each array element to be examined in sequential order to locate the maximum value. Program 8.5 illustrates the use of `findMax()` in a complete program.

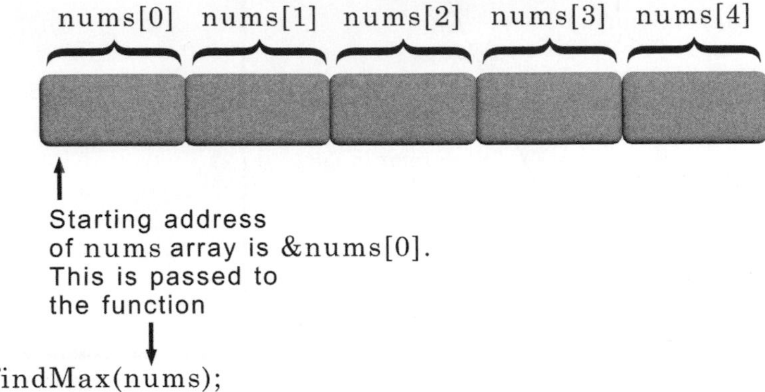

Figure 8.8 The starting address of the array is passed

Program 8.5

```
#include <stdio.h>
int findMax(int [], int); /* function prototype */

int main()
{
  #define MAXELS 5
  int nums[MAXELS] = {2, 18, 1, 27, 16};

  printf("The maximum value is %d\n", findMax(nums, MAXELS));

  return 0;
}

int findMax(int vals[], int numels)
{
  int i, max = vals[0];

  for (i = 1; i < numels; i++)
    if (max < vals[i])
      max = vals[i];
```

```

   return (max);
}
```

The output displayed when Program 8.5 is executed is

```
The maximum value is 27
```

EXERCISES 8.3

Short Answer Questions

1. The following declaration was used to create the `prices` array:

   ```
   double prices[500];
   ```

   Write two different function header lines for a function named `sortArray()` that accepts the `prices` array as a parameter named `inArray` and returns no value.

2. The following declaration was used to create the `keys` array:

   ```
   char keys[256];
   ```

   Write two different function header lines for a function named `findKey()` that accepts the `keys` array as a parameter named `select` and returns no value.

3. The following declaration was used to create the `rates` array:

   ```
   double rates[256];
   ```

   Write two different function header lines for a function named `prime()` that accepts the `rates` array as a parameter named `rates` and returns a double-precision value.

Programming Exercises

1. a. Modify the `findMax()` function in Program 8.5 to locate the minimum value of the passed array. Rename the function `findMin()`.
   b. Include the function written in Exercise 1a in a complete program and run the program on a computer.

2. Write a program that has a declaration in `main()` to store the following numbers into an array named `rates`: 6.5, 8.2, 8.5, 8.3, 8.6, 9.4, 9.6, 9.8, 10.0. There should be a function call to `show()` that accepts the `rates` array as a parameter named `rates` and then displays the numbers in the array.

3. a. Write a program that has a declaration in `main()` to store the string "`Vacation is near`" into an array named `message`. There should be a function call to `display()` that accepts `message` in a parameter named `strng` and then displays the contents of the message.
   b. Modify the `display()` function written in Exercise 3a to display the first eight elements of the `message` array.

4. Write a program that declares three one-dimensional arrays named `price`, `quantity`, and `amount`. Each array should be declared in `main()` and should be capable of holding 10 double-precision numbers. The numbers that should be stored in `price` are 10.62, 14.89, 13.21, 16.55, 18.62, 9.47, 6.58, 18.32, 12.15, 3.98. The numbers that should be stored in `quantity` are 4, 8.5, 6, 8.35, 9, 15.3, 3, 5.4, 2.9, 4.8. Your program should pass these three arrays to a function called `extend()`, which should calculate the elements in the `amount` array as the product of the equivalent elements in the `price` and `quantity` arrays (for example, `amount[1] = price[1] * quantity[1]`). After `extend()` has put values into the `amount` array, the values in the array should be displayed from within `main()`.

5. Write a C program that includes two functions named `calcAvg()` and `variance()`. The `calcAvg()` function should calculate and return the average of the values stored in an array named `testvals`. The array should be declared in `main()` and include the values 89, 95, 72, 83, 99, 54, 86, 75, 92, 73, 79, 75, 82, 73. The `variance()` function should calculate and return the variance of the data. The variance is obtained by subtracting the average from each value in `testvals`, squaring the differences obtained, adding their squares, and dividing by the number of elements in `testvals`. The values returned from `calcAvg()` and `variance()` should be displayed using `printf()` function calls in `main()`.

8.4 Case Study: Computing Averages and Standard Deviations

The following application is presented to both illustrate array processing and further your understanding of using arrays as function arguments. In this application two statistical functions are created to determine the average and standard deviation, respectively of an array of numbers.

Requirements Specification

Two functions are to be developed; the first function is to determine the average and the second function is to determine the standard deviation of a list of integer numbers. Each function must be capable of accepting the numbers as an array and returning their calculated values to the calling function.

We now apply the top-down development procedure to developing the required functions.

Analyze the Problem

Using the software development process presented in Section 1.4, we now analyze the requirements specification by explicitly listing the provided input data, required output, and the algorithms that relate the inputs to the outputs.

a. Determine the Input Items The input item defined in the problem statement is a list of integer numbers.

b. Determine the Desired Outputs The statement of the problem indicates that two functions are to be developed. The first function is to return an average and the second function a standard deviation.

c. List the Algorithms Relating the Inputs and Outputs The first function is to return the average of the numbers in a passed array and the second function the standard deviation. These items are determined using the following algorithms:

Average Function:
Calculate the average by adding the grades and dividing by the number of grades that were added.

Standard Deviation Function:

1. ***Subtract the average from each individual grade. This results in a set of new numbers, each of which is called a deviation.***
2. ***Square each deviation found in Step 1.***
3. ***Add the squared deviations and divide the sum by the number of deviations.***
4. ***The square root of the number found in Step 3 is the standard deviation.***

Notice that the calculation of the standard deviation requires the average, which means that the standard deviation can be calculated only after the average has been computed. Thus, in addition to requiring the array of integers and the number of values in the array, the standard deviation function also will require that the average be passed to it. This is the advantage of specifying algorithms, in detail, before any coding is done; it ensures that all necessary inputs and requirements are discovered early in the programming process.

To ensure that we understand the required processing, we will do a hand calculation. For this calculation we will arbitrarily assume that the average and standard deviation of the following 10 grades are to be determined: 98, 82, 67, 54, 78, 83, 95, 76, 68, and 63.

The average of this data is determined as

$$\text{Average} = (98 + 82 + 67 + 54 + 78 + 83 + 95 + 76 + 68 + 63)/10 = 76.4$$

The standard deviation is calculated by first determining the sum of the squared deviations. The standard deviation is then obtained by dividing the resulting sum by 10 and taking its square root.

$$\begin{aligned}\text{Sum of squared deviations} &= (98 - 76.4)^2 + (82 - 76.4)^2 \\ &+ (67 - 76.4)^2 + (54 - 76.4)^2 \\ &+ (78 - 76.4)^2 + (83 - 76.4)^2 \\ &+ (95 - 76.4)^2 + (76 - 76.4)^2 \\ &+ (68 - 76.4)^2 + (63 - 76.4)^2 \\ &= 1730.400700\end{aligned}$$

$$\text{Standard Deviation} = \sqrt{1730.4007/10} = \sqrt{173.04007} = 13.154470$$

Because the size of the list is not specified in the problem statement and to make our functions as general as possible, we will design both functions to handle any size list passed to them. This requires that the exact number of elements in the array must also be passed to each function at the time of the function call. From each function's viewpoint this means that it must be capable of receiving at least two input items as arguments: an array of arbitrary size and an integer number corresponding to the number of elements in the passed array. Additionally, the function used to determine the standard deviation must also be capable of receiving the average that is computed by the first function.

Historical Note

Statistics

The sum, the sum of squares, and the average of a list of numbers are commonly used quantities in statistics. In fact, some of the most important applications of mathematics and computing to the real world involve statistics. Whether you are in business, engineering, politics, government, weather forecasting, sports, education, or virtually any other field you can name, being able to handle statistics will give you a decided advantage. So by all means, take one or more courses in statistics.

It has been claimed that "statistics don't lie, but some statisticians do," and this is true. Statistical methods and data are sometimes misused by people to convince others—people who do not understand statistics—of something the statistics really do not support.

Select an Overall Solution Algorithm

Once again, the Problem-Solver Algorithm presented in Section 1.4 can be used as the basis for solving this programming problem. As applied to this problem, the algorithm becomes

Initialize an array of integers
Call the average function
Call the standard deviation function
Display the returned value of the average function
Display the returned value of the standard deviation function

Write the Functions

In writing functions it is convenient to concentrate initially on the header line. The body of the function can then be written to process the input arguments correctly to produce the desired results.

Naming our averaging function `findAvg()`, and arbitrarily selecting the argument names `nums`, and `numel` for the passed array and the number of elements, respectively, the function header becomes

```
double findAvg(int nums[], int numel)
```

This begins the definition of the averaging function as accepting an array of integer values and an integer number. As illustrated by our previous hand calculation, the average of a set of integer numbers can be a double-precision number; therefore, the function is defined as returning a double-precision value. The body of the function calculates the average as described by the algorithm developed in the analysis of the problem. Thus, the completed `findAvg()` function becomes

```
double findAvg(int nums[], int numel)
{
  int i;
  double sumnums = 0.0;

  for (i = 0; i < numel; i++)  /* calculate the sum of the grades */
    sumnums = sumnums + nums[i];

  return (sumnums/numel);     /* calculate and return the average */
}
```

In the body of the function is a `for` loop that is used to sum the individual numbers. Notice also that the termination value of the loop counter in the `for` loop is `numel`, the number of integers in the array that is passed to the function through the argument list. The use of this argument gives the function its generality and allows it to be used for input arrays of any size. For example, calling the function with the statement

```
findAvg(values,10)
```

tells the function that `numel` is 10 and the values array consists of 10 values, while the statement

```
findAvg(values,1000)
```

tells `findAvg()` that `numel` is 1000 and that the values array consists of 1000 numbers. In both calls the actual argument named `values` corresponds to the parameter named `nums` within the `findAvg()` function.

Using similar reasoning as that for the averaging function, the function header for the standard deviation routine, which we will name `stdDev()` becomes

```
double stdDev(int nums[], int numel, double av)
```

This header begins the definition of the `stdDev()` function. It defines the function as returning a double-precision value and accepting an array of integers, an integer value, and a double-precision value as inputs to the function. The body of the `stdDev()` function must calculate the standard deviation as described in the analysis of the problem. The complete standard deviation function becomes

```
double stdDev(int nums[], int numel, double av)
{
  int i;
  double sumdevs = 0.0;

  for (i = 0; i < numel; i++)
    sumdevs = sumdevs + pow((nums[i] - av),2.0);

  return(sqrt(sumdevs/numel));
}
```

Test and Debug the Functions

Testing a function requires writing a `main()` program unit to call the function and display the returned results. Program 8.6 uses such a `main()` unit to set up a `values` array with the data previously used in our hand calculation and to call the `findAvg()` and `stdDev()` function.

Program 8.6

```
#include <stdio.h>
#include <math.h>

double findAvg(int [], int);          /* function prototype */
double stdDev(int [], int, double);   /* function prototype */

```

```
int main()
{
  #define NUMELS 10
  int values[NUMELS] = {98, 82, 67, 54, 78, 83, 95, 76, 68, 63};
  double average, stddev;

  average = findAvg(values, NUMELS); /* call the function */
  stddev = stdDev(values, NUMELS, average); /* call the function */

  printf("The average of the numbers is %5.2f\n", average);
  printf("The standard deviation of the numbers is %5.2f\n", stddev);

  return 0;
}

double findAvg(int nums[], int numel)
{
  int i;
  double sumnums = 0.0;

  for (i = 0; i < numel; i++)  /* calculate the sum of the grades */
    sumnums = sumnums + nums[i];

  return (sumnums / numel);    /* calculate and return the average */
}

double stdDev(int nums[], int numel, double av)
{
  int i;
  double sumdevs = 0.0;

  for (i = 0; i < numel; i++)
    sumdevs = sumdevs + pow((nums[i] - av),2);

  return(sqrt(sumdevs/numel));
}
```

A test run using Program 8.6 produced the following display:

```
The average of the numbers is 76.40
The standard deviation of the numbers is 13.15
```

Although this result agrees with our previous hand calculation, testing is really not complete without verifying the calculation at the boundary points. In this case such a test consists of checking the calculation with all of the same values, such as all 0s and all 100s. Another simple test would be to use five 0s and five 100s. We leave these tests as an exercise.

EXERCISES 8.4

Programming Exercises

1. Modify Program 8.6 so that the grades are entered into the `values` array using a function named `entvals()`.

2. Rewrite Program 8.6 to determine the average and standard deviation of the following list of 15 grades: 68, 72, 78, 69, 85, 98, 95, 75, 77, 82, 84, 91, 89, 65, 74.

3. Modify Program 8.6 so that a high function is called that determines the highest value in the passed array and returns this value to the main program unit for display.

4. Modify Program 8.6 so that a function named `sort` is called after the call to the `stdDev` function. The `sort` function should sort the grades into increasing order for display by `main()`.

5. a. Write a C program that reads a list of double-precision grades from the keyboard into an array named `grades`. The grades are to be counted as they are read, and entry is to be terminated when a negative value has been entered. Once all of the grades have been input, your program should find and display the sum and average of the grades. The grades should then be listed with an asterisk (*) in front of each grade that is below the average.

   b. Extend the program written for Exercise 5a to display each grade and its letter equivalent. Assume the following scale:

   A grade between 90 and 100 is an A.

   A grade greater than or equal to 80 and less than 90 is a B.

   A grade greater than or equal to 70 and less than 80 is a C.

   A grade greater than or equal to 60 and less than 70 is a D.

   A grade less than 60 is an F.

6. Define an array named `PeopleTypes` that can store a maximum of 50 integer values that will be entered at the keyboard. Enter a series of 1s, 2s, 3s, and 4s into the array, where a 1 represents an infant, a 2 represents a child, a 3 represents a teenager, and a 4 represents an adult who was present at a local school function. Any other integer value should not be accepted as valid input and data entry should stop when a negative value has been entered.

   Your program should count the number of each 1, 2, 3, and 4 in the array and output a list of how many infants, children, teenagers, and adults were at the school function.

7. Write a program that initially accepts a set of numerical grades from the keyboard into an array. The maximum number of grades is 50 and data entry should be terminated when a negative number has been entered. Have your program sort and print the grades in *descending* order.

8. Write and test a function that returns the position of the largest and smallest values in an array of double-precision numbers.

9. Given a one-dimensional array of integer numbers, write and test a function that prints the elements in reverse order.

10. a. Write a C program that keeps track of the frequency of occurrence of each vowel as lines of text are typed at the keyboard. The end of the text should be signified by entry of an EOF (see Section 5.3) marker (Ctrl z for DOS and Ctrl d for Unix). The output of your program should be a count of each vowel encountered in the input text.
    b. Add a function to the program written for Exercise 10a that displays a histogram of the number of each vowel encountered. For example, if your program detected the letter a five times, the letter e three times, the letter i two times, the letter o four times, and the letter u 1 time, the histogram should appear as

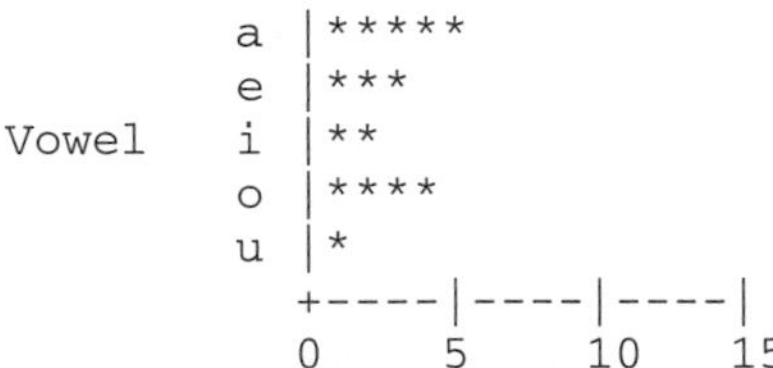

```
            a  |*****
            e  |***
Vowel       i  |**
            o  |****
            u  |*
               +----|----|----|
               0    5    10   15
```

11. a. Define an array with a maximum of 20 integer values and fill the array with numbers either input from the keyboard or assigned by the program. Then write a function named `split()` that reads the array and places all 0 or positive numbers into an array named `positive` and all negative numbers into an array named `negative`. Finally, have your program call a function that displays the values in both the positive and negative arrays.
    b. Extend the program written for Exercise 11a to sort the positive and negative arrays into ascending order before they are displayed.

12. Using the `rand()` C library functions, fill an array of 1000 double-precision numbers with random numbers that have been scaled to the range 1 to 100. Then determine and display the number of random numbers having values between 1 and 50 and the number having values greater than 50. What do you expect the output counts should be?

13. In many statistical analysis programs, data values that are considerably outside the range of the majority of values are simply dropped from consideration. Using this information, write a C program that accepts up to 10 double-precision values from a user and determines and displays the average and standard deviation of the input values. All values that are more than four standard deviations away from the computed average are to be displayed and dropped from any further calculation, and a new average and standard deviation should be computed and displayed.

14. Given a one-dimensional array of double-precision numbers named `num`, write a function that determines the sum of the numbers
    a. using repetition.
    b. using recursion. (*Hint:* If n = 1, then the sum is `num[0]`; otherwise, the sum is `num[n]` plus the sum of the first (n - 1) elements.)

8.5 Two-Dimensional Arrays

A two-dimensional array, which is sometimes referred to as a table, consists of both rows and columns of elements. For example, the array of numbers

```
8 16 9 52
3 15 27 6
14 25 2 10
```

is a two-dimensional array of integers. This array consists of three rows and four columns. To reserve storage for this array, both the number of rows and the number of columns must be included in the array's declaration. Calling the array `val`, the appropriate declaration for this two-dimensional array is

```
#define NUMROWS 3
#define NUMCOLS 4
int val[NUMROWS][NUMCOLS];
```

Similarly, the declarations

```
#define NUMROWS 10
#define NUMCOLS 5
double prices[NUMROWS][NUMCOLS];
```

and

```
#define NUMROWS 6
#define NUMCOLS 26
char code[NUMROWS][NUMCOLS];
```

declare that the array `prices` consists of 10 rows and 5 columns of double-precision numbers and that the array `code` consists of 6 rows and 26 columns of characters.

Each element in a two-dimensional array is identified by its position in the array. As illustrated in Figure 8.9, the term `val[1][3]` uniquely identifies the element in row 1, column 3. As with one-dimensional array variables, double-dimensional array variables can be used anywhere that scalar variables are valid. Examples that use elements of the `val` array are

```
num = val[2][3];
val[0][0] = 62;
newnum = 4 * (val[1][0] - 5);
sumrow0 = val[0][0] + val[0][1] + val[0][2] + val[0][3];
```

The last statement causes the values of the four elements in row 0 to be added and the sum to be stored in the scalar variable `sumrow0`.

As with single-dimensional arrays, two-dimensional arrays can be initialized from within their declaration statements. This is done by listing the initial values within braces and separating them by commas. Additionally, braces can be used to separate individual rows. For example, the declaration

```
#define NUMROWS 3
#define NUMCOLS 4
int val[NUMROWS][NUMCOLS] = { {8,16,9,52},
                              {3,15,27,6},
                              {14,25,2,10} };
```

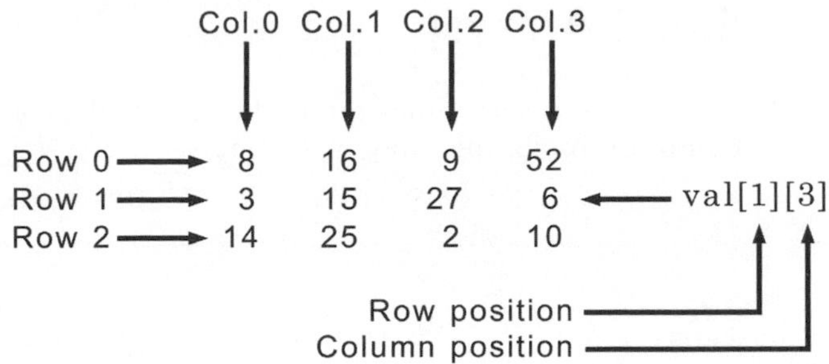

Figure 8.9 Each array element is identified by its row and column

declares `val` to be an array of integers with three rows and four columns, with the initial values given in the declaration. The first set of internal braces contains the values for row 0 of the array, the second set of braces contains the values for row 1, and the third set contains the values for row 2.

Although the commas in the initialization braces are always required, the inner braces can be omitted. Thus, the initialization for `val` may be written as

```
int val[NUMROWS][NUMCOLS] = { 8,16,9,52,
                              3,15,27,6,
                             14,25,2,10};
```

The separation of initial values into rows in the declaration statement is not necessary because the compiler assigns values beginning with the `[0][0]` element and proceeds row by row to fill in the remaining values. Thus, the initialization

```
int val[3][4] = {8,16,9,52,3,15,27,6,14,25,2,10};
```

is equally valid but does not clearly illustrate to another programmer where one row ends and another begins.

As illustrated in Figure 8.10, the initialization of a two-dimensional array is done in row order. First the elements in the first row are initialized, then the elements in the second row are initialized, and so on until the initializations are completed. This row ordering is also the same ordering used to store two-dimensional arrays. That is, array `element[0][0]` is stored first, followed by `element[0][1]`, followed by `element[0][2]`, and so on. Following the first row's elements are the second row's elements, and so on for all the rows in the array.

As with one-dimensional arrays, double-dimensional arrays may be displayed by individual element notation or by using loops (either `while` or `for`). This is illustrated by Program 8.7, which displays all the elements of a three-by-four two-dimensional array using two different techniques.

Initialization starts with this element

val[0][0] = 8 → val[0][1] = 16 → val[0][2] = 9 → val[0][3] = 52

val[1][0] = 3 → val[1][1] = 15 → val[1][2] = 27 → val[1][3] = 6

val[2][0] = 14 → val[2][1] = 25 → val[2][2] = 2 → val[2][3] = 10

Figure 8.10 Storage and initialization of the `val[]` array

Program 8.7

```
#include <stdio.h>
int main()
{
  #define NUMROWS 3
  #define NUMCOLS 4
  int val[NUMROWS][NUMCOLS] = {8,16,9,52,3,15,27,6,14,25,2,10};
  int i, j;

  printf("\nDisplay of val array by explicit element");
  printf("\n%2d %2d %2d %2d",
         val[0][0],val[0][1],val[0][2],val[0][3]);
  printf("\n%2d %2d %2d %2d",
         val[1][0],val[1][1],val[1][2],val[1][3]);
  printf("\n%2d %2d %2d %2d",
         val[2][0],val[2][1],val[2][2],val[2][3]);

  printf("\n\nDisplay of val array using a nested for loop");
  for (i = 0; i < NUMROWS; i++)
  {
    printf("\n"); /* start a new line for each row */
    for (j = 0; j < NUMCOLS; j++)
      printf("%2d ", val[i][j]);
  }
  printf("\n");

  return 0;
}
```

The display produced by Program 8.7 is

```
Display of val array by explicit element
8 16 9 52
3 15 27 6
14 25 2 10

Display of val array using a nested for loop
8 16 9 52
3 15 27 6
14 25 2 10
```

The first display of the `val` array produced by Program 8.7 is constructed by explicitly designating each array element. The second display of array element values, which is identical to the first, is produced using a nested `for` loop. Nested loops are especially useful when dealing with two-dimensional arrays because they allow the programmer to easily designate and cycle through each element. In Program 8.7, the variable `i` controls the outer loop and the variable `j` controls the inner loop. Each pass through the outer loop corresponds to a single row, with the inner loop supplying the appropriate column elements. After a complete row is printed, a new line is started for the next row. The effect is a display of the array in a row-by-row fashion.

Once two-dimensional array elements have been assigned, array processing can begin. Typically, `for` loops are used to process two-dimensional arrays because, as previously noted, they allow the programmer to easily designate and cycle through each array element. For example, the nested `for` loop in Program 8.8 is used to multiply each element in the `val` array by the scalar number 10 and display the resulting value.

Program 8.8

```
#include <stdio.h>
int main()
{
  #define NUMROWS 3
  #define NUMCOLS 4
  int val[NUMROWS][NUMCOLS] = {8,16,9,52,3,15,27,6,14,25,2,10};
  int i, j;

  /* multiply each element by 10 and display it */
  printf("\nDisplay of multiplied elements\n");
  for (i = 0; i < NUMROWS; i++)
  {
    printf("\n"); /* start a new line */
    for (j = 0; j < NUMCOLS; ++j)
    {
      val[i][j] = val[i][j] * 10;
      printf("%3d ", val[i][j]);
    } /* end of inner loop */
```

```
  } /* end of outer loop */
  printf("\n");

  return 0;
}
```

The output produced by Program 8.8 is

```
Display of multiplied elements

80 160 90 520
30 150 270 60
140 250 20 100
```

Passing two-dimensional arrays into functions is a process identical to passing one-dimensional arrays. The called function receives access to the entire array. For example, the function call `display(val);` makes the complete `val` array available to the function named `display()`. Thus, any changes made by `display()` are made directly to the `val` array. Assuming that the following two-dimensional arrays named `test`, `code`, and `stocks` are declared as:

```
int test[7][9];
char code[26][10];
double stocks[256][52];
```

the following function calls are valid:

```
findMax(test);
obtain(code);
price(stocks);
```

On the receiving side, the called function must be alerted that a two-dimensional array is being made available. For example, suitable function header lines for the previous functions are

```
int findMax(int nums[7][9])
char obtain(char key[26][10])
void price(double names[256][52])
```

In each of these function headers, the parameter names chosen are local to the function. However, the internal parameter names used by the function still refer to the original array created outside the function. If the array is a global one, there is no need to pass the array because the function could access the array by its global name. Program 8.9 illustrates passing a local, two-dimensional array into a function that displays the array's values.

Program 8.9

```c
#include <stdio.h>
#define ROWS 3
#define COLS 4

void display(int [ROWS][COLS]); /* function prototype */

int main()
{
  int val[ROWS][COLS] = {8,16,9,52,
                         3,15,27,6,
                         14,25,2,10};

  display(val);

  return 0;
}

void display(int nums[ROWS][COLS])
{
  int rowNum, colNum;

  for (rowNum = 0; rowNum < ROWS; rowNum++)
  {
    for(colNum = 0; colNum < COLS; colNum++)
      printf("%4d",nums[rowNum][colNum]);
    printf("\n");
  }
}
```

Only one array is created in Program 8.9. This array is known as `val` in `main()` and as `nums` in `display()`. Thus, `val[0][2]` refers to the same element as `nums[0][2]`.

Notice the use of the nested `for` loop in Program 8.9. Nested `for` statements are especially useful when dealing with multidimensional arrays because they allow the programmer to cycle through each element. In Program 8.9, the variable `rowNum` controls the outer loop and the variable `colNum` controls the inner loop. For each pass through the outer loop, which corresponds to a row, the inner loop makes one pass through the column elements. After a complete row is printed, the `\n` escape sequence causes a new line to be started for the next row. The effect is a display of the array in a row-by-row fashion

```
8 16 9 52
3 15 27 6
14 25 2 10
```

The parameter declaration for nums in display() contains extra information not required by the function. The declaration for nums can omit the row size of the array. Thus, an alternative function prototype is

```
void display(int[][COLS]);
```

and an alternative function header line is

```
void display(int nums[][4])
```

The reason the column size must be included whereas the row size is optional becomes obvious when you consider how the array elements are stored in memory. Starting with element val[0][0], each succeeding element is stored consecutively, row by row, as val[0][0], val[0][1], val[0][2], val[0][3], val[1][0], val[1][1], etc., as illustrated in Figure 8.11.

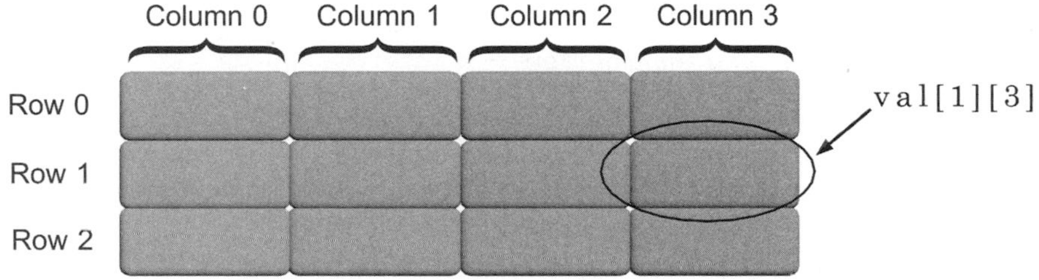

Figure 8.11 Storage of the val array

As with all array accesses, an individual element of the val array is obtained by adding an offset to the starting location of the array. For example, assuming an integer requires 4 bytes of storage, the element val[1][3] is located at an offset of 28 bytes from the start of the array. Internally, the computer uses the row subscript, columns subscript, and column size to determine this offset using the calculation shown in Figure 8.12. The number of columns is necessary in the offset calculation so that the computer can determine the number of positions to skip over to get to the desired row.

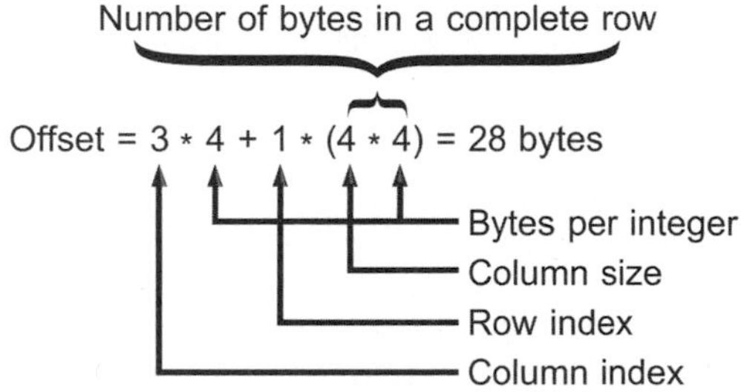

Figure 8.12 Determining an element's offset

Internal Array Element Location Algorithm [Optional][5]

Internally, each individual element in an array is obtained by adding an offset to the starting address of the array. Thus, the memory address of each array element is internally calculated as

Address of element i = starting array address + the offset

For single-dimensional arrays, the offset to the element with index `i` is calculated as

Offset = i * the size of an individual element

For two-dimensional arrays, the same address calculation is made, except that the offset is determined as follows:

Offset = column index value * the size of an individual element
+ row index value * number of bytes in a complete row

where the number of bytes in a complete row is calculated as

number of bytes in a complete row =
maximum column specification * the size of an individual element

For example, for an array of integers where each integer is stored using 4 bytes, the offset to the element whose index value is 5 is 5 * 4 = 20. Using the address operator, &, we can check this address algorithm. For example, consider Program 8.10.

Program 8.10

```
#include <stdio.h>
#define NUMELS 20
int main()
{
  int numbers[NUMELS];

  printf("The starting address of the numbers array is: %d\n",
                                                &(numbers[0]));
  printf("The storage size of each array element is: %d\n",
                                                  sizeof(int));
  printf("The address of element numbers[5] is : %d\n", &(numbers[5]));

  printf("The starting address of the array,\n");
  printf("  using the notation numbers, is: %d\n", numbers);

  return 0;
}
```

[5] This topic is optional and may be omitted without loss of subject continuity.

A sample output produced by Program 8.10 is

```
The starting address of the numbers array is: 1244808
The storage size of each array element is: 4
The address of element numbers[5] is: 1244828
The starting address of the array,
  using the notation numbers, is: 1244808
```

Notice that the addresses have been displayed in decimal form using the `%d` control sequence (using the control sequence `%p`, which is the sequence intended for addresses, results in the addresses being displayed in hexadecimal format) and that element 5 is, indeed, located 20 bytes beyond the starting address of the array. Also notice that the starting address of the array is the same as the address of element 0, which is coded as `&numbers[0]` in the first `printf()` call. Alternatively, as illustrated by the last `printf()` call, the starting array address can also be obtained as numbers, which is the name of the array. This is because an array name is a pointer constant, which is an address. (The close association of array names and pointers is explained in depth in Chapter 11.)

Larger Dimensional Arrays

Although arrays with more than two dimensions are not commonly used, C does allow any number of dimensions to be declared. This is done by listing the maximum size of all dimensions for the array. For example, the declaration `int response[4][10][6];` declares a three-dimensional array. The first element in the array is designated as `response[0][0][0]` and the last element as `response[3][9][5]`.

A three-dimensional array can be viewed as a book of data tables. Using this analogy, the first subscript can be thought of as the location of the desired row in a table, the second subscript value as the desired column, and the third subscript value, which is often called the **rank**, as the page number of the selected table.

Similarly, arrays of any dimension can be declared. Conceptually, a four-dimensional array can be represented as a shelf of books where the fourth dimension is used to declare a desired book on the shelf. A five-dimensional array can be viewed as a bookcase filled with books where the fifth dimension refers to a selected shelf in the bookcase. A six-dimensional array can be considered a row of bookcases where the sixth dimension references the desired bookcase in the row. A seven-dimensional array can be considered multiple rows of bookcases where the seventh dimension references the desired row, and so on. Alternatively, arrays of three, four, five, six, or more dimensions can be viewed as mathematical *n*-tuples of order three, four, five, six, and so on, respectively.

EXERCISES 8.5

Short Answer Questions

1. Write appropriate declaration statements for the following:
   a. An array of integers with 6 rows and 10 columns
   b. An array of integers with 2 rows and 5 columns
   c. An array of characters with 7 rows and 12 columns
   d. An array of characters with 15 rows and 7 columns
   e. An array of double-precision numbers with 10 rows and 25 columns
   f. An array of double-precision numbers with 16 rows and 8 columns

Programming Exercises

1. Write a function that multiplies each element of a 7-by-10 array of integers by a scalar number. Both the array name and the number by which each element is to be multiplied are to be passed into the function as arguments. Assume the array is an array of integers.

2. Write a C function that adds the values of all elements in a two-dimensional array that is passed to the function, Assume that the array is an array of double-precision numbers having 4 rows and 5 columns.

3. Write a C function that adds respective values of two double-dimensional arrays named `first` and `second`. Both arrays have 2 rows and 3 columns. For example, element `[1][2]` of the resulting array should be the sum of `first[1][2]` and `second[1][2]`. Assume the arrays are arrays of integers. The first and second arrays should be initialized as follows:

First	Second
`16 18 23`	`24 52 77`
`54 91 11`	`16 19 59`

4. a. Write a C function that finds and displays the maximum value in a two-dimensional array of integers. The array should be declared as a 10-row-by-20-column array of integers in `main()`, and the starting address of the array should be passed to the function.
   b. Modify the function written in Exercise 4a so that it also displays the row and column number of the element with the maximum value.
   c. Can the function you wrote for Exercise 4a be generalized to handle any size two-dimensional array?

5. Write a C function that can be used to sort the elements of a 10-by-20 two-dimensional array of integers. (*Hint:* Use the `swap()` function in Program 7.10 to swap array elements.)

6. a. A professor has constructed a two-dimensional array of double-precision numbers having 35 rows and 4 columns. This array currently contains the numerical grades of the students in the professor's four classes. Write a C program that determines the total number of grades in the ranges less than 60, greater than or equal to 60 and less than 70, greater than or equal to 70 and less than 80, greater than or equal to 80 and less than 90, and greater than or equal to 90.
   b. How might the function you wrote for Exercise 6a be modified to include the case where no grade is present? That is, what grade could be used to indicate an invalid grade, and how does your function have to be modified to exclude counting such a grade?

7. a. Write a function that finds and displays the maximum value in a two-dimensional array of integers. The array should be declared as a 10-by-20 array of integers in `main()`.
   b. Modify the function written in Exercise 7a so that it also displays the row and column number of the element with the maximum value.
   c. Can the function you wrote for Exercise 7a be generalized to handle any size two-dimensional array?

8.6 Common Programming and Compiler Errors

In using the material presented in this chapter, be aware of the following possible programming and compiler errors:

Programming Errors

1. Forgetting to declare the array. This error results in a compiler error message equivalent to "invalid indirection" each time a subscripted variable is encountered within a program.

2. Using a subscript that references a nonexistent array element. For example, declaring the array to be of size 20 and using a subscript value of 25. This error is not detected by most C compilers. However, it causes a run-time error that results either in a program "crash" or a value that has no relation to the intended element being accessed from memory. In either case it is usually an extremely troublesome error to locate. The only solution to this problem is to make sure, either by specific programming statements or by careful coding, that each subscript references a valid array element.

3. Not using a large enough conditional value in a `for` loop counter to cycle through all the array elements. This error usually occurs when an array is initially specified to be of size `n` and there is a `for` loop within the program of the form `for (i = 0; i < n; i++)`. The array size is then expanded but the programmer forgets to change the interior `for` loop parameters. Using a symbolic constant both to declare an array's size and for the maximum subscript value in the `for` statement eliminates this error.

4. Forgetting to initialize the array. Although many compilers automatically set all elements of integer and real valued arrays to 0 and all elements of character arrays to blanks, it is up to the programmer to ensure that each array is correctly initialized before the processing of array elements begins.

Compiler Errors

The following table summarizes common errors that will result in compilation errors and the typical error messages provided by Unix- and Windows-based compilers.

Error	Typical Unix-based Compiler Error Message	Typical Windows-based Compiler Error Message
Designating a variable as an `extern` in one file, without declaring the variable as a `global` in another file	`ERROR: Undefined symbol: ex` (Note: use the `-bloadmap` or `–bnoquiet` option to obtain more information about the error.)	`Link error: unresolved external symbol …`
Applying the indirection operator to a nonpointer variable	`(S) Operand of indirection operator must be a pointer expression.`	`error: illegal indirection`
Not passing an address in a call to a function whose parameter is declared as a pointer	`(W) Function argument assignment between types "int*" and "int" is not allowed.`	`error: function cannot convert parameter from dataType to dataType*`
Assigning a value, rather than an address, to a pointer	`(W) Operation between types "int*" and "int" is not allowed.`	`error: cannot convert parameter from dataType to dataType*`
Attempting to take the address of a constant	`(W) Operation between types "int" and "const int*" is not allowed.`	`error: & on constant`
Attempting to use a variable that is not within scope	`(S) Undeclared identifier…`	`error: undeclared identifier …`

8.7 Chapter Summary

1. A single-dimensional array is a data structure that can be used to store a list of values of the same data type. Such arrays must be declared by giving the data type of the values that are stored in the array and the array size. For example, the declaration
   ```
   int num[100];
   ```
   creates an array of 100 integers. A preferable approach is first to use a named constant for the array size and then use this constant in the definition of the array. For example
   ```
   #define MAXSIZE 100
   ```
   and
   ```
   int num[MAXSIZE];
   ```
2. Array elements are stored in contiguous locations in memory and referenced using the array name and a subscript, for example, `num[22]`. Any nonnegative integer value expression can be used as a subscript and the subscript 0 always refers to the first element in an array.
3. Single-dimensional arrays may be initialized when they are declared. This is accomplished by listing the initial values, in a row-by-row manner, within braces and separating them with commas. For example, the declaration
   ```
   int nums[] = {3, 7, 8, 15};
   ```
4. Single-dimensional arrays are passed to a function by passing the name of the array as an argument. The value actually passed is the address of the first array storage location. Thus, the called function receives direct access to the original array and not a copy of the array elements. Within the called function, a parameter must be declared to receive the passed array name. The declaration of the parameter can omit the size of the array.
5. A two-dimensional array is declared by listing both a row and a column size with the data type and name of the array. For example, the declarations
   ```
   #define ROWS  5
   #define COLS 7
   int mat[ROWS][COLS];
   ```
   create a two-dimensional array consisting of five rows and seven columns of integer values.
6. Two-dimensional arrays may be initialized when they are declared. This is accomplished by listing the initial values, in a row-by-row manner, within braces and separating them with commas. For example, the declaration
   ```
   int vals[ROWS][COLS] = { {1, 2},
                            {3, 4},
                            {5, 6} };
   ```
   produces the following three-row-by-two-column array:
   ```
   1 2
   3 4
   5 6
   ```

As C uses the convention that initialization proceeds in row-wise order, the inner braces can be omitted. Thus, an equivalent initialization is provided by the statement
`int vals[ROWS][COLS] = {1, 2, 3, 4, 5, 6};`

7. Two-dimensional arrays are passed to a function by passing the name of the array as an argument. Within the called function, a parameter must be declared to receive the passed array name. The declaration of the parameter can omit the row size of the array.

8.8 Chapter Supplement: Searching and Sorting Methods

Most programmers encounter the need both to sort and search a list of data items at some time in their programming careers. For example, experimental results might have to be arranged in either increasing (ascending) or decreasing (descending) order for statistical analysis, lists of names may have to be sorted in alphabetical order, or a list of dates may have to be rearranged in ascending date order. Similarly, a list of names may have to be searched to find a particular name, or a list of dates may have to be searched to locate a particular date. In this section, we introduce the fundamentals of both searching and sorting lists. (Note: It is not necessary to sort a list before searching it, although, as we shall see, much faster searches are possible if the list is in sorted order.)

Search Algorithms

A common requirement of many programs is to search a list for a given element. For example, in a list of names and telephone numbers, we might search for a specific name so that the corresponding telephone number can be printed, or we might wish to search the list simply to determine if a name is there. The two most common methods of performing such searches are the **linear** and **binary search algorithms**.

Linear Search In a linear search, which is also known as a **sequential search**, each item in the list is examined in the order it occurs until the desired item is found or the end of the list is reached. This is analogous to looking at every name in the phone directory, beginning with Aardvark, Aaron, until you find the one you want or until you reach Zzxgy, Zora. Obviously, this is not the most efficient way to search a long alphabetized list. However, the advantages of the linear search are that

1. The algorithm is simple.
2. The list need not be in any particular order.

In a linear search, the search begins at the first item and continues sequentially, item by item, through the list. The pseudocode for a function performing a linear search is

Set a "found" flag to FALSE
Set an index value to -1
Begin with the first item in the list
While there are still items in the list AND the "found" flag is FALSE
    Compare the item with the desired item
    If the item was found
        Set the "found" flag to TRUE
        Set the index value to the item's position in the list

EndIf
EndWhile
Return the index value

Notice that the function's return value indicates whether the item was found. If the return value is -1, the item was not in the list; otherwise, the return value provides the index of where the item is located within the list.

The function `linearSearch()` illustrates this procedure as a C function

```
linearSearch(int list[], int size, int key)
/* this function returns the location of key in the list */
/* a -1 is returned if the value is not found */
{
  int index, found, i;
  index = -1;
  found = FALSE;

  i = 0;
  while (i < size && !found)
  {
    if (list[i] == key)
    {
      found = TRUE;
      index = i;
    }
    i++; /* move to next item in the list */
  }
  return (index);
}
```

In reviewing `linearSearch()` notice that the `while` loop is simply used to access each element in the list, from first element to last, until a match is found with the desired item. If the desired item is located, the logical variable `found` is set to `true`, which causes the loop to terminate; otherwise, the search continues until the end of the list is encountered.

To test this function, we have written a `main()` driver function to call it and display the results returned by `linearSearch()`. The complete test program is illustrated in Program 8.11.

Program 8.11

```
#include <stdio.h>
#define TRUE 1
#define FALSE 0
#define NUMEL 10

int linearSearch (int [], int, int);

```

```
int main()
{
  int nums[NUMEL] = {5,10,22,32,45,67,73,98,99,101};
  int item, location;

  printf("Enter the item you are searching for: ");
  scanf("%d", &item);

  location = linearSearch(nums, NUMEL, item);

  if (location > -1)
    printf("The item was found at index location %d\n",
                                                   location);
  else
    printf("The item was not found in the list\n");

  return 0;
}

linearSearch(int list[], int size, int key)
/* this function returns the location of key in the list */
/* a -1 is returned if the value is not found */
{
  int index, found, i;
  index = -1;
  found = FALSE;

  i = 0;
  while (i < size && !found)
  {
    if (list[i] == key)
    {
      found = TRUE;
      index = i;
    }
    i++; /* move to next item in the list */
  }
  return (index);
}
```

The following are sample runs using Program 8.11:

```
Enter the item you are searching for: 101
The item was found at index location 9
```

and

```
Enter the item you are searching for: 65
The item was not found in the list
```

As has already been pointed out, an advantage of linear searches is that the list does not have to be in sorted order to perform the search. Another advantage is that if the desired item is located toward the front of the list, only a small number of comparisons are done. The worst case, of course, occurs when the desired item is at the end of the list. On average, however, and assuming that the desired item is equally likely to be anywhere within the list, the number of required comparisons are `N/2`, where `N` is the number of items in the list. Thus, for a 10-element list, the average number of comparisons needed for a linear search is 5, and for a 10,000-element list, the average number of comparisons is 5000. As we show next, this number can be significantly reduced using a binary search algorithm.

Binary Search In a binary search, the list must be in sorted order to begin with. Starting with an ordered list, the desired item is first compared to the element in the middle of the list (for lists with an even number of elements, either of the two middle elements can be used). Three possibilities present themselves once the comparison is made: (1) the desired item may be equal to the middle element, (2) it may be greater than the middle element, or (3) it may be less than the middle element.

In the first case, the search has been successful, and no further searches are required. In the second case, because the desired item is greater than the middle element, if it is found at all, it must be in the upper part of the list. This means that the lower part of the list, consisting of all elements from the first to the midpoint element, can be discarded from any further search. In the third case, because the desired item is less than the middle element, if it is found at all, it must be found in the lower part of the list. For this case the upper part of the list, consisting of all elements from the midpoint element to the last element, can be discarded from any further search.

The algorithm for implementing this search strategy is illustrated in Figure 8.13 and defined by the following pseudocode:

```
Set an index value to -1
Set a "found" flag to FALSE
Set the lower index to 0
Set the upper index to one less than the size of the list
Begin with the first item in the list
While the lower index is less than or equal to the upper index and a match is not yet
found
  Set the midpoint index to the integer average of the lower and upper index values
  Compare the desired item to the midpoint element
  If the desired element equals the midpoint element
    the item has been found
  Else if the desired element is greater than the midpoint element
    set the lower index value to the midpoint value plus 1
  Else if the desired element is less than the midpoint element
    set the upper index value to the midpoint value less 1
  EndIf
EndWhile
Return the index value
```

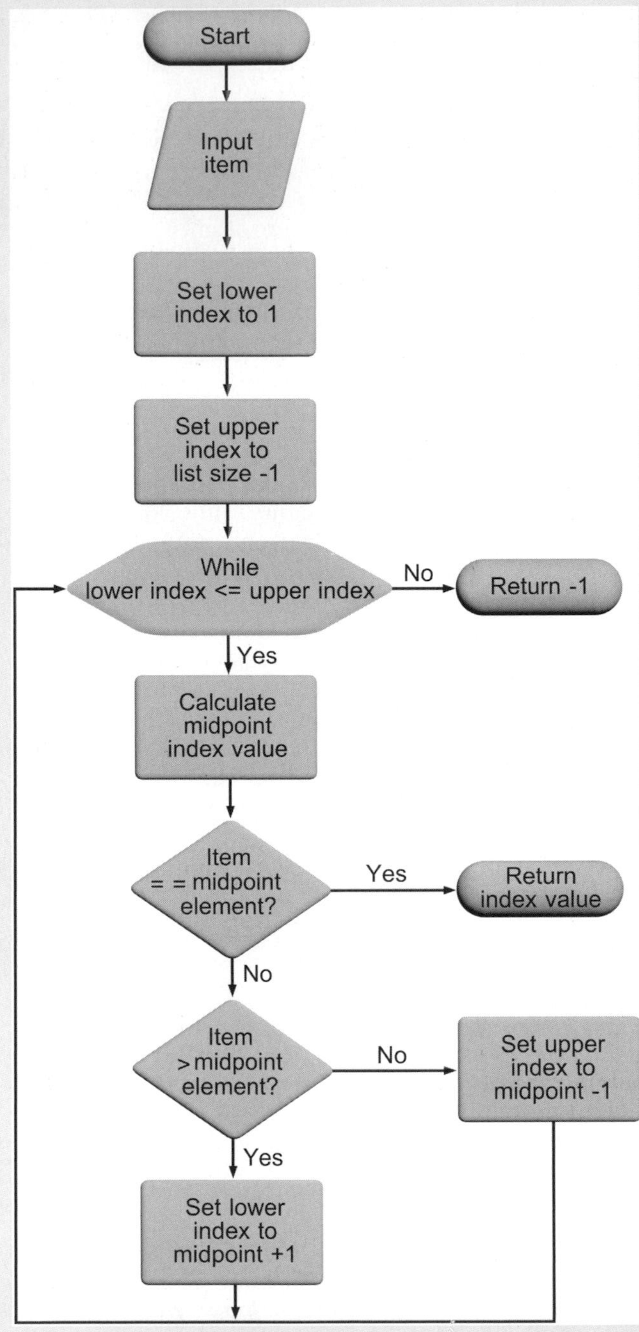

Figure 8.14 The binary search algorithm

As illustrated by both the pseudocode and the flowchart, a `while` loop is used to control the search. The initial list is defined by setting the lower index value to 0 and the upper index value to one less than the number of elements in the list. The midpoint element is then taken as the integerized average of the lower and upper values. Once the comparison to the midpoint element is made, the search is subsequently restricted by moving either the lower index to one integer value above the midpoint, or by moving the upper index one integer value below the midpoint. This process is continued until the desired element is found or the lower and upper index values become equal. The function `binarySearch()` presents the C version of this algorithm. In this function the variables named `left` and `right` correspond to the lower and upper indices, respectively.

```
binarySearch(int list[], int size, int key)
/* this function returns the location of key in the list */
/* a -1 is returned if the value is not found */
{
int index, found, left, right, midpt;

  index = -1;
  found = FALSE;
  left = 0;
  right = size -1;
  while (left <= right && !found)
  {
    midpt = (int) ((left + right) / 2);
    if (key == list[midpt])
    {
      found = TRUE;
      index = midpt;
    }
    else if (key > list[midpt])
      left = midpt + 1;
    else
      right = midpt - 1;
  }
  return (index);
}
```

For purposes of testing this function, we use Program 8.12.

Program 8.12

```
#include <stdio.h>
#define NUMEL 10

int binarySearch(int [], int, int);   /* function prototype */

int main()
```

```
{
  int nums[NUMEL] = {5,10,22,32,45,67,73,98,99,101};
  int item, location;

  printf("Enter the item you are searching for: ");
  scanf("%d", &item);

  location = binarySearch(nums, NUMEL, item);

  if (location > -1)
    printf("The item was found at index location %d\n", location);
  else
    printf("The item was not found in the list\n");

  return 0;
}

#define TRUE 1
#define FALSE 0
binarySearch(int list[], int size, int key)
/* this function returns the location of key in the list */
/* a -1 is returned if the value is not found */
{
  int index, found, left, right, midpt;

  index = -1;
  found = FALSE;
  left = 0;
  right = size -1;
  while (left <= right && !found)
  {
    midpt = (int) ((left + right) / 2);
    if (key == list[midpt])
    {
      found = TRUE;
      index = midpt;
    }
    else if (key > list[midpt])
      left = midpt + 1;
    else
      right = midpt - 1;
  }
  return (index);
}
```

A sample run using Program 8.12 yielded the following:

```
Enter the item you are searching for: 101
The item was found at index location 9
```

The value in using a binary search algorithm is that the number of elements that must be considered is cut in half each time through the `while` loop. Thus, the first time through the loop, N elements must be considered; the second time through the loop, N/2 of the elements have been eliminated and only N/2 remain. The third time through the loop, another half of the remaining elements have been eliminated and so on.

In general, after p passes through the loop, the number of values remaining to be searched is $N/(2^p)$. In the worst case, the search can continue until there are less than or equal to 1 element remaining to be searched. Mathematically, this can be expressed as $N/(2^p) \leq 1$. Alternatively, this may be rephrased as p is the smallest integer such that $2^p \geq N$. For example, for a 1000-element array, `N` is 1000 and the maximum number of passes, p, required for a binary search is 10. Table 8.1 compares the number of loop passes needed for a linear and binary search for various list sizes. As illustrated the maximum number of loop passes for a 50-item list is almost 10 times more for a linear search than for binary search, and even more spectacular for larger lists. As a rule of thumb, 50 elements are usually taken as the switchover point: For lists smaller than 50 elements, linear searches are acceptable; for larger lists, a binary search algorithm should be used.

Table 8.1 A Comparison of `while` loop Passes for Linear and Binary Searches

Array Size	**10**	**50**	**500**	**5,000**	**50,000**	**500,000**	**5,000,000**	**50,000,000**
Average Linear Search Passes	5	25	250	2,500	25,000	250,000	2,500,000	25,000,000
Maximum Linear Search Passes	10	50	500	5,000	50,000	500,000	5,000,000	50,000,000
Maximum Binary Search Passes	4	6	9	13	16	19	23	26

Big O Notation

On average, over a large number of linear searches with N items in a list, we expect to examine half (`N/2`) of the items before locating the desired item. In a binary search, the maximum number of passes, p, occurs when $N/2^P = 1$. This relationship can be algebraically manipulated to $2^P = N$, which yields $p = \log_{10} N$, which approximately equals $3.33 \log_{10} n$.

For example, finding a particular name in an alphabetical directory with `N = 1000` names would require an average of `500 = (N/2)` comparisons using a linear search. With a binary search, only about $10 (\approx 3.33 * \log_{10} 1000)$ comparisons are required.

A common way to express the number of comparisons required in any search algorithm using a list of `N` items is to give the order of magnitude of the number of comparisons required, on average, to locate a desired item. Thus, the linear search is said to be of order N and the binary search of order $\log_2 N$. In Big O notation, this is expressed as O(N) and $O(\log_2 N)$, where the O is read as "the order of" and the notation is called Big O notation.

Sort Algorithms

For sorting data, two major categories of sorting techniques exist, called internal and external sorts, respectively. **Internal sorts** are used when the data list is not too large and the complete list can be stored within the computer's memory, usually in an array. **External sorts** are used for much larger data sets that are stored in large external disk or tape files, and cannot be accommodated within the computer's memory as a complete unit. Here we present two internal sort algorithms. The algorithms shown are commonly used when sorting lists with less than approximately 50 elements. For larger lists more sophisticated sorting algorithms, such as the Quicksort algorithm, are typically employed.

The Selection Sort One of the simplest sorting techniques is the **selection sort.** In a selection sort, the smallest value is initially selected from the complete list of data and exchanged with the first element in the list. After this first selection and exchange, the next smallest element in the revised list is selected and exchanged with the second element in the list. The smallest element is thus already in the first position in the list, so the second pass need consider only the second through last elements. For a list consisting of *N* elements, this process is repeated *N-1* times, with each pass through the list requiring one less comparison than the previous pass.

For example, consider the list of numbers in Figure 8.14. The first pass through the initial list results in the 32 being selected and exchanged with the first element in the list. The second pass, made on the reordered list, results in the 155 being selected from the second through fifth elements. This value is then exchanged with the second element in the list. The third pass selects 307 from the third through fifth elements in the list and exchanges this value with the third element. Finally, the fourth and last pass through the list selects the remaining minimum value and exchanges it with the fourth list element. Although each pass in this example resulted in an exchange, no exchange is made in a pass if the smallest value is already in the correct location.

Initial List	Pass 1	Pass 2	Pass 3	Pass 4
690	32	32	32	32
307	307	155	144	144
32	690	690	307	307
155	155	307	690	426
426	426	426	426	690

Figure 8.15 A sample selection sort

In pseudocode, the selection sort is described as

Set interchange count to zero (not required; done just to keep track of the interchanges)
For each element in the list from first to next-to-last
  Find the smallest element from the current element being referenced to the last element by:
    Setting the minimum value equal to the current element
    Saving (storing) the index of the current element
    For each element in the list from the current element + 1 to the last element in the list
      If element[inner loop index] < minimum value

Set the minimum value = element[inner loop index]
Save the index of the new found minimum value
EndIf
EndFor
Swap the current value with the new minimum value
Increment the interchange count
EndFor
Return the interchange count

The function `selectionSort()` incorporates this procedure into a C function.

```
int selectionSort(int num[], int numel)
{
  int i, j, min, minidx, temp, moves = 0;

  for ( i = 0; i < (numel - 1); i++)
  {
    min = num[i]; /* assume minimum is first element in sublist */
    minidx = i; /* index of minimum element */
    for(j = i + 1; j < numel; j++)
    {
      if (num[j] < min) /* if we've located a lower value */
      {                 /* capture it */
        min = num[j];
        minidx = j;
      }
    }
    if (min < num[i]) /* check if we have a new minimum */
    {                 /* and if we do, swap values */
      temp = num[i];
      num[i] = min;
      num[minidx] = temp;
      moves++;
    }
  }
  return (moves);
}
```

The `selectionSort()` function expects two parameters: the list to be sorted and the number of elements in the list. As specified by the pseudocode, a nested set of `for` loops performs the sort. The outer `for` loop causes one less pass through the list than the total number of data items in the list. For each pass, the variable `min` is initially assigned the value `num[i]`, where `i` is the outer `for` loop's counter variable. Because `i` begins at 0 and ends at one less than `numel`, each element in the list, except the last, is successively designated as the current element.

The inner loop cycles through the elements below the current element and is used to select the next smallest value. Thus, this loop begins at the index value `i+1` and continues through the end of the list. When a new minimum is found, its value and position in the list are stored in the variables named `min` and `minidx`, respectively. Upon completion of the inner loop, an exchange is made only if a value less than that in the current position was found.

Program 8.13 was constructed for purposes of testing `selectionSort()`. This program implements a selection sort for the same list of 10 numbers that was previously used to test our search algorithms. For later comparison to the other sorting algorithm that is presented, the number of actual moves made by the program to get the data into sorted order is counted and displayed.

Program 8.13

```
#include <stdio.h>
#define NUMEL 10

int selectionSort(int [], int);

int main()
{
  int nums[NUMEL] = {22,5,67,98,45,32,101,99,73,10};
  int i, moves;

  moves = selectionSort(nums, NUMEL);

  printf("The sorted list, in ascending order, is:\n");
  for (i = 0; i < NUMEL; i++)
    printf("%d ",nums[i]);
  printf("\n %d moves were made to sort this list\n", moves);

  return 0;
}

int selectionSort(int num[], int numel)
{
  int i, j, min, minidx, temp, moves = 0;

  for ( i = 0; i < (numel - 1); i++)
  {
    min = num[i]; /* assume minimum is first element in sublist */
    minidx = i; /* index of minimum element */
    for(j = i + 1; j < numel; j++)
    {
      if (num[j] < min) /* if we've located a lower value */
      {                 /* capture it */
        min = num[j];
        minidx = j;
      }
    }
```

```
      if (min < num[i]) /* check if we have a new minimum */
      {                 /* and if we do, swap values */
        temp = num[i];
        num[i] = min;
        num[minidx] = temp;
        moves++;
      }
    }
    return (moves);
}
```

Following is the output produced by Program 8.13:

```
The sorted list, in ascending order, is:
5 10 22 32 45 67 73 98 99 101
8 moves were made to sort this list
```

Clearly, the number of moves displayed depends on the initial order of the values in the list. An advantage of the selection sort is that the maximum number of moves that must be made is N-1, where N is the number of items in the list. Further, each one is a final move that results in an element residing in its final location in the sorted list.

A disadvantage of the selection sort is that N(N-1)/2 comparisons are always required, regardless of the initial arrangement of the data. This number of comparisons is obtained as follows: The last pass always requires one comparison, the next-to-last pass requires two comparisons, and so on, to the first pass, which requires N-1 comparisons. Thus, the total number of comparisons is

$$1 + 2 + 3 + \ldots N-1 = N(N-1)/2 = N2-N/2.$$

For large values of N, the N^2 dominates, and the order of the selection sort is $O(N^2)$.

An Exchange ("Bubble") Sort In an exchange sort, adjacent elements of the list are exchanged with one another in such a manner that the list becomes sorted. One example of such a sequence of exchanges is provided by the **bubble sort,** where successive values in the list are compared, beginning with the first two elements. If the list is to be sorted in ascending (from smallest to largest) order, the smaller value of the two being compared is always placed before the larger value. For lists sorted in descending (from largest to smallest) order, the smaller of the two values being compared is always placed after the larger value.

For example, assuming that a list of values is to be sorted in ascending order, if the first element in the list is larger than the second, the two elements are interchanged. Then the second and third elements are compared. Again, if the second element is larger than the third, these two elements are interchanged. This process continues until the last two elements have been compared and exchanged, if necessary. If no exchanges were made during this initial pass through the data, the data is in the correct order and the process is finished; otherwise, a second pass is made through the data, starting from the first element and stopping at the next-to-last element. The reason for stopping at the next-to-last element on the second pass is that the first pass always results in the most positive value "sinking" to the bottom of the list.

As a specific example of this process, consider the list of numbers in Figure 8.15. The first comparison results in the interchange of the first two element values, 690 and 307. The next comparison, between elements 2 and 3 in the revised list, results in the interchange of values between the second and third elements, 690 and 32. This comparison and possible switching of adjacent values are continued until the last two elements have been compared and possibly switched. This process completes the first pass through the data and results in the largest number moving to the bottom of the list. As the largest value sinks to its resting place at the bottom of the list, the smaller elements slowly rise, or "bubble," to the top of the list. As a result, the exchange sort is also sometimes called a *bubble sort.*

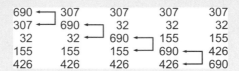

690	307	307	307	307
307	690	32	32	32
32	32	690	155	155
155	155	155	690	426
426	426	426	426	690

Figure 8.16 First pass of an exchange sort

Because the first pass through the list ensures that the largest value always moves to the bottom of the list, the second pass stops at the next-to-last element. This process continues with each pass stopping at one higher element than the previous pass, until either N-1 passes through the list have been completed or no exchanges are necessary in any single pass. In both cases the resulting list is in sorted order. The pseudocode describing this sort is

Set interchange count to zero (not required; done just to keep track of the interchanges)
For the first element in the list to one less than the last element (i index)
  For the second element in the list to the last element (j index)
    If num[j] < num[j-1]
      Swap num[j] with num[j-1]
      Increment interchange count
    EndIf
  EndFor
EndFor
Return interchange count

This sort algorithm is coded in C as the function `bubbleSort()`, and is tested in Program 8.14. This program tests `bubbleSort()` with the same list of 10 numbers used in Program 8.13 to test `selectionSort()`. For comparison to the earlier selection sort, the number of adjacent moves (exchanges) made by `bubbleSort()` is also counted and displayed.

Program 8.14

```
#include <stdio.h>
#define NUMEL 10

int bubbleSort(int [], int);  /* function prototype */

int main()
```

```
{
  int nums[NUMEL] = {22,5,67,98,45,32,101,99,73,10};
  int i, moves;

  moves = bubbleSort(nums, NUMEL);

  printf("The sorted list, in ascending order, is:\n");
  for (i = 0; i < NUMEL; i++)
    printf("%d ",nums[i]);
  printf("\n %d moves were made to sort this list\n", moves);

  return 0;
}

int bubbleSort(int num[],int numel)
{
  int i, j, temp, moves = 0;

  for ( i = 0; i < (numel - 1); i++)
  {
    for(j = 1; j < numel; j++)
    {
      if (num[j] < num[j-1])
      {
        temp = num[j];
        num[j] = num[j-1];
        num[j-1] = temp;
        moves++;
      }
    }
  }
  return (moves);
}
```

Following is the output produced by Program 8.14:

```
The sorted list, in ascending order, is:
5 10 22 32 45 67 73 98 99 101
18 moves were made to sort this list
```

As with the selection sort, the number of comparisons using a bubble sort is $O(N^2)$, and the number of required moves depends on the initial order of the values in the list. In the worst case, when the data are in reverse sorted order, the selection sort performs better than the bubble sort. Here, both sorts require N(N-1)/2 comparisons, but the selection sort needs only N-1 moves while the exchange sort needs N(N-1)/2 moves. The additional moves required by the exchange sort result from the intermediate exchanges between adjacent elements to "settle" each element into its final position. In this regard, the selection sort is superior because no intermediate moves are necessary. For random data, such as those used in Programs 8.13 and 8.14, the selection sort generally performs as well as or better than the bubble sort.

A modification to the bubble sort that causes the sort to terminate whenever no exchanges have been made in a pass, which indicates that the list is in order, can make the bubble sort operate as an O(N) sort in specialized cases.

The Quicksort The selection and exchange sorts both require $O(N^2)$ comparisons, which make them very slow for long lists. The **Quicksort algorithm,** which is also called a **"partition" sort,** divides a list into two smaller sublists and sorts each sublist by portioning into smaller sublists, and so on.[6] The order of a Quicksort is $N\log_2N$. Thus, for a 1000-item list, the total number of comparisons for a Quicksort is in the order of $1000(3.3 \log_{10}1000) = 1000(10) = 10{,}000$ compared to $1000(1000) = 1{,}000{,}000$ for a selection or exchange sort.

The Quicksort puts a list into sorted order by a partitioning process. At each stage the list is partitioned into sublists so that a selected element, called the **pivot,** is placed in its correct position in the final sorted list. To understand the process consider the list illustrated in Figure 8.16.

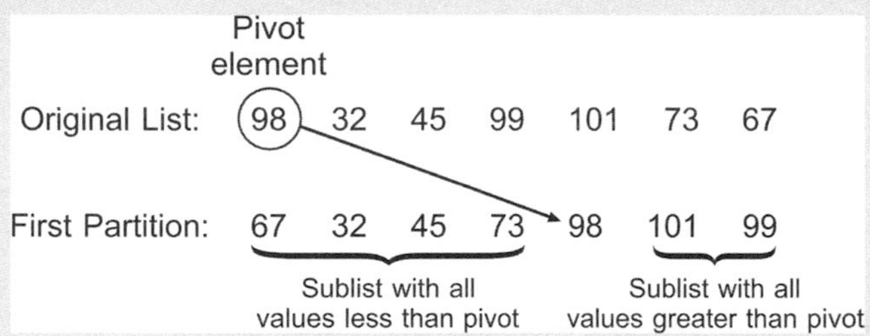

Figure 8.17 A first Quicksort Partition

As illustrated in Figure 8.16, the original list consists of seven numbers. Designating the first element in the list, 98, as the pivot element, the list is rearranged as shown in the first partition. Notice that this partition results in all values less than 98 residing to its left and all values greater than 98 to its right. For now, disregard the exact order of the elements to the left and right of the 98 (in a moment we will see how the arrangement of the numbers came about).

The numbers to the left of the pivot constitute one sublist and the numbers to the right another sublist, which individually must be reordered by a partitioning process. The pivot for the first sublist is 67 and the pivot for the second sublist is 101. Figure 8.17 shows how each of these sublists is partitioned using their respective pivot elements. The partitioning process stops when a sublist has only one element. In the case illustrated in Figure 8.17, a fourth partition is required for the sublist containing the values 45 and 32, because all other sublists have only one element. Once this last sublist is partitioned, the Quicksort is completed and the original list is in sorted order.

As we have illustrated, the key to the Quicksort is its partitioning process. An essential part of this process is that each sublist is rearranged in place; that is, elements are rearranged

[6] This algorithm was developed by C.A.R. Hoare and first described by him in an article entitled "QuickSort" in *Computer Journal* (vol. 5, pp. 10–15) in 1962. This sorting algorithm was so much faster than previous algorithms that it became known as *the* Quicksort.

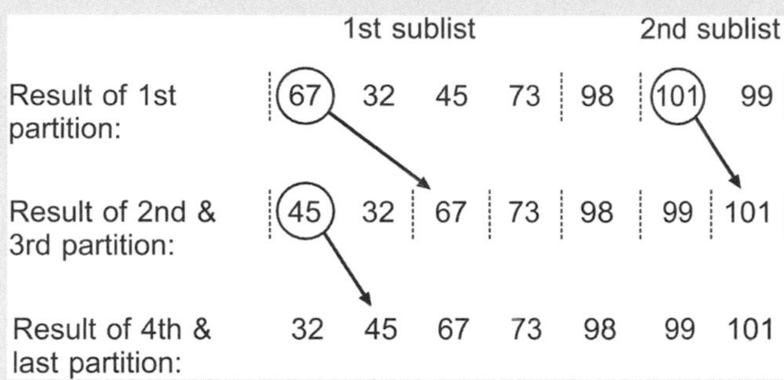

Figure 8.18 The initial list

within the existing list. This rearrangement is facilitated by first saving the value of the pivot, which frees its slot to be used by another element. The list is then examined from the right, starting with the last element in the list, for a value less than the pivot; when one is found, it is copied to the pivot slot. This copy frees a slot at the right of the list for use by another element. The list is now examined from the left for any value greater than the pivot; when one is found it is copied to the last freed slot. This right-to-left and left-to-right scan is continued until the right and left index values meet. The saved pivot element is then copied into this slot. At that point all values to the left of the index are smaller than the pivot value and all values to the right are greater. Before providing the pseudocode for this process, we will show all of the steps required to complete one partition using our previous list of numbers.

Consider Figure 8.18, which shows our original list of Figure 8.16 and the positions of the initial left and right indexes. As shown in the figure, the pivot value has been saved into a variable named `pivot`, the right index points to the last list element and is the active index. Using this index the scan for elements less than the pivot value of 98 begins.

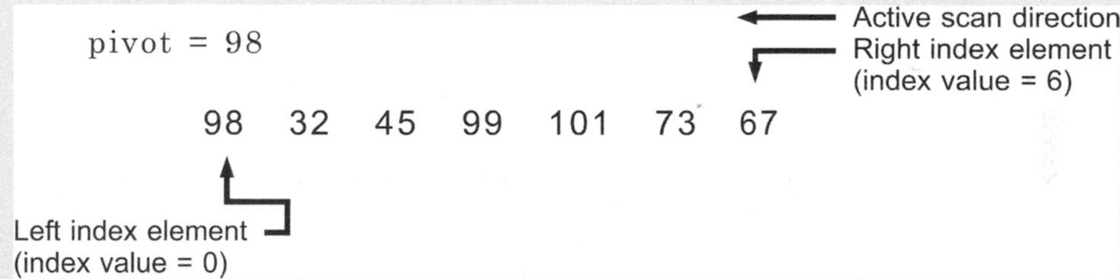

Figure 8.19 Start of the scanning process

Because 67 is less than the pivot value of 98, the 67 is moved into the pivot slot (the pivot value is not lost because it has been assigned to the variable `pivot`) and the left index is incremented. This results in the arrangement shown in Figure 8.19.

Notice in Figure 8.19 that the element pointed to by the right index is now available for the next copy, because its value, 67, has been reproduced as the first element. (This will always be the case. When a scan stops, its index will indicate the position available for the next move.)

Scanning of the list shown in Figure 8.19 continues from the left for a search of all values greater than 98. This occurs when the 99 is reached. Because 99 is greater than the pivot

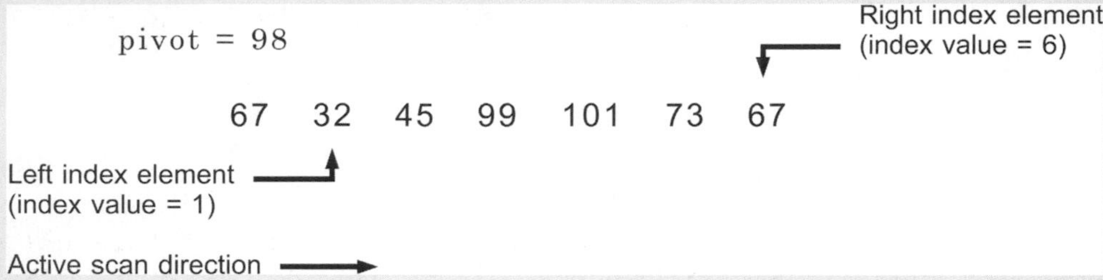

Figure 8.20 List after the first copy

value of 98, the scan stops and the 99 is copied into the position indicated by the right index. The right index is then incremented, which produces the situation illustrated in Figure 8.20.

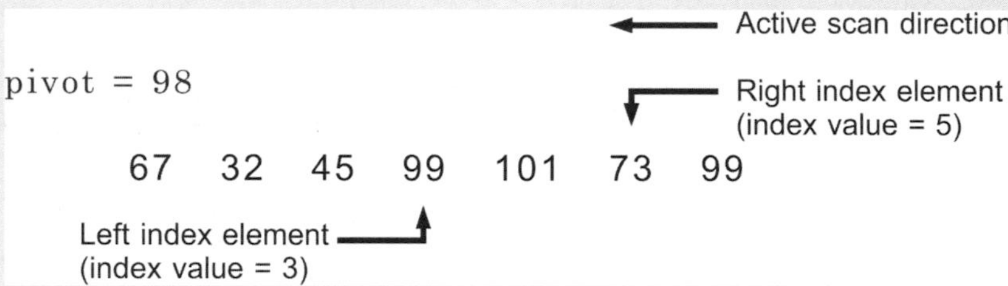

Figure 8.21 Start of second right-side scan

Scanning of the list shown in Figure 8.20 now continues from the right in a search for values less than the pivot. Because 73 qualifies, the right scan stops, the 73 is moved into the position indicated by the left index, and the left index is incremented. This results in the list shown in Figure 8.21.

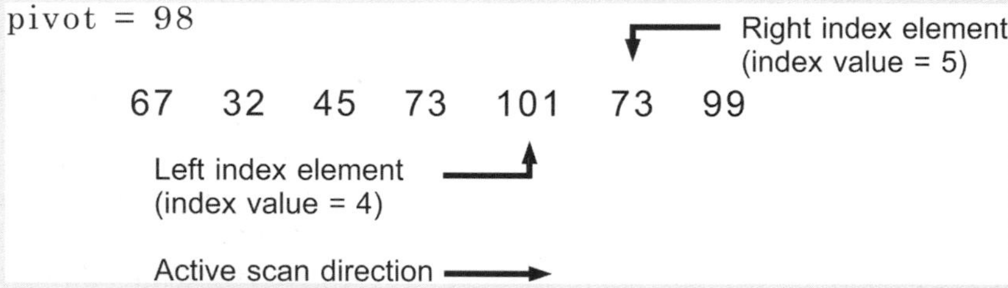

Figure 8.22 Start of second left-side scan

Scanning of the list shown in Figure 8.21 now resumes from the left in a search for values greater than 98. Because 101 qualifies this scan stops and the 101 is moved into the slot indicated by the right index, and the right index is incremented. This results in the list illustrated in Figure 8.22.

Notice in Figure 8.22 that left and right indices are equal. This is the condition that stops all scanning and indicates the position where the pivot should be placed. Doing so results in completion of this partition with the list in the order: 67 32 45 73 98 101 99.

Compare this list with the one previously shown for the first partition in Figure 8.17. As is seen, they are the same. Here the pivot has been placed so that all elements less than it

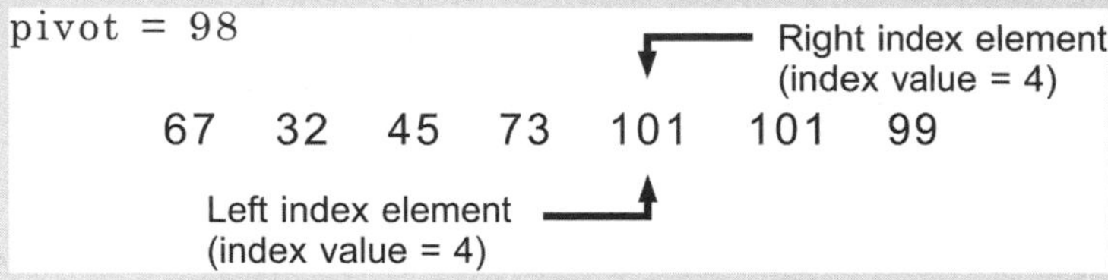

Figure 8.23 Position of list elements after the 101 is moved

are to its left and all values greater than it are to its right. The same partitioning process would now be applied to the sublists on either side of the partition.

The pseudocode describing this partitioning process is

```
Set the pivot to the value of the first list element
Initialize the left index to the index of the first list element
Initialize the right index to the index of the last list element
While (left index < right index)
   /* scan from the right, skipping over larger values */
  While (right index element >= pivot && left < right) /* skip over larger values */
    Decrement right index
  EndWhile
  If (right index != left index)
    Move the lower value into the slot indicated by the left index
    Increment the left index
  EndIf
   /* scan from the left, skipping over smaller values */
  While (left index element <= pivot && left < right) /* skip over smaller values */
    Increment left index
  EndWhile
  If right index != left index)
   Move the higher value into the slot indicated by the right index
   Decrement the right index
  EndIf
EndWhile
Move the pivot into the slot indicated by the left (or right) index (they are equal here)
Return the left (or right) index (the two are the same value at this point)
```

The function partition, contained within Program 8.15, codes this algorithm in C.

Program 8.15

```
 #include <stdio.h>
#define NUMEL 7

int main()
{
  int nums[NUMEL] = {98,32,45,99,101,73,67};
  int i, pivot;
```

```
  int partition(int [], int, int); /* function prototype */

  pivot = partition(nums, 0, NUMEL-1);

  printf("The returned pivot index is %d\n", pivot);
  printf("The list is now in the order:\n");
  for (i = 0; i < NUMEL; i++)
    printf("%d  ",nums[i]);
  printf("\n");

  return 0;
}

int partition(int num[], int left, int right)
{
  int pivot, temp;

  pivot = num[left];  /* "capture" the pivot value, which frees up one slot */
  while (left < right)
  {
    /* scan from right to left */
    while(num[right] >= pivot && left < right)  /* skip over larger or equal values */
      right--;
    if (right != left)
    {
      num[left] = num[right];   /* move the higher value into the available slot */
      left++;
    }
    /* scan from left to right */
    while (num[left] <= pivot && left < right) /* skip over smaller or equal values */
      left++;
    if (right != left)
    {
      num[right] = num[left];  /* mover lower value into the available slot */
      right--;
    }
  }
  num[left] = pivot;  /* move pivot into correct position */
  return(left);       /* return the pivot index */
}
```

Program 8.15 is simply used to test the function. Notice that it contains the same list that we have used in our hand calculation.

A sample run using Program 8.15 produced the output

```
The returned pivot index is 4
The list is now in the order:
67  32  45  73  98  101  99
```

Notice that this output produces the result previously obtained by our hand calculation. The importance of the returned pivot index is that it defines the sublists that will be subsequently partitioned. The first sublist consist of all elements from the first list element to the element whose index is 3 (one less than the returned pivot index) and the second sublist consists of all elements starting at index value 5 (one more than the returned pivot index) and ending at the last list element.

The Quicksort uses the returned pivot value in determining whether additional calls to partition are required for each sublist defined by the list segments to the left and right of the pivot index. This is done using the following recursive logic:

```
quicksort(list, lower index, upper index)
  Calculate a pivot index calling partition(list, lower index, upper index)
  If (lower index < pivot index)
    quicksort(list, lower, pivot index - 1)
  If (upper index > pivot index)
    quicksort(list, upper, pivot index + 1)
```

The C code for this logic is described by the Quicksort function contained within Program 8.16. As indicated, Quicksort requires partition to both rearrange lists and return its pivot value.

Program 8.16

```
#include <stdio.h>
#define NUMEL 7

int main()
{
  int nums[NUMEL] = {67,32,45,73,98,101,99};
  int i;
  void quicksort(int [], int, int);

  quicksort(nums, 0, NUMEL-1);

  printf("The sorted list, in ascending order, is:\n");
  for (i = 0; i < NUMEL; i++)
    printf("%d  ",nums[i]);
  printf("\n");

```

```
  return 0;
}

void quicksort(int num[], int lower, int upper)
{
  int pivot;
  int partition(int [], int, int);

  pivot = partition(num, lower, upper);

  if (lower < pivot)
    quicksort(num, lower, pivot - 1);
  if (upper > pivot)
    quicksort(num, pivot + 1, upper);
  return;
}

int partition(int num[], int left, int right)
{
  int pivot, temp;

  pivot = num[left];  /* "capture" the pivot value, which frees up one slot */
  while (left < right)
  {
    /* scan from right to left */
    while(num[right] >= pivot && left < right)  /* skip over larger or equal values */
      right--;
    if (right != left)
    {
      num[left] = num[right];   /* move the higher value into the available slot */
      left++;
    }
    /* scan from left to right */
    while (num[left] <= pivot && left < right) /* skip over smaller or equal values */
      left++;
    if (right != left)
    {
      num[right] = num[left];  /* move lower value into the available slot */
      right--;
    }
  }
  num[left] = pivot;  /* move pivot into correct position */
  return(left);       /* return the pivot index */
}
```

Following is the output produced by Program 8.16:

```
The sorted list, in ascending order, is:
32  45  67  73  98  99  101
```

As indicated by this output, Quicksort correctly sorts the test list of numbers. Figure 8.23 shows the sequence of calls made to Quicksort by Program 8.16. In this figure left-pointing arrows indicate calls made because the first `if` condition (lower < pivot) was true and right-pointing arrows indicate calls made because the second `if` condition (upper > pivot) was true.

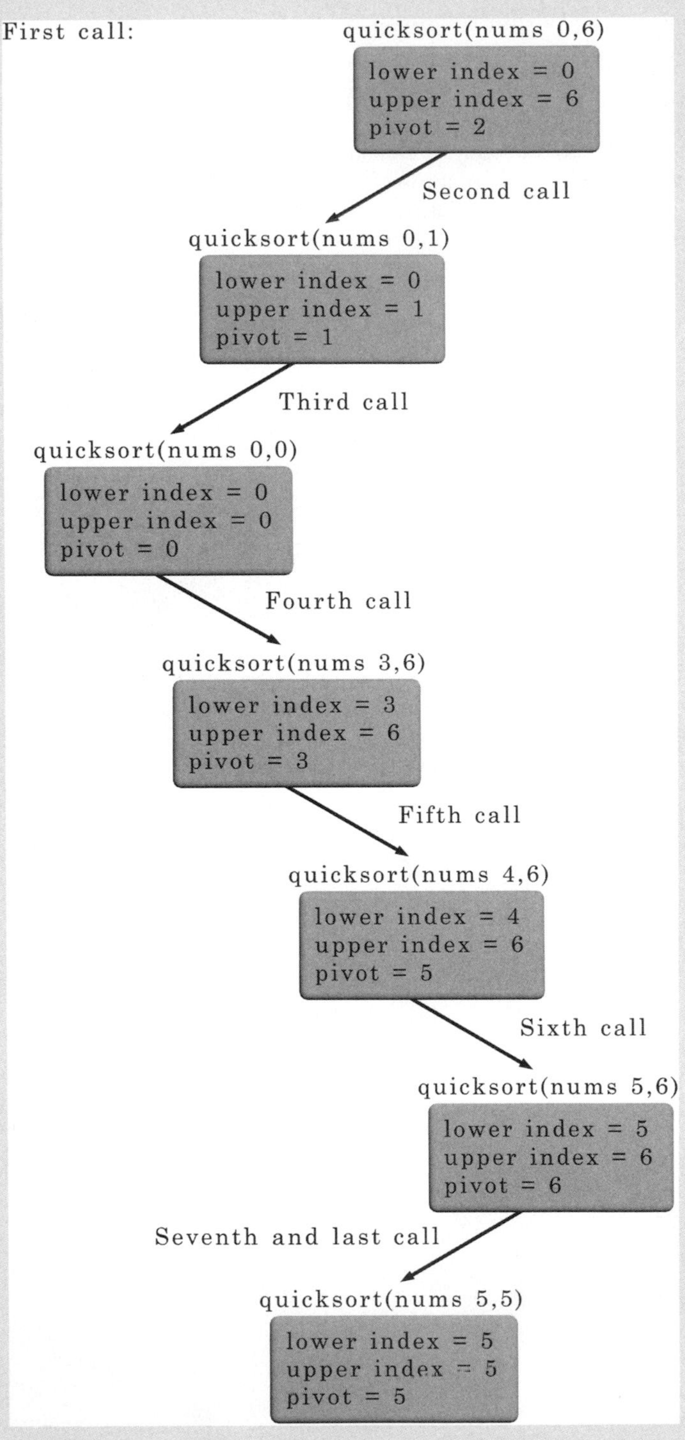

Figure 8.24 Sequence of calls made by Program 8.16

EXERCISES 8.8

Programming Exercises

1. a. Modify Program 8.13 to use a list of 100 randomly generated numbers and determine the number of moves required to put the list in order using a selection sort. Display both the initial list and the reordered list.
   b. Redo Exercise 1a using a bubble sort.

2. For the functions `selectionSort()`, `bubbleSort()`, and `quicksort()`, the sorting can be done in decreasing order by a simple modification. In each case identify the required changes and then rewrite each function to accept a flag indicating whether the sort should be in increasing or decreasing order. Modify each routine to receive and use this flag argument correctly.

3. a. The selection and bubble sort both use the same technique for swapping list elements. Replace the code in these two functions that performs the swap by a call to a function named swap. The prototype for swap should be `void swap(int *, int*)`. The `swap()` function should be constructed using the algorithm presented in Section 7.4.
   b. Describe why the function `quicksort()` does not require the swapping algorithm used by the selection and bubble sorts.

4. An alternate form of the bubble sort is presented in the following program:

```
#define TRUE 1
#define FALSE 0
int main()
{
  int nums[10] = {22,5,67,98,45,32,101,99,73,10};
  int i, temp, moves, npts, outord;

  moves = 0;
  npts = 10;
  outord = TRUE;
  while (outord && npts > 0)
  {
    outord = FALSE;
    for ( i = 0; i < npts - 1; i++)
      if (nums[i] > nums[i+1])
      {
        temp = nums[i+1];
     nums[i+1] = nums[i];
     nums[i] = temp;
        outord = TRUE;
     moves++;
      }
    npts--;
    }
  printf("The sorted list, in ascending order, is:\n");
  for (i = 0; i < 10; i++)
```

```
    printf("%d  ",nums[i]);
  printf("\n %d moves where made to sort this list\n", moves);
}
```

An advantage of this version of the bubble sort is that processing is terminated whenever a sorted list is encountered. In the best case, when the data is in sorted order to begin with, an exchange sort requires no moves (the same for the selection sort) and only N-1 comparisons (the selection sort always requires N(N-1)/2 comparisons).

After you have run this program, to convince yourself that it correctly sorts a list of integers, rewrite the sort algorithm it contains as a function named `newbubble()`, and test your function using the driver function contained in Program 8.14.

5. **a.** Modify Program 8.16 to use a larger test list consisting of 20 numbers.
b. Modify Program 8.16 to use a list of 100 randomly selected numbers.

6. A company currently maintains two lists of part numbers, where each part number is an integer. Write a C program that compares these lists of numbers and displays the numbers, if any, that are common to both. (*Hint:* Sort each list prior to making the comparison.)

7. Redo Exercise 6, but display a list of part numbers that are only on one list, but not both.

8. Rewrite the binary search algorithm to use recursion rather than iteration.

Chapter 9

Character Strings

Besides their primary purpose, representing text, strings are used extensively in C for validating user input and creating format strings. They are also extremely useful in studying pointers, because each character that is pointed to can be immediately displayed and recognized.

In C, a string is constructed as a one-dimensional array of characters. As such, it can be manipulated using standard element-by-element array-processing techniques. On a higher level, string library functions are available for treating strings as complete entities. This chapter explores the input, manipulation, and output of strings using both approaches. We will also examine the particularly close connection between string-handling functions and pointers and then use strings for user-input validation and creating format strings.

9.1 String Fundamentals

As we have already seen in Chapter 2, as well as throughout this text, a **string literal** is any sequence of characters enclosed in double quotes. A string literal is also referred to as a **string constant** and **string value**, and more conventionally as a **string**. For example, `"This is a string"`, `"Hello World!"`, and `"xyz 123 *!#@&"` are all strings.

In C, a string is stored as an array of characters terminated by a special end-of-string symbolic constant named `NULL`. The value assigned to the `NULL` constant is the escape sequence '\0' and is the sentinel marking the end of the string. For example, Figure 9.1 illustrates how the string `"Good Morning!"` is stored in memory. The string uses 14 storage locations, with the last character in the string being the end-of-string marker `'\0'`. The double quotes are not stored as part of the string.

Figure 9.1 Storing a string in memory

Because a string is stored as an array of characters, the individual characters in the array can be input, manipulated, or output using standard array-handling techniques utilizing either subscript or pointer notations. The end-of-string `NULL` character is useful for detecting the end of the string when handling strings in either of these ways.

String Input and Output

Inputting a string from a keyboard and displaying a string always requires some reliance on standard library functions. Table 9.1 lists the commonly available library functions for both character-by-character and complete string input and output.

Table 9.1 Standard String and Character Library Functions

Input	Output
`gets()`	`puts()`
`scanf()`	`printf()`
`getchar()`	`putchar()`

The `gets()` and `puts()` functions deal with strings as complete units. Both are written using the more elemental routines `getchar()` and `putchar()`. The `getchar()` and `putchar()` routines provide for the input and output of individual characters. Programs that access any of these four routines must include the `stdio.h` header file.

Program 9.1 illustrates the use of `gets()` and `puts()` to input and output a string entered at the user's terminal. Within `main()`, in line 5, the character array declared to store the string has been set to accept a maximum of 80 user-input characters, which will be terminated by the `NULL` character, for a total size of 81 characters. Although this size is arbitrary, it does correspond to a typical maximum line length.

Program 9.1

```
#include <stdio.h>
int main()
{
  #define MSIZE 81
  char message[MSIZE]; /* enough storage for 80 characters plus '\0' */

  printf("Enter a string:\n");
  gets(message);
  printf("The string just entered is:\n");
  puts(message);

  return 0;
}
```

The following is a sample run of Program 9.1:

```
Enter a string:
This is a test input of a string of characters.
The string just entered is:
This is a test input of a string of characters.
```

The `gets()` function used in Program 9.1 continuously accepts and stores the characters typed at the terminal into the character array named message. Pressing the Enter key at the terminal generates a newline character, \n, which is interpreted by `gets()` as the end-of-character entry. All the characters encountered by `gets()`, except the newline character, are stored in the message array. Before returning, the `gets()` function appends the `NULL` character to the stored set of characters, as illustrated in Figure 9.2a. The `puts()` function is then used to display the string. As illustrated in Figure 9.2b, the `puts()` function automatically sends a newline escape sequence to the display terminal after the string has been printed.

In general, a `printf()` function call can always be used in place of a `puts()` function call. For example, the statement `printf("%s\n",message);` is a direct replacement for the statement `puts(message);` used in Program 9.1. The newline escape sequence in the `printf()` function call substitutes for the automatic newline generated by `puts()` after the string is displayed. This one-to-one correspondence between the output functions `printf()` and `puts()` is not duplicated by the input functions `scanf()` and `gets()`. This is because the `scanf()` function reads a set of characters up to either a blank space or a newline character, whereas `gets()` stops accepting characters only when a newline is detected. Thus, trying to enter the characters `This is a string` using the statement `scanf("%s",message);` results in the word `This` being assigned to the message array.

If the `scanf()` function *is* used for inputting string data, the & is not used before the array name. Because an array name is a pointer constant equivalent to the address of the first storage location reserved for the array, the expressions `message` and `&message[0]`are equivalent. Thus, the function call `scanf("%s", &message[0])` can be replaced by `scanf("%s", message)`. In both cases `scanf()` will accept a string of characters and store this text starting at the same memory location.

(a)

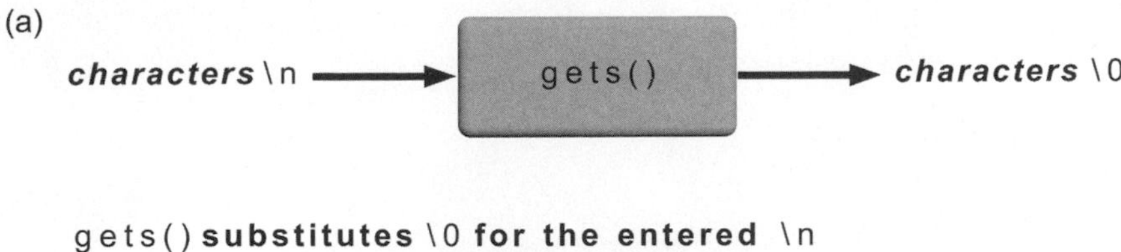

(b)

puts() substitutes \n when \0 is encountered

Figure 9.2 (a) `gets()` substitutes `\0` for the entered `\n`
(b) `puts()` substitutes `\n` when `\0` is encountered

String Processing

Strings can be manipulated using either standard library functions or standard array-processing techniques. The library functions typically available for use are presented in the Section 9.2. For now, we concentrate on processing a string in a character-by-character fashion. This allows us to understand how the standard library functions are constructed and to create our own library functions. For a specific example, consider the function `strcopy()`, which copies the contents of `string2` to `string1`.[1]

```
/* copy string2 to string1 */
void strcopy(char string1[], char string2[]) /* two arrays are passed */
{
  int i = 0; /* i will be used as a subscript */

  while (string2[i] != '\0') /* check for the end-of-string */
  {
    string1[i] = string2[i]; /* copy the element to string1 */
    i++;
  }
  string1[i] = '\0'; /* terminate the copied string */

  return;
}
```

[1]Because of its name, this becomes a programmer-defined version of an existing string library function that has the same name.

Although this string copy function can be shortened considerably and written more compactly, the function illustrates the main features of string manipulation. The two strings are passed to `strcopy()` as arrays. Each element of `string2` is then assigned to the equivalent element of `string1` until the end-of-string marker is encountered. The detection of the `NULL` character forces the termination of the `while` loop controlling the copying of elements. Because the `NULL` character is not copied from `string2` to `string1`, the last statement in `strcopy()` appends an end-of-string character to `string1`. Within `strcopy()`, the subscript `i` is used successively to access each character in the array named `string2` by "marching along" the string one character at a time. Prior to calling `strcopy()`, the programmer must ensure that sufficient space has been allocated for the `string1` array to store the elements of the `string2` array.

Program 9.2 includes the `strcopy()` function in a complete program. Notice that the function prototype in line 3 declares that the function expects to receive two character arrays. Within `main()`, in lines 8 and 9, the character arrays declared to store the string have been set to accept a maximum of 80 user-input characters, which will be terminated by the `NULL` character, for a total size of 81 characters. Although this size is again arbitrary, it does correspond to a typical maximum line length.

Program 9.2

```
 1  #include <stdio.h>
 2
 3  void strcopy(char [], char []); /* expects two arrays of chars */
 4
 5  int main()
 6  {
 7    #define LSIZE 81
 8    char message[LSIZE];   /* enough storage for 80 characters plus '\0' */
 9    char newMessage[LSIZE]; /* enough storage for a copy of message */
10
11    printf("Enter a sentence: ");
12    gets(message);
13
14    strcopy(newMessage, message); /* pass two array addresses */
15
```

```
16    puts(newMessage);
17
18    return 0;
19  }
20
21  /* copy string2 to string 1 */
22  void strcopy (char string1[], char string2[]) /* two arrays are passed */
23  {
24    int i = 0;   /* i will be used as a subscript */
25
26    while (string2[i] != '\0') /* check for the end-of-string */
27    {
28      string1[i] = string2[i]; /* copy the element to string1 */
29      i++;
30    }
31    string1[i] = '\0'; /* terminate the copied string */
32  }
```

The following is a sample run of Program 9.2:

```
Enter a sentence: How much wood could a woodchuck chuck.
How much wood could a woodchuck chuck.
```

As indicated by this output, the input string has been successfully copied to a second string and subsequently displayed.

Detecting the `NULL` Character An experienced C programmer would modify Program 9.2's `strcopy()` function in one of two ways. As you will almost always see these two types of coding conventions, it is worthwhile that you become familiar with them.

First notice that the `while` statement in line 26 of `strcopy()` tests each character to ensure that the end of the string has not been reached.

```
26  while (string2[i] != '\0') /* check for the end-of-string */
```

As with all relational expressions, the tested expression, `string2[i] != '\0'`, must be either true or false. Using the string illustrated in Figure 9.3 as an example, as long as `string[i]` does not access the end-of-string NULL character, the value of the expression `string2[i] != '\0'` is non-0 and is considered to be true. The expression is false only when the value of the expression is 0, and this occurs only when the last element in the string is accessed.

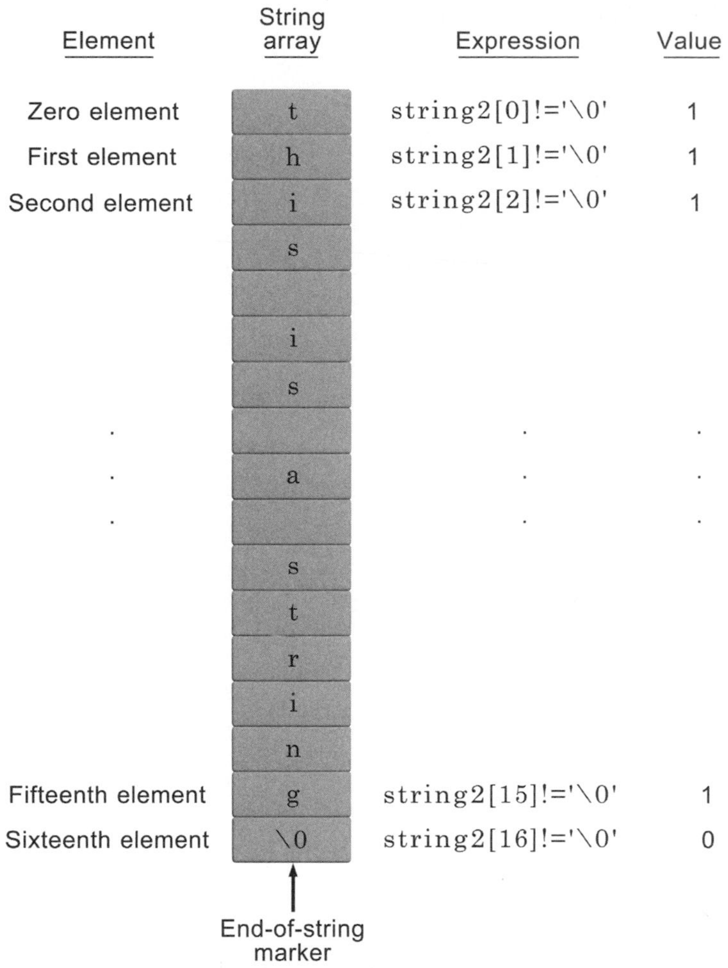

Element	String array	Expression	Value
Zero element	t	string2[0]!='\0'	1
First element	h	string2[1]!='\0'	1
Second element	i	string2[2]!='\0'	1
	s		
	i		
	s		
.		.	.
.	a	.	.
.		.	.
	s		
	t		
	r		
	i		
	n		
Fifteenth element	g	string2[15]!='\0'	1
Sixteenth element	\0	string2[16]!='\0'	0

End-of-string marker

Figure 9.3 The `while` test becomes false at the end of the string

Recall that C defines false as 0 and true as anything else. Thus, the expression `string2[i] != '\0'` becomes 0, or false, when the end of the string is reached. It is non-0, or true, everywhere else. However, because the `NULL` character has an internal value of 0 by itself, the comparison to `'\0'` is not necessary at all. This is because when `string2[i]` accesses the end-of-string character, the value of `string2[i]` is 0. When `string2[i]` accesses any other character, the value of `string[i]` is the value of the code used to store the character, which is always non-0. Figure 9.4 lists the ASCII codes for the string `this is a string`. As seen in the figure, each element has a non-0 value except for the `NULL` character.

Because the expression `string2[i]` is only 0 at the end of a string and non-0 for every other character, the expression `while (string2[i] != '\0')` can be replaced by the simpler expression `while (string2[i])`. Although this may appear confusing at first, the revised test expression is certainly more compact than the longer version.

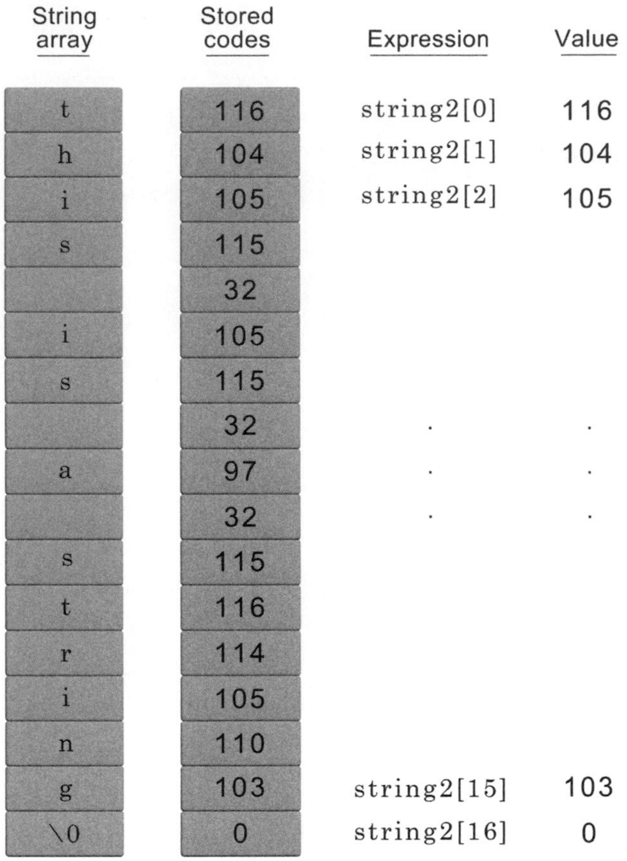

String array	Stored codes	Expression	Value
t	116	string2[0]	116
h	104	string2[1]	104
i	105	string2[2]	105
s	115		
	32		
i	105		
s	115		
	32	.	.
a	97	.	.
	32	.	.
s	115		
t	116		
r	114		
i	105		
n	110		
g	103	string2[15]	103
\0	0	string2[16]	0

Figure 9.4 The ASCII codes used to store this is a string

End-of-string tests are frequently written by professional C programmers in this shorter form, so it is worthwhile to become familiar with it. Including this shorter test expression in `strcopy()` results in the following version, where the only change has been made to line 26:

```
21 /* copy string2 to string1 */
22 void strcopy(char string1[], char string2[])
23 {
24   int i = 0;
25
26   while (string2[i])
27   {
28     string1[i] = string2[i]; /* copy the element to string1 */
29     i++;
30   }
31   string1[i] = '\0'; /* terminate the first string */
32 }
```

Programming Note

The Character `'\n'` and the String `"\n"`

Both `'\n'` and `"\n"` are recognized by the compiler as containing the newline character. The difference is in the data types being used. Formally, `'\n'` is a character literal, while `"\n"` is a string literal. From a practical standpoint, both cause the same thing to happen: a new line is placed on the output display. In encountering the character value `'\n'`, however, the compiler translates it using the single byte code 00001010 (see Table 2.5). In encountering the string value `"\n"`, the compiler translates this string using the correct character code, but also adds one additional character, the `NULL` character, that indicates the end of the string.

Good programming practice requires that you end the last output display with a newline escape sequence, usually as the single character `'\n'`. This ensures that the first line of output from one program does not end up on the last line displayed by the previously executed program

The second modification that would be made to this string copy function by an experienced C programmer is to include the assignment inside the test portion of the `while` statement. Our new version of the string copy function is

```
/* copy string2 to string1 */
void strcopy(char string1[], char string2[]) /* copy string2 to string1 */
{
  int i = 0;

  while (string1[i] = string2[i])
    i++;
}
```

Notice that including the assignment statement within the test part of the `while` statement eliminates the necessity of separately terminating the first string with the `NULL` character. The assignment within the parentheses ensures that the `NULL` character is copied from the second string to the first string. The value of the assignment expression becomes 0 only after the `NULL` character is assigned.

Character-by-Character Input Just as strings can be processed using character-by-character techniques, they can also be entered and displayed in this manner. For example, consider Program 9.3, which uses the character-input function `getchar()` to enter a string one character at a time. The shaded portion of Program 9.3 essentially replaces the `gets()` function previously used in Program 9.2.

Program 9.3

```
#include <stdio.h>
int main()
{
```

```
4       #define LSIZE 81
5       char message[LSIZE];   /* enough storage for 80 characters plus '\0' */
6       char c;
7       int i;
8
9       printf("Enter a string:\n");
10      i = 0;
11      while(i < (LSIZE-1) && (c = getchar()) != '\n')
12      {
13        message[i] = c; /* store the character entered */
14        i++;
15      }
16      message[i] = '\0'; /* terminate the string */
17      printf("The string just entered is: \n");
18      puts(message);
19
20      return 0;
21    }
```

The following is a sample run of Program 9.3:

```
Enter a string:
This is a test input of a string of characters.
The string just entered is:
This is a test input of a string of characters.
```

The `while` statement in Program 9.3 in line 11 causes characters to be read, as long as the number of characters entered is fewer than 80 and the character returned by `getchar()` is not the newline character.

```
11  while(i < (LSIZE-1) && (c = getchar()) != '\n')
```

The parentheses around the expression `c = getchar()` in this statement are necessary to assign the character returned by `getchar()` to the variable `c` prior to comparing it to the newline escape sequence. Otherwise, the comparison operator, `!=`, which takes precedence over the assignment operator, causes the entire expression to be equivalent to

```
c = (getchar() != '\n')
```

This has the effect of first comparing the character returned by `getchar()` to `'\n'`. The value of the relational expression `getchar() != '\n'` is either 0 or 1, depending on whether `getchar()` received the newline character. The value assigned to `c` then would also be either 0 or 1, as determined by the comparison.

Program 9.3 also illustrates a very useful technique for developing functions. The shaded statements constitute a self-contained unit for entering a complete line of characters from a terminal. As such, these statements can be removed from `main()` and placed together as a new function. Program 9.4 illustrates placing these statements in a new function called `getline()`.

Programming Note

Why the `char` Data Type Uses Integer Values

In C, a character is stored as an integer value, which is sometimes confusing to beginning programmers. The reason for this is that, in addition to the standard English letters and characters, a program needs to store special characters that have no printable equivalents. One of these is the end-of-file sentinel that all computer systems use to designate the end of a file of data. These end-of-file sentinels can also be transmitted from the keyboard. For example, on Unix-based systems it is generated by pressing the Ctrl and D keys at the same time, whereas on Windows-based systems, it is generated by simultaneously pressing the Ctrl and Z keys. Both of these sentinels are stored as the integer number −1, which has no equivalent character value. You can check this by displaying the integer value of each entered character (see Program 3.10) and typing either Ctrl + D or Ctrl + Z, depending on the system you are using.

A very important consequence of using integer codes for string characters is that characters can be easily compared for alphabetical ordering. For example, as long as each subsequent letter in an alphabet has a higher value than its preceding letter, the comparison of character values is reduced to the comparison of numeric values. If characters are stored in sequential numerical order, it ensures that adding one to a letter will produce the next letter in the alphabet.

Program 9.4

```
#include <stdio.h>
void getline(char []); /* function prototype */
#define LSIZE 81

int main()
{
  char message[LSIZE];  /* enough storage for 80 characters plus '\0' */

  printf("Enter a string: \n");
  getline(message);
  printf("The string just entered is:\n");
  puts(message);

  return 0;
}

void getline(char strng[])
{
  int i = 0;
  char c;

```

```
  while(i < (LSIZE-1) && (c = getchar()) != '\n')
  {
    strng[i] = c; /* store the character entered */
    i++;
  }
  strng[i] = '\0'; /* terminate the string */
}
```

We can go further with `getline()` and write it more compactly by having the character returned by `getchar()` assigned directly to the `strng` array. This eliminates the need for the local variable `c` and results in the following version:

```
void getline (char strng[])
{
  int i = 0;

  while(i < (LSIZE-1) && (strng[i++] = getchar()) != '\n')
     ;
  strng[i] = '\0'; /* terminate the string */
}
```

In addition to assigning the returned character from `getchar()` directly to the `strng` array, the assignment expression `strng[i++] = getchar()` increments the subscript `i` using the postfix operator, `++`. The `NULL` statement, `;` , then fulfills the requirement that a `while` loop contain at least one statement. Both versions of `getline()` are suitable replacements for `gets()` and show the interchangeability of user-written and library functions.

C's enormous flexibility is evidenced by its ability to replace a library function with a user-written version and by its ability to have functions written in various ways. Neither version of `getline()` is "more correct" from a programming standpoint. Each version presented (and more versions can be created) has its advantage and disadvantages. While the second version is more compact, the first version is clearer to beginning programmers. In creating your own C programs, select a style that is comfortable and remain with it until your growing programming expertise dictates modifications to your style.

EXERCISES 9.1

Short Answer Questions

1. What data type does C use to store strings?
2. What character is used to terminate all C strings?
3. What character corresponds to `message[3]` for the declaration

   ```
   char message[] = "Hello there";
   ```

4. What will be displayed by the statement

`printf("%s\n", &message[6]);` assuming that message has been declared as

```
char message[] = "Hello there";
```

Programming Exercises

1. a. The following function can be used to select and display all vowels contained within a user-input string:

```
void vowels(char strng[])
{
  int i = 0;
  char c;

  while ((c = strng[i++]) != '\0')
  switch(c)
  {
    case 'a':
    case 'e':
    case 'i':
    case 'o':
    case 'u':
      putchar(c);
  } /* end of switch */
  putchar('\n');

  return;
}
```

Notice that the `switch` statement in `vowels()` uses the fact that selected cases "drop through" in the absence of `break` statements. Thus, all selected cases result in a `putchar()` function call. Include `vowels()` in a working program that accepts a user-input string and then displays all vowels in the string. In response to the input `How much is the little worth worth?`, your program should display `ouieieoo`.

   b. Modify the `vowels()` function to count and display the total number of vowels contained in the string passed to it.

2. Modify the `vowels()` function given in Exercise 1a to count and display the individual numbers of each vowel contained in the string.

3. a. Write a C function to count the total number of characters, including blanks, contained in a string. Do not include the end-of-string `NULL` marker in the count.

   b. Include the function written for Exercise 3a in a complete working program.

4. Write a C program that accepts a string of characters from a terminal and displays the hexadecimal equivalent of each character.

5. Write a C program that accepts a string of characters from a terminal and displays the string one word per line.

6. Write a C function that reverses the characters in a string. (*Hint:* This can be considered as a string copy starting from the back end of the first string.)

7. Write a C function named `delChar()` that can be used to delete characters from a string. The function should accept three arguments: the string name, the number of characters to delete, and the starting position in the string where characters should be deleted. For example, the function call `delChar(strng,13,5)`, when applied to the string `all enthusiastic people`, should result in the string `all people`.

8. Write a C function named `addChar()` to insert one string of characters into another string. The function should accept three arguments: the string to be inserted, the original string, and the position in the original string where the insertion should begin. For example, the call `addChar("for all",message,6)` should insert the characters `for all` in `message` starting at `message[5]`.

9. **a.** Write a C function named `toUpper()` that converts individual lowercase letters into uppercase letters. The expression `ch - 'a' + 'A'` can be used to make the conversion for any lowercase character stored in `ch`.
   b. Add a data input check to the function written in Exercise 9a to verify that a valid lowercase letter is passed to the function. A character is lowercase if it is greater than or equal to `a` and less than or equal to `z`. If the character is not a valid lowercase letter, have the function `toUpper()` return the passed character unaltered.
   c. Write a C program that accepts a string from a terminal and converts all lowercase letters in the string to uppercase letters.

10. Write a C program that accepts a string from a terminal and converts all uppercase letters in the string to lowercase letters.

11. Write a C program that counts the number of words in a string. A word is encountered whenever a transition from a blank space to a nonblank character is encountered. Assume the string contains only words separated by blank spaces.

9.2 Library Functions

C does not provide built-in operations for complete arrays, such as array assignments or array comparisons. Because a string is just an array of characters terminated with a `'\0'` character and not a data type in its own right, this means that assignment and relational operations *are not* provided for strings. Extensive collections of string- and character-handling functions are, however, included in C's standard library. The more commonly used string functions were previously listed in Section 6.4, and for convenience are repeated within the more extensive listing provided in Table 9.2.

Table 9.2 String Library Routines (Required Header File is `string.h`)

Name	Description	Example
`strcpy(str1, str2)`	Copies `str2` to `str1`, including the `'\0'`	`strcpy(test, "efgh")`
`strcat(str1, str2)`	Appends `str2` to the end of `str1`	`strcat(test, "there")`

Table 9.2 String Library Routines (Required Header File is `string.h`) (continued)

Name	Description	Example
`strlen(string)`	Returns the length of `string`. Does not include the `'\0'` in the length count.	`strlen("Hello World!")`
`strcmp(str1, str2)`	Compares `str1` to `str2`. Returns a negative integer if `str1 < str2`, 0 if `str1 == str2`, and a positive integer if `str1 > str2`.	`strcmp("Beb", "Bee")`
`strncpy(str1, str2,n)`	Copies at most `n` characters of `str2` to `str1`. If `str2` has fewer than `n` characters, it pads `str1` with `'\0'`s.	`strncpy(str1, str2, 5)`
`strncmp(str1, str2,n)`	Compares at most `n` characters of `str1` to `str2`. Returns the same values as `strcmp()` based on the number of characters compared.	`strncmp("Beb", "Bee", 2)`
`strchr(string, char)`	Locates the position of the first occurrence of the **char** within `string`. Returns the address of the character.	`strchr("Hello", 'l')`
`strtok(string, char)`	Parses `string` into tokens. Returns the next sequence of **char** contained in `string` up to but not including the delimiter character.	`strtok("Hi Ho Ha", ' ')`

String library functions are called in the same manner as all C functions. This means that the appropriate declarations for these functions, which are contained in the standard header file `string.h`, must be included in your program before the function is called.

The most commonly used functions listed in Table 9.2 are the first four. The `strcpy()` function copies a source string expression, which consists of either a string literal or the contents of a string variable, into a destination string variable. For example, in the function call `strcpy(string1, "Hello World!")`, the source string literal `"Hello World!"` is copied into the destination string variable `string1`. Similarly, if the source string is a string

Programming Note

Initializing and Processing Strings

Each of the following declarations produce the same result:

```
char test[5] = "abcd";
char test[] = "abcd";
char test[5] = {'a', 'b', 'c', 'd', '\0'};
char test[] = {'a', 'b', 'c', 'd', '\0'};
```

Each declaration creates storage for exactly five characters and initializes this storage with the characters `'a'`, `'b'`, `'c'`, `'d'`, and `'\0'`. Since a string literal is used for initialization in the first two declarations, the compiler automatically supplies the end-of-string `NULL` character.

String variables declared in either of these ways shown preclude the use of any subsequent assignments, such as `test = "efgh";`, to the character array. In place of an assignment, you can use the `strcpy()` function, such as `strcpy(test,"efgh")`. The only restriction on using `strcpy()` is the size of the declared array, which in this case is five elements. Attempting to copy a larger string value into `test` causes the copy to overflow the destination array beginning with the memory area immediately following the last array element. This overwrites whatever was in these memory locations and typically causes a run-time crash when the overwritten areas are accessed via their legitimate identifier name(s).

The same problem can arise when using the `strcat()` function. It is your responsibility to ensure that the concatenated string will fit into the original string.

An interesting situation arises when string variables are defined using pointers (see Section 11.5). In these situations assignments can be made after the declaration statement.

variable named `srcString`, the function call `strcpy(string1, srcString)` copies the contents of `srcString` into `string1`. In both cases, it is the programmer's responsibility to ensure that `string1` is large enough to contain the source string (see this section's Programming Note).

The `strcat()` function appends a string expression onto the end of a string variable. For example, if the contents of a string variable named `destString` are `"Hello"`, then the function call `strcat(destString, " there World!")` results in the string value `"Hello there World!"` being assigned to `destString`. As with the `strcpy()` function, it is the programmer's responsibility to ensure that the destination string has been defined large enough to hold the additional concatenated characters.

The `strlen()` function returns the number of characters in its string argument but does not include the terminating `NULL` character in the count. For example, the value returned by the function call `strlen("Hello World!")` is 12.

Finally, two string expressions may be compared for equality using the `strcmp()` function. Each character in a string is stored as a binary number using either the ASCII or Unicode codes. The first 128 characters of the Unicode code are identical to the complete 128-character ASCII code. In both of them, a blank precedes (is less than) all letters and numbers, the letters of the alphabet are stored in order from A to Z, and the digits are stored in order from 0 to 9.

When two strings are compared, their individual characters are evaluated a pair at a time (both first characters, then both second characters, and so on). If no differences are found, the strings are equal; if a difference is found, the string with the first lower character is considered the smaller string. Thus,

"Good Bye" is less than "Hello" because the first 'G' in Good Bye is less than the first 'H' in Hello.
"Hello" is less than "hello" because the first 'H' in Hello is less than the first 'h' in hello.
"Hello" is less than "Hello " because the '\0' terminating the first string is less than the ' ' in the second string.
"SMITH" is greater than "JONES" because the first 'S' in SMITH is greater than the first 'J' in JONES.
"123" is greater than "122" because the third character, '3', in 123 is greater than the third character, '2', in 122.
"1237" is greater than "123" because the fourth character, '7', in 1237 is greater than the fourth character, '\0', in 123.
"Behop" is greater than "Beehive" because the third character, 'h', in Behop is greater than the third character, 'e', in Beehive.

Program 9.5 uses the string functions we have discussed within the context of a complete program.

Program 9.5

```
#include <stdio.h>
#include <string.h> /* required for the string function library */

int main()
{
  #define MAXELS 50
  char string1[MAXELS] = "Hello";
  char string2[MAXELS] = "Hello there";
  int n;

  n = strcmp(string1, string2);

  if (n < 0)
    printf("%s is less than %s\n\n", string1, string2);
  else if (n == 0)
    printf("%s is equal to %s\n\n", string1, string2);
  else
    printf("%s is greater than %s\n\n", string1, string2);

  printf("The length of string1 is %d characters\n", strlen(string1));
```

```
  printf("The length of string2 is %d characters\n\n", strlen(string2));

  strcat(string1," there World!");

  printf("After concatenation, string1 contains the string value\n");
  printf("%s\n", string1);
  printf("The length of this string is %d characters\n\n",
                                                    strlen(string1));
  printf("Type in a sequence of characters for string2:\n");
  gets(string2);

  strcpy(string1, string2);

  printf("After copying string2 to string1");
  printf(" the string value in string1 is:\n");
  printf("%s\n", string1);
  printf("The length of this string is %d characters\n\n",
                                                  strlen(string1));
  printf("\nThe starting address of the string1 string is: %d\n",
                                                  (void *) string1);
  return 0;
}
```

A sample output produced by Program 9.5 is

```
Hello is less than Hello there

The length of string1 is 5 characters
The length of string2 is 11 characters

After concatenation, string1 contains the string value
Hello there World!
The length of this string is 18 characters

Type in a sequence of characters for string2:
It's a wonderful day
After copying string2 to string1, the string value in string1 is:
It's a wonderful day
The length of this string is 20 characters

The starting address of the string1 string is: 1244836
```

Except for the last displayed line, the output of Program 9.5 follows the discussion presented for the string library functions. As demonstrated by this output, supplying a string variable or string constant as an argument to `printf()` forces the contents of the string to be displayed and requires the control string `%s`. Sometimes, however, we really want to see the address of the string. As shown in Program 9.5, this can be done by casting the string variable name using the expression `(void *)`. Another method is to use the expression `&string1[0]` as an argument to `printf()`. This expression is read as "the address of the `string[0]`element," which is also the starting address of the complete character array.

Character Routines

In addition to string manipulation functions, the standard C library includes the character-handling routines listed in Table 9.3. The prototypes for each of these routines are contained in the header file `ctype.h`, which should be included in any program that uses these routines.

Table 9.3 Character Library Routines (Required Header File is `ctype.h`)

Required Prototype	Description	Example
`int isalpha(char)`	Returns a non-0 number if the character is a letter; otherwise, it returns 0.	`isalpha('a')`
`int isupper(char)`	Returns a non-0 number if the character is uppercase; otherwise, it returns 0.	`isupper('a')`
`int islower(char)`	Returns a non-0 number if the character is lowercase; otherwise, it returns 0.	`islower('a')`
`int isdigit(char)`	Returns a non-0 number if the character is a digit (0 through 9); otherwise, it returns 0.	`isdigit('a')`
`int isascii(char)`	Returns a non-0 number if the character is an ASCII character; otherwise, it returns 0.	`isascii('a')`
`int isspace(char)`	Returns a non-0 number if the character is a space; otherwise, it returns 0.	`isspace(' ')`
`int isprint(char)`	Returns a non-0 number if the character is a printable character; otherwise, it returns 0.	`isprint('a')`
`int iscntrl(char)`	Returns a non-0 number if the character is a control character; otherwise, it returns 0.	`iscntrl('a')`
`int ispunct(char)`	Returns a non-0 number if the character is a punctuation character; otherwise, it returns 0.	`ispunct('!')`
`int toupper(char)`	Returns the uppercase equivalent if the character is lowercase; otherwise, it returns the character unchanged.	`toupper('a')`
`int tolower(char)`	Returns the lowercase equivalent if the character is uppercase; otherwise, it returns the character unchanged.	`tolower('A')`

All of the routines listed in Table 9.3 except for the last two, return a non-0 integer (that is, a true value) if the character meets the desired condition and a 0 integer (that is, a false value) if the condition is not met; therefore, these functions can be used directly within an `if` statement. For example, consider the following code segment:

```
char ch;

printf("Enter a single character: ");
ch = getchar(); /* get a character from the keyboard */
if(isdigit(ch))
    printf("The character just entered is a digit\n");
else if(ispunct(ch))
  printf("The character just entered is a punctuation mark\n");
```

Notice that the character routine is included as a condition within the `if` statement because the function effectively returns either a true (non-0) or false (0) value.

Program 9.6 illustrates the use of the `toupper()` routine within the function `convertToUpper()`, which is used to convert all lowercase string characters into their uppercase form.

Program 9.6

```
#include <stdio.h>
#include <ctype.h> /* required for the character function library */

int main()
{
  #define MAXCHARS 100
  char message[MAXCHARS];
  void convertToUpper(char []);   /* function prototype */

  printf("\nType in any sequence of characters:\n");
  gets(message);

  convertToUpper(message);

  printf("The characters just entered, in uppercase are:\n%s\n", message);

  return 0;
}

// this function converts all lowercase characters to uppercase
void convertToUpper(char message[])
{
  int i;
  for(i = 0; message[i] != '\0'; i++)
    message[i] = toupper(message[i]);
}
```

The output produced by Program 9.6

```
Type in any sequence of characters:
this is a test OF 12345.
The characters just entered, in uppercase are:
THIS IS A TEST OF 12345.
```

Notice that the `toupper()` library function only converts lowercase letters and that all other characters are unaffected.

Conversion Routines

The last group of standard C-string library routines, listed in Table 9.4, is used to convert C strings to and from integer and double-precision data types. The prototypes for each of these routines are contained in the header file `stdlib.h`, which should be included in any program that uses these routines.

Table 9.4 Conversion Routines (Required Header File is `stdlib.h`)

Prototype	Description	Example
`int atoi(string)`	Converts an ASCII string to an integer. Conversion stops at the first noninteger character.	`atoi("1234")`
`double atof(string)`	Converts an ASCII string to a double-precision number. Conversion stops at the first character that cannot be interpreted as a double.	`atof("12.34")`
`char[] itoa(string)`	Converts an integer to an ASCII string. The space allocated for the returned string must be large enough for the converted value.	`itoa(1234)`

Program 9.7 illustrates using the `atoi()` and `atof()` functions.

Program 9.7

```
#include <stdio.h>
#include <string.h>
#include <stdlib.h> // required for test conversion function library

int main()
{
#define MAXELS 20
  char test[MAXELS] = "1234";
  int num;
  double dnum;

```

☞

```
  num = atoi(test);
  printf("The string %s as an integer number is %d\n", test,num);
  printf("This number divided by 3 is: %d\n", num/3);

  strcat(test, ".96");

  dnum = atof(test);
  printf("\nThe string %s as a double number is: %f\n", test,dnum);
  printf("This number divided by 3 is: %f\n", dnum/3);

  return 0;
}
```

The output produced by Program 9.7 is

```
The string "1234" as an integer number is: 1234
This number divided by 3 is: 411

The string "1234.96" as a double number is: 1234.960000
This number divided by 3 is: 411.653333
```

As this output illustrates, once a string has been converted to either an integer or double-precision value, mathematical operations on the numerical value are valid.

EXERCISES 9.2

Short Answer Questions

1. True or false: The string `"april"` is greater than the string `"April"`.
2. What is the length of the string message where message has been declared as

   ```
   char message[10] = "Wow!";
   ```

3. What is the value of the expression `isdigit('a');`?
4. What character routine would you use to convert the string `"78.45"` to a double-precision numeric value?

Programming Exercises

1. Enter and execute Program 9.5 on your computer.
2. Enter and execute Program 9.6 on your computer.

3. a. Write a C function named `trimfrnt()` that deletes all leading blanks from a string.
   b. Write a simple `main()` function to test the `trimfrnt()` function written for Exercise 3a.

4. a. Write a C function named `trimrear()` that deletes all trailing blanks from a string.
   b. Write a simple `main()` function to test the `trimrear()` function written for Exercise 4a.

5. a. Write a C function named `chartype()` that determines the ASCII type of any integer in the range 0 to 127. If the number represents a printable ASCII character, print the character with one of the following appropriate messages:
   - `The ASCII character is a lowercase letter.`
   - `The ASCII character is an uppercase letter.`
   - `The ASCII character is a digit.`
   - `The ASCII character is a punctuation mark.`
   - `The ASCII character is a space.`

   If the ASCII character is a nonprintable character, display its ASCII code in decimal format and the message, `The ASCII character is a nonprintable character.`
   b. Write a simple `main()` function to test the function written for Exercise 5a. The `main()` function should generate 20 random numbers in the range 0 to 127 and call `chartype()` for each generated number.

6. a. Include the string library functions `strlen()`, `strcat()`, and `strncat()` within a function having the prototype `int concat(char string1[], char string2[], int maxlength)`. The `concat()` function should perform a complete concatenation of `string2` to `string1` only if the length of the concatenated string does not exceed `maxlength`, which is the maximum length defined for `string1`. If the concatenated string exceeds `maxlength`, concatenate only the characters in `string2` so that the maximum combined string length is equal to `maxlength - 1`, which provides enough room for the end-of-string `NULL` character.
   b. Write a simple `main()` function to test the `concat()` function written for Exercise 6a.

7. a. Write a function named `countlets()` that return the number of letters in an entered string. Digits, spaces, punctuation, tabs, and newline characters should not be included in the returned count.
   b. Write a simple `main()` function to test the `countlets()` function written for Exercise 7a.

9.3 Input Data Validation

One of the major uses of strings in programs is validating user input, an essential part of any program. Even though a program prompts the user to enter a specific type of data, such as an integer, this does not ensure that the user will comply. What a user enters is, in fact, totally out of the programmer's control. What is in your control is how your program deals with the entered data.

It certainly does no good to tell a frustrated user, "The program clearly tells you to enter an integer and you entered a date." Rather, successful programs always try to anticipate invalid data and isolate such data from being accepted and processed. This is typically accomplished by first validating that the data is of the correct type. If it is, the data is accepted; otherwise, the user is requested to re-enter the data, with a possible explanation of why the entered data was invalid.

One of the most common methods of validating input data is to accept all numbers as strings. Each character in the string can then be checked to ensure that it complies with the data type being requested. Only after this check is made and the data is verified for the correct type is the string converted to either an integer or double-precision value using one of the conversion functions previously listed in Table 9.4.

As an example, consider the input of an integer number. To be valid, the data entered must adhere to the following conditions:

- The data must contain at least one character.
- If the first character is a + or - sign, the data must contain at least one digit.
- Only digits from 0 to 9 are acceptable following the first character.

The following function, named `isvalidInt()`, can be used to check that an entered string complies with these conditions. This function returns an integer value of 1, if the conditions are satisfied; otherwise, it returns an integer value of 0.

```
#define TRUE 1
#define FALSE 0
int isvalidInt(char val[])
{
  int start = 0;
  int i;
  int valid = TRUE;
  int sign = FALSE;

  /* check for an empty string */
  if (val[0] == '\0') valid = FALSE;

  /* check for a leading sign */
  if (val[0] == '-' || val[0] == '+')
  {
    sign = TRUE;
    start = 1;  /* start checking for digits after the sign */
  }

  /* check that there is at least one character after the sign */
  if(sign == TRUE && val[1] == '\0')
    valid = FALSE;

  /*now check the string, which we know has at least one non-sign char */
  i = start;
  while(valid == TRUE && val[i] != '\0')
  {
    if (val[i] < '0' || val[i] > '9') /* check for a non-digit */
      valid = FALSE;
    i++;
  }

  return valid;
}
```

In the code for the `isvalidInt()` method, pay attention to the conditions that are being checked. These are commented in the code and consist of checking the following:

- The string is not empty (lines 10 and 11).
- The presence of a valid sign symbol (+ or -) (lines 13 through 18).
- If a sign symbol is present, at least one digit follows it (lines 20 through 22).
- All of the remaining characters are valid digits. A valid digit is any character between 0 and 9, while any character less than 0 or greater than 9 is not a digit (lines 24 through 31).

Only if all of these conditions are met does the function return a value of 1. Once this value is returned, the string can be safely converted into an integer with the assurance that no unexpected value will result to hamper further data processing. Program 9.8 uses this method within the context of a complete program.

Program 9.8

```
#include <stdio.h>
#include <stdlib.h>  /* needed to convert a string to an integer */
#define MAXCHARS 40
#define TRUE 1
#define FALSE 0

int isvalidInt(char []);  /* function prototype */

int main()
{

  char value[MAXCHARS];
  int number;

  printf("Enter an integer: ");
  gets(value);

  if (isvalidInt(value)== TRUE)
  {
    number = atoi(value);
    printf("The number you entered is %d\n", number);
  }
  else
    printf("The number you entered is not a valid integer.\n");

  return 0;
}

```

```
int isvalidInt(char val[])
{
  int start = 0;
  int i;
  int valid = TRUE;
  int sign = FALSE;

  /* check for an empty string */
  if (val[0] == '\0') valid = FALSE;

  /* check for a leading sign */
  if (val[0] == '-' || val[0] == '+')
  {
    sign = TRUE;
    start = 1;  /* start checking for digits after the sign */
  }

  /* check that there is at least one character after the sign */
  if(sign == TRUE && val[1] == '\0') valid = FALSE;

  /*now check the string, which we know has at least one non-sign char */
  i = start;
  while(valid == TRUE && val[i] != '\0')
  {
    if (val[i] < '0' || val[i] > '9') /* check for a non-digit */
        valid = FALSE;
    i++;
  }

  return valid;
 }
```

Two sample runs using Program 9.8 produced the following:

```
Enter an integer: 12e45
The number you entered is not a valid integer.
```

and

```
Enter an integer: -12345
The number you entered is -12345
```

As illustrated by this output, the program successfully determines that an invalid character was entered in the first run. The `isvalidInt()` function can be written more compactly using pointers, which, as they relate to string arrays, are described in Chapter 11.

Having created the function `isvalidInt()` to successfully detect whenever a valid integer number has been entered, we can now incorporate this function within a loop that continually requests an integer until a valid integer value is entered. The algorithm that we will use to accept the user's input is

Set an integer variable named isanInt to 0
do
    Accept a string value
    If the string value does not correspond to an integer
        Display the error message "Invalid integer - Please re-enter: "
        Send control back to expression being tested by the do-while statement
    Set isanInt to 1 (this causes the loop to terminate)
while(isanInt is 0)
Return the integer corresponding to the entered string

The code corresponding to this algorithm is highlighted in Program 9.9 (lines 27 through 39).

Program 9.9

```
 1  #include <stdio.h>
 2  #include <stdlib.h>
 3
 4  int getanInt();   /* function prototype */
 5
 6  int main()
 7  {
 8    int value;
 9
10    printf("Enter an integer value: ");
11    value = getanInt();
12    printf("The integer entered is: %d\n", value);
13
14    return 0;
15  }
16
17  #define TRUE 1
18  #define FALSE 0
19  #define MAXCHARS 40
20  int getanInt()
21  {
22    int isvalidInt(char []);  /* function prototype */
23
24    int isanInt = FALSE;
25    char value[MAXCHARS];
26
27    do
28    {
```

```
      gets(value);
      if (isvalidInt(value) == FALSE)
      {
        printf("Invalid integer - Please re-enter: ");
        continue; /* send control to the do-while expression test */
      }
      isanInt = TRUE;
    }while (isanInt == FALSE);

    return (atoi(value));  /* convert to an integer */
}

int isvalidInt(char val[])
{
    int start = 0;
    int i;
    int valid = TRUE;
    int sign = FALSE;

    /* check for an empty string */
    if (val[0] == '\0') valid = FALSE;

    /* check for a leading sign */
    if (val[0] == '-' || val[0] == '+')
    {
      sign = TRUE;
      start = 1;  /* start checking for digits after the sign */
    }

    /* check that there is at least one character after the sign */
    if(sign == TRUE && val[1] == '\0') valid = FALSE;

    /*now check the string, which we know has at least one non-sign char */
    i = start;
    while(valid == TRUE && val[i] != '\0')
    {
      if (val[i] < '0' || val[i] > '9') /* check for a non-digit */
          valid = FALSE;
      i++;
    }

     return valid;
}
```

Following is a sample output produced by Program 9.9:

```
Enter an integer value: abc
Invalid integer - Please re-enter: 12.
Invalid integer - Please re-enter: 12e
Invalid integer - Please re-enter: 120
The integer entered is: 120
```

As shown by this output, the `getanInt()` function works correctly. It continuously requests input until a valid integer is entered.

Creating a Personal Library

The functions `isvalidInt()` and `getanInt()` are useful in many situations because they can be used in any program requesting a user-entered integer value. For such functions programmers typically create their own libraries of these functions. This permit the functions to be incorporated in any program without further expenditure of coding time.

At this stage in your programming career, you can also begin to build your own library of useful functions, starting with `isvalidInt()` and `getanInt()`. The procedure for doing so is to store the desired functions in a file. Typically, each file would also contain related functions. Thus, one file might contain data validation functions, while other files would contain functions related in other ways.

For example, applications in both the financial and engineering scheduling fields require specialized date-handling functions. These include finding the number of business days between two dates that take into account weekends and holidays. It also requires functions that implement prior date and next date algorithms that take into account leap years and the actual number of days in each month.

Once such functions have been coded, tested, and placed into their own files, they can be incorporated in any program without further expenditures of coding time by using a `#include` statement. For example, assuming that the two functions, `isvalidInt()` and `getanInt()` have been stored in a file named `dataChecks.h` on the C drive within the directory `mylibrary`, either of the following statements can be used to include the functions within a program:

```
#include <C:\\mylibrary\\dataChecks.h>
```

or

```
#include "C:\\mylibrary\\dataChecks.h"
```

Both statements provide the full path name for the new header file. Notice that a full name requires that two backslashes be used to separate individual directory and filenames. As indicated, the `dataChecks.h` source file is contained within a directory named `mylibrary`. The only time that backslashes are not required is when the library code resides in the same directory as the program being executed. The angle brackets, <>, tell the compiler to begin searching for the included file in the C compiler system library directory, while the double quotes, `""`, tell the compiler to start looking in the default directory where the program file is located. Providing a full path name redirects the compiler, in both cases, to go to the designated directory starting at the root directory. Thus, providing a full path name makes both statements equivalent. In either case, the `#include` statement for `dataChecks.h` would have to be placed *after* the `#include` statements for the `stdio.h` and `stdlib.h` header files. This is required because the functions in the `dataChecks.h` header file require `stdio.h` and `stdlib.h` functions to correctly compile.

Appendix F provides a personal library that includes a number of very useful, general-purpose functions that include `isvalidInt()` and `getanInt()` written more compactly using pointers.

EXERCISES 9.3

Short Answer Questions

1. In terms of user-input validation, why is it convenient to enter a number as a string?
2. List a number of data checks that should be made on a user-entered date.
3. List at least four functions that you think would be useful in a personal library.

Programming Exercises

1. Enter and execute Program 9.8 five times. The first time you run the program, enter a valid integer number, the second time enter a double-precision number, and the third time enter a character. Next, enter the value 12e34 and then 31234.
2. Modify Program 9.8 to display any invalid characters that were entered.
3. Write a function that checks each digit as it is entered, rather than checking the completed string, as done in Program 9.8.
4. Write a C program that accepts a name as first name last name and then displays the name as last name, first name. For example, if the user entered `Gary Bronson`, the output should be `Bronson, Gary`.
5. Store the functions `isvalidInt()` and `getanInt()` provided in this section in a header file named `dataChecks.h`. Next, rewrite Program 9.9 to use this header file.
6. Write a C function named `isvalidReal()` that checks for a valid double-precision number. This kind of number can have an optional + or – sign, at most one decimal point, which can also be the first character, and at least one digit between 0 and 9 inclusive. The function should return an integer value of 1 if the entered number is a real number; otherwise, it should return an integer value of 0.

9.4 Formatting Strings (Optional)

The standard library provided with your C compiler includes some special string-handling functions. In addition, both the `printf()` and `scanf()` functions have string-formatting capabilities. Two related functions, `sprintf()` and `sscanf()`, provide further string-processing features. In this section you'll learn about these string-processing features.

Field-width specifiers can be included in a `printf()` control sequence to control the spacing of integers and decimal numbers. These specifiers can also be used with the `%s` control sequence to control the display of a string. For example, the statement

```
printf("|%25s|","Have a Happy Day");
```

displays the message `Have a Happy Day`, right-justified, in a field of 25 characters, as follows:

```
|∧∧∧∧∧∧∧∧∧ Have a Happy Day|
```

We have placed a bar (|) at the beginning and end of the string field to clearly delineate the field being printed. Placing a minus sign (-) in front of the field-width specifier forces the string to be left-justified in the field. For example, the statement

```
printf("|%-25s|","Have a Happy Day");
```

causes the display

```
|Have a Happy Day ∧∧∧∧∧∧∧∧∧|
```

where we have used ∧to denote a blank space.

If the field-width specifier is too small for the string, the specifier is ignored and the string is displayed using sufficient space to accommodate the complete string.

The precision specifier used for determining the number of digits displayed to the right of a decimal number can also be used as a string specifier. When used with strings, the precision specifier determines the maximum number of characters that will be displayed. For example, the statement

```
printf("|%25.12s|","Have a Happy Day");
```

causes the first 12 characters in the string to be displayed, right justified, in a field of 25 characters. This produces the display

```
|∧∧∧∧∧∧∧∧∧∧∧∧∧ Have a Happy|
```

Similarly, the statement

```
printf("|%-25.12s|","Have a Happy Day");
```

causes 12 characters to be left justified in a field of 25 characters. This produces the display

```
|∧∧∧∧∧∧∧∧∧∧∧∧∧ Have a Happy|
```

When a precision specifier is used with no field-width specifier, the indicated number of characters is displayed in a field sufficiently large to hold the designated number of characters. Thus, the statement

```
printf("|%.12s|","Have a Happy Day");
```

causes the first 12 characters in the string to be displayed in a field of 12 characters, which produces the output

```
Have a Happy
```

If the string has less than the number of characters designated by the precision specifier, the display is terminated when the end-of-string is encountered.

Programming Note

Data Type Conversions

Converting from character data to numerical data, in all languages, requires some thought. One neat "trick" that can be applied in C is to use the `sscanf()` function to make the conversions for you. For example, assume you need to extract the month, day, and year from the string 07/01/94, which is stored in a character array named `date`. The simple statement

```
sscanf(date,"%d/%d/%d", &month, &day, &year);
```

extracts the data and converts it into integer form. Such ASCII-to-number conversions really become simple in C! Of course, like other languages, C also provides library functions for simple conversions. The function `atoi()` converts a string to a single integer value, and the function `atof()` converts a string to a double-precision value. Some compilers provide `itoa()` and `ftoa()` functions, for converting a single integer and double-precision number, respectively, to their ASCII representations. But if these functions are not available, a call to `sprint()` can be used for these numeric-to-string conversions.

In-Memory String Conversions

While `printf()` displays data to the standard device used by your computer for output and `scanf()` scans, the standard device used for input, the `sprintf()` and `sscanf()` functions provide similar capabilities for writing and scanning strings to and from memory variables. For example, the statement

```
sprintf(disStrn,"%d %d", num1, num2);
```

writes the numerical values of `num1` and `num2` into `disStrn` rather than displaying the values on the standard output terminal. Here, `disStrn` is a programmer-selected variable name that must be declared as either an array of characters, sufficiently large to hold the resulting string, or as a pointer to a string.

Typically, the `sprintf()` function is used to "assemble" a string from smaller pieces until a complete line of characters is ready to be written, either to the standard output device or to a file (writing data to a file is described in Chapter 10). For example, another string could be concatenated to `disStrn` using the `strcat()` function and the complete string displayed using the `printf()` function.

In contrast to `sprintf()`, the string scan function `sscanf()` may be used to "disassemble" a string into smaller pieces. For example, if the string "$23.45 10" were stored in a character array named data, the statement

```
sscanf(data,"%c%lf %d",&dol,&price,&units);
```

would scan the string stored in the data array and "strip off" three data items. The dollar sign would be stored in the variable named `dol`, the 23.45 would be converted to a double-precision number and stored in the variable named price, and the 10 would be converted to an integer value and stored in the variable named units. For a useful result, the variables `dol`, `price`, and `units` would have to be declared as the appropriate data types. In this way `sscanf()` provides a helpful means of converting parts of a string into other data types.

Typically, the string being scanned by `sscanf()` is used as a working storage area, or buffer, for storing a complete line from either a file or the standard input. Once the string has been filed, `sscanf()` disassembles the string into component parts and suitably converts each data item into the designated data type. For programmers familiar with COBOL, this is equivalent to first reading data into a working storage area before moving the data into smaller fields.

Format Strings

When you use any of the four functions, `printf()`, `scanf()`, `sprintf()`, or `sscanf()`, the control string containing the conversion control sequences need not be explicitly contained within the function. For example, the control string `"$%5.2f %d"` contained within the function call

```
printf("$%5.2f %d",num1,num2);
```

can itself be stored as a string and the address of the string can be used in the call to `printf()`. If either of the following declarations for `fmat` are made:

```
char *fmat = "$%5.2f %d";
```

or

```
char fmat[] = "$%5.2f %d";
```

the function call, `printf(fmat,num1,num2);` can be made in place of the previous call to `printf()`. Here, `fmat` is a pointer that contains the address of the control string used to determine the output display.

The technique of storing and using control strings in this manner is very useful for clearly listing format strings with other variable declarations at the beginning of a function. If a change to a format must be made, it is easy to find the desired control string without the necessity of searching through the complete function to locate the appropriate `printf()` or `scanf()` function call. Restricting the definition of a control string to one place is also advantageous when the same format control is used in multiple function calls.

EXERCISES 9.4

Short Answer Questions

1. Determine the display produced by each of the following statements:
   a. `printf("!%10s!","four score and ten");`
   b. `printf("!%15s!","Home!");`
   c. `printf("!%-15s!","Home!");`
   d. `printf("!%15.2s!","Home!");`
   e. `printf("!%-15.2s!","Home!");`

2. a. Assuming that the following declaration has been made

   ```
   char *text = "Have a nice day!";
   ```

determine the display produced by the statements

```
printf("%s", text);
printf("%c", *text);
```

b. Because both `printf()` function calls in Question 2a display characters, determine why the indirection operator is required in the second call but not in the first.

Programming Exercises

1. Write a C program that accepts three user-entered numbers as one string. Once the string has been accepted, have the program pass the string and the addresses of three single-precision variables to a function called `separate()`. The `separate()` function should extract the three floating-point values from the passed string and store them using the passed variable addresses.

2. Modify the program written for Exercise 1 to display the input string using the format `"%6.2f %6.2f %6.2f"`.

3. Write a C program that accepts a string and two integer numbers from a user. Each of these inputs should be preceded by a prompt and stored using individual variable names. Have your program call a function that assembles the input data into a single string. Display the assembled string using a `puts()` call.

9.5 Case Study: Character and Word Counting

In this section we will focus on constructing two string-processing functions. The first function will be used to count the number of characters in a string. The purpose of this problem is to reinforce our concept of a string and how characters can be accessed one at a time. The second function will be used to count words. Although this seems a simple problem at first glance, it is more typical in that it brings up a set of subissues that must be addressed before a final algorithm can selected. Chief among these subissues is determining a suitable criteria for what constitutes a word. This is necessary so that the function can correctly identify and count a word when it encounters one.

Program Requirement: Character Counting

In this problem we want to pass a string to a function and have the function return the number of characters in the string. For our current purposes any character in the string, be it a blank, printable, or nonprintable character, is to be counted. The end-of-string `NULL` character is not to be included in the final count.

Analyze the Problem

This problem has the following input and output.

a. Determine the Input Data The input data, which in this case is a string of characters, becomes the arguments supplied to the function. Because a string in C is simply an array of characters, we can pass the string to our function simply by passing a character array.

b. Determine the Required Outputs The output data, which in this case is an integer that corresponds to the number of characters in the string, is the value returned by the function. Because the function is to return an integer value it will be defined as returning an `int`.

c. List the Algorithm(s) Relating the Inputs to the Outputs Here, the algorithm relating inputs to outputs becomes the code within the body of the function. Once the function receives the character array it must start at the beginning of the array and keep count of each character it encounters as it "marches along" to the end of the string. Because each string is terminated by a `'\0'` character, we can use this as a sentinel to tell us when the count should stop. As illustrated in Figure 9.5, we examine each character by indexing through the array until the sentinel is reached.

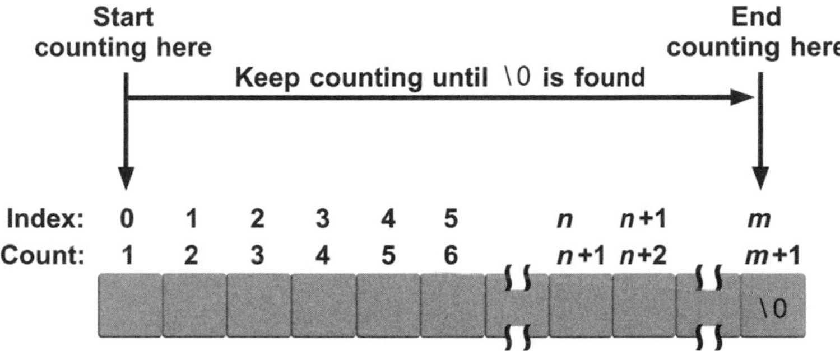

Figure 9.5 Counting characters in a string

The pseudocode describing our character counting algorithm is

```
Accept the string as an array argument
Initialize a count to 0
For all the characters in the array
  increment the count
EndFor
Return the count
```

Code the Function

The C code corresponding to our pseudocode solution is

```
int countchar(char list[])
{
  int i, count = 0;

  for(i = 0; list[i] != '\0'; i++)
    count++;

  return(count);
}
```

Notice that we have used a `for` loop within `countchar()`. We could just as easily replaced this with a `while` loop.

Test and Debug the Function

To test the function, we create a main driver function whose sole purpose is to exercise `countchar()`. Program 9.10 includes both the `main` driver and `countchar()`.

Program 9.10

```
#include <stdio.h>
#define MAXNUM 1000

int countchar(char []);   /* function prototype */

int main()
{
  char message[MAXNUM];
  int numchar;

  printf("\nType in any number of characters: ");
  gets(message);
  numchar = countchar(message);
  printf("The number of characters just entered is %d\n", numchar);

  return 0;
}

int countchar(char list[])
{
  int i, count = 0;

  for(i = 0; list[i] != '\0'; i++)
    count++;

  return(count);
}
```

A sample run using Program 9.10 follows:

```
Type in any number of characters: This is a test of character counts
The number of characters just entered is 34
```

Although this is not an exhaustive test of `countchar()`, it does verify that the function appears to be working correctly.

Requirement Specification: Word Counting

The issue of word counting is more complicated than the previous problem because we must first determine a criteria for identifying a word. At first glance, since each word is followed by a blank space, we might be tempted to simply count spaces. For example, consider the situation pictured in Figure 9.6.

Figure 9.6 A sample line of words

The problem with this approach is that the last word will not have a trailing blank. Even more troublesome are the cases where more than one blank is used between words and leading blanks are used before the first word. We will have to keep these situations in mind when we develop a solution for counting words.

Analyze the Problem

Using the software development process presented in Section 1.4, we now analyze the requirements specification by explicitly listing the provided input data, required output, and the algorithms that relate the inputs to the outputs.

a. Determine the Input Items A string of characters serves as the input data, which becomes the argument supplied to the function. Because a string in C is simply an array of characters, we can pass the string to our function simply by passing the character array.

b. Determine the Required Outputs The value returned to the function is an integer that corresponds to the number of words in the string. Because the function is to return an integer value the function will be defined as returning an `int`.

c. List the Algorithm(s) Relating the Inputs and Outputs Next, we create the algorithm, which becomes the code within the body of the function. As we have seen in Figure 9.6, we must come up with a criteria for determining when to increment our word counter. That is, we must algorithmically define what constitutes a word. Counting spaces will not work without modification to account for extra blanks. An alternative is to increment a counter only when the first character of a word is detected. This approach has the advantages of a positive test for a word and is the approach we will take.

Once this character is found, we can set a flag indicating that we are in a word. This flag can stay on until we come out of a word, which is signified by detecting a blank space. At this point we set the flag to not-in-a-word. The not-in-a-word condition will remain true until a nonblank character is again detected. A pseudocode description of this algorithm is

Set an integer variable named inaword to the symbolic constant NO
Set the word count to 0
For all the characters in the array
   If the current character is a blank
      set inaword to NO
   Else if (inaword equals NO)
      set inaword to the symbolic constant YES

increment the word count
EndIf
EndFor
Return the count

The key to this algorithm is the `if/else` condition. If the current character is a blank, the `inaword` variable is set to `NO`, *regardless* of what it was on the previous character. The `else` condition is only checked when the current character is not a blank. It then checks if we were not in a word. Thus, the `else` condition will only be true when the current character is not a blank and we are not in a word, which means we must be making the transition from a blank to a nonblank character. Because this is the criteria for determining that we are in a word, the word count is incremented and the `inaword` variable is set to `YES`.

Code the Function

The C code corresponding to our solution is

```
int countword(char list[])
#define YES 1
#define NO 0
{
  int i, inaword, count = 0;

  inaword = NO;
  for(i = 0; list[i] != '\0'; i++)
  {
    if (list[i] == ' ')
      inaword = NO;
    else if (inaword == NO)
    {
      inaword = YES;
      count++;
    }
  }
  return(count);
}
```

Test and Debug the Function

To test the function, we create a main driver function whose sole purpose is to exercise `countword()`. Program 9.11 includes both the `main` driver and `countchar()`.

Program 9.11

```
#include <stdio.h>
#define MAXNUM 1000

int countword(char []);   /* function prototype */

```

```
int main()
{
  char message[MAXNUM];
  int numchar;

  printf("\nType in any number of words: ");
  gets(message);
  numchar = countword(message);
  printf("The number of words just entered is %d\n", numchar);

  return 0;
}

int countword(char list[])
#define YES 1
#define NO 0
{
  int i, inaword, count = 0;

  inaword = NO;
  for(i = 0; list[i] != '\0'; i++)
  {
    if (list[i] == ' ')
      inaword = NO;
    else if (inaword == NO)
    {
      inaword = YES;
      count++;
    }
  }

  return(count);
}
```

A sample run using Program 9.11 follows:

```
Type in any number of words: This is a test line with a bunch of words
The number of words just entered is 10
```

Further tests that should be performed using Program 9.11 are

- Enter words with multiple spaces between them.
- Enter words with leading spaces before the first word.
- Enter words with trailing spaces after the last word.
- Enter a sentence that ends in a period or question mark.

EXERCISES 9.5

Programming Exercises

1. Modify the `countchar()` function in Program 9.10 to omit blank spaces from the count.
2. Create a function named `cvowels()` that counts and returns the number of vowels in a passed string.
3. Create a function that counts both characters and words. (*Hint:* Refer to Section 7.3 on how to return multiple values.)
4. Modify the `countword()` function in Program 9.11 to also count the number of letters in each word and then return the average number of characters per word. Name the modified function `avgCharPerWord()`.
5. Write a function to count the number of lines entered. (*Hint:* You will not be able to use `gets()` to input the lines, because `gets()` ends input on receipt of the first newline character.)
6. Write a function to count the number sentences entered; assume a sentence ends in either a period, question mark, or exclamation point. (*Hint:* You will not be able to use `gets()` to input the sentences, because `gets()` ends input on receipt of the first newline character.)
7. Modify the function written for Exercise 6 to count the number of words as well as the number of sentences. The function should return the average words per sentence.
8. The Fog Index is an index that can be used to determine the approximate reading grade level of an article. It is determined by measuring both sentence length and the fraction of words with three or more syllables, without taking into account either the article's conceptual difficulty or its clarity. The index is determined using the following steps:

   Step 1: ***Select a sample of at least 100 words.***
   Step 2: ***Count the number of sentences. Any clause that is separated by a semicolon or colon should be counted as a separate sentence.***
   Step 3: ***Count the number of words containing three or more syllables; but do not include words that reach three or more syllables because of either "es" or "ed" endings, or because they are compounds of simple words, such as everything or seventeen.***
   Step 4: ***Calculate the Fog Index using the formula:***

$$FogIndex = 0.4\left(\frac{NumberOfWords}{NumberOfSentences} + 100\frac{NumberOfBigWords}{NumberOfWords}\right)$$

For this exercise obtain samples of at least 10 sentences from a variety of sources, such as children's books, high school textbooks, college textbooks, or a number of different newspapers. For each of these samples, manually determine the number of words and big words contained in the sample. Then write a C function that: accepts the number of words, accepts the number of sentences, accepts the number of big words, calculates a Fog Index, and returns the calculated value. Verify the value returned by your function against your hand calculations.

9.6 Common Programming and Compiler Errors

In using the material presented in this chapter, be aware of the following possible programming and compiler errors.

Programming Errors

1. Forgetting to take into account the terminating `NULL` character, `'0'`, when processing existing strings in a character-by-character manner.
2. Forgetting to terminate a newly created character string with the `NULL` character, '0'.
3. Forgetting that the newline character, `'\n'`, is a valid data input character.
4. Forgetting to include the `string.h`, `ctype.h`, and `stdlib.h` header files when using the string library, character library, and conversion library functions, respectively.

Compiler Errors

The following table summarizes common errors that will result in compilation errors and the typical error messages provided by Unix- and Windows-based compilers.

Error	Typical Unix-based Compiler Error Message	Typical Windows-based Compiler Error Message
Attempting to assign a single character into an element of the array using double, rather than single quotes. For example, `message[5] = "A";`	`(W) Operation between types "unsigned char" and "unsigned char*" is not allowed.`	`error : cannot convert from 'const char [2]' to 'char'`
Not using a system predefined constant in all capital letters. For example, `message[10] = NULL;`	`(S) Undeclared identifier NULL.`	`error: 'NULL' : undeclared identifier`
Forgetting to insert a length in the Size of the Array without initializers. For example, `char message[];`	`(S) Explicit dimension specification or initializer required for an auto or static array.`	`error: 'message' : unknown size`

Error	Typical Unix-based Compiler Error Message	Typical Windows-based Compiler Error Message
Comparing against an escape sequence that is inside double quotes. For example, `while((c = getchar()) != "\n")`	`(W) Operation between types "int" and "unsigned char*" is not allowed.`	`error: '!=' : no conversion from 'const char *' to 'int'`
Providing an incorrect path for including header files. For example, `#include "c:\\stdio.h"`	`(S) #include file "c:\\stdio.h" not found.`	`fatal error: Cannot open include file: 'c:\\stdio.h': No such file or directory`

9.7 Chapter Summary

1. A string is an array of characters that is terminated by the `NULL` (`'\0'`) character.

2. Character arrays can be initialized using a string assignment of the form
   ```
   char *arrayName[] = "text";
   ```
   This initialization is equivalent to
   ```
   char *arrayName[] = {'t','e','x','t','\0'};
   ```

3. Strings can always be processed using standard array-processing techniques. The input and display of a string, however, always require reliance on a standard library function.

4. The `gets()`, `scanf()`, and `getchar()` library functions can be used to input a string. The `scanf()` function tends to be of limited usefulness for string input because it terminates input when a blank is encountered.

5. The `puts()`, `printf()`, and `putchar()` functions can be used to display strings.

6. Many standard library functions exist for processing strings as a complete unit. Internally, these functions manipulate strings in a character-by-character manner, and are included in the `string.h` header file.

7. The standard C library also includes individual character-handling functions in the `ctype.h` header file.

8. One of the major uses of strings in programs is validating user input, which is an essential part of any program. Strings are extremely useful for this purpose because they easily permit the inspection of each individual character that is entered by the user.

9. The conversion routines `atoi()` and `atof()` are provided in the `stdlib.h` header file for converting strings to integer and double-precision numeric values. These routines are typically applied to user-input data after the data has been validated for the input data type expected by the application.

Chapter 10

Data Files

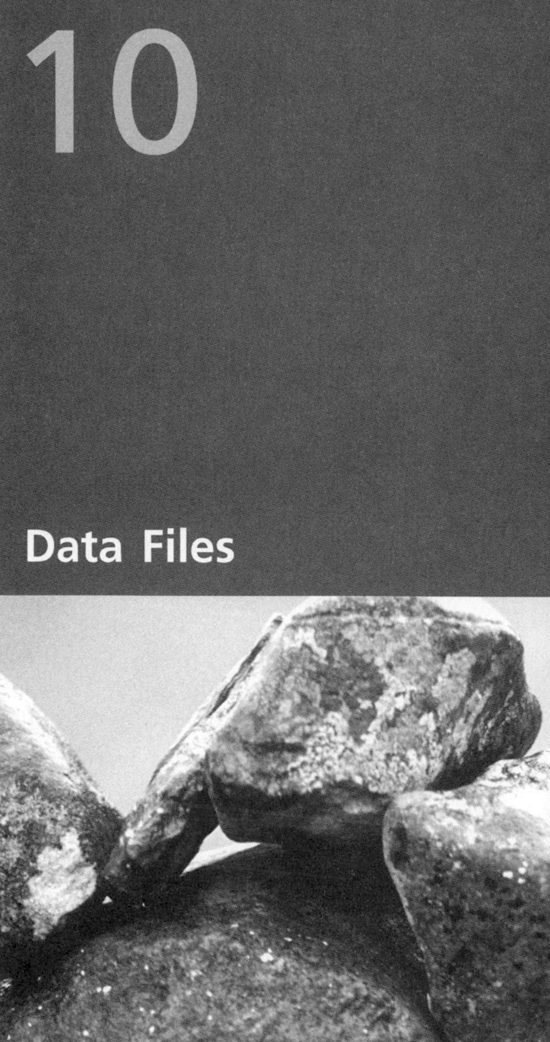

The data for the programs we have seen so far has either been assigned internally within the programs or entered by the user during program execution. As such, the data used in these programs is stored only in the computer's main memory, and ceases to exist once the program finishes executing. This type of data entry is fine for small amounts of data. Imagine, however, a company having to pay someone to type in the names and addresses of hundreds or thousands of customers every month each time bills are prepared and sent.

As you'll learn in this chapter, it makes more sense to store such data outside of a program, on a convenient storage medium. Data that is stored together under a common name on a storage medium other than the computer's main memory is called a **data file**. Typically data files are stored on disks, tapes, or CD-ROMs. Besides providing a permanent storage for the data, another advantage of data files is that they can be shared between programs. Thus, data output by one program can be stored in a data file that is then input directly to another program.

You'll begin this chapter by learning how data files are created and maintained in C. Because one major concern about using data files has to do with ensuring that your programs open and connect correctly to them before any data processing begins, you'll also learn how to use error checking for this task. This type of error detection and correction is a major part of all professionally written programs.

10.1 Declaring, Opening, and Closing File Streams

To store and retrieve data outside a C program, you need two items:

- A file
- A file stream

Files

A **file** is a collection of data that is stored together under a common name, usually on a disk, magnetic tape, or CD-ROM. For example, the C programs that you store on disk are examples of files. The stored data in a program file is the program code that becomes input data to the C compiler. In the context of data processing, however, the C program is not usually considered data, and the term file, or data file, is typically used to refer only to external files that contain the data used in a C program.

A file is physically stored on an external medium such as a disk. Each file has a unique filename referred to as the file's **external name**. The external name is the name of the file as it is known by the operating system. When you review the contents of a directory or folder (for example, in Windows Explorer), you see files listed by their external names. Each computer operating system has its own specification as to the maximum number of characters permitted for an external filename. Table 10.1 lists these specifications for the more commonly used operating systems.

To ensure that the examples presented in this text are compatible with all of the operating systems listed in Table 10.1, we will generally, but not exclusively, adhere to the more restrictive DOS specification. If you are using one of the other operating systems, however, you should take advantage of the increased length specification to create descriptive filenames. Very long filenames should be avoided, however, because they take more time to type and can result in typing errors. A manageable length for a filename is 12 to 14 characters, with an outside maximum of 25 characters.

Table 10.1 Maximum Allowable Filename Characteristics

Operating System	Maximum Length
DOS	8 characters plus an optional period and 3-character extension
Windows 98, 2000, XP	255 characters
Unix Early Versions Current Versions	 14 characters 155 characters

Using the DOS convention then, the following are all valid computer data filenames:

```
prices.dat        records        info.txt
exper1.dat        scores.dat     math.mem
```

When choosing filenames, select names that indicate both the type of data in the file and the application for which it is used. Frequently, the first eight characters describe the data

Historical Note

Privacy, Security, and Files

Data files have been around a long time, mainly on paper stored in filing cabinets. Terms, such as *open*, *close*, *records*, and *lookup*, which we use in handling computer files, are reminders of older techniques for accessing paper files stored in drawers.

Today most files are stored electronically, and the amount of information that is collected and stored proliferates wildly. Because it is easier to transmit bits and bytes than to ship paper folders, serious problems of security have arisen with concerns over people's privacy.

Whenever an individual fills out a government form or a credit application, submits a mail order, applies for a job, writes a check, or uses a credit card, an electronic data trail is created. Each time those files are shared among government agencies or private enterprises, the individual loses more of his or her privacy.

To help protect U.S. citizens' constitutional rights, the Fair Credit Reporting Act was passed in 1970, followed by the Federal Privacy Act in 1974. These acts specify that it is illegal for a business to keep secret files, that you are entitled to examine and correct any data collected about you, and that government agencies and contractors must show justification for accessing your records. Efforts continue to create mechanisms that will serve to preserve an individual's security and privacy.

themselves, and an extension (the characters after the decimal point) describes the application. For example, the Excel spreadsheet program automatically applies an extension of `xls` to all spreadsheet files; Microsoft's Word and the WordPerfect word processing programs use the extensions `doc` and `wpx` (where `x` refers to the version number), respectively; and most C compilers require a program file to have either the extension `c` or `cpp`. When creating your own filenames, you should adhere to this practice. For example, using the DOS convention, the name `exper1.dat` is appropriate in describing a file of data corresponding to experiment number one.

There are two basic types of files: **text files**, which are also known as **character-based files**, and **binary files**. Both file types store data using a binary code; the difference is in what the codes represent. Briefly, text files store each individual character, such as a letter, digit, dollar sign, decimal point, and so on, using an individual character code (typically ASCII). The use of a character code allows such files to be displayed by a word processing program or text editor, so that a person can read them independently of any C program.

Binary files use the same code as your computer processor uses internally for C's primitive data types. This means that numbers are stored in true binary form (typically two's complement, as described in Section 1.8 and Appendix E), while only strings retain their ASCII character form. The advantage of binary files is typically speed, because no conversion to and from text to binary numbers is needed, and compactness, because it typically takes less space to store most numbers using their binary code than as individual character values. The default type in C, however, is always a text file, and is the type (except for Section 10.6) presented in this chapter.

File Streams

A **file stream** is a one-way transmission path that is used to connect a file stored on a physical device, such as a disk or CD-ROM, to a program. Each file stream has its own mode, which determines the direction of data on the transmission path—that is, whether the path will move data from a file into a program or whether the path will move data from a program to a file. A file stream that receives (that is, reads) data from a file into a program is referred to as an **input file stream**. A file stream that sends (that is, writes) data to a file is referred to as an **output file stream**. Notice that the direction is always defined in relation to the program and not the file; data that go into a program are considered input data, and data sent out from the program are considered output data. Figure 10.1 illustrates the data flow from and to a file using input and output streams.

Programming Note

Input and Output File Streams

A stream is a one-way transmission path between a source and destination. What gets sent down this transmission path is a stream of bytes. A good analogy to the "stream of bytes" is a stream of water that provides a one-way transmission path of water from a source to a destination.

Two streams that we have used extensively are the standard input stream, which is used by all `printf()` function calls, and standard output streams, which are used by all `scanf()` function calls. The `scanf()` function automatically uses the standard input stream, named `stdin`, which provides a transmission path from keyboard to program, while all `printf()` functions use the standard output stream, named `stdout`, which provides a transmission path from program to terminal screen. These two streams, `stdin` and `stdout`, are automatically opened each time a C program begins execution.

File streams provide the same capabilities as `stdin` and `stdout`, except that they connect a program to a file rather than the keyboard or terminal screen. Also, file streams must be explicitly declared. Once declared, they are physically attached to a specific external file using an `fopen()` function call.

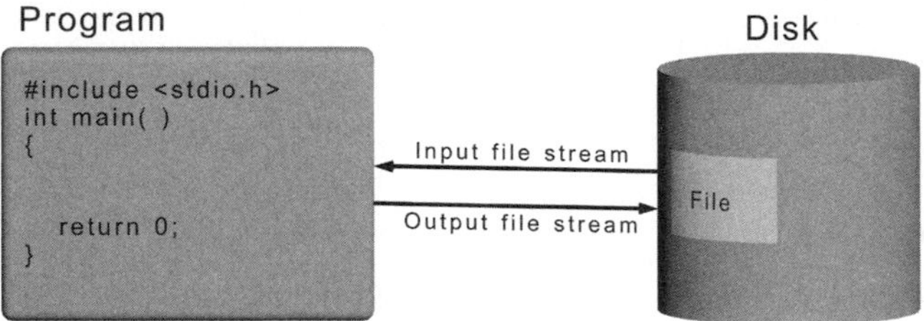

Figure 10.1 Input and output file streams

For each file that your program uses, regardless of the file's type (text or binary), a distinct file stream must be named and created. The naming and creation of a file stream is accomplished using declaration and open statements.

Declaring a File Stream

Naming a file stream is accomplished by declaring a variable name to be of type `FILE`. Once the file stream in declared, the name of the stream becomes the name of the file within a C program. This name need not be, and is usually not, the same as the external name used by the computer to store the file. Examples of such variable declarations are

```
FILE *inFile;
FILE *prices;
FILE *fp;
```

Notice that each file stream name, when it is declared, is preceded by an asterisk, *.[1] In each of these declarations, the variable name is selected by the programmer. It is the name of the data file as it will be referenced to internally, within your C program.

The term `FILE` in each declaration is the type of a special data structure used by C for storing information about a file, including whether the file is available for reading or writing, the next available character in the file, and where this character is stored. The actual declaration of this structure is contained in the `stdio.h` standard header file, which must be included at the top of each program that uses a data file. Once the file stream is declared, it is, for all practical purposes, the name of the file, as used by the program. Therefore, we shall refer to this file stream name as the data file's internal name. It is this name that is used within a C program.

Opening a File Stream

Opening a file stream, a process referred to as opening the file, accomplishes two purposes, only one of which is directly pertinent to the programmer. First, opening a file stream establishes the physical communication link between the program and the data file. Because the specific details of this link are handled by the computer's operating system and are transparent to the program, the programmer normally need not consider them.

From a programming perspective, the second purpose of opening a file stream is relevant. Besides establishing the actual physical connection between a program and a data file (that is, the actual stream over which the data will pass), the open statement also equates a specific external filename to the name declared in the `FILE` declaration statement, which is the name that is subsequently used within a program to access the file.

Appropriately enough, the file open function is called `fopen()` and is available in the standard C library in the `stdio.h` header file. As such, this header file should be included by any program using `fopen()`. (An alternative is just to provide a prototype for the `fopen()` function.) The first argument is the file's external name. The second argument is the mode in which the file is to be used, which must be placed in double quotes. Permissible modes are `r`, `w`, or `a`, which represent reading, writing, or appending to a file.[2]

A file opened for writing creates a new file and makes the file available for output by the function opening the file. If a file exists with the same name as a file opened for writing, the old file is erased. For example, the statement

```
outFile = fopen("prices.bnd","w");
```

opens an external file named `prices.bnd` that can now be written to. Once this file has been opened, the program accesses the file using the internal pointer name `outFile`, while the computer saves the file under the external name `prices.bnd`.

A file opened for appending makes an existing file available for data to be added to the end of the file. If the file opened for appending does not exist, a new file with the designated name is created and made available to receive output from the program. For example, the statement

```
outFile = fopen("prices.bnd","a");
```

opens a file named `prices.bnd` and makes it available for data to be appended to the end of the file.

---

[1]The file stream name is actually a pointer, described in detail in Section 7.3, hence the need for the asterisk.

[2]Additionally, the modes `r+`, `w+`, and `a+` are available. The `r+` mode opens an existing file for reading and writing existing records; the `w+` mode erases an existing file and opens a blank file for reading and writing; and the `a+` mode allows reading, writing, and appending to a file.

Programming Note

Mode Indicators

When using the `fopen()` function, two arguments are required: a file's external name and a mode indicator. Permissible mode indicators are described in the following table:

Indicator	Description
"r"	Open an existing text file for reading (input mode).
"w"	Create a text file for writing (output mode); if a file exists, its contents are discarded.
"a"	Open a text file for writing (output mode), where text is written at the end of the existing file; if there is no existing file, a new file is created for writing.
"r+"	Open an existing text file for reading and writing; if a file exists, its contents are discarded.
"w+"	Create a text file for reading and writing.
"a+"	Open a text file for reading and writing, where text is written at the end of the file; if there is no existing file, a new file is created for reading and writing.

A file opened in `"w"` mode creates a new file and makes the file available for writing. If a file exists with the same name as a file opened for output, the old file is erased. For example, assuming that `fileOut` has been declared as being of type `FILE` using the statement

```
FILE *fileOut;
```

then the statement

```
fileOut = fopen("prices.dat","w");
```

attempts to open the file named `prices.dat` for output. Once this file has been opened, the program accesses the file using the internal name `fileOut`, while the computer saves the file under the external name `prices.dat`.

A file opened in `"a"` mode means that an existing file is available for data to be added to the end of the file. If the file opened for appending does not exist, a new file with the designated name is created and made available to receive output from the program. For example, again assuming that `fileOut` has been declared to be of type `FILE`, the statement

```
fileOut = fopen("prices.dat","a");
```

attempts to open a file named `prices.dat` and makes it available for data to be appended to the end of the file.

continued...

Programming Note

Mode Indicators (continued)

Finally, a file opened in "r" mode means that an existing external file has been connected and its data is available as input. For example, assuming that fileIn has been declared to be of type FILE, the statement

```
fileIn = fopen("prices.dat","r");
```

attempts to open a file named prices.dat for input.

The mode indicators can include a "b" designation as the last letter, as in "wb" or "r+b", which specifies a binary file (see Section 10.6). For example, the statement

```
fileOut = fopen("prices.dat", "wb");
```

creates the prices.dat file, as an output binary file.

The only difference between a file opened in write mode and one opened in append mode is where the data is physically placed in the file. In write mode, the data is written starting at the beginning of the file, while in append mode the data is written starting at the end of the file. For a new file, the two modes are identical.

For files opened in either write or append mode, the functions needed to write data to it are similar to the printf(), puts(), and putchar() functions used for displaying data on a terminal. These functions are described in the next section. A file opened in read mode retrieves an existing file and makes its data available as input to the program. For example, the open statement

```
inFile = fopen("prices.bnd","r");
```

opens the file named prices.bnd and makes the data in the file available for input. Within the function opening the file, the file is read using the pointer name inFile. The functions used to read data from a file are similar to the scanf(), gets(), and getchar() functions used for inputting data from the keyboard. These functions are also described in the next section.

If a file opened for reading does not exist, the fopen() function returns the NULL address value. This is the same NULL address previously described in Section 9.1. It can be used to test that an existing file has, in fact, been opened.

Notice that in all the open statements, both the external filename and the mode arguments passed to fopen() were strings contained between double quotes. If the external filename is first stored in either an array of characters or as a string, the array or string name, without quotes, can be used as the first argument to fopen().

Program 10.1 illustrates the statements required to open a file for input, including an error-checking routine to ensure that a successful open was obtained. A file opened for input is said to be in read mode.

Program 10.1

```
#include <stdio.h>
#include <stdlib.h>  /* needed for exit() */

int main()
{
    FILE *inFile;

  inFile = fopen("prices.dat","r"); /* open the file having the */
                                    /* external name prices.dat */
  if (inFile == NULL)
  {
    printf("\nThe file was not successfully opened.");
    printf("\nPlease check that the file currently exists.\n");
    exit(1);
  }
  printf("\nThe file has been successfully opened for reading.\n");

  return 0;
}
```

A sample run using Program 10.1 produced the output

```
The file has been successfully opened for reading.
```

The `exit()` function used in Program 10.1 is a systems call that passes its integer argument directly to the operating system and then terminates program operation. It requires the header file `stdlib.h`.

A slightly different check is required for output files, because if a file exists having the same name as the file to be opened for writing, the existing file is erased and all its data is lost. To avoid this situation, the file can first be opened in input mode, simply to see if it exists. If it does, the user is given the choice of explicitly permitting it to be overwritten when it is subsequently opened in output mode. The code used to accomplish this is highlighted in Program 10.2.

Program 10.2

```
#include <stdio.h>
#include <stdlib.h>  /* needed for exit() */

int main()
{
```

☞

```
  char response;
  FILE *outFile;

  outFile = fopen("prices.dat","r"); /* open the file having the */
                                     /* external name prices.dat */
  if (outFile != NULL) /* check for a successful open*/
  {
    printf("\nA file by the name prices.dat exists.");
    printf("\nDo you want to continue and overwrite it");
    printf("\n with the new data (y or n): ");
    scanf("%c", &response);
    if (response == 'n')
    {
      printf("\nThe existing file will not be overwritten.\n");
      exit(1);
    }
  }
  outFile = fopen("prices.dat","w");  /* now open the file */
                                      /* for writing */

  if(outFile == NULL)  /* check for an unsuccessful opening */
  {
    printf("\nThe file was not successfully opened.\n");
    exit(1);
  }

  printf("\nThe file has been successfully opened for output.\n");

  return 0;
}
```

Following are two runs made with Program 10.2. The output of the first run is

```
A file by the name prices.dat exists.
Do you want to continue and overwrite it
with the new data (y or n): n

The existing file will not be overwritten.
```

The output of the second run is

```
A file by the name prices.dat exists.
Do you want to continue and overwrite it
with the new data (y or n): y

The file has been successfully opened for output.
```

Programming Note

Checking `fopen()`'s Return Value

It is important to check the return value when making an `fopen()` call because the call is really a request to the operating system to open a file. For a variety of reasons, the open call can fail. (One of the reasons this can happen is that a request is made to open an existing file for reading that the operating system cannot locate.) If the operating system cannot satisfy the open request, you need to know about it and either correct the error or terminate your program. Failure to do so almost always results in some abnormal program behavior or a program crash.

There are two styles of coding for checking the return value. The first style is the one coded in Program 10.1. It is used to clearly illustrate the request for the opening as distinct from the return value check, and is repeated below for convenience:

```
/* here is the request to open the file */
inFile = fopen("prices.dat","r");

/* here we check that the file was successfully opened */
if (inFile == NULL)
{
    printf("\nThe file was not successfully opened.");
    printf("\nPlease check that the file currently exists.\n");
    exit(1);
}
```

Alternatively, the open request and check can be combined together within the `if` statement as:

```
if ((inFile = fopen("test.dat","r")) == NULL)
{
  printf("\nFailed to open the data file.\n");
  exit(1);
}
```

Use the style with which you are initially more comfortable. As you gain experience in programming, however, be prepared to adopt the second style. It is the one used almost universally by advanced programmers.

Although Programs 10.1 and 10.2 can be used to open an existing file for reading and writing, respectively, both programs lack statements to actually perform a read or write. These topics are discussed in the next section. Before leaving these programs, however, it is worthwhile noting that it is possible to combine the `fopen()` call and its check for a returned `NULL` into a single statement. For example, the two statements in Program 10.1

```
inFile = fopen("prices.dat","r");
if (inFile == NULL)
```

can be combined into the single statement

```
if ((inFile = fopen("prices.dat","r")) == NULL )
```

Embedded and Interactive Filenames

Two practical problems with Programs 10.1 and 10.2 are:

1. The external filename is embedded within the program code.
2. There is no provision for a user to enter the desired filename while the program is executing.

In both programs before the filename can change, the programmer must modify the external filename in the call to `fopen()` and recompile the program. This can be avoided by assigning the filename to a string variable.

A string variable, as we have used it throughout the text (see especially Chapter 9), is a variable that can hold a string value, which is any sequence of zero or more characters enclosed within double quotes. For example, `"Hello World"`, `"prices.dat"`, and `""` are all strings. Notice that strings are always written with double quotes that delimit the beginning and end of a string but are not stored as part of the string.

Once a string variable is declared to store a filename, it can be used in one of two ways. First, as shown in Program 10.3a, it can be placed at the top of a program to clearly identify a file's external name, rather than embed it within an `fopen()` function call.

Program 10.3a

```
#include <stdio.h>
#include <stdlib.h>   /* needed for exit() */

int main()
{
  FILE *inFile;
  char fileName[13] = "prices.dat";

  inFile = fopen(fileName,"r"); /* open the file */
  if (inFile == NULL)
  {
    printf("\nThe file %s was not successfully opened.", fileName);
    printf("\nPlease check that the file currently exists.\n");
    exit(1);
  }
  printf("\nThe file has been successfully opened for reading.\n");

  return 0;
}
```

In reviewing Program 10.3a, notice that we have declared and initialized the string named `fileName` at the top of `main()` for easy file identification. Next, notice that when a string variable is used, as opposed to a string literal, the variable name *is not* enclosed within double quotes in the `fopen()` method call. Finally, notice that when the file fails to open, the file's external name is displayed by inserting the string's name in the `printf()` function call that alerts the user that the open was not successful. For all of these reasons we will continue to identify the external names of files in this manner.

Another extremely useful role played by strings is to permit the user to enter the filename as the program is executing. For example, the code

```
gets(fileName);
inFile = fopen(fileName,"r"); /* open the file */
```

allows a user to enter a file's external name at run time. The only restriction in this code is that the user must not enclose the entered string value in double quotes, which is a plus.

Program 10.3b uses this code in the context of a complete program.

Program 10.3b

```
#include <stdio.h>
#include <stdlib.h>  /* needed for exit() */

int main()
{
  FILE *inFile;
  char fileName[13];

  printf("\nEnter a file name: ");
  gets(fileName);
  inFile = fopen(fileName,"r"); /* open the file */
  if (inFile == NULL)
  {
    printf("\nThe file %s was not successfully opened.", fileName);
    printf("\nPlease check that the file currently exists.\n");
    exit(1);
  }
  printf("\nThe file has been successfully opened for reading.\n");

  return 0;
}
```

Following is a sample output provided by Program 10.3b:

```
Enter a file name: foobar

The file named foobar was not successfully opened.
Please check that the file currently exists.
```

Programming Note

Using Strings as Filenames

If you choose to use a string to store an external filename, you must be aware of the following restrictions. The maximum length of the string must be specified within brackets immediately after it is declared. For example, in the declaration

```
char filename[21]
```

the number 21 limits the number of characters that can be stored in the string. The number in brackets, in this example, 21, always represents one fewer than the maximum number of characters that can be assigned to the variable. This is because the compiler always adds a final end-of-string character to terminate the string. Thus, the string value `"prices.dat"`, which consists of 10 characters, is actually stored as 11 characters. The extra character is the end-of-string marker, `'\0'`, automatically supplied by the compiler. In our example, the maximum string value assignable to the string variable `filename` is a string value consisting of 20 characters.

Closing a File Stream

A file stream is closed using the `fclose()` function. This function breaks the link between the file's external and internal names, releasing the internal file pointer name, which can then be used for another file. For example, the statement

```
fclose(inFile);
```

closes the `inFile` file. The argument to `fclose()` always should be the pointer name used when the file was opened.

Because all computers have a limit on the maximum number of files that can be open at one time, closing files that are no longer needed makes good sense.[3] Any open files existing at the end of normal program execution are also automatically closed by the operating system.

EXERCISES 10.1

Short Answer Questions

1. Write individual declaration and open statements that link the following external data filenames to their corresponding internal names. Assume that all the files are text files.

External Name	Internal Name	Mode
`coba.mem`	`memo`	`output`

[3]The maximum number of files that can be opened at one time is defined by the system symbolic constant `FOPEN_MAX`.

External Name	Internal Name	Mode
`book.let`	`letter`	`output`
`coupons.bnd`	`coups`	`append`
`yield.bnd`	`yield`	`append`
`prices.dat`	`priFile`	`input`
`rates.dat`	`rates`	`input`

2. a. Write a set of two statements that opens each of these external files as input text files, using internal filenames of your own choosing: `Data.txt`, `prices.txt`, `coupons.dat`, and `exper.dat`.
   b. Rewrite the two statements for Question 2a using a single statement.

3. a. Write a set of two statements that opens each of these external files as output text files, using internal filenames of your own choosing: `Data.txt`, `prices.txt`, `coupons.dat`, and `exper.dat`.
   b. Rewrite the two statements for Question 3a using a single statement.

4. Would it be appropriate to call a saved C program a file? Why or why not?

5. Using the reference manuals provided with your computer's operating system, determine the maximum number of characters that can be used to name a file for storage by the computer system.

6. Search the `stdio.h` header file and locate the symbolic constants `FILENAME_MAX` and `FOPEN_MAX`, to determine, respectively, the maximum number of characters permitted for an internal filename and the maximum number of files that can be open within a C program.

Programming Exercises

1. Enter and execute Program 10.1 on your computer.

2. Enter and execute Program 10.2 on your computer.

3. a. Enter and execute Program 10.3a on your computer.
   b. Add an `fclose()` function to Program 10.3a and then execute the program.

4. a. Enter and execute Program 10.3b on your computer.
   b. Add an `fclose()` function to Program 10.3b and then execute the program.

5. Write individual declaration and open statements to link the following external data filenames to their corresponding internal names. Note that all files are binary, not text.

External Name	Internal Name	Mode
coba.mem	memo	binary and output
coupons.bnd	coups	binary and append
prices.dat	priFile	binary and input

10.2 Reading from and Writing to Text Files

Reading or writing to an open text file involves almost the identical standard library functions for reading input from a terminal and writing data to a display screen. For writing to a text file, use the functions described in the following table.

Function	Description
`fputc(c,filename)`	Write a single character to the file.
`fputs(string,filename)`	Write a string to the file.
`fprintf(filename,"format",args)`	Write the values of the arguments to the file according to format.

The function prototypes for these functions are contained in `stdio.h`. In each of these functions, the filename is the internal pointer name specified when the file is opened. For example, if `outFile` is the internal pointer name of a file opened in either the write or append modes, the following output statements are valid:

```
fputc('a',outFile); /* write an a to the file */
fputs("Hello world!",outFile); /* write the string to the file */
fprintf(outFile,"%s %n",descrip,price);
```

Notice that the `fputc()`, `fputs()`, and `fprintf()` file functions are used in the same manner as the equivalent `putchar()`, `puts()`, and `printf()` functions, with the addition of a filename as an argument. The filename simply directs the output to a specific file instead of to the standard display device. Program 10.4 illustrates the use of the file write function `fprintf()` to write a list of descriptions and prices to a file.

Program 10.4

```
#include <stdio.h>
#include <stdlib.h>  /* needed for exit() */

int main()
{
  int i;
  FILE *outFile; /* FILE declaration */
  double price[] = {39.25,3.22,1.03}; /* a list of prices */
  char *descrip[] = { "Batteries", /* a list of */
                      "Bulbs",     /* descriptions */
                      "Fuses"};

  outFile = fopen("prices.dat","w"); /* open the file */

  if (outFile == NULL)
```

☞

```
  {
    printf("\nFailed to open the file.\n");
    exit(1);
  }
  for(i = 0; i < 3; i++)
    fprintf(outFile,"%-9s %5.2f\n",descrip[i],price[i]);
  fclose(outFile);

  return 0;
}
```

When Program 10.4 is executed, a file named `prices.dat` is created and saved by the computer. The file is a sequential file consisting of the following three lines:

```
Batteries 39.25
Bulbs      3.22
Fuses      1.03
```

The prices in the file line up one after another because the control sequence `%-9s` in the `printf()` function call forces the descriptions to be left-justified in a field of nine character positions. Similarly, the prices are right-justified in a field of five characters, beginning one space away from the end of the description field.

The actual storage of characters in the file depends on the character codes used by the computer. Although only 45 characters appear to be stored in the file, corresponding to the descriptions, blanks, and prices written to the file, the file actually contains 48 characters. The extra characters consist of the newline escape sequence at the end of each line.

Assuming characters are stored using ASCII code, the `prices.dat` file is physically stored as illustrated in Figure 10.2. For convenience, the character corresponding to each hexadecimal code is listed below the code. A code of 20 represents the blank character. Additionally, C appends the low-value hexadecimal byte 0x00 as the end-of-file (EOF) sentinel when the file is closed. This end-of-file sentinel is never counted as part of the file.

```
42 61 74 74 65 72 69 65 73 20 33 39 2e 32 35 0a 42 75 6c 62 73
 B  a  t  t  e  r  i  e  s     3  9  .  2  5 \n  B  u  l  b  s

20 20 20 20 20 20 33 2e 32 32 0a 46 75 73 65 73 20 20 20 20 20
                   3  .  2  2 \n  F  u  s  e  s

20 31 2e 30 33 0a
    1  .  0  3 \n
```

Figure 10.2 The `prices.dat` file as stored by a typical computer

Programming Note

Using Full Path Names

During program development data files are usually placed in the same directory as the program. Therefore, an expression such as `fopen("prices.dat","r")` causes no problems to the operating system. In production systems, however, it is not uncommon for data files to reside in one directory while program files reside in another. For this reason it is always a good idea to include the full path name of any file opened.

For example, if the `prices.dat` file resides in the directory `\test\files`, the `fopen()` statement should include the full path name, as follows:

```
fopen("\\test\\files\\prices.dat", "r")
```

Then, no matter where the program is run, the operating system will know where to locate the file.

Another important convention is to list all filenames at the top of a program instead of embedding the names deep within the code. This can easily be accomplished by using a string variable for each filename. For example, if a declaration such as

```
char fileName[50] = "\\test\\files\\prices.dat";
```

is placed at the top of a program file, it clearly lists both the name of the desired file and its location. Then, if some other file is to be tested, all that is required is a simple, one-line change at the top of the program.

Using a string variable to store the file's name is also useful for the return code check. For example, consider the following code:

```
if ((inFile = fopen(fileName,"r")) == NULL)
{
  printf("\nFailed to open the data file named %s.\n", inFile);
  exit(1);
}
```

Here, if the file is not successfully opened, the name of the offending file is printed as part of the error message without explicitly rewriting the full path name a second time.

Reading from a Text File

Reading data from a file is almost identical to reading data from a standard keyboard, with the addition of the filename to indicate where the data is coming from. The file functions available for reading from a file are explained in the following table:

Function	Description
`fgetc(`*`filename`*`)`	Read a character from the file.
`fgets(`*`stringname,n,filename,`*`)`	Read *n* –1 characters from the file and store the characters in the given string name.
`fscanf(`*`filename,"format",&args`*`)`	Read values for the listed arguments from the file, according to the format.

For example, if `inFile` is the internal pointer name of a file opened in read mode, the following statements could be used to read data from the file:

```
fgetc(inFile); /* Read the next character in the file */
fgets(message,10,inFile); /* Read the next 9 characters from */
                          /* the file into message */
fscanf(inFile,"%lf",&price); /* Read a double-precision number */
```

The function prototypes for all of these input functions are contained in `stdio.h`. All the input functions correctly detect the end-of-file marker. The functions `fgetc()` and `fscanf()`, however, return the named constant `EOF` when the marker is detected. The function `fgets()` returns a `NULL('\0')` when it detects the end of a file. Both of these named constants, `EOF` and `NULL`, are useful sentinels for detecting the end of a file being read, depending on the function used.

Reading data from a file requires that the programmer knows how the data appears in the file. This is necessary for correct "stripping" of the data from the file into appropriate variables for storage. All files are read sequentially so that once an item is read, the next item in the file becomes available for reading.

Program 10.5 illustrates reading the `prices.dat` file that was created in Program 10.4. The program also illustrates using the `EOF` marker, which is returned by `fscanf()` when the end of the file is encountered.

Program 10.5

```
#include <stdio.h>
#include <stdlib.h>  /* needed for exit() */

int main()
{
  char descrip[10];
  double price;
  FILE *inFile;

  inFile = fopen("prices.dat","r");
  if (inFile == NULL)
  {
    printf("\nFailed to open the file.\n");
    exit(1);
  }
  while (fscanf(inFile, "%s %lf",descrip,&price) != EOF)
    printf("%-9s %5.2f\n",descrip,price);
  fclose(inFile);

  return 0;
}
```

Program 10.5 continues to read the file until the EOF has been detected. Each time the file is read, a string and a double-precision number are input to the program. The display produced by Program 10.5 is

```
Batteries 39.25
Bulbs      3.22
Fuses      1.03
```

In place of the `fscanf()` function used in Program 10.5, an `fgets()` function call can be used. The `fgets()` function call requires three arguments: an address where the first character read will be stored, the maximum number of characters to be read, and the name of the input file. For example, the function call

```
fgets(line,81,inFile);
```

causes a maximum of 80 characters (one fewer than the specified number) to be read from the file named `inFile` and stored starting at the address contained in the pointer named `line`. The `fgets()` function call continues reading characters until 80 characters have been read or a newline character has been encountered. If a newline character is encountered, it is included with the other entered characters before the string is terminated with the end-of-string marker, `\0`. The `fgets()` function call also detects the end-of-file marker, but returns the `NULL` character when the end of the file is encountered. Program 10.6 illustrates the use of `fgets()` in a working program.

Program 10.6

```
#include <stdio.h>
#include <stdlib.h>  /* needed for exit() */

int main()
{
  char line[81],descrip[10];
  double price;
  FILE *inFile;

  inFile = fopen("prices.dat","r");
  if (inFile == NULL)
  {
    printf("\nFailed to open the file.\n");
    exit(1);
  }
  while (fgets(line,81,inFile) != NULL)
    printf("%s",line);

  fclose(inFile);
  printf("\nThe file has been successfully written.\n");
```

```

}
```

Program 10.6 is really a line-by-line text-copying program, reading a line of text from the file and then displaying it on the terminal. Thus, the output of Program 10.6 is identical to the output of Program 10.5. If it were necessary to obtain the description and price as individual variables, either Program 10.5 should be used or the string returned by `fgets()` in Program 10.6 must be processed further using the string scan function, `sscanf()`. For example, the statement

```
sscanf(line,"%s %lf",descrip,&price)
```

could be used to extract the description and price from the string stored in the `line` character array (see Section 9.5 for a description of in-memory string formatting).

Standard Device Files

The data file pointers we have used have all been logical file pointers. A logical file pointer is one that references a file of related data that has been saved under a common name; that is, it "points to" a data file. In addition to logical file pointers, C also supports physical file pointers. A physical file pointer "points to" a hardware device, such as a keyboard, screen, or printer.

The actual physical device assigned to your program for data entry is formally called the standard input file. Usually this is a keyboard. When a `scanf()` function call is encountered in a C program, the computer automatically goes to this standard input file for the expected input. Similarly, when a `printf()` function call is encountered, the output is automatically displayed or "written to" a device that has been assigned as the standard output file. For most systems this is a CRT screen, although it can be a printer.

When a program is run, the keyboard used for entering data is automatically opened and assigned to the internal file pointer name `stdin`. Similarly, the output device used for display is assigned to the file pointer named `stdout`. These file pointers are always available for programmer use.

The similarities between `printf()` and `fprintf()`, and `scanf()` and `fscanf()` are not accidental. The `printf()` function is a special case of `fprintf()` that defaults to the standard output file, and `scanf()` is a special case of `fscanf()` that defaults to the standard input file. Thus,

```
fprintf(stdout,"Hello World!");
```

causes the same display as the statement

```
printf("Hello World!");
```

In the same vein,

```
fscanf(stdin,"%d",&num);
```

is equivalent to the statement

```
scanf("%d",&num);
```

In addition to the `stdin` and `stdout` file pointers, a third pointer named `stderr` is assigned to the output device used for system error messages. Although `stderr` and `stdout` frequently refer to the same device, the use of `stderr` provides a means of redirecting any error messages away from the file being used for normal program output, as described in Appendix D.

Just as `scanf()` and `printf()` are special cases of `fscanf()` and `fprintf()`, respectively, the functions `getchar()`, `gets()`, `putchar()`, and `puts()` are also special cases of the more general file functions listed in Table 10.2.

Table 10.2 Correspondence between Selected I/O Functions

Function	General Form
`putchar(`*character*`)`	`fputc(`*character*`,stdout)`
`puts(`*string*`)`	`fputs(`*string*`,stdout)`
`getchar()`	`fgetc(stdin)`
`gets(`*stringname*`)`	`fgets(`*stringname*`,`*n*`,stdin)`

The character function pairs listed in Table 10.2 can be used as direct replacements for each other. This is not true for the string-handling functions. The differences between the string-handling functions are described below.

At input, as previously noted, the `fgets()` function reads data from a file until a newline escape sequence or a specified number of characters has been read. If `fgets()` encounters a newline escape sequence, as we saw in Program 10.6, it is stored with the other characters entered. The `gets()` function, however, does not store the newline escape sequence in the final string. Both functions terminate the entered characters with an end-of-string `NULL` character.

At output, both `puts()` and `fputs()` write all the characters in the string except for the terminating end-of-string `NULL`. The `puts()` function, however, automatically adds a newline sequence at the end of the transmitted characters while `fputs()` does not.

Other Devices

The keyboard, display, and error-reporting devices are automatically opened and assigned the internal filenames `stdin`, `stdout`, and `stderr`, respectively, whenever a C program begins execution. Additionally, other devices can be used for input or output if the name assigned by the system is known. For example, most IBM or IBM-compatible personal computers assign the name `prn` to the printer connected to the computer. For these computers, the statement `fprintf("prn","Hello World!");` causes the string `Hello World!` to be printed directly at the printer. As with `stdin`, `stdout`, and `stderr`, `prn` is the name of a physical device. Unlike `stdin`, `stdout`, and `stderr`, `prn` is not a pointer constant but the actual name of the device; as such, it must be enclosed in double quotes when used in a statement.

EXERCISES 10.2

Short Answer Questions

1. What additional argument is required when using `fprintf()` and `fscanf()`, as opposed to `printf()` and `scanf`?
2. List three functions that can be used to write data to a file.
3. List three functions that can be used to read data from a file.
4. What is the device that corresponds to `stdin`?
5. What is the device that corresponds to `stdout`?

Programming Exercises

1. **a.** Using the `gets()` and `fputs()` functions, write a C program that accepts lines of text from the keyboard and writes each line to a file named `text.dat` until an empty line is entered. An empty line is a line with no text—just a new line caused by pressing the Enter key.
   b. Replace the `gets()` function in the program written for Exercise 1a with an equivalent call to `fgets()`.
   c. Modify Program 10.6 to read and display the data stored in the `text.dat` file created in Exercise 1a.

2. Determine the operating system command or procedure provided by your computer to display the contents of a saved file. Compare its operation with the program developed for Exercise 1c. (*Hint:* In keyboard-driven operating systems, such as DOS and Unix, the operating system command is typically `dir`, `list`, `type`, or `cat`.)

3. **a.** Create a file named `employee.dat` containing the following data:

Anthony	A.J.	10031	7.82	12/18/62
Burrows	W.K.	10067	9.14	6 /9/63
Fain	B.D.	10083	8.79	5/18/59
Janney	P.	10095	10.57	9/28/62
Smith	G.J.	10105	8.50	12/20/61

   b. Write a program called `fcopy` to read the `employ.dat` file created in Exercise 3a and produce a duplicate copy of the file named `employ.bak`.
   c. Modify the program written in Exercise 3b to accept the names of the original and duplicate files as user input.
   d. Since `fcopy` always copies data from an original file to a duplicate file, can you think of a better method of accepting the original and duplicate filenames than prompting the user for them each time the program is executed?

4. a. Write a program that opens a file and displays the contents of the file with associated line numbers. That is, the program should print 1 before displaying the first line, 2 before displaying the second line, and so on for each line in the file.
   b. Modify the program written in Exercise 4a to list the contents of the file on the printer assigned to your computer.

5. a. Create a file containing the following data:

H.Baker	614 Freeman St.	Orange	NJ
D.Rosso	83 Chambers St.	Madison	NJ
K.Tims	891 Ridgewood Rd.	Millburn	NJ
B.Williams	24 Tremont Ave.	Brooklyn	NY

   b. Write a program to read and display the data file created in Exercise 5a using the following output format:

```
Name:
Address:
City, State:
```

6. a. Create a file containing the following names, Social Security numbers, hourly rate, and hours worked:

B.Caldwell	555-98-4182	7.32	37
D.Memcheck	555-53-2147	8.32	40
R.Potter	555-32-9826	6.54	40
W.Rosen	555-09-4263	9.80	35

   b. Write a C program that reads the data file created in Exercise 6a and computes and displays a payroll schedule. The output should list the Social Security number, name, and gross pay for each individual.

7. a. Create a file containing the following car numbers, number of miles driven, and number of gallons of gas used by each car:

Car No.	Miles Driven	Gallons Used
54	250	19
62	525	38
71	123	6
85	1,322	86
97	235	14

   b. Write a C program that reads the data in the file created in Exercise 7a and displays the car number, miles driven, gallons used, and the miles per gallon for each car. The output should additionally contain the total miles driven, total gallons used, and average miles per gallon for all the cars. These totals should be displayed at the end of the output report.

8. a. Create a file with the following data containing the part number, opening balance, number of items sold, and minimum stock required:

Part Number	Initial Amount	Quantity Sold	Minimum Amount
QA310	95	47	50
CM145	320	162	200
MS514	34	20	25
EN212	163	150	160

   b. Write a C program to create an inventory report based on the data in the file created in Exercise 8a. The display should consist of the part number, current balance, and amount that is necessary to bring the inventory to the minimum level.

9. a. Create a file containing the following data:

Name	Rate	Hours
Callaway, G.	6.00	40
Hanson, P.	5.00	48
Lasard, D.	6.50	35
Stillman, W.	8.00	50

   b. Write a C program that uses the information contained in the file created in Exercise 9a to produce the following pay report for each employee:

```
Name    Rate    Hours    Regular Pay    Overtime Pay    Gross Pay
```

   Any hours worked above 40 hours are paid at time and a half. Additionally, the program should display the totals of the regular, overtime, and gross pay columns.

10. a. Store the following data in a file:

```
5 96 87 78 93 21 4 92 82 85 87 6 72 69 85 75 81 73
```

   b. Write a C program to calculate and display the average of each group of numbers in the file created in Exercise 10a. The data is arranged in the file so that each group of numbers is preceded by the number of data items in the group. Thus, the first number in the file, 5, indicates that the next five numbers should be grouped together. The number 4 indicates that the following four numbers are a group, and the 6 indicates that the last six numbers are a group. (*Hint:* Use a nested loop. The outer loop should terminate when the `EOF` marker is encountered.)

10.3 Random File Access

File organization refers to the way data is stored in a file. All the files we have used have sequential organization. This means that the characters in the file are stored sequentially, one after another. Additionally, we have read the file in a sequential manner. The way data from a file is accessed is called file access. The fact that the characters in the file are stored sequentially, however, does not force us to access the file sequentially.

The standard library functions `rewind()`, `fseek()`, and `ftell()` can be used to provide random access to a file. In random access any character in the file can be read immediately, without first having to read all the characters stored before it.

The `rewind()` function resets the current position to the start of the file. The only argument required by `rewind()` is the file's name. For example, the statement

```
rewind(inFile):
```

resets the file so that the next character accessed will be the first character in the file. A `rewind()` is done automatically when a file is opened in read mode.

The `fseek()` function allows the programmer to move to any position in the file. To understand this function, you must first clearly comprehend how data is referenced in the file.

Each character in a data file is located by its position in the file. The first character in the file is located at position 0, the next character at position 1, and so on. This is identical to the way data is stored in a single-dimensional array. As with elements in an array, a character's position in a file is also referred to as its offset from the start of the file. Thus, the first character has an offset value of 0, the second character has an offset of 1, and so on for each character in the file.

The `fseek()` function requires three arguments: the pointer name of the file; the offset, as a long integer; and the position from which the offset is to be calculated. The general form of `fseek()` is

```
fseek(fileName, offset, origin)
```

The values of the origin argument can be either 0, 1, or 2. These are defined in the `stdio.h` as header file as the named constants SEEK_SET, SEEK_CUR, and SEEK_END, respectively. An origin of SEEK_SET means the offset is relative to the start of the file. An origin of SEEK_CUR means the offset is relative to the current position in the file, and an origin of SEEK_END means the offset is relative to the end of the file. A positive offset means move forward in the file and a negative offset means move backward. Examples of `fseek()` are

```
fseek(inFile,4L,SEEK_SET); /* go to the fifth character in the file */
fseek(inFile,4L,SEEK_CUR); /* move ahead five characters */
fseek(inFile,-4L,SEEK_CUR); /* move back five characters */
fseek(inFile,0L,SEEK_SET); /* go to start of file-same as rewind() */
fseek(inFile,0L,SEEK_END); /* go to end of file */
fseek(inFile,-10L,SEEK_END); /* go to 10 characters before the file's end */
```

In these examples, `inFile` is the name of the file pointer used when the data file was opened. Notice that the offset passed to `fseek()` must be a long integer. The appended `L` tells the compiler to convert the number to a long integer.

The last function, `ftell()`, simply returns the offset value of the next character that will be read or written. For example, if 10 characters have already been read from a file named `inFile`, the function call

```
ftell(inFile);
```

returns the long integer 10. This means that the next character to be read is offset 10 byte positions from the start of the file and is the 11th character in the file.

Program 10.7 illustrates the use of `fseek()` and `ftell()` to read a file in reverse order, from last character to first. Each character is also displayed as it is read.

Program 10.7

```
#include <stdio.h>
#include <stdlib.h>  /* needed for exit() */

int main()
{
  int ch, n;
  long int offset, last;
  FILE *inFile;

  inFile = fopen("text.dat","r");
  if (inFile == NULL)
  {
    printf("\nFailed to open the test.dat file.\n");
    exit(1);
  }
  fseek(inFile,0L,SEEK_END); /* move to the end of the file */
  last = ftell(inFile); /* save the offset of the last character */
  for(offset = 0; offset <= last; offset++)
  {
    fseek(inFile, -offset, SEEK_END); /* move back to the */
                                      /* next character */
    ch = getc(inFile); /* get the character */
    switch(ch)
    {
      case '\n': printf("LF : ");
                 break;
      case EOF : printf("EOF: ");
                 break;
      default : printf("%c : ",ch);
                break;
    }
  }
```

```
    fclose(inFile);

    return 0;
}
```

Assuming the file `text.dat` contains the following data:

```
Bulbs 3.12
```

the output of Program 10.7 is

```
EOF : 2 : 1 : . : 3 : : s : b : l : u : B :
```

Program 10.7 initially goes to the last character in the file. The offset of this character, which is the end-of-file character, is saved in the variable `last`. Since `ftell()` returns a long integer, `last` has been declared as a long integer. The function prototype for `ftell()` is contained in `stdio.h`.

Starting from the end of the file, `fseek()` is used to position the next character to be read, referenced from the back of the file. As each character is read, the character is displayed and the offset adjusted to access the next character.

EXERCISES 10.3

Short Answer Questions

1. How is the data organized in a file that has sequential organization?
2. If a file is organized sequentially, does this mean that file access must be sequential? Why or why not?
3. What function can be used to position the file pointer to any position in the file?
4. Determine the value of the offset returned by `ftell()` in Program 10.7. Assume that the file `text.dat` contains the data

   ```
   Bulbs 3.12
   ```

Programming Exercises

1. Rewrite Program 10.7 so that the origin for the `fseek()` function used in the `for` loop is the start of the file rather than the end. The program should still print the file in reverse order.
2. The function `fseek()` returns 0 if the position specified has been reached, or 1 if the position specified was beyond the file's boundaries. Modify Program 10.7 to display an error message if `fseek()` returns 1.

3. Write a C program that will read and display every second character in a file named `test.dat`.

4. Using the `fseek()` and `ftell()` functions, write a C function named `totChars()` that returns the total number of characters in a file.

5. a. Write a C function named `readBytes()` that reads and displays *n* characters starting from any position in a file. The function should accept three arguments: a file pointer, the offset of the first character to be read, and the number of characters to be read.
   b. Modify the `readBytes()` function written in Exercise 5a to store the characters read into a string or an array. The function should accept the address of the storage area as a fourth argument.

6. Assume that a data file consisting of a group of individual lines has been created. Write a C function named `printLine()` that will read and display any desired line of the file. For example, the function call `printLine(fileName,5);` should display the fifth line of the filename passed to it.

10.4 Passing and Returning Filenames

Internal filenames are passed to a function using the same procedures for passing all function arguments. For passing a filename this requires declaring the passed argument as a pointer to a `FILE`. For example, in Program 10.8 a file named `outFile` is opened in `main()` and the filename is passed to the function `inOut()`, which is then used to write five lines of user-entered text to the file.

Program 10.8

```
#include <stdio.h>
#include <stdlib.h>  /* needed for exit() */

void inOut(FILE *); /* function prototype */

int main()
{
  FILE *outFile;

  outFile = fopen("prices.dat","w");
  if (outFile == NULL)
  {
    printf("\nFailed to open the file.\n");
    exit(1);
  }

```

```
  inOut(outFile);  /* call the function */

  fclose(outFile);
  printf("\nThe file has been successfully written.\n");

  return 0;
}

void inOut(FILE *fname) /* fname is a pointer to a FILE */
{
  int count;
  char line[81]; /* enough storage for one line of text */

  printf("Please enter five lines of text:\n");
  for (count = 0; count < 5; count++)
  {
    gets(line);
    fprintf(fname,"%s\n",line);
  }
}
```

Within `main()` the file is known as `outFile`. The value in `outFile`, which is an address, is passed to the `inOut()` function. The function `inOut()` stores the address in the parameter named `fname` and correctly declares `fname` to be a pointer to a `FILE`. Notice that the function prototype for `inOut()` declares that the function expects to receive a pointer to a `FILE`.

Returning a filename from a function also requires following the same rules used to return any value from a function. This means including the data type of the returned value in the function header, making sure the correct variable type is actually returned from the function, and alerting the calling function to the returned data type. For example, assume that the function `getOpen()` is called with no arguments. The purpose of this function is to prompt a user for a filename, open the file for output, and pass the filename back to the calling function. Since `getOpen()` returns a filename that is actually a pointer to a `FILE`, the correct function declaration for `getOpen()` is

```
FILE *getOpen()
```

This declaration specifically declares that the function `getOpen()` expects no argument and will return a pointer to a `FILE`. It is consistent with the pointer declarations that have been made previously.

Once a function has been declared to return a pointer to a `FILE`, there must be at least one variable or parameter in the function consistent with this declaration that can be used for the actual returned value. Consider Program 10.9. In this program `getOpen()` returns a filename to `main()`.

Program 10.9 is simply a modified version of Program 10.8 that now allows the user to enter a filename from the standard input device. It also illustrates the correct function declaration for returning a filename. The `getOpen()` function declaration defines the function as returning a pointer to a FILE. Within getOpen(), the returned variable, fname, is the correct data type. Finally, main() is alerted to the returned value by the function prototype for the getOpen() function.

The function getOpen() is a "bare bones" function in that it does not check the file being opened for output. If the name of an existing data file is entered, the file will be destroyed when it is opened in write mode. A useful trick to prevent this type of mishap is to open the entered filename in read mode. Then, if the file exists, the fopen() function returns a non-0 pointer value to indicate that the file is available for input. This can be used to alert the user that a file with the entered name currently exists in the system and to request confirmation that the data in the file can be destroyed and the filename used for the new output file. Before the file can be reopened in write mode, of course, it would have to be closed.

Program 10.9

```
#include <stdio.h>
#include <stdlib.h>  /* needed for exit() */

FILE *getOpen();     /* function prototype */
void inOut(FILE *); /* function prototype */

int main()
{
  FILE *outFile;

  outFile = getOpen();  /* call the function */
  inOut(outFile);       /* call the function */

  fclose(outFile);
  printf("\nThe file has been successfully written.\n");

  return 0;
}

FILE *getOpen() /* getOpen() returns a pointer to a FILE */
{
  FILE *fname;
  char name[13];

  printf("\nEnter a file name: ");
  gets(name);
  fname = fopen(name,"w");
  if (fname == NULL)
  {
```

```
    printf("\nFailed to open the file %s.\n", name);
    exit(1);
  }

  return(fname);
}

void inOut(FILE *fname) /* fname is a pointer to a FILE */
{
  int count;
  char line[81]; /* enough storage for one line of text */

  printf("Please enter five lines of text:\n");
  for (count = 0; count < 5; count++)
  {
    gets(line);
    fprintf(fname,"%s\n",line);
  }
}
```

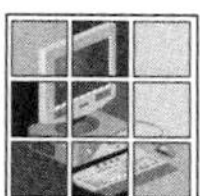

EXERCISES 10.4

Short Answer Questions

1. A function named `pFile()` is to receive a filename as an argument. What declarations are required to pass a filename to `pFile()`?

2. a. A function named `getFile()` is to return a filename. What declarations are required in the function header and internal to the file?
   b. What declaration statement is required for each function that calls `getFile()`? Under what conditions can this declaration be omitted?

Programming Exercises

1. Write a C function named `fcheck()` that checks whether a file exists. The function should be passed a filename. If the file exists, the function should return a value of 1; otherwise the function should return a value of 0.

2. Rewrite the function `getOpen()` used in Program 10.9 to incorporate the file-checking procedures described in the text. Specifically, if the entered filename exists, an appropriate message should be displayed. The user should then be presented with the option of entering a new filename or allowing the program to overwrite the existing file, append to it, or exit.

10.5 Case Study: Creating and Using a Table of Constants

A common real-world programming requirement is creating and maintaining a small file of constants, reading and storing these constants into a list, and then providing functions for checking data against the constants in the list. For example, a scientific program might require a set of temperatures at which various elements freeze or change state, or an engineering program might require a set of material densities for various grades of steel and iron ore. In financial and scheduling programs, this requirement takes the form of reading a set of holiday dates and then checking a date against each date in the table. This determination is important in many applications to ensure that contractual settlement dates and delivery dates are not scheduled on a holiday.

Requirements Specification

Our objective in this section is to create a set of functions that determines if a given date is a holiday, using concepts that are equally applicable to any program that needs to check data against a list of constants, such as temperatures, densities, or other parameters. Specifically, two functions are developed. The first function constructs a list of holidays, which is referred to as a **holiday table**, and consists of legal holiday dates that have been previously stored in a file. The second function compares any given date to the dates in the table and determines if there is a match.

Analysis for the First Function

The creation of a list of holidays requires reading data from a file that contains the necessary dates. Because these dates change each year, a separate maintenance program would be required to maintain the holiday dates. Typically, toward the latter part of December, a function would automatically send a reminder to the user to update the holiday dates. In this program, we will use the North American holidays listed in Table 10.3 for our dates.

Table 10.3 North American Government Holidays

Holiday	Date
New Year's Day	1/1/2007
Martin Luther King Jr.'s Birthday	1/15/2007
Presidents' Day	2/19/2007
Good Friday	4/6/2007
Easter	4/9/2007
Cinco de Mayo	5/5/2007
Victoria Day	5/21/2007
Memorial Day	5/30/2007
Canada Day	7/1/2007
Independence Day	7/4/2007
Labor Day	9/3/2007
Columbus Day	10/8/2007

Table 10.3 North American Government Holidays (continued)

Holiday	Date
Canadian Thanksgiving	10/8/2007
United States Thanksgiving	11/22/2007
Christmas	12/25/2007

We assume that the holiday dates listed in Table 10.3 are stored and available in a file named `Holidays.txt`. Such a file can be created using either a text editor, copying the file from the Web site provided for this text, or writing a program that accepts the dates from a user and writes the dates to a file. Table 10.4 illustrates the 15 holiday dates, one per line, as they are stored in the `Holidays.txt` file.

Table 10.4 Holiday Dates Stored in the Holidays.txt File

```
1/1/2007
1/15/2007
2/19/2007
4/6/2007
4/9/2007
5/5/2007
5/21/2007
5/30/2007
7/1/2007
7/4/2007
9/3/2007
10/8/2007
10/8/2007
11/22/2007
12/25/2007
```

Our first task will be to develop a function that reads the dates in the `Holidays.txt` file and stores them in a table.

a. Determine the Input Items

The input item is the `Holidays.txt` file listed in Table 10.4.

b. Determine the Required Outputs

The required output is a table of the dates that are stored in the `Holidays.txt` file. This table should have global scope so that it is available for all subsequent functions that require access to the dates. In creating this table, we must first decide how to store the month, day, and year values contained within each line of the `Holidays.txt` file. Rather than storing each date as a month, day, and year value, we will make use of the fact that a date can be stored as a single integer in the form yyyymmdd. For example, using this format, a date such as 12/25/2007 would be stored as 20071225. Using this single-integer date value has a number of advantages.

First, storing dates in this manner means that the table can be created as a single-dimensioned array with one element per date. Doing this avoids the necessity of using three arrays: one for the month, one for the day, and one for the year. Second, this format makes comparing two dates for equality rather easy, in that only one number has to be compared, rather than comparing month to month, day to day, and year to year. And finally, this format makes it quite easy to determine which of two dates occurs either earlier or later; the date with the higher single-integer value occurs later than the date with the smaller integer value. It is for all of these reasons that many applications that use dates convert them to a single number.

c. List the Algorithms Relating the Inputs to the Outputs

For our purposes, we will construct the table as an array whose size is slightly larger than the number of entries in the file. Doing this permits the array size to accept the number of dates being stored automatically, which can change over time as new holidays are declared, and vary for each country. As the `Holidays.txt` file currently has 15 entries, we will arbitrarily set the maximum number of dates that we can store at 20. This provides for an increase of 5 more official holidays, which should be ample for all conceivable additional official holidays that might be declared in the future. (An alternative is to first count the number of entries in the file, and then create an array of the exact size. This solution, which is certainly valid, requires two file reads: the first to determine how many entries are in the file and the second to store each date as it is read.)

Converting a date provided as a month, day, and year to a single-date integer is accomplished using the formula

*dateInteger = yearValue *10000 + monthValue * 100 + dayValue.*

Finally, simply as a useful check, we will develop our file-reading function to return the number of holidays actually read and stored. The pseudocode for this algorithm becomes

Create an array large enough to hold all holiday dates
  While there are dates in the file
      Read a Date
      Convert the Date to a single integer
      Store the date in the date array
EndWhile

d. Perform a Hand Calculation

Any date can be used for this calculation. We will use the second date in the file, 1/15/2007, because, unlike the first date, it has a different day and month value As a single-date integer this becomes

```
2007 * 10000 + 1 * 100 * 15 = 20070000 + 100 + 15 = 20070115
```

Notice that the multiplications essentially shift the year and month values so that the month value gets placed as a two-digit number immediately after the year, and the day value gets placed as a two-digit number immediately after the month.

Code the Function

Based on these considerations the pseudocode describing the algorithm for our file retrieval function becomes

```
Create an array capable of storing 20 integers
Set a counter to 0
Open the Holidays.txt file, checking that a successful open occurred
While there are dates in the file
    Read a date as a month, day, and year
    Convert the date to an integer having the form yyyymmdd
    Assign the integer date to the Holiday array
    Add 1 to the counter
EndWhile
Close the Holidays.txt file
Return the value of the counter
```

Naming our function `getHolidays()`, the following C code corresponds to this algorithm:

```c
#include <stdio.h>
#include <stdlib.h>  /* needed for exit() */
#define HOLIDAYS 20
int htable[HOLIDAYS];  /* a global holiday array */

int getHolidays()
{
  char HolidayFile[] = "c:\\csrccode\\Holidays.txt";  /* change this to the */
  int i = 0;                                   /* path where the file is stored on */
  int mo, day, yr;                             /* your computer */
  char del1, del2;
  FILE *inFile;

  inFile = fopen(HolidayFile,"r");  /* open the file */
  /* check for a successful open */
  if (inFile == NULL)
  {
    printf("\nFailed to open the file.\n");
    exit(1);
  }

  /* read, convert, and store each date */
  while (fscanf(inFile, "%d%c%d%c%d", &mo, &del1, &day, & del2, &yr) != EOF)
    htable[i++] = yr * 10000 + mo * 100 + day;

  fclose(inFile);

  return i;
}
```

The coding of `getHolidays()` is rather straightforward once its underlying algorithm is understood. The first important point to notice is that the separation of a date into a month, day, and year depends on the stored dates within the `Holidays.txt` file being written in the form month/day/year that uses a single character, the forward slash, to delimit individual values. Thus, in parsing these values from the input data, this single delimiter is accepted as a character, and then simply ignored. This is accomplished in line 23 each time that a date is read from the file

```
23  while (fscanf(inFile, "%d%c%d%c%d", &mo, &del1, &day, &del2, &yr) != EOF)
```

Here, the first delimiter that separates the month and day values is stored in the character variable `del1` and the second delimiter that separates the day and year value is stored in the character variable `del2`, both of which are then ignored in any further processing.[4]

Once values for a month, day, and year are obtained, they are immediately converted to a single integer and stored in the `htable` array using the assignment statement in line 24

```
24  htable[i++] = yr * 10000 + mo * 100 + day;
```

Notice that this statement also increments the value of `i` so that that next value that is read will be correctly assigned to the next position in the `htable` array. After the function detects that there are no additional entries in the `Holidays.txt` file, the `while` loop is exited and the file closed. Finally, the number of data items that have been read and assigned to the `htable` array is returned by the function.

Test and Debug the Function

Once the `getHolidays()` function has been coded, we can test its operation. Program 10.10 performs this testing by first calling the `getHolidays()` function and then displaying the dates retrieved from the `Holidays.txt` file and stored in the `htable` array.

Program 10.10

```
#include <stdio.h>
#include <stdlib.h>  /* needed for exit() */
#define HOLIDAYS 20
int htable[HOLIDAYS];   /* a global holiday array */

int main()
{
int getHolidays();  /* function prototype */
int i, numHolidays;

numHolidays = getHolidays();

/* verify the input and storage of the Holidays */
printf("The Holiday array contains %d holidays\n", numHolidays);
printf(" and contains the elements:\n");
for(i = 0; i < numHolidays; i++)
```

[4]An alternative is to use the function call `fscanf(inFile, "%d/%d/%d", &mo, &day, &yr)`, which tells the function to use the slash as a delimiter between integer values.

```
printf("%d\n", htable[i]);

return 0;
}

int getHolidays()
{
  char HolidayFile[] = "c:\\csrccode\\Holidays.txt";  /* change this to the */
  int i = 0;                               /* path where the file is stored on */
  int mo, day, yr;                           /* your computer */
  char del1, del2;
  FILE *inFile;

  inFile = fopen(HolidayFile,"r");  /* open the file */
  /* check for a successful open */
  if (inFile == NULL)
  {
    printf("\nFailed to open the file.\n");
    exit(1);
  }

  /* read, convert, and store each date */
  while (fscanf(inFile, "%d%c%d%c%d", &mo, &del1, &day, &del2, &yr) != EOF)
    htable[i++] = yr * 10000 + mo * 100 + day;

  fclose(inFile);

  return i;
}
```

The output produced by Program 10.10 is

```
The Holiday array contains 15 holidays
 and contains the elements:
20070101
20070115
20070219
20070406
20070409
20070505
20070521
20070530
20070701
20070704
```

```
20070903
20071008
20071008
20071122
20071225
```

As indicated by this output, the file's data has been successfully read, converted to a single-integer data value, and stored in the `htable` array by `getHolidays()`.

Analysis for the Second Function

The requirement for this function is that it accepts a date and checks it against the dates stored in the program's global `htable` array. If a matching date is found, the function should return a value of 1, which corresponds to the C value for true; otherwise, it should return a 0, which corresponds to a C value for false. Before this check is made, however, the function must first determine if the table is empty; if it is, the `getHolidays()` function should be called to create a valid table.

a. Determine the Input Items

The input items are the `htable` array produced by `getHoliday()` and a date whose value is to be checked against each entry in the array until either a match is found or the end of the array is reached.

b. Determine the Required Outputs

The output is a return value of 1 if a match; otherwise 0 must be returned.

c. List the Algorithms Relating the Inputs to the Outputs

The algorithm describing our function is

```
If the holiday table is empty
    Call getHolidays()
EndIf
For all Holidays in the table
  Retrieve the holiday from the table
  Compare the date being tested to the date retrieved from the array
  If there is a match
    Return 1
EndFor
Return 0
```

Code the Function

Naming our function `isHoliday()`, the C code for this algorithm becomes

```
int isHoliday(int testDate)
{
  int getHolidays();  /* function prototype */
  #define TRUE 1
  #define FALSE 0
  int i;

```

```
8    /* read the Holiday file if the Holiday array is empty */
9    if (htable[0] == 0)
10     getHolidays();
11
12   /* search the Holiday array for the given date */
13   for(i = 0; i < HOLIDAYS; i++)
14     if (testDate == htable[i])
15       return TRUE;
16
17   return FALSE;
18 }
```

If there is a match (line 14), the function breaks out of the loop and returns a value of 1; otherwise, if the loop exits normally, indicating that no match was found, a value of 0 is returned. Notice that the function expects to receive the date that is being checked as an integer argument that will have the same format as the dates stored in the `htable` array.

Test and Debug the Function

A suitable test of the `isHoliday()` function is obtained by including the function within Program 10.11. Specifically, Program 10.11 verifies `isHoliday()` by testing for one holiday and one nonholiday date.

Program 10.11

```
#include <stdio.h>
#include <stdlib.h>  /* needed for exit() */
#define HOLIDAYS 20
int htable[HOLIDAYS];  /* a global holiday array */

int main()
{
  int isHoliday(int);  /* function prototype */
  int mo, day, yr, testDate;

  printf("Enter a month, day, and year: ");
  scanf("%d %d %d", &mo, &day, &yr);
  testDate = yr * 10000 + mo * 100 + day;

  if (isHoliday(testDate))
    printf("This date is a holiday.\n");
  else
    printf("This date is not a holiday.\n");

  return 0;
}
```

```

int isHoliday(int testDate)
{
  int getHolidays();  /* function prototype */
  #define TRUE 1
  #define FALSE 0
  int i;

  /* read the Holiday file if the Holiday array is empty */
  if (htable[0] == 0)
    getHolidays();

  /* search the Holiday array for the given date */
  for(i = 0; i < HOLIDAYS; i ++)
    if (testDate == htable[i])
      return TRUE;

  return FALSE;
}

int getHolidays()
{
  char HolidayFile[] = "c:\\csrccode\\Holidays.txt";
  int i = 0;
  int mo, day, yr;
  char del1, del2;
  FILE *inFile;

  inFile = fopen(HolidayFile,"r");  /* open the file */
  /* check for a successful open */
  if (inFile == NULL)
  {
    printf("\nFailed to open the file.\n");
    exit(1);
  }

  /* read, convert, and store each date */
  while (fscanf(inFile, "%d%c%d%c%d", &mo, &del1, &day, &del2, &yr) != EOF)
    htable[i++] = yr * 10000 + mo * 100 + day;

  fclose(inFile);

  return i;
}
```

The output produced by two runs of Program 10.11 is

```
Enter a month, day, and year: 1 5 2007
This date is not a holiday.
```

and

```
Enter a month, day, and year: 12 25 2007
This date is a holiday.
```

As indicated by this output, the `isHoliday()` function appears to be working correctly.

EXERCISES 10.5

Short Answer Questions

1. The dates in the `Holidays.txt` file can be stored in three separate arrays, one for the day, one for the month, and one for the year.
   a. What is an advantage of storing the dates in this manner?
   b. What is a disadvantage of storing the dates in this manner?

2. Devise an algorithm for converting a date in the form of yyyymmdd into a day, month, and year value. For example, the date 20071225 should provide a day, month, and year value of 12, 25, and 2007, respectively.

3. In addition to the `isHoliday()` function presented in Program 10.11, what other functions might be useful when dealing with dates?

Programming Exercises

1. Enter, compile, and execute Program 10.10.

2. Enter and execute Program 10.11 on your computer.

3. Create a function named `setHolidays()` that reads and displays the current list of holidays and then lets the user change, add, or delete holidays from the list. After a holiday has been modified, the function should sort the holidays and display the new list. Finally, the function should ask the user whether the new list should be saved; if the user responds affirmatively, the function should write the new data to the existing `Holdiays.txt` file, overwriting the contents of the existing file.

4. Pollen count readings, which are taken from August through September in the northeastern region of the United States, measure the number of ragweed pollen grains in the air. Pollen counts in the range of 10 to 200 grains per cubic meter of air are typical during this time of year. Pollen counts above 10 begin to affect a small percentage of hay fever sufferers, counts in the range of 30 to 40 will noticeably bother approximately 30 percent of hay fever sufferers, and counts between 40 and 50 adversely affect more than 60 percent of all hay fever sufferers.

Write a C program that updates a file containing the 10 most recent pollen counts. Add each new count to the end of the file. As you add a new count to the end of the file, delete the oldest count, which is the first value in the file. Your program should also calculate and display the averages of the data for the old and new files.

To test your program, first create a file named `Pollen.dat` that contains the following pollen count data: 30, 60, 40, 80, 90, 120, 150, 130, 160, 170. Here the first value, 30, corresponds to the oldest pollen count, and the last value, 170, corresponds to the most recent pollen count. The pseudocode for the file update program is

Display a message indicating what the program does
Request the name of the data file
Request a new pollen count reading
Open the data file as an input file
Do for 10 data items
   Read a value into an array
   Add the value to a total
EndDo
Close the file
Open the file as an output file
Calculate and display the old 10-day average
Calculate and display the new 10-day average
Write the nine most recent pollen counts from the array to the file
Write the new pollen count to the file
Close the file

10.6 Writing and Reading Binary Files (Optional)[5]

An alternative to a text file, where each character in the file is represented by a unique code, is a binary file. Although, at a basic level, all files are stored using binary numbers, files that are referred to as **binary files** store numerical values using the computer's internal numerical code. For example, assuming that your C compiler stores integers using 32 bits (4 bytes), the integer numbers 125 and −125 are represented as listed in Table 10.5.

Table 10.5 Binary and Hexadecimal Representations of Integer Numbers

Integer	Binary Representation	Hexadecimal Equivalent
125	0000 0000 0000 0000 0000 0000 0111 1101	0x00 00 00 7D
−125	1111 1111 1111 1111 1111 1111 1000 0010	0xFF FF FF 83

Because a binary file's storage codes match the computer's internal storage codes, no intermediary conversions are required for storing or retrieving the data. This means that there is no number-to-character conversion required when writing a number to a file and no character-to-number conversion required when a value is read from the file. For files consisting predominantly of numerical data, this is a distinct advantage and can improve program efficiency. The resulting file frequently requires less storage space than its character-based counterpart. The disadvantage is that the file can no longer be inspected using either a word processing or text editing program, which means that the ability to see

[5]This topic requires familiarity with the computer storage concepts presented in Section 1.8.

the numerical values as textual information is lost. In this section, the creation of a binary file is presented first, followed by a number of examples for reading such a file.

The specification for explicitly creating and writing to a binary file is made by appending a 'b' to the mode indicator when the file is opened. For example, the following two statements can be used to open a binary file named prices.bin as an output file:

```
FILE *outFile;
open("prices.bin", "wb");
```

As with text files, an output stream for a binary file creates a new file and makes the file available for writing. If a file exists with the same name as a file opened for output, the old file is erased.

A binary file opened in append mode means that any data written to the file will be added to the end of the file. If the file opened for appending does not exist, a new file with the designated name is created and data is written starting at the beginning of the file.

Finally, a binary file opened in input mode means that an existing external file has been connected and its data is available as input. For example, the following two statements can be used to open a binary file named prices.bin as an input file:

```
FILE *inFile;
open("prices.bin", "rb");
```

Once opened, the actual writing of data to a binary file takes a rather simple, but convoluted form. Program 10.12 illustrates the required procedure after the file is correctly opened as an output binary file.

Program 10.12

```
#include <stdio.h>
#include <stdlib.h>  /* needed for exit() */

int main()
{
  char response;
  char fileName[20] = "prices.bin";
  FILE *outFile;
  int num1 = 125;
  long num2 = -125;
  double num3 = 1.08;

  /* check that a file by the given name does not already exist */
  outFile = fopen(fileName,"r"); /* open the file */
  if (outFile != NULL) /* check for a successful open*/
  {
    printf("\nA file by the name %s exists.", fileName);
    printf("\nDo you want to continue and overwrite it");
    printf("\n with the new data (y or n): ");
```

```
    scanf("%c", &response);
    if (response == 'n')
    {
      printf("\nThe existing file %s will not be overwritten.\n",
                                                          fileName);
      fclose(outFile);
      exit(1);  /* terminate program execution */
    }
  }

  /* okay to proceed */
  outFile = fopen(fileName,"wb");  /* now open the file */
                                   /* for writing */
  if(outFile == NULL)  /* check for an unsuccessful opening */
  {
    printf("\nThe file %s was not successfully opened.\n", fileName);
    exit(1);
  }
  /* write to the file */
  fwrite(&num1, sizeof(num1), 1, outFile);
  fwrite(&num2, sizeof(num2), 1, outFile);
  fwrite(&num3, sizeof(num3), 1, outFile);

  fclose(outFile);
  printf("\nThe file %s has successfully been written as a binary file.\n",
                                                                fileName);
  return 0;
}
```

In reviewing Program 10.12, first notice that the filename has been designated as a `FILE` object at the top of `main()` function in the same manner as was done for text files. Next, notice that the open statement is also identical to that for a text file, with the addition of the mode indicator specifying that the file is to be a binary file.

Finally, concentrate on the three highlighted statements used to write data to the file. Notice that all of these statements use this syntax:

```
fwrite(&variable, sizeof(variable), n, file);
```

In this syntax the first method argument is always the address operator, &, and a variable name. The second argument uses the `sizeof()` operator to determine the number of bytes to be written. The third argument indicates how many items are to be written, which in this case is one, and the last argument tells `fwrite()` which file stream to place the data on. Thus, starting from the first byte stored in the variable, which is provided by the first argument, the exact number of bytes in each variable is then written to the file. This places the internal binary code for each variable, byte by byte, into the file.

The binary file created by Program 10.12 is illustrated in Figure 10.3, which uses hexadecimal values to indicate the equivalent binary values. Although Figure 10.3 separates the file's data into three individual lines, with bars, `|`, used to distinguish individual items, in actuality the file is stored as a consecutive sequence of bytes. As indicated in the figure, each integer value consists of 4 bytes, and the double-precision number is 8 bytes.

```
            |00 00 00 7D| <--- corresponds to  125
            |FF FF FF 83| <--- corresponds to -125
|3F F1 47 AE 14 7A E1 48| <--- corresponds to  1.08
```

Figure 10.3 The stored binary data in the `prices.bin` file and their decimal equivalents

The specific bit patterns for the two integers in Figure 10.3 can be converted to decimal notation using a hexadecimal to decimal conversion. This can be accomplished by first converting each hexadecimal digit to its binary form using the conversions provided in Table 10.6, and then using the two's complement value box presented in Section 1.8 to convert from binary to decimal (direct conversion from hexadecimal to decimal can also be used). Converting a double-precision number requires using the real number storage specification presented in Appendix E.

Table 10.6 Hexadecimal Digits to Binary Conversions

Hexadecimal Digit	Binary Equivalent
0	0000
1	0001
2	0010
3	0011
4	0100
5	0101
6	0110
7	0111
8	1000
9	1001
A	1010
B	1011
C	1100
D	1101
E	1110
F	1111

Reading a binary file, similar to the one illustrated in Figure 10.3, requires constructing an input binary stream and then using appropriate input methods.

Program 10.13 illustrates the opening of a binary input stream object, the input of the data stored in the file created in Program 10.12, and the display of this data. In reviewing the actual input of the data, notice that the individual data items are read in almost the identical manner in which they were written.

Program 10.13

```
#include <stdio.h>
#include <stdlib.h>  /* needed for exit() */

int main()
{
  FILE *inFile;
  char fileName[13] = "prices.bin";
  int num1;
  long num2;
  double num3;

  inFile = fopen(fileName,"rb"); /* open the file */
  if (inFile == NULL)
  {
    printf("\nThe file %s was not successfully opened.", fileName);
    printf("\nPlease check that the file currently exists.\n");
    exit(1);
  }

  /* read the binary data from the file */
  fread(&num1, sizeof(num1), 1, inFile);
  fread(&num2, sizeof(num2), 1, inFile);
  fread(&num3, sizeof(num3), 1, inFile);

  fclose(inFile);
  printf("The data input from the %s file is: ", fileName);
  printf("%d %ld %lf", num1, num2, num3);
  printf("\n");

  return 0;
}
```

The output produced by Program 10.13 is

```
The data input from the prices.bin file is: 125 -125 1.080000
```

EXERCISES 10.6

Short Answer Questions

1. Describe the difference between a text file and a binary file.
2. Show the binary codes that would be used to store the number 25 in an ASCII text file (see Appendix B) and how the same number would be stored in a binary file using two's complement representations (see Section 1.8).
3. Repeat Exercise 2 using the number -25.

Programming Exercises

1. Enter and execute Program 10.12. Once the `prices.bin` file has been written, execute Program 10.12 a second time to verify that it does not overwrite the existing file without your permission.
2. Enter and execute Program 10.13 on your computer.
3. Write, compile, and run a C program that writes the numbers 92.65, 88.72, 77.46, and 82.93 as double-precision values to a binary file named `results.bin`. After writing the data to the file, the program should read the data from the file, determine the average of the four numbers read, and display the average. Verify the output produced by the program by manually calculating the average of the four input numbers.
4. a. Write, compile, and execute a C program that creates a binary file named `points` and writes the following numbers to the file:

6.3	8.2	18.25	24.32
4.0	4.0	10.0	-5.0
-2.0	5.0	4.0	5.0

   b. Using the data in the `points` file created in Exercise 4a, write, compile, and run a C program that reads four numbers using a `for` loop and interprets the first and second numbers in each record as the coordinates of one point and the third and fourth numbers as the coordinates of a second point. Have the program compute and display the slope and midpoint of each pair of entered points.

5. a. Write, compile, and run a C program that creates a binary file named `grades.bin` and writes the following five lines of data to the file:

90.3	92.7	90.3	99.8
85.3	90.5	87.3	90.8
93.2	88.4	93.8	75.6
82.4	95.6	78.2	90.0
93.5	80.2	92.9	94.4

b. Using the data in the `grades.bin` file created in Exercise 5a, write, compile, and run a C program that reads, computes, and displays the average of each group of four grades.

10.7 Common Programming and Compiler Errors

In using the material presented in this chapter, be aware of the following possible programming and compiler errors.

Programming Errors

1. Using a file's external name in place of the internal file pointer variable name when accessing the file. The only standard library function that uses the data file's external name is the `fopen()` function. All the other standard functions presented in this chapter require the pointer variable assigned to the file when it was initially opened.

2. Omitting the file pointer name altogether. Programmers used to `scanf()` and `printf()` that access the standard input and output devices, where a specific file pointer is not required, sometimes forget to include a filename when accessing data files.

3. Opening a file for output without first checking that a file with the given name already exists. Not checking for a preexisting filename ensures that the file will be overwritten.

4. Not understanding the end of a file is only detected until after the `EOF` sentinel has either been read or passed over.

5. Attempting to detect the end of a file using character variable for the `EOF` marker. Any variable used to accept the EOF must be declared as an integer variable. For example, if `ch` is declared as a character variable, the expression

   ```
   while ( (ch = in.file.peek()) ! EOF )
   ```

   produces an infinite loop. This occurs because a character variable can never take on an EOF code. EOF is an integer value (usually -1) that has no character representation. This ensures that the EOF code can never be confused with any legitimate character encountered as normal data in the file. To terminate the loop created by the above expression, the variable `ch` must be declared as an integer variable.

6. Supplying an integer argument offset to the `seekg()` and `seekp()` functions. This offset must be a long integer constant or variable. Any other value passed to these functions can result in an unpredictable effect.

7. Not using the `sizeof()` operator when specifying the number of bytes to be written when writing a binary file.

8. Not using the `sizeof()` operator when specifying the number of bytes to be read when reading a binary file.

Compiler Errors

The following table summarizes common errors that will result in compilation errors and the typical error messages provided by Unix- and Windows-based compilers.

Error	Typical Unix-based Compiler Error Message	Typical Windows-based Compiler Error Message

Not using a `FILE` pointer when trying to open a file. For example:
`int *f;`
`f=fopen("test.txt","a");`
	`(W) Operation between types "int*" and "struct {...}*" is not allowed.`
	`(W) Function argument assignment between types "struct {...}*" and "int*" is not allowed.`
		`:error: '=' : cannot convert from 'FILE *' to 'int *'`

Not including the file permissions inside double quotes. For example:
`FILE *f;`
`f=fopen("test.txt", a);`
	`(S) Undeclared identifier a.`	`:error: '=' : cannot convert from 'FILE *' to 'int *'`

Not capitalizing the symbolic constant `FILE`. For example:
`file *f;`
`f=fopen("test.txt", "a");`
	`(S) Undeclared identifier file.`
	`(S) Undeclared identifier f.`
		`: error C2065: 'file' : undeclared identifier :error C2065: 'f' : undeclared identifier`

Not supplying a `FILE` argument to `fprintf()`. For example:
`FILE *f;`
`f=fopen("test.txt", "a"); fprintf("Hello!");`
	`(W) Function argument assignment between types "struct {...}*" and "unsigned char*" is not allowed. (E) Missing argument(s).`	`:error: 'fprintf' : function does not take 1 arguments`

Not providing `fclose()` with a `FILE` ptr. For example: `fclose();`	`(E) Missing argument(s).`	`:error: 'fclose' : function does not take 0 arguments`

10.8 Chapter Summary

1. A data file is any collection of data stored together in an external storage medium under a common name.
2. Data files can be stored as either character-based or binary files. A character-based file, also referred to as a text file, stores each individual digit, letter, and symbol with a separate code. This permits the file to be viewed and manipulated with a word processor or editor program.

   A binary file stores numbers using the internal binary code (typically two's complement) used by the computer's internal processing unit.
3. A data file is opened using the `fopen()` standard library function. This function connects a file's external name with an internal pointer name. After the file is opened, all subsequent accesses to the file require the internal pointer name. The default file type in C is text. Binary files are designated by including a `"b"` in the mode indicator, which is the second argument required by `fopen()`.
4. A file can be opened for reading, writing, or appending. A file opened for writing creates a new file and erases any existing file having the same name as the opened file. A file opened for appending makes an existing file available for data to be added to the end of the file. If the file does not exist it is created. A file opened for reading makes an existing file's data available for input.
5. An internal filename must be declared as a pointer to a `FILE`. This means that a declaration similar to

   ```
   FILE *fileName;
   ```

   must be included with the declarations in which the file is opened. In this declaration, `filename` can be replaced with any user-selected variable name.
6. In addition to any files opened within a function, the standard files `stdin`, `stdout`, and `stderr` are automatically opened when a program is run. The symbolic constant `stdin` is the pointer name of the physical file used for data entry by `scanf()`, `stdout` is the pointer name of the physical file device used for data display by `printf()`, and `stderr` is the pointer name of the physical file device used for displaying system error messages.
7. Data files can be accessed randomly using the `rewind()`, `fseek()`, and `ftell()` functions.
8. Table 10.7 lists the standard file library functions.

Table 10.6 Standard File Library Functions

Function Name	Purpose
`fopen()`	Open or create a file
`fclose()`	Close a file
`fgetc()`	Character input
`getchar()`	Character input from `stdin`
`fgets()`	String input
`gets()`	String input from `stdin`
`fscanf()`	Formatted input
`scanf()`	Formatted input from `stdin`
`fputc()`	Character output
`putchar()`	Character output to `stdout`
`fputs()`	String output
`puts()`	String output to `stdout`
`fprintf()`	Formatted output
`printf()`	Formatted output to `stdout`
`fseek()`	File positioning
`rewind()`	File positioning
`ftell()`	Position reporting

10.9 Chapter Supplement: Control Codes

In addition to responding to the codes for letters, digits, and special punctuation symbols, which are collectively referred to as printable characters, physical device files such as printers and CRT screens can also respond to a small set of control codes. These codes, which convey control information to the physical device, have no equivalent characters that can be displayed and are called nonprintable characters.

Two of these codes, which are extremely useful in applications, are the clear and bell control codes. When the clear control code is sent to a printer, the printer ejects a page of paper and begins printing on the next sheet of paper. For dot-matrix printers, if you take care to align the printer to the top of a new page when printing begins, the clear control character can be used as a "top-of-page" command. For laser printers the clear code acts as a straight page-eject code. When the equivalent clear code is sent to a CRT display, the screen is cleared of all text and the cursor is positioned at the left-hand corner of the screen.

Sending control codes to an output device is done in a manner similar to sending a printable character to a file. Recall that sending a printable character to a file requires two pieces of information: the filename and the character being written to the file. For example, the statement `fputc('a',outFile);` causes the letter *a* to be written to the file named `outFile`. Instead of including the actual letter as an argument to `fputc()`, we can substitute the numerical code for the letter. For computers that use the ASCII code, this amounts to substituting the equivalent ASCII numerical value for the appropriate letter. Referring to Appendix B, we see that in the ASCII code the value for *a* is 97 as a decimal number, 61 as a hexadecimal number, and 141 as an octal number. Any one of these numerical values can be used in place of the letter *a* in the previous `fputc()` function call. Thus, the following four statements are all equivalent:

```
fputc('a',outFile);
fputc(97, outFile);
fputc(0x61, outFile);
fputc('\141',outFile);
```

Note that in each of these statements we have adhered to the notation used in C to identify decimal and hexadecimal numbers. A number with no leading zero is considered a decimal number and a number with a leading `0x` is considered a hexadecimal value. Octal character codes must, however, be preceded by a backslash and enclosed in single apostrophes. The backslash identifies the number as an octal value, allowing us to omit the normal leading zero associated with octal values. Because most control codes, by convention, are listed as octal values using three significant digits, we will retain this convention in all further examples.

The importance of substituting the numerical code for the letter is only realized when a control code rather than a character code must be sent. Because no equivalent character exists for control codes, the actual code for the command must be used. Although each computer can have its own code for clearing the CRT screen, the bell code and the code for clearing a printer are fairly universal. To activate the bell, the octal code 07 is used. The octal clear code for most printers is 014. Thus, if the file `outFile` has been opened as the printer in write mode, the statement

```
fputc('\014',outFile);
```

causes the printer to eject the current page. Similarly, if `scrn` has been opened as the CRT screen in write mode, the statement

```
fputc('\07',scrn);
```

causes the bell to be activated for a short "beep."

For PC desktop and laptop computers, the CRT screen has its own clear code. For your computer, check the manual for the CRT screen to obtain the proper clear-screen control code. You must also check the name by which your computer "knows" the printer and CRT screen. For PCs the printer has the name `prn` and the CRT screen the name `con` (short for console). Program 10.14 illustrates the use of control codes to eject a page of paper from the printer and alert the user with a "beep" if the printer is not turned on. Using `#define` commands, the appropriate codes have been equated to more readable symbolic names.

Program 10.14

```
#include <stdio.h>
#include <stdlib.h>  /* needed for exit() */

#define BELL '\07'
#define TOP_OF_PAGE '\014' /* page eject code */
```

```
void check(FILE *); /* function prototype */

int main()
{
  FILE *printer;

  printer = fopen("prn", "w");
  check(printer);

  return 0;
}

/* make sure printer is ready and eject a page */
void check(FILE *printer)
{
  if(printer == 0) /* check that the file has been opened */
  {
    fputc(BELL,stdout);
    printf("The printer cannot be opened for output.");
    printf("\nPlease check the printer is on and ready for use.");
    exit(1);
  }
  else
    fputc(TOP_OF_PAGE,printer);
}
```

The statements in the function `check()` are used to ensure that the printer has been opened and is ready for output. The symbolic constants `BELL` and `TOP_OF_PAGE` can be used freely within the `check()` function because they have been defined globally at the top of the program. Each of these constants is sent using a `fputc()` function call. Because the CRT screen is the standard output device for the computer used to run Program 10.14, the CRT did not have to be opened as a new file. Instead, the filename `stdout` was used to send the `BELL` constant to the screen.

In addition to the `BELL` code, all CRT screens have control codes to position the cursor directly at different screen locations. This enables the programmer to place messages anywhere on the screen. Because these codes differ for various CRT models, you should check the manual for your computer to determine the proper codes. Additionally, many C compilers for personal computers include standard library functions that provide the same cursor-positioning capabilities.

Part Four

Additional Topics

Chapter 11

Arrays, Addresses, and Pointers

One of C's advantages is that it allows the programmer access to the addresses used by a program. This is not the case with other high-level languages. Nevertheless, generally unknown to programmers of these other languages, addresses run rampant throughout the executable versions of their programs. These addresses are used by the program to keep track of where data and instructions are kept.

So far in our C programs, we have used addresses in calling the `scanf()` function and in passing arguments by reference. Addresses are also extremely useful in dealing with arrays, strings, and other data structure elements. In this chapter we explore the exceptionally strong connection that exists among arrays, addresses, and pointers. The programming techniques learned in this chapter are then extended in the following chapters to strings and data structures.

11.1 Array Names as Pointers

Pointers, both as variables and function parameters, are used to store addresses. (You may want to review the introduction to pointers in Section 7.3.) They are, however, also closely associated with array names. In this section we describe this association in detail.

Figure 11.1 illustrates the storage of a single-dimensional array named `grade`, which contains five integers. Assume that each integer requires 4 bytes of storage.

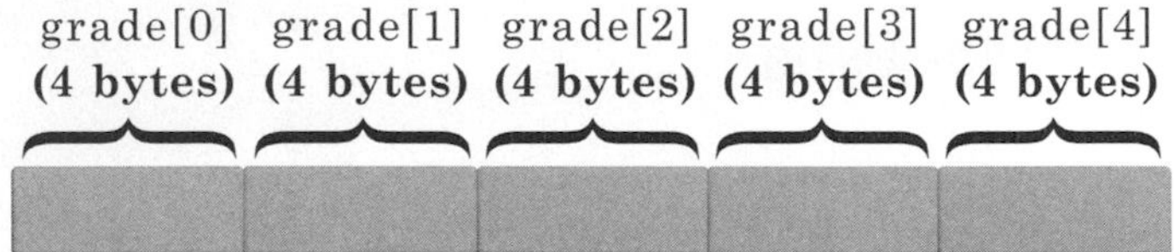

Figure 11.1 The `grade` array in storage

Using subscripts, the fourth integer stored in the `grade` array is referenced as `grade[3]`. The use of a subscript, however, conceals the extensive use of addresses by the computer. Internally, the computer immediately uses the subscript to calculate the address of the desired element based on both the base address of the array, which is the address of the first memory location used to store the array, and the amount of storage used by each array element. Calling the fourth stored integer `grade[3]` forces the computer, internally, into an address computation (assuming 4 bytes for each integer). That is

```
&grade[3] = &grade[0] + (3 * 4)
```

Remembering that the address operator, &, means "the address of," this last statement is read "the address of `grade[3]` equals the address of `grade[0]` plus 12." Figure 11.2 illustrates the address computation used to locate `grade[3]`, assuming 4 bytes of storage for each integer element in the array.

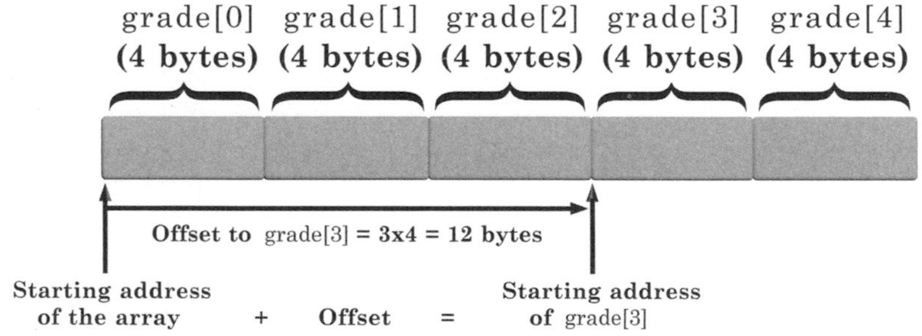

Figure 11.2 Using a subscript to obtain an address

Recall that a pointer is either a variable or function parameter that is used to store addresses. If we create a pointer as a variable to store the address of the first integer stored in the `grade` array, we can mimic the operation used by the computer to access the array elements. Before we do this, let us first consider Program 11.1.

Program 11.1

```
#include <stdio.h>
#define NUMELS 5
int main()
{
  int i;
  int grade[] = {98, 87, 92, 79, 85};

  for (i = 0; i < NUMELS; i++)
    printf("Element %d is %d\n", i, grade [i]);

  return 0;
}
```

When Program 11.1 is run, the following display is obtained:

```
Element 0 is 98
Element 1 is 87
Element 2 is 92
Element 3 is 79
Element 4 is 85
```

Program 11.1 displays the values of the array `grade` using standard subscript notation. Now, let us store the address of array element 0 in a pointer. Then, using the indirection operator, `*`, we can use the address in the pointer to access each array element. For example, if we store the address of `grade[0]` in a pointer named `gPtr` (using the assignment statement `gPtr = &grade[0];`), then, as illustrated in Figure 11.3, the expression `*gPtr`, which means "the variable pointed to by `gPtr`," references `grade[0]`.

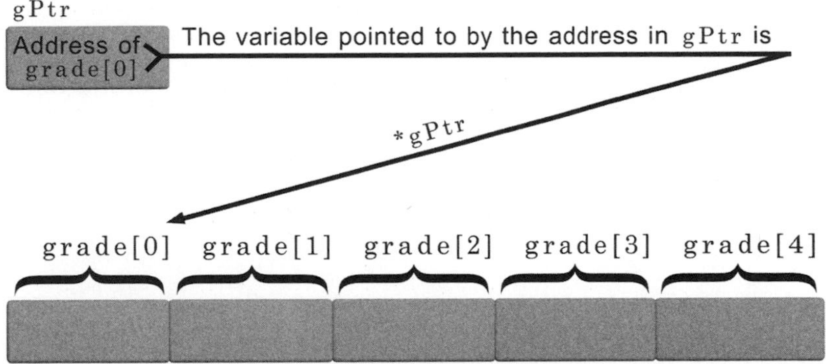

Figure 11.3 The variable pointed to by `*gPtr` is `grade[0]`

One unique feature of pointers is that **offsets** may be included in expressions using pointers. For example, the `1` in the expression `*(gPtr + 1)` is an offset. The complete expression accesses the integer variable that is one beyond the integer pointed to by `gPtr`.[1] Similarly, as illustrated in Figure 11.4, the expression `*(gPtr + 3)` references the variable that is three integers beyond the variable pointed to by `gPtr`. This is the variable `grade[3]`.

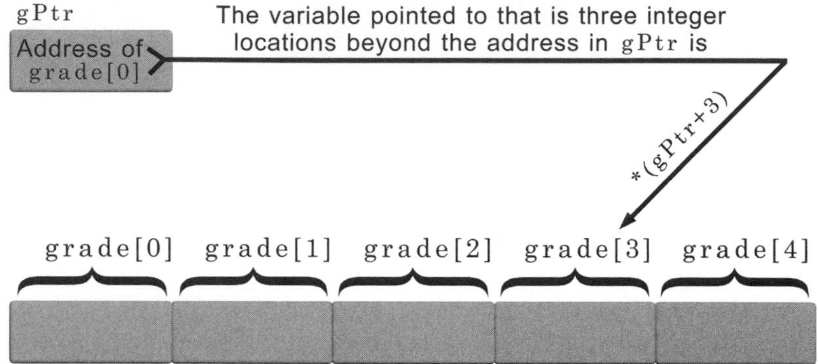

Figure 11.4 An offset of three from the address in `gPtr`

Table 11.1 lists the complete correspondence between elements referenced by subscripts and by pointers and offsets. The relationships listed in Table 11.1 are illustrated in Figure 11.5.

Table 11.1 Array Elements May be Accessed in Two Ways

Array Element	Subscript Notation	Pointer Notation
Element 0	`grade[0]`	`*gPtr`
Element 1	`grade[1]`	`*(gPtr + 1)`
Element 2	`grade[2]`	`*(gPtr + 2)`
Element 3	`grade[3]`	`*(gPtr + 3)`
Element 4	`grade[4]`	`*(gPtr + 4)`

Using the correspondence between pointers and subscripts illustrated in Figure 11.5, the array elements previously accessed in Program 11.1 using subscripts can now be accessed using pointers. This is done in Program 11.2.

Program 11.2

```
#include <stdio.h>
#define NUMELS 5
int main()
```

[1]The offset tells the number of variables that are to be skipped over. The correspondence between the number of bytes and number of variables is handled by the compiler.

```
{
  int *gPtr; /* declare a pointer to an int */
  int i;
  int grade[] = {98, 87, 92, 79, 85};

  /* store the starting array address */
  gPtr = &grade[0];

  for (i = 0; i < NUMELS; i++)
    printf("Element %d is %d\n", i, *(gPtr + i) );

  return 0;
}
```

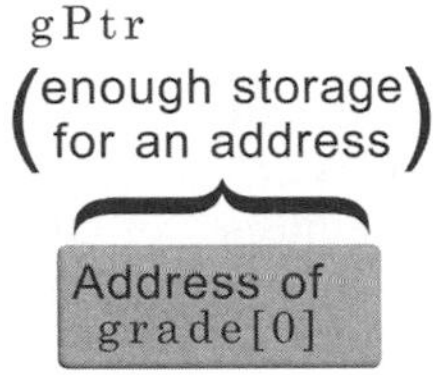

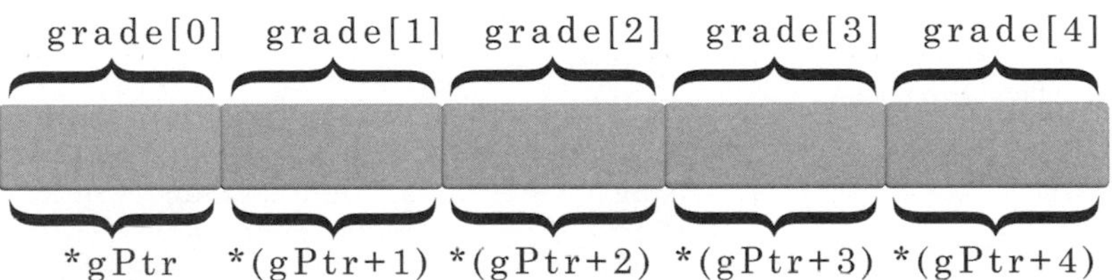

Figure 11.5 The relationship between array elements and pointers

The following display is obtained when Program 11.2 is run:

```
Element 0 is 98
Element 1 is 87
Element 2 is 92
Element 3 is 79
Element 4 is 85
```

Notice that this is the same display produced by Program 11.1.

The method used in Program 11.2 to access *individual* array elements simulates how the computer internally accesses *all* array elements. Any subscript used by a programmer is automatically converted to an equivalent pointer expression by the compiler. In our case, because the declaration of `gPtr` included the information that integers are pointed to, any offset added to the address in `gPtr` is automatically scaled by the size of an integer. For example, `*(gPtr + 3)` refers to the address of `grade[0]` plus an offset of 12 bytes `(3 * 4)`. This is the address of `grade[3]` illustrated in Figure 11.2.

> ## Historical Note
>
> **Admiral Grace Hopper, USN**
>
> Grace Hopper received a Ph.D. degree from Yale University and joined the Naval Reserve in 1943. In her assignment to the Bureau of Ordinance Computation Project at Harvard University, she programmed the Mark I, the first large-scale, electro-mechanical, digital computer. Later she applied her outstanding talents in mathematics as senior programmer of the UNIVAC I.
>
> Commodore Hopper became a pioneer in the development of computer languages and served on the Conference of Data Systems Languages (CODASYL) committee. She helped develop COBOL and is credited with producing the first practical program in that language. In 1959 she developed a COBOL compiler, which allowed programs written in a standardized language to be transported between different computers for the first time.
>
> An interesting sidelight to her career was that her entry into her logbook, dated September 19, 1945, at 15:45 hours recorded: "First actual case of bug being found." It was a real insect that had shorted a relay in the Mark I.
>
> Admiral Hopper remained a colorful figure in the computing community even after her retirement from active duty in the U.S. Navy in August 1986 at the age of 79.

The parentheses in the expression `*(gPtr + 3)` are necessary to access the desired array element correctly. Omitting the parentheses results in the expression `*gPtr + 3`. This expression adds 3 to "the variable pointed to by `gPtr`." Since `gPtr` points to `grade[0]`, this expression adds the value of `grade[0]` and 3 together. Note also that the expression `*(gPtr + 3)` does not change the address stored in `gPtr`. Once the computer uses the offset to locate the correct variable from the starting address in `gPtr`, the offset is discarded and the address in `gPtr` remains unchanged.

Although the pointer `gPtr` used in Program 11.2 was specifically created to store the starting address of the `grade` array, this was, in fact, unnecessary. When an array is created, the compiler automatically creates an internal **pointer constant** for it and stores the base address of the array in this pointer. A pointer constant is equivalent to a symbolic constant, in that the address stored in the pointer constant cannot be changed once it is set.

For each array created, the name of the array becomes the name of the pointer constant created by the compiler for the array, and the starting address of the first location reserved for the array, which is the base address for the array, is stored in this pointer. Thus, declaring the `grade` array in Programs 11.1 and 11.2 actually reserved enough storage for five integers, created an internal pointer named `grade`, and stored the address of `grade[0]` in the pointer. This is illustrated in Figure 11.6.

The implication is that every access to `grade` using a subscript can be replaced by an equivalent access using `grade` as a pointer. Thus, wherever the expression `grade[i]`is used, the expression `*(grade + i)` can also be used. This is illustrated in Program 11.3, where `grade` is used as a pointer to access all of its elements.

Program 11.3 produces the same output as Program 11.1 and Program 11.2. However, using `grade` as a pointer made it unnecessary to declare and initialize the pointer `gPtr` used in Program 11.2.

grade

&grade[0]

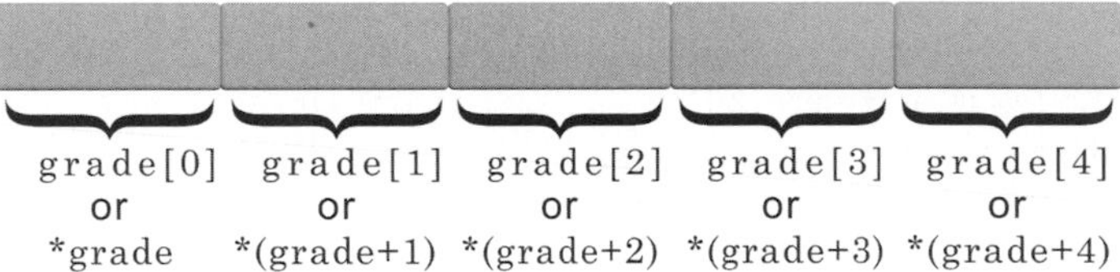

Figure 11.6 Creating an array also creates a pointer

Program 11.3

```
#include <stdio.h>
#define NUMELS 5
int main()
{
  int i;
  int grade[] = {98, 87, 92, 79, 85};

  for (i = 0; i < NUMELS; i++)
    printf("Element %d is %d\n", i, *(grade + i) );

  return 0;
}
```

In most respects an array name and a pointer can be used interchangeably. An array name, however, is actually a pointer constant; as such, the address stored in the array name cannot be changed by an assignment statement. Thus, a statement such as `grade = &grade[2];` is invalid. This should come as no surprise. Because the whole purpose of an array name is to correctly locate the base address of the array, allowing a programmer to change this base address would defeat this purpose and lead to havoc whenever array elements were referenced. Additionally, attempting to assign the address of an array name is invalid. Thus, trying to store the address of `grade` using the expression `&grade` results in a compiler error.

An interesting sidelight to the observation that elements of an array can be accessed using pointers is that a pointer access can always be replaced using subscript notation. For example, if `numPtr` is declared as a pointer variable, the expression `*(numPtr + i)` can also be written as `numPtr[i]`. This is true even though `numPtr` is not created as an array. As before, when the compiler encounters the subscript notation, it replaces it internally with the pointer notation. One advantage of using pointers directly is that they are more efficient than using subscripts for array processing because the internal conversion from subscripts to addresses is avoided.

EXERCISES 11.1

Short Answer Questions

1. Replace each of the following subscripted variables using pointer notation.
   a. `prices[5]`
   b. `grades[2]`
   c. `yield[10]`
   d. `dist[9]`
   e. `mile[0]`
   f. `temp[20]`
   g. `celsius[16]`
   h. `num[50]`
   i. `time[12]`

2. Replace each of the following pointer notations with a subscript notation.
   a. `*(message + 6)`
   b. `*amount`
   c. `*(yrs + 10)`
   d. `*(stocks + 2)`
   e. `*(rates + 15)`
   f. `*(codes + 19)`

3. a. List the three specific tasks that the declaration statement `double prices[5];` causes the compiler to do.
   b. If each double-precision number uses 4 bytes of storage, how much storage is set aside for the `prices` array?
   c. Draw a diagram similar to Figure 11.6 for the `prices` array.
   d. Determine the byte offset relative to the start of the `prices` array corresponding to the offset in the expression `*(prices + 3)`.

Programming Exercises

1. a. Write a declaration to store the string `"This is a sample"` in an array named `samtest`. Include the declaration in a program that displays the values in `samtest` in a `for` loop that uses a pointer to access each element in the array.
   b. Modify the program written in Exercise 1a to display only array elements 10 through 15 (these are the letters `s`, `a`, `m`, `p`, `l`, and `e`).

2. Write a declaration to store the following values in a static array named `rates`: 12.9, 19.6, 11.4, 13.7, 9.5, 15.2, 17.6. Include the declaration in a program that displays the values in the array using pointer notation.

3. Repeat Programming Exercise 1 in Section 8.2, but use pointer references to access all array elements.

4. Repeat Programming Exercise 2 in Section 8.2, but use pointer references to access all array elements.

11.2 Manipulating Pointers

A pointer, constructed either as a variable or function parameter, contains a value. With pointers, however, the stored value is an address. Thus, by adding numbers to and subtracting numbers from pointers, we can obtain different addresses. Additionally, the addresses in pointers can be compared using any of the relational operators (==, !=, <, >, etc.) that are valid for comparing other variables. Another characteristic of pointers, shared with all variables, is that they can be initialized when they are declared. In this section you will first learn how to perform some arithmetic calculations with pointers. You will also learn more about initializing pointers.

Pointer Arithmetic

In performing arithmetic on pointers, we must be careful to produce addresses that point to something meaningful. In comparing pointers, we must also make comparisons that make sense. Consider the declarations

```
int nums[100];
int *nPtr;
```

To set the address of `nums[0]` in `nPtr`, either of the following two assignment statements can be used:

```
nPtr = &nums[0];
nPtr = nums;
```

The two assignment statements produce the same result because `nums` is a pointer constant that itself contains the address of the first location in the array (that is, the address `nums[0]`). Figure 11.7 illustrates the allocation of memory resulting from the previous declaration and assignment statements, assuming that each integer requires 4 bytes of memory and that the location of the beginning of the `nums` array is at address 18934.

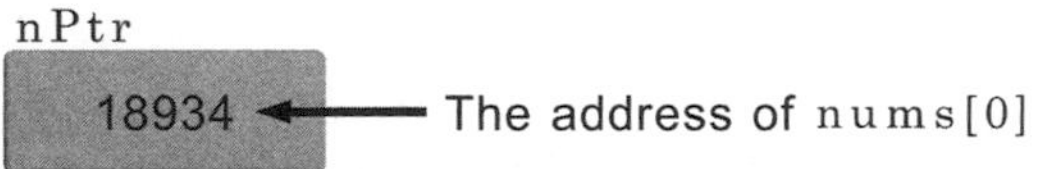

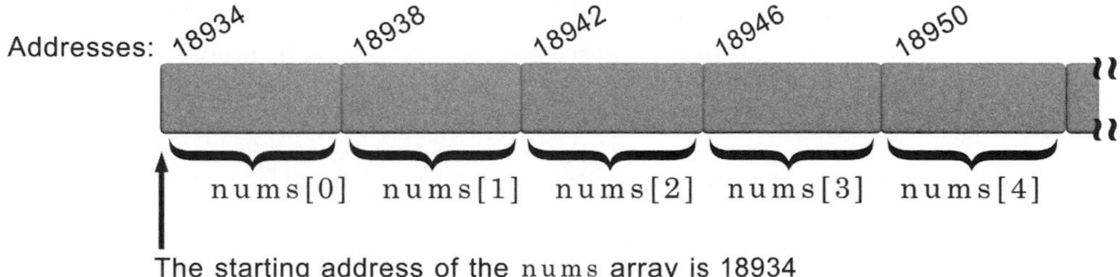

Figure 11.7 The `nums` array in memory

Once `nPtr` contains a valid address, values can be added to and subtracted from the address to produce new addresses. When adding or subtracting numbers to pointers, the computer automatically adjusts the number to ensure that the result still "points to" a value of the original data type. For example, the statement `nPtr = nPtr + 2;` forces the computer to scale the 2 by the correct number to ensure that the resulting address is the address of an integer. Assuming that each integer requires 4 bytes of storage, as illustrated in Figure 11.7, the computer multiplies 2 by 4 and then adds the calculated value of 8 to the address in `nPtr`. The resulting address is 18942, which is the correct address of `nums[2]`.

This correct scaling when numbers are added to pointers is automatically accomplished because the compiler converts the arithmetic operation `pointer + number` to

```
pointer + number * sizeof(data type being pointed to)
```

This automatic scaling ensures that the expression `nPtr + i`, where `i` is any positive integer, correctly points to the *i*th element beyond the one currently being pointed to by `nPtr`. Thus, if `nPtr` initially contains the address of `nums[0]`, `nPtr + 2` is the address of `nums[2]`, `nPtr + 4` is the address of `nums[4]`, and `nPtr + i` is the address of `nums[i]`. Although we have used actual addresses in Figure 11.7 to illustrate the scaling process, the programmer need never know or care about the actual addresses used by the computer.

Addresses can also be incremented or decremented using both prefix and postfix increment and decrement operators. Adding 1 to a pointer causes the pointer to point to the next element of the original data type being pointed to. Decrementing a pointer causes the pointer to point to the previous element. For example, if the pointer variable `p` is a pointer to an integer, the expression `p++` causes the address in the pointer to be incremented to point to the next integer. This is illustrated in Figure 11.8.

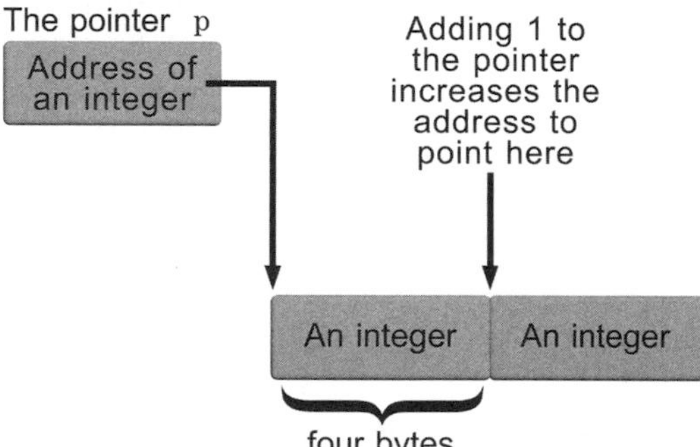

Figure 11.8 Increments are scaled when used with pointers

In reviewing Figure 11.8, notice that the increment added to the pointer is correctly scaled to account for the fact that the pointer is used to point to integers. It is, of course, up to the programmer to ensure that the correct type of data is stored in the new address contained in the pointer.

The increment and decrement operators can be applied as both prefix and postfix pointer operators. All of the following combinations using pointers are valid:

```
*ptNum++    /* use the pointer and then increment it */
*++ptNum    /* increment the pointer before using it */
*ptNum--    /* use the pointer and then decrement it */
*--ptNum    /* decrement the pointer before using it */
```

Of the four possible forms, the most commonly used is the first, `*ptNum++`. This is because such an expression allows each element in an array to be accessed as the address is "marched along" from the starting address of the array to the address of the last array element. To see the use of the increment operator, consider Program 11.4. In this program each element in the `nums` array is retrieved by successively incrementing the address in `nPtr`.

Program 11.4

```
#include <stdio.h>
#define NUMELS 5
int main()
{
  int nums[NUMELS] = {16, 54, 7, 43, -5};
  int i, total = 0, *nPtr;

  nPtr = nums; /* store address of nums[0] in nPtr */
  for (i = 0; i < NUMELS; i++)
    total = total + *nPtr++;
  printf("The total of the array elements is %d\n", total);

  return 0;
}
```

The output produced by Program 11.4 is

```
The total of the array elements is 115
```

The expression `total = total + *nPtr++` used in Program 11.4 is a standard accumulating expression and can be replaced by the expression `total += *nPtr++` . Within this expression, the term `*nPtr++` first causes the program to retrieve the integer pointed to by `nPtr`. This is done by the `*nPtr` part of the term. The postfix increment, `++`, then adds 1 to the address in `nPtr` so that `nPtr` now contains the address of the next array element. The increment is, of course, scaled by the compiler so that the actual address in `nPtr` is the correct address of the next element.

Pointers may also be compared. This is particularly useful when dealing with pointers used to access elements in the same array. For example, rather than using a counter in a `for` loop to correctly access each element in an array, the address in a pointer can be compared to the starting and ending address of the array itself. The expression

```
nPtr <= &nums[4]
```

is true (non-0) as long as the address in `nPtr` is less than or equal to the address of `nums[4]`. Because `nums` is a pointer constant that contains the address of `nums[0]`, the term `&nums[4]` can be replaced by the equivalent term `nums + 4`. Using either of these forms, Program 11.4 can be rewritten as Program 11.5 to continue adding array elements while the address in `nPtr` continues to point to a valid array element.

Program 11.5

```
#include <stdio.h>
#define NUMELS 5
int main()
{
  int nums[NUMELS] = {16, 54, 7, 43, -5};
  int total = 0, *nPtr;

  nPtr = nums; /* store address of nums[0] in nPtr */
  while (nPtr < nums + NUMELS)
    total += *nPtr++;
  printf("The total of the array elements is %d\n", total);

  return 0;
}
```

Notice that in Program 11.5 the compact form of the accumulating expression, `total += *nPtr++`, was used in place of the longer form, `total = total + *nPtr++`. Also, the expression `nums + NUMELS` does not change the address in `nums`. Because `nums` is an array name and not a pointer variable, its value cannot be changed. The expression `nums + NUMELS` first retrieves the address in `nums`, adds 5 to this address (appropriately scaled) and uses the result for comparison purposes. Expressions such as `*nums++`, which attempt to change the address, are incorrect here. Expressions such as `*nums` or `*(nums + i)`, which use the address without attempting to alter it, are valid.

Historical Note

Numerosophy

The ancient Greeks attached great philosophical and religious significance to numbers. They considered the natural (counting) numbers, 1, 2, 3, ..., to be examples of perfection, and rations of whole numbers (fractions) as somewhat suspect. Diophantus (third century B.C.) called negative numbers "absurd."

According to tradition, Hipparchus (second century B.C.) was drowned when he discussed the scandalous irrational nature of the square root of 2 outside of the Pythagorean Society. The first mention of the square root of a negative number was by Heron of Alexandria (third century A.D.). Such concepts were treated with disbelief and even considered wicked. Today, of course, it is not unusual to use negative, irrational, "artificial," and complex numbers all at once to represent such concepts as vectors and points in a plane. The Greeks of that Golden Age would probably regard our modern mathematics as truly degenerate.

Pointer Initialization

Like all variables, pointers can be initialized when they are declared. When initializing pointers, however, you must be careful to set an address in the pointer. For example, an initialization such as

```
int *ptNum = &miles;
```

is only valid if `miles` itself is declared as an integer variable before `ptNum` is declared. Here we are creating a pointer to an integer and setting the address in the pointer to the address of an integer variable. If the variable `miles` is declared after `ptNum` is declared, as follows:

```
int *ptNum = &miles;
int miles;
```

an error occurs. This is because the address of `miles` is used before `miles` has even been defined. Since the storage area reserved for `miles` has not been allocated when `ptNum` is declared, the address of `miles` does not yet exist.

Pointers to arrays can be initialized within their declaration statements. For example, if `prices` has been declared as an array of double-precision numbers, either of the following two declarations can be used to initialize the pointer named `zing` to the address of the first element in `prices`:

```
double *zing = &prices[0];
double *zing = prices;
```

The last initialization is correct because `prices` is itself a pointer constant containing an address of the proper type. (The variable name `zing` was selected in this example to reinforce the idea that any variable name can be selected for a pointer.)

EXERCISES 11.2

Short-Answer Questions

1. Using the indirection operator, write expressions for the following:
   a. The variable pointed to by `xAddr`
   b. The variable whose address is in `yAddr`
   c. The variable pointed to by `ptMiles`
   d. The variable whose address is in `pdate`
   e. The variable pointed to by `distPtr`
   f. The variable whose address is in `hoursPt`

2. Write English sentences for the following declarations:
   a. `char *keyAddr;`
   b. `int *ptDate;`
   c. `double *yldAddr;`
   d. `long *yPtr;`
   e. `float *p_cou;`

3. For the following declarations,

```
int *xPt, *yAddr;
long *ptAddr;
double *pt_z;
int a;
long b;
double c;
```

   determine which of the following statements is valid.
   a. `yAddr = &a;`
   b. `yAddr = &b;`
   c. `yAddr = &c;`
   d. `yAddr = a;`
   e. `yAddr = b;`
   f. `yAddr = c;`
   g. `ptAddr = &a;`
   h. `ptAddr = &b;`
   i. `ptAddr = &c;`
   j. `ptAddr = a;`
   k. `ptAddr = b;`
   l. `ptAddr = c;`

Programming Exercises

1. Replace the `while` statement in Program 11.5 with a `for` statement.

2. a. Write a C program that stores the following numbers in an array named `rates`: 6.25, 6.50, 6.8, 7.2, 7.35, 7.5, 7.65, 7.8, 9.2, 9.4, 9.6, 9.8, 9.0. Display the values in the array by changing the address in a pointer called `dispPt`. Use a `for` statement in your program.
   b. Modify the program written in Exercise 2a to use a `while` statement.

3. a. Write a program that stores the string `"Hooray for All of Us"` in an array named `strng`. Use the declaration `char strng[] = "Hooray for All of Us";`, which ensures that the end-of-string escape sequence `\0` is included in the array. Display the characters in the array by changing the address in a pointer called `messPtr`. Use a `for` statement in your program.
   b. Modify the program written in Exercise 3a to use the `while` statement `while (*messPtr != '\0')`.
   c. Modify the program written in Exercise 3a to start the display with the word `All`.

4. Write a C program that stores the following numbers in an array named `miles`: 15, 22, 16, 18, 27, 23, 20. Have your program copy the data stored in `miles` to another array named `dist` and then display the values in the `dist` array.

5. Write a program that stores the following letters in the array named `message`: `This is a test`. Have your program copy the data stored in `message` to another array named `mess2` and then display the letters in the `mess2` array.

6. Write a program that declares three single-dimensional arrays named `miles`, `gallons`, and `mpg`. Each array should be capable of holding 10 elements. In the `miles` array, store the numbers 240.5, 300.0, 189.6, 310.6, 280.7, 216.9, 199.4, 160.3, 177.4, 192.3. In the `gallons` array, store the numbers 10.3, 15.6, 9.7, 14, 16.3, 15.7, 14.9, 10.7, 9.3, 9.4. Each element of the `mpg` array should be calculated as the corresponding element to the `miles` array divided by the equivalent element of the `gallons` array; for example, `mpg[0] = miles[0]/gallons[0]`. Use pointers when calculating and displaying the elements of the `mpg` array.

11.3 Passing and Using Array Addresses

When an array is passed to a function, an address is the only item actually passed. That is, the address of the first location used to store the array is passed, as illustrated in Figure 11.9. Because the first location reserved for an array corresponds to element 0 of the array, the "address of the array" is also the address of element 0.

An array is a series of memory locations

The address of the first location is passed as an argument and stored in a pointer parameter

Figure 11.9 The address of an array is the address of the first location reserved for the array

For a specific example in which an array is passed to a function, consider Program 11.6. In this program the `nums` array is passed to the `findMax()` function using conventional array notation.

The output displayed when Program 11.6 is executed is

```
The maximum value is 27
```

Program 11.6

```
#include <stdio.h>
int findMax(int[], int); /* function prototype */

int main()
```

```
{
#define NUMELS 5
  int nums[NUMELS] = {2, 18, 1, 27, 16};

  printf("The maximum value is %d\n", findMax(nums,NUMELS));

  return 0;
}

int findMax(int vals[], int numEls) /* find the maximum value */
{
  int i, max = vals[0];
  for (i = 1; i < numEls; i++)
    if (max < vals[i])
      max = vals[i];

  return (max);
}
```

The parameter named `vals` in the header line for `findMax()` actually receives the address of the array `nums`. Hence, `vals` is really a pointer, because pointers are variables (or parameters) used to store addresses. Because the address passed into `findMax()` is the address of an integer, another suitable header line for `findMax()` is

```
findMax(int *vals, int numEls) /* vals declared as a pointer to an integer */
```

The declaration `int *vals` in the header line declares that `vals` is used to store an address of an integer. The address stored is, of course, the location of the beginning of an array. The following is a rewritten version of the `findMax()` function that uses the new pointer declaration for `vals` but retains the use of subscripts to refer to individual array elements:

```
int findMax(int *vals, int numEls) /* find the maximum value */
/* vals declared as a pointer to an integer */
{
  int i, max = vals[0];

  for (i = 1; i < numEls; i++)
    if (max < vals[i])
      max = vals[i];

  return(max);
}
```

One further observation needs to be made. Regardless of how `vals` is declared in the function header or how it is used within the function body, it is truly a pointer parameter. Thus, the address in `vals` may be modified. This is not true for the name `nums`. Since `nums` is the name of the originally created array, it is a pointer constant. As described in Section 11.1, this means that the address in nums cannot be changed and that the expression &nums is invalid. No such restrictions, however, apply to the pointer parameter named `vals`. All the address arithmetic that we learned in the previous section can be legitimately applied to `vals`.

We shall write two additional versions of `findMax()`, both using pointers instead of subscripts. In the first version, we simply substitute pointer notation for subscript notation. In the second version, we use address arithmetic to change the address in the pointer.

As previously stated, a reference to an array element using the subscript notation `arrayName[i]` can always be replaced by the pointer notation `*(arrayName + i)`. In our first modification to `findMax()`, we make use of this correspondence by simply replacing all notations of the form `vals[i]` with the equivalent notation `*(vals + i)`.

```
int findMax(int *vals, int numEls) /* find the maximum value */
/* vals declared as a pointer to an integer */
{
  int i, max = *vals;

  for (i = 1; i < numEls; i++)
    if (max < *(vals + i))
      max = *(vals + i);

  return(max);
}
```

Our second version of `findMax()` makes use of the fact that the address stored in `vals` can be changed. After each array element is retrieved using the address in `vals`, the address itself is incremented by 1 in the altering list of the `for` statement. The expression `*vals++` used initially to set max to the value of `vals[0]` also adjusts the address in `vals` to point to the second integer stored in the array. The element obtained from this expression is the array element pointed to by `vals` before `vals` is incremented. The postfix increment, ++, does not change the address in `vals` until after the address has been used to retrieve the first integer in the array.

```
1  int findMax(int *vals, int numEls) /* find the maximum value */
2  /* vals declared as a pointer */
3  {
4    int i, max;
5    max = *vals++; /* get the first element and increment */
6
7    for (i = 1; i < numEls; i++, vals++)
8      if (max < *vals)
9        max = *vals;
10
11   return(max);
12 }
```

Let us review this version of `findMax()`. Initially, the maximum value is set to "the thing pointed to by `vals`" in line 5

```
5  max = *vals++; /* get the first element and increment */
```

Because `vals` initially contains the address of element zero in the array passed to `findMax()`, the value of this initial element is now stored in max. The address in `vals` is then incremented by 1. The 1 that is added to `vals` is automatically scaled by the number of bytes used to store integers. Thus, after the increment, the address stored in `vals` is the address of the next array element. This is illustrated in Figure 11.10. The value of this next element is compared to the maximum, and the address is again incremented, this time from within the altering list of the `for` statement. This process continues until all the array elements have been examined.

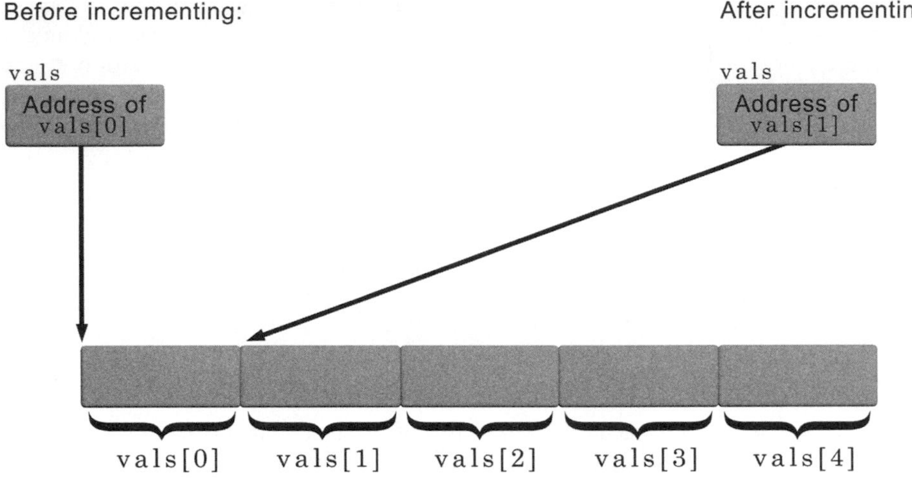

Figure 11.10 Pointing to different elements

The version of `findMax()` that appeals to you is a matter of personal style and taste. Generally, beginning programmers feel more at ease using subscripts than using pointers. Also, if the program uses an array as the natural storage structure for the application and data at hand, an array access using subscripts is more appropriate to clearly indicate the intent of the program. However, as we learn about strings and data structures, the use of pointers becomes an increasingly useful and powerful tool in its own right. In other situations, such as the dynamic allocation of memory (see Section 13.1), there is no simple or easy equivalence using subscripts.

One further "neat trick" can be gleaned from our discussion. Because passing an array to a function really involves passing an address, we can just as well pass any valid address. For example, the function call

```
findMax(&nums[2],3)
```

passes the address of `nums[2]` to `findMax()`. Within `findMax()` the pointer `vals` stores the address and the function starts the search for a maximum at the element corresponding to this address. Thus, from `findMax()`'s perspective, it has received an address and proceeds appropriately.

Advanced Pointer Notation[2]

Access to multidimensional arrays can also be made using pointer notation, although the notation becomes more and more cryptic as the array dimensions increase. An extremely useful application of this notation occurs with arrays whose elements are strings, which are presented in Section 11.5. Here we consider pointer notation for two-dimensional numeric arrays. For example, consider the declaration

```
#define ROWS 2
#define COLS 3
int nums[ROWS][COLS] = { {16,18,20},
                         {25,26,27} };
```

This declaration creates an array of elements and a set of pointer constants named nums, nums[0], and nums[1]. The relationship between these pointer constants and the elements of the nums array is illustrated in Figure 11.11.

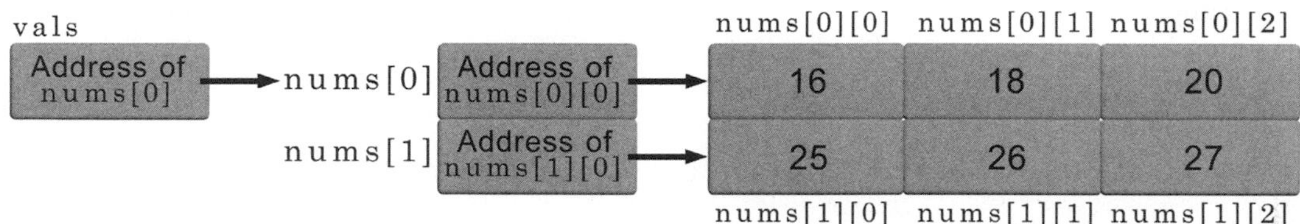

Figure 11.11 Storage of the nums array and associated pointer constants

The availability of the pointer constants associated with a two-dimensional array allows us to access array elements in a variety of ways. One way is to consider the two-dimensional array as an array of rows, where each row is itself an array of three elements. Considered in this light, the address of the first element in the first row is provided by nums[0] and the address of the first element in the second row is provided by nums[1]. Thus, the variable pointed to by nums[0] is nums[0][0] and the variable pointed to by nums[1] is nums[1][0]. Once the nature of these constants is understood, each element in the array can be accessed by applying an appropriate offset to the appropriate pointer. Thus, the following notations are equivalent:

Pointer Notation	Subscript Notation	Value
*(*nums)	nums[0][0]	16
*(*nums + 1)	nums[0][1]	18
*(*nums + 2)	nums[0][2]	20
((nums + 1))	nums[1][0]	25
((nums + 1) + 1)	nums[1][1]	26
((nums + 1) + 2)	nums[1][2]	27

We can now go even further and replace nums[0] and nums[1] with their respective pointer notations, using the address of nums itself. As illustrated in Figure 11.11, the variable

[2]This topic may be omitted with no loss of subject continuity.

pointed to by nums is nums[0]. That is, *nums is nums[0]. Similarly, *(nums + 1) is nums[1]. Using these relationships leads to the following equivalences:

Pointer Notation	Subscript Notation	Value
*nums[0]	nums[0][0]	16
*(nums[0] + 1)	nums[0][1]	18
*(nums[0] + 2)	nums[0][2]	20
*nums[1]	nums[1][0]	25
*(nums[1] + 1)	nums[1][1]	26
*(nums[1] + 2)	nums[1][2]	27

The same notation applies when a two-dimensional array is passed to a function. For example, assume that the two-dimensional array nums is passed to the function calc() using the call calc(nums);. Here, as with all array arguments, an address is passed. A suitable function header for the function calc() is

```
calc(int pt[2][3])
```

As we have already seen, the parameter declaration for pt can also be

```
int pt[][3]
```

Using pointer notation, another suitable declaration is

```
int (*pt)[3]
```

In this last declaration, the parentheses are required to create a single pointer to objects of three integers. Each object is, of course, equivalent to a single row of the nums array. By suitably offsetting the pointer, each element in the array can be accessed. Notice that without the parentheses the parameter declaration becomes

```
int *pt[3]
```

which creates an array of three pointers, each one pointing to a single integer.

Once the correct declaration for pt is made (any of the three valid declarations), the following notations within the function calc() are all equivalent:

Pointer Notation	Subscript Notation	Value
*(*pt)	pt[0][0]	16
*(*pt+1)	pt[0][1]	18
*(*pt+2)	pt[0][2]	20
((pt+1))	pt[1][0]	25
((pt+1)+1)	pt[1][1]	26
((pt+1)+2)	pt[1][2]	27

Finally, two additional notations using pointers are encountered in more advanced C programs. The first of these occurs because functions can return any valid C scalar data type, including pointers to any of these data types. If a function returns a pointer, the data type being pointed to must be declared in the function's header line and prototype. For example, the header line

```
int *calc()
```

declares that `calc()` returns a pointer to an integer value. This means that *an address* of an integer variable is returned. Similarly, the header line

```
double *taxes()
```

declares that `taxes()` returns a pointer to a double-precision value. This means that *an address* of a double-precision variable is returned.

In addition to declaring pointers to integers, double-precision numbers, and C's other data types, pointers can also be declared that point to (contain the address of) a function. Pointers to functions are possible because function names, like array names, are themselves pointer constants. For example, the header line

```
int (*calc)()
```

declares `calc` to be a pointer to a function that returns an integer. This means that `calc` contains the address of a function, and the function whose address is in the variable `calc` returns an integer value. If, for example, the function `sum()` returns an integer, the assignment `calc = sum;` is valid.

EXERCISES 11.3

Short Answer Questions

1. The following declaration was used to create the `prices` array:

   ```
   double prices[500];
   ```

   Write three different header lines for a function named `sortArray()` that accepts the `prices` array as a parameter named `inArray` and returns no value.

2. The following declaration was used to create the `keys` array:

   ```
   char keys[256];
   ```

   Write three different header lines for a function named `findKey()` that accepts the `keys` array as a parameter named `select` and returns no value.

3. The following declaration was used to create the `rates` array:

   ```
   double rates[256];
   ```

   Write three different header lines for a function named `prime()` that accepts the `rates` array as a parameter named `rates` and returns a double-precision value.

4. In the last version of `findMax()` presented in this section, `vals` was incremented inside the altering list of the `for` statement. Instead, suppose that the incrementing was done within the condition expression of the `if` statement as follows:

```
int findMax(int *vals, int numEls) /* incorrect version */
{                                 /* vals declared as a pointer */
  int i, max = *vals++; /* get the first element and increment */

  for (i = 1; i < numEls; i++)
    if (max < *vals++)
      max = *vals;

  return (max);
}
```

This version produces an incorrect result. Determine why.

5. a. Determine the output of the following program:

```
#include <stdio.h>
void arr(int[][3]);
int main()
{
  int nums[2][3] = {{33,16,29},
                    {54,67,99}};

  arr(nums);
  return 0;
}
void arr(int (*val)[3])
{
  printf("\n %d",*(*val) );
  printf("\n %d",*(*val + 1) );
  printf("\n %d",*(*(val + 1) + 2) );
  printf("\n %d",*(*val) + 1 );
  return;
}
```

b. Given the declaration for `val` in the `arr()` function, would the notation `val[1][2]` be valid within the function?

Programming Exercises

1. Modify the `findMax()` function to locate the minimum value of the passed array. Write the function using only pointers and rename the function `findMin()`.

2. a. Write a C program that has a declaration in `main()` to store the following numbers into an array named `rates`: 6.5, 7.2, 7.5, 9.3, 9.6, 9.4, 9.6, 9.8, 10.0. There should be a function call to `show()` that accepts `rates` in a parameter named rates and then displays the numbers using the pointer notation `*(rates + i)`.

   b. Modify the `show()` function written in Exercise 2a to alter the address in `rates`. Use the expression `*rates` rather than `*(rates + i)` to retrieve the correct element.

3. a. Write a C program that includes a declaration in `main()` that stores the string `"Vacation is near"` in an array named `message`. Include a function call to `display()` that accepts `message` in a parameter named `strng` and then displays the message using the pointer notation `*(strng + i)`.
   b. Modify the `display()` function written in Exercise 3a to alter the address in `message`. Use the expression `*strng` rather than `*(strng + i)` to retrieve the correct element.

4. Write a C program that declares three single-dimensional arrays named `price`, `quantity`, and `amount`. Each array should be declared in `main()` and be capable of holding 10 double-precision numbers. The numbers to be stored in `price` are 10.62, 14.89, 13.21, 16.55, 19.62, 9.47, 6.58, 19.32, 12.15, 3.99. The numbers to be stored in `quantity` are 4, 9.5, 6, 7.35, 9, 15.3, 3, 5.4, 2.9, 4.9. Have your program pass these three arrays to a function called `extend()`, which calculates the elements in the `amount` array as the product of the equivalent elements in the `price` and `quantity` arrays (for example, `amount[1] = price[1] * quantity[1]`). After `extend()` has put values into the amount array, display the values in the array from within `main()`. Write the `extend()` function using pointers.

11.4 Processing Strings Using Pointers

Pointers are exceptionally useful in constructing string-handling functions. When pointer notation is used in place of subscripts to access individual characters in a string, the resulting statements are both more compact and more efficient. In this section, we describe the equivalence between subscripts and pointers when accessing individual characters in a string.

Consider the last version of `strcopy()` function introduced in Section 9.1 to copy the characters from one array to another array, one character at a time. For convenience, this function is reproduced below.

```
/* copy string2 to string1 */
void strcopy(char string1[], char string2[]) /* copy string2 to string1 */
{
  int i = 0;

  while (string1[i] = string2[i])
    i++;
}
```

Notice that including the assignment statement within the test part of the `while` statement copies all elements of the `string2` array, which includes terminating the `NULL` character. The value of the assignment expression becomes 0 only after the `Null` character is assigned to `string1`, at which point the `while` loop is terminated.

The conversion of `strcopy()` from subscript notation to pointer notation is now straightforward. Although each subscript version of `strcopy` can be rewritten using pointer notation, the following is the equivalent of our last subscript version:

Historical Note

Anagrams and Palindromes

Some of the most challenging and fascinating word games are played with anagrams and palindromes.

An **anagram** is a rearrangement of the letters in a word or phrase that makes another word or phrase. Although the letters of the word *door* can be rearranged to spell *orod* and *doro*, it is more exciting to discover the words *odor* and *rood*. A word, phrase, or sentence that reads the same forward and backward, such as *top spot* is a **palindrome**.

The origins of most known anagrams and palindromes are lost in anonymity. Here are some collected by Richard Manchester in *The Mammoth Book of Fun and Games* (Hart Publishing Co. Inc., New York City, 1977; pages 229–231).

Apt Anagrams

- The Mona Lisa →No hat, a smile
- The United States of America →Attaineth its cause: freedom!

Interesting Palindromes

- Live not on evil!
- 'Tis Ivan on a visit.
- Yreka Bakery
- Able was I ere I saw Elba.
- Madam, I'm Adam.
- A man, a plan, a canal: Panama!

Computers can be programmed to detect palindromes and find anagrams, but the human brain may be more efficient for doing this.

```
void strcopy(char *string1, char *string2)
               /* copy string2 to string1 */
{
  while (*string1 = *string2)
  {
    string1++;
    string2++;
  }

  return;
}
```

In both the subscript and pointer versions of `strcopy()`, the function receives the name of the array being passed. Recall that passing an array name to a function actually passes the address of the first location of the array. In our pointer version of `strcopy()`, the two passed addresses are stored in the pointer parameters `string1` and `string2`, respectively.

The declarations `char *string2;` and `char *string1;` used in the pointer version of `strcopy()` indicate that `string2` and `string1` are both pointers containing the address of a character and stress the treatment of the passed addresses as pointer values rather than array names. These declarations are equivalent to the declarations `char string2[]` and `char string1[]`, respectively.

Internal to `strcopy()`, the pointer expression `*string2`, which refers to *the element whose address is in* `string2`, replaces the equivalent subscript expression `string2[i]`. Similarly, the pointer expression `*string1` replaces the equivalent subscript expression `string1[i]`. The expression `*string1 = *string2` causes the element pointed to by `string2` to be assigned to the element pointed to by `string1`. Because the starting addresses of both strings are passed to `strcopy()` and stored in `string2` and `string1`, respectively, the expression `*string2` initially refers to `string2[0]` and the expression `*string1` initially refers to `string1[0]`.

Consecutively incrementing both pointers in `strcopy()` with the expressions `string2++` and `string1++` simply causes each pointer to "point to" the next consecutive character in the respective string. As with the subscript version, the pointer version of `strcopy` steps along, copying element by element, until the end of the string is copied.

One final change to the string copy function can be made by including the pointer increments as postfix operators within the test part of the while statement. The final form of the string copy function is

```
void strcopy(char *string1, char *string2) /* copy string2 to string1 */
{
  while (*string1++ = *string2++)
    ;
  return;
}
```

There is no ambiguity in the expression `*string1++ = *string2++` even though the indirection operator, *, and increment operator, ++, have the same precedence. Here, the character pointed to is accessed before the pointer is incremented. Only after completion of the assignment `*string1 = *string2` are the pointers incremented to point correctly to the next characters in the respective strings.

The string copy function included in the standard library supplied with C compilers is typically written exactly like our pointer version of `strcopy()`.

EXERCISES 11.4

Short Answer Questions

1. Determine the value of `*text`, `*(text + 3)`, and `*(text + 10)`, assuming that text is an array of characters and the following has been stored in the array:
   a. `now is the time`
   b. `rocky raccoon welcomes you`
   c. `Happy Holidays`
   d. `The good ship`

Programming Exercises

1. a. The following function, `convert()`, "marches along" the string passed to it and sends each character in the string one at a time to the `toUpper()` function until the NULL character is encountered.

```
char toUpper(char); /* function prototype */
void convert(char strng[]) /* convert a string to uppercase letters*/
{
  int i = 0;

  while (strng[i] != '\0');
  {
    strng[i] = toUpper(strng[i]);
    i++;
  }

  return;
}
```

```
char toUpper(char letter) /* convert a character to uppercase */
{
  if( letter >= 'a' && letter <= 'z')
    return (letter - 'a' + 'A');
  else
    return (letter);
}
```

The `toUpper()` function takes each character passed to it and first examines it to determine if the character is a lowercase letter (a lowercase letter is any character between *a* and *z*, inclusive). Assuming that characters are stored using the standard ASCII character codes, the expression `letter - 'a' + 'A'` converts a lowercase letter to its uppercase equivalent. Rewrite the `convert()` function using pointers.

b. Include the `convert()` and `toUpper()` functions in a working program. The program should prompt the user for a string and echo the string back to the user in uppercase letters. Use `gets()` and `puts()` for string input and display.

2. Using pointers, repeat Programming Exercise 1 from Section 9.1.

3. Using pointers, repeat Programming Exercise 2 from Section 9.1.

4. Using pointers, repeat Programming Exercise 3 from Section 9.1.

5. Write a function named `remove()` that deletes all occurrences of a character from a string. The function should take two arguments: the string name and the character to be removed. For example, if `message` contains the string `HappyHolidays`, the function call `remove(message,'H')` should place the string `appyolidays` into `message`.

6. Using pointers, repeat Programming Exercise 6 from Section 9.1.

7. Write a program using the `getchar()`, `toupper()`, and `putchar()` library functions that echo back each letter entered in its uppercase form. The program should terminate when the digit 1 key is pressed.

8. Write a function that uses pointers to add a single character at the end of an existing string. The function should replace the existing `\0` character with the new character and append a new `\0` at the end of the string.

9. Write a C function that uses pointers to delete a single character from the end of a string. This is effectively achieved by moving the `\0` character one position closer to the start of the string.

10. Write a C function named `trimfrnt()` that deletes all leading blanks from a string. Write the function using pointers.

11. Write a C function named `trimrear()` that deletes all trailing blanks from a string. Write the function using pointers.

Programming Note

Allocating Space for a String

Because the declaration

```
char *message = "abcdef";
```

is valid, many beginning programmers make the mistake of assuming the following code is also valid:

```
char *message;    /* a declaration for a pointer */
strcpy(message,"abcdef");   /* an INVALID copy here */
```

The `strcpy` is invalid here because the declaration of the pointer only reserves sufficient space for one value—an address. No space has been allocated for a string, and `message` has not been initialized to point to a valid set of character locations. This is not the case for the first declaration of `message`, which actually reserves two sets of locations—one for a pointer variable named `message` and one for a string consisting of seven characters. The latter are then initialized to the characters `a`, `b`, `c`, `d`, `e`, `f`, and `\0` and the former to the address of the letter `a`. Once this first declaration has been made, a statement such as `strcpy(message,"ghijkl");` is now valid because `message` points to a set of memory locations sufficiently large enough to hold the new string. The lesson here is to consciously ensure allocating enough storage for any string being copied.

11.5 Creating Strings Using Pointers

The definition of a string automatically involves a pointer. For example, the definition `char message1[81];` both reserves storage for 81 characters and automatically creates a pointer constant, `message1`, that contains the address of `message1[0]`. As a pointer constant, the address associated with the pointer cannot be changed—it must always "point to" the beginning of the created array.

Instead of initially creating a string as an array, however, it is also possible to create a string using a pointer. This is similar in concept to declaring a passed array as either an array or a pointer parameter internal to the receiving function. For example, the definition `char *message2;` creates a pointer to a character. In this case, `message2` is a true pointer variable. Once a pointer to a character is defined, assignment statements, such as `message2 = "this is a string";`, can be made. In this assignment, `message2` receives the address of the first location used by the computer to store the string.

Although `message` points to a string sufficiently large enough to hold the new string "`ghijkl`", *strings cannot be copied using an assignment operator*. The main difference in the definitions of `message1` as an array and `message2` as a pointer is the way the pointer is created. Defining `message1` using the declaration `static char message1[81]` explicitly calls for a fixed amount of storage for the array. This causes the compiler to create a pointer constant. Defining `message2` using the declaration `char *message2` explicitly creates a pointer variable first. This pointer is then used to hold the address of a string when the string is actually specified. This difference in definitions has both storage and programming consequences.

From a programming perspective, defining `message2` as a pointer to a character allows string assignments, such as `message2 = "this is a string";`, to be made. Similar assignments are not allowed for strings defined as arrays. Thus, the statement `message1 = "this is a string";` is not valid. Both definitions, however, allow initializations to be made using a string assignment. For example, both of the following initializations are valid:

```
char message1[81] = "this is a string";
char *message2 = "this is a string";
```

The initialization of the `message1` array is straightforward and follows the pattern previously presented for initializing an array of characters (see Section 9.2's Programming Note).The same is not true for `message2`. The initialization of `message2` consists of setting an initial address into a pointer variable.

From a storage perspective, the allocation of space for `message1` and `message2` is different, as illustrated in Figure 11.12. As shown in the figure, both initializations cause the computer to store the same string internally. In the case of `message1`, a specific set of 81 storage locations is reserved and the first 17 locations are initialized. For `message1`, different strings can be stored, but each string will overwrite the previously stored characters. The same is not true for `message2`.

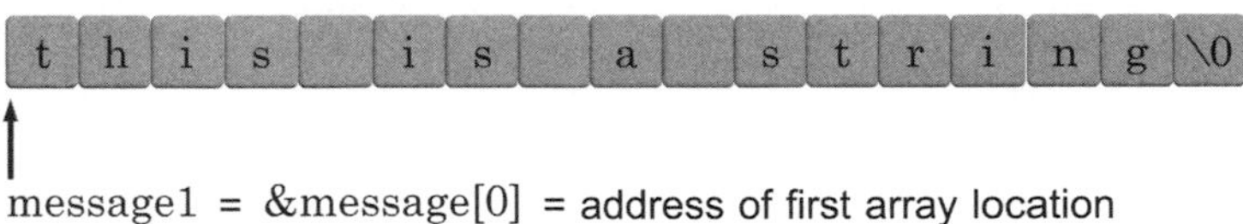

a. Storage allocation for a string defined as an array

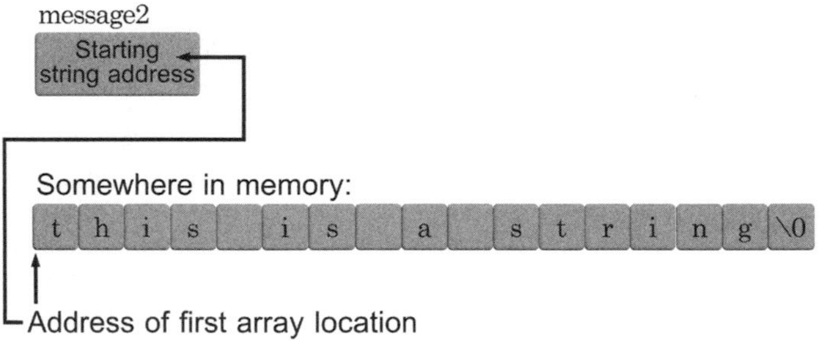

b. Storage of a string using a pointer

Figure 11.12 String storage allocation

The definition of `message2` reserves enough storage for one pointer. The initialization then causes the string to be stored and the address of the string's first character, in this case, the address of the `t`, to be loaded into the pointer. If a later assignment is made to `message2`, the initial string remains in memory and new storage locations are allocated to the new string. Program 11.7 uses the `message2` character pointer successively to "point to" two different strings. A key point to note is that access to the original string is lost. (Access can certainly be kept if a second pointer is used to store the original address.)

Program 11.7

```
#include <stdio.h>
int main()
{
  char *message2 = "this is a string";

  printf("\nThe string is %s", message2);
  printf("\n The base address of this string is %p\n", message2);

  message2 = "A new message";
  printf("\nThe string is now: %s", message2);
  printf("\n The base address of this string is %p\n", message2);

  return 0;
}
```

A sample output for Program 11.7 is[3]

```
The string is: this is a string
 The base address of this string is 00420094

The string is now: A new message
 The base address of this string is 00420038
```

In Program 11.7 the variable `message2` is initially created as a pointer variable and loaded with the starting storage address of the first string. The `printf()` function is then used to display this string. When the `%s` conversion control sequence is encountered by `printf()`, it alerts the function that a string is being referenced. The `printf()` function then expects either a string constant or a pointer containing the address of the first character in the string. This pointer can be either an array name or a pointer variable. The `printf()` function uses the address provided to correctly locate the string, and then continues accessing and displaying characters until it encounters a null character. As illustrated by the output, the hexadecimal address of the first character in the first string is 00420094.

After the first string and its starting address are displayed, the next assignment statement in Program 11.7 causes the computer to store a second string and change the address in

[3]The actual addresses used by this program for the storage of the messages are machine dependent.

message2 to point to the starting location of this new string. The printf() function then displays this string and its starting storage address.

It is important to realize that the second string assigned to message2 does not overwrite the first string but simply changes the address in message2 to point to the new string. As illustrated in Figure 11.13, both strings are stored inside the computer. Any additional string assignment to message2 results in the additional storage of the new string and a corresponding change in the address stored in message2.

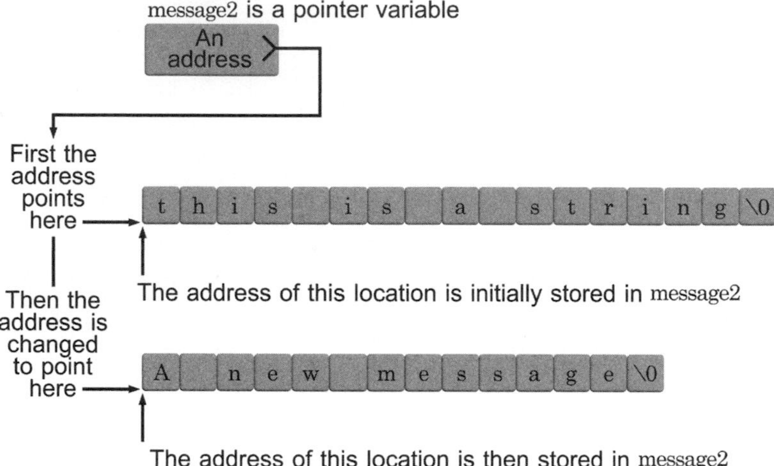

Figure 11.13 Storage allocation for Program 11.7

Pointer Arrays

The declaration of an array of character pointers is an extremely useful extension to single-string pointer declarations. For example, the declaration

```
char *seasons[4];
```

creates an array of four elements, where each element is a pointer to a character. As individual pointers, each pointer can be assigned to point to a string using string assignment statements. Thus, the statements

```
seasons[0] = "Winter";
seasons[1] = "Spring";
seasons[2] = "Summer";
seasons[3] = "Fall";
```

set appropriate addresses into the respective pointers. Figure 11.14 illustrates the addresses loaded into the pointers for these assignments.

As illustrated in Figure 11.14, the seasons array does not contain the actual strings assigned to the pointers. These strings are stored elsewhere in the computer, in the normal data area allocated to the program. The array of pointers contains only the address of the starting location for each string.

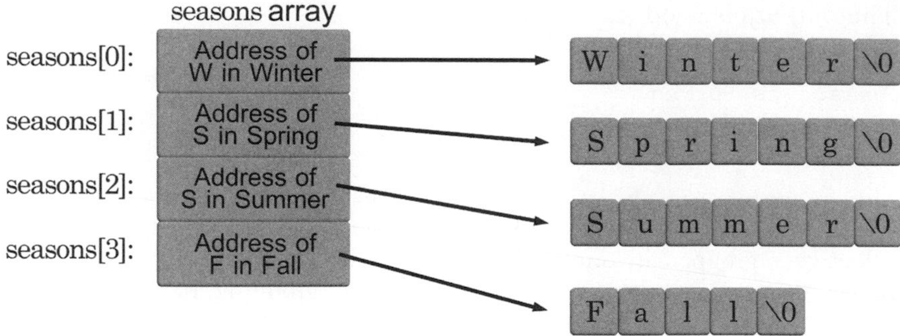

Figure 11.14 The addresses contained in the `seasons[]` pointers

The initializations of the `seasons` array can also be incorporated directly within the definition of the array as follows:

```
char *seasons[4] = {"Winter",
                    "Spring",
                    "Summer",
                    "Fall"};
```

This declaration both creates an array of pointers and initializes the pointers with appropriate addresses. Once addresses have been assigned to the pointers, each pointer can be used to access its corresponding string. Program 11.8 uses the `seasons` array to display each season using a `for` loop.

Program 11.8

```
#include <stdio.h>
int main()
{
  int n;
  char *seasons[] = {"Winter",
                     "Spring",
                     "Summer",
                     "Fall"};

  for(n = 0; n < 4; n++)
    printf("The season is %s.\n",seasons[n]);

  return 0;
}
```

The output obtained from Program 11.8 is

```
The season is Winter.
The season is Spring.
The season is Summer.
The season is Fall.
```

The advantage of using a list of pointers is that logical groups of data headings can be collected together and accessed with one array name. For example, the months in a year can be collectively grouped in one array called `months`, and the days in a week collectively grouped together in an array called `days`. The grouping of like headings allows the programmer to access and print an appropriate heading by simply specifying the correct position of the heading in the array. Program 11.9 uses the `seasons` array to identify and display correctly the season corresponding to a user-input month.

Program 11.9

```
#include <stdio.h>
int main()
{
  int n;
  char *seasons[] = {"Winter",
                      "Spring",
                      "Summer",
                       "Fall"};

  printf("\nEnter a month (use 1 for Jan., 2 for Feb., etc.): ");
  scanf("%d", &n);
  n = (n % 12) / 3; /* create the correct subscript */
  printf("The month entered is a %s month.\n",seasons[n]);

  return 0;
}
```

Except for the expression `n = (n % 12) / 3`, Program 11.9 is rather straightforward. The program requests the user to input a month and accepts the number corresponding to the month using a `scanf()` function call.

The expression `n = (n % 12) / 3` uses a common programming "trick" to scale a set of numbers into a more useful set. In this case, the first set is the numbers 1 through 12 and the second set is the numbers 0 through 3. The months of the year, which correspond to the numbers 1 through 12, are thus adjusted to correspond to the correct season subscript using this expression. First the expression `n % 12` adjusts the month entered to lie within the range 0 through 11, with 0 corresponding to December, 1 corresponding to January, etc. Dividing by 3 then causes the resulting number to range between 0 and 3, corresponding to the possible `seasons` elements. The result of the division by 3 is assigned to the integer variable n. The months 0, 1, and 2, when divided by 3, are set to 0; the months 3, 4, and 5 are set to 1; the months 6, 7, and 8 are set to 2; and the months 9, 10, and 11 are set to 3. This is equivalent to the following assignments:

Months	Season
December, January, February	Winter
March, April, May	Spring
June, July, August	Summer
September, October, November	Fall

The following is a sample output obtained for Program 11.9:

```
Enter a month (use 1 for Jan., 2 for Feb., etc.): 12
The month entered is a Winter month.
```

EXERCISES 11.5

Short Answer Questions

1. Write two declaration statements that can be used in place of the declaration `char text[] = "Hooray!";`.

2. Determine the value of `*text`, `*(text + 3)`, and `*(text + 7)` for each of the following sections of code:

   a. `char *text;`
   ```
   char message[] = "the check is in the mail";
   text = message;
   ```

   b. `char *text;`
   ```
   char formal[] = {'t', 'h', 'i', 's', ' ', 'i', 's', ' ',
                    'a', 'n', ' ', 'i', 'n', 'v', 'i', 't',
                    'a', 't', 'i', 'o', 'n', '\0'};
   text = &formal[0];
   ```

   c. `char *text;`
   ```
   char more[] = "Happy Holidays";
   text = &more[4];
   ```

   d. `char *text, *second;`
   ```
   char blip[] = "The good ship";
   second = blip;
   text = second++;
   ```

3. Determine the error in the following program:

```
#include <stdio.h>
int main()
{
  int i = 0;
  char message[] = {'H', 'e', 'l', 'l', 'o', '\0'};

  for( ; i < 5; i++)
  {
    putchar(*message);
    message++;
  }

  return 0;
}
```

Programming Exercises

1. a. Write a C function that displays the day of the week corresponding to a user-entered input number between 1 and 7. That is, in response to an input of 2, the program displays the name `Monday`. Use an array of pointers in the function.
   b. Include the function written for Exercise 1a in a complete working program.

2. Modify the function written in Exercise 1a so that the function returns the address of the character string containing the proper day to be displayed.

3. Write a C function that will accept 6 lines of user-input text and store the entered lines as 6 individual strings. Use a pointer array in your function.

11.6 Common Programming and Compiler Errors

In using the material presented in this chapter, be aware of the following possible programming and compiler errors.

Programming Errors

1. Using a pointer to reference nonexistent array elements. For example, if `nums` is an array of 10 integers, the expression `*(nums + 60)` points 50 integer locations beyond the last element of the array. As C does not do any bounds checking on array references, this type of error is not caught by the compiler. This is the same error as using a subscript to reference an out-of-bounds array element disguised in its pointer notation form.

2. Incorrectly applying the address and indirection operators. For example, if `pt` is a pointer variable, the expressions

```
pt = &45
pt = &(miles + 10)
```

are both invalid because they attempt to take the address of a value. Notice that the expression `pt = &miles + 10`, however, is valid. Here, 10 is added to the address of miles. Again, it is the programmer's responsibility to ensure that the final address "points to" a valid data element.

3. Addresses of pointer constants cannot be taken. For example, given the declarations

```
int nums[25];
int *pt;
```

the assignment

```
pt = &nums;
```

is invalid. Here, `nums` is a pointer constant that is itself equivalent to an address. The correct assignment is `pt = nums`.

4. Not providing sufficient space for the end-of-string `NULL` character when a string is defined as an array of characters and not including the `\0 NULL` character when the array is initialized.

5. Misunderstanding the terminology. For example, if `text` is defined as

```
char *text;
```

the variable `text` is sometimes referred to as a string. Thus, the terminology "store the characters `Hooray for the Hoosiers` into the `text` string" may be encountered. Strictly speaking, calling `text` a string or a string variable is incorrect. The variable `text` is a pointer that contains the address of the first character in the string. Nevertheless, referring to a character pointer as a string occurs frequently enough that you should be aware of it.

6. The final common error that occurs is one common to pointer usage in general. The situation always arises when the beginning C programmer becomes confused about whether a variable *contains* an address or *is an* address. Pointer variables and pointer arguments contain addresses. Although a pointer constant is synonymous with an address, it is useful to treat pointer constants as pointer variables with two restrictions:

   - The address of a pointer constant cannot be taken.
   - The address "contained in" the pointer constant cannot be altered.

   Except for these two restrictions, pointer constants and variables can be used almost interchangeably. Therefore, when an address is required any of the following can be used:

   - a pointer variable name
   - a pointer argument name
   - a pointer constant name
   - a nonpointer variable name preceded by the address operator (e.g., `&variable`)
   - a nonpointer argument name preceded by the address operator (e.g., `&argument`)

   Some of the confusion surrounding pointers is caused by the cavalier use of the word pointer. For example, the phrase "a function requires a pointer argument" is more clearly understood when it is realized that the phrase really means "a function requires an address as an argument." Similarly, the phrase "a function returns a pointer" really means "a function returns an address." Since an address is returned, a suitably declared pointer must be available to store the returned address. If you are ever in doubt as to what is really contained in a variable, or how it should be treated, use the `printf()` function to display the contents of the variable, the "thing pointed to," or "the address of the variable." Seeing what is displayed frequently helps sort out what is really in the variable.

Compiler Errors

The following table summarizes typical compiler error messages in Unix and Windows.

Error	Typical Unix-based Compiler Error Message	Typical Windows-based Compiler Error Message

Attempting to initialize a pointer to a variable that has not been declared yet.
For example:
`int *inum = #`
`int num = 7;`
	`(S) Undeclared identifier num.`	`:error: 'num' : undeclared identifier`

Attempting to dereference a variable that is not a pointer.
For example:
`int num = 7;`
`printf("%d",*num);`
	`(S) Operand of indirection operator must be a pointer expression.`	`:error: illegal indirection`

Incorrectly applying the address operator.
For example:
`int *num;`
`int val;`
`num =&(val+10);`
	`(S) Operand of address operator must be an lvalue or function designator.`	`:error C2102: '&' requires l-value`

Attempting to take the address of a pointer constant.
For example:
`int nums[] = {16,18};`
`int *numsPtr;`
`numsPtr =&nums;`
	`(W) Operation between types "int*" and "int(*)[2]" is not allowed.`	`:error C2440: '=' : cannot convert from 'int (*__w64 )[2]' to 'int *'`

11.7 Chapter Summary

1. An array name is a pointer constant. The value of the pointer constant is the address of element zero in the array. Thus, if `val` is the name of an array, `val` and `&val[0]` can be used interchangeably.

2. Any access to an array element using subscript notation can always be replaced using pointer notation. That is, the notation `a[i]` can always be replaced by the notation `*(a + i)`. This is true whether `a` was initially declared explicitly as an array or as a pointer.

3. Arrays are passed to functions by address, not by value. The called function always receives direct access to the originally declared array elements.

4. When a single-dimensional array is passed to a function, the parameter declaration for the array can be either an array declaration or a pointer declaration. Thus, the following parameter declarations are equivalent:
   ```
   double a[]
   double *a
   ```

5. In place of subscripts, pointer notation and pointer arithmetic are especially useful for manipulating string elements.

6. String storage can be created by declaring an array of characters or a pointer to be a character. A pointer to a character can be assigned a string directly. String assignment to an array of characters is invalid except when done in a declaration statement.

7. Pointers can be incremented, decremented, and compared. Numbers added to or subtracted from a pointer are automatically scaled. The scale factor used is the number of bytes required to store the data type originally pointed to.

Chapter 12

Structures

In the broadest sense, the term "structure" refers to how individual elements of a group are arranged or organized. For example, a corporation's structure consists of the organization of the departments and people in the company. In programming, "structure" refers to the way individual data items are arranged to form a cohesive and related unit.

To make the discussion more tangible, consider data items that might be stored for a video game character, as illustrated in Figure 12.1.

Each of the individual data items listed in Figure 12.1 is an entity by itself that is referred to as a **data field**. Taken together, all the data fields form a single unit that is referred to as a **record**.[1] In C, a record is referred to as a **structure,** and we use these terms interchangeably.

Although there could be hundreds of characters in a video game, each with its individual characteristics, the form of each character's structure within an individual game would be identical. Thus, in dealing with structures, it is important to distinguish between a structure's form and its contents.

[1]This is the same as an individual record that is stored in a file.

A structure's **form** consists of the symbolic names, data types, and arrangement of individual data fields in the record. The structure's **contents** consist of the actual data stored in the symbolic names. Figure 12.2 shows acceptable contents for the record form in Figure 12.1.

```
Name:
Type:
Location in Dungeon:
Strength Factor:
Intelligence Factor:
Type of Armor:
```

Figure 12.1 Typical components of a video game character

```
Name: Golgar
Type: Monster
Location in Dungeon: G7
Strength Factor: 78
Intelligence Factor: 15
Type of Armor: Chain Mail
```

Figure 12.2 The form and contents of a structure

In this chapter, we describe the C statements required to create, fill, use, and pass structures between functions.

12.1 Single Structures

Using structures involves the same two steps needed for using any C variable. First the structure must be declared. Then specific values can be assigned to the individual structure's data items. To declare a structure, you must list its data types, data names, and arrangement of data items. For example, the definition

```
struct
{
  int month;
  int day;
  int year;
} birth;
```

gives the form of a structure named `birth` and reserves storage for the individual data items listed in the structure. The `birth` structure consists of three data items, which are called **members of the structure**.

Assigning actual data values to the data items of a structure is called **populating the structure.** This is a relatively straightforward procedure. Each member of a structure is accessed by giving both the structure name and individual data item name, separated by a period. Thus, `birth.month` refers to the first member of the `birth` structure, `birth.day` refers to the second member of the structure, and `birth.year` refers to the third member. Program 12.1 illustrates the process of assigning values to the individual members of the `birth` structure.

Program 12.1

```
1  #include <stdio.h>
2  int main()
3  {
4    struct
5    {
6      int month;
7      int day;
8      int year;
9    } birth;
10
11   birth.month = 12;
12   birth.day = 28;
13   birth.year = 1987;
14   printf("My birth date is %d/%d/%d\n",
15              birth.month,birth.day,birth.year % 100);
16
17   return 0;
18 }
```

The output produced by Program 12.1 is

```
My birth date is 12/28/87
```

Notice that although we have stored the year as a four-digit number in line 13 as follows

```
13  birth.year = 1987
```

the output displays the year in conventional two-digit form.

As in most C statements, the spacing of a structure definition is not rigid. For example, the `birth` structure could just as well have been defined as follows:

```
struct {int month; int day; int year;} birth;
```

Also, as with all C definition statements, multiple variables can be defined in the same statement. For example, the definition statement

```
struct {int month; int day; int year;} birth, current;
```

creates two structures having the same form. Members of the first structure are accessed by the individual names `birth.month`, `birth.day`, and `birth.year`, whereas members of the second structure are accessed by the individual names `current.month`, `current.day`, and `current.year`. Notice that the form of this particular structure definition statement is identical to the form used in defining any program variable: the data type is followed by a list of variable names.

When defining structures, it is common to list the form of the structure with no following variable names. In this case, however, the list of structure members must be preceded by a user-selected **structure type name**. For example, in the declaration

```
struct Date
{
  int month;
  int day;
  int year;
};
```

the term Date is a structure type name. That is, it creates a new structure type of the declared form. By convention the first letter of user-selected structure type names is uppercase, as in the name Date, which helps to identify them when they are used in subsequent definition statements. Here, the declaration for the Date structure creates a new data type without actually reserving any storage locations. As such, it is not a definition statement. It simply declares a Date structure type and describes how individual data items are arranged within the structure. Actual storage for the members of the structure is reserved only when specific variable names are assigned. For example, the definition statement

```
struct Date birth, current;
```

reserves storage for two Date structure variables named birth and current, respectively. Each of these individual structures has the form previously declared for the Date structure.

Like all variable declarations, a structure may be declared globally or locally. Program 12.2 illustrates the global declaration of a Date structure. Internal to main(), the variable birth is defined as a local variable of Date type.

Program 12.2

```
#include <stdio.h>
struct Date
{
  int month;
  int day;
  int year;
};

int main()
{
  struct Date birth;

  birth.month = 12;
  birth.day = 28;
  birth.year = 1987;
  printf("My birth date is %d/%d/%d\n",
  birth.month,birth.day,birth.year % 100);

  return 0;
}
```

Programming Note

Homogeneous and Heterogeneous Data Structures

Both arrays and structures are structured data types. The difference between these two data structures are the types of elements they contain. An array is a **homogeneous** data structure, which means that each of its components must be of the same type. A record is a **heterogeneous** data structure, which means that each of its components can be of different data types. Thus, an array of records is a homogeneous data structure whose elements are of the same heterogeneous type.

The output produced by Program 12.2 is identical to the output produced by Program 12.1.

The initialization of structures follows the same rules as for the initialization of arrays: Structures may be initialized by following the definition with a list of initializers.[2] For example, the definition statement

```
struct Date birth = {12, 28, 1987};
```

can be used to replace the first four statements internal to `main()` in Program 12.2.

Notice that the initializers are separated by commas, not semicolons. The individual members of a structure are not restricted to integer data types, as they are in the `Date` structure. Any valid C data type can be used. For example, consider an employee record consisting of the following data items:

```
Name:
Identification Number:
Regular Pay Rate:
Overtime Pay Rate:
```

A suitable declaration for these data items is

```
struct PayRecord
{
  char name[20];
  int idNum;
  double regRate;
  double otRate;
};
```

Once the `PayRecord` structure type is declared, a specific structure variable using this type can be defined and initialized. For example, the definition

```
struct PayRecord employee = {"H. Price",12387,15.89,25.50};
```

creates a structure named `employee` of the `PayRecord` type. The individual members of `employee` are initialized with the respective data listed between braces in the definition statement.

[2]This is true for ANSI C compilers. For non-ANSI C compilers, the keyword `static` must be placed before the keyword `struct` for initialization within a local declaration statement. This is because static local structures may be initialized, whereas automatic local structures cannot be initialized in non-ANSI C compilers.

Notice that a single structure is simply a convenient method for combining and storing related items under a common name. Although a single structure is useful in explicitly identifying the relationship among its members, the individual members could be defined as separate variables. The real advantage to using structures is realized only when the same structure type is used in a list many times over. Creating lists with the same structure type is the topic of the next section.

Before leaving the topic of single structures, it is worth noting that because any valid C data type can serve as an individual member of a structure, individual members can also be arrays and structures. For example, an array of characters was used as a member of the `employee` structure defined previously. Accessing an element of a member array requires giving the structure's name, followed by a period, followed by the array designation. For example, `employee.name[4]` refers to the fifth character in the `employee` structure's `name` array.

Including a structure within a structure follows the same rules for including any data type in a structure. For example, assume that a structure is to consist of a name and a date of birth, where a `Date` structure has been declared as

```
struct Date
{
  int month;
  int date;
  int year;
};
```

A suitable definition of a structure that includes a name and a `Date` structure is

```
struct
{
  char name[20];
  struct Date birth;
} person;
```

Notice that in declaring this structure, the term `Date` is a structure type name. In defining the `person` variable, `person` is the name of a specific structure. The same is true of the variable named `birth`. This is the name of a specific structure having the form of `Date`. Individual members in the `person` structure are accessed by preceding the desired member with the structure name followed by a period. For example, `person.birth.month` refers to the `month` variable in the `birth` structure contained in the `person` structure.

EXERCISES 12.1

Short Answer Questions

1. List the data items found on your driver's license.

2. Declare a structure type named `Stemp` for each of the following records:
   a. A student record consisting of a student identification number, number of credits completed, and cumulative grade point average
   b. A student record consisting of a student's name, date of birth, number of credits completed, and cumulative grade point average
   c. A mailing list consisting of a person's name and address (street, city, state, and zip code)

d. A stock record consisting of the stock's name, the price of the stock, and the date of purchase
e. An inventory record consisting of an integer part number, part description, number of parts in inventory, and an integer reorder number

3. For the individual structure types declared in Question 2, define a suitable structure variable name and initialize each structure with the following data:
a.
```
Identification Number: 4672
Number of Credits Completed: 68
Grade Point Average: 3.01
```
b.
```
Name: Rhona Karp
Date of Birth: 8/4/1980
Number of Credits Completed: 96
Grade Point Average: 3.89
```
c.
```
Name: Kay Kingsley
Street Address: 614 Freeman Street
City: Indianapolis
State: IN
Zip Code: 47030
```
d.
```
Stock:IBM
Price: 115.375
Date Purchased: 12/7/1999
```
e.
```
Part Number: 16879
Description: Battery
Number in Stock: 10
Reorder Number: 3
```

Programming Exercises

1. a. Write a C program that prompts a user to input the current month, day, and year. Store the data entered in a suitably defined structure and display the date in an appropriate manner.
b. Modify the program written in Programming Exercise 1a to accept the current time in hours, minutes, and seconds.

2. Write a program that uses a structure for storing the name of a stock, its estimated earnings per share, and its estimated price-to-earnings ratio. Have the program prompt the user to enter these items for five different stocks, each time using the same structure to store the entered data. When the data have been entered for a particular stock, have the program compute and display the anticipated stock price based on the entered earnings and price-per-earnings values. For example, if a user entered the data XYZ 1.56 12, the anticipated price for a share of XYZ stock is *(1.56)*(12) = $18.72.*

3. Write a C program that accepts a user-entered time in hours and minutes. Have the program calculate and display the time one minute later.

4. a. Write a C program that accepts a user-entered date. Have the program calculate and display the date of the next day. For purposes of this exercise, assume that all months consist of 30 days.
b. Modify the program written in Exercise 4a to account for the actual number of days in each month.

12.2 Arrays of Structures

The real power of structures is realized when they are used in an array. For example, assume that the data shown in Figure 12.3 must be processed.

Employee number	Employee name	Employee pay rate
32479	Abrams, B.	6.72
33623	Bohm, P.	7.54
34145	Donaldson, S.	5.56
35987	Ernst, T.	5.43
36203	Gwodz, K.	8.72
36417	Hanson, H.	7.64
37634	Monroe, G.	5.29
38321	Price, S.	9.67
39435	Robbins, L.	8.50
39567	Williams, B.	7.20

Figure 12.3 A list of employee data

Clearly, the employee numbers can be stored together in an array of long integers, the names in an array of pointers, and the pay rates in an array of floating-point numbers. In organizing the data in this fashion, each column in Figure 12.3 is considered as a separate list, which is stored in its own array. Using arrays, the correspondence between items for each individual employee is maintained by storing an employee's data in the same array position in each array. Such arrays are known as parallel arrays, and are discussed at the end of this section.

The separation of the complete list into three individual arrays is unfortunate, because all of the items relating to a single employee constitute a natural organization of data into records, as illustrated in Figure 12.4.

	Employee Number	Employee Name	Employee Pay Rate
1st Structure →	32479	Abrams, B.	6.72
2nd Structure →	33623	Bohm, P.	7.54
3rd Structure →	34145	Donaldson, S.	5.56
4th Structure →	35987	Ernst, T.	5.43
5th Structure →	36203	Gwodz, K.	8.72
6th Structure →	36417	Hanson, H.	7.64
7th Structure →	37634	Monroe, G.	5.29
8th Structure →	38321	Price, S.	9.67
9th Structure →	39435	Robbins, L.	8.50
10th Structure →	39567	Williams, B.	7.20

Figure 12.4 A list of records

Programming Note

Using a typedef Statement

A commonly used programming technique when dealing with structure declarations is to use a `typedef` statement. This provides a simple method for creating a new and typically shorter name for an existing structure type (see Section 14.1 for a complete description of `typedef`). For example, assuming the following global structure declaration has been made

```
struct Date
{
  int month;
  int day;
  int year;
};
```

then the `typedef` statement

```
typedef struct Date DATE;
```

makes the name `DATE` a synonym for the terms `struct Date`. Now, whenever a variable is to be declared as a `struct Date`, the term `DATE` can be used instead. Thus, for example, the declaration

```
struct Date a, b, c;
```

can be replaced by the statement

```
DATE a, b, c;
```

Similarly, if a record structure named `PayRecord` has been declared and the statement

```
typedef struct PayRecord PAYRECS
```

had been made, the declaration

```
PAYRECS employee[10];
```

could be used in place of the longer declaration

```
struct PayRecord employee[10];
```

By convention all `typedef` names are written in uppercase but this is not mandatory. The names used in a `typedef` statement can be any name that conforms to C's identifier naming rules.

Using a structure, the integrity of the data organization as a record can be maintained and reflected by the program. Under this approach, the lists illustrated in Figure 12.4 can be processed as a single array of 10 structures. Declaring an array of structures is the same as declaring an array of any other variable type. For example, if the structure type `PayRecord` is declared as

```
struct PayRecord {int idnum; char name[20]; double rate;};
```

then an array of 10 such structures can be defined as

```
struct PayRecord employee[10];
```

This definition statement constructs an array of 10 elements, each of which is a structure of the type PayRecord. Notice that the creation of an array of 10 structures has the same form as the creation of any other array. For example, creating an array of 10 integers named employee requires the following declaration:

```
int employee[10];
```

In this declaration the data type is integer, while in the former declaration for employee the data type is a structure of the PayRecord form.

Once an array of structures is declared, a particular data item is accessed by giving the position of the desired structure in the array followed by a period and the appropriate structure member. For example, the variable employee[0].rate accesses the rate member of the first structure in the employee array. Including structures as elements of an array permits a list of records to be processed using standard array programming techniques. Program 12.3 displays the first five employee records illustrated in Figure 12.4.

Program 12.3

```
#include <stdio.h>
#define NUMRECS 5
struct PayRecord /* construct a global structure type */
{
  int id;
  char name[20];
  double rate;
};

int main()
{
  int i;
  struct PayRecord employee[NUMRECS] = {{32479, "Abrams, B.", 6.72},
                                         {33623, "Bohm, P.", 7.54},
                                         {34145, "Donaldson, S.", 5.56},
                                         {35987, "Ernst, T.", 5.43},
                                         {36203, "Gwodz, K.", 8.72}
                                        };

  for (i = 0; i < NUMRECS; i++)
    printf("%d %-20s %4.2f\n",
           employee[i].id,employee[i].name,employee[i].rate);

  return 0;
}
```

The output displayed by Program 12.3 is

```
32479 Abrams, B.           6.72
33623 Bohm, P.             7.54
34145 Donaldson, S.        5.56
35987 Ernst, T.            5.43
36203 Gwodz, K.            8.72
```

In reviewing Program 12.3, notice the initialization of the array of structures in lines 13 through 18:

```
13  struct PayRecord employee[NUMRECS] = {{32479, "Abrams, B.", 6.72},
14                                         {33623, "Bohm, P.", 7.54},
15                                         {34145, "Donaldson, S.", 5.56},
16                                         {35987, "Ernst, T.", 5.43},
17                                         {36203, "Gwodz, K.", 8.72}
18                                        };
```

Although the initializers for each structure have been enclosed in inner braces, these are not strictly necessary because all members have been initialized. As with all external and static variables, in the absence of explicit initializers, the numeric elements of both static and external arrays or structures are initialized to 0 and their character elements are initialized to nulls. The `%-20s` format included in the `printf()` function call forces each name to be displayed left-justified in a field of 20 spaces.

An inferior alternative to an array of structures, but one that you may encounter, is parallel arrays. **Parallel arrays** are two or more arrays, where each array has the same number of elements and the elements in each array are directly related by their position in the arrays. For example, the single `employee` array of `PayRecord` structures used in Program 12.3 could be represented as a set of three parallel arrays—one array for the identification number, one array for the name, and one array for the pay rate. Within this set of parallel arrays, all of the elements with the same subscript value would refer to information corresponding to the same individual.

The problem with parallel arrays is that the correspondence between data items is easily lost if only one of the arrays is reordered. An example of this is provided in Programming Exercise 5. Parallel arrays are rarely used anymore because almost all programming languages currently provide structures. However, in languages that did not provide structures, such as earlier versions of Fortran, parallel arrays were used instead.

EXERCISES 12.2

Short Answer Questions

1. Define an array of 500 structures that can be used to store the following data on boats docked in a marina: boat owner's last name, boat license number, boat length, and dock number where the boat is currently docked.

2. Define arrays of 100 structures for each of the structures described in Exercise 2 of Section 12.1.

3. Using the following declaration

```
struct MonthDays
{
  char name[10];
  int days;
};
```

define an array of 12 structures of type `MonthDays`. Name the array `convert[]`, and initialize the array with the names of the 12 months in a year and the number of days in each month.

Programming Exercises

1. Include the array created in Short Answer Question 3 in a program that displays the names and number of days in each month.

2. Using the structure defined in Short Answer Question 3, write a C program that accepts a month from a user in numeric form and displays the name of the month and the number of days in the month. Thus, in response to an input of 3, the program displays `March has 31 days`.

3. **a.** Declare a single structure type suitable for an employee record consisting of an integer identification number, a last name (consisting of a maximum of 20 characters), a floating-point pay rate, and a floating-point number of hours worked.
   b. Using the structure type declared in Programming Exercise 3a, write a C program that interactively accepts the following data into an array of six structures:

ID Number	Name	Pay Rate	Hours Worked
3462	Jones	4.62	40.0
6793	Robbins	5.83	38.5
6985	Smith	5.22	45.5
7834	Swain	6.89	40.0
8867	Timmins	6.43	35.5
9002	Williams	4.75	42.0

   Once the data have been entered, the program should create a payroll report listing each employee's name, number, and gross pay. Include the total gross pay of all employees at the end of the report.

4. **a.** Declare a single structure type suitable for a car record consisting of an integer car identification number, an integer value for the miles driven by the car, and an integer value for the number of gallons used by each car.

b. Using the structure type declared for Programming Exercise 4a write a C program that interactively accepts the following data into an array of five structures:

Car Number	Miles Driven	Gallons Used
25	1,450	62
36	3,240	136
44	1,792	76
52	2,360	105
68	2,114	67

Once the data have been entered, the program should create a report listing each car number and the miles per gallon achieved by the car. At the end of the report, include the average miles per gallon achieved by the complete fleet of cars.

5. a. Construct a set of parallel arrays consisting of 10 integer identification numbers and 10 pay rates. Then, determine the identification number that corresponds to the highest pay rate. Make sure to locate the highest pay rate by sorting the pay rate array so that the highest pay rate has a subscript value of 0.

b. What problems did you encounter in determining the correct identification number when you sorted the pay rate array, as specified in Programming Exercise 5a.

12.3 Passing and Returning Structures

Individual structure members may be passed to a function in the same manner as any scalar variable. For example, given the structure definition

```
struct
{
  int idNum;
  double payRate;
  double hours;
} emp;
```

the statement

```
display(emp.idNum);
```

passes a copy of the structure member `emp.idNum` to a function named `display()`. Similarly, the statement

```
calcPay(emp.payRate,emp.hours);
```

passes copies of the values stored in structure members `emp.payRate` and `emp.hours` to the function `calcPay()`. Both functions, `display()` and `calcPay()`, must declare the correct data types of their respective parameters.

On most compilers, complete copies of all members of a structure can also be passed to a function by including the name of the structure as an argument to the called function. For example, the function call

```
calcNet(emp);
```

passes a copy of the complete emp structure to `calcNet()`. Internal to `calcNet()`, an appropriate declaration must be made to receive the structure. Program 12.4 declares a global structure type for an employee record. This type is then used by `main()`, in line 13 as follows:

```
13 struct Employee emp = {6787, 8.93, 40.5};
```

It is also used in `calcNet()`, in line 23, as follows:

```
23 double calcNet(struct Employee temp)
```

In these lines, it is used to define specific structures with the names emp and temp, respectively.

Program 12.4

```
1  #include <stdio.h>
2  struct Employee /* declare a global structure type */
3  {
4    int idNum;
5    double payRate;
6    double hours;
7  };
8
9  double calcNet(struct Employee); /* function prototype */
10
11 int main()
12 {
13   struct Employee emp = {6787, 8.93, 40.5};
14   double netPay;
15
16   netPay = calcNet(emp); /* pass copies of the values in emp */
17   printf("The net pay of employee %d is $%6.2f\n",
18                                          emp.idNum,netPay);
19
20   return 0;
21 }
22
23 double calcNet(struct Employee temp)
24 /* temp is of data type struct Employee */
25 {
```

```
26    return(temp.payRate * temp.hours);
27  }
```

The output produced by Program 12.4 is

```
The net pay of employee 6787 is $361.66
```

In reviewing Program 12.4, observe that both `main()` and `calcNet()` use the same global structure type to define their individual structures. The structure subsequently defined in `main()` in line 13, and the structure defined in `calcNet()` in line 23, are two completely different structures. Any changes made to the local `temp` structure in `calcNet()` are not reflected in the `emp` structure of `main()`. In fact, because both structures are local to their respective functions, the same structure name could have been used in both functions with no ambiguity.

The function `calcNet()` is called by `main()` in line 16 as follows:

```
16 netPay = calcNet(emp); /* pass copies of the values in emp */
```

As a result, copies of emp's structure values are passed to the `temp` structure. The `calcNet()` function then uses two of the passed member values to calculate a value, which is returned to `main()`.

Although the structures in both `main()` and `calcNet()` use the same globally defined structure type, this is not strictly necessary. For example, the structure variable in `main()` could have been defined directly as

```
struct
{
  int idNum;
  double payRate;
  double hours;
} emp = {6787, 8.93, 40.5};
```

Similarly, the structure variable in `calcNet()` could have been defined as

```
struct
{
  int idNum;
  double payRate;
  double hours;
} temp;
```

The global declaration of the `Employee` structure type provided in Program 12.4 is highly preferable to these latter two individual structure specifications because the global structure type centralizes the declaration of the structure's organization. Any change that must subsequently be made to the structure need only be made once to the global declaration. Making changes to individual structure definitions requires that all occurrences of the structure definition be located in every function defining the structure. For larger programs, this usually results in an error when a change to one of the structure definitions is inadvertently omitted.

An alternative to passing a copy of a structure is to pass the address of the structure. This, of course, allows the called function to make changes directly to the original structure. For example, referring to Program 12.4, the call to `calcNet()` can be modified to

```
calcNet(&emp);
```

In this call, an address is passed. To correctly store this address, `calcNet()` must declare its parameter as a pointer. A suitable function header line for `calcNet()` to accept this address is

```
double calcNet(struct Employee *pt)
```

Here, the declaration for `pt` declares this parameter as a pointer to a structure of type `Employee`. The pointer variable, `pt`, receives the starting address of a structure whenever `calcNet()` is called. Within `calcNet()`, this pointer is used to directly access any member in the structure. For example, `(*pt).idNum` refers to the `idNum` member of the structure, `(*pt).payRate` refers to the `payRate` member of the structure, and `(*pt).hours` refers to the `hours` member of the structure. These relationships are illustrated in Figure 12.5.

The parentheses around the expression `*pt` in Figure 12.5 are necessary to initially access "the structure whose address is in `pt`." This is followed by an identifier to access the desired member within the structure. In the absence of the parentheses, the structure member operator . takes precedence over the indirection operator `*`. Thus, the expression `*pt.hours` is another way of writing `*(pt.hours)`, which refers to *the variable whose address is in the* `pt.hours` *variable*. This last expression clearly makes no sense because there is no structure named `pt`, and `hours` does not contain an address.

As illustrated in Figure 12.5, the starting address of the `emp` structure is also the address of the first member of the structure. Thus, the expressions `*pt` and `(*pt).idNum` both refer to the `idNum` member of the `emp` structure.

The use of pointers is so common with structures that a special notation exists for them. The general expression *(*pointer).member* can always be replaced with the notation *pointer->member*, where the -> operator is constructed using a minus sign followed by a greater-than symbol. Either expression can be used to locate the desired member. For example, the following expressions are equivalent:

```
(*pt).idNum can be replaced by pt->idNum
(*pt).payRate can be replaced by pt->payRate
(*pt).hours can be replaced by pt->hours
```

Program 12.5 illustrates passing a structure's address and using a pointer with the new notation to access the structure directly.

The name of the pointer parameter, `pt`, is declared in line 23 of Program 12.5 as follows:

```
23 double calcNet(struct Employee *pt)
```

This pointer name is, of course, selected by the programmer. When `calcNet()` is called, emp's starting address is passed to the function. Using this address as a starting point, individual members of the structure are accessed by including their names with the pointer.

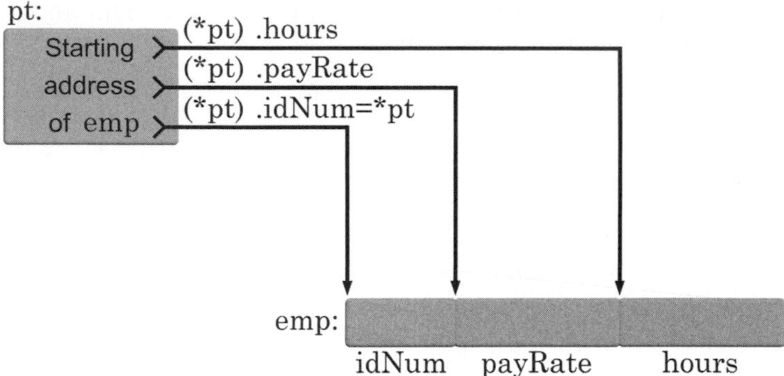

Figure 12.5 A pointer can be used to access structure members

Program 12.5

```
#include <stdio.h>
struct Employee /* dcclare a global structure type */
{
  int idNum;
  double payRate;
  double hours;
};

double calcNet(struct Employee *); /* function prototype */

int main()
{
  struct Employee emp = {6787, 8.93, 40.5};
  double netPay;

  netPay = calcNet(&emp); /* pass an address*/
  printf("The net pay for employee %d is $%6.2f\n",
                                    emp.idNum, netPay);

  return 0;
}

double calcNet(struct Employee *pt) /* pt is a pointer to a */
{                             /* structure of Employee type */

  return(pt->payRate * pt->hours);
}
```

As with all C expressions that access a variable, the increment and decrement operators can also be applied to them. For example, the expression

```
++pt->hours
```

adds one to the `hours` member of the `emp` structure. Because the `->` operator has a higher priority than the increment operator, the `hours` member is accessed first and then the increment is applied.

Alternatively, the expression `(pt++)->hours` uses the postfix increment operator to increment the address in `pt` after the `hours` member is accessed. Similarly, the expression `(++pt)->hours` uses the prefix increment operator to increment the address in `pt` before the `hours` member is accessed. In both of these cases, however, there must be sufficient defined structures to ensure that the incremented pointers actually point to legitimate structures.

As an example, Figure 12.6 illustrates an array of three structures of type `Employee`. Assuming that the address of `emp[1]` is stored in the pointer `pt`, the expression `++pt` changes the address in `pt` to the starting address of `emp[2]`, while the expression `--pt` changes the address to point to `emp[0]`.

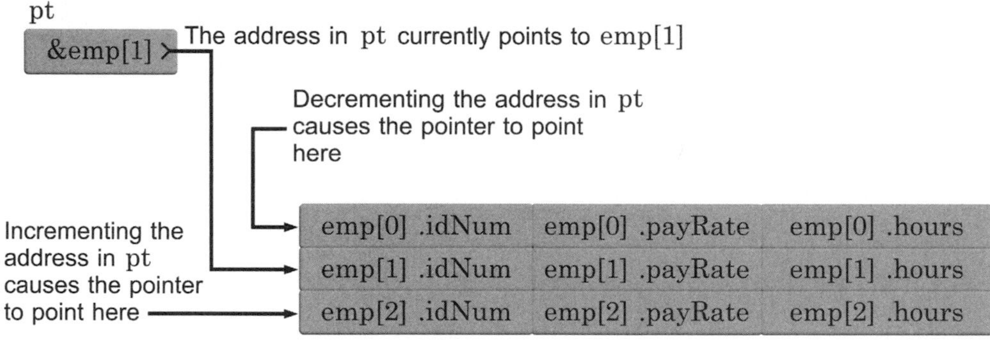

Figure 12.6 Changing pointer addresses

Returning Structures

In practice, most structure-handling functions gain direct access to a structure by receiving the address of the structure as an argument when the function is called. Then any changes can be made directly by the function using pointer notation. If you want to have a function return a separate structure, however, and your compiler supports this option, you must follow the same procedures for returning complete structures as for returning scalar values. These include both declaring the function appropriately and alerting any calling function to the type of structure being returned. For example, in Program 12.6, the `return` statement in line 31 in the `getValues() function`,

```
31 return (newemp);
```

returns a complete structure to `main()`.

Program 12.6

```
1  #include <stdio.h>
2  struct Employee /* declare a global structure type */
3  {
4    int idNum;
5    double payRate;
6    double hours;
7  };
8
9  struct Employee getValues(); /* function prototype */
10
11 int main()
12 {
13   struct Employee emp;
14
15   emp = getValues();
16   printf("\nThe employee id number is %d\n", emp.idNum);
17   printf("The employee pay rate is $%5.2f\n", emp.payRate);
18   printf("The employee hours are %5.2f\n", emp.hours);
19
20   return 0;
21 }
22
23 struct Employee getValues()
24 {
25   struct Employee newemp;
26
27   newemp.idNum = 6789;
28   newemp.payRate = 16.25;
29   newemp.hours = 38.0;
30
31   return (newemp);
32 }
```

The following output is displayed when Program 12.6 is run:

```
The employee id number is 6789
The employee pay rate is $16.25
The employee hours are 38.00
```

Because the `getValues()` function returns a structure, the function header for `getValues()` must specify the type of structure being returned. As `getValues()` does not receive any arguments, the function header has no parameter declarations and consists of the line

```
23  struct Employee getValues()
```

Within `getValues()`, the variable `newemp` is defined in line 25 as a structure of the type to be returned

```
25  struct Employee newemp;
```

After values have been assigned to the `newemp` structure, the structure values are returned by including the structure name within the parentheses of the `return` statement.

On the receiving side, `main()` must be alerted that the function `getValues()` will be returning a structure. This is handled by the function prototype for `getValues()` in line 9

```
9  struct Employee getValues(); /* function prototype */
```

Notice that these steps for returning a structure from a function are identical to the procedures for returning scalar data types previously described in Section 6.2.

EXERCISES 12.3

Short Answer Questions

1. In Section 10.5 a file of holiday dates was entered into an array of integers. For these holiday dates, declare a suitable array of structures that could be used to hold each holiday using a day, month, and year field.
2. **a.** What data type can be used to store a single record in a file?
   b. What data type can be used to store all of the records in a file?

Programming Exercises

1. Write a C function named `days()` that determines the number of days from the date 1/1/1900 for any date passed as a structure. Use the following `Date` structure:

```
struct Date
{
  int month;
  int day;
  int year;
};
```

   In writing the `days()` function, use the convention that all years have 360 days and each month consists of 30 days. The function should return the number of days for any date structure passed to it.

2. Write a C function named `difDays()` that calculates and returns the difference between two dates. Each date is passed to the function as a structure using the following global structure:

```
struct Date
{
  int month;
  int day;
```

```
   int year;
};
```

The `difDays()` function should make two calls to the `days()` function written for Programming Exercise 1.

3. Rewrite the `days()` function written for Programming Exercise 1 so that it directly accesses a `Date` structure, as opposed to receiving a copy of the structure.

4. a. Write a C function named `larger()` that returns the later date of any two dates passed to it. For example, if the dates 10/9/2001 and 11/3/2001 are passed to `larger()`, the second date would be returned.
   b. Include the `larger()` function that was written for Programming Exercise 4a in a complete program. Store the date structure returned by `larger()` in a separate date structure and display the member values of the returned date.

5. a. Modify the function `days()` written for Programming Exercise 1 to account for the actual number of days in each month. Assume, however, that each year contains 365 days (that is, do not account for leap years).
   b. Modify the function written for Programming Exercise 5a to account for leap years.

6. Rewrite Program 10.10 to read the `Holidays.txt` file into an array of structures where each individual structure consists of an integer day, month, and year member.

12.4 Unions[3]

A **union** is a data type that reserves the same area in memory for two or more variables, each of which can be a different data type. A variable that is declared as a union data type can be used to hold a character variable, an integer variable, a double-precision variable, or any other valid C data type. Each of these types, but only one at a time, can actually be assigned to the union variable.

The declaration for a union is identical in form to a structure declaration, with the reserved word `union` used in place of the reserved word `struct`. For example, the declaration

```
union
{
  char key;
  int num;
  double price;
} val;
```

creates a union variable named `val`. If `val` were a structure, it would consist of three individual members. As a union, however, `val` contains a single member that can be either a character variable named `key`, an integer variable named `num`, or a double-precision variable named `price`. In effect, a union reserves sufficient memory locations to accommodate its largest member's data type. This same set of locations is then accessed by different variable names depending on the data type of the value currently residing in the reserved locations. Each value stored overwrites the previous value, using as many bytes of the reserved memory area as necessary.

---

[3]This topic may be omitted without loss of subject continuity.

Individual union members are accessed using the same notation as structure members. For example, if the val union is currently used to store a character, the correct variable name to access the stored character is val.key. Similarly, if the union is used to store an integer, the value is accessed by the name val.num, and a double-precision value is accessed by the name val.price. With union members, it is the programmer's responsibility to ensure that the correct member name is used for the data type currently residing in the union.

Typically, a second variable keeps track of the current data type stored in the union. For example, the following code could be used to select the appropriate member of val for display. Here, the value in the variable uType determines the currently stored data type in the val union.

```
switch(uType)
{
  case 'c': printf("%c", val.key);
            break;
  case 'i': printf("%d", val.num);
            break;
  case 'd': printf("%f", val.price);
            break;
   default : printf("Invalid type in uType : %c", uType);
}
```

Because they are in structures, a type name can be associated with a union to create templates. For example, the declaration

```
union DateTime
{
  long days;
  double time;
};
```

provides a union type without actually reserving any storage locations. The type name can then be used to define any number of variables. For example, the definition

```
union DateTime first, second, *pt;
```

creates a union variable named first, a union variable named second, and a pointer that can be used to store the address of any union having the form of DateTime. Once a pointer to a union has been declared, the same notation used to access structure members can access union members. For example, if the assignment pt = &first; is made, then pt->days refers to the days member of the union named first.

Unions may themselves be members of structures and arrays; correspondingly, structures, arrays, and pointers may be members of unions. In each case, the notation used to access a member must be consistent with the nesting employed. For example, in the structure defined by

```
struct
{
  char uType;
  union
  {
    char *text;
    double rate;
  } uTax;
} flag;
```

the variable `rate` is referenced as

```
flag.uTax.rate
```

Similarly, the first character of the string whose address is stored in the pointer `text` is accessed as follows:

```
*flag.uTax.text
```

EXERCISES 12.4

Short Answer Questions

1. Assume that the following definition has been made:

```
union
{
  double rate;
  double taxes;
  int num;
} flag;
```

For this union write appropriate `printf()` function calls to display the various members of the union.

2. Define a union variable named `car` that contains an integer named `year`, an array of 10 characters named `name`, and an array of 10 characters named `model`.

3. Define a union variable named `lang` that allows a double-precision number to be accessed by both the variable names `interest` and `rate`.

4. Declare a union with the type name `amt` that contains an integer variable named `intAmt`, a double-precision variable named `dblAmt`, and a pointer to a character named `ptKey`.

Programming Exercises

1. a. Determine the display produced by the following section of code:

```
union
{
  char ch;
  double btype;
} alt;
alt.ch = 'y';
printf("%f", alt.btype);
```

   b. Include the code presented in Exercise 1a in a program and run the program to verify your answer to Exercise 1a.

12.5 Common Programming and Compiler Errors

In using the material presented in this chapter, be aware of the following possible programming and compiler errors.

Programming Errors

Three common errors are often made when using structures or unions.

1. Attempting to use structures and unions, as complete entities, in relational expressions. For example, even if `TeleType` and `PhoneType` are two structures of the same type, the expression `TeleType == PhoneType` is invalid. Individual members of a structure or union can, of course, be compared using any of C's relational operators.
2. Assigning an incorrect address to a pointer that is a member of a structure or union. Whenever a pointer is a member of a structure or a union, make sure to assign an address to the pointer that "points to" the pointer's declared data type. Should you be confused about just what is being pointed to, remember, "If in doubt print it out."
3. Storing one data type in a union and accessing it by the wrong variable name can result in an error that is particularly troublesome to locate. Because a union can store only one of its members at a time, you must be careful to keep track of the currently stored variable.

Compiler Errors

The following table summarizes common errors that will result in compilation errors and the typical error messages provided by Unix- and Windows-based compilers.

Error	Typical Unix-based Compiler Error Message	Typical Windows-based Compiler Error Message

Using the wrong type of braces when declaring a structure.
For example:
`struct`
`[`
`  int month;`
`  int day;`
`  int year;`
`] birth;`
	The following error will be reported on each line containing a brace:
	`(S) Syntax error.`
		`:error: syntax error : missing ';' before '[' : error: syntax error : missing ']' before ';`

<table>
<tr><th>Error</th><th>Typical Unix-based Compiler Error Message</th><th>Typical Windows-based Compiler Error Message</th></tr>
<tr><td>Attempting to initialize the elements of a structure inside the declaration.
For example:
<code>struct</code>
<code>{</code>
<code> int month = 6;</code>
<code> int day;</code>
<code> int year;</code>
<code>} birth;</code></td><td><code>S) Syntax error: possible missing ';' or ','?</code></td><td><code>:error: 'month' : only const static integral data members can be initialized inside a class or struct</code></td></tr>
<tr><td>Assigning a pointer to a structure rather than the address of the structure.
For example:
<code>int main()</code>
<code>{</code>
<code> struct Date *ptr;</code>
<code> struct Date birth;</code>
<code> ptr = birth;</code>
<code>}</code></td><td><code>(S) Operation between types "struct Date*" and "struct Date" is not allowed.</code></td><td><code>:error: '=' : cannot convert from 'Date' to 'Date *'</code></td></tr>
</table>

12.6 Chapter Summary

1. A structure allows individual variables to be grouped under a common variable name. Each variable in a structure is accessed by its structure name, followed by a period, followed by its individual variable name. Another term for a structure is a record. The general form for declaring a structure is

```
struct
{
  individual member declarations;
} structureVariableName;
```

2. A structure type name can be used to create a generalized structure type describing the form and arrangement of elements in a structure. This declaration has the syntax

```
struct StructureTypeName
{
  individual member declarations;
};
```

   Individual structure variables may then be defined as this `StructureTypeName`. By convention, the first letter of a `StructureTypeName` is always capitalized.

3. Structures are particularly useful as elements of arrays. Used in this manner, each structure becomes one record in a list of records.

4. Individual members of a structure are passed to a function in the manner appropriate to the data type of the member being passed. Most ANSI C compilers allow complete structures to be passed, in which case the called function receives a copy of each element in the structure. The address of a structure may also be passed, which provides the called function with direct access to the structure.

5. Structure members can be any valid C data type, including structures, unions, arrays, and pointers. When a pointer is included as a structure member, a linked list can be created. Such a list uses the pointer in one structure to "point to" (contain the address of) the next logical structure in the list.

6. Unions are declared in the same manner as structures. The definition of a union creates a memory overlay area, with each union member using the same memory storage locations. Thus, only one member of a union may be active at a time.

Chapter 13

Dynamic Data Structures

The scalar, array, and structure variables that we have used so far all have had memory space reserved at compile time. As the compiler determines the correct memory allocation for each variable defined in a program, sufficient storage for the variable (scalar, structure, or array) is assigned from a pool of available computer memory. Once specific memory locations have been reserved, these locations are fixed for the life of that variable, whether they are used or not. For example, if a function requests storage for an array of 500 integers, the storage for the array is allocated and fixed from the point of the array's definition. If the application requires fewer than 500 integers, the unused allocated storage is not released until the array goes out of existence. If, on the other hand, the application requires more than 500 integers, the size of the array must be increased and the function defining the array recompiled.

An alternative to fixed memory allocation is dynamic memory allocation in which memory space grows or diminishes under program control at run time. **Dynamic memory allocation**, which is also known as **run-time allocation,** makes it unnecessary to reserve a fixed amount of memory for a scalar, array, or structure variable in advance. Instead, requests are made for allocation and release of memory space while the program is running. In this chapter we will see how this is accomplished. We will also investigate three types of lists that commonly use dynamic memory allocation in their construction: stacks, queues, and dynamically linked lists. We begin by examining the structure of a statically linked list, which provides the real-world motivation for the majority of dynamic memory allocation applications. A statically linked list is one in which all structures in the list have been allocated at compile time.

13.1 Introduction to Linked Lists

To understand linked lists and their need for dynamic memory allocation, consider the alphabetical list of names and telephone numbers shown in Figure 13.1. Each name and telephone number pair makes up one structure. Assume that we must write code that adds new structures to this list in the proper alphabetical sequence, and deletes existing structures in such a way that the storage spaced originally assigned to deleted structures is freed up for other uses.

Acme, Sam
(555) 898-2392

Dolan, Edith
(555) 682-3104

Lanfrank, John
(555) 718-4581

Mening, Stephanie
(555) 382-7070

Zemann, Harold
(555) 219-9912

Figure 13.1 A telephone list in alphabetical order

Although an array of structures can be used to insert and delete ordered structures, this is not an efficient use of memory. Deleting a structure from the array creates an empty slot in the array. To close this empty slot, you need to include code that either marks the deleted structure as no longer in active use or that shifts up all elements below the deleted structure to close the empty slot. Similarly, adding a structure to the array requires that either all structures below the addition be shifted down to make room for the new entry or that the new structure be added at the bottom of the existing array and then the array be resorted to restore the proper alphabetical order of the names. Thus, either adding or deleting structures to such a list requires restructuring and rewriting the list—a cumbersome, time-consuming, and inefficient practice.

A linked list provides a convenient method for maintaining a constantly changing list without the need to reorder and restructure the complete list continually. A **linked list** is a set of structures in which each structure contains at least one member whose value is the address of the next logically ordered structure in the list. Rather than requiring each structure to be physically stored in the proper order, each new structure is physically added either to the end of the existing list, or wherever the computer has free space in its storage area. The structures are "linked" together by including the address of the next structure in the structure immediately preceding it. From a programming standpoint, the current structure being processed contains the address of the next structure, no matter where the next structure is actually stored. Such structures are also known as **self-referencing structures.**

Figure 13.2 conceptually illustrates how the telephone list from Figure 13.1 could be constructed as a linked list. Although the actual data for the Lanfrank structure illustrated in the figure may be physically stored anywhere in the computer, the address included at the end of the Dolan structure maintains the proper alphabetical order. This address, which is stored in a pointer, provides the starting address of the location where the Lanfrank structure is stored.

To see the usefulness of the pointer in the Dolan structure, let us insert a record for June Hagar into the alphabetical list shown in Figure 13.2. The data for June Hagar is stored in a data structure using the same template as that used for the existing structures. To ensure that the telephone number for Hagar is correctly displayed after the Dolan telephone number, the address in the Dolan structure must be altered to point to the Hagar structure,

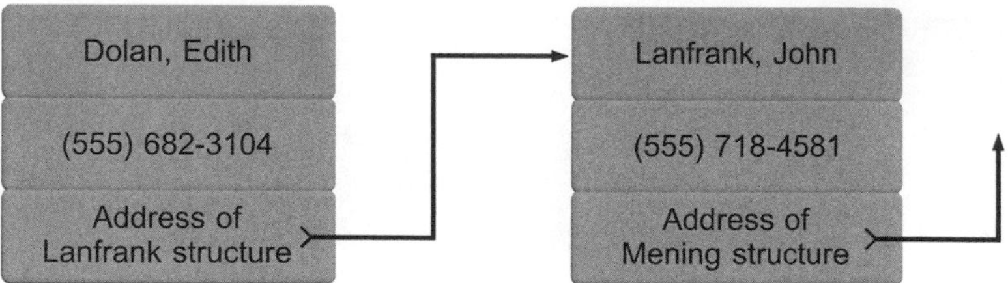

Figure 13.2 Using pointers to link structures

and the address in the Hagar structure must be set to point to the Lanfrank structure. This is illustrated in Figure 13.3.

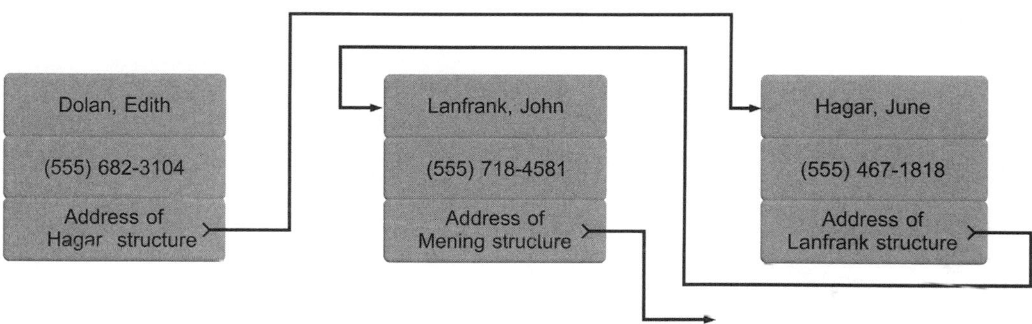

Figure 13.3 Adjusting addresses to point to appropriate structures

Notice that the pointer in each structure simply points to the location of the next ordered structure, even if that structure is not physically located in the correct order. Removal of a structure from the ordered list is the reverse process of adding a structure. The actual structure is logically removed from the list by simply changing the address in the structure preceding it to point to the structure immediately following the deleted structure.

Each structure in a linked list has the same format; however, it is clear that the last structure cannot have a valid pointer value that points to another structure, because there is none. To accommodate this situation, all programming languages that support pointers provide a special pointer value, known as both `NULL` and `NIL`, that acts as a sentinel or flag to indicate when the last structure has been processed. In C, this special pointer value is a `NULL` pointer value that, like its end-of-string counterpart, has a numerical value of 0.

In addition to an end-of-list sentinel value, we must provide a special pointer for storing the address of the first structure in the list. Figure 13.4 illustrates the complete set of pointers and structures for a list consisting of three names.

The need for a pointer in a structure should not surprise you. As we discovered in Section 12.1, a structure can contain any C data type. For example, the structure declaration

```
struct Test
{
  int idNum;
  double *ptPay;
};
```

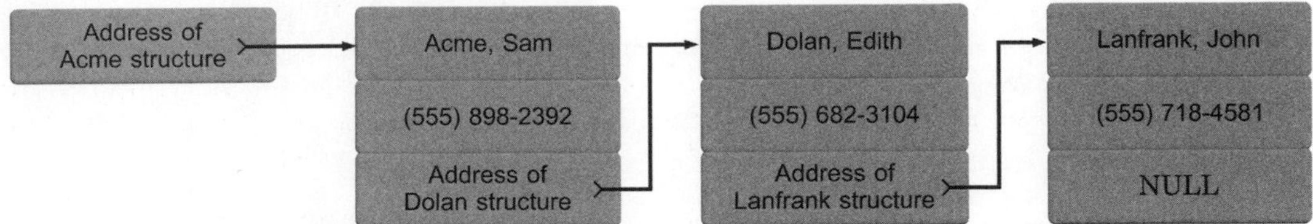

Figure 13.4 Use of the initial and final pointer values

declares a structure template consisting of two members. The first member is an integer variable named `idNum`, and the second variable is a pointer named `ptPay`, which is a pointer to a double-precision number. Program 13.1 illustrates that the pointer member of a structure is used like any other pointer variable.

Program 13.1

```
#include <stdio.h>

struct Test
{
  int idNum;
  double *ptPay;
};

int main()
{
  struct Test emp;
  double pay = 456.20;

  emp.idNum = 12345;
  emp.ptPay = &pay;

  printf("Employee number %d was paid $%6.2f\n", emp.idNum,
                                                  *emp.ptPay);
  return 0;
}
```

The output produced by executing Program 13.1 is

```
Employee number 12345 was paid $456.20
```

Figure 13.5 illustrates the relationship between the members of the `emp` structure defined in Program 13.1 and the variable named `pay`. The value assigned to `emp.idNum` is the number 12345 and the value assigned to `pay` is 456.20. The address of the `pay` variable is assigned to the structure member `emp.ptPay`. Because this member has been defined as a pointer to a double-precision number, placing the address of the double-precision variable `pay` in it is a correct use of this member. Finally, because the dot operator (`.`) has a higher precedence than the indirection operator (`*`) the expression used in the printf call in Program 13.1 is correct. The expression `*emp.ptPay` is equivalent to the expression `*(emp.ptPay)`, which is translated as "the variable whose address is contained in the member `emp.ptPay`.

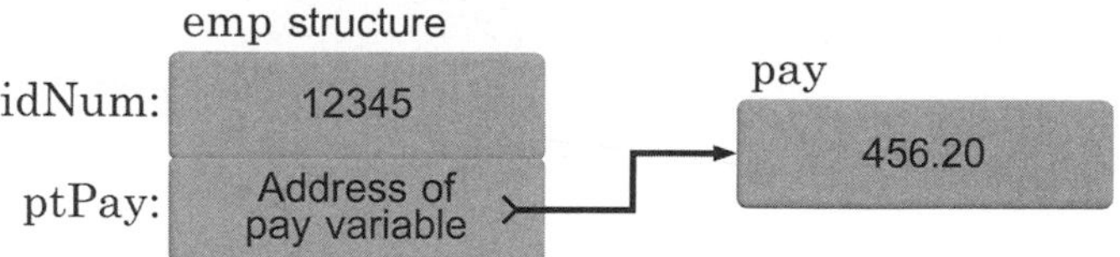

Figure 13.5 Storing an address in a structure member

Although the pointer defined in Program 13.1 has been used in a rather trivial fashion, the program does illustrate the concept of including a pointer in a structure. This concept can be easily extended to create a linked list of structures suitable for storing the names and telephone numbers previously listed in Figure 13.1. The following declaration creates a template for such a structure:

```
struct TeleType
{
  char name[30];
  char phoneNum[15];
  struct TeleType *nextaddr;
};
```

The `TeleType` template consists of three members. The first member is an array of 30 characters, suitable for storing names with a maximum of 29 letters and an end-of-string `NULL` marker. The next member is an array of 15 characters, suitable for storing telephone numbers with their respective area codes. The last member is a pointer suitable for storing the address of a structure of the `TeleType` type.

Program 13.2 illustrates the use of the `TeleType` template by specifically defining three structures having this form. The three structures are named `t1`, `t2`, and `t3`, respectively, and the name and telephone members of each of these structures are initialized when the structures are defined, using the data previously listed in Figure 13.1.

Program 13.2

```
#include <stdio.h>
#define MAXNAME 30
#define MAXPHONE 15

struct TeleType
{
  char name[MAXNAME];
  char phoneNum[MAXPHONE];
  struct TeleType *nextaddr;
```

```
10  };
11
12  int main()
13  {
14    struct TeleType t1 = {"Acme, Sam","(555) 898-2392"};
15    struct TeleType t2 = {"Dolan, Edith","(555) 682-3104"};
16    struct TeleType t3 = {"Lanfrank, John","(555) 718-4581"};
17    struct TeleType *first;    /* create a pointer to a structure */
18
19    first = &t1;               /* store t1's address in first */
20    t1.nextaddr = &t2;         /* store t2's address in t1.nextaddr */
21    t2.nextaddr = &t3;         /* store t3's address in t2.nextaddr */
22    t3.nextaddr = NULL;        /* store the NULL address in t3.nextaddr */
23
24    printf("%s\n%s\n%s\n",first->name,t1.nextaddr->name,t2.nextaddr->name);
25
26    return 0;
27  }
```

The output produced by Program 13.2 is

```
Acme, Sam
Dolan, Edith
Lanfrank, John
```

Program 13.2 demonstrates the use of pointers to create and access a linked list of structure members. As illustrated in Figure 13.6, each structure contains the address of the next structure in the list.

The initialization of the names and telephone numbers for each of the structures defined in Program 13.2 is straightforward. Although each structure consists of three members, only the first two members of each structure are initialized. As both of these members are arrays of characters, they can be initialized with strings. The remaining member of each structure is a pointer. To create a linked list, each structure pointer must be assigned the address of the next structure in the list. The four assignment statements in Program 13.2 in lines 19 through 22 perform the correct assignments.

```
19  first = &t1;             /* store t1's address in first */
20  t1.nextaddr = &t2;       /* store t2's address in t1.nextaddr */
21  t2.nextaddr = &t3;       /* store t3's address in t2.nextaddr */
22  t3.nextaddr = NULL;      /* store the NULL address in t3.nextaddr */
```

The expression `first = &t1`, in line 19, stores the address of the first structure in the list in the pointer variable named `first`. The expression `t1.nextaddr = &t2`, in line 20, stores the starting address of the `t2` structure in the pointer member of the `t1` structure. Similarly, the expression `t2.nextaddr = &t3`, in line 21, stores the starting address of the `t3` structure in the pointer member of the `t2` structure. To end the list, the value of the `NULL` pointer, which is 0, is stored in line 22 in the pointer member of the `t3` structure.

Once values have been assigned to each structure member and correct addresses have been stored in the appropriate pointers, the addresses in the pointers are used to access each structure's name member. For example, the expression `t1.nextaddr->name`, in line 24,

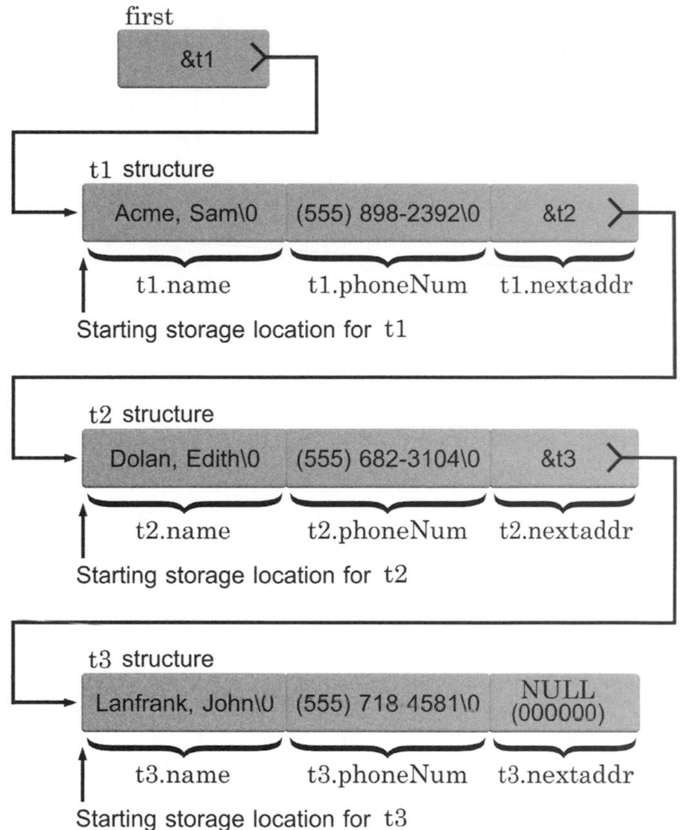

Figure 13.6 The relationship between structures in Program 13.2

refers to the name member of the structure whose address is in the `nextaddr` member of the `t1` structure.

```
printf("%s\n%s\n%s\n", first->name, t1.nextaddr->name,t2.nextaddr->name);
```

The precedence of the member operator, `.`, and the structure pointer operator, `->`, are equal, and are evaluated from left to right. Thus, the expression `t1.nextaddr->name` is evaluated as `(t1.nextaddr)->name`. Because `t1.nextaddr` contains the address of the `t2` structure, the proper name is accessed.

The expression `t1.nextaddr->name` can, of course, be replaced by the equivalent expression `(*t1.nextaddr).name`, which explicitly uses the indirection operator. This expression also refers to "the name member of the variable whose address is in `t1.nextaddr`."

The addresses in a linked list of structures can be used to loop through the complete list. As each structure is accessed, it can be either examined to select a specific value or used to print out a complete list. For example, the `display()` function in Program 13.3 illustrates the use of a `while` loop (lines 32–36), which uses the address in each structure's pointer member to cycle through the list and successively display data stored in each structure.

Program 13.3

```
#include <stdio.h>
#define MAXNAME 30
#define MAXPHONE 15

struct TeleType
{
  char name[MAXNAME];
  char phoneNum[MAXPHONE];
  struct TeleType *nextaddr;
};

int main()
{
  struct TeleType t1 = {"Acme, Sam","(555) 898-2392"};
  struct TeleType t2 = {"Dolan, Edith","(555) 682-3104"};
  struct TeleType t3 = {"Lanfrank, John","(555) 718-4581"};
  struct TeleType *first;   /* create a pointer to a structure */
  void display(struct TeleType *);       /* function prototype */

  first = &t1;         /* store t1's address in first */
  t1.nextaddr = &t2;  /* store t2's address in t1.nextaddr */
  t2.nextaddr = &t3;  /* store t3's address in t2.nextaddr */
  t3.nextaddr = NULL; /* store the NULL address in t3.nextaddr */

  display(first);      /* send the address of the first structure */

  return 0;
}

void display(struct TeleType *contents) /* contents is a pointer */
{                                 /* to a structure of type TeleType */
  while (contents != NULL)  /* display till end of linked list */
  {
    printf("%-30s %-20s\n",contents->name, contents->phoneNum);
    contents = contents->nextaddr;      /* get next address */
  }
}
```

The output produced by Program 13.3 is

```
Acme, Sam                   (555) 898-2392
Dolan, Edith                (555) 682-3104
Lanfrank, John              (555) 718-4581
```

Historical Note

Dr. Lukasiewicz and RPN

Dr. Jan Lukasiewicz, born in 1878, studied and taught mathematics at the University of Lvov in Poland before becoming a respected professor at the University of Warsaw. He received an appointment in 1919 to the post of Minister of Education in Poland and, with Stanislaw Lesniewski, founded the Warsaw School of Logic.

After World War II, Dr. Lukasiewicz and his wife, Regina, found themselves exiled in Belgium. When he was offered a professorship at the Royal Academy in Dublin, they moved to Ireland, where they remained until his death in 1956.

In 1951, Dr. Lukasiewicz developed a new set of postfix algebraic notation, which was critical in the design of early microprocessors in the 1960s and 1970s.

The actual implementation of postfix algebra was done using stack arithmetic, in which data were pushed on a stack and popped off when an operation needed to be performed. Such stack handling instructions require no address operands and made it possible for very small computers to handle large tasks effectively.

Stack arithmetic, which is based on Dr. Lukasiewicz's work, reverses the more commonly known prefix algebra and became known as Reverse Polish Notation (RPN). Early pocket calculators developed by the Hewlett-Packard Corporation were especially notable for their use of RPN and made stack arithmetic the favorite of many scientists and engineers.

Program 13.3 demonstrates the important technique of using the address in one structure to access members of the next structure in the list. When the `display()` function is called, it receives the value stored in the variable named `first`. Because the variable named `first` is a pointer variable, the actual value passed is an address (the address of the `t1` structure). The `display()` function accepts the passed value in the argument named `contents`. To store the passed address correctly, `contents` is declared as a pointer to a structure of the `TeleType` type.

Within `display()`, a `while` loop is used to cycle through the linked structures, starting with the structure whose address is in `contents`. The condition tested in the `while` statement compares the value in `contents`, which is an address, to the `NULL` value. For each valid address the name and phone number members of the addressed structure are displayed. The address in `contents` is then updated with the address in the pointer member of the current structure. The address in `contents` is then retested, and the process continues while the address in `contents` is not equal to the `NULL` value. The `display()` function "knows" nothing about the names of the structures declared in `main()` or even how many structures exist. It simply cycles through the linked list, structure by structure, until it encounters the end-of-list `NULL` address. Because the value of `NULL` is 0, the tested condition can be replaced by the equivalent expression `!contents`.

A disadvantage of Program 13.3 is that exactly three structures are defined in `main()` by name, and storage for them is reserved at compile time. Should a fourth structure be required, the additional structure would have to be declared and the program recompiled. In the next four sections, we show how to combine data structures containing pointer members with dynamic memory allocation to create three different types of dynamically expanding and contracting lists: stacks, queues, and dynamically linked lists.

EXERCISES 13.1

Short-Answer Questions

1. Using the linked list of structures illustrated in Figure 13.6, write the sequence of steps necessary to delete the structure for Edith Dolan from the list.

2. Generalize your answer to Question 1 to describe the sequence of steps necessary to remove the nth structure from a list of linked structures. The *n*th structure is preceded by the (*n*-1)st structure and followed by the (*n*+1)st structure. Make sure to store all pointer values correctly.

Programming Exercises

1. Enter and execute Program 13.1.

2. Enter and execute Program 13.2.

3. Modify Program 13.3 to prompt the user for a name. Have the program search the existing list for the entered name. If the name is in the list, display the corresponding phone number; otherwise display the message: `The name is not in the current phone directory.`

4. Write a program containing a linked list of 10 integer numbers. Have the program display the numbers in the list.

5. a. A doubly linked list is a list in which each structure contains a pointer to both the following and previous structures in the list. Define an appropriate template for a doubly linked list of names and telephone numbers.
   b. Using the template defined in Programming Exercise 5a, modify Program 13.3 to list the names and phone numbers in reverse order.

13.2 Dynamic Memory Allocation

Now that you are familiar with linked lists, you can learn how to dynamically (that is, at run time) allocate space for new structures in a linked list and how to deallocate space for structures that have been deleted from such a list.

C provides the four functions, `malloc()`, `calloc()`, `realloc()`, and `free()`, listed in Table 13.1, to control the dynamic allocation and release of memory space. The function prototypes for these functions are contained in the `stdlib.h` header file.

Table 13.1 Functions to Dynamically Allocate and Deallocate Memory Space

Function Name	Description
`malloc()`	Reserves the number of bytes requested by the argument passed to the function. Returns the address of the first reserved location, as an address of a `void` data type, or `NULL` if sufficient memory is not available.
`calloc()`	Reserves space for an array of n elements of the specified size. Returns the address of the first reserved location and initializes all reserved bytes to 0s, or returns a `NULL` if sufficient memory is not available.
`realloc()`	Changes the size of previously allocated memory to a new size. If the new size is larger than the old size, the additional memory space is uninitialized and the contents of the original allocated memory remain unchanged; otherwise, the new allocated memory remains unchanged up to the limits of the new size.
`free()`	Releases a block of bytes previously reserved. The address of the first reserved location is passed as an argument to the function.

Although, in practice, the `malloc()` and `calloc()` functions can frequently be used interchangeably, we will use the `malloc()` function exclusively because it is the more general purpose of the two functions.[1] In requesting a new allocation of storage space using `malloc()`, the programmer must provide the function with an indication of the amount of storage needed. This may be done by either requesting a specific number of bytes or, more commonly, by requesting enough space for a particular type of data. For example, the function call `malloc(10 * sizeof(char))` requests enough memory to store 10 characters, while the function call `malloc(sizeof(int))` requests enough storage to store one integer number.

In a similar manner and of more usefulness is the dynamic allocation of arrays and structures. For example, the expression

```
malloc(200 * sizeof(int))
```

reserves a sufficient number of bytes to store 200 integers.[2] Although we have used the constant 200 in this example declaration, a variable or symbolic constant is more typically used. The space allocated by `malloc()` comes from the computer's free storage area, which is formally known as the **heap.** The heap consists of unallocated memory that can be allocated to a program, as requested, while the program is executing. All such allocated memory is returned to the heap, either explicitly using the `free()` function or automatically when the program requesting additional memory is finished executing.[3]

In allocating storage dynamically, we have no advance indication as to where the computer system will physically reserve the requested number of bytes, and we have no explicit name to access the newly created storage locations. To provide access to these locations, `malloc()` returns the address of the first location that has been reserved. This address must, of course, be assigned to a pointer. The return of a pointer by `malloc()` is

---

[1]The advantage to the `calloc()` function is that it initializes all newly allocated numeric memory to 0 and character allocated memory to NULL.
[2]The equivalent `calloc()` call is `calloc(200,sizeof(int))`.
[3]In a similar fashion, the compiler automatically provides the same type of dynamic allocation and deallocation of memory for all auto variables and function arguments. In these cases, however, the allocation and deallocation is made from the stack storage area.

especially useful for creating either arrays or a set of data structures. Before illustrating the actual dynamic allocation of both an array and structure, we need to consider one logistical problem created by `malloc()`. The `malloc()` function always returns the address of the first byte of storage reserved, where the returned address is declared as a pointer to a `void`.

Because the returned address is always a pointer to a `void`, regardless of the data type requested, the returned address must always be reinterpreted as pointing to the desired type. To use this address to reference the correct data type, it must be reinterpreted as pointing to the correct type using a cast. For example, if the variable `grades` is to be a pointer to an integer, but has been created by `malloc()` using the statement

```
grades = malloc(sizeof(int));
```

you would first have to redefine grades, which `malloc()` always creates as a pointer to a `void`, as the address of an integer. This is accomplished by the statement

```
(int *)grades;
```

The address in `grades` is not changed physically, but any subsequent reference using the address in `grades` will now cause the correct number of bytes to be accessed for an integer value. For example, consider the following section of code, which can be used to create an array of integers whose size is determined by the user at run time as an input value:

```
int *grades;        /* define a pointer to an integer */

printf("\nEnter the number of grades to be processed: ");
scanf("%d", &numgrades);

 /* here is where the request for memory is made */
grades = (int *) malloc(numgrades * sizeof(int));
```

In this sequence of instructions, the actual size of the array that is created depends on the number input by the user. Since pointer and array names are related, each value in the newly created storage area can be accessed using standard array notation, such as `grades[i]`, rather than the equivalent pointer notation `*(grades + i)`. Program 13.4 illustrates this sequence of code within the context of a complete program.

Program 13.4

```
#include <stdio.h>
#include <stdlib.h>

int main()
{
  int numgrades, i;
  int *grades;

  printf("\nEnter the number of grades to be processed: ");
  scanf("%d", &numgrades);
```

```
11
12     /* here is where the request for memory is made */
13     grades = (int *) malloc(numgrades * sizeof(int));
14
15     /* here we check that the allocation was satisfied */
16     if (grades == (int *) NULL)
17     {
18       printf("\nFailed to allocate grades array\n");
19       exit(1);
20     }
21
22     for(i = 0; i < numgrades; i++)
23     {
24       printf("  Enter a grade: ");
25       scanf("%d", &grades[i]);
26     }
27
28     printf("\nAn array was created for %d integers", numgrades);
29     printf("\nThe values stored in the array are:\n");
30
31     for (i = 0; i < numgrades; i++)
32       printf(" %d\n", grades[i]);
33
34     free(grades);
35
36     return 0;
37   }
```

Following is a sample run using Program 13.4:

```
Enter the number of grades to be processed: 4
  Enter a grade: 85
  Enter a grade: 96
  Enter a grade: 77
  Enter a grade: 92

An array was created for 4 integers
The values stored in the array are:
 85
 96
 77
 92
```

As seen by this output, dynamic storage allocation successfully created storage for four integer values.

Although the call to `malloc()` in Program 13.4 is rather simple, two important concepts related to the call should be noted. First, notice the code in lines 15 to 20 (repeated in the following for convenience), which is made immediately after the call to `malloc()`.

Programming Note

Checking `malloc()`'s Return Value

It is very important to check return values when making `malloc()` and `realloc()` function calls. You need to make sure that your program will terminate gracefully if the operating system cannot satisfy the allocation request. Otherwise, if the memory was not allocated and a subsequent program statement attempts to use the memory, your program will crash. There are two styles of coding that you can use to check the return value and therefore avoid this problem.

The first style is the one coded in Program 13.4, which is repeated below for convenience. Notice that it clearly separates the request for memory from the subsequent check of the returned value.

```
/* here is where the request for memory is made */
grades = (int *) malloc(numgrades * sizeof(int));

/* here we check that the allocation was satisfied */
if (grades == (int *) NULL)
{
  printf("\nFailed to allocate grades array\n");
  exit(1);
}
```

Alternatively, the request and check can be combined together within the `if` statement as

```
if ( (grades = (int *) malloc(numgrades * sizeof(int))) == (int *) NULL)
{
  printf("\nFailed to allocate grades array\n");
  exit(1);
}
```

```
/* here we check that the allocation was satisfied */
if (grades == (int *) NULL)
{
  printf("\nFailed to allocate grades array\n");
  exit(1);
}
```

This section of code tests `malloc()`'s return value to ensure that the memory request was successfully satisfied. If `malloc()` cannot obtain the desired memory space, it returns a `NULL`, which in Program 13.4 would be cast into a pointer to an integer by the statement making the `malloc()` call. Thus, `grades` must subsequently be compared to `(int *) NULL` in the `if` statement. In making requests for dynamic memory allocation, it is extremely important to always check the return value; otherwise, the program will crash when a subsequent access to nonexistent memory is made.

Next, notice that Program 13.4 uses the `free()` function in line 34 to restore the allocated block of storage back to the operating system at the end of the program.[4]

```
34   free(grades);
```

The only address required by `free()` is the starting address of the block of storage that was dynamically allocated. Thus, any address returned by `malloc()` subsequently can be used by `free()` to restore the reserved memory back to the computer. The `free()` function does not alter the address passed to it, but simply makes the previously allocated storage available for future memory allocation calls.

In addition to requesting data space for arrays, as is done in Program 13.4, `malloc()` is more typically used for dynamically allocating memory for structures. For example, consider that we have declared a data structure named `OfficeInfo` as

```
struct OfficeInfo
{
  any number of data members declared in here;
};
```

Regardless of the number and type of data members declared in `OfficeInfo`, the call `malloc(sizeof(struct OfficeInfo))` requests enough storage for one structure of the `OfficeInfo` type. To use the return pointer value provided by `malloc()` once again requires us to cast the return address into a pointer of the correct structure type. Typically this is done using a sequence of statements similar to the following:[5]

```
struct OfficeInfo *Off;  /* create a pointer to store the allocated address */

/*  request space for one structure */
Off = (struct OfficeInfo *) malloc(sizeof(struct OfficeInfo));

/* check that space was allocated */
if (Off == (struct OfficeInfo*) NULL)
{
  printf("\nAllocation of office info structure failed\n");
  exit(1);
}
```

This type of dynamic allocation is extremely useful in a variety of advanced programming situations. One of these is in the construction and maintenance of software stacks, queues, and dynamically linked lists. All of these applications are specific cases of linked lists that require each data structure in the list to contain at least one pointer to a data member and are the topics of the next three sections.

---

[4]The allocated storage would automatically be returned to the heap when the program has completed execution. It is, however, good practice to restore explicitly the allocated storage back to the heap using `free()` when the memory is no longer needed. This is especially true for larger, longer-running programs that make numerous requests for additional storage areas.

[5]Again, for clarity, we have separated the request for memory allocation from the verification that the request was successfully satisfied. These, however, can be combined as

```
if ((Off = (struct OfficeInfo *) malloc(sizeof(struct OfficeInfo))) == (struct OfficeInfo) *NULL)
{
  printf("\nAllocation of office info structure failed\n");
  exit(1);
}
```

EXERCISES 13.2

Short Answer Questions

1. Describe what the `malloc()`, `calloc()`, `realloc()`, and `free()` functions do?
2. Why do you think that the `malloc()` function returns an address? What does this address represent? Why is a cast typically used on the returned address?
3. Write `malloc()` function calls to do the following:
   a. Reserve space for an integer variable
   b. Reserve space for an array of 50 integer variables
   c. Reserve space for a floating-point variable
   d. Reserve space for an array of 100 floating-point variables
   e. Reserve space for a structure of type `NameRec`
   f. Reserve space for an array of 150 structures of type `NameRec`
4. Write `calloc()` function calls for Questions 3b, 3d, and 3f.

Programming Exercises

1. Enter and execute Program 13.4.

13.3 Stacks

A stack is a special type of linked list in which objects can only be added to and removed from the top of the list. As such, it is a `last-in, first-out` (LIFO) list; that is, a list in which the last item added to the list is the first item that can be removed. An example of this type of operation is a stack of dishes in a cafeteria, where the last dish placed on top of the stack is the first dish removed. Another example is the "in basket" on a desk, where the last paper placed in the basket is typically the first one removed. In computer programming, stacks are used in all function calls to store and retrieve data input to and retrieved from the function, respectively.

As a specific stack example, consider Figure 13.7, which illustrates an existing list of three last names. As shown, the top name on this list is Barney.

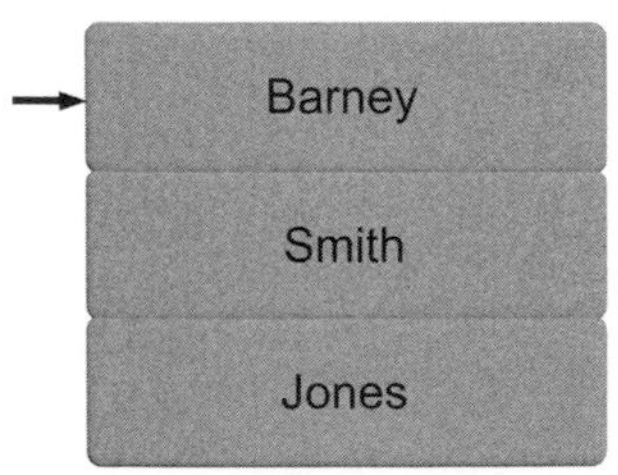

Figure 13.7 A list of last names

If we now restrict access to the list so that names can only be added and removed from the top of the list, then the list becomes a stack. This requires that we clearly designate which end of the list is the top and which is the bottom. Since the name Barney is physically placed above the other names in Figure 13.7, by implication, this is considered the top of the list. To signify this explicitly, however, we have used an arrow to clearly indicate the list's top.

Figure 13.8 (which consists of six parts, labeled a through f) illustrates how the stack expands and contracts as names are added and deleted. For example, in part b, the name Ventura has been added to the list. By part c, a total of two new names have been added and the top of the list has changed accordingly. By removing the top name,

Lanfrank, from the list in part c, the stack shrinks to that shown in part d, where Ventura now resides at the top of the stack. As names continue to be removed from the list (parts e and f), the stack continues to contract.

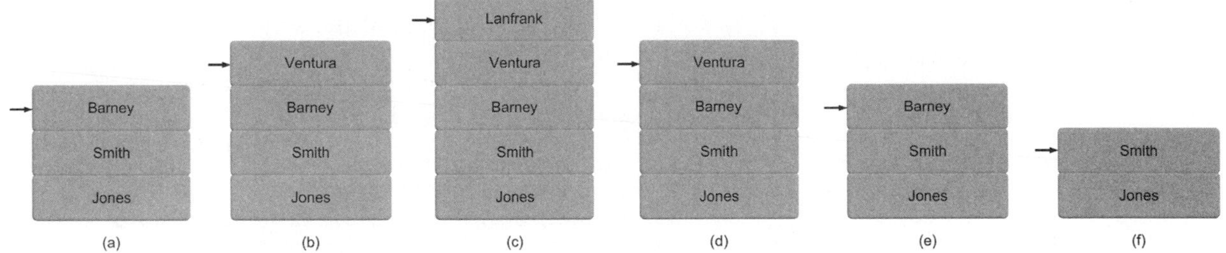

Figure 13.8 An expanding and contracting stack of names

Although Figure 13.8 is an accurate representation of a list of names, it contains additional information that is not provided by a true stack object. When adding names to a stack or removing them, no count is kept of how many names have been added or deleted, or of how many items the stack actually contains at any one time.

For example, in examining each part of Figure 13.8, you can determine how many names are on the list. In a true stack, the only item that can be seen and accessed is the top item on the list. To find out how many items the list contains would require continual removal of the top item until no more items exist.

Stack Implementation

Creating a stack requires the following four components:

- A structure definition
- A method of designating the current top stack structure
- An operation for placing a new structure on the stack
- An operation for removing a structure from the stack

PUSH and POP

The operation of placing a new structure on the top of a stack is called a PUSH and removing a structure from a stack is called a POP. Let's see how these operations are implemented in practice.

> **Historical Note**
>
> **Stacking the Deque**
>
> Stacks and queues are two special forms of a more general data object called a deque (pronounced "deck"). The term "deque" stands for "double-ended queue."
>
> In a deque object, data can be handled in one of four ways:
>
> 1. Insert at the beginning and remove from the beginning. This is the last-in, first-out (LIFO) stack.
> 2. Insert at the beginning and remove from the end. This is the first-in, first-out (FIFO) queue.
> 3. Insert at the end and remove from the end, which represents an inverted LIFO technique.
> 4. Insert at the end and remove from the beginning, which represents an inverted FIFO queue.
>
> Implementation 1 (stack object) is presented in this section and implementation 2 (queue object) is presented in the next section. Implementations 3 and 4 are sometimes used for keeping track of memory addresses, such as when programming is done in machine language or when objects are handled in a file. When a high-level language, such as C, manages the data area automatically, users may not be aware of where the data are being stored or of which type of deque is being applied.

Figure 13.9 illustrates a stack consisting of three structures. As shown, each structure consists of a name member and a pointer member containing the address of the previous structure stored on the stack. In addition, there is a separate stack pointer, which we will call the top-of-stack pointer (`tosp`), that contains the address of the last structure added to the stack.

PUSHing a new structure on a stack, such as that shown in Figure 13.9, involves the following algorithm:

PUSH (add a new structure to the stack)
  Dynamically create a new structure
  Put the address in the top-of-stack pointer into
    the address field of the new structure
  Fill in the remaining fields of the new structure
  Put the address of the new structure into the top-of-stack pointer

For example, if we were to PUSH a new structure onto the stack illustrated in Figure 13.9, the resulting stack would appear as shown in Figure 13.10.

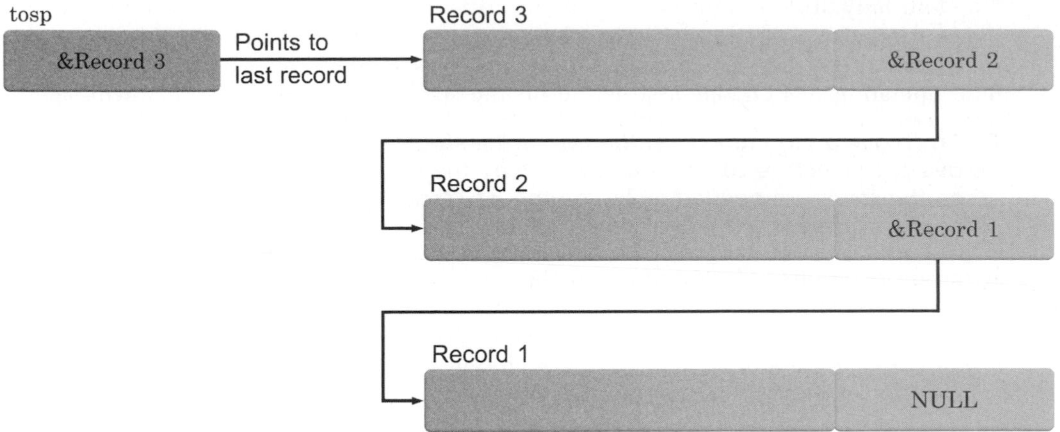

Figure 13.9 A stack consisting of three structures

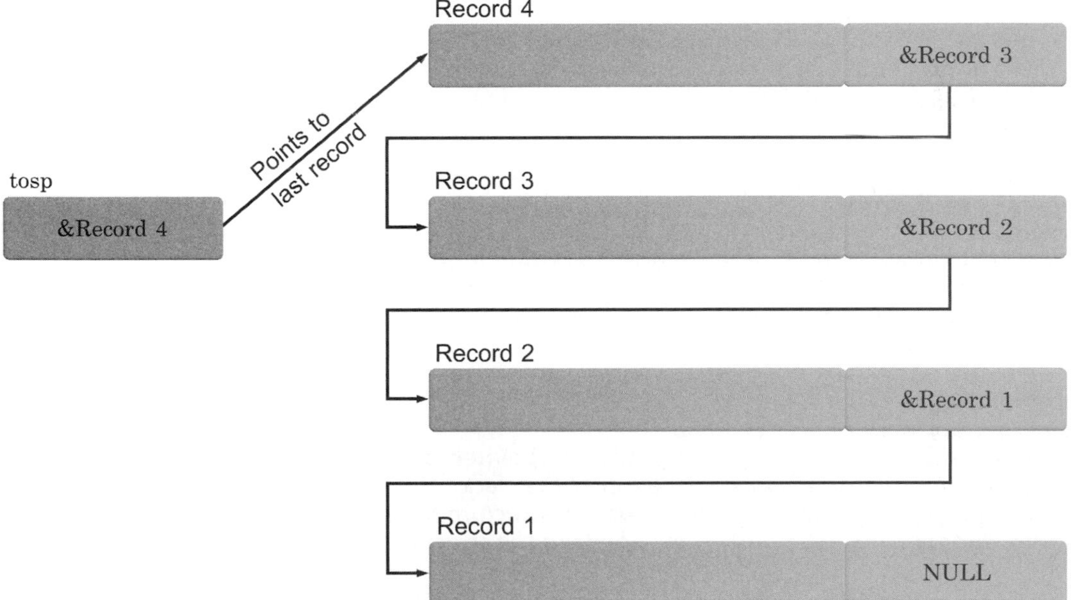

Figure 13.10 The stack after a PUSH

The only structure that can be removed from a stack is always the topmost structure. Thus, for the stack shown in Figure 13.10, the next structure that can be removed is structure four. After this structure is removed ("POPped"), structure three can be removed, and so on. The operation of POPping a structure off the stack is defined by the following algorithm:

POP (remove a structure from the top of the stack)
Move the structure contents pointed to by the top-of-stack pointer into a work area
Free the structure pointed to by the top-of-stack pointer
Move the address in the work area address field into the top-of-stack pointer

If these operations are carried out on the stack illustrated in Figure 13.10, the stack would revert to that shown in Figure 13.9.

As a specific demonstration of a dynamically allocated stack, assume that the structure type of data to be stored on the stack is declared as

```
#define MAXCHARS 30
struct NameRec
{
  char name[MAXCHARS];
  struct NameRec *priorAddr;
};
```

This is simply a structure consisting of a name and a pointer member of the type illustrated in Figures 13.9 and 13.10. The PUSH and POP stack operations for this particular structure type can now be described[6] as follows:

Function PUSH(a name)
Allocate a new structure space
Assign a value to the name field
Assign the address value from the top-of-stack-pointer to the pointer field
(thus, each structure contains a pointer that points to the previous structure location)
Assign the address of the new structure space to top-of-stack-pointer

Function POP(a name)
If top-of-stack-pointer is not a `NULL`
Assign field values referenced by top-of-stack-pointer to a temporary structure
Deallocate the structure space on the top of the stack
Assign the pointer member of the temporary structure to the top-of-stack-pointer
(thus, the top-of-stack-pointer now points to the structure preceding the structure just popped)

The two functions, `push()` and `pop()`, described by this pseudocode are included within Program 13.5. Within this program, the top-of-stack pointer is named `tosp`.

[6]A function named `isempty()`, which returns a 1 if the stack is empty and a 0 if the stack in not empty is also typically defined. This function is then used to determine when POPs should terminate.

Program 13.5

```
#include <stdio.h>
#include <stdlib.h>
#include <string.h>
#define MAXCHARS 30
#define DEBUG 0

/* here is the declaration of a stack structure */
struct NameRec
{
  char name[MAXCHARS];
  struct NameRec *priorAddr;
};

/* here is the definition of the top-of-stack pointer */
struct NameRec *tosp;

int main()
{
  void readPush();  /* function prototypes */
  void popShow();

  tosp = NULL;     /* initialize the top-of-stack pointer */
  readPush();
  popShow();

  return 0;
}

/* get a name and push it onto the stack */
void readPush()
{
  char name[MAXCHARS];
  void push(char *);

  printf("Enter as many names as you wish, one per line");
  printf("\nTo stop entering names, enter a single x\n");
  while (1)
  {
    printf("Enter a name: ");
    gets(name);
    if (strcmp(name,"x") == 0)
      break;
    push(name);
```

```
  }
}

/* pop and display names from the stack */
void popShow()
{
  char name[MAXCHARS];
  void pop(char *);

  printf("\nThe names popped from the stack are:\n");
  while (tosp != NULL)  /* display till end of stack */
  {
    pop(name);
    printf("%s\n",name);
  }
}

void push(char *name)
{
  struct NameRec *newaddr;  /* pointer to structure of type NameRec */

  if (DEBUG)
    printf("Before the push the address in tosp is %p", tosp);

  newaddr = (struct NameRec *) malloc(sizeof(struct NameRec));
  if (newaddr == (struct NameRec *) NULL)
  {
    printf("\nFailed to allocate memory for this structure\n");
    exit(1);
  }
  strcpy(newaddr->name,name);  /* store the name */
  newaddr->priorAddr = tosp;   /* store address of prior structure */
  tosp = newaddr;              /* update the top-of-stack pointer */

  if (DEBUG)
    printf("\n  After the push the address in tosp is %p\n", tosp);
}

void pop(char *name)
{
  struct NameRec *tempAddr;

  if (DEBUG)
    printf("Before the pop the address in tosp is %p\n", tosp);

```

```
    strcpy(name,tosp->name);  /* retrieve the name from the top-of-stack */
    tempAddr = tosp->priorAddr;  /* retrieve the prior address */
    free(tosp);                  /* release the structure's memory space */
    tosp = tempAddr;             /* update the top-of-stack pointer */

    if (DEBUG)
      printf("  After the pop the address in tosp is %p\n", tosp);
  }
```

In general, Program 13.5 is straightforward. The function `readPush()` allows the user to enter names and PUSHes the names on the stack by calling `push()`. Similarly, the function `popShow()` POPs the names from the stack by calling `pop()` and then displays the names. Notice that the address of a name is used as an argument in both `push()` and `pop()`. A sample run using Program 13.5 produced the following:

```
Enter as many names as you wish, one per line
To stop entering names, enter a single x
Enter a name: Jane Jones
Enter a name: Bill Smith
Enter a name: Jim Robinson
Enter a name: x

The names popped from the stack are:
Jim Robinson
Bill Smith
Jane Jones
```

EXERCISES 13.3

Short Answer Questions

1. **a.** Describe the steps necessary to perform a PUSH operation on a stack.
   b. Describe the steps necessary to perform a POP operation on a stack.
   c. What value should the top-of-stack pointer contain when the stack is empty?

2. Assume that the first structure allocated by Program 13.5 is allocated at memory location 100, the second at memory location 150, and the third at memory location 200. Using this information, construct a figure similar to Figure 13.9 showing the values in the `tosp` pointer and each structure after the third name has been pushed onto the stack.

3. State whether a stack structure would be appropriate for each of the following tasks. Indicate why or why not.
   a. A word processor must remember a line of up to 80 characters. Pressing the Backspace key deletes the previous character, and pressing Ctrl/Backspace deletes the entire line. Users must be able to undo deletion operations.
   b. Customers must wait one to three months for delivery of their new automobiles. The dealer creates a list that will determine the "fair" order in which customers should get their cars; the list is to be prepared in the order in which customers placed their requests for a new car.
   c. You are required to search downward in a pile of magazines to locate the issue for last January. Each magazine was placed on the pile as soon as it was received.
   d. A programming team accepts jobs and prioritizes them on the basis of urgency.
   e. Passengers form a line at a bus stop.

Programming Exercises

1. Modify Program 13.5 so that the arguments transmitted to both `push()` and `pop()` are a structure name rather than a single field variable name.

2. Write a stack program that accepts a structure consisting of an integer identification number and a floating-point hourly pay rate.

3. Add a menu function to Program 13.5 that gives the user a choice of adding a name to the stack, removing a name from the stack, or listing the contents of the stack without removing any structures from it.

13.4 Queues

A second important data structure that relies on linked structures is called a **queue** (pronounced "cue"). Items are removed from a queue in the order in which they were entered. Thus, a queue is a first in, first out (FIFO) structure.

As an example of a queue, consider a waiting list of people who want to purchase season tickets to a professional football team. The first person on the list is to be called for the first set of tickets that becomes available, the second person should be called for the second available set, and so on. For purposes of illustration assume that the names of the people currently on the list are shown in Figure 13.11.

```
Harriet Wright  <---  last name on the queue (queueIn)
Jim Robinson
Bill Smith
Jane Jones      <---  first name on the queue (queueOut)
```

Figure 13.11 A queue with its pointers

As illustrated on Figure 13.11, the names have been added in the same fashion as on a stack; that is, as new names are added to the list, they have been stacked on top of the existing names. The difference between a stack and a queue is in how the names are popped off the list. Clearly the people on this list expect to be serviced in the order that they were placed on the list—that is first in, first out. Thus, unlike a stack, the most recently added name to the list *is not* the first name removed. Rather, the oldest name on the list is always the next name removed.

To keep the list in proper order, where new names are added to one end of the list and old names are removed from the other end, it is convenient to use two pointers: one that points to the front of the list for the next person to be serviced, and one that points to the end of the list where new people will be added. The pointer that points to the front of the list where the next name is to be removed will be referred to as the `queueOut` pointer. The second pointer, which points to the last person in line and indicates where the next person entering the list is to be placed, will be called the `queueIn` pointer. Thus, for the list shown in Figure 13.11, `queueOut` points to Jane Jones and `queueIn` to Harriet Wright. If Jane Jones were now removed from the list and Lou Hazlet and Teresa Filer were added, the queue and its associated pointers would appear as in Figure 13.12.

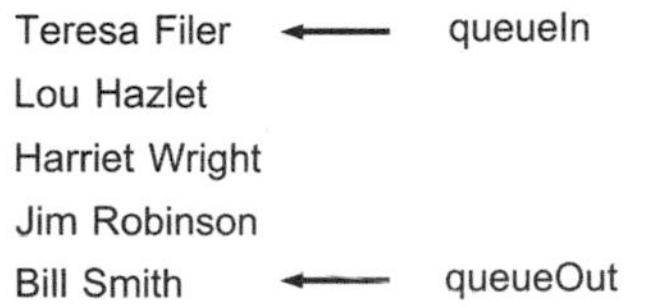

Figure 13.12 The updated queue pointers

Enque and Serve

Placing a new item on top of the queue is formally referred to as **enqueueing** and the operation of removing an item from a queue is formally referred to as **serving**. Except for the pointers involved, enqueueing on a queue is similar to pushing on one end of a stack. Serving from a queue is similar to popping from the other end of a stack. Let's see how these operations are implemented for a queue.

Figure 13.13 illustrates a queue consisting of three structures. As shown, each structure consists of a name member and a pointer member. Unlike a stack, where the pointer member points to the previous structure in the list, in a queue each pointer member points to the next list structure. In addition, there are two separate queue pointers, the `queueIn` pointer, which contains the address of the last structure added to the queue, and the `queueOut` pointer, which contains the address of the first structure stored on the queue.

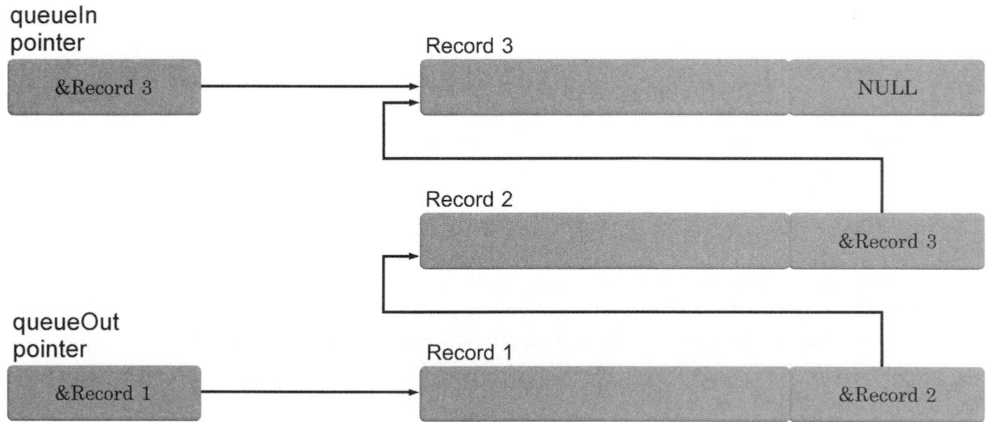

Figure 13.13 A queue consisting of three structures

Enqueueing (PUSHing) a new structure onto an existing queue, such as the queue shown in Figure 13.13, involves the following algorithm:

Enqueue (add a new structure to an existing queue)
Dynamically create a new a structure
Set the address field of the new structure to a `NULL`
Fill in the remaining fields of the new structure
Set the address field of the prior structure (which is pointed to by the `queueIn` pointer) to the address of the newly created structure
Update the address in the `queueIn` pointer with the address of the newly created structure

For example, if we were to add a new structure onto the queue illustrated in Figure 13.13, the resulting queue would appear as shown in Figure 13.14.

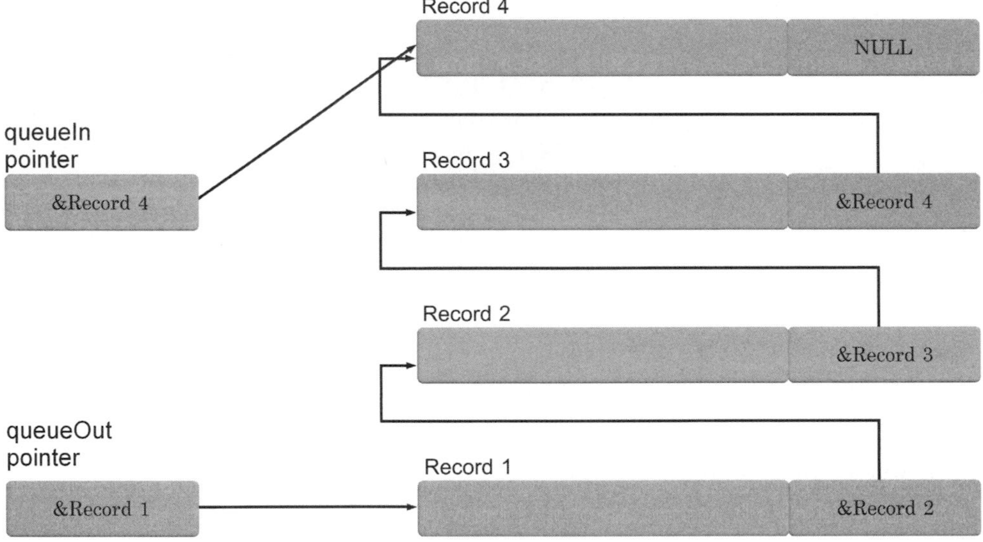

Figure 13.14 The queue after an enqueue (PUSH)

The only structure that can be removed from a queue is always the earliest structure placed on the queue. Thus, for the queue shown in Figure 13.14, the next structure that can be removed is Record 1. After this structure is removed (served), structure two can be removed, and so on. The operation of serving (POPping) a structure from an existing queue is defined by the algorithm:

Serve (remove a structure from an existing queue)
Move the contents of the structure pointed to by the `queueOut` pointer into a work area
Free the structure pointed to by the `queueOut` pointer
Move the address in the work area address field into the `queueOut` pointer

If these operations are carried out on the queue illustrated in Figure 13.14, the queue would consist of the structures and pointers shown in Figure 13.15.

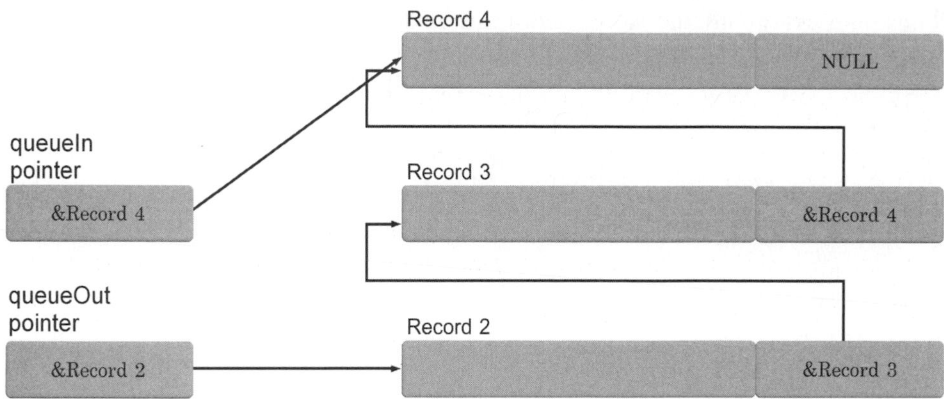

Figure 13.15 The queue after a serve (POP)

As a specific demonstration of a dynamically allocated queue, assume that the structure type of data to be stored on the queue is declared as

```
#define MAXCHARS 30
struct NameRec
{
  char name[MAXCHARS];
  struct NameRec *nextAddr;
};
```

This is simply a structure consisting of a name and a pointer member of the type illustrated in Figures 13.13 through 13.15. The enqueue and serve queue operations for this particular structure type can now be described.

```
Enqueue (a name)
  Dynamically create a new a structure
  Set the address field of the new structure to a NULL
  Assign a value to the name field
  If this is the first structure pushed onto the queue (that is, queueOut contains a NULL)
       Update the address in the queueOut pointer with the address of the newly created structure
  If the queue is not empty (that is, queueIn does not contain a NULL)
       Set the address field of the prior structure (which is pointed to by the queueIn pointer) to the
       address of the newly created structure (thus, each structure contains a pointer that points to the next
       structure in the queue)
  Update the address in the queueIn pointer with the address of the newly created structure
```

```
Serve (a name)
  If queueOut is not a NULL
    Move the contents of the structure pointed to by the queueOut pointer into a work area
    Free the structure pointed to by the queueOut pointer
    Move the address in the work area address field into the queueOut pointer
```

These are essentially the same algorithms as described previously, with the addition of the proper procedure to account for the special case where the queue is empty.[7] For this case, both `queueIn` and `queueOut` pointers will contain `NULL`s. The two functions, `enque()` and `serve()`, described by this pseudocode are included within Program 13.6.

Program 13.6

```
#include <stdio.h>
#include <stdlib.h>
#include <string.h>
#define MAXCHARS 30
#define DEBUG 0

/* here is the declaration of a queue structure */
struct NameRec
{
  char name[MAXCHARS];
  struct NameRec *nextAddr;
};

/* here is the definition of the top and bottom queue pointers */
struct NameRec *queueIn, *queueOut;

int main()
{
  void readEnque();  /* function prototypes */
  void serveShow();
  queueIn = NULL;      /* initialize queue pointers */
  queueOut = NULL;
  readEnque();
  serveShow();
}
/* get a name and enque it onto the queue */
void readEnque()
{
  char name[MAXCHARS];
  void enque(char *);

  printf("Enter as many names as you wish, one per line");
  printf("\nTo stop entering names, enter a single x\n");
  while (1)
```

[7]In practice the functions `isempty()` and `isfull()` also would be defined to simplify the code for servicing and enqueueing, respectively.

```
  {
    printf("Enter a name: ");
    gets(name);
    if (strcmp(name,"x") == 0)
      break;
    enque(name);
  }
}
/* serve and display names from the queue */
void serveShow()
{
  char name[MAXCHARS];
  void serve(char *);

  printf("\nThe names served from the queue are:\n");
  while (queueOut != NULL)  /* display till end of queue */
  {
    serve(name);
    printf("%s\n",name);
  }
}

void enque(char *name)
{
  struct NameRec *newaddr;  /* pointer to structure of type NameRec */

  if (DEBUG)
  {
    printf("Before the enque the address in queueIn is %p", queueIn);
    printf("\nand the address in queueOut is %p", queueOut);
  }

  newaddr = (struct NameRec *) malloc(sizeof(struct NameRec));
  if (newaddr == (struct NameRec *) NULL)
  {
    printf("\nFailed to allocate memory for this structure\n");
    exit(1);
  }

  /* the next two if statements handle the empty queue initialization */
  if (queueOut == NULL)
    queueOut = newaddr;
  if (queueIn != NULL)
    queueIn->nextAddr = newaddr; /* fill in prior structure's address field */
```

```
  strcpy(newaddr->name,name);   /* store the name */
  newaddr->nextAddr = NULL;    /* set address field to NULL */
  queueIn = newaddr;           /* update the top-of-queue pointer */

  if (DEBUG)
  {
    printf("\n  After the enque the address in queueIn is %p\n", queueIn);
    printf("  and the address in queueOut is %p\n", queueOut);
  }
}

void serve(char *name)
{
  struct NameRec *nextAddr;

  if (DEBUG)
    printf("Before the serve the address in queueOut is %p\n", queueOut);

  /* retrieve the name from the bottom-of-queue */
  strcpy(name,queueOut->name);

  /* capture the next address field */
  nextAddr = queueOut->nextAddr;

  free(queueOut);

  /* update the bottom-of-queue pointer */
  queueOut = nextAddr;
  if (DEBUG)
    printf("  After the serve the address in queueOut is %u\n",
                                                          queueOut);
}
```

In general, Program 13.6 is straightforward: the function `readEnque()` allows the user to enter names and pushes the names on the queue by calling `enque()`. Similarly, the function `serveShow()` pops the names from the queue by calling `serve()` and then displays them. Notice that the address of a name is used as an argument in both `enque()` and `serve()`. This was done for convenience and to keep the example simple. More generally, the name of a structure containing the data to be pushed onto the queue would be passed to `enque()` and the name of the structure that will contain the data popped from the queue would be passed to `serve()`. A sample run using Program 13.6 produced the following:

```
Enter as many names as you wish, one per line
To stop entering names, enter a single x
```

```
Enter a name: Jane Jones
Enter a name: Bill Smith
Enter a name: Jim Robinson
Enter a name: x

The names served from the queue are:
Jane Jones
Bill Smith
Jim Robinson
```

EXERCISES 13.4

Short Answer Questions

1. a. Describe the steps necessary to add a structure to an existing queue.
   b. Describe the steps necessary to remove a structure from an existing queue.
   c. What value should the `queueIn` and `queueOut` pointers contain when a queue is empty?

2. Assume that the first structure allocated by Program 13.6 is allocated at memory location 100, the second at memory location 150, and the third at memory location 200. Using this information, construct a figure similar to Figure 13.13 showing the values in the queue pointers and each structure after the third name has been pushed onto the queue.

3. State whether a queue, a stack, or neither structure would be appropriate for each of the following tasks. Indicate why or why not.
   a. A waiting list of customers to be seated in a restaurant
   b. A group of student tests waiting to be graded
   c. An address book listing names and telephone numbers in alphabetical order
   d. Patients waiting for service in a doctor's office

Programming Exercises

1. Modify Program 13.6 so that the arguments to both `enque()` and `serve()` are a structure name rather than a single field variable.

2. Write a queue program that accepts a structure consisting of an integer identification number and a floating-point hourly pay rate.

3. Add a menu function to Program 13.6 that gives the user a choice of adding a name to the queue, removing a name from the queue, or listing the contents of the queue without removing any structures from it.

13.5 Dynamically Linked Lists

Both stacks and queues are examples of linked lists in which elements can only be added to and removed from the ends of the list. In a dynamically linked list, this capability is extended to permit adding or deleting a structure from anywhere within the list. Such a capability is extremely useful when structures must be kept within a specified order, such as alphabetically, and the list must expand as new structures are added and contracted as structures are removed from the list.

In Section 13.1 we saw how to construct a fixed set of linked lists. In this section we show how to dynamically allocate and free structures from such a list. For example, in constructing a list of names, the exact number of structures ultimately needed may not be known in advance. Nevertheless, we may want to maintain the list in alphabetical order by last name regardless of how many names are added or removed from the list. A dynamically allocated list that can expand and contract is ideally suited for this type of list maintenance.

INSERT and DELETE

The operation of adding a new structure to a dynamically linked list is called an INSERT and removing a structure from such a list is called a DELETE. Let's see how these operations are implemented in practice.

Figure 13.16 illustrates a linked list consisting of three structures. As shown, each structure consists of a name member and a pointer member containing the address of the next structure in the list. Several observations about this list apply to all dynamically maintained linked lists.

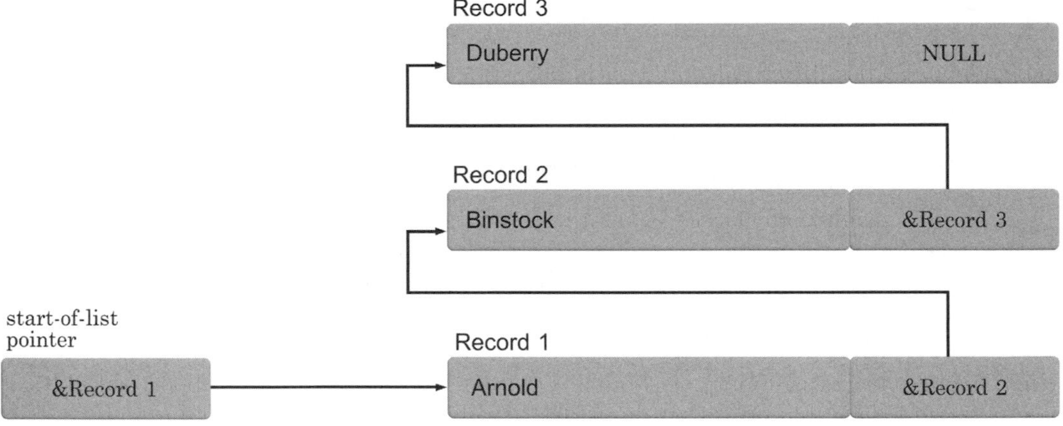

Figure 13.16 The initial linked list

First, notice that each structure shown in Figure 13.16 contains one pointer member, which is the address of the next structure in the list. Also notice that the list one pointer contains the address of the first structure in the list and that the pointer member of the last structure is a NULL address. This configuration is required of all dynamically linked lists regardless of any other data members present in each structure.

Next, notice that the structures illustrated in Figure 13.16 are in alphabetical order. In general, every dynamically linked list is maintained based on the value of a particular field in each structure. The field on which the list is ordered is referred to as the **key field**, and insertions and deletions are always made to preserve the ordering of this field.

Now assume that we want to insert the name Carter into the list. After dynamically allocating new memory space for the Carter structure, the structure addresses would have to be adjusted as shown in Figure 13.17 to maintain the proper alphabetical ordering.

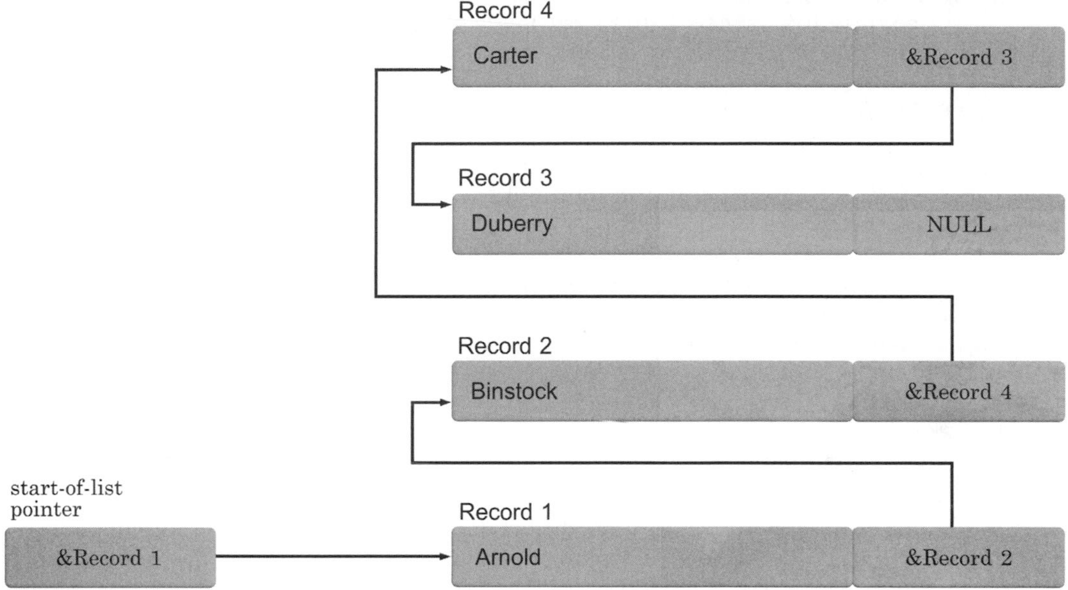

Figure 13.17 Adding a new name to the list

The algorithm for performing an insertion into a linked list is as follows:

```
INSERT (add a new structure into a linked list)
  Dynamically allocate space for a new structure
  If no structures exist in the list
    Set the address field of the new structure to a NULL
    Set the address in the first structure pointer to the address of the newly created structure
  Else /* we are working with an existing list */
    Locate where this new structure should be placed
    If this structure should be the new first structure in the list
      Copy the current contents of the first structure pointer into
        the address field of the newly created structure
     Set the address in the first structure pointer to the address of the newly created structure
    Else
      Copy the address in the prior structure's address member into the address field of the  newly created
       structure
      Set the address field of the prior structure's address member to the address of the newly created structure
    EndIf
 EndIf
```

This algorithm provides the steps for correctly updating the pointer members of each structure in a list such as shown in Figure 13.17, including the first structure pointer when necessary. The algorithm does not, however, indicate how to locate the exact position in the list where the insertion should be made. The location of the insertion point can be made by a linear search (see Section 8.8) of the existing list. The pseudocode for a linear search to determine the correct insertion point is

LINEAR LOCATION for INSERTING a NEW STRUCTURE
If the key field of the new structure is less than the first
structure's key field the new structure should be the new first structure
Else
While there are still more structures in the list
Compare the new structure's key value to each structure key
Stop the comparison when the new structure key either falls
between two existing structures or belongs at the end of the existing list
EndWhile
EndIf

As a specific demonstration of insertions into a linked list, assume that the structure type of data stored in the list is declared as

```
#define MAXCHARS 30
struct NameRec
{
  char name[MAXCHARS];
  struct NameRec *nextAddr;
};
```

This is simply a structure consisting of a name and pointer member of the type illustrated in Figures 13.16 and 13.17. The INSERT and LINEAR LOCATION algorithms are included within Program 13.7.

Program 13.7

```
#include <stdio.h>
#include <stdlib.h>
#include <string.h>
#define MAXCHARS 30
#define DEBUG 0

/* here is the declaration of a linked list structure */
struct NameRec
{
  char name[MAXCHARS];
  struct NameRec *nextAddr;
};

/* here is the definition of the first structure pointer */
struct NameRec *firstRec;

```

```
int main()
{
  void readInsert();  /* function prototypes */
  void display();

  firstRec = NULL;      /* initialize list pointer */
  readInsert();
  display();

  return 0;
}

/* get a name and insert it into the linked list */
void readInsert()
{
  char name[MAXCHARS];
  void insert(char *);

  printf("\nEnter as many names as you wish, one per line");
  printf("\nTo stop entering names, enter a single x\n");
  while (1)
  {
    printf("Enter a name: ");
    gets(name);
    if (strcmp(name,"x") == 0)
      break;
    insert(name);
  }
}

void insert(char *name)
{
  struct NameRec *linear Locate(char *);  /* function prototype */
  struct NameRec *newaddr, *here;  /* pointers to structure
                                      of type NameRec */


  newaddr = (struct NameRec *) malloc(sizeof(struct NameRec));
  if (newaddr == (struct NameRec *) NULL)  /* check the address */
  {
    printf("\nCould not allocate the requested space\n");
    exit(1);
  }

  /* locate where the new structure should be placed and */
```

```
  /* update all pointer members */
  if (firstRec == NULL)  /* no list currently exists */
  {
    newaddr->nextAddr = NULL;
    firstRec = newaddr;
  }
  else if (strcmp(name, firstRec->name) < 0) /* a new first structure */
  {
    newaddr->nextAddr = firstRec;
    firstRec = newaddr;
  }
  else  /* structure is not the first structure of the list */
  {
    here = linear Locate(name);
    newaddr->nextAddr = here->nextAddr;
    here->nextAddr = newaddr;
  }

  strcpy(newaddr->name,name);  /* store the name */
}

/* This function locates the address of where a new structure
   should be inserted within an existing list.
   It receives the address of a name and returns the address of a
   structure of type NameRec
*/
struct NameRec *linear Locate(char *name)
{
  struct NameRec *one, *two;
  one = firstRec;
  two = one->nextAddr;

  if (two == NULL)
    return(one);  /* new structure goes after the existing single structure */
  while(1)
  {
    if(strcmp(name,two->name) < 0) /* if it is located within the list */
      break;
    else if(two->nextAddr == NULL)  /* it goes after the last structure */
    {
      one = two;
      break;
    }
    else  /* more structures to search against */
    {
```

```
        one = two;
        two = one->nextAddr;
      }
    }   /* the break takes us here */

    return(one);
  }
  /* display names from the linked list */
  void display()
  {
    struct NameRec *contents;

    contents = firstRec;
    printf("\nThe names currently in the list, in alphabetical");
    printf("\norder, are:\n");
    while (contents != NULL)  /* display till end of list */
    {
      printf("%s\n",contents->name);
      contents = contents->nextAddr;
    }
  }
```

Adequately testing Program 13.7 requires entering names to a new list and then adding names that should be inserted before the first name, after the last name, and between two existing names. The following sample run shows the results of these tests:

```
Enter as many names as you wish, one per line
To stop entering names, enter a single x
Enter a name: Binstock
Enter a name: Arnold
Enter a name: Duberry
Enter a name: Carter
Enter a name: x

The names currently in the list, in alphabetical
order, are:
Arnold
Binstock
Carter
Duberry
```

Notice that the first name entered forces `insert()` to construct the list, while the second name forces `insert()` to place this new name at the beginning of the list. The third name, Duberry, forces `locate()` to correctly determine that this name should be placed at the end of the list, while the last name, Carter, forces `locate()` to correctly position the name between two existing names.

Deleting a structure in a linked list is essentially the reverse process of inserting a structure. That is, a deletion requires determining where the selected structure currently resides; at the beginning, at the end, or within the list; adjusting all pointer values accordingly and then freeing the structure space of the deleted structure. We leave the detailed construction of the deletion algorithm as an exercise (Programming Exercise 1).

Historical Note

Artificial Intelligence

One of the major steps toward creating dynamic machines that "learn" as they work is the development of dynamic data structures.

In 1950, Alan Turing proposed a test in which an expert enters questions at an isolated terminal and then waits for an answer. Presumably, artificial intelligence (AI) is achieved when the expert cannot discern whether the answers returned to the screen have been produced by a human or by a machine. Although there are problems with the Turing test, its concepts have spawned numerous research efforts.

By the mid 1960s, many AI researchers believed the efforts to create "thinking machines" were futile. Today, however, much lively research and development is focused on such topics as dynamic problem solving, computer vision, parallel processing, natural language processing, and speech and pattern recognition; all of which are encompassed within the field of artificial intelligence.

Development of techniques that allow machines to emulate humans have proliferated in recent years with the development of computers that are smaller, faster, more powerful, and less expensive. Most people agree that computers could never replace all human decision making. There is also general agreement that society must remain alert and remain in control of important decisions that require human compassion, ethics, and understanding.

EXERCISES 13.5

Short Answer Questions

1. Draw a diagram that illustrates how the linked list created by Program 13.7 looks as each name is inserted into the list. Make sure to include the first structure pointer in your diagram.

2. Write the pseudocode for deleting an existing structure from the linked list of structures created by Program 13.7. The algorithm for deleting a linked structure should follow the sequence developed for deleting a structure developed in your answer to Short Answer Question 2 in Section 13.1.

Programming Exercises

1. Write a C code for the algorithm developed in Short Answer Question 2.

2. Write a function named `modify()` that can be used to modify the `name` member of the structures created in Program 13.7. The argument passed to modify should be the address of the structure to be modified. The modify function should first display the existing name in the selected structure and then request new data for this member.

3. Write a C program that initially presents a menu of choices for the user. The menu should consist of the following choices:
   a. Create an initial linked list of names.
   b. Insert a new structure into the linked list.
   c. Modify an existing structure in the linked list.
   d. Delete an existing structure from the list.
   e. Exit the program.

   Upon the user's selection, the program should execute the appropriate functions to satisfy the request.

13.6 Common Programming and Compiler Errors

In using the material presented in this chapter, be aware of the following possible programming and compiler errors.

Programming Errors

The five most common programming errors in using dynamically allocated storage areas are:

1. Not checking the return codes provided by `malloc()` and `realloc()`. If either of these functions return a `NULL` pointer, the user should be notified that the allocation did not take place and the normal program operation must be altered in an appropriate way. You simply cannot assume that all calls to `malloc()` and `realloc()` will result in the requested allocation of memory space.

2. Not correctly updating all relevant pointer addresses when adding or removing structures from dynamically created stacks, queues, and linked lists. Unless extreme care is taken in updating all addresses, each of these dynamic data structures can quickly become corrupted.

3. Forgetting to free previously allocated memory space when the space is no longer needed. This is typically only a problem in a large application program that is expected to run continuously and can make many requests for allocated space based on user demand.

4. Not preserving the integrity of the addresses contained in the top-of-stack pointer, queue-in, queue-out, and list pointer when dealing with a stack, queue, and dynamically linked list, respectively. As each of these pointers locates a starting position in their respective data structures, the complete list will be lost if the starting addresses are incorrect.

5. Related to the previous error is the equally disastrous one of not correctly updating internal structure pointers when inserting and removing structures from a stack, queue, or dynamically linked list. Once an internal pointer within a singly linked list contains an incorrect address, it is almost impossible to locate and reestablish the missing set of structures.

Compiler Errors

The following table summarizes typical compiler error messages in Unix and Windows:

Error	Typical Unix-based Compiler Error Message	Typical Windows-based Compiler Error Message

Forgetting to provide `malloc()` with a memory size argument when allocating memory.
For example:
`#include <stdlib.h>`
`int main()`
`{`
`  int *p;`
 	
`  p = (int *)malloc();`
`  return 0;`
`}`
	`(E) Missing argument(s).`	`: error: 'malloc' : function does not take 0 arguments`

Error	Typical Unix-based Compiler Error Message	Typical Windows-based Compiler Error Message

Forgetting to include the stdlib.h header file whenever malloc() is used in a program.
For example:
#include <stdio.h>
int main()
{
  int *p;
 	
  p = (int
*)malloc(sizeof(int));
  return 0;
}
	(W) Operation between types "int*" and "int" is not allowed.	:error: 'malloc': identifier not found, even with argument-dependent lookup

Forgetting to pass a pointer argument to the free() function.
For example:
#include <stdio.h>
int main()
{
  int *p;
 	
  p = (int
*)malloc(sizeof(int));
  free();
  return 0;
}
	(E) Missing argument(s).	: error: 'free' : function does not take 0 arguments

Forgetting to include the indirection operator when creating a pointer member to the structure.
For example:
struct NR
{
  char name[30];
  struct NR nameRec;
};
rather than
struct NR
{
  char name[30];
  struct NR *nameRec;
};
	(E) "struct NR" uses "struct NR" in its definition.	:error C2460: 'NR::nameRec' : uses 'NR', which is being defined

13.7 Chapter Summary

1. An alternative to fixed memory allocation for variables at compile time is the dynamic allocation of memory at run time. This dynamic allocation, which is also known as a run-time allocation, allocates and deallocates memory storage under program control and is extremely useful when dealing with a list of data that can expand and contract as items are added and deleted from the list. In C, the functions that are used for dynamic memory allocation are `malloc()`, `calloc()`, `realloc()`, and `free()`.

2. The `malloc()` function reserves a requested number of bytes and returns a pointer to the first reserved byte. For example, the expression `malloc(50 * sizeof(int))` reserves a sufficient number of bytes to store 50 integers. The `malloc()` function will either return a pointer to the first byte of reserved storage or return a `NULL` pointer if the request cannot be satisfied. Since the returned pointer always "points to" a `void`, it must always be cast into a pointer of the desired type. Thus, this specific request for storage would be made using the expression

   ```
   pointerToInt = (int *) malloc(50 * sizeof(int))
   ```

   where `pointerToInt` has been declared as a pointer to an integer.

   In using `malloc()` you should always check its return value to ensure that a `NULL` pointer was not returned, which would indicate that the request for memory space was not satisfied. Continuing with our example, this check would take the form

   ```
   if (pointerToInt == (int *)NULL))
   {
      do an error procedure in here-
      typically an exit
   }
   ```

3. The `realloc()` function operates in a similar fashion as the `malloc()` function except it is used to expand or contract an existing allocated space. If the new size is larger than the previously allocated space, only the additional space remains uninitialized and the previously allocated space retains its contents; otherwise, the new space retains its prior contents up to its new limits. As with `malloc()`, the return address provided by `realloc()` should always be checked.

4. The `free()` function is used to deallocate previously allocated memory space.

5. A stack is a list consisting of structures that can only be added and removed from the top of the list. Such a structure is a last in, first out (LIFO) list in which the last structure added to the list is the first structure removed. The pointer member of each structure in a stack always points to the prior structure in the list. Additionally, one pointer variable is always required to contain the address of the current top-of-stack structure.

6. A queue is a list consisting of structures that are added to the top of the list and removed from the bottom of the list. Such a structure is a first in, first out (FIFO) list in which structures are removed in the order in which they were added. The pointer member of each structure in a queue always points to the next structure in the list. Additionally, one pointer is always required to contain the address of the current top-of-queue structure and one pointer to contain the current bottom-of-queue structure.

7. A dynamically linked list consists of structures that can be added or removed from any position in the list. Such lists are used to keep structures in a specified order, such as alphabetically. The pointer member of each structure in a dynamically linked list always points to the next structure in the list. Additionally, one pointer is always required to contain the address of the first structure in the list.

Chapter 14

Additional Capabilities

Previous chapters have presented C's basic capabilities, statements, and structure. The variations on each of these, which are almost endless, are a source of delight to many programmers, who continuously find new possibilities of expression using variations of the basic language building blocks. This chapter presents additional capabilities that you will find useful as you progress in your understanding and use of C. For completeness we also include one statement that is part of the C language but is almost never used by knowledgeable C programmers.

14.1 Additional Features

In this section five additional features are presented. Of these, only the `typedef` declaration and conditional preprocessor directives are used extensively.

The typedef Declaration Statement

The typedef declaration statement permits constructing alternate names for an existing C data type name. These alternate names are known as **aliases**. For example, the statement

```
typedef double REAL;
```

makes the name REAL an alias (that is, a synonym) for double. The name REAL can now be used in place of the term double anywhere in the program after the alias has been declared. For example, the definition

```
REAL val;
```

is equivalent to the definition

```
double val;
```

The typedef statement does not create a new data type; it creates a new name for an existing data type. Using uppercase names in typedef statements is not mandatory. It is done simply to alert the programmer to a user-specified name, similar to uppercase names in #define statements. In fact, the equivalence produced by a typedef statement can frequently be produced equally well by a #define statement. The difference between the two, however, is that typedef statements are processed directly by the compiler while #define statements are processed by the preprocessor. Compiler processing of typedef statements allows for text replacements that are not possible with the preprocessor. For example the statement

```
typedef double REAL;
```

actually specifies that REAL is a placeholder that will be replaced with another variable name. A subsequent declaration such as

```
REAL val;
```

has the effect of substituting the variable named val for the placeholder named REAL in the terms following the word typedef. Substituting val for REAL in the typedef statement and retaining all terms after the reserved word typedef results in the equivalent declaration double val;.

Once the mechanics of the replacement are understood, more useful equivalences can be constructed. Consider the statement

```
typedef int ARRAY[100];
```

Here, the name ARRAY is actually a placeholder for any subsequently defined variables. Thus, a statement such as ARRAY first, second; is equivalent to the two definitions int first[100]; and int second[100];. Each of these definitions is obtained by replacing the name ARRAY with the variable names first and second in the terms following the reserved word typedef.

As another example, consider the following statement:

```
typedef struct
{
  char name[20];
  int idNum;
} empRecord;
```

Here empRecord is a convenient placeholder for any subsequent variable. For example, the declaration empRecord employee[75]; is equivalent to the declaration

```
struct
{
  char name[20];
  int idNum;
} employee[75];
```

This last declaration is obtained by directly substituting the term employee[75] in place of the word empRecord in the terms following the word typedef in the original typedef statement.

Conditional Preprocessor Directives

In addition to the #include directive, the preprocessor provides a number of other valuable directives. Two of the more useful of these are the conditional directives, #ifndef, which means "if not defined," and #ifdef, which means "if defined." These directives work in almost the same manner as the if and else statements. For example, the syntax of the #ifndef statement is

```
#ifndef condition
  compile the statements placed here
#else
  compile the statements placed here
#endif
```

As with the if/else statement, the #else directive is optional.

Both the #ifndef and #ifdef directives permit **conditional compilation** in that the statements immediately following these directives, up to either the #else or #endif directives, are compiled only if the condition is true, whereas the statements following the #else are compiled only if the condition is false.

By far, #ifndef is the most frequently used conditional preprocessor directive. Its most common usage is in the form

```
#ifndef header-file
  #include <header-file>
#endif
```

For example,

```
#ifndef stdio.h
  #include <stdio.h>
#endif
```

This statement checks whether the stdio.h header file has already been included. Only if it has not been previously defined is the #include directive executed. This prevents multiple inclusions of the stdio.h header file.

The #ifdef works in a manner similar to the #ifndef, except that the statements immediately following the #ifdef, up to either the #else or #endif directives, are only executed if the tested condition has been defined.

The relationship between the #ifdef and #ifndef directives is that the expression #ifndef condition performs the same task as the expression #ifdef !condition, and these two expressions can be used interchangeably.

Enumerated Constants

In addition to equating a single constant to a named constant, sets of related integer values can be equated to an equivalent set of constants using an enumerated list. Enumerated lists are identified by the reserved word enum followed by an optional, user-selected name and a required list of one or more constants. For example, consider the enumeration

```
enum {Mon, Tue, Wed, Thr, Fri, Sat, Sun};
```

By default, the first enumerated name in an enumerated list has a value of 0. Thus, the previous list is equivalent to the following list of #define statements:

```
#define Mon 0
#define Tue 1
#define Wed 2, and so on.
```

Alternatively, explicit values can be assigned to each enumerated constant, with unspecified values automatically continuing the integer sequence from the last specified value. Thus, the enumerated list

```
enum {Mon = 1, Tue, Wed, Thr, Fri, Sat, Sun};
```

equates Mon with 1, Tue with 2, Wed with 3, and so on.

Additionally, any integer constant can be equated to enumerated names; they need not be in sequence, and an optional enumerated list name can be used. For example, the enumeration

```
enum escsequences {BELL = '\a',BACKSPACE = '\b',NEWLINE = '\n',
                                             RETURN = '\r', TAB ='\t'};
```

identifies the list as escsequences, and assigns character constants to each enumerated name. Notice that the enumerated constants can be any valid user-created identifier, but each name in the list must be unique. It is valid, however, for two constants to be equated to the same integer value.

Conditional Expressions

In addition to expressions formed with the arithmetic, relational, logical, and bit operators, C provides a conditional expression. A conditional expression uses the conditional operator, ?: and provides an alternate way of expressing a simple if-else statement.

The general form of a conditional expression is

```
expression1 ? expression2 : expression3
```

If the value of *expression1* is non-0 (true), *expression2* is evaluated, otherwise *expression3* is evaluated. Thus, the value of the complete conditional expression is the value of either *expression2* or *expression3*, depending on which expression was evaluated. As always, the value of the exprssion may be assigned to a variable.

Conditional expressions are most useful in replacing simple `if-else` statements. For example, the `if-else` statement

```
if (hours > 40)
  rate = 0.045;
else
  rate = 0.02;
```

can be replaced with the one-line conditional statement

```
rate = (hours > 40) ? 0.045 : 0.02;
```

Here, the complete conditional expression

```
(hours > 40) ? 0.045 : 0.02
```

is evaluated before any assignment is made to `rate`, because the conditional operator, `?:`, has a higher precedence than the assignment operator. Within the conditional expression, the expression `hours > 40` is evaluated first. If this expression has a non-0 value, which is equivalent to a logical true value, the value of the complete conditional expression is set to 0.045. Otherwise the conditional expression has a value of 0.02. Finally, the value of the conditional expression, either 0.045 or 0.02, is assigned to the variable `rate`.

The conditional operator, `?:`, is unique in C in that it is a **ternary** operator. This means that the operator connects three operands. The first operand is always evaluated first. It is usually a conditional expression that uses logical operators.

The next two operands are any other valid expressions, which can be single constants, variables, or more general expressions. The complete conditional expression consists of all three operands connected by the condition operator symbols, `?` and `:`.

Conditional expressions are only useful in replacing `if-else` statements when the expressions in the equivalent `if-else` statement are not long or complicated. For example, the statement

```
maxVal = a > b ? a : b;
```

is a one-line statement that assigns the maximum value of the variables `a` and `b` to `maxVal`. A longer, equivalent form of this statement is

```
if (a > b)
  maxVal = a;
else
   maxVal = b;
```

Because of the length of the expressions involved, a conditional expression would not be useful in replacing the following `if-else` statement:

```
if (amount > 20000)
  taxes = 0.025(amount - 20000) + 400;
else
  taxes = 0.02 * amount;
```

The goto Statement

The goto statement provides an unconditional transfer of control to some other statement in a program. The general form of a goto statement is

```
goto label;
```

where *label* is any unique name chosen according to the rules for creating variable names. The label name must appear, followed by a colon, in front of any other statement in the function that contains the goto statement. For example, the following section of code transfers control to the label named err if division by 0 is attempted:

```
if (denom == 0.0)
  goto err;
else
  result = num /denom;
    .
    .
    .
err:  printf("Error - Attempted Division by Zero");
```

The astute reader will realize that in this case goto provides a cumbersome solution to the problem. It would require a second goto above the printf() statement to stop this statement from always being executed. Generally, it is much easier either to call an error routine for unusual conditions or to use a break statement if this is necessary.

Theoretically, a goto statement is never required because C's normal structures provide sufficient flexibility to handle all possible flow control requirements. Also, gotos tend to complicate programs. For example, consider the following code:

```
if (a == 100)
  goto first;
else
  x = 20;
goto sec;

first: x = 50;
sec: y = 10;
```

Written without a goto this code is

```
if (a == 100)
  x = 50;
else
  x = 20;
y = 10;
```

Both sections of code produce the same result; however, the second version is clearly easier to read. It is worthwhile to convince yourself that the two sections of code do, in fact, produce the same result by running the code on your computer. This will let you experience the sense of frustration when working with goto-invaded code.

Using even one goto statement in a program is almost always a sign of bad programming structure. Possibly the only case that conceivably might use a goto is in a nested loop where some error condition requires escape from both the inner and outer loop structure (a break will only exit from the inner loop). If such an escape was ever used in developing a program, the code should ultimately be rewritten as a function where the escape is replaced by an exit from the function.

EXERCISES 14.1

Short Answer Questions

1. Write enumerated lists for the following:
   a. The enumerated names `TRUE` and `FALSE` are to be equated to the integers `1`, and `0`, respectively.
   b. The enumerated names `JAN.`, `FEB.`, `MARCH`, `APRIL`, `MAY`, `JUNE`, `JULY`, `AUG.`, `SEPT.`, `OCT.`, `NOV.`, and, `DEC.` are to be equated to the integers `1`, `2`, `3`, and so on.

2. Determine the errors in the following enumerated lists:
   a. `enum {SUMMER, SPRING, WINTER, FALL}`
   b. `enum (RED = 1, YELLOW = 5, GREEN = 3, BLUE = 1)`
   c. `enum {RED = 1, BLUE = 2, GREEN = 3, RED = 4, YELLOW = 5}`

3. Rewrite each of the following `if-else` statements using a conditional expression:
   a.
   ```
   if (a < b);
     minVal = a;
   else
     minVal = b;
   ```
   b.
   ```
   if (num < 0)
     sign = -1;
   else
     sign = 1;
   ```
   c.
   ```
   if (flag == 1)
     val = num;
   else
     val = num * num;
   ```
   d.
   ```
   if (credit == plus)
     rate = prime;
   else
     rate = prime + delta
   ```
   e.
   ```
   if (!bond)
     cou = .075;
   else
     cou = 1.1;
   ```

14.2 Bit Operations

C operates with complete data entities that are stored as 1 or more bytes, such as character, integer and double-precision constants, and variables. In addition, C provides for the manipulation of individual bits of character and integer constants and variables.

The operators that are used to perform these bit operations are known as **bit operators**. They are listed in Table 14.1.

Table 14.1 Bit Operators

<table>
<tr><th>Operator</th><th>Description</th></tr>
<tr><td>&</td><td>Bit-by-bit AND</td></tr>
<tr><td>|</td><td>Bit-by-bit inclusive OR</td></tr>
<tr><td>^</td><td>Bit-by-bit exclusive OR</td></tr>
<tr><td>~</td><td>Bit-by-bit one's complement</td></tr>
<tr><td><<</td><td>Left shift</td></tr>
<tr><td>>></td><td>Right shift</td></tr>
</table>

All the operators listed in Table 14.1 are binary operators, requiring two operands. In using the bit operators, each operand is treated as a binary number consisting of a series of individual 1s and 0s. The respective bits in each operand are then compared on a bit-by-bit basis, and the result is determined based on the selected operation.

The AND Operator

The AND operator, &, causes a bit-by-bit AND comparison between its two operands. The result of each bit-by-bit comparison is a 1 only when both bits being compared are 1s, otherwise the result of the AND operation is a 0. For example, assume that the following two 8-bit numbers are to be ANDed:

```
1 0 1 1 0 0 1 1
1 1 0 1 0 1 0 1
```

To perform an AND operation, each bit in one operand is compared to the bit occupying the same position in the other operand. Figure 14.1 illustrates the correspondence between bits for these two operands. AND comparisons are determined by the following rule: *The result of an AND comparison is 1 when both bits being compared are 1s; otherwise the result is a 0.* The result of each comparison is, of course, independent of any other bit comparison.

```
 10110011
&11010101
---------
 10010001
```

Figure 14.1 A sample AND operation

Program 14.1 illustrates the use of an AND operation. In this program, the variable op1 is initialized to the octal value 325, which is the octal equivalent of the binary number 11010101, and the variable op2 is initialized to the octal value 263, which is the octal representation of the binary number 10110011. These are the same two binary numbers illustrated in Figure 14.1.

Program 14.1

```
#include <stdio.h>
int main()
{
  int op1 = 0325, op2 = 0263;

  printf("%o ANDed with %o is %o\n", op1, op2, op1 & op2);

```

```
  return 0;
}
```

Program 14.1 produces the following output:

```
325 ANDed with 263 is 221
```

The result of ANDing the octal numbers 325 and 263 is the octal number 221. The binary equivalent of 221 is the binary number 10010001, which is the result of the AND operation illustrated in Figure 14.1.

AND operations are extremely useful in **masking**, or eliminating, selected bits from an operand. This is a direct result of the fact that ANDing any bit (1 or 0) with a 0 forces the resulting bit to be a 0, while ANDing any bit (1 or 0) with a 1 leaves the original bit unchanged. For example, assume that the variable op1 has the arbitrary bit pattern xxxxxxxx, where each x can be either 1 or 0, independent of any other x in the number. The result of ANDing this binary number with the binary number 00001111 is

```
  op1 = x x x x x x x x
  op2 = 0 0 0 0 1 1 1 1
--------------------------
Result = 0 0 0 0 x x x x
```

As can be seen from this example, the 0s in op2 effectively mask, or eliminate, the respective bits in op1, while the ones in op2 **filter**, or pass, the respective bits in op1 through with no change in their values. In this example, the variable op2 is called a **mask**. By choosing the mask appropriately, any individual bit in an operand can be selected, or filtered, out of an operand for inspection. For example, ANDing the variable op1 with the mask 00000100 forces all the bits of the result to be 0, except for the third bit. The third bit of the result will be a copy of the third bit of op1. Thus, if the result of the AND is 0, the third bit of op1 must have been 0, and if the result of the AND is a non-0 number, the third bit must have been a 1.

The Inclusive OR Operator

The inclusive OR operator, |, performs a bit-by-bit comparison of its two operands in a fashion much like that of the bit-by-bit AND. Inclusive OR comparisons, however, are determined by the following rule: *The result of an inclusive OR comparison is 1 if either bit being compared is a 1; otherwise the result is a 0.* As with all bit operations, the result of each comparison is, of course, independent of any other comparison. Figure 14.2 illustrates an inclusive OR operation.

```
 10110011
:11010101
---------
 11110111
```

Figure 14.2 A sample OR operation

Program 14.2 illustrates an inclusive OR operation using the octal values of the operands illustrated in Figure 14.2.

Program 14.2

```
#include <stdio.h>
int main()
{
int op1 = 0325, op2 = 0263;

  printf("%o ORed with %o is %o\n", op1, op2, op1 | op2);

  return 0;
}
```

Program 14.2 produces the following output:

```
325 ORed with 263 is 367
```

The result of inclusive ORing the octal numbers 325 and 263 is the octal number 367. The binary equivalent of 367 is 11110111, which is the result of the inclusive OR operation illustrated in Figure 14.2.

Inclusive OR operations are extremely useful in forcing selected bits to take on a 1 value or for passing through other bit values unchanged. This is a direct result of the fact that inclusive ORing any bit (1 or 0) with a 1 forces the resulting bit to be a 1, while inclusive ORing any bit (1 or 0) with a 0 leaves the original bit unchanged. For example, assume that the variable op1 has the arbitrary bit pattern xxxxxxxx, where each x can be either 1 or 0, independent of any other x in the number. The result of inclusive ORing this binary number with the binary number 11110000 is

```
   op1 = x x x x x x x x
   op2 = 1 1 1 1 0 0 0 0
------------------------
Result = 1 1 1 1 x x x x
```

As can be seen from this example, the 1s in op2 force the resulting bits to 1, while the 0s in op2 filter, or pass, the respective bits in op1 through with no change in their values. Thus, inclusive OR and AND perform similar masking operations, except that in OR operations the masked bits are set to 1s rather than cleared to 0s. Another way of looking at this is to say that inclusive ORing with a 0 has the same effect as ANDing with a 1.

The Exclusive OR Operator

The exclusive OR operator, ^, performs a bit-by-bit comparison of its two operands. The result of the comparison is determined by the following rule: *The result of an exclusive OR comparison is 1 if one and only one of the bits being compared is a 1; otherwise the result is 0.*

Figure 14.3 illustrates an exclusive OR operation. As shown in the figure, when both bits being compared are the same value (both 1 or both 0), the result is a 0. Only when both bits have different values (one bit a 1 and the other a 0) is the result a 1. Again, each pair or bit comparison is independent of any other bit comparison

```
 10110011
^11010101
---------
 01100110
```

Figure 14.3 A sample exclusive OR operation

An exclusive OR operation can be used to create the opposite value, or complement, of any individual bit in a variable. This is a direct result of the fact that exclusive ORing any bit (1 or 0) with a 1 forces the resulting bit to be of the opposite value of its original state, while exclusive ORing any bit (1 or 0) with a 0 leaves the original bit unchanged. For example, assume that the variable op1 has the arbitrary bit pattern xxxxxxxx, where each x can be either 1 or 0, independent of any other x in the number. Using the notation that $\bar{x}$ is the complement (opposite) value of x, the result of exclusive ORing this binary number with the binary number 01010101 is

$$\begin{array}{lcl} \text{op1} & = & x\ x\ x\ x\ x\ x\ x\ x \\ \text{op2} & = & 0\ 1\ 0\ 1\ 0\ 1\ 0\ 1 \\ \hline \text{Result} & = & x\ \bar{x}\ x\ \bar{x}\ x\ \bar{x}\ x\ \bar{x} \end{array}$$

As can be seen from this example, the 1s in op2 force the resulting bits to be the complement of their original bit values, while the 0s in op2 filter, or pass, the respective bits in op1 through with no change in their values.

The Complement Operator

The complement operator, ~, is a unary operator that changes each 1 bit in its operand to 0 and each 0 bit to 1. For example, if the variable op1 contains the binary number 11001010,~op1 replaces this binary number with the number 00110101. The complement operator is used to force any bit in an operand to 0, independent of the actual number of bits used to store the number. For example, the statement

```
op1 = op1 & ~07;
```

or its shorter form,

```
op1 &= ~07;
```

both set the last 3 bits of op1 to 0, regardless of how op1 is stored within the computer. Either of these two statements can, of course, be replaced by ANDing the last 3 bits of op1 with 0s, if the number of bits used to store op1 is known. In a computer that uses 16 bits to store integers, the appropriate AND operation is

```
op1 = op1 & 0177770;
```

For a computer that uses 32 bits to store integers, the above AND sets the leftmost or higher-order 16 bits to 0 also, which is an unintended result. The correct statement for 32 bits is

```
op1 = op1 & 027777777770;
```

Using the complement operator in this situation frees the programmer from having to determine the storage size of the operand and, more importantly, makes the program portable between machines using different integer storage sizes.

Different-Sized Data Items

When the bit operators &, |, and ^ are used with operands of different sizes, the shorter operand is always increased in bit size to match the size of the larger operand. Figure 14.4 illustrates the extension of a 16-bit unsigned integer into a 32-bit number.

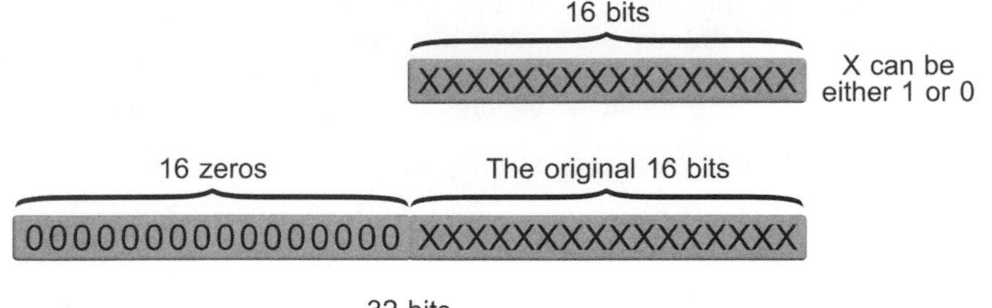

Figure 14.4 Extending 16-bit unsigned data to 32 bits

As the figure shows, the additional bits are added to the left of the original number and filled with 0s. This is the equivalent of adding leading 0s to the number, which has no effect on the number's value.

When extending signed numbers, the original leftmost bit is reproduced in the additional bits that are added to the number. As illustrated in Figure 14.5, if the original leftmost bit is 0, corresponding to a positive number, 0 is placed in each of the additional bit positions. If the leftmost bit is 1, which corresponds to a negative number, 1 is placed in the additional bit positions. In either case, the resulting binary number has the same sign and magnitude of the original number.

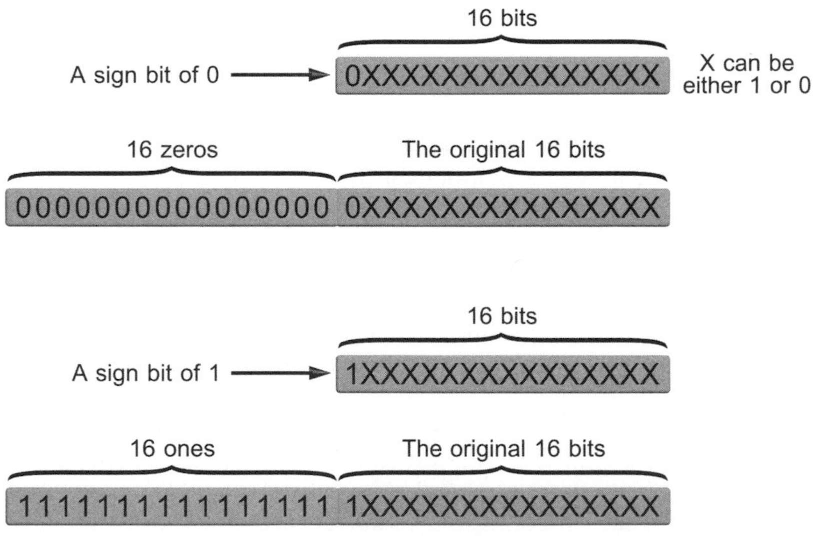

Figure 14.5 Extending 16-bit signed data to 32 bits

The Shift Operators

The left shift operator, <<, causes the bits in an operand to be shifted to the left by a given amount. For example, the statement

```
p1 = op1 << 4;
```

causes the bits in op1 to be shifted 4 bits to the left, filling any vacated bits with a 0. Figure 14.6 illustrates the effect of shifting the binary number 1111100010101011 to the left by 4 bit positions.

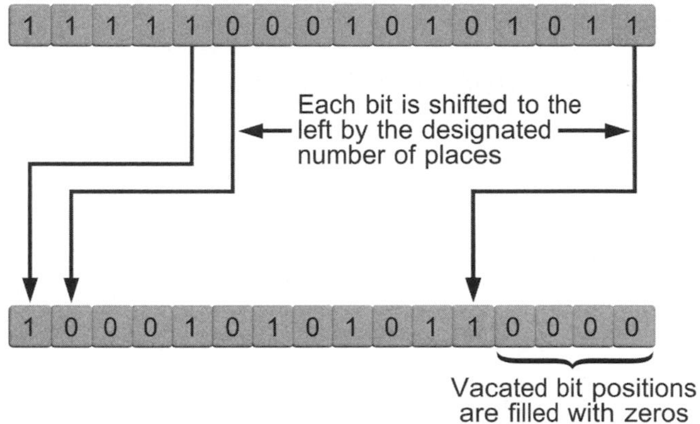
1 1 1 1 1 0 0 0 1 0 1 0 1 0 1 1
Each bit is shifted to the left by the designated number of places
1 0 0 0 1 0 1 0 1 0 1 1 0 0 0 0
Vacated bit positions are filled with zeros

Figure 14.6 An example of a left shift

For unsigned integers, each left shift corresponds to multiplication by 2. This is also true for signed numbers using two's complement representation, as long as the leftmost bit does not switch values. Since a change in the leftmost bit of a two's complement number represents a change in both the sign and magnitude represented by the bit, such a shift does not represent a simple multiplication by 2.

The right shift operator, >>, causes the bits in an operand to be shifted to the right by a given amount. For example, the statement

```
op1 = op1 >> 3;
```

causes the bits in op1 to be shifted to the right by 3 bit positions. Figure 14.7a illustrates the right shift of the unsigned binary number 1111100010101011 by 3 bit positions. As illustrated, the 3 rightmost bits are shifted "off the end" and are lost.

For unsigned numbers, the leftmost bit is not used as a sign bit. For this type of number, the vacated leftmost bits are always filled with 0s. This is the case that is illustrated in Figure 14.7a.

For signed numbers, what is filled in the vacated bits depends on the computer. Most computers reproduce the original sign bit of the number. Figure 14.7b illustrates the right shift of a negative binary number by 4 bit positions, where the sign bit is reproduced in the vacated bits. Figure 14.7c illustrates the equivalent right shift of a positive signed binary number.

The type of fill illustrated in Figures 14.7b and 14.7c, where the sign bit is reproduced in vacated bit positions, is known as an **arithmetic right shift**. In an arithmetic right shift, each single shift to the right corresponds to a division by 2.

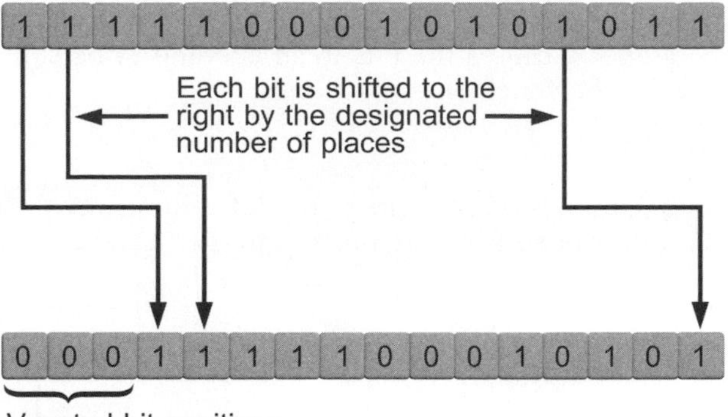
1 1 1 1 1 0 0 0 1 0 1 0 1 0 1 1
Each bit is shifted to the right by the designated number of places
0 0 0 1 1 1 1 1 0 0 0 1 0 1 0 1
Vacated bit positions are filled with zeros

Figure 14.7a An unsigned arithmetic right shift

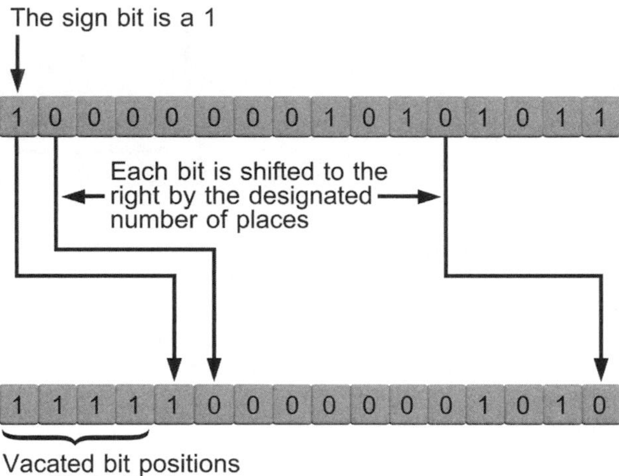
The sign bit is a 1
1 0 0 0 0 0 0 0 1 0 1 0 1 0 1 1
Each bit is shifted to the right by the designated number of places
1 1 1 1 1 0 0 0 0 0 0 0 1 0 1 0
Vacated bit positions are filled with 1s

Figure 14.7b The right shift of a negative binary number

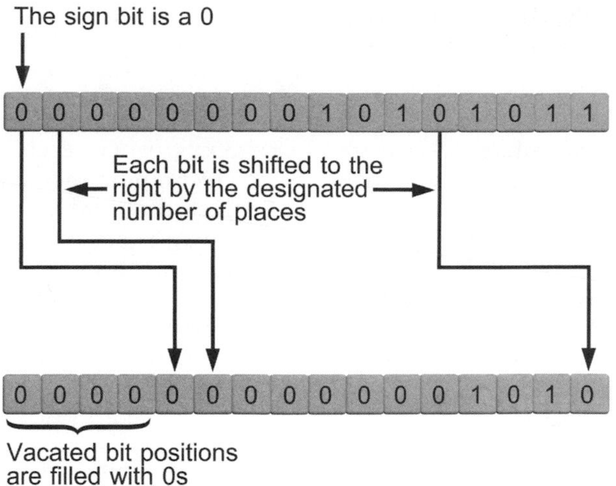
The sign bit is a 0
0 0 0 0 0 0 0 0 1 0 1 0 1 0 1 1
Each bit is shifted to the right by the designated number of places
0 0 0 0 0 0 0 0 0 0 0 0 1 0 1 0
Vacated bit positions are filled with 0s

Figure 14.7c The right shift of a positive binary number

Instead of reproducing the sign bit in right-shifted signed numbers, some computers automatically fill the vacated bits with 0s. This type of shift is known as a **logical shift**. For positive signed numbers, where the leftmost bit is 0, both arithmetic and logical right shifts produce the same result. The results of these two shifts are only different when negative numbers are involved.

EXERCISES 14.2

Short Answer Questions

1. Determine the results of the following operations:

   a.
   ```
     11001010
   & 10100101
   ----------
   ```

   b.
   ```
     11001010
   | 10100101
   ----------
   ```

   c.
   ```
     11001010
   ^ 10100101
   ----------
   ```

2. Write the octal representations of the binary numbers given in Question 1.

3. Determine the octal results of the following operations, assuming unsigned numbers:
   a. the octal number 0157 shifted left by 1 bit position
   b. the octal number 0701 shifted left by 2 bit positions

c. the octal number 0673 shifted right by 2 bit positions
d. the octal number 067 shifted right by 3 bit positions

4. Repeat Question 3 assuming that the numbers are treated as signed values.

5. a. Assume that the arbitrary bit pattern *xxxxxxxx*, where each *x* can represent either 1 or 0, is stored in the integer variable `flag`. Determine the octal value of a mask that can be ANDed with the bit pattern to reproduce the third and fourth bits of `flag` and set all other bits to 0. The rightmost bit in `flag` is considered bit 0.
   b. Determine the octal value of a mask that can be inclusively `OR`ed with the bit pattern in `flag` to reproduce the third and fourth bits of `flag` and set all other bits to 1. Again, consider the rightmost bit in `flag` to be bit 0.
   c. Determine the octal value of a mask that can be used to complement the values of the third and fourth bits of `flag` and leave all other bits unchanged. Determine the bit operation that should be used with the mask value to produce the desired result.

6. a. Write the two's complement form of the decimal number -1 using 8 bits. (*Hint:* Refer to Section 1.8 for a review of two's complement numbers.)
   b. Repeat Question 6a using 16 bits to represent the decimal number -1 and compare your answer to your previous answer. Could the 16-bit version have been obtained by sign-extending the 8-bit version?

Programming Exercises

1. Write a C program that displays the first 8 bits of each character value input into a variable named `ch`. (*Hint:* Assuming each character is stored using 8 bits, start by using the hexadecimal mask 80, which corresponds to the binary number `10000000`. If the result of the masking operation is a 0, display a 0; else display a 1. Then shift the mask one place to the right to examine the next bit, and so on until all bits in the variable `ch` have been processed.)

2. Write a C program that reverses the bits in an integer variable named `okay` and store the reversed bits in the variable named `revOkay`. For example, if the bit pattern `11100101`, corresponding to the octal number 0345, is assigned to `okay`, the bit pattern `10100111`, corresponding to the octal number 0247, should be produced and stored in `revOkay`.

14.3 Macros

In its simplest form, the `#define` preprocessor is used to equate constants and operators to symbolic names. For example, the statement

```
#define SALESTAX 0.05
```

equates the symbolic name `SALESTAX` to the number `0.05`. When `SALESTAX` is used in any subsequent statement or expression, the equivalent value of `0.05` is substituted for the symbolic name. The substitutions are made by the C preprocessor just prior to program compilation.

C places no restrictions on the equivalences that can be established with the #define statement. Thus, in addition to using #define preprocessor statements for simple equivalences, these statements can also be used to equate symbolic names to text, a partial or complete expression, and may even include arguments. When the equivalence consists of more than a single value, operator, or variable, the symbolic name is referred to as a **macro**, and the substitution of the text in place of the symbolic name is called a **macro expansion** or **macro substitution**. The word *macro* refers to the direct, in-line expansion of one word into many words. For example, the equivalence established by the statement

```
#define FORMAT "The answer is %f\n"
```

enables us to write the statement

```
printf(FORMAT, 15.2);
```

When this statement is encountered by the preprocessor, the symbolic name FORMAT is replaced by the equivalent text "The answer is %f\n". The compiler always receives the expanded version after the text has been inserted in place of the symbolic name by the preprocessor.

In addition to using #define statements for straight text substitutions, these statements can also be used to define equivalences that use arguments. For example, in the equivalence statement

```
#define SQUARE(x) x * x
```

x is an argument. Here, SQUARE(x) is a true macro that is expanded into the expression x * x, where x is itself replaced by the variable or constant used when the macro is utilized. For example, the statement

```
y = SQUARE(num);
```

is expanded into the statement

```
y = num * num;
```

The advantage of using a macro such as SQUARE(x) is that since the data type of the argument is not specified, the macro can be used with any data type argument. If num, for example, is an integer variable, the expression num * num produces an integer value. Similarly, if num is a double-precision variable, the SQUARE(x) macro produces a double-precision value. This is a direct result of the text substitution procedure used in expanding the macro and is an advantage of making SQUARE(x) a macro rather than a function.

Care must be taken when defining macros with arguments. For example, in the definition of SQUARE(x), there must be no space between the symbolic name SQUARE and the left parenthesis used to enclose the argument. There can, however, be spaces within the parentheses if more than one argument is used.

Additionally, because the expression of a macro involves direct text substitution, unintended results may occur if you do not use macros carefully. For example, the assignment statement

```
val = SQUARE(num1 + num2);
```

does not assign the value of $(\text{num1 + num2})^2$ to val. Rather, the expansion of

```
SQUARE(num1 + num2)
```

results in the equivalent statement

```
val = num1 + num2 * num1 + num2;
```

This statement results from the direct text substitution of the term `num1 + num2` for the argument `x` in the expression `x * x` that is produced by the preprocessor.

To avoid unintended results, always place parentheses around all macro arguments wherever they appear in the macro. For example, the definition

```
#define SQUARE(x) (x) * (x)
```

ensures that a correct result is produced whenever the macro is invoked. Now the statement

```
val = SQUARE(num1 + num2);
```

is expanded to produce the desired assignment

```
val = (num1 + num2) * (num1 + num2);
```

Macros are extremely useful when the calculations or expressions they contain are relatively simple and can be kept to one or at most two lines. Larger macro definitions tend to become cumbersome and confusing and are better written as functions. If necessary, a macro definition can be continued on a new line by typing a backslash character, \, before the Enter key is pressed. The backslash acts as an escape character that causes the preprocessor to treat the Enter literally and not include it in any subsequent text substitutions.

The advantage of using a macro instead of a function is an increase in execution speed. Because the macro is directly expanded and included in every expression or statement using it, there is no execution time loss due to the call and return procedures required by a function. The disadvantage is the increase in required program memory space when a macro is used repeatedly. Each time a macro is used, the complete macro text is reproduced and stored as an integral part of the program. Thus, if the same macro is used in 10 places, the final code includes 10 copies of the expanded text version of the macro. A function, however, is stored in memory only once. No matter how many times the function is called, the same code is used. The memory space required for one copy of a function used extensively throughout a program can be considerably less than the memory required for storing multiple copies of the same code defined as a macro.

EXERCISES 14.3

Short Answer Questions

1. Define a macro named `NEGATE(x)` that produces the negative of its argument.
2. Define a macro named `ABSVAL(x)` that produces the absolute value of its argument.
3. Define a macro named `CIRCUM(r)` that determines the circumference of a circle of radius `r`. The circumference is determined from the relationship *circumference* = 2.0 * *PI* * *radius*, where PI = 3.1416.

4. Define a macro named `MIN(x,y)` that determines the minimum value of its two arguments.

5. Define a macro named `MAX(x,y)` that determines the maximum value of its two arguments.

Programming Exercises

1. Include the `NEGATE(x)` macro defined in Short Answer Question 1 in a complete C program and run the program to confirm proper operation of the macro for various cases.

2. Include the `ABSVAL(x)` macro defined in Short Answer Question 2 in a complete C program and run the program to confirm proper operation of the macro for various cases.

3. Include the `CIRCUM(r)` macro defined in Short Answer Question 3 in a complete C program and run the program to confirm proper operation of the macro for various cases.

4. Include the `MIN(x,y)` macro defined in Short Answer Question 4 in a complete C program and run the program to confirm proper operation of the macro for various cases.

5. Include the `MAX(x,y)` macro defined in Short Answer Question 5 in a complete C program and run the program to confirm proper operation of the macro for various cases.

14.4 Command-Line Arguments

Arguments can be passed to any function in a program, including the `main()` function. In this section we describe the procedures for passing arguments to `main()` when a program is initially invoked and having `main()` correctly receive and store the arguments passed to it. Both the sending and receiving sides of the transaction must be considered. Fortunately, the interface for transmitting arguments to a `main()` function has been standardized in C, so both sending and receiving arguments can be done almost mechanically.

All the programs that have been run so far can be invoked by typing the name of the executable version of the program after the operating system prompt is displayed. The command line for these programs consists of a single word, which is the name of the program. For computers that use the Unix operating system, the prompt is usually the `$` symbol and the executable name of the program is `a.out`. For these systems, the simple command line

```
$a.out
```

begins program execution of the last compiled source program currently residing in `a.out`.

If you are using a Windows-based C compiler, the equivalent operating system prompt in a DOS Window is typically `C>`, and the name of the executable program is the same name as the source program with an `.exe` extension rather than either a `.cpp` or `.c` extension. Assuming that you are using a DOS Window with the `C>` operating system prompt, the complete command line for running an executable program named `pgm14.3.exe` is `C> pgm14.3`. As illustrated in Figure 14.8, this command line causes the `pgm14.3` program to begin execution with its `main()` function, but no arguments are passed to `main()`.

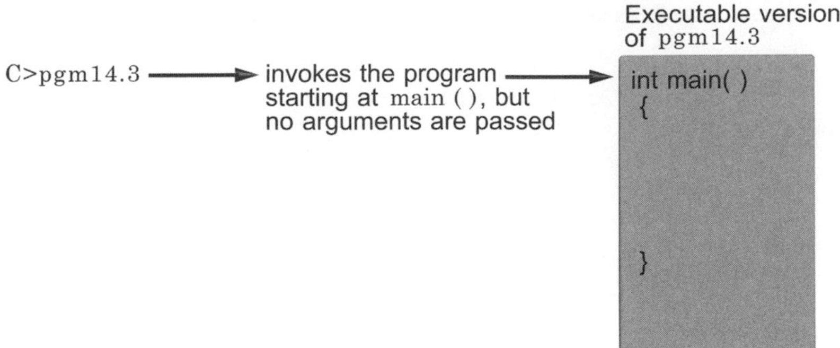

Figure 14.8 Invoking Program `pgm14.3.exe`

Now assume that we want to pass the three separate string arguments `three blind mice` directly into `pgm14.3`'s `main()` function. Sending arguments into a `main()` function is extremely easy. It is accomplished by including the arguments on the command line used to begin program execution. Because the arguments are typed on the command line, they are, naturally, called **command-line arguments**. To pass the arguments `three blind mice` directly into the `main()` function of the `pgm14.3` program, we only need to add the desired words after the program name on the command line

```
C:>pgm14.3 three blind mice
```

Upon encountering the command line `pgm14.3 three blind mice`, the operating system stores it as a sequence of four strings. Figure 14.9 illustrates the storage of this command line, assuming that each character uses 1 byte of storage. As shown in the figure, each string terminates with the standard C null character `\0`.

p	g	m	1	4	.	3	\0	t	h	r	e	e	\0	b	l	i	n	d	\0	m	i	c	e	\0

Figure 14.9 The command line stored in memory

Sending command-line arguments to `main()` is always this simple. The arguments are typed on the command line, and the operating system nicely stores them as a sequence of separate strings. We must now handle the receiving side of the transaction and let `main()` know that arguments are being passed to it.

Arguments passed to `main()`, like all function arguments, must be declared as part of the function's definition. To standardize arguments passing to a `main()` function, only two items are allowed: a number and an array. The number is an integer variable, which must be named `argc` (short for *argument counter*), and the array is a one-dimensional list, which must be named `argv` (short for *argument values*). Figure 14.10 illustrates these two arguments.

The integer passed to `main()` is the total number of items on the command line. In our example, the value of `argc` passed to `main()` is four, which includes the name of the program plus the three command-line arguments. The one-dimensional list passed to `main()` is a list of pointers containing the starting storage address of each string typed on the command line, as illustrated in Figure 14.11.[1]

[1]If the full path name of the program is stored, `pgm14.3` in Figure 14.11 should be replaced by its full path name.

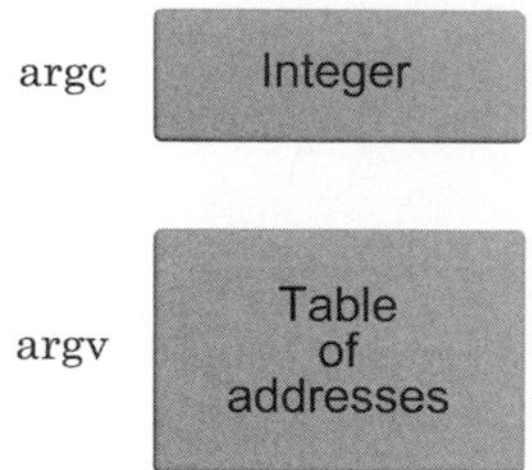

Figure 14.10 An integer and an array are passed to `main()`

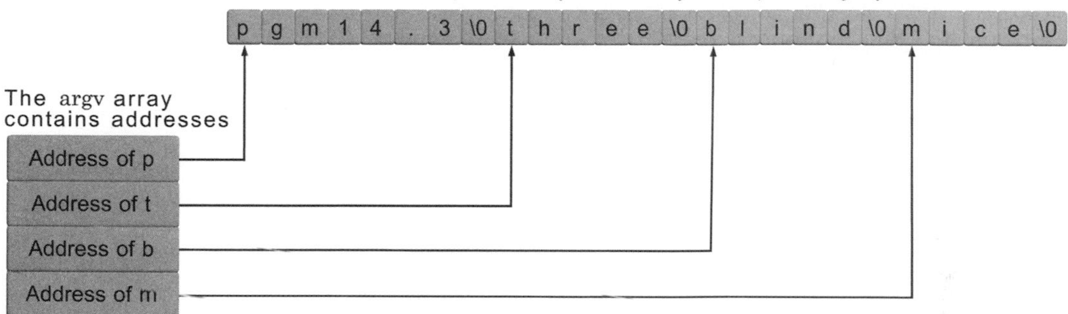

Figure 14.11 Addresses are stored in the `argv` array

We can now write the complete function definition for `main()` to receive arguments by declaring their names and data types. For `main()`'s two arguments, C requires that they be named `argc` and `argv`, respectively. Because `argc` is an integer, its declaration will be `int argc`. Because `argv` is the name of an array whose elements are addresses that point to where the actual command-line arguments are stored, its proper declaration is `char *argv[]`. This is nothing more than the declaration of an array of pointers. It is read "`argv` is an array whose elements are pointers to characters." Putting all this together, the full function header of a `main()` function that will receive command-line arguments is

```
int main(int argc, char *argv[]) /* complete main() header line */
```

No matter how many arguments are typed on the command line, `main()` only needs the two standard pieces of information provided by `argc` and `argv`: the number of items on the command line and the list of starting addresses indicating where each argument is actually stored.

Program 14.3 verifies our description by printing the data actually passed to `main()`. The variable `argv[i]` used in Program 14.3 contains an address. The notation `*argv[i]` refers to "the character pointed to" by the address in `argv[i]`.

Program 14.3

```
1   #include <stdio.h>
2   int main(int argc, char *argv[])
3   {
4     int i;
5
6     printf("\nThe number of items on the command line is %d\n\n",argc);
7     for (i = 0; i < argc; i++)
8     {
9       printf("The address stored in argv[%d] is %u\n", i, argv[i]);
10      printf("The character pointed to is %c\n", *argv[i]);
11    }
12
13    return 0;
14  }
```

Assuming that the executable version of Program 14.3 is named `pgm14.3.exe`, a sample output for the command line `pgm14.3 three blind mice` is:[2]

```
The number of items on the command line is 4

The address stored in argv[0] is 3280036
The character pointed to is p
The address stored in argv[1] is 3280044
The character pointed to is t
The address stored in argv[2] is 3280050
The character pointed to is b
The address stored in argv[3] is 3280056
The character pointed to is m
```

The addresses displayed by Program 14.3 depend, of course, on the machine used to run the program. The `%u` control sequence in line 9 causes these addresses to be displayed as unsigned integers. Figure 14.12 illustrates the storage of the command line whose values are displayed by this output. As anticipated, the addresses in the `argv` array "point" to the starting characters of each string typed on the command line.

Once command-line arguments are passed to a C program, they can be used like any other C strings. Program 14.4 causes its command-line arguments to be displayed from within `main()`.

[2]If the full path name of the program is stored, the first character displayed is the disk drive designation, which is usually C.

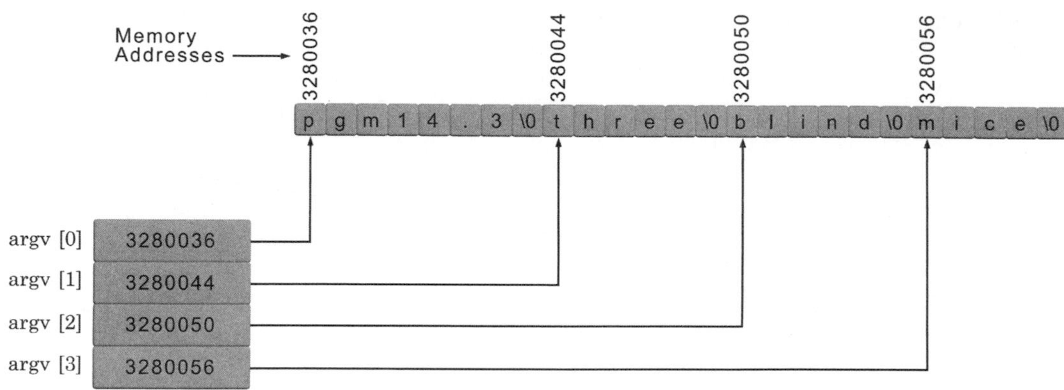

Figure 14.12 The command line stored in memory

Program 14.4

```
/* A program that displays command line arguments */
#include <stdio.h>
int main(int argc, char *argv[])
{
int i;

  printf("\nThe following arguments were passed to main(): ");
  for (i = 1; i < argc; i++)
    printf("%s ", argv[i]);
  printf("\n");

  return 0;
}
```

Assuming that the name of the executable version of Program 14.4 is `a.out`, the output of this program for the command line `a.out three blind mice` is

```
The following arguments were passed to main(): three blind mice
```

Notice that when the addresses in `argv[]` are passed to the `printf()` function in Program 14.4, the strings pointed to by these addresses are displayed. When these same addresses were passed to the `printf()` function in Program 14.3, the actual values of the addresses were printed. The difference in displays is caused by the `printf()` function. When a `%s` control sequence is used in `printf()`, as it is in Program 14.4, it alerts the function that a string will be accessed. The `printf()` function then expects the address of the first character in the string; this is exactly what each element in `argv[]` supplies. Once `printf()` receives the address, the function performs the required indirection to locate the actual string that is displayed.

One final comment about command-line arguments is in order. Any argument typed on a command line is considered to be a string. To pass numerical data to `main()`, you must convert the passed string into its numerical counterpart. This is seldom an issue, however, since most command-line arguments are used as flags to pass appropriate processing control signals to an invoked program.

EXERCISES 14.4

Short Answer Questions

1. What is the name of data passed to the main function when it is called for execution?
2. What is the data type of the arguments named `argc` and `argv`?
3. a. What information does `argc` provide to `main()`?
   b. What information does `argv` provide to `main()`?
4. Must the variable names `argc` and `argv` be used if data is passed to `main()` when it is called for execution?

Programming Exercises

1. a. Write a program that accepts the name of a data file as a command-line argument. Have your program open the data file and display its contents, line by line, on the monitor screen.
   b. Would the program written for Exercise 1a work correctly for a program file?
2. a. Modify the program written for Exercise 1a so that each line displayed is preceded by a line number.
   b. Modify the program written for Exercise 2a so that the command-line argument `-p` will cause the program to list the contents of the file on the printer attached to your system.
3. Write a program that accepts a command-line argument as the name of a data file. Given the name, your program should display the number of characters in the file. (*Hint:* Use the `fseek()` and `ftell()` library functions discussed in Section 10.3.)
4. Write a program that accepts two integer values as command-line arguments. The program should multiply the two values entered and display the result. (*Hint:* The command line must be accepted as string data and converted to numerical values before multiplication.)

14.5 Common Programming and Compiler Errors

In using the material presented in this chapter, be aware of the following possible programming and compiler errors.

Programming Errors

1. Forgetting that enumerated constants are a set of symbolic constants that equate to integers.
2. Using the relational operators, > and <, in place of the shift operators, >> and <<.
3. Forgetting that each argument passed to `main()` is passed as a string value. As such, if it is intended to be used as a numerical value, the argument must be converted to a numerical data type.

Compiler Errors

The following table summarizes common errors that will result in compilation errors and the typical error messages provided by Unix- and Windows-based compilers.

Error	Typical Unix-based Compiler Error Message	Typical Windows-based Compiler Error Message

Placing a space between the words type and def.
For example:
`type def double REAL;`
instead of
`typedef double REAL;`
	`(S) Definition of function type requires parentheses.`
	`(S) Syntax error: possible missing '{'?`
		`:error: 'def': undeclared identifier`
		`:error: 'type': undeclared identifier`

Using an assignment statement when defining a macro.
For example:
`#define SQUARE(X)= X*X;`
instead of
`#define SQUARE(X) X*X;`
	`(S) Unexpected text '=' encountered.`	No error reported, as the substitution is acceptable. You will, however, get a compile error, when you use the macro.

Declaring `argc` within `main()` when it is used as a parameter to accept command line arguments.	`(S) Identifier argc has already been defined`	`:error: redefinition of formal parameter 'argc'`
Forgetting to end a `#ifdef` Conditional Preprocessor directive with an `#endif`.	`(S) #if, #else, #elif, #ifdef, #ifndef block must be ended with #endif.`	`:fatal error: mismatched #if/#endif pair in file`

14.6 Chapter Summary

1. A `typedef` statement creates synonym names, which are known as aliases, for any C data type name. For example, the statement

   ```
   typedef int WHOLENUM;
   ```

   makes `WHOLENUM` a synonym for `int`.

2. A conditional expression provides an alternate way of expressing a simple `if-else` statement. The general form of a conditional expression is

   ```
   expression1 ? expression2 : expression3
   ```

   The equivalent `if-else` statement for this is

   ```
   if (expression1)
     expression2;
   else
     expression3;
   ```

3. C also provides a `goto` statement. In theory this statement need never be used. In practice it produces confusing and unstructured code, and should be used only in a very limited and controlled manner, if at all.

4. Individual bits of character and integer variables and constants can be manipulated using C's bit operators. These are the `AND`, inclusive `OR`, exclusive `OR`, complement, left shift, and right shift operators.

5. The `AND` and inclusive `OR` operators are useful in creating masks. These masks can be used to pass or eliminate individual bits from the selected operand. The exclusive `OR` operator is useful in complementing an operand's bits.

6. When the `AND` and `OR` operators are used with operands of different sizes, the shorter operand is always increased in bit size to match the size of the larger operand.

7. The shift operators produce different results depending on whether the operand is a signed or an unsigned value.

8. Using the `#define` command, complete expressions can be equated to symbolic names. When these expressions include arguments, they are referred to as macros.

9. Arguments passed to `main()` are termed command-line arguments. C provides a standard argument-passing procedure in which `main()` can accept any number of arguments passed to it. Each argument passed to `main()` is considered a string and is stored using a pointer array named `argv`. The total number of arguments on the command line is stored in an integer variable named `argc`.

Chapter 15

A Brief Introduction to C++

This chapter presents a brief introduction to C++. More detailed information on the topics introduced in this chapter can be found in Chapters 16 and 17, which are provided on the Course Technology Web site, at *www.course.com.*

The similarities and differences between C and C++ are described in Table 15.1. The similarities are presented in the first eight rows of the table, which illustrate the almost one-to-one relationship between C and C++ statements and operators. The last row in the table explains the major difference between the two languages, a difference that has to do with the design and programming approach of the two languages. Other similarities and differences are described in detail in the Chapters 16 and 17 (the two chapters provided on the Web). However, a C programmer can easily begin coding in C++ if he or she is familiar with the topics listed in the first eight rows of Table 15.1.

From a programmer's viewpoint, the first eight items in Table 15.1 are essentially syntactical; that is, they are just different ways of coding the same operations. It is the last item in Table 15.1 that clearly distinguishes the two languages, because the object-oriented design philosophy of C++ represents a fundamental shift in how a program is constructed.

Table 15.1 Correspondence Between C and C++

Topic	C Statements, Operators, and Approach	C++ Statements, Operators, and Approach
Standard input and output header files	#include <stdio.h>	#include <iostream> using namespace std;
Standard input	scanf() function For example: scanf("%d", &price);	cin object For example: cin >> price;
Basic mathematical and assignment operators	+, -, *, /, =	+, -, *, /, =
Standard output	printf() function For example: printf("Hello World");	cout object For example: cout << "Hello World";
Formatted output	Control sequences For example: printf("%5.2f", 2.756);	Format manipulators (requires the header file iomanip) For example: cout << fixed << setw(5) << setprecision(2) << 2.756;
Comment delimiters	/* */	/* */ and //
New line designation	'\n'	'\n' and endl
Indirect addressing	Pointers	Pointers and references
Program design	Procedural	Object-oriented

15.1 Procedural Programming in C++

The first eight items in Table 15.1 represent basic C statements and operations that are easily translated into equivalent C++ statements and operations. As we have seen throughout this text, C is a procedural language whose statements are used to produce C functions. Because C++ was created from C, it should come as no surprise that all such C functions can also be constructed in C++.

The procedural nature of C++ is implicitly indicated in Table 15.1, where the equivalent C++ approach is placed side-by-side with its C forerunner. That is why C++ is sometimes referred to as "a better C," because it both incorporates aspects of C while adding a number of useful procedural features (such as function overloading described in Chapter 16). This is also one of the reasons that many introductory C++ courses are taught using procedural programs initially, because doing so permits any student with a procedural programming background to convert to C++ code rather easily.[1] As an example of this easy transference of C procedural code to C++ code, consider Programs 15.1 and 15.2.

[1]This is the approach taken by the author's *A First Book of C++ and Program Development* and *Design Using C++*. A second approach, which starts immediately with object-oriented design, is taken by the author's *Object-Oriented Program Design Using C++*. Both books are published by Course Technology.

Program 15.1 illustrates a C program that prompts the user for two values and returns the product of the numbers entered. This same task is performed by the equivalent C++ program in 15.2, with almost a one-to-one correspondence between statements from one program to another.

Program 15.1

```
/* this is a C procedural program */
#include <stdio.h>



int main()
{
  double price, total;
  int units;

  printf("Enter the price: ");
  scanf("%lf", &price);
  printf("Enter the number sold: ");
  scanf("%d", &units);

  total = price * units;
  printf("The total for the %d units is $%4.2f\n", units, total);

  return 0;
}
```

Program 15.2

```
// this is a C++ procedural program
#include <iostream>
#include <iomanip>   // needed for formatting
using namespace std;

int main()
```

```
 7  {
 8    double price, total;
 9    int units;
10
11    cout << "Enter the price: ";
12    cin  >> price;
13    cout <<  "Enter the number sold: ";
14    cin  >> units;
15
16    total = price * units;
17    cout << "The total for the " << units << " units is $"
18         << fixed << setw(4) << setprecision(2)
19         << total << endl;
20
21    return 0;
22  }
23
```

The output produced by a sample run for both of these programs, using the same input data for both is:

```
Enter the price: 23.36
Enter the number sold: 15
The total for the 15 units is $350.40
```

In reviewing the code for these two programs, note the following correspondence, starting with the comment line 1 in Program 15.1:

```
1  /* this is a C procedural program */
```

This code will also work in C++. However, for single-line comments C++ provides a simpler alternative that begins with a double slash, //. Any text after this delimiter, but only to the end of the current line, is taken to be a comment in C++. This is used in line 1 of Program 15.2.

```
1  // this is a C++ procedural program
```

The header files in C++ are different from those in C, but perform the same task and occupy similar positions in a C++ program that they occupy in a C program. Thus, while the standard I/O header line is provided by statement 2 in Program 15.1,

```
2  #include <stdio.h>
```

the header files in Program 15.2 require the code listed as lines 2 and 3

```
2 #include <iostream>
3 #include <iomanip>    // needed for formatting
4 using namespace std;
```

Starting with line 6 in both programs, the one-to-one correspondence between C and C++ code becomes even more pronounced for all of the remaining statements, with the exception of line 17, which is discussed in a moment. For example, compare lines 6 through 16 in both programs, which are repeated below and aligned side-by-side.

C Program 15.1

```
6   int main()
7   {
8     double price, total;
9     int units;
10
11    printf("Enter the price: ");
12    scanf("%lf", &price);
13    printf("Enter the number sold: ");
14    scanf("%d", &units);
15
16    total = price * units;
```

C++ Program 15.2

```
6   int main()
7   {
8     double price, total;
9     int units;
10
11    cout << "Enter the price: ";
12    cin  >> price;
13    cout <<  "Enter the number sold: ";
14    cin  >> units;
15
16    total = price * units;
```

Notice that the code for the shaded lines, which include the function header line (line 6), the opening brace of the `main()` function (line 7), the declaration statements (lines 8 and 9), and the assignment statement (line 16) are identical in both programs. The remaining statements (lines 11 through 14) are actually simpler in C++ than in C, where `cout` is used in place of `printf()` and `cin` is used in place of `scanf()`. Additionally, on input, C++'s `cin` does not require the address operator needed for C's `scanf()` function.

The only real difference in the two languages, as far as Programs 15.1 and 15.2 are concerned, is how they format output values. Here, the formatting control sequence used in line 17 of the C program

```
17 printf("The total for the %d units is $%4.2f\n", units, total);
```

is replaced by the following format syntax used in lines 17 through 19 of the C++ program.

```
17  cout << "The total for the " << units << " units is $"
18       << fixed << setw(4) << setprecision(2)
19       << total << endl;
```

Finally, notice that C++ uses `endl` to signify a new line. This is equivalent to C's newline sequence `'\n'` (which is also available in C++) followed by a `flush()` function call.

The close relationship between Programs 15.1 and 15.2 should begin to convince you that a C programmer can easily begin to code procedural programs in C++. This correspondence between the languages makes learning C++ procedural programs relatively simple for C programmers and is the approach taken in the two Web-based chapters provided with this text. With your knowledge of C, you should be ready to understand and quickly adapt to a C++ environment using these two Web-based C++ chapters.

EXERCISES 15.1

Short Answer Questions

1. Rewrite the following C statements with their equivalent C++ counterparts:
   a. `printf("Hello World");`
   b. `printf("Enter an integer value");`
   c. `printf ("The sum of %d and %d is %d", 5, 6, 5 + 6);`
   d. `printf("%d plus %d is %d", num1, num2, num1+num2);`

2. Rewrite the following C formatted statements with their equivalent C++ counterparts:
   a. `printf("%4d", 5);`
   b. `printf("%3d", result);`
   c. `printf ("The sum of %3d and %3d is %3d", num1, num2, num1+num2);`
   d. `printf("%5.2f", 2.756);`

3. Rewrite the following C input statements with their equivalent C++ counterparts:
   a. `scanf("%d", &units);`
   b. `scanf("%f", &price);`
   c. `scanf("%d %f", &units, &price);`

4. What is the fundamental difference between C and C++?

Programming Exercises

1. a. Design, write, compile, and execute a C++ program to calculate the dollar amount contained in a piggy bank. The bank currently contains 12 half dollars, 20 quarters, 32 dimes, 45 nickels, and 27 pennies.
   b. Check the values computed by your program by hand. After you have verified that your program is working correctly, modify it to determine the dollar value of a bank containing no half dollars, 17 quarters, 19 dimes, 10 nickels, and 42 pennies.

2. a. Design, write, compile, and execute a C++ program to calculate the elapsed time it took to make a 183.67-mile trip. The equation for computing elapsed time is

   elapsed time = total distance / average speed

   Assume that the average speed during the trip was 58 miles per hour.
   b. Check the values computed by your program by hand. After you have verified that your program is working correctly, modify it to determine the elapsed time it takes to make a 372-mile trip at an average speed of 67 miles per hour.

3. a. Design, write, compile, and execute a C++ program to calculate the sum of the numbers from 1 to 100. The formula for calculating this sum is

   $sum = (n/2)[2\,a + (n - 1)d]$

   where n = number of terms to be added, a = the first number, and d = the difference between each number.

b. Check the values computed by your program by hand. After you have verified that your program is working correctly, modify it to determine the sum of the integers from 100 to 1000.

4. a. Write, compile, and execute a C++ program that displays the following prompt:

```
Enter the radius of a circle:
```

After accepting a value for the radius, your program should calculate and display the circumference of the circle using the formula *circumference = 2 * pi * radius.*

b. Check the values computed by your program using a test input radius of 3 inches.

After manually determining that the result produced by your program is correct, use your program to determine the circumference for the following data:

Data set 1: radius = 1.0

Data set 2: radius = 1.5

Data set 3: radius = 2.0

Data set 4: radius = 2.5

Data set 5: radius = 3.0

Data set 6: radius = 3.5

5. a. Write, compile, and execute a C++ program that displays the following prompts:

```
Enter the miles driven:
Enter the gallons of gas used:
```

After each prompt is displayed, your program should use a `cin` statement to accept data from the keyboard for the displayed prompt. After the gallons of gas used number has been entered, your program should calculate and display miles per gallon obtained. This value should be included in an appropriate message and calculated using the equation *miles per gallon = miles / gallons used.*

b. Check the values computed by your program using data of 176 miles and 10 gallons. After manually determining that the result produced by your program is correct, use your program to determine the miles-per-gallon for the following data:

Data set 1: miles = 250, gas = 16.5 gallons

Data set 2: miles = 275, gas = 18.00 gallons

Data set 3: miles = 312, gas = 19.54 gallons

Data set 4: miles = 296, gas = 17.39 gallons

6. a. Write, compile, and execute a C++ program that displays the following prompts:

```
Enter a number:
Enter a second number:
Enter a third number:
Enter a fourth number:
```

After each prompt is displayed, your program should use a `cin` statement to accept a number from the keyboard for the displayed prompt. After the fourth number has been entered, your program should calculate and display the average of the numbers. The average should be included in an appropriate message.

b. Check the values computed by your program using the numbers 100, 0, 100, 0. After manually determining that the result produced by your program is correct, use your program to determine the average for the following data:

Data set 1: 100, 100, 100, 100

Data set 2: 92, 98, 79, 85

Data set 3: 86, 84, 75, 86

Data set 4: 63, 85, 74, 82

15.2 Object-Oriented C++

One of the driving forces in the creation of object-oriented languages was the inability of procedurally structured code to be extended easily without extensive revisions, retesting, and reevaluations. Object-oriented languages, which are based on three features not found in procedural languages, make it easier to reuse code in a manner that significantly increases software productivity. The three features required for an object-oriented language are class construction, inheritance, and polymorphism.

Class construction is the ability to create programmer-defined data types. As we learned in Section 2.3, a data type provides both a set of values and a set of operations that can be applied to these values. In a programmer-defined data type, which is known as a **class**, the values defined for the data type can only be accessed and operated on by functions specified as part of the class. The basic structures used in C++ to create classes are presented in detail in Sections 16.4 and 16.5. Additional class features, such as class scope and conversions from class types to built-in data types, are presented in Sections 17.1 though 17.4.

Inheritance is the capability of deriving one class from another. This feature permits existing code, which has been thoroughly tested, to be reused efficiently without the need for extensive retesting. A derived class is a completely new data type that incorporates all of the data values and operations of one class with new data and operations that create a different and expanded class. For example, the class defined as all real numbers can be expanded to create a complex number class. The initial class is known as the **parent** or **base class**, while the derived class is known as the **child** or **subclass**. The concept of inheritance is presented in Section 17.5.

Finally, **polymorphism** permits the same operation to invoke one set of results on data values of a base class and a different set of results on data values of a derived class. For example, the operation of addition as applied to a real number would produce a different result than the addition of a complex number.

Using polymorphism, existing operations on a base class can be left alone, without the need to retest and reverify them, while they are extended to a derived class. Thus, only the extensions, rather than the complete base class, needs to be tested and verified. Polymorphism is presented in Section 17.5.

Once these three key features have been incorporated into a language, the benefits of creating reusable source code can be more easily realized. As a specific example, consider the source code needed for creating a dynamically created array, stack, or queue. Assume that a single program needs to use three arrays: an array of characters, an array of integers, and an array of double-precision numbers. Coding these as three different arrays requires both an initial programming effort and additional time required for fully testing and verifying code that is essentially the same for each array. Clearly, it makes more sense to implement each array from a single, fully tested generic array class that comes complete with operations for processing the array, such as sorting, inserting, finding maximum and minimum values, locating values, randomly shuffling values, copying arrays, comparing arrays, and dynamically expanding and contracting the array, as needed.

Such generic data types are available in C++, which not only incorporates a generic, dynamically created array type, but six other generic data structures as well. This particular library of data types is contained in a library of classes known as the Standard Template Library (STL).[2]

Finally, it should be noted that in a true object-oriented language all programs would have to adhere to an object-oriented structure. This is not true in C++ because the language, as we have seen in Section 15.1, can be used to construct procedure-oriented programs that do not make use of classes at all. For this reason, C++ is sometimes known as a hybrid language.

EXERCISES 15.2

Short Answer Questions

1. What was one of the prime motivations for creating object-oriented languages?
2. What three characteristics must a language have to be classified as object-oriented?
3. Define the following terms:
   a. class
   b. inheritance
   c. polymorphism
4. If one class is derived from another class, which is the base class and which is the subclass?
5. What does the Standard Template Library (STL) of classes provide?

15.3 Common Programming and Compiler Errors

In using the material presented in this chapter, be aware of the following possible programming and compiler errors.

Programming Errors

1. Misspelling the name of a function or C++ supplied name; for example, typing `cot` instead of `cout`.
2. Forgetting to close a string to be displayed by `cout` with a double quote symbol.

[2]The STL is described more fully in all of the author's C++ texts.

3. Forgetting to separate individual data items in a cout statement with the << symbol.
4. Forgetting to separate individual data items in a cin statement with the >> symbol.
5. Omitting the semicolon at the end of each C++ statement.
6. Not including the C++ header lines

```
#include <iostream>
using namespace std;
```

at the top of a C++ program.

Compiler Errors

The following table summarizes typical compiler error messages in Unix and Windows.

Error	Typical Unix-based Compiler Error Message	Typical Windows-based Compiler Error Message
Forgetting to include the statement: using namespace std;	S) The name lookup for "cout" did not find a declaration. (S) The name lookup for "cin" did not find a declaration. (S) The name lookup for "fixed" did not find a declaration.	:error: 'cin' : undeclared identifier :error: 'cout' : undeclared identifier
Using #include<stdio.h> instead of #include <iostream>	(S) The name lookup for "cout" did not find a declaration. (S) The name lookup for "cin" did not find a declaration.	:error: 'cin' : undeclared identifier :error: 'cout' : undeclared identifier
Forgetting to use the "put to" symbol, <<, when placing a variable onto the output stream. For example: cout << "sum = " sum;	(S) The text "sum" is unexpected.	:error: syntax error : missing ';' before identifier 'sum'

Error	Typical Unix-based Compiler Error Message	Typical Windows-based Compiler Error Message
Incorrectly typing the << symbol as < when using cout. For example: cout < "Enter price: "	(S) The call does not match any parameter list for "operator<". (I) "template <class _T1, class _T2> std::operator<(const pair<_T1,_T2> &, const pair<_T1,_T2> &)" is not a viable candidate. (I) "template <class _RI> std::operator<(const reverse_iterator<_RI> &, const reverse_iterator<_RI> &)" is not a viable candidate.	The following warning, not an error, is triggered. :warning: '<' : operator has no effect; expected operator with side-effect
Incorrectly typing the >> symbol as > when using cin.	(S) The call does not match any parameter	:error: binary '>' : no operator found which takes a right-hand operand of type 'int' (or there is no acceptable conversion)
Forgetting to use the "get from" symbol, >>, when using the input stream: For example: cin units;	(S) The text "units" is unexpected.	:error: syntax error : missing ';' before identifier 'units'

15.4 Chapter Summary

1. C++ is an object-oriented language that also supports procedural programming.
2. Creating a C-like procedural program using C++ essentially involves changing syntax for the input and output statements. Instead of printf() and scanf() used in C, C++ uses cout and cin. Additionally, C++ requires a different set of header files than those used in C.

3. All object-oriented languages, including C++, must provide the ability to create classes and provide for inheritance and polymorphism.
4. A class is a programmer-defined data type that includes specification of data values and operations that can be performed on these values.
5. Inheritance is the ability to create a new class by extending the definition of an existing class.
6. Polymorphism is the ability to have the same function perform different tasks depending on the class it is a member of.
7. Every variable in a C++ program must be declared as to the type of value it can store. Declarations within a function may be placed anywhere within a function, although a variable can only be used after it is declared. Variables may also be initialized when they are declared. Additionally, variables of the same type may be declared using a single declaration statement. Variable declaration statements have the general form:

   ```
   dataType variableName(s);
   ```

8. A simple C++ program containing declaration statements typically has the form:

   ```
   #include <iostream>
   using namespace std;

   int main()
   {
     declaration statements;

     other statements;

     return 0;
   }
   ```

   Although declaration statements may be placed anywhere within the function's body, a variable may only be used after it is declared.
9. The general form of a statement using `cout` to display output from a C++ program is

   ```
   cout << expression1 << expression2 . . . << expressionn;
   ```

   where all expressions are either strings, variables, or specific values.
10. The general form of a statement using `cin` to accept data input from the keyboard is

    ```
    cin >> variable1 >> variable2 . . . >> variablen;
    ```

    where each variable must be preceded by the >> symbol.
11. It is good programming practice to display a message, prior to a `cin` statement, that alerts the user as to the type and number of data items to be entered. Such a message is called a prompt.
12. The use of `cout` and `cin` within a program requires that the header lines

    ```
    #include <iostream>
    using namespace std;
    ```

    be placed at the top of the program.

Appendix A

Operator Precedence Table

Table A.1 presents the symbols, precedence, descriptions, and associativity of C's operators. Operators toward the top of the table have a higher precedence than those toward the bottom. Operators within each box have the same precedence and associativity.

Table A.1 Summary of C Operators

Operator	Description	Associativity
`()`	Function call	Left to right
`[]`	Array element	
`->`	Structure member pointer reference	
`.`	Structure member reference	

Table A.1 Summary of C Operators (continued)

Operator	Description	Associativity

`++`
`--`
`-`
`!`
`~`
`(type)`
`sizeof`
`&`
`*`
	Increment
	Decrement
	Unary minus
	Logical negation
	One's complement
	Type conversion (cast)
	Storage size
	Address of
	Indirection
		Right to left

`*`
`/`
`%`
	Multiplication
	Division
	Modulus (remainder)
		Left to right

`+` `-`	Addition Subtraction	Left to right
`<<` `>>`	Left shift Right shift	Left to right

`<`
`<=`
`>`
`>=`
	Less than
	Less than or equal to
	Greater than
	Greater than or equal to
		Left to right

`==` `!=`	Equal to Not equal to	Left to right
`&`	Bitwise AND	Left to right
`^`	Bitwise exclusive OR	Left to right
`|`	Bitwise inclusive OR	Left to right
`&&`	Logical AND	Left to right
`||`	Logical OR	Left to right
`?:`	Conditional expression	Right to left

`=`
`+= -= *=`
`/= %= &=`
`^= |=`
`<<= >>=`
	Assignment
	Assignment
	Assignment
	Assignment
	Assignment
		Right to left

`,`	Comma	Left to right

Appendix B

ASCII Character Codes

Key(s)	Dec	Oct	Hex
Ctrl 1	0	0	0
Ctrl A	1	1	1
Ctrl B	2	2	2
Ctrl C	3	3	3
Ctrl D	4	4	4
Ctrl E	5	5	5
Ctrl F	6	6	6
Ctrl G	7	7	7
Ctrl H	8	10	8
Ctrl I	9	11	9
Ctrl J (\n)	10	12	A
Ctrl K	11	13	B
Ctrl L	12	14	C

Key(s)	Dec	Oct	Hex
Return	13	15	D
Ctrl N	14	16	E
Ctrl O	15	17	F
Ctrl P	16	20	10
Ctrl Q	17	21	11
Ctrl R	18	22	12
Ctrl S	19	23	13
Ctrl T	20	24	14
Ctrl U	21	25	15
Ctrl V	22	26	16
Ctrl W	23	27	17
Ctrl X	24	30	18
Ctrl Y	25	31	19
Ctrl Z	26	32	1A
Esc	27	33	1B
Ctrl <	28	34	1C
Ctrl /	29	35	1D
Ctrl =	30	36	1E
Ctrl -	31	37	1F
Space	32	40	20
!	33	41	21
″	34	42	22
#	35	43	23
$	36	44	24
%	37	45	25
&	38	46	26
′	39	47	27
(	40	50	28
)	41	51	29
*	42	52	2A
+	43	53	2B
,	44	54	2C
-	45	55	2D
.	46	56	2E
/	47	57	2F
0	48	60	30
1	49	61	31
2	50	62	32
3	51	63	33
4	52	64	34
5	53	65	35

Key(s)	Dec	Oct	Hex
6	54	66	36
7	55	67	37
8	56	70	38
9	57	71	39
:	58	72	3A
;	59	73	3B
<	60	74	3C
=	61	75	3D
>	62	76	3E
?	63	77	3F
@	64	100	40
A	65	101	41
B	66	102	42
C	67	103	43
D	68	104	44
E	69	105	45
F	70	106	46
G	71	107	47
H	72	110	48
I	73	111	49
J	74	112	4A
K	75	113	4B
L	76	114	4C
M	77	115	4D
N	78	116	4E
O	79	117	4F
P	80	120	50
Q	81	121	51
R	82	122	52
S	83	123	53
T	84	124	54
U	85	125	55
V	86	126	56
W	87	127	57
X	88	130	58
Y	89	131	59
Z	90	132	5A
[	91	133	5B
\	92	134	5C
]	93	135	5D
^	94	136	5E

Key(s)	Dec	Oct	Hex
_	95	137	5F
'	96	140	60
a	97	141	61
b	98	142	62
c	99	143	63
d	100	144	64
e	101	145	65
f	102	146	66
g	103	147	67
h	104	150	68
i	105	151	69
j	106	152	6A
k	107	153	6B
l	108	154	6C
m	109	155	6D
n	110	156	6E
o	111	157	6F
p	112	160	70
q	113	161	71
r	114	162	72
s	115	163	73
t	116	164	74
u	117	165	75
v	118	166	76
w	119	167	77
x	120	170	78
y	121	171	79
z	122	172	7A
{	123	173	7B
|	124	174	7C
}	125	175	7D
~	126	176	7E
Del	127	177	7F

Appendix C

The Standard C Library

The standard C library is defined by the ANSI C standard and is composed of the functions, definitions, and macros that are declared in 15 header files. These header files and the types of routines that they provide are listed in Table C.1.

Table C.1 Standard C Library Header Files

Name	Type of Routines
`<assert.h>`	Diagnostic
`<ctype.h>`	Single-character testing
`<errno.h>`	Error detection
`<float.h>`	System-defined floating-point limits
`<limits.h>`	System-defined integer limits
`<locale.h>`	Country definitions
`<math.h>`	Mathematical
`<stjump.h>`	Nonlocal function calls
`<signal.h>`	Exception handling and interrupt signals

Table C.1 Standard C Library Header Files (continued)

Name	Type of Routines
<stdarg.h>	Variable-length argument processing
<stddef.h>	System constants
<stdio.h>	Input/output
<stdlib.h>	Miscellaneous utilities
<string.h>	String manipulation
<time.h>	Time and date functions

Of these 15 header files, the most commonly used file is <stdio.h>, which contains approximately one-third of all standard library functions and macros. The next most commonly used headers consist of <ctype.h>, <math.h>, <stdlib.h>, and <string.h>. The most commonly used routines contained in each of these five header files are presented in this appendix.

<stdio.h>

The functions, macros, and data types defined in <stdio.h> are concerned with input and output. The most commonly used are:

Prototype	Description
`int fclose(FILE *)`	Close a file
`int fflush(FILE *)`	Causes any buffered but unwritten output data to be written on output; undefined for input
`int fgetc(FILE *)`	Return the next character from the file (converted to an int) or `EOF` if end of file is encountered
`char fgets(char *s, int n, FILE *)`	Read at most `n-1` characters into the `s` array; stops at a newline, which is included in the array. The array is automatically terminated with a `\0`

Prototype	Description
`FILE *fopen(char *fname, char *mode)`	Open the file named `fname` in the designated mode, which can be: "r" open a file for reading "w" open a file for writing; old contents discarded if file exists "a" open a file for writing at the end of the file; a new file is created if one does not exist "r+" open a text file for reading and writing "w+" create a text file for update; old contents discarded if file exists "a+" open a text file for writing at the end of the file; a new file is created if one does not exist
`int fprintf(FILE *, char *format, args)`	Write the `args` to the file under control of the format string
`int fputc(intc, FILE *)`	Write `c`, converted to an unsigned char, to the file
`int fputs(char *s,FILE*)`	Write string `s` to the file
`int fscanf(FILE *, char *format, &args)`	Read from the file under control of the format string
`int fseek(FILE *, long offset, intorigin)`	Set the file position; the position is set to offset characters from the origin; the origin may be `SEEK_SET`, `SEEK_CUR`, or `SEEK_END`, which is the beginning, current position, or end of the file, respectively
`long ftell(file *)`	Return the current file position of a `-1L` if an error
`int getc(FILE *)`	`fgetc()` written as a macro
`int getchar(void)`	Same as `getc(stdin)`

Prototype	Description
`char *gets(char *s)`	Read the next input line into `s` array, replacing the newline with `\0`
`void perror(char *s)`	Print the string `s` and a compiler-defined error message corresponding to the last error number (`errno`) reported
`int printf(char *format, args)`	Write output to standard output under control of the format string; equivalent to `fprintf(stdout, char *format, args)`
`int putc(intc, FILE *)`	`fputc()` written as a macro
`int putchar(intc)`	Same as `putc (c, stdout)`
`int puts(char *s)`	Write the string `s`, followed by a newline character to `stdout`
`rewind(FILE *)` `int scanf(char *format, &args)`	Read from standard input under control of the format string; equivalent to `fscanf(stdin, char *format, args)`
`int sscanf(char *s, char *format, &args)`	Equivalent to `scanf()` except that input is taken from the `s` string
`sprintf(char *s, char *format, args)`	Equivalent to `printf()` except that output is written to the `s` string; the string is terminated with a `\0` and must be large enough to hold the data
`int ungetc(intc, FILE *)`	Push `c` (converted to an unsigned char) back onto the file stream

<ctype.h>

Each function declared in <ctype.h> returns a non-0 (true) integer if the argument satisfies the condition or a 0 (false) value if it does not. The argument must have a value representable as an unsigned char.

Prototype	Description
`int isalnum(intc)`	Is `c` alphanumeric `(isalpha || isdigit)`
`int isalpha(intc)`	Is `c` alphabetic
`int iscntrl(intc)`	Is `c` a control character
`int isdigit(intc)`	Is `c` a digit
`int isgraph(intc)`	Is `c` printable (excluding space)
`int islower(intc)`	Is `c` lowercase
`int isprint(intc)`	Is `c` printable (including space)
`int ispunct(intc)`	Is `c` printable except a space, letter, or digit
`int isspace(intc)`	Is `c` a space, formfeed, newline, carriage return, or tab
`int isupper(intc)`	Is `c` uppercase
`int isxdigit(intc)`	Is `c` a hexadecimal digit
`int tolower(intc)`	Convert `c` to lowercase
`int toupper(intc)`	Convert `c` to uppercase

<math.h>

This header file contains mathematical functions and macros.

Prototype	Description
`double acos(double x)`	Arc cosine of `x`
`double asin(double x)`	Arc sine of `x`
`double atan(double x)`	Arc tangent of `x`
`double ceil(double x)`	Smallest integer not less than `x`
`double cos(double x)`	Cosine of `x`
`double cosh(double x)`	Hyperbolic cosine of `x`
`double exp(double x)`	e^x
`double fabs(double x)`	Absolute value of `x`
`double floor(double x)`	Largest integer not greater than `x`
`double fmod(double x, double y)`	Remainder of `x/y`, with the sign of `x`
`double ldexp(x,n)`	$x.2^n$
`double log(double x)`	ln(x)
`double log10(double x)`	log10(x)
`double mod(double x, double *ip)`	Fraction part of `x`, with the sign of `x` Integer part of `x`, with the sign of `x`, is pointed to by `ip`
`double pow(x,y)`	x^y

Prototype	Description
`double sin(double x)`	Sine of `x`
`double sinh(double x)`	Hyperbolic sine of `x`
`double sqrt(double x)`	Square root of `x`
`double tan(double x)`	Tangent of `x`
`double tanh(double x)`	Hyperbolic tangent of `x`

<stdlib.h>

This header declares number conversion and storage allocation functions.

Prototype	Description
`int abs(intn)`	Absolute value of integer
`long labs(long n)`	Absolute value of long integer
`double atof(char *s)`	Convert `s` to double
`int atoi(char *s)`	Convert `s` to int
`int atol(char *s)`	Convert `s` to long
`int rand(void)`	Pseudo-random integer
`void srand(unsigned int seed)`	Seed for pseudo-random integers
`void *calloc(size_n, size_n)`	Allocate space for an array of `n` objects, each of size `n`. Initialize all allocated bytes to 0
`void *malloc(size_tn)`	Allocate space for an object of size `n`
`void *realloc(void *p, size_n)`	Reallocate space to size `n`, contents remain the same for old contents up to the new size
`void free(void *p)`	Deallocate space pointed to
`void exit(int status)`	Normal program termination

<string.h>

This header contains string-handling functions. All functions starting with the letters `str` assume `NULL` terminated strings as arguments and return a `NULL`-terminated string. The functions starting with the letters `mem` do not assume a `NULL`-terminated string and process data in memory.

Prototype	Description
`char *strcat(char *d, char*s)`	Concatenate string `s` to string `d`
`char *strncat(char *d, char *s, int n)`	Concatenate at most `n` characters of string `s` to string `d`
`char *strcpy(char *d, char *s)`	Copy string `s` to string `d`

Prototype	Description
char *strncpy(char *d, char *s, int n)	Copy at most n characters of string s to string d; pad with \0s if s has fewer than n characters
char *strcmp(char *d, char *s)	Compare string d to string s; return <0 if d < s, 0 if d == s, and > 0 if d > s
char *strncmp(char *d, char *s, int n)	Compare at most n characters of string d to string s; return < 0 if d < s, 0 if d == s, and > 0 if d > s
char *strchr(char *d, char c)	Return a pointer to the first occurrence of c in string d or a NULL if c is not found
char *strrchr(char *d, char c)	Return a pointer to the last occurrence of c in string d or a NULL if c is not found
char *strstr(char *d, char *s)	Return a pointer to the first occurrence of string s in string d or a NULL if s is not found
intstrlen(char *d)	Return the length of string d, not including the terminating NULL
void *memcpy(void *d, void *s, int n)	Copy n characters from s to d
void *memmove(void *d, void *s, int n)	Same as memcpy but works even if d overlaps s
void *memcmp(void *d, void *s, int n)	Compare the first n characters of d to s; same return as strcmp
void *memchr(void *d, char c, int n)	Return a pointer to the first occurrence of c in the n characters pointed to by d or a NULL if c is not found
void *memset(void *d, char c, int n)	Fill d with n occurrences of c

Appendix D

Input, Output, and Standard Error Redirection

The display produced by the `printf()` function is normally sent to the terminal where you are working. This terminal is called the *standard output device* because it is where the display is automatically directed, in a standard fashion, by the interface between your C program and your computer's operating system.

On most systems it is possible to redirect the output produced by `printf()` to some other device, or to a file, using the output redirection symbol, >, at the time the program is invoked. In addition to this symbol, you must specify where you want the displayed results to be sent.

For purposes of illustration, assume that the command to execute a compiled program named `salestax`, without redirection, is

```
salestax
```

This command is entered after your computer's system prompt is displayed on your terminal. When the salestax program is run, any `printf()` function calls within it automatically cause the appropriate display to be sent to your terminal. Suppose we would like to have the display produced by the program sent to a file named `results`. To do this requires the command

```
salestax > results
```

The redirection symbol, >, tells the operating system to send any display produced by `printf()` directly to a file named `results` rather than to the standard output device used by the system. The display sent to `results` can then be examined by using either an editor program or issuing another operating system command. For example, on Unix-based systems, the command

```
cat results
```

causes the contents of the file `results` to be displayed on your terminal. The equivalent command on Windows-based systems is

```
type results
```

In redirecting an output display to a file, the following rules apply:

1. If the file does not exist, it will be created.
2. If the file exists, it will be overwritten with the new display.

In addition to the output redirection symbol, the output append symbol, >>, can also be used. The append symbol is used in the same manner as the redirection symbol, but causes any new output to be added to the end of a file. For example, the command

```
salestax >> results
```

causes any output produced by `salestax` to be added to the end of the `results` file. If the `results` file does not exist, it will be created.

Besides having the display produced by `printf()` redirected to a file, using either the > or >> symbols, the display can also be sent to a physical device connected to your computer, such as a printer. You must, however, know the name used by your computer for accessing the desired device. For example, on an IBM PC or compatible computer, the name of the printer connected to the terminal is designated as `prn` and on a Unix system it is typically `lpr`. Thus, if you are working on an IBM or compatible machine, the command

```
salestax > prn
```

causes the display produced in the salestax program to be sent directly to the printer connected to the terminal. In addition to `printf()`, output redirection also affects the placement of displays produced by the `puts()` and `putchar()` functions and any other function that uses the standard output device for display.

Corresponding to output redirection, it is also possible to redesignate the standard input device for an individual program run using the input redirection symbol, <. Again, the new source for input must be specified immediately after the input redirection symbol.

Input redirection works much like output redirection but affects the source of input for the `scanf()`, `gets()`, and `getchar()` functions. For example, the command

```
salestax < dataIn
```

causes any input functions within salestax that normally receive their input from the keyboard to receive it from the dataIn file instead. This input redirection, like its output counterpart, is only in effect for the current execution of the program. As you might expect, the same run can have both an input and output redirection. For example, the command

```
salestax < dataIn > results
```

causes an input redirection from the file dataIn and an output redirection to the file results.

In addition to standard input and output redirection, the device to which all error messages are sent can also be redirected. On many systems this file is given an operating system designation as device file 2. Thus, the redirection

```
2> err
```

causes any error messages that would normally be displayed on the standard error device, which is usually your terminal, to be redirected to a file named err. As with standard input and output redirection, standard error redirection can be included on the same command line used to invoke a program. For example, the command

```
salestax < dataIn > show 2> err
```

causes the compiled program named salestax to receive its standard input from a file named dataIn, write its results to a file named show, and send any error messages to a file named err.

As the redirection of input, output, and error messages is generally a feature of the operating system used by your computer and not typically part of your C compiler, you must check the manuals for your particular operating system to ensure that these features are available.

Appendix E

Floating-Point Number Storage

The two's complement binary code used to store integer values was presented in Section 1.8. In this appendix, we present the binary storage format typically used in C++ to store single- and double-precision numbers, which are stored as floats and doubles, respectively. Collectively, both single- and double-precision values are commonly referred to as floating-point values.

Like their decimal number counterparts that use a decimal point to separate the integer and fractional parts of a number, floating-point numbers are represented in a conventional binary format with a binary point. For example, consider the binary number 1011.11. The digits to the left of the binary point (1011) represent the integer part of the number and the digits to the right of the binary point (11) represent the fractional part.

To store a floating-point binary number, a code similar to decimal scientific notation is used. To obtain this code the conventional binary number format is separated into a mantissa and an exponent. The following examples illustrate floating-point numbers expressed in this scientific notation:

Conventional binary notation	Binary scientific notation
1010.0	1.01 exp 011
-10001.0	-1.0001 exp 100
0.001101	1.101 exp -011
-0.000101	-1.01 exp -100

In binary scientific notation, the term "exp" stands for "exponent." The binary number in front of the exp term is the mantissa and the binary number following the exp term is the exponent value. Except for the number 0, the mantissa always has a single leading 1 followed immediately by a binary point. The exponent represents a power of 2 and indicates the number of places the binary point should be moved in the mantissa to obtain the conventional binary notation. If the exponent is positive, the binary point is moved to the right. If the exponent is negative, the binary point is moved to the left. For example, the exponent 011 in the number

1.01 exp 011

means move the binary point three places to the right, so that the number becomes 1010. The -011 exponent in the number

1.101 exp -011

means move the binary point three places to the left, so that the number becomes

.001101

Table E.1 IEEE Standard 754-1985 Floating-Point Specification

Data format	Sign bits	Mantissa bits	Bits
Single-precision	1	23	8
Double-precision	1	52	11
Extended-precision	1	64	15

In storing floating-point numbers, the sign, mantissa, and exponent are stored individually within separate fields. The number of bits used for each field determines the precision of the number. Single-precision (32 bit), double-precision (64 bit), and extended-precision (80 bit) floating-point data formats are defined by the Institute of Electrical and Electronics Engineers (IEEE) Standard 754-1985 to have the characteristics given in Table E.1. The format for a single-precision, floating-point number is illustrated in Figure E.1.

The sign bit shown in Figure E.1 refers to the sign of the mantissa. A sign bit of 1 represents a negative number and a 0 sign bit represents a positive value. Since all mantissas, except for the number 0, have a leading 1 followed by their binary points, these two items are never stored explicitly. The binary point implicitly resides immediately to the left of mantissa bit 22, and a leading 1 is always assumed. The binary number 0 is specified by setting all mantissa and exponent bits to 0. For this case only, the implied leading mantissa bit is also 0.

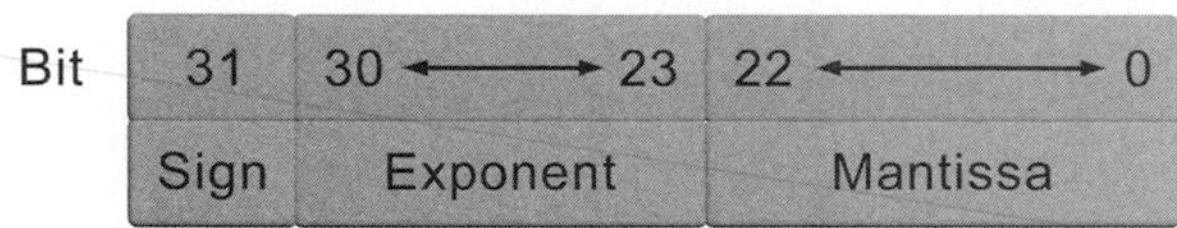

Figure E.1 Single-precision, floating-point number storage format

The exponent field contains an exponent that is biased by 127. For example, an exponent of 5 would be stored using the binary equivalent of the number 132 (127 + 5). Using 8 exponent bits, this is coded as 100000100. The addition of 127 to each exponent allows negative exponents to be coded within the exponent field without the need for an explicit sign bit. For example, the exponent -011, which corresponds to -3, would be stored using the binary equivalent of +124 (127 - 3).

Figure E.2 illustrates the encoding and storage of the decimal number -59.75 as a 64-bit single-precision binary number.

1	10000100	11011110000000000000000

Figure E.2 The encoding and storage of the decimal number -59.75

The sign, exponent, and mantissa are determined as follows. The conventional binary equivalent of

-59.75

is

-111011.11

Expressed in binary scientific notation this becomes

-1.1101111 exp 101

The minus sign is signified by setting the sign bit to 1. The mantissa's leading 1 and binary point are omitted and the 23-bit mantissa field is encoded as

11011110000000000000000

The exponent field encoding is obtained by adding the exponent value of 101 to 1111111, which is the binary equivalent of the 127_{10} bias value

1 1 1 1 1 1 1 = 127_{10}
+ 1 0 1 = 5_{10}
1 0 0 0 0 1 0 0 = 132_{10}

Appendix F

Creating a Personal Library

Most C programmers create and store source code that they find useful in their work in a separate folder or directory that is referred to as the programmer's personal library of functions. Two such functions, `getanInt()` and `isvalidInt()`, that are used to accept and verify a user-entered integer value, were introduced in Section 9.3.

Additional functions that you will find useful in your work include the following:

- Functions to accept and verify that a user-entered value is a double-precision number
- A function that deletes leading spaces from an entered string
- A function that deletes trailing spaces from an entered string

Table F.1 presents the prototypes for these functions, including the two integer functions previously presented in Section 9.3. The source code for each of these functions is available at *www.course.com*. Note that the source code for the `isvalidInt()` function is more robust than that presented in Section 9.3, because it first removes all leading and trailing blanks from the entered string before checking the remaining characters.

Although the functions listed in Table F.1 are all general-purpose functions, the last four are included because they are required by one or both of the first two functions. Thus, `getanInt()` calls the functions `trimleft()`, `trimright()`, and `isvalidInt()`, while `getaDouble()` calls the functions `trimleft()`, `trimright()`, and `isvalidDouble()`.

For accepting a user-entered value, both the `getanInt()` and `getaDouble()` functions are used in the same manner. For example, a statement such as

```
number = getaDouble();
```

reads user-entered data at the keyboard. If the data represents a valid double-precision value, the data is accepted and stored in the variable named `number`. Here `number` can be any programmer-selected variable name that has been declared to be of type `double`. If the entered data does not correspond to a valid double-precision value, the function will display an error message and request that the user reenter a value. Clearly, the `getaDouble()` function can also be used to accept a floating-point value by casting the returned number to a float.

Similarly, the `getanInt()` function is used to accept a valid integer number. For example, a statement such as

```
years =  getanInt();
```

reads and stores a valid user-entered integer into the variable named `years`. Once again, the variable's name is programmer-selectable, but should be declared as an integer variable.

Table F.1 Useful C Functions Provided with This Text

Prototype	Description
`int getanInt()`	Returns a valid integer entered by the user
`double getaDouble()`	Returns a valid double-precision number entered by the user
`int isvalidInt(char [])`	If the character array (string) passed to the function can be converted to a valid integer, the function returns a 1; otherwise, it returns a 0
`int isvalidDouble(char [])`	If the character array (string) passed to the function can be converted to a valid double-precision value, the function returns a 1; otherwise, it returns a 0
`void trimleft(char [])`	Deletes all leading spaces in the character array (string) passed to the function
`void trimright(char [])`	Deletes all trailing spaces in the character array (string) passed to the function

Appendix G

Solutions to Short Answer Questions

Chapter 1

Exercises 1.1

Short Answer Questions

1. A bit is the smallest and most basic data item. It is a switch (typically a transistor) that can be in one of two states; open or closed. As such, a bit can represent the values 0 and 1.
2. A byte is a grouping of 8 bits. A byte can assume 256 distinct patterns.
3. A byte uses a pattern of 8 bits, such as 00110011, to represent characters in a computer.
4. A word is a single unit combination of 1 or more bytes. Word sizes for some common computers include: a single byte for early personal computers, such as the Apple IIe and Commodore machines; 2 bytes for the first IBM PCs; 4 bytes for the more current Intel-based PCs.
5. The two principal parts of the CPU are the Control Unit and the Arithmetic and Logic

Unit (ALU). The Control Unit monitors the overall operation of the computer while the ALU performs all the arithmetic and logic functions provided by the system.

6. The main difference between RAM and ROM is that RAM is volatile while ROM is nonvolatile. Both RAM and ROM are random access which means that every section of memory can be accessed randomly as quickly as any other section.
7. a. The input/output unit is the interface that provides access to and from the computer to which peripheral devices are attached.
   b. Three devices that would be connected to the input/output unit include keyboards, monitors, and printers.
8. Secondary storage is a permanent storage area for programs and data. Three examples of secondary storage include magnetic tapes, magnetic disks, and CD-ROMS.
9. The difference between sequential storage and direct access storage is that sequential storage allows data to be written or read in one sequential stream from beginning to end, while direct access storage allows data to be written or read from any one file or program independent of its position on the storage medium. Direct access storage allows the computer to jump directly to the desired point in storage, rather than passing through all intervening points like sequential storage would require. In other words, the data can be accessed more quickly.
10. A microprocessor is a single microchip CPU. In everyday life, microprocessors are used in notebook and desktop computers, calculators, and even digital watches.

Exercises 1.2

Short Answer Questions

1. a. *computer program*—a self-contained set of instructions and data used to operate a computer to produce a specific result
   b. *programming*—the process of developing and writing a program
   c. *programming language*—the set of data and instructions that can be used to construct a program
   d. *high-level language*—language in which the instructions resemble human languages, such as English, and can be run on a variety of computer types
   e. *low-level language*—language that uses instructions that are directly tied to one type of computer
   f. *machine language*—a programming language consisting of the binary codes that can be executed by a computer
   g. *assembly language*—a programming language that uses symbolic names for operations and memory addresses
   h. *procedure-oriented language*—high-level language in which the instructions are only used to create self-contained units referred to as procedures
   i. *object-oriented language*—high-level language which defines and manipulates objects to produce results
   j. *source program*—program written in a computer language
   k. *compiler*—program which translates high-level languages as a complete unit before any individual statement is executed
   l. *assembler*—a program that converts, or translates, assembly language programs into machine language

2. a. A high-level language can be translated to run on a variety of computer types, while a low-level language is directly tied to one type of computer.
   b. Procedure-oriented languages create logically consistent sets of instructions, or procedures, to produce a specific result, while object-oriented languages create and manipulate objects to produce specific results.
3. An assembler translates assembly language programs, while both compilers and interpreters translate high-level source programs. A compiler translates a high-level source program as a complete unit before any one statement is actually executed, while an interpreter translates individual source program statements one at a time into executable statements. Each interpreted statement is executed immediately after translation.
4. a. Add the data in memory location 1 to the data in memory location 2.

   Multiply the data in memory location 3 by the data in memory location 2.

   Subtract the data in memory location 4 from the data in memory location 3.

   Divide the data in memory location 3 by the data in memory location 5.
   b. 3 + 5 = 8

   6 * 3 = 18

   6 – 14 = -8

   6 / 4 = 1.5
5. ADD 1, 2

   MUL 3, 2

   SUB 4, 3

   DIV 3, 5
6. (10 + 20) * .6 = 18

Exercises 1.3

Short Answer Questions

1. a. *Fix a flat tire*

   Stop vehicle in a safe, level location

   Set the parking brake

   Get jack, lug-wrench, and spare tire

   Check air pressure in spare tire

   Use jack to raise vehicle so that damaged tire is clear of ground

   Remove hubcap

   Use lug-wrench to loosen each individual lug nut

   Place lug nuts into hubcap

   Remove tire from axle

   Place spare tire onto axle

   Restore each lug nut, and tighten by hand

   Tighten all lug nuts securely with lug-wrench

   Replace hubcap

Release jack

Return jack, lug-wrench, and damaged tire to trunk of vehicle

(Note: an alternative solution is to place a call to someone else and have them come and fix the flat tire.)

b. ***Make a telephone call***

Lift telephone receiver

Dial a number

Wait for answer

Speak to person, or respond to electronic instructions

c. ***Go to the store and purchase a loaf of bread***

Transport yourself to the store

Find bakery department

Select an appropriate loaf of bread

Proceed to checkout area

Exchange money for the loaf of bread

d. ***Roast a turkey***

Clean turkey thoroughly, removing giblets

Place turkey into roasting pan

Stuff with dressing, if desired

Insert meat thermometer deeply into turkey breast

Cover turkey with foil

Roast in 325-degree oven for 4–5 hours, until appropriate internal temp is reached

Remove foil

Roast until outer surfaces of turkey are browned

2. Label cups: #1, #2, and #3, with #3 being the empty cup

Rinse #3

Pour contents of #1 into #3

Rinse #1

Pour contents of #2 into #1

Rinse #2

Pour contents of #3 into #2

Rinse #3

3. Multiply h by 50, and remember this number as hTotal.

Multiply q by 25, and remember this number as qTotal.

Multiply d by 10, and remember this number as dTotal.

Multiply n by 5, and remember this number as nTotal.

Add hTotal to qTotal to dTotal to nTotal to p, and remember this number as Total.

Divide Total by 100 to get the dollar amount.

4. Compare first and second

   If first < second, then compare second and third

   If second < third, then first is smallest

   If second > third, then compare first and third

   If first < third, then first is smallest

   If first > third, then third is smallest

   If first > second, then compare second and third

   If second > third, then third is smallest

   If second < third, then second is smallest

5. a. If the number is greater than 100, keep subtracting 100 from the number.

      The number of times 100 was subtracted is the number of 100 bills needed.

      If the remaining number is greater than 50, keep subtracting 50 from the number until the number is less than 50. The number of times 50 was subtracted is the number of 50 bills needed.

      If the remaining number is greater than 20, keep subtracting 20 from the number until the number is less than 20. The number of times 20 was subtracted is the number of 20 bills needed.

      If the remaining number is greater than 10, keep subtracting 10 from the number until the number is less than 10.The number of times 10 was subtracted is the number of 10 bills needed.

      If the remaining number is greater than 5, keep subtracting 5 from the number until the number is less than 5.The number of times 5 was subtracted is the number of 5 bills needed.

      The remaining number is then number of $1 bills needed.

   b. Total multiplied by 1 is product1

      Product1 is the number of $1 bills

6. a. Compare the first letter of the word JONES with the first letter of each word.

      If the first letter is a match, compare the second letters in each word.

      If the second letter is a match, compare the third letters.

      If the third letters match, compare the fourth.

      If the fourth letters match, compare the fifth.

      If the fifth letters match, the words match.

      If a letter is not a match, proceed to the next word in the list and repeat this comparison.

   b. If the names are in alphabetical order, you will not need to go through each name from the beginning of the list. You can jump to the names that begin with J, or even just jump straight to where JONES would be stored.

7. Step 1: Look at the first letter. If it is an 'e', then set COUNT to 1; else set COUNT to 0.

   Step 2: Look at the next letter. If it is 'e', then add 1 to COUNT.

   Step 3: Continue to repeat Step 2 until a period '.' is encountered.

8. Step 1: Compare the number in the first position to that in the second position.
   If the number in the first position is greater than the number in the second position, switch the numbers.

   Step 2: Compare the number currently in the second position to that in the third position.
   If the number in the second position is greater than the number in the third position, switch the numbers.

   Step 3: Compare the number currently in the first position to that currently in the second position.
   If the number in the first position is greater than the number in the second position, switch the numbers.

Exercises 1.4

Short Answer Questions

1. 1). *Specify the program's requirements*: Ensure that the program requirement is clearly stated and that you understand what is to be achieved.

   2) *Design and Development*: This includes analyzing the problem, developing a solution, coding the solution, and testing and correcting the program.

   3) *Documentation*: Provide adequate user documentation for people who will use the program and programmer documentation for people who will have to maintain the program.

   4) *Maintenance*: Keep the solution up to date by making modifications required, whether due to changes in requirements or because errors are found during program execution.

2. a. Find out exactly what the inventory problem is and what is expected of the solution.
   b. Contact Ms. R. Karp to either define the problem more specifically or to introduce you to other people and/or documents that can define the problem more specifically.

3. a. One output: the dollar amount
   b. Five inputs: half dollars, quarters, dimes, nickels, pennies
   c. Dollar amount = 0.50 * half dollars + 0.25 * quarters + 0.10 * dimes + 0.05 * nickels + 0.01 * pennies
   d. Dollar amount = 0.50 * 0 + 0.25 * 17 + 0.10 * 24 + 0.05 * 16 + 0.01 * 12 = 7.57

4. a. One output: distance
   b. Two inputs: rate, elapsed time
   c. Distance = Rate * Time
   d. Distance = 55 * 2.5 = 137.5
   e. Divide time in minutes by 60 to convert to time in hours.

5. a. One output: the amount of Ergies
   b. Two inputs: Fergies, Lergies
   c. Ergies = Fergies * Lergies
   d. Ergies = 14.65 * 4 = 58.6

6. a. Three lines of output
   b. Three lines of input
   c. Each input becomes a line of output.

7. a. One output: distance
   b. Three inputs: s, d, and t
   c. Distance = s*t-0.5 * d * t * t
   d. Distance = ((60*5280)/3600 * 10) – 0.5 * 12 * 10 * 10 = 280 ft

   (*Note:* You mist first convert the 60 mph to feet/second.)

8. Generally, people envision only the part of the problem they are concerned with and in terms they are familiar with. Once they see the effects of the code on the screen, other possibilities immediately present themselves. However, once you have coded an application, making changes to it are generally very time consuming and in many cases take more time to redo than the original coding took to complete. This is very difficult to explain to a client, who generally expects the additional costs to be less than the original coding costs. In some cases the client may tell you that you should have anticipated the problems. It is almost always better to lay out what the program will and will not do before beginning to code the solution.

9. A fixed fee is a good choice if you have experience in exactly what is wanted, are selling an existing program to a new client, or both you and the client are in total agreement as to what will be produced; otherwise, it is generally a bad choice for both parties. A positive is that you do know how much you will receive for your work and the client knows how much they will pay. The disadvantage is that unless you both are very clear as to what will be produced, you may end up doing double and triple the amount of work contracted for, with very little if any additional funding. This occurs because after the client sees the program, new features immediately present themselves. You, as a programmer, may claim these are additional features, while the client may claim them as normal features that you should have incorporated as part of a useful program. No matter how the issue is resolved, generally, one or both sides may feel they have been deceived.

10. An hourly rate is generally preferable when the exact nature and scope of the work is not known or clearly specified in advance. This is typically a good arrangement for new projects. When a clear understanding, in writing, is available describing what will be produced, or you are selling an application that you have previously developed, a fixed fee is generally used.

11. A clearly written statement of programming work to be done is generally a good idea. The user will know exactly what the programmer is expected to do. Once the programmer completes the program according to the specifications, his job is done. You, as the programmer, will know exactly what you need to do to fulfill your obligation. The user can't decide at the last minute that he wants you to add additional features or functionality without hiring you for additional work. The disadvantage is that this will limit the amount of freedom you have as a programmer. You may have a better idea of how to make the program more user-friendly or easier to handle, but unless this is specified in the agreement, you need to stick with what the user originally asked for. The user also, has less freedom. Unless you both agree on any proposed changes to the agreement, the user needs to stick with what was originally specified.

12. (100 char/sale) × (15 sales/day) × (6 days/week) × (52 weeks/year) × 2 years = 936,000 characters, or approximately 1 million characters. Since each character is stored using 1 byte, the minimum storage is 1 million bytes (1 MB).

13. Assuming that the average typist can type 50 words per minute and that the average word consists of 5 characters, the time it takes to enter all of the sales is [300 (char/sale) × (200 sales)] / [(50 words/minute) × (5 char/word)] = (60,000 char) / (250 char/min) = 240 minutes = 4 hours of nonstop typing.

Exercises 1.5

Short Answer Questions

1.
```
#include <stdio.h>

int main()
{
  double rad, cir;  /* declare an input and output item */
  rad = 2.0;     /* set a value for the radius */
  cir = 2.0 * 3.1416 * rad;  /* calculate the circumference */
  printf("The circumference of the circle is f", cir);

  return 0;
}
```

2. If the area of a circle was required output, the following modifications would have to be made to Program 1.1: Declare a variable to hold the value of the area. Add a line to calculate the area. Add a line to output the value of the area. Modify comments to reflect these changes.

3. a. The value in miles of a distance given in kilometers is calculated using the formula miles = 0.625 * kilometers. Using this information, write a C program to calculate the value in miles of 86 kilometers.
   b. The output required is a value in miles.
   c. The program will have one input (86 kilometers).
   d. miles = 0.625 * kilometers
   e. miles = 0.625 * 86 = 53.75 miles
   f. Get the input kilometers value.

      Calculate miles = 0.625 * kilometers value.

      Display the resulting miles value.

4. a. The final balance of an investment with interest compounded annually is given by the formula balance = principal * (1.0 + rate)(final year - initial year). Using this information, write a C program to calculate the final balance in 2006 of an investment initiated in 1627 with a principal of $24 and an interest rate of 5% compounded annually.
   b. One output: balance
   c. Four inputs: principal, rate, initial year, final year
   d. balance = principal * (1.0 + rate)(final year initial year)
   e. balance = 24 * (1.0 + 0.05)(2006-1627) = 24 * 1.05 * 379 = 9550.80
   f. Get the input values principal, rate, final year, and initial year.

      Calculate balance = principal * (1.0 + rate)(final year initial year).

      Display the resulting balance value.

5. a. Four outputs: the weekly gross and net pay of each individual
   b. Gross pay = Hourly rate * Hours worked

      The general formula for calculating Net pay is:

      Net pay = Gross pay - Tax rate * Gross pay - Medical benefits rate * Gross pay

      = Gross pay * (1 - Tax rate -Medical benefits rate)

      If the tax and benefits rates are considered as fixed numbers that will not change, this formula can be written as:

      Net pay = Gross pay (1 - 0.2 - 0.02) = 0.78 * Gross pay
   c. Eight inputs: the hourly rate, hours worked, income tax rate, and medical benefits rate for each individual (*Note:* If you consider the tax and benefits rates as fixed, then there are four inputs)
   d. Gross Pay1 = $8.43 * 40 = $337.20

      Net Pay1 = 0.78 * $337.20 = $263.02

      Gross Pay2 = $5.67 * 35 = $198.45

      Net Pay2 = 0.78 * $198.45 = $154.79
   e. Get the input values Hourly rate1, Hourly rate2, Hours worked1, and Hours worked2.

      Calculate Gross pay for each worker as Gross pay = Hourly rate * Hours worked.

      Calculate Net pay for each worker as Net pay = 0.78 * Gross pay.

      Display the Gross pay and Net pay values for both workers.
6. a. One output: z
   b. Three inputs: x, u, and s
   c. z = (x u) / s
   d. z = (85.3 80) / 4 = 1.325
   e. Get the three input values of x, u, and s.

      Calculate the value of the standard normal deviate (z) using the formula z = (x-u)/s.

      Display the z value returned by the calculation.
7. a. One output: the value of y
   b. One input: the value of x
   c. $y = e^x$
   d. $y = 2.718^{10} = 22003.64$
   e. Get the input values of e and x.

      Calculate the value of y using the formula $y = e^x$.

      Display the value of y.

Chapter 2

Exercises 2.1

Short Answer Questions

1. `m1234()`	Valid. Not a mnemonic.
`power()`	Valid. A mnemonic.
`add5()`	Valid. Could be a mnemonic.
`taxes()`	Valid. A mnemonic.

`invoices()`	Valid. A mnemonic.
`salestax()`	Valid. A mnemonic.
`newBalance()`	Valid. A mnemonic.
`a2b3c4d5()`	Valid. Not a mnemonic.
`abcd()`	Valid. Not a mnemonic.
`do()`	Invalid. Violates rule 3; is a reserved word.
`newBal()`	Valid. A mnemonic.
`absVal()`	Valid. A mnemonic.
`A12345()`	Valid. Not a mnemonic.
`while()`	Invalid. Violates rule 3; is a reserved word.
`netPay()`	Valid. A mnemonic.
`amount()`	Valid. A mnemonic.
`1A2345()`	Invalid. Violates rule 1; starts with a number.
`int()`	Invalid. Violates rule 3; is a reserved word.
`12345()`	Invalid. Violates rule 1; starts with a number.
`$taxes()`	Invalid. Violates rule 1; starts with a special character.

2. These functions might be used to determine the billing for an order of goods purchased. The purpose of each function, as indicated by its name, is given in the comment statements (/* . . . */) for each function call shown below:

```
input(); /* input the items purchased */
salestax(); /* compute required salestax */
balance(); /* determine balance owed */
calcbill(); /* determine and output bill */
```

3. a. `maxVal()`
   b. `minVal()`
   c. `lowerToUpper()`
   d. `upperToLower()`
   e. `sortNums()`
   f. `sortNames()`
4. Carriage return and line feed

Exercises 2.2

Short Answer Questions

1. a. Yes.
   b. It is not in standard form. To make programs more readable and easier to debug, the standard form presented in Section 2.2 of the text should be used.
2. a. Two backslashes in a row results in one backslash being displayed.
   b. `printf("\\ is a backslash.\n");`

Exercises 2.3

Short Answer Questions

1. The combination of a set of values and a set of operations
2. a. A built-in data type is one that is provided as integral part of the language.
   b. integer and floating point
3. a. int and char
   b. floating point
4. a. float or double
   b. integer
   c. float or double
   d. integer
   e. float or double
   f. character
5. 634,000

   195.162

   83.95

   .00295

   .0004623
6. 1.26e2

   6.5623e2

   3.42695e3

   4.8932e3

   3.21e-1

   1.23e-2

   6.789e-3
7. 8 bytes for KINGSLEY, as follows:

```
|<----------------------- 8 bytes of storage ------------------------>|
01001011 01001001 01001110 01000111 01010011 01001100 01000101 01011001
    K        I        N        G        S        L        E        Y
```

8. You should provide a figure similar to the one provided in Exercise 7 for your own name. However, because each letter requires one byte of storage, the number of bytes required to store your name will be the same number as the total letters in your name.
9. A computer will use variables and declaration statements to let the computer know what types of values it will be using. For example, if the program requires integer types, it will declare variables of the `int` data type.

Exercises 2.4

Short Answer Questions

1. a. (2 * 3) + (4 * 5)
   b. (6 + 18)/2

c. 4.5/(12.2-3.1)
d. 4.6*(3.0+14.9)
e. (12.1 + 18.9) * (15.3 - 3.8)

2. a. 27
b. 8
c. 0
d. 220
e. 23
f. 20
g. 6
h. 2
i. 10
j. 1

3. a. 27.0
b. 8.0
c. 1.0
d. 220.0
e. 22.667
f. 19.778
g. 6.0
h. 2.0

4. a. 21.3 (double) f. 65 (int)
b. 21.8 (double) g. 19.7 (double)
c. 8.0 (double) h. 6.0 (double)
d. 8.0 (double) i. 16 (int)
e. 23.0 (double)

5. a. n / p + 3 = 5
b. m / p + n - 10 * amount = 10
c. m - 3 * n + 4 * amount = 24
d. amount / 5 = 0
e. 18 / p = 3
f. -p * n = -50
g. -m / 20 = -2
h. (m + n) / (p + amount) = 10
i. m + n / p + amount = 53

6. a. n / p + 3 = 5.0
b. m / p + n - 10 * amount = 10.0
c. m - 3 * n + 4 * amount = 24.0
d. amount / 5 = 0.2
e. 18 / p = 3.6
f. -p * n = -50.0
g. -m / 20 = -2.5
h. (m + n) / (p + amount) = 10.0
i. m + n / p + amount = 53.0

7. a. `printf("%d", 15);`
b. `printf("%d", 33);`
c. `printf("%f %d", 526.768, 33);`

8. answer1 is the integer 5
   answer2 is the integer 2
9. The remainder of 9 divided by 4 is 1.
   The remainder of 17 divided by 3 is 2.
10. a. 'm' - 5 = 'h'
    b. 'm' + 5 = 'r'
    c. 'G' + 6 = 'M'
    d. 'G' - 6 = 'A'
    e. 'b' - 'a' = 1
    f. 'g' - 'a' + 1 = 6 + 1 = 7
    g. 'G' - 'A' + 1 = 6 + 1 = 7
11. The value of the decimal number 9 in octal is 11.
    The value of the decimal number 9 in hexadecimal is 9.
    The value of the decimal number 14 in octal is 16.
    The value of the decimal number 14 in hexadecimal is E.

Exercises 2.5

Short Answer Questions

1. `proda` Valid.
   `newbal` Valid.
   `9ab6` Invalid. Begins with a number.
   `c1234` Valid.
   `while` Invalid. C++ keyword.
   `sum.of` Invalid. Decimal point not allowable.
   `abcd` Valid.
   `$total` Invalid. Begins with special character.
   `average` Valid.
   `c3` Valid.
   `newbal` Invalid. Contains a space.
   `grade1` Valid.
   `12345` Invalid. Begins with a number.
   `a1b2c3d4` Valid.
   `finGrad` Valid.
2. `Salestax` Valid.
   `Harry` Valid. Not meaningful.
   `Maximum` Valid.
   `3sum` Invalid. Begins with a number.
   `a234` Valid. Not meaningful.
   `sue` Valid. Not meaningful.

`okay`	Valid.
`for`	Invalid. C++ keyword.
`r2d2`	Valid. Not meaningful.
`c3p0`	Valid. Not meaningful.
`a`	Valid. Not meaningful.
`tot.al`	Invalid. Contains decimal point.
`firstNum`	Valid.
`average`	Valid.
`awesome`	Valid. Not meaningful.
`c$five`	Invalid. Contains special character.
`ccA1`	Valid. Not meaningful.
`sum`	Valid.
`goforit`	Valid. Not meaningful.
`netpay`	Valid.

3. a. `intcount;`
   b. `floatgrade;`
   c. `doubleyield;`
   d. `charinitial;`
4. a. `intnum1, num2, num3;`
   b. `floatgrade 1, grade2, grade3, grade4;`
   c. `doubletempa, tempb, tempc;`
   d. `charch, let1, let2, let3, let4;`
5. a. `intfirstnum, secnum;`
   b. `floatprice, yield, coupon;`
   c. `doublematurity;`
6. a.
   ```
   intmonth;
   intday = 30;
   intyear;
   ```
   b.
   ```
   doublehours;
   doublerate;
   doubleotime= 15.62;
   ```
   c.
   ```
   floatprice;
   floatamount;
   floattaxes;
   ```
   d.
   ```
   charin _key;
   charch;
   charchoice = 'f';
   ```
7. a.
   ```
   #include <stdio.h>
   int main()
   {
   int num1; /* declare the integer variable num1 */
   int num2; /* declare the integer variable num2 */
   ```

```
int total; /* declare the integer variable total */

num1 = 25; /* assign the integer 25 to num1 */
num2 = 30; /* assign the integer 30 to num2 */
      /* assign the sum of num1 and num2 to total */
      total = num1 + num2;
      printf("The total of %d and %d is %d.\n",num1,num2,total");
               /* this prints: The total of 25 and 30 is 55. */

return 0;
    }
```

b. Output: `The total of 25 and 30 is 55.`

8. Every variable has type (e.g., `int`, `float`, etc.), a value, and an address in memory where it is stored.

9. a. All definitions are declarations but not all declarations are definitions.
   b. Definition statements reserve storage areas in memory for the variables. In this sense variables are created (come into existence) by definition statements. Before a variable is used it must exist. Thus, definition statements must precede any statement that uses the variables.

Chapter 3

Exercises 3.1

Short Answer Questions

1. a. The listing as written is missing variable declarations, missing a semicolon in the width assignment, missing a value for the length variable, and missing the closing parenthesis and semicolon on the `printf` statement. Corrected listing:

```
#include <stdio.h>
int main()
{
int length, width, area;

width = 15;
length = 20; /* must be assigned some value */

area = length * width;
printf("The area is %d", area);

return 0;
}
```

   b. The listing as written contains an area calculation that should be positioned after the value assignments to length and width. Also, there is no closing bracket '}'. Corrected listing:

```
#include <stdio.h>
int main()
{
```

```
int length, width, area;

length = 20;
width = 15;

area = length * width;
printf("The area is %d", area);

return 0;
}
```

c. The listing as written contains a semicolon where there should be a comma in the variable declaration statement, and the assignment of the area variable is reversed. Corrected listing:

```
#include <stdio.h>
int main()
{
int length = 20, width = 15, area;

area = length * width;
printf("The area is %d", area);

return 0;
}
```

2. a. 10
   b. 13
   c. -3
   d. 23
   e. 19.68
   f. 19.58
   g. 19

3. The second expression is correct because the assignment of 25 to b is done before the subtraction. Without the parentheses the subtraction has the higher precedence, and the expression a – b is calculated, yielding a value, say 10. The subsequent attempt to assign the value of 25 to this value is incorrect and is equivalent to the expression 10 = 25. Values can only be assigned to variables.

Exercises 3.2

Short Answer Questions

1. a. `sqrt(6.37);`
   b. `sqrt(x-y);`
   c. `pow(3.62,3);`
   d. `pow(81,.24);`
   e. `abs(pow(a, 2.0) - pow(b, 2.0))` -or- `abs(a*a - b*b);`
   f. `exp(3.0);`

2. a. `c = sqrt((a * a) + (b * b));` -or- `c = sqrt( pow (a,2.0) + pow (b,2.0))`
   b. `p = sqrt( abs(m-n));`
   c. `sum = (a * ( pow (r, n) - 1)) / (r-1);`

Exercises 3.3

Short Answer Questions

1. a. `scanf("%d", & firstnum );`
   b. `scanf("%f", &grade);`
   c. `scanf("%lf", & secnum ); /* the lf is required here */`
   d. `scanf("%c", & keyval );`
   e. `scanf("%d %d %f", &month, &years, &average);`
   f. `scanf("%c %d %d %lf % lf",&ch , &num1, &num2, &grade1, &grade2);`
   g. `scanf("%f %f %f %lf % lf",&interest , &principal, &capital, &price, &yield);`
   h. `scanf("%c %c %c %d %d % d",&ch , &letter1, &letter2, &num1,&num2, &num3);`
   i. `scanf("%f %f %f %lf %lf %lf",&temp1, &temp2, &temp3,&volts1, &volts2);`

2. a. `int day;`
   b. `char firChar;`
   c. `float grade;`
   d. `double price;`
   e.
   ```
   int num1;
   int num2;
   char ch1;
   ```
   f.
   ```
   float firstnum;
   float secnum;
   int count;
   ```
   g.
   ```
   char ch1;
   char ch2;
   int flag;
   doubl eaverage;
   ```

3. a. Missing & operator in front of num1. The correct form is

   ```
   scanf("%d", &num1);
   ```

   b. Missing & operator in front of firstnum and wrong control sequence for price. The correct form is

   ```
   scanf("%d %f %lf", &num1, &firstnum, &price);
   ```

   c. The wrong control sequence for num1 and secnum. The correct form is

   ```
   scanf("%d %f %lf", &num1, &secnum, &price);
   ```

   d. Missing & operators in front of all the variables. The correct form is

   ```
   scanf("%d %d %lf", &num1, &num2, &yield);
   ```

   e. Missing control string entirely. The correct form is

   ```
   scanf("%d %d", &num1, &num2);
   ```

   f. Reversed address and control string. The correct form is

   ```
   scanf("%d", &num1);
   ```

Exercises 3.4

Short Answer Questions

1. The output of the program is:

```
answer1 is the integer 5
answer2 is the integer 2
```

2. The output of the program is:

```
The remainder of 9 divided by 4 is 1
The remainder of 17 divided by 3 is 2
```

3. a. The comma is within the control string and the statement is not terminated with a semicolon. This statement will generate a compiler error, even if the semicolon is appended to the statement.
   b. The statement uses a floating-point control sequence with an integer argument. The statement will compile and print an unpredictable result.
   c. The statement uses an integer control sequence with a floating-point constant. The statement will compile and print an unpredictable result.
   d. The statement has no control sequences for the numerical arguments. The statement will compile and print the letters a b c. The numerical values are ignored.
   e. The statement uses a floating-point control sequence with an integer argument. The statement will compile and print an unpredictable result.
   f. The f conversion character has been omitted from the control string. The statement will compile and print %3.6. The second numerical value has no effect.
   g. The formatting string must come before the arguments. The statement will compile and produce no output.

4. a. |5|
   b. | 5|
   c. |56829|
   d. | 5.26|
   e. | 5.27|
   f. |53.26|
   g. |534.26|
   h. |534.00|

5. a. The number is 26.27

   The number is 682.30

   The number is 1.97

   b.
```
$  26.27
  682.30
    1.97
 --------
$ 710.54
```
   c.
```
$  26.27
  682.30
    1.97
  --------
$ 710.54
```

d. 34.16
10.00

44.17

Exercises 3.5

Short Answer Questions

1. a. #define TRUE 1
   #define FALSE 2
   b. #define AM 0
   #define PM 1
   c. #define Rate 3.25
2. a. Terminal semicolon not required.
   b. Value and symbolic constant name are reversed.
   c. Value must be a number.

Chapter 4

Exercises 4.1

Short Answer Questions

1. a. True. Value is 1.
   b. True. Value is 1.
   c. True. Value is 1.
   d. True. Value is 1.
   e. True. Value is 1.
   f. Value is 10.
   g. Value is 4.
   h. Value is 0.
   i. Value is 10.
2. a.
```
a % b * c && c % b * a
= ((a % b) * c) && ((c % b) * a)
= ((5 % 2) * 4) && ((4 % 2) * 5)
= (1 * 4) && (0 * 5)
= 4 && 0                    /* same as True AND False */
= 0
```
   b.
```
a% b * c || c % b * a
=((a % b) * c) || ((c % b) * a)
= ((5 % 2) * 4) || ((4 % 2) * 5)
= (1 * 4) || (0 * 5)
= 4 || 0                    /* same as True OR False */
= 1
```

c.
```
b% c * a && a % c * b
=((b % c) * a) && ((a % c) * b)
= ((2 % 4) * 5) && ((5 % 4) * 2)
= (2 * 5) && (1 * 2)
= 10 && 2                   /* same as True AND True */
= 1
```

d.
```
b% c * a || a % c * b
= ((b % c) * a) || ((a % c) * b)
= ((2 % 4) * 5) || ((5 % 4) * 2)
= (2 * 5) || (1 * 2)
= 10 || 2                   /* same as True OR True */
= 1
```

3. a. `age == 30`
   b. `temp> 98.6`
   c. `height< 6.0`
   d. `month== 12`
   e. `letter_in== 'm'`
   f. `age== 30 && height > 6.0`
   g. `day== 15 && month == 1`
   h. `age> 50 || years_empl>= 5`
   i. `id< 500 && age > 55`
   j. `length > 2 && length < 3`

4. a. 1
   b. 0
   c. 1

Exercises 4.2

Short Answer Questions

1. a.
```
if (angle == 90)
       printf("The angle is a right angle");
   else
       printf("The angle is not a right angle");
```

b.
```
if(temperature > 100)
       printf("above the boiling point of water");
   else
       printf("below the boiling point of water");
```

c.
```
if(number > 0)
       positiveSum = number + positiveSum;
   else
       negativeSum = number + negativeSum;
```

d.
```
if(slope < .5)
       flag = 0;
   else
       flag = 1;
```

e.
```
if((num1 - num2) < .001)
        approx = 0;
    else
        approx = (num1 - num2)/2.0;
```

f.
```
if((temp1 - temp2) > 2.3)
        error = (temp1 - temp2) * factor;
```

g.
```
if((x > y) && (z < 20))
        scanf("%d", &p);
```

h.
```
if((distance > 20) && (distance < 35))
        scanf("%d", &time);
```

2. a.
```
if (score > 70)
        pass = pass + 1;
    else
        fail = fail + 1;
```

b.
```
if(c == 15)
    {
        credit = 10;
        limit = 1000;
    }
    else
    {
        credit = 5;
        limit = 400;
    }
```

c.
```
if(id > 22)
        factor = 0.7;
```

d.
```
if(count == 10)
        average = sum / count;
        printf("%f", average);
```

3. The error is that the intended relational expression letter == 'm' has been written as the assignment expression letter = 'm'. When the expression is evaluated, the character 'm' is assigned to the variable letter and the value of the expression itself is the value of 'm'. Since this is a non-0 value, it is taken as true and the message is displayed.

Another way of looking at this is to realize that the `if` statement, as written in the program, is equivalent to the following two statements:

```
letter = 'm';
if(letter) printf("Hello there!");
```

A correct version of the program is

```
#include <stdio.h>
int main()
{
char letter;
printf("Enter a letter: ");
scanf("%c", &letter);
if (letter == 'm') printf("Hello there!");
return 0;
 }
```

Exercises 4.3

Short Answer Questions

1. The program output is "`The if part is true`"
2. factor = 1.06
3. a.
```
if (grade == 'A')
{
  if (weight > 35)
    bin = 1;
  else   t = s + a;
    }
```

   b.
```
sum= 0;
 if (count < 5)
 {
   if (grade < 50)
     fail = fail + 1;
 }
```

4. a. Yes.
   b. Program 4.5 is a better program because fewer calculations would typically be made. For example, if 45000 were entered for `monthlySales` in Program 4.5, the first `if` statement is executed and found to be false. The first `else-if` statement is then executed, found to be true, and further execution of the chain stops. This is not true for the Exercise program. Here, all `if` statements are executed, regardless of which has a true condition. Program 4.5 also requires fewer comparisons, using simpler relational expressions.
5. a. This program will run. It will not, however, produce the correct result.
   b and c. This program evaluates correct incomes for `monthlySales` less than 20000.00 only. If 10000.00 or more were entered, the first `else if` statement would be executed and all others would be ignored. That is, for 10000.00 or more, the income for >= 10000.00 would be calculated and displayed. Had `if` statements been used in place of the `else if` statements, the program would have worked correctly, but inefficiently.

Exercises 4.4

Short Answer Questions

1.
```
switch(material)
{
case 1:
   factor = 1.5;
   density = 2.76;
   break;
case 3:
   factor = 2.5;
   density = 2.85;
   break;
```

```
case 7:
   factor = 3.5;
   density = 3.14;
   break;
default:
   factor = 1.0;
   density = 1.25;
}
```

2.
```
switch(letterGrade)
  {
case 'A':
   printf("The numerical grade is between 90 and 100");
   break;
case 'B':
   printf("The numerical grade is between 80 and 89.9");
   break;
case 'C':
   printf("The numerical grade is between 70 and 79.9");
   break;
case 'D':
   printf("How are you going to explain this one");
   break;
default:
   printf("Of course I had nothing to do with the grade.");
   printf("\nThe professor was really off the wall.");
}
```

3.
```
switch(bondType)
  {
  case 1:
    inData();
    check();
    break;
  case 2:
    dates();
    leapYr();
    break;
  case 3:
    yield();
    maturity();
    break;
  case 4:
    price();
    roi();
    break;
  case 5:
    files();
    save();
    break;
  case 6:
    retrieve();
    screen();
    break;
}
```

Chapter 5

Exercises 5.1

Short Answer Questions

1. The repetition statements are the `while` statement, `for` statement, and `do-while` statement.
2. The four elements are the repetition statement, a condition that must be evaluated, a statement that initially sets the condition being tested, and a statement within the repeating section of code that alters the condition so that it eventually becomes false.
3. a. An entrance-controlled loop, also known as a pretest loop, is a loop in which the condition being tested is evaluated at the beginning of the repeating section of code (at the beginning of the loop).
   b. `while`, `for`
4. a. An exit-controlled loop, also known as a posttest loop, is a loop in which the condition being tested is evaluated at the end of the repeating section of code (at the end of the loop).
   b. `do-while`
5. a. A pretest loop is a loop in which the condition being tested is evaluated at the beginning of the repeating section of code, while a posttest loop is one in which the condition is evaluated at the end of the repeating section of code.
   b. If the condition is initially false, then the statements in a pretest loop will never be executed.
   c. If the condition is initially false, then the statements in a posttest loop will execute only once.
6. In a counter-controlled loop, the number of repetitions is known before the loop executes, whereas in a condition-controlled loop the number of repetitions is not known and instead terminates according to some set condition.

Exercises 5.2

Short Answer Questions

1. `while` statements produce entrance-controlled loops because the condition is evaluated before the repeating section of code.
2.
```
int count = 10;
while (count <= 20)
{
printf("%d ",count);
count++;
}
```
3.
```
int count = 10;
while (count <= 20)
{
printf("%d ",count);
count = count + 2;
}
```

4.
```
int count = 20;
while (count >= 10)
{
printf("%d ",count);
count--;
}
```

5.
```
int count = 20;
while (count >= 10)
{
printf("%d ",count);
count = count-  2;
}
```

6. 21 numbers are displayed with 1 as the first and 21 as the last.

Exercises 5.3

Short Answer Questions

1. accumulating statement
2. A sentinel is a specific value or start of a range of values that will cause a loop to terminate.
3. A `break` statement causes an immediate exit from a repetition or selection statement, while a `continue` statement causes an immediate re-evaluation of the condition being tested in a repetition or selection statement.
4. The program yields the correct average; it also yields all intermediate averages, none of which are displayed. From a programming perspective, only one average should be calculated, which is the final average after all numbers have been input. Thus, Program 5.7 is a more correct program in that it does not calculate unnecessary results.

Exercises 5.4

Short Answer Questions

1. a. `for(i= 1; i<= 20; i++)`
   b. `for(icount= 1; icount<= 21; icount+= 2)`
   c. `for(J = 1; J <= 100; J += 5)`
   d. `for(icount= 20; icount>= 1; icount--)`
   e. `for(icount= 21; icount>= 1; icount-= 2)`
   f. `for(count = 1.0; count <= 16.2; count += 0.2)`
   g. `for(xcnt= 20.0; xcnt>= 10.0; xcnt-= 0.5)`
2. a. 20
   b. 10
   c. 20
   d. 20
   e. 10
   f. 77
   g. 21

3. a. 10
   b. 1024
   c. 75
   d. -5
   e. 40320
   f. 0.031250
4. 20 16 12 8 4 0

Chapter 6

Exercises 6.1

Short Answer Questions

1. a. requires one int value
   b. requires 3 values, an int and two floats, in that order
   c. requires 3 values, an int and two doubles, in that order
   d. requires 3 values, a char and two floats, in that order
   e. requires 2 floats
   f. requires 6 values, 2 ints, 2 chars and 2 floats, in that order
   g. requires 3 values, 2 ints and a char, in that order
2. a. `void check(int num1, float num2, float num3)`
   b. `void findAbs(float num )`
   c. `void mult(float num1, float num2)`
   d. `void sqrIt(int num )`
   e. `void powFun(int num, intpower )`
   f. `void makeTable()`
3. a. `void check(int, float, float);`
   b. `void findAbs(float);`
   c. `void mult(float, float);`
   d. `void sqrIt(int);`
   e. `void powFun(int, int);`
   f. `void makeTable();`

Exercises 6.2

Short Answer Questions

1. a. requires one int value and returns an int value
   b. requires 3 values, an int and two doubles, in that order, and returns a double
   c. requires 3 values, an int and two doubles, in that order, and returns a double
   d. requires 3 values, a char and two floats, in that order, and returns a char
   e. requires 2 floats and returns an int
   f. requires 6 values, 2 ints, 2 chars and 2 floats, in that order, and returns a float
   g. requires 3 values, 2 ints and a char, in that order, and does not return a value

2. a. `void check(int num1, float num2, double num3)`
   b. `float findAbs(float num )`
   c. `float mult(float num1, float num2)`
   d. `long sqrIt(intnum)`
   e. `void makeTable()`

Chapter 7

Exercises 7.1

Short Answer Questions

1. a.

Variable name	Data type	Scope
`price`	integer	global to `main()`, `roi()`, and `step()`
`years`	long integer	global to `main()`, `roi()`, and `step()`
`yield`	float	global to `main()`, `roi()`, and `step()`
`bondtype`	integer	local to `main()`
`integererest`	float	local to `main()`
`coupon`	float	local to `main()`
`mat1`	integer	local to `roi()`
`mat2`	integer	local to `roi()`
`count`	integer	local to `roi()`
`effectiveInt`	float	local to `roi()`
`first`	float	local to `step()`
`last`	float	local to `step()`
`numofyrs`	integer	local to `step()`
`fracpart`	float	local to `step()`

b. See boxes around the code below.

```
int price;
long int years;
float yield;

int main()
{
  int bondtype;
  float interest, coupon;
      .
      .

  return 0;
}

float roi(int mat1, int mat2)
{
  int count;
  float effectiveInt;
      .
      .
  return(effectiveInt);
}

int step(float first, float last)
{
  int numofyrs;
  float fracpart;
      .
      .
  return(10*numofyrs);
}
```

c. roi() – expected: 2 integer values; returns: a float value
step() – expected: 2 float values; returns: an integer value

2. a.

Variable name	Data type	Scope
`key`	character	global to `main()`, `func1()`, and `func2()`
`number`	long integer	global to `main()`, `func1()`, and `func2()`
`a, b, c`	integer	local to `main()`
`x, y`	float	local to `main()`
`secnum`	float	global to `func1()`, and `func2()`
`num1, num2`	integer	local to `func1()`
`o, p`	integer	local to `func1()`
`q`	float	local to `func1()`
`first, last`	float	local to `func2()`

`a, b, c, o, p`	integer	local to `func2()`
`r`	float	local to `func2()`
`s, t, x`	float	local to `func2()`

b. The boxes appear below.

```
char key;
long int number;

int main()
{
  int a,b,c;
  float x,y;
     .
     .

  return 0;
}

float secnum;

int func1(int num1, int num2)
{
  int o,p;
  float q;
     .
     .
  return(p);
}

float func2(float first, float last)
{
  int a,b,c,o,p;
  float r;
  float s,t,x;
     .
     .
  return(s * t);
}
```

c. `func1()` – expected: 2 int values; returns: an int value

`func2()` – expected: 2 float values; returns: a float value

3. All function parameters have local scope with respect to their defined function. *Note:* Although function parameters assume a value which is dependent on the calling function, these parameters can change values within their respective functions. This makes them behave as is they were local variables within the called function.

4. The output of the program is:

```
The value of firstnum is 20
The value of firstnum is now 10
```

Exercises 7.2

Short Answer Questions

1. a. The storage categories available to local variables are automatic, static, and register. It is important to realize, however, that not all variables declared inside functions are necessarily local. An example of this is an external variable.
   b. The storage categories available to global variables are external and static.
2. A local automatic variable is unique to the function in which it is declared. Every time the function is called, the automatic variable is recreated, as if it never existed before. A local static variable is also unique to the function where it is declared. However, a static variable retains its last value and is not recreated when its function is called again.
3. The first function declares `yrs` to be a static variable and assigns a value of 1 to it only once when the function is compiled. Each time the function is called thereafter, the value in `yrs` is increased by 2. The second function also declares `yrs` to be static, but assigns it the value 1 every time it is called, and the value of `yrs` after the function is finished will always be 3. By resetting the value of `yrs` to 1 each time it is called, the second function defeats the purpose of declaring the variable to be static.
4. a. A static global variable is declared outside of the body of any function (but not necessarily at the top of the file) and may always be initialized. If it is not explicitly initialized, it is implicitly initialized to 0 or to a null value (for character or character arrays) by the compiler. The definition of a static global variable also creates storage for the variable. A global `extern` declaration does not create storage for the variable and, therefore, can never be used to initialize a variable. The `extern` declaration simply alerts the compiler that the variable was created (defined) elsewhere. Additionally, static global variables are private to the file in which they are defined. Thus, static global variables may not be made `extern` in another file. Both `static` and `extern` declarations can be made within a function, in which case they are no longer global declarations.
   b. If a variable is declared with `extern`, then there must be one and only one global definition for the same variable somewhere in the program. This can be in any file that is part of the program.
5. The location of the variable declaration determines its scope.
6. a. `extern char choice; /* place at the top of file2 */`
   b. `extern int flag; /* placed w/in pduction () */`
   c. `extern long date; /* placed above pduction () but below roi () */`
   d. `extern long date; /* placed w/in roi () */`
   e. `extend double coupon; /* placed w/in roi () */`
   f. `extern char bondType ; /* placed at the top of file1 */`
   g. `extern double maturity; /* above price() but below main() */`

Exercises 7.3

Short Answer Questions

1. `&average` means "the address of the variable named average"
2. The address of a variable is always its starting location.

   Therefore:

   `&temp` is 16892

   `&dist` is 16896

   `&date` is 16900

   `&miles` is 16908
3. An address is stored in a pointer.
4. a. `float *amount;`
   b. `double *price;`
   c. `int *minutes;`
   d. `char *key;`
   e. `int *yield;`
   f. `float *coupon;`
   g. `double *rate;`
   h. `char *securityType;`
   i. `int *datePt;`
   j. `double *yldAddr;`
   k. `float *amtPpt;`
   l. `char *ptrchr;`
5. All pointer declarations must have an asterisk. Therefore, c, e, g, and i are pointer declarations.
6. a. `void whatNow(char *m1Ptr, char *m2Ptr, float *m3Ptr, float *m4Ptr, int *m5Ptr)`
   b. `void whatNow(char *, char *, float *, float *, int *);`

Exercises 7.4

Short Answer Questions

1. `voidtime(int& sec, int& min, int& hours)`
2. In `main()` the variables `min` and `hour` refer to integer quantities, while in `time()` the variables `min` and `hours` are pointers to integers. Thus, there are four distinct variables in all, two of which are known in `main()` and two of which are known in `time()`. The computer (actually, the compiler) keeps track of each variable with no confusion. The effect on a programmer, however, may be quite different.
3. When used in `main()`, the programmer must remember to use the names `min` and `hour` as integer variables. When in `time()` the programmer must "switch" viewpoints and use the same names as pointer variables. Debugging such a program can be quite frustrating because the same names are used in two different contexts. It is, therefore, more advisable to avoid this type of situation by adopting different names for pointers than those used for other variables. A useful trick is to either prepend each pointer name with a `ptr` notation or append each pointer name with `Addr`.

4. The precedence of the indirection operator is higher than the multiplication operator and is therefore performed first. Using parentheses will make the expression clearer

```
(*pt1) * (*pt2)
```

Chapter 8

Exercises 8.1

Short Answer Questions

1. a.
```
#define SIZE 60
  double rate[SIZE];
```
   b.
```
#define SIZE 30
  double temp[SIZE];
```
   c.
```
#define SIZE 25
  char code[SIZE];
```
   d.
```
#define SIZE 100
  int year[SIZE];
```
   e.
```
#define SIZE 26
  double rate[SIZE];
```
   f.
```
#define SIZE 1000
  double distance[SIZE];
```
   g.
```
#define SIZE 20
  int code[SIZE];
```

2. a. grade[0] refers to the first item stored in the array.
   grade[2] refers to the third item stored in the array.
   grade[6] refers to the seventh item stored in the array.
   b. grade[0] refers to the first item stored in the array.
   grade[2] refers to the third item stored in the array.
   grade[6] refers to the seventh item stored in the array.
   c. amps[0] refers to the first item stored in the array.
   amps[2] refers to the third item stored in the array.
   amps[6] refers to the seventh item stored in the array.
   d. dist[0] refers to the first item stored in the array.
   dist[2] refers to the third item stored in the array.
   dist[6] refers to the seventh item stored in the array.
   e. velocity[0] refers to the first item stored in the array.
   velocity[2] refers to the third item stored in the array.
   velocity[6] refers to the seventh item stored in the array.
   f. time[0] refers to the first item stored in the array.
   time[2] refers to the third item stored in the array.
   time[6] refers to the seventh item stored in the array.

3. a. a) `scanf ("%d %d %d", &grade[0], &grade[2], &grade[6]);`
   b) `scanf ( "%lf %lf %lf", &grade[0], &grade[2], &grade[6]);`
   c) `scanf ( "%lf %lf %lf", &s[0], &s[2], &s[6]);`
   d) `scanf ( "%lf %lf %lf", &dist[0], &dist[2], &dist[6]);`
   e) `scanf ( "%lf %lf %lf", &velocity[0], &velocity[2], &velocity[6]);`
   f) `scanf ( "%lf %lf %lf", &time[0], &time[2], &time[6]);`

   b.
```
#define MAXGRADES 20
     int grade[MAXGRADES];
     int i;

     /* input the grades */
     for (i = 0; i < MAXGRADES; i++)    {
     printf("Enter a grade: ");
     scanf("%d", &grade[i]);
     }
```

4. a.
```
a) printf("%d, %d, %d" grade[0], grade[2], grade[6]);
b) printf("%lf, %lf, %lf" grade[0], grade[2], grade[6]);
c) printf("%lf, %lf, %lf" amps[0], amps[2], amps[6]);
d) printf("%lf, %lf, %lf" dist[0], dist[2], dist[6]);
e) printf("%lf, %lf, %lf" velocity[0], velocity[2], velocity[6]);
f) printf("%lf, %lf, %lf" time[0], time[2], time[6]);
```

   b.
```
for( i= 0; i< 20; i++ )
printf ( "%d\n", grade[i] );
```

5. a. a[1] a[2] a[3] a[4] a[5]
   b. a[1] a[3] a[5]
   c. b[3] b[4] b[5] b[6] b[7] b[8] b[9] b[10]
   d. b[3] b[6] b[9] b[12]
   e. c[2] c[4] c[6] c[8] c[10]

Exercises 8.2

Short Answer Questions

1. a.
```
#define SIZE 10
int grade[SIZE] = {89, 75, 82, 93, 78, 95, 81, 88, 77, 82};
```

   b.
```
# define SIZE 5
double  amount[SIZE] = {10.62, 13.98, 18.45, 12.68, 14.76};
```

   c.
```
# define SIZE 100
double  rate[SIZE] = {6.29, 6.95, 8.25, 8.35, 8.40, 8.42};
```

   d.
```
# define SIZE 64
double  temp[SIZE] = {78.2, 69.6, 68.5, 83.9, 55.4, 68.0, 49.8, 58.3, 62.5, 71.6};
```

   e.
```
# define SIZE 15
char code[SIZE] = { 'f', 'j', 'm', 'q', 't', 'w', 'z' };
```

2.
```
char  string[13] = "Good Morning";
char  string[]   = {' G','o','o','d ',' ', ' M','o','r','n','i','n','g ', '\0'};
char  string[13] = {' G','o','o','d ',' ', ' M','o','r','n','i','n','g ', '\0'};
```

Exercises 8.3

Short Answer Questions

1. `void sortArray(double inArray[500])`
   `void sortArray(double inArray [])`
2. `void findKey(char select [256])`
   `void findKey(char select [])`
3. `double prime (double rates [256])`
   `double prime (double rates [])`

Exercises 8.5

Short Answer Questions

1. a. `intarray[6][10];`
   b. `intcodes[2][5];`
   c. `charkeys[7][12];`
   d. `charletter[15][7];`
   e. `doublevals[10][25];`
   f. `doubletest[16][8];`

Chapter 9

Exercises 9.1

Short Answer Questions

1. `char`
2. NULL, or `'\0'`
3. `message[3]` corresponds to the second `'l'` in `"Hello there"`
4. The output is:
   `there`

Exercises 9.2

Short Answer Questions

1. true
2. 4 characters
3. 0
4. `atof()`

Exercises 9.3

Short Answer Questions

1. When a number is entered as a string, each character in the string can be checked to ensure that it complies with the data type requested (`int, float, double`).
2. Data type checks could ensure that the month, day, and year were all entered as integers. Some simple reasonableness checks would ensure that a month was between 1 and 12, a day between 1 and 31, and a year between reasonable limits for the application. More complex reasonableness checks might check that a day in months 1, 3, 5, 7, 8, 10, and 12 were between 1 and 31, those in months 4, 6, 9, and 11 between 1 and 30, and those in month 2 between 1 and 28, except if the year is a leap year, in which case the day must be between 1 and 29 in month 2.
3. Answers will vary. Students may want to include such functions as `isvalidInt()` and `getanInt()` among others.

Exercises 9.4

Short Answer Questions

1. a. `!four score and ten!`
   b. `! Home!!`
   c. `!Home! !`
   d. `! Ho!`
   e. `!Ho!`
2. a. First output: `Have a nice day!`

   Second output: `H`

   b. In the first output, `%s` format expects a string variable, which is supplied with the name of the string array, `text`. In the second output, `%c` expects a single character from the string; the data contained in the first element of `text` or `*text`.

Chapter 10

Exercises 10.1

Short Answer Questions

1. i)
```
FILE *memo;
memo = fopen("coba.mem","w");
```
   ii)
```
FILE *letter;
letter = fopen("book.let","w");
```
   iii)
```
FILE *coups;
coups = fopen("coupons.bnd","a");
```
   iv)
```
FILE *yield;
yield = fopen("yield.bnd","a");
```

v)
```
FILE *priFile;
priFile = fopen("prices.dat","r");
```
vi)
```
FILE *rates;
rates = fopen("rates.dat","r");
```
2. a. i)
```
FILE *data;
data = fopen("Data.txt","r");
```
ii)
```
FILE *prices;
prices = fopen("prices.txt","r");
```
iii)
```
FILE *coups;
coups = fopen("coupons.dat","r");
```
iv)
```
FILE *exper;
exper = fopen("exper.dat","r");
```
b. i) `FILE *data = fopen("Data.txt","r");`

ii) `FILE *prices = fopen("prices.txt","r");`

iii) `FILE *coups = fopen("coupons.dat","r");`

iv) `FILE *exper = fopen("exper.dat","r");`

3. a. i)
```
FILE *data;
data = fopen("Data.txt","w");
```
ii)
```
FILE *prices;
prices = fopen("prices.txt","w");
```
iii)
```
FILE *coups;
coups = fopen("coupons.dat","w");
```
iv)
```
FILE *exper;
exper = fopen("exper.dat","w");
```
b. i) `FILE *data = fopen("Data.txt","w");`

ii) `FILE *prices = fopen("prices.txt","w");`

iii) `FILE *coups = fopen("coupons.dat","w");`

iv) `FILE *exper = fopen("exper.dat","w");`

4. A saved C program is a file; it contains a collection of characters stored under a common name on a secondary storage medium.

5. Answers may vary depending on what system the student is using. On DOS, VMX, and Windows 3.1 systems, a filename may have up to 8 characters, and optionally a decimal point followed by 3 more characters. On Windows 95/NT/2000/XP, or a Mac OS X system, a filename may consist of up to 255 characters. On early versions of Unix systems, filenames could be a maximum of 14 characters and on more current versions a filename may consist of up to 255 characters.

6. FILENAME_MAX = 260

FOPEN_MAX = 20

Exercises 10.2

Short Answer Questions

1. `fprintf()` requires an external file pointer and `fscanf()` requires an internal file pointer.
2. `fputc(c,filename)`, `fputs(string,filename)`, `fprintf(filename,"format",args)`
3. `fgetc(filename)`, `fgets(stringname,n,filename,)`, `fscanf(filename,"format",&args)`
4. keyboard
5. display (monitor)

Exercises 10.3

Short Answer Questions

1. The characters in the file are stored sequentially, one after another.
2. The fact that the characters in the file are stored sequentially does not force us to access the file sequentially. The standard library functions `rewind()`, `fseek()`, and `ftell()` can be used to provide random access to a file.
3. `fseek()`
4. The `fseek()` function call moves the character pointer to the last character in the file, which is the `EOF` character at offset position 10. The `ftell()` function reports the offset of the character currently pointed to. This is the `EOF` character. Thus, a 10 is returned by `ftell()`.

Exercises 10.4

Short Answer Questions

1. Passing a filename requires declaring the passed argument as a pointer to a `FILE`. The definition of `pFile()` is `pfile(fname)`

   ```
   FILE *fname;
   ```

2. a. `FILE *getFile()`

      There must be at least one variable in the function consistent with this declaration that can be used as the returned value. For example:

      ```
      File *fname;
      ```

   b. `FILE *file;`

      This can be omitted if the function calling `getFile()` is using a global variable to get the value returned.

Exercises 10.5

Short Answer Questions

1. a. The advantage of storing dates in three separate arrays is that no computation is needed to store the dates or display the dates. To get the date, just pull the month, day, and year from the respective arrays.
   b. Storing dates in this manner means that three separate arrays have to be used. This takes up computational time and memory. This manner also makes comparing and calculating dates a little more difficult, since you have to work with three arrays, rather than just one single dimensional array.
2.
```
year = date/10000
date = date % 10000
month = date/100
date = date%100
day = date
```
3. Answers will vary.

   An `isWeekday()`, or `isWeekend()` function may be useful.

   A `compareDate()` function might be useful to compare two dates. This function could return -1 if the first date is later than the second date, 0 if they are equal, and 1 if the second date is later that the first.

   A `dateAdd()` function might be useful to add a certain amount of times (possibly in days) to a date and return the new date, just as a `dateSubtract()` function may be useful.

Exercises 10.6

Short Answer Questions

1. A text file is one in which each character in the file is represented by a unique code, while a binary file is one in which data is stored using the computer's internal numerical code.
2. 25 in a text file: 5053

   25 in a binary file: 00011001
3. -25 in a text file: 455053

   -25 in a binary file: 11100111

Chapter 11

Exercises 11.1

Short Answer Questions

1. a. `*(prices + 5)`
   b. `*(grades + 2)`
   c. `*(yield + 10)`

d. `*(dist + 9)`
e. `*mile`
f. `*(temp + 20)`
g. `*(celsius + 16)`
h. `*(num + 50)`
i. `*(time + 12)`

2. a. `message[6]`
   b. `amount[0]`
   c. `yrs[10]`
   d. `stocks[2]`
   e. `rates[15]`
   f. `codes[19]`

3. a. The declaration statement `double prices[5];` causes storage space for five double-precision numbers, creates a `pointer` constant named `prices`, and equates the pointer constant to the address of the first element (`&prices[0]`).
   b. Each element in `prices` contains 4 bytes, and there are five elements for a total of 20 bytes.
   c. prices

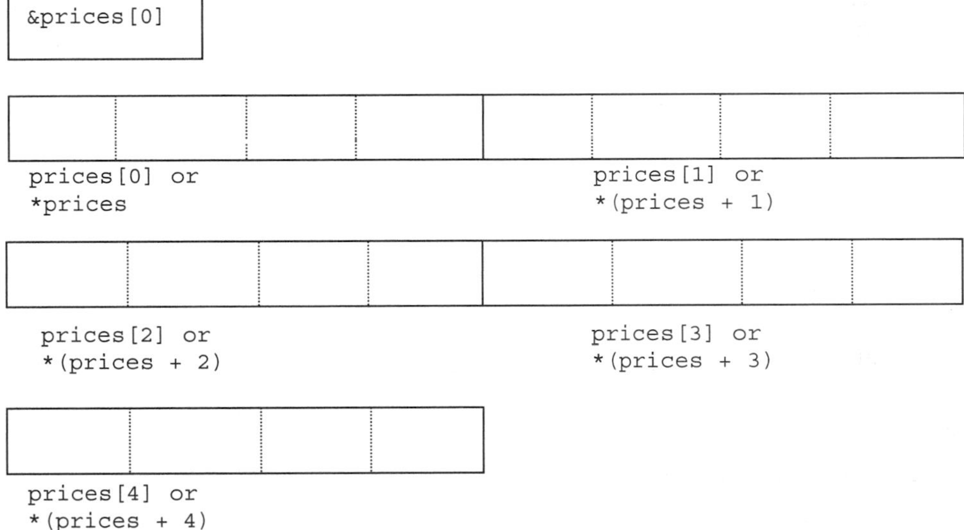

   d. The byte offset for this element, from the beginning of the array is 3 * 4 = 12 bytes.

Exercises 11.2

Short Answer Questions

1. a. `*xAddr`
   b. `*yAddr`
   c. `*ptYld`
   d. `*ptMiles`

e. `*mptr`
f. `*pdate`
g. `*disPtr`
h. `*tabTp`
i. `*hoursPt`

2. For this problem any number of descriptions can be given. Sample solutions are:
   a. keyAddr is a pointer to a character.

      keyAddr points to a character.

      The variable whose address is in keyAddr is a character.
   b. ptDate is a pointer to an integer.

      ptDate points to an integer.

      The variable whose address is in ptDate is an integer.
   c. yldAddr is a pointer to a double.

      yldAddr points to a double.

      The variable whose address is in yldAddr is a double.
   d. yPtr is a pointer to a long integer.

      yPtr points to a long integer.

      The variable whose address is in yPtr is a long integer.
   e. p_cou is a pointer to a float.

      p_cou points to a float.

      The variable whose address is in p_cou is a float

3. Only a and h are valid assignment statements.

Exercises 11.3

Short Answer Questions

1.
```
void sortArray(double inArray[500])
void sortArray(double inArray[])
void sortArray(double *inArray)
```

2.
```
void findKey(char select[256])
void findKey(char select[])
void findKey(char *select)
```

3.
```
double prime(double rates[256])
double prime (double rates[])
double prime (double * rates)
```

4. The problem with this method lies in the statement

```
if(max < *vals++)
      max = *vals;
```

   This statement compares the correct value to max, but then increments the address in the pointer before any assignment is made. Thus, the element assigned to max by the expression max = *vals is one element beyond the element pointed to within the parentheses.

5. a. 33
16
99
34

b. Yes, the notation `val[1][2]` is valid within the function. *Note:* This is equivalent to `*(*(val+ 1) + 2)`.

Exercises 11.4

Short Answer Questions

1. a.
```
*text = 'n'
*(text + 3) = ' '
*(text + 10) = ' '
```
b.
```
*text = 'r'
*(text + 3) = 'k'
*(text + 10) = 'o''
```
c.
```
*text = 'H'
*(text + 3) = 'p'
*(text + 10) = 'd'
```
d.
```
*text = 'T'
*(text + 3) = ' '
*(text + 10) = 'h'
```

Exercises 11.5

Short Answer Questions

1.
```
char* text = "Hooray!";
char text[] = {'H', 'o', 'o', 'r', 'a', 'y', '!', '\0'};
```
2. a.
```
*text = 't'
*text + 3) = ' '
*(text + 7) = 'c'
```
b.
```
*text = 't'
*(text + 3) = 's'
*(text + 7) = ' '
```
c.
```
*text = 'y'
*(text + 3) = 'o'
*(text + 7) = 'a'
```
d.
```
*text = 'T'
*(text + 3) = ' '
*(text + 7) = 'd'
```

3. `message` is a pointer constant. Therefore, the statement `message++`, which attempts to alter its address, is invalid. A correct statement is

```
putchar(*(message + i));
```

Here the address in `message` is unaltered and the character pointed to is in the character offet `i` bytes from the address corresponding to `message`.

Chapter 12

Exercises 12.1

Short Answer Questions

1. Answers may vary. Data items found a driver's license could include name, age, height, weight, eye color, date of birth, and address.

2. a.
```
struct Stemp
{
      int idNum;
      int credits;
      float avg;
};
```

b.
```
struct Stemp
{
      char name[40];
      int month;
      int day;
      int year;
      int credits;
      float avg;
};
```

c.
```
struct Stemp
{
      char name[40];
      char street[80];
      char city[40];
      char state[2];
      char zip[10];
};
```

d.
```
struct Stemp
{
      char name[40];
      float price;
      char date[10]; /* Assumes a date in the form
      mm/dd/yyyy */
};
```

e.
```
struct Stemp
{
     int partNum;
     char desc[100];
     int quant;
     int reorder;
};
```

3. a. `StempstudentRec= { 4672, 68, 3.01};`
   b. `StempstudentRec= {"RhonaKarp", 8, 4, 1980, 96, 3.89};`
   c. `StempmailList= {"Kay Kingsley", "614 Freeman Street", "Indianapolis", "IN", 47030};`
   d. `Stempstock = {"IBM", 115.375, "12/7/1999"};`
   e. `StempInven= {16879, "Battery", 10, 3};`

Exercises 12.2

Short Answer Questions

1.
```
structStemp
{
     char lastName[40];
     int boatNumber;
     int length;
     int dockNumber;
};

struct Stemp boats[500];
```

2. a. `structStempstudent[100];`
   b. `structStempstudent[100];`
   c. `structStempaddress[100];`
   d. `structStempstock[100];`
   e. `structStempinven[100];`

3.
```
struct MonthDays convert[MONTHS] = { "January", 31, "February",
28,"March", 31, "April", 30, "May", 31, "June", 30, "July", 31,
"August", 31, "September", 30, "October", 31, "November", 30,
"December", 31 };
```

Exercises 12.3

Short Answer Questions

1.
```
structDate
{
     int month;
     int day;
     int year;
};

struct Date holidays[20];
```

2. a. A `struct` can store a single record from a file.
   b. An array of `struct`s can store all of the records from a file.

Exercises 12.4

Short Answer Questions

1.
```
printf("\nTherate is %f",flag.rate);
printf("\ntaxes are %f",flag.taxes);
printf("\nnum is %d",flag.num);
```

2.
```
union
{
  int year;
  char name[10];
  char model[10];
} car;
```

3.
```
union
{
  double interest;
  double rate;
} lang;
```

4.
```
unionamt
{
   int intAmt;
   double dblAmt;
   char* ptKey;
};
```

5. a. Since a value has not been assigned to `alt.btype`, the display produced is unpredictable (the code for 'y' resides in the storage locations overlapped by the variables `alt.ch` and `alt.btype`). Thus, either a garbage value will be displayed or the program could even crash.

Chapter 13

Exercises 13.1

Short Answer Questions

1. To delete the Edith Dolan record, `t2`, the pointer in the Sam Acme recond, `t1.nextaddr`, must be changed to point to the John Lanfrank record, `t3`.
2. To delete the nth record, a check should be performed to see if the record is the first, last, or one in the middle. If the record is the first one, a pointer should be re-assigned to point to the second record. If the record to be deleted is the last one, then the (n - 1) record should contain the NULL pointer. Finally, if the record is neither the first or last record, the (n - 1) record should point to the (n + 1) record.

Exercises 13.2

Short Answer Questions

1. `malloc()` reserves the number of bytes requested by the argument passed to it and returns the address of the first reserved location. `calloc()` reserves space for an array of *n* elements of the specified size and returns the address of the first reserved location and initializes all reserved bytes to 0. `realloc()` changes the size of the previously allocation memory to a new size. `free()` releases a block of previously reserved bytes.
2. The `malloc()` function returns an address in order for the program to know where the computer system physically reserved the requested number of bytes. The address represents the address of the first location that has been reserved. A cast is typically used on the return address because the return address is always a pointer to a `void`, regardless of the data type requested.
3. a. `malloc(sizeof(int))`
   b. `malloc(50 * sizeof(int))`
   c. `malloc(sizeof(float))`
   d. `malloc(100 * sizeof(float))`
   e. `malloc(sizeof(structNameRec))`
   f. `malloc(150 * sizeof(structNameRec))`
4. `calloc(50, sizeof(int))`, `calloc(100, sizeof(float))`, `calloc(150, sizeof(structNameRec))`

Exercises 13.3

Short Answer Questions

1. a. PUSH operation steps:

      Dynamically create a new a structure.

      Put the address in the top-of-stack pointer into the address field of the new structure.

      Fill in the remaining fields of the new structure.

      Put the address of the new structure into the top-of-stack pointer.

   b. POP operation steps:

      Move the structure contents pointed to by the top-of-stack pointer into a work area.

      Free the structure pointed to by the top-of-stack pointer.

      Move the address in the work area address field into the top-of-stack pointer.

   c. When the stack is empty the top-of-stack pointer value is NULL.

2. *Note:* The following figure assumes the names Jane Jones, Bill Smith, and Jim Robinson were added to the stack in that order:

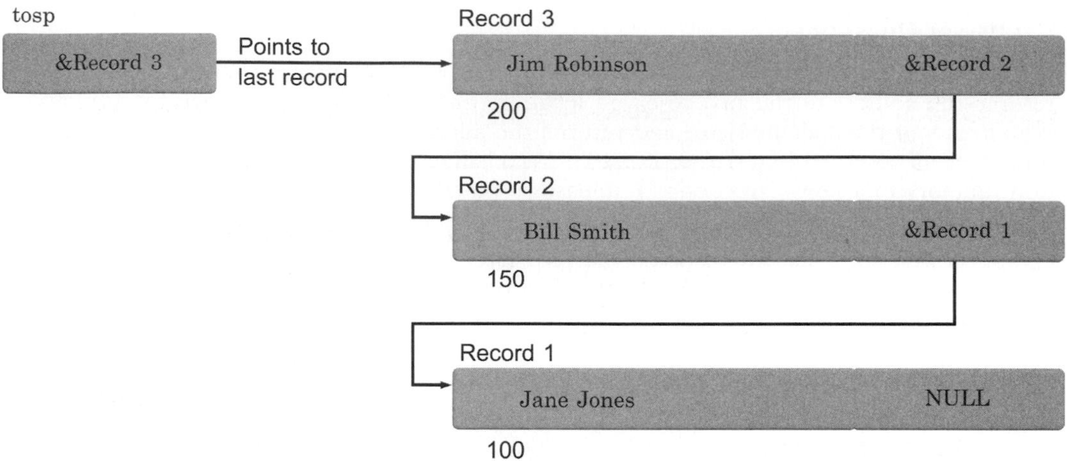

3. a. As the problem is stated, this is ideal for a stack because the last characters typed in are the first out when deletions are made. Also, the deletions can be stored in a stack for the undo operation.
   b. No, because in stack order the last person on the list would be the first to receive a car.
   c. Yes, because the search is from the most recent to the oldest.
   d. No, in a stack the priority is last in, first out.
   e. No, because the first one in line is the first on the bus, which is not the last in, first out order used in a stack.

Exercises 13.4

Short Answer Questions

1. a. Enqueue (add a new structure to an existing queue) steps:

   Dynamically create a new a structure.

   Set the address field of the new structure to a NULL.

   Fill in the remaining fields of the new structure.

   Set the address field of the prior structure (which is pointed to by the queueIn pointer) to the address of the newly created structure.

   Update the address in the queueIn pointer with the address of the newly created structure.

   b. Serve (remove a structure an existing queue) steps:

   Move the contents of the structure pointed to by the queueOut pointer into a work area.

   Free the structure pointed to by the queueOut pointer.

   Move the address in the work area address field into the queueOut pointer.

   c. When the queue is empty queueIn and queueOut will be NULL.

2. *Note:* The following figure assumes the name Jane Jones, Bill Smith, and Jim Robinson were added to the stack in that order.

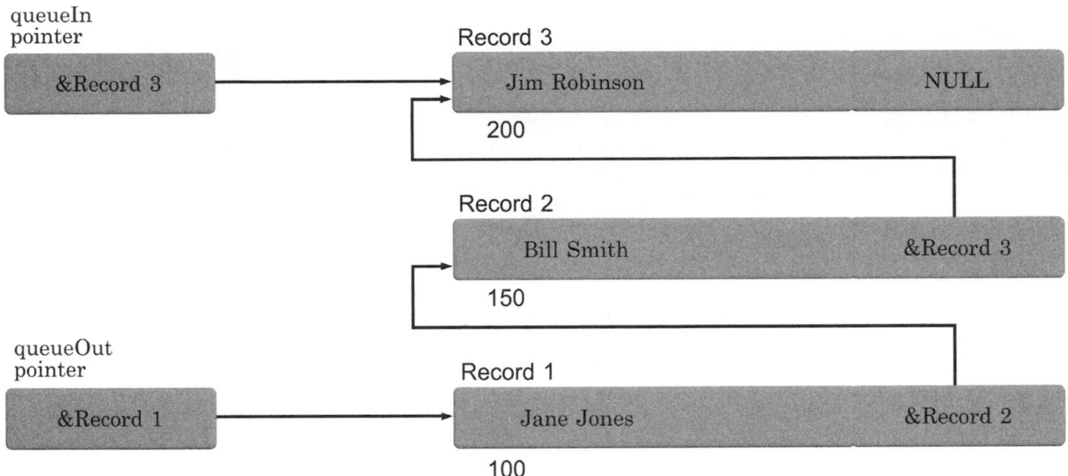

3. a. Queue, because this represents a first in, first out situation.
   b. Queue, because this is also a first in, first out situation.
   c. Neither, because the order of retrieval is neither first in, first out nor last in, first out.
   d. Queue, because this is also a first in, first out situation.

Exercises 13.5

Short Answer Questions

1. The student should draw a diagram similar to Figure 13.16 and Figure 13.17.
2. If the structure is the first, set `firstrec` to `firstrec->nextAddr`.

   If the structure is the last, set the previous structures pointer to `NULL`.

   If the structure is in the middle, set the prior structure's pointer to the next structure.

   Free the structure.

Chapter 14

Exercises 14.1

Short Answer Questions

1. a. `enum{FALSE, TRUE};`
   b. `enum{JAN=1, FEB, MARCH, APRIL, MAY, JUNE, JULY, AUG, SEPT, OCT, NOV, DEC}`
2. a. Missing semicolon
   b. Number 1 is assigned twice, the () should be {}, and missing semicolon
   c. Symbolic name RED is used twice and there is a missing semicolon

3. a. `minVal= (a < b) ? a :b;`
   b. `sign= (num < 0) ? -1 :1;`
   c. `val= (flag == 1) ? num :num * num;`
   d. `rate= (credit == plus) ? prime :prime + delta;`
   e. `cou= (!bond) ? .075 : 1.1;`

Exercises 14.2

Short Answer Questions

1. a. 10000000
   b. 11101111
   c. 01101111

2. To obtain the octal representation, starting from the right, take groups of 3 bits and convert each group into a decimal number from 0 to 7. The last group will consist of only 2 bits, not 3.

```
11001010 = 11 001 010 = 312
  10100101 = 10 100 101 = 245
  10000000 = 10 000 000 = 200
  11101111 = 11 101 111 = 347
  01101111 = 01 101 111 = 137
```

3. a.
```
0157 = 001 101 111
       001 101 111 << 1 = 011 011 110 = 0336
```
   b.
```
0701 = 111 000 001
       111 000 001 << 2 = 100 000 100 = 0404
```
   c.
```
0673 = 110 111 011
       110 111 011 >> 2 = 001 101 110 = 0156
```
   d.
```
067 =110 111
      110 111 >> 3 = 000 110 = 06
```

4. a. 0336
   b. 0404
   c. 0756
   d. 076

5. a. 014
   b. 363
   c. 014 using the exclusive OR

6. a. 11111111
   b. 1111111111111111

Exercises 14.3

Short Answer Questions

1. `#define NEGATE(x) (x)`
2. `#define ABSVAL(x) ((x) < 0 ?(-x) :(x))`

3. `#define CIRCUM(r)  (2.0 * 3.1416*(r))`
4. `#define MIN(x,y)  ((x) < (y) ? (x) :(y))`
5. `#define MAX(x,y)  ((x) > (y) ? (x) :(y))`

Exercises 14.4

Short Answer Questions

1. Command-line arguments
2. argc is an integer and argv is an array char pointer.
3. a. argc provides the number of items on the command line.
   b. argv provides the list of started addresses indicating where each argument is actually stored.
4. Yes, the variable names argc and argv must be used.

Chapter 15

Exercises 15.1

Short Answer Questions

1. a. `cout<< "Hello World";`
   b. `cout<< "Enter an integer value";`
   c. `cout<< "The sum of " << 5 << " + " << 6 << " is " << (5+6);`
   d. `cout<< num1 << " plus " << num2 << " is " << num1+num2;`
2. a. `cout<< setw(4) << 5; printf("%4d", 5);`
   b. `cout<< setw(3) << result; printf("%3d", result);`
   c. `cout<< "The sum of " << setw(3) << num1 << " and " << setw(3) << num2 << " is " << setw(3) << num1+num2;`
   d. `cout<< fixed << setw(5) << setprecision(2) << 2.756;`
3. a. `cin>> units;`
   b. `cin>> price;`
   c. `cin>> units >> price;`
4. C is a procedural language while C++ is an object-oriented language. One of the main syntactical differences between the languages is how input and output is formatted, as seen in Programs 15.1 and 15.2.

Exercises 15.2

Short Answer Questions

1. One of the prime motivations was the inability of procedurally structured code to be easily extended without extensive revision, retesting, and reevaluations.
2. To be classified as object-oriented, a language must have the following features: class construction, inheritance, and polymorphism.

3. a. *class*—a programmer defined data type
   b. *inheritance*—the capacity of deriving one class from another
   c. *polymorphism*—the ability to use the same operation to invoke one set of results on data values of a base class and a different set of results on data values of a derived class
4. The initial (first) class is known as the base class, while the subclass (second) class is known as the subclass.
5. The Standard Template Library (STL) of classes provides generic data types of available in C++, such as an array class.

Index

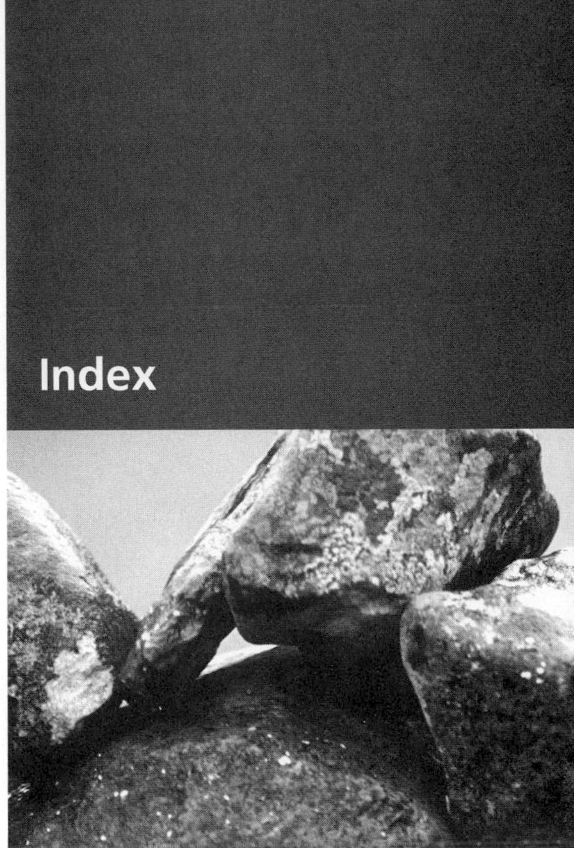